Social Welfare

Seventh Edition

Social Welfare

POLITICS AND PUBLIC POLICY

Diana M. DiNitto
The University of Texas at Austin

Allyn & Bacon

Boston   Columbus   Indianapolis   New York   San Francisco   Upper Saddle River
Amsterdam   Cape Town   Dubai   London   Madrid   Milan   Munich   Paris   Montreal   Toronto
Delhi   Mexico City   Sao Paulo   Sydney   Hong Kong   Seoul   Singapore   Taipei   Tokyo

Executive Editor: Ashley Dodge
Editorial Product Manager: Carly Czech
Senior Marketing Manager: Wendy Albert
Marketing Assistant: Patrick M. Walsh
Production Editor: Pat Torelli
Manufacturing Buyer: Debbie Rossi
Editorial Production and Composition Service: Laserwords Maine
Cover Designer: Joel Gendron

Library of Congress Cataloging-in-Publication Data

DiNitto, Diana M.
  Social welfare : politics and public policy / Diana M. DiNitto. — 7th ed.
    p. cm.
  Includes bibliographical references and index.
  ISBN-13: 978-0-205-79384-6
  ISBN-10: 0-205-79384-3
    1. Public welfare—United States. 2. United States—Social policy. I. Title.

  HV95.D56 2011
  361.6'130973—dc22
                                                    2010031421

10 9 8 7 6 5 4 3 2 1 EB 14 13 12 11 10

Allyn & Bacon
is an imprint of

www.pearsonhighered.com

ISBN 10:   0-205-79384-3
ISBN 13: 978-0-205-79384-6

Dedication

In loving memory of my father, Vincent J. DiNitto (1918–2008),
for always putting his family first.

CONTENTS

PREFACE

I can hardly believe that nearly three decades have gone by since publication of the first edition of *Social Welfare: Politics and Public Policy.* Like previous editions, the seventh edition is intended to introduce students to the major social welfare policies and programs in the United States and to stimulate them to think about major conflicts in social welfare today. The book focuses on issues and emphasizes that social welfare in the United States involves a series of political questions about what should be done for those who are poor, near poor, and not poor and other individuals and groups—or whether anything should be done at all.

Social Welfare: Politics and Public Policy describes the major social welfare programs—their histories, trends, and current problems and prospects. But more importantly, it tackles the difficult conflicts and controversies that surround these programs. Social welfare policy is not presented as a series of solutions to social problems. Instead, social policy is portrayed as public conflict over the nature and causes of social welfare problems, over what, if anything, should be done about them, over who should do it, and over who should decide about it.

Some of the major policies and programs covered in this book are the following:

Social Security
Unemployment insurance
Workers' compensation
Supplemental Security Income
Vocational rehabilitation
The Americans with Disabilities Act
Individuals with Disabilities Education Act
Child support enforcement
Temporary Assistance for Needy Families
Supplemental Nutrition Assistance Program
Community action programs
No Child Left Behind Act
Job training
Minimum wage legislation
Mental health services
The Older Americans Act
Child welfare services
Medicare
Medicaid
Civil rights legislation
Affirmative action
Immigration legislation
Abortion policy
Gay rights legislation
Voting rights legislation

Although it is impossible to capture all the complexities of social welfare in a single volume, and this book is not a legal guide to benefits, these policies and programs are described and analyzed, and alternative proposals and reforms are considered.

This book is designed for undergraduate and beginning graduate courses in social welfare policy. It does not require prior knowledge of social welfare. Hopefully, it will spur further interest in social welfare policies and programs.

Many texts on social policy treat social insurance, public assistance, and social service programs descriptively; by so doing, they tend to obscure important conflicts and issues. Other books treat these programs prescriptively; by so doing, they imply that there is a "right" way to resolve social problems. *Social Welfare: Politics and Public Policy* views social policy as a continuing political struggle over the issues posed by poverty and other social welfare problems in society—different goals and objectives, competing definitions of problems, alternative approaches and strategies, multiple programs and policies, competing proposals for reform, and different ideas about how social welfare policy decisions should be made. An instructor's manual, test bank, PowerPoint slides, and a MySocialWorkLab are available to accompany the text.

I owe a special debt to Thomas R. Dye, Emeritus Professor of Political Science at Florida State University. Although he no longer appears as a coauthor of the book, without him there would never have been a book at all. The seventh edition might not have been completed without the work of David Johnson, Mary Margaret Just, Peter Kindle, Melissa Radey, and Jessica Ritter, who took the lead in writing several chapters in this seventh edition. I am grateful to each of them for their meticulous work and the many hours they invested in this project. Thanks again to Linda Cummins, who took on the task of helping with the sixth edition of this book. I wish to thank the reviewers who commented on previous editions, in particular Professor Robert B. Hudson of Boston University, who provided very helpful comments through the years, and Professor Miguel Ferguson of the University of Texas at Austin for his comments in recent years. Thanks also to Mark Cederburg, University of Kansas; Elwood Hamlin, Florida Atlantic University; Katharine Hill, University of St. Thomas; Charles Lewis, Howard University; Jeanne Saunders, University of Iowa; Maria Spence, University of Akron; and Jim Stafford, University of Mississippi, all of whom reviewed this edition. I thank my mother and Craig for their patience during the many hours it took to complete this project and friends and members of the WRD group for their support. My thanks to graduate assistants Lauren Alper, Ayla Pintchovski, and Chris Babb for their help. My appreciation also goes to Dean Barbara White and the faculty and staff of The University of Texas at Austin School of Social Work for their continued support and encouragement of my work.

A number of users of the book, both faculty and students, have communicated with me about previous editions. I appreciate their interest and look forward to further contacts with readers.

D. M. D.

Social Welfare

INTRODUCTION: POLITICS, RATIONALISM, AND SOCIAL WELFARE POLICY

No one is happy with the nation's social welfare system—not the taxpayers who must support it, not the social welfare professionals who must administer it, and certainly not the needy who must live under it. The nation's social insurance, public assistance, and social service programs are sources of intense controversy. Since the Social Security Act of 1935, the federal government has tried to develop a rational social welfare system for the entire nation. Today a wide variety of federal programs serve people who are aged, poor, disabled, sick, or have other social service needs. Social welfare programs are the federal government's largest expenditure, far surpassing national defense. The Social Security Administration and the U.S. Department of Health and Human Services have the largest budgets of any federal agencies, and other agencies administer many additional social welfare programs. After 75 years of large-scale, direct federal involvement, social welfare policy remains a central issue in U.S. politics.

This book describes the country's major social welfare policies and programs, but it is also concerned with the causes of social welfare policy—why policy is what it is. To understand contemporary social welfare policy, it is necessary to learn about some of the social, economic, and political forces that have shaped social welfare policy in the United States. This book looks at how social welfare policies have developed and changed over time. It considers the consequences of social welfare policies—their effects on target groups and on society in general. The chapters that follow also consider alternative policies—possible changes, reforms, improvements, or phaseouts—and how those involved in the policy process develop, analyze, and evaluate these proposals.

Policymaking is frequently portrayed as a *rational* process in which policymakers identify social problems, explore all the solutions to a problem, forecast all the benefits and costs of each solution, compare benefits to costs for each solution, and select the best ratio of benefits to costs. In examining social welfare policy, this book considers both the strengths and weaknesses of this rational model of policymaking and demonstrates that the political barriers to rational policy-making are indeed very great.

In so doing, this book presents social welfare policy as a series of continuing political conflicts over the nature and causes of poverty and other social problems and what should be done for groups such as the poor, near-poor, or nonpoor—or whether anything should be done at all. The real problems in social welfare are not problems of organization, administration, or service delivery. Rather, they involve different ideas about the nature and causes of inequality in society, government's role in society, the burdens that taxpayers should carry, the appropriate strategies for coping with social problems, the need for reform in specific social welfare programs, the importance of one's own needs and aspirations in relation to those of others, the nature of the decision-making process itself, and about the ability of government to do anything "rationally." In short, we present social welfare policy as a continuing political struggle over the issues of poverty, inequality, and other social problems in society.

WHAT IS SOCIAL WELFARE POLICY?

Social welfare policy is anything a government chooses to do, or not to do, that affects the quality of life of its people. Broadly conceived, social welfare policy includes nearly everything government does—from taxation, national defense, and energy conservation, to healthcare, housing, and public assistance. More elaborate definitions of social welfare policy are available.[1] Most of them refer to actions of government that have an "impact on the welfare of citizens by providing them with services or income."[2] By government, we mean the legislative, executive, and judicial branches. Agency administrators and judges influence social welfare policy as much as elected officials.

Some scholars have insisted that government activities must have "a goal, objective, or purpose," in order to be labeled a "policy."[3] This definition implies a difference between governmental actions in general and an overall plan of action toward a specific goal. The problem, however, in insisting that government actions must have goals in order to be labeled as "policy" is that we can never be sure what the goal of a particular government action is. We generally assume that if a government chooses to do something, there must be a goal, objective, or purpose, but often we find that bureaucrats who helped write the law, lobbyists who pushed for its enactment, and members of Congress who voted for it all had different goals, objectives, and purposes in mind. Multiple goals are not necessarily a bad thing, especially when they mean that more people stand to benefit from a policy, but any of the intentions of a law (stated or not) may also be quite different from what government agencies actually do. All we can really observe is what governments choose to do or not do.

Political scientists Heinz Eulau and Kenneth Prewitt supply still another definition of public policy: "Policy is defined as a 'standing decision' characterized by behavioral consistency and repetitiveness on the part of those who make it and those who abide by it."[4] It might be a wonderful thing if government activities were characterized by such consistency—that they seem to have "rhyme and reason"—but it is doubtful that we would ever find a public policy in government if we insisted on these criteria. As you shall see, much of what government does is not consistent, and government policies often conflict with each other.

Note that this book focuses not only on government action but also on government *inaction*—that is, on what governments choose *not* to do. Government inaction can have just as important an impact on society as government action.

Lengthy discussions of the definition of social welfare policy are unnecessary, often futile, and even exasperating, since few people can agree on a single definition of social welfare policy. Moreover, these discussions divert attention away from the study of specific social welfare policies.

The boundaries of social welfare policy are indeed fuzzy. For practical purposes, much of the discussion presented in this book concerns government policies that directly affect the income, services, and opportunities available to people who are aged, poor, disabled, ill, or otherwise vulnerable. Specifically, the major government policies and programs addressed are:

Income maintenance
   Social Security
   Unemployment insurance
   Workers' compensation
   Supplemental Security Income (SSI)
   Temporary Assistance for Needy Families (TANF)
   Child support
   Minimum wage legislation
   Earned income tax credit

Health
   Medicare
   Medicaid
   State Children's Health Insurance Program (SCHIP)
   Public health

Nutrition
   Supplemental Nutrition Assistance Program (SNAP) (formerly the Food Stamp Program)
   Nutrition programs for older adults

Social services
   Child and adult protective services
   Family preservation services
   Community mental health services
   Day care
   Independent living services
   Long-term care services

Employment
   Employment services (job finding)
   Job training

       Vocational rehabilitation

       Ticket to Work

    Housing

       Public housing

       Housing vouchers

       Mortgage assistance

       Homeless shelters

    Education

       Preschool education

       No Child Left Behind Act

       Individuals with Disabilities Education Act

       Public school funding

       Financial aid for higher education

Some of these social welfare programs are called *public assistance* because people must be poor (according to legal standards) in order to receive benefits, and benefits are paid from general-revenue funds. Public assistance programs (what most people call "welfare") include TANF, SNAP, Medicaid, SSI, public housing, and school lunches and breakfasts. These programs are also called *residual* because benefits are provided only *after* people experience economic difficulties.

Other social welfare programs are called *social insurance* because they are designed to *prevent* poverty. Workers and/or their employers pay into these programs. Upon retirement, disability, or unemployment, those who paid in are entitled to benefits, regardless of their wealth. Social insurance programs include Social Security, Medicare, unemployment insurance, and workers' compensation. These programs are also called *universal* or *institutional* because almost all Americans participate or are entitled to do so no matter their income or wealth.

Still other social welfare programs are labeled *social services* because they provide care, counseling, education, or other forms of assistance to children, older adults, people with disabilities, and others with particular needs. Child protective services, daycare, independent living services, and mental health care are all examples of social services. Social services are also provided in areas like employment, housing, and education.

This book also addresses a number of social justice or rights policies that affect social welfare. Civil rights legislation, the Americans with Disabilities Act, affirmative action, and other provisions bear directly on the status of women, people of color, immigrants, gay men and lesbians, and other groups.

SOCIAL WELFARE POLICY: A RATIONAL APPROACH

Ideally, social welfare policy ought to be rational. A policy is rational if the ratio between the values it achieves and the values it sacrifices is positive and higher than any other policy alternative. This might be viewed as a strictly economic (cost-benefit) approach, but we should not measure benefits and costs only in a narrow dollar-and-cents framework while ignoring basic social values. The idea of rationalism involves the calculation of *all* social, political, and economic values sacrificed or achieved by a public policy, not just those that can be measured in dollars.

Rationalism has been proposed as an "ideal" approach to both studying and making public policy[5] and even as a single "model of choice" that can be applied to all kinds of problems, large and small, public and private.[6] Most government policies are far from being entirely rational. Even so, the model remains important because it helps identify barriers to rationality. It also helps us ask why policymaking is not a more rational process.

Steps in the Rational Process

Let's consider the conditions for rational policymaking more closely:

1. Society must be able to identify and define social problems and agree there is a need to resolve these problems.
2. All the values of society must be known and weighed.
3. All possible alternative policies must be identified and considered.
4. The consequences of each alternative must be fully understood in terms of both costs and benefits, for the present and for the future, and for target groups and the rest of society.
5. Policymakers must calculate the ratio of benefits to costs for each alternative.
6. Policymakers must choose the policy that maximizes *net* values—the alternative that achieves the greatest benefit at the lowest cost.

Because this notion of rationality assumes that the values of society as a whole can be known and weighed, it is not enough to know some groups' values but not others. There must be a common understanding of societal values. Rational policymaking also requires information about alternative policies and the capacity to accurately predict the consequences of each alternative. Rationality requires the intelligence to calculate correctly the ratio of costs to benefits for each policy alternative. This means calculating all present and future benefits and costs to both the target groups (those for whom the policy is intended) and nontarget groups. Finally, rationalism requires a policymaking system that facilitates rationality in policy formation and implementation.

The Limits of Rationality

This type of *comprehensive rationality* not only fails to occur in the political environment, it may actually not be rational. Herbert A. Simon, a Nobel Prize winner for his studies of the decision-making process in large organizations, noted this apparent contradiction many years ago. It is so costly and time-consuming to learn about *all* the policy alternatives available to decision makers, to investigate *all* the possible consequences of each alternative, and to calculate the cost-benefit ratio of *every* alternative, that the improvement in the policy selected is not worth the extra effort required to make a comprehensive rational selection. Simon's theory of *bounded rationality* recognizes the practical limits to complete rationality:

> It is impossible for the behavior of a single, isolated individual to reach any high degree of rationality. The number of alternatives . . . [to] explore is so great, the information . . . to evaluate them so vast that even an approximation to objective rationality is hard to conceive.[7]

In contrast to completely rational decision making, Simon's notion of bounded rationality means that policymakers consider a limited number of alternatives, estimate these consequences using the best available means, and select the alternative that appears to achieve the most important values without incurring unacceptable costs. Instead of maximizing the ratio of benefits to costs, policymakers search for a "satisfying" choice—an alternative that is good enough to produce the desired benefits at a reasonable cost. Policymakers do not try to create the best of all possible worlds; rather they seek to get by, to come out all right, to avoid trouble, to compromise.

Rationalism presents an ideal model of policymaking—in social welfare and in other policy fields—even though policymaking in "the real world" is not usually a rational process. Policymaking occurs in a political context that places severe limits on rationality, especially in an increasingly partisan political environment. Anyone who has witnessed the various rounds in the country's debate over health insurance knows this is true.

SOCIAL WELFARE POLICY: A POLITICAL APPROACH

Social welfare policy is political because it arises out of conflict over the nature of the problems confronting society and what actions, if any, governments should take to address them. The word politics itself is almost synonymous with the word conflict.

Political scientist Harold Lasswell described politics as "who gets what, when, and how."[8] Politics is an activity through which people try to get more of whatever there is to get—money, jobs, prestige, prosperity, respect, and power itself. "Politics . . . consists of the activities—for example, reasonable discussion, impassioned oratory, balloting, and street fighting—by which conflict is carried on."[9] Conflict over the allocation of values in society is central to politics and policymaking. In the United States this conflict more often takes the form of balloting and debate than violence.

Why do we expect conflict in society over who gets what? Why can't we agree on "a theory of justice" according to which everyone would agree on what is fair for all members of society, particularly those who are most vulnerable to social problems?[10] Why can't we have a harmonious, loving, caring, sharing society of equals? Philosophers have pondered these questions for centuries. James Madison, perhaps the first American to write seriously about politics, believed that the causes of "faction" (conflict) are found in human diversity—"a zeal for different opinions concerning religion, concerning government, and many other points . . . [and] an attachment to different leaders ambitiously contending for preeminence and power." More importantly, according to Madison, "the most common and durable source of faction has been the various and unequal distribution of property. Those who hold and those who are without property have ever formed distinct interests in society."[11] In short, class differences among people, particularly in the sources and amount of their wealth, are the root cause of social conflict.

A critical task of government is to regulate conflict. It does so by (1) establishing and enforcing general rules by which conflict is carried on, (2) arranging compromises and balancing interests in public policy, and (3) imposing settlements that the parties to a dispute must accept. Governments arrange settlements in the form of public policies that allocate values in such a way that both "winners" and "losers" will accept them, at least temporarily. Governments impose these settlements by enforcing public policy through the promise of rewards or threat of punishment.

From a political perspective, public policy is the outcome of conflicts in government over who gets what, and when and how they get it. A policy may be considered "politically rational" when it succeeds in winning enough support to be enacted into law, implemented by executive agencies, and enforced by the courts. Or it may be considered politically rational if it is supported by influential groups and believed to be popular among the voters. But this certainly differs from the type of rationality described in the rational model.

The political approach raises serious questions about rationality in policymaking. It suggests that:

1. Few social values are generally agreed on; more often there are only the values of specific groups and individuals, many of which are conflicting. For example, even if there is agreement that all Americans should have health insurance, deciding the role of the public and private sectors in accomplishing this goal is a major public policy issue that has defied a rational solution. On many issues, there is no fundamental agreement on the value to be achieved. For example, there is little likelihood that antiabortion and prochoice forces will ever agree on the issue of access to abortion. Moreover, it seems that policymakers are increasingly coming to the table with such strongly held philosophical positions or partisan loyalties that there is less and less room for compromise.

2. Problems cannot be defined, because people do not agree on what the problems are. And what is a problem to one group may be a benefit to another group. Consider discussions of what causes poverty. Explanations range from the willful behavior of those who prefer not to work, to discrimination and structural barriers to participation in gainful, economic activity. Remedies include low public assistance payments that provide a very meager standard of living for the poor, but save taxpayers' money, at least in the short run. Meager welfare payments may also force unemployed people to accept low-wage jobs benefitting industries that rely on this cheap labor pool. Or consider that saving the spotted owl is viewed as a great benefit to some environmentalists but represents a serious cost to those who rely on the logging industry for a living.

3. Many conflicting costs and values cannot be compared or weighed. For example, how can we compare the value of individual dignity with the cost of a general tax increase? Policymakers at all levels—local, state, and federal—face these challenges every day. A city or county government may choose to fund a residential program for people with developmental disabilities rather than a drug detoxification program. Perhaps they view people with developmental disabilities as a more deserving clientele; perhaps they believe that program will be better administered. But they do not really know if their choice will achieve greater social values. In fact, local governments may appoint citizen advisory groups to recommend allocations of human service funding, because it takes the political pressure off elected officials in trying to distinguish one seemingly good cause from another.

4. Policymakers, even with most advanced analytic techniques, cannot accurately forecast or predict the consequences of various policy alternatives or calculate their cost-benefit ratios when many diverse social, economic, and political values are involved. Perhaps the best example of this concerns difficulties in economic forecasting. We may try to predict the effects of a general tax cut or an economic stimulus payment on consumer buying power, but other economic forces that cannot be foreseen well in advance—downturns in particular sectors of the economy (auto, steel, high tech) or a rise in fuel costs—may offset any beneficial effects on the country's overall economic well-being. Many other events happen over which we have no control, such as earthquakes in California, tornadoes in the Midwest, or hurricanes on the Gulf Coast. Even though federal, state, and local governments try to respond rationally to these natural disasters, they may divert funds and attention from other activities already in place. Finally, there is fallout from events that perhaps could be predicted, but were ignored—events leading to city riots during the civil rights unrest of the 1960s and the sub-prime mortgage debacle and stock market failures that shook the U.S. economy in 2008.

5. The environment of policymakers, particularly the political system of power and influence, makes it virtually impossible to discern all social values, particularly those that do not have active or powerful proponents in or near government.   Those who are homeless, ill, or lack sophisticated communication skills may have little access to governmental representation, even though their needs may be great. Children in the United States face high rates of poverty, abuse, and neglect, yet they have no direct voice in the political arena. Cynicism has grown that without substantial financial resources it is difficult to influence public policy.

6. Policymakers are not necessarily motivated to make decisions on the basis of social values. Instead they often seek to maximize their own rewards—power, status, reelection, money, and so on.   Policymakers have their own needs, ambitions, and inadequacies, all of which can prevent them from performing in a highly rational manner. For instance, although the federal debt may place a severe strain on the country, Congress members often do little about it, because any tax increase or budget cut may mean lost votes for some senator or representative anxious for reelection. Most Congress members also do their best to support "earmarks"—pet projects in their districts—to gain favor with constituents, regardless of whether these projects have value for the nation as a whole.

7. Large, segmented government bureaucracies create barriers to coordinated policymaking.   It is difficult to bring all the interested individuals, groups, and experts together at the point of decision. Governmental decision making is so disjointed that it is a wonder how any legislation gets passed and any programs get implemented. Anyone who remembers the diagrams of "How a Bill Becomes a Law" from middle school civics classes knows that the maze of readings and calendars works to prevent most proposals from ever being seriously considered. Even when proposed legislation is considered, lawmakers use many tactics to pass or to defeat it, from filibusters to riders attached to other, sometimes unrelated, bills. Generally, both the 435 members of the U.S. House of Representatives and the 100 members of the U.S. Senate must consider a bill and both chambers must pass an identical version of the bill for it to become law. With the two major political parties vying for their philosophies to prevail and with these 535 Congress members representing constituencies that have many diverse interests, the process is daunting. Only a tiny fraction of legislation that is introduced to Congress and state legislatures ever makes it through the gauntlet (see the Illustration I.1 "Tips for the Legislative Process"). The process of implementing public policy once it is enacted is no less challenging.

ILLUSTRATION I.1:
Tips for the Legislative Process

Very few of the bills introduced in any body become law. In the U.S. Congress as well as most states, only about 10 to -15 percent of the bills introduced become law. A classic study by Ron Dear and Rino Patti of the bills introduced over several years in the Washington state legislature yielded seven tactics that were likely to improve a bill's chances of success. The bills that made it out of committee and onto the floor tended to share the following characteristics.

FACTORS THAT FOSTER SUCCESS
Early Introduction

If your state allows bills to be prefiled before the session formally begins, that's a good time to get your bill introduced. It means there will be more time to consider it, hold hearings on it, build for it, raise and answer questions about it.

Multiple Sponsors

A bill that has several sponsors from the outset tends to look more like a winner. Bills with only one sponsor, by contrast, are sometimes assumed to be introduced just to please a constituent or do somebody a favor but not as a serious legislative proposal. Multiple sponsors increase credibility and also the number of advocates working for its success.

Bipartisan Sponsorship

It is always essential to have sponsors from the party in the majority, but unless the legislature is overwhelmingly dominated by one party, it helps a bill's credibility and chances if its sponsors come from both parties. (On the national level, and anywhere that margins are close or party discipline is unreliable, bipartisan sponsorship is essential.)

Support of Governor and Relevant Executive Agency

Since the executive branch will have to administer the resulting program (and in any case tends to have data, information, and expertise), legislators often are influenced by their support or opposition. If support is out of the question, the next best option is executive branch neutrality. The worst posture is outright opposition.

Influential Sponsors

The job of getting a bill through hearings and out to the floor will be much easier if the chair or highest ranking minority members of the subcommittees and committees are sponsors of the bill. If they, or highly respected senior members of the body, become sponsors and use their influence on its behalf, that's half the battle.

Open Hearings

Hearings are a good opportunity to make a public record, bring an issue before the public, get questions and points of opposition out in the open and dealt with, and to give the advocacy groups a rallying point.

Amendments

Some advocates think their proposal has to be enacted exactly as they conceived it. That rarely happens. In fact, bills that are not amended tend to die. That's because everyone who amends a proposal has to be familiar with it and develops a bit of "ownership," a stake in its future if you will. Encourage amendments; they'll increase your bill's chances of success.

Ultimately, even these seven tactics are no guarantee of success. Bills are more likely to pass if they involve low costs, noncontroversial beneficiaries and purposes, and little significant change. Bills to create "National Tuna Week" or name a building have an easier time than bills to provide comprehensive health or human services to low-income families. Knowing the process won't ensure victory, but not knowing it makes it hard to even be a player.

Just keep reminding yourself: Laws will be passed with you or without you. The choice is yours.

Source: Nancy Amidei, *So You Want to Make a Difference: Advocacy Is the Key* (Washington, DC: OMB Watch, June 1991), pp. 19–20. Based on Ronald B. Dear and Rino J. Patti, "Legislative Advocacy: Seven Effective Tactics," *Social Work*, Vol. 26, No. 4, 1981, pp. 289–296. Copyright 1981, National Association of Social Workers, Inc. Reprinted by permission of OMB Watch.

Incrementalism

How can we bridge the differences between an ideal model of rational policymaking and the realization that policymaking is a political activity? Political scientist Charles E. Lindblom first presented an **incremental model** of policymaking as a critique of the rational model.[12] Lindblom observed that government policymakers do *not* annually review the entire range of existing and proposed policies, identify all of society's goals, or research the benefits and costs of all alternative policies to achieve these goals. They, therefore, do not make their selections on the basis of *all* relevant information. Limits of time, knowledge, and costs pose innumerable obstacles in identifying the full range of policy alternatives and predicting their consequences. Political limitations prevent the establishment of clear-cut societal goals and the accurate calculation of cost-benefit ratios. The incremental model recognizes the impracticality of comprehensive rational policymaking and describes a more conservative process of public decision making.

Incremental policymaking considers existing policies, programs, and expenditures as a base. It concentrates attention on newly proposed policies and programs and on increases, decreases, or other modifications in existing programs. Incrementalism is conservative in that policymakers generally accept the legitimacy of established policies and programs. The focus of attention is on proposed changes in these policies and programs. This narrows policymakers' attention to a limited number of new initiatives and increases or decreases in the budget.

There are important political advantages to incrementalism in policymaking. Conflict is reduced if the items in dispute are only increases or decreases in existing budgets or modifications of existing programs. Conflict is greater when policymaking focuses on major policy shifts involving great gains or losses for various groups in society or "all or nothing," "yes or no" policy decisions. To reconsider existing policies every year would generate a great deal of conflict; it is easier politically to continue previously accepted policies. Policymakers may also continue existing policies because of uncertainty about the consequences of completely new or different policies. It is safer to stick with known programs when the consequences of new programs cannot be accurately predicted. Under conditions of uncertainty, policymakers continue past policies or programs regardless of whether they have proven effective.

Policymakers also realize that individuals and organizations—executive agencies, congressional committees, special interest groups—accumulate commitments to existing policies and programs. For example, it is accepted wisdom in Washington that bureaucracies persist over time regardless of their utility, that they develop routines that are difficult to alter, and that individuals develop a personal stake in the continuation of organizations and programs. These commitments are serious obstacles to major change. It is politically easier for policymakers to seek alternatives that involve only a minimum of budgetary, organizational, or administrative change.

In the absence of generally agreed-on social goals or values, it is also politically expedient for governments to pursue a variety of different programs and policies simultaneously, even if some of them are overlapping or even conflicting. In this way, a wider variety of individuals and groups in society are "satisfied." Comprehensive policy planning for specific social goals may maximize some people's values, but it may also generate extreme opposition from others. A government that pursues multiple policies may be politically more suitable to a pluralistic society comprised of people with varying values. In the last few decades, others have proposed theories of the policy process, but virtually all pay homage to Simon's concept of bounded rationality and Lindblom's concept of incrementalism.[13]

Policy Punctuations

Incrementalism explains much, but not all, policymaking. Major policy changes, sometimes called "policy punctuations," can emerge when more minor events add up over time.[14] When the Aid to Dependent Children (ADC) program was established as part of the Social Security Act in 1935, the idea was that as Social Security covered more families, ADC would diminish in importance. That is not what happened. Caseloads grew over time until Congress took heed of experiments by some states and passed legislation in 1996 to cut the program's rolls dramatically.

Occasionally, major policy changes do occur in shorter order. In crisis situations, political decision makers may consider new and untried policies over existing ones. Following the stock market crash of 1929 and the ensuing Great Depression, President Roosevelt led the federal government to take unprecedented steps in entering the social welfare arena with programs such as Social Security and Aid to Dependent Children. After the terrorist attacks of September 11, 2001, Congress passed the USA Patriot Act, giving the federal government unprecedented powers in the areas of surveillance and detainment to thwart subsequent attacks. Following the national economic crisis that erupted in the fall of 2008, President George W. Bush and Congress took steps to bail out troubled financial institutions in a way that had never been seen before. Upon taking office, President Barack Obama also saw that an economic stimulus bill of unprecedented proportions was passed. These actions of the president and Congress were major changes, but the problems that built up to them had accumulated over time until they reached what Malcolm Gladwell calls a *tipping point*—"that one dramatic moment . . . when everything can change all at once."[15]

"Policy entrepreneurs"[16]—groups and individuals who seek more than incremental change in public policy—may also try to generate a crisis atmosphere. For example, some people portray Social Security as on the verge of bankruptcy and believe that current workers would be better off if they were allowed to invest some of their Social Security taxes in the private market. Policy entrepreneurs may also try to focus attention on problems such as drug crime in order to generate support for their policy ideas, such as private prisons focused on rehabilitation.

Policy punctuations can also occur due to shifts in political leadership. President Ronald Reagan ushered in an era of "supply side" or "trickle down" economics that had far-reaching effects by reducing taxes, especially on the wealthiest Americans, and by retrenchment in social welfare programs. In contrast, President Obama has encouraged infusions of federal funds that have boosted government spending on a wide variety of programs from infrastructure projects (roads and bridges) to social welfare programs like SNAP (food stamps) and mortgage assistance.

In the chapters ahead we focus first on policy processes—developing and analyzing policies; enacting policies through laws, administrative rulemaking, and court decisions; implementing policies; and evaluating them to see what, if any, effects they have had. We then use the lenses of rationalism and politics to study specific social welfare policies and programs allowing you, the reader, to consider just what social welfare policy should be.

Summary

Although there are elements of rationalism in policy-making, the policy process is largely political. Our abilities to develop policies rationally are limited because we cannot agree on what constitute social problems and on what, if anything, should be done to alleviate these problems. We usually hesitate to take bold, new directions in the social welfare system, because we fear making large, costly errors that may be difficult to reverse. Occasionally, new policy directions do emerge. Social welfare policymaking is the focus of considerable attention by policymakers, social welfare advocates, and the public.

Discussion Questions and Class Activities

Track a bill or bills of interest to you through the U.S. Congress or your state legislature. If this legislative body is currently in session, you may wish to track the bill in "real" time. If not, you may wish to look at a bill and how it fared by looking back in time. Websites of the Library of Congress (see the section called "Thomas"), U.S. Senate, U.S. House of Representatives, and your state legislature contain tools to help in this process. You may also wish to consult a librarian for help. Hold a class discussion to compare what class members learned about how the bills chosen fared.

Websites

Thomas, http://www.thomas.gov/links, named for statesman Thomas Jefferson, provides federal legislative information and many related resources to the public at the Library of Congress website.

U.S. House of Representatives, http://www.house.gov, provides information on House members, committees, legislation, and votes.

U.S. Senate, http://www.senate.gov, provides information on Senate members, committees, legislation, and votes.

Notes

1. See, for example, David G. Gil, "A Systematic Approach to Social Policy Analysis," *Social Service Review*, Vol. 44, December 1970, pp. 411–426.
2. T. H. Marshall, *Social Policy* (London: Hutchison University Library, 1955), p. 7. Also see the discussion in Neil Gilbert and Paul Terrell, *Dimensions of Social Welfare Policy*, 5th ed. (Boston: Allyn and Bacon, 2002), Chapter 1. The distinction between social policy and social welfare policy is discussed in George Rohrlich, "Social Policy and Income Distribution," in Robert Morris, Ed., *Encyclopedia of Social Work*, 16th ed. (New York: National Association of Social Workers, 1971), pp. 1385–1386.
3. See Carl T. Friedrich, *Man and His Government* (New York: McGraw-Hill, 1963), p. 70; Harold Lasswell and Abraham Kaplan, *Power and Society* (New Haven, CT: Yale University Press, 1970), p. 71.
4. Heinz Eulau and Kenneth Prewitt, *Labyrinths of Democracy* (Indianapolis: Bobbs-Merrill, 1973), p. 465.
5. For an introduction to other major theoretical approaches to the study of public policy (institutionalism, incrementalism, group theory, elite theory, public choice theory, and game theory) see Thomas R. Dye, *Understanding Public Policy*, 12th ed. (Upper Saddle River, NJ: Pearson Prentice Hall, 2008), especially Chapter 2. Another set of theories or frameworks (institutional rational choice, multiple streams framework, social construction, network approach, punctuated equilibrium, and advocacy coalition) is discussed in Paul A. Sabatier, Ed., *Theories of the Policy Process*, 2nd ed. (Boulder, CO: Westview Press, 2007).
6. Edith Stokey and Richard Zeckhauser, *A Primer of Policy Analysis* (New York: Norton, 1978).
7. Herbert A. Simon, *Administrative Behavior* (New York: Macmillan, 1945), p. 79. See also his *Models of Man* (New York: Wiley, 1957) and *The Sciences of the Artificial* (New York: Wiley, 1970). Simon was trained as a political scientist; he won the Nobel Prize in economics in 1978.
8. Harold Lasswell, *Politics: Who Gets What, When, How* (New York: Free Press, 1936).
9. Edward C. Banfield and James Q. Wilson, *City Politics* (Cambridge, MA: Harvard University Press, 1963), p. 7.
10. See John Rawls, *A Theory of Justice*, rev. ed. (Cambridge, MA: Belknap Press of Harvard University Press, 1999).
11. James Madison, *The Federalist, No. X*, November 23, 1787, reprinted in *The Federalist of the New Constitution* (London: Dent, 1911), pp. 41–48.
12. Charles E. Lindblom, "The Science of 'Muddling Through,'" *Public Administration Review*, Vol. 19, Spring 1959, pp. 79–88.
13. See, for example, various chapters in Sabatier, *Theories of the Policy Process*, 2nd ed.
14. James L. True, Bryan D. Jones, and Frank R. Baumgartner, "Punctuated-Equilibrium Theory: Explaining Stability and Change in Public Policymaking," in Sabatier, *Theories of the Policy Process*, 2nd ed., pp. 155–187.
15. Malcolm Gladwell, *The Tipping Point* (New York: Little, Brown and Company, 2002), p. 9.
16. John W. Kingdon, *Agendas, Alternatives, and Public Policies*, 2nd ed. (New York, Longman, 2003).

1

POLITICS AND THE POLICYMAKING PROCESS

This chapter looks more closely at the steps in the policymaking process. Perhaps more importantly, it looks at how different ideologies shape social welfare policy, how people attempt to influence policy, and how governments acquire the funds to support their functions. Politics intervenes at every step in the policymaking process.

THE POLICYMAKING PROCESS

Policymaking involves a combination of processes. Although not always clear-cut or easily distinguishable, political scientists have identified these processes for purposes of analysis.[1] They include the following:

- *Identifying policy problems:* Publicized demands for government action can lead to identification of policy problems.
- *Formulating policy proposals:* Policy proposals can be formulated through political channels by policy-planning organizations, interest groups, government bureaucracies, state legislatures, and the president and Congress.

- *Legitimizing public policy:* Policy is legitimized as a result of the public statements or actions of government officials, both elected and appointed—the president, Congress, state legislators, agency officials, and the courts. This includes executive orders, budgets, laws and appropriations, rules and regulations, and decisions and interpretations that have the effect of setting policy directions.
- *Implementing public policy:* Policy is implemented through the activities of public bureaucracies and the expenditure of public funds.
- *Evaluating public policy:* Policies are formally and informally evaluated by government agencies, by outside consultants, by interest groups, by the mass media, and by the public.

Although this *stages* or *phases* approach to policymaking has been criticized for being too simplistic, insufficiently explicating that some phases may occur together, and not saying much about why policy turns out as it does,[2] it does provide a way to discuss many of the ways policy is constructed, carried out, evaluated, and made again. It also provides a framework for introducing theories that do suggest more about why policy turns about the way it does. All these activities include both attempts at rational problem solving and political conflict.

Identifying Policy Problems

Many factors influence the identification of policy problems. They include the methods of getting issues on the political agenda as well as keeping them off the agenda. Political ideology and special interests, the mass media, and public opinion all play roles in problem identification.

AGENDA SETTING   "Agenda setting," that is, deciding what is to be decided, is the first critical step in the policymaking process. To get on the agenda, problems must come to policymakers' attention. Problem indicators (e.g., the number of people affected by a particular problem) are often insufficient to promote policy change.[3] Some issues, such as healthcare, are already highly visible, because they affect us all, while other times crises or "focusing events" (e.g., levees breaking in New Orleans) are needed to bring problems to light.

Think of all the conditions that existed for many years that remained "nonissues," that is, they were not identified as problems for governments' consideration. The "separate but equal" doctrine that gave legitimacy to segregation by condoning the establishment of separate facilities for whites and blacks remained in place for decades until the civil rights movement swept the country. Poverty has always been with us, but it became a political issue in the 1960s with the help of television documentaries. Abortion and domestic violence would not have become part of the policy agenda without the rise of the women's movement. Without political pressure, some conditions might worsen, but they would never be identified as public problems, they would never get on policymakers' agenda, and governments would never be forced to decide what, if anything, to do about them.

Most policy issues do not just happen. Creating an issue, dramatizing it, calling attention to it, and pressuring government to do something about it are important political tactics. Influential individuals and ordinary citizens, organized interest groups, think tanks and policy-planning organizations, political candidates, and officeholders all employ the tactics of agenda setting, usually through attempts to get the mass idea to publicize the issue.

NONDECISIONS   Preventing certain conditions in society from becoming policy issues is also an important political tactic. "Nondecision making" occurs when influential individuals or groups act to prevent the emergence of challenges to their own interests in society. According to political scientists Peter Bachrach and Morton Baratz:

> Non-decision making is a means by which demands for change in the existing allocation of benefits and privileges in the community can be suffocated before they are even voiced; or kept covert; or killed before they gain access to the relevant decision-making arena; or failing all these things, maimed or destroyed in the decision-implementing stage of the policy process.[4]

Nondecision making occurs when powerful individuals, groups, or organizations act to suppress an issue because they fear that if public attention is focused on it, their best interests may suffer. Nondecision making also occurs when political candidates, officeholders, or administrative officials anticipate that powerful individuals or groups will not favor a particular idea. They therefore do not pursue the idea because they don't want to rock the boat. Such was the case with publicly supported health insurance. Until the 1960s, powerful medical lobbies were successful in blocking serious consideration of initiatives that came to be known as Medicare and Medicaid. Powerful healthcare lobbies continue to try to block proposals for government-sponsored national health insurance.

POLITICAL IDEOLOGY   Political ideology is a driving force in agenda setting. The *New Political Dictionary* defines a *conservative* as "a defender of the status quo"; "the more rigid conservative generally opposes virtually all government regulation of the economy, . . . favors local and state action over federal action, and emphasizes fiscal responsibility, most notably in the form of balanced budgets."[5] Of course, not all conservatives are this rigid. Federal deficits have ballooned under recent conservative Republican presidential administrations.

A *liberal* can be defined as "one who believes in more government action to meet individual need."[6] Liberals often want the government to do much more to promote *distributive justice*, economic as well as social. Conservatives fear that the government has already done too much in this regard, destroying individual initiative and promoting economic and other social problems. Many Americans fall somewhere in between the extremes of liberal and conservative, but it is often the most zealous individuals who organize and attempt to influence the political agenda.

A June 2009 Gallup poll found that 46 percent of Americans thought that the Democratic Party was too liberal, while 43 percent see the Republican party as too conservative.[7] Nevertheless, 42 percent of Americans said the "Democrats' ideology is 'about right,' while 34 percent say the Republicans' ideology is 'about right.'"

The Republican party platform has become highly conservative, especially on social issues such as abortion and gay rights. The 1984 Republican Contract with America was an attempt to set a socially conservative political agenda for the country. Republican members of Congress have resisted initiatives like broad-scale healthcare reform, preferring a more incremental and narrowly targeted approach, and one that focuses on private rather than public sector strategies.

Political ideology is not always pure. For example, some Republicans may favor their party's ideology on spending and taxing matters, while they may be unhappy with the party's stance on abortion and gay rights. Meanwhile, many people who espouse the liberal agenda, which remains consistent in its prochoice and pro gay rights stances, have become more cautious about government spending.

Although the term *liberal* (sometimes referred to as the "L" word) is most often associated with the Democratic party, some authors claim that liberalism is dead.[8] Democrats of more moderate or conservative persuasions may align themselves with the need for strengthening some social programs, but there are Democrats whose religious and moral convictions persuade them that access to abortion and gay rights are not issues they can support. Except for the most strident of ideologies, the lines between liberal and conservative, Democrat and Republican can be difficult to draw.

Americans have long debated the effects that out-of-wedlock births, divorce, and desertion have on the country's moral fiber. The Republican platform on traditional family matters sits quite well with the "religious right" of this country. Not content to focus on matters of religion alone, this movement, the so-called *moral majority,* has taken a high-profile stance on certain political issues, especially abortion. For example, the Christian Coalition, founded by preacher Pat Robertson, is dedicated to mobilizing Christians for political action. As one source described it, the religious right believes that "government should enforce scriptural law," while "most mainstream religious people support the separation of church and state to ensure freedom of religion and speech for all."[9] Conservative jurist Robert Bork makes the counterclaim that "all participants in politics want to 'impose' on others as much of their morality as possible, and no group is more insistent on that than liberals."[10]

Although much of the religious right would like to see less government involvement in issues such as education and public assistance, it would like more government intervention to outlaw abortion and restrict the rights of gay men and lesbians. The ranks of the religious right feel that they hold the ideal for family values in the United States, even if public opinion polls show that a majority of Americans support access to abortion on some level.[11] The public's support for marriage between same sex partners has also grown.[12]

Libertarians generally believe that governments should have very limited functions, primarily police and military protection. They are strong supporters of free market capitalism and believe that the government has no place in making laws about personal behavior—reproduction, homosexuality, and drug use—unless there is threat of harm to others. Libertarians provide a third voice in U.S. politics.

Centrists believe that political partisanship and polarization have prevented compromise that could result in more effective public policy. Centrists see themselves as encouraging moderation and compromise. President Bill Clinton fashioned himself a centrist or "New Democrat." Clinton, a Southern Baptist, was well informed about scripture. He called for a "new covenant" for social welfare that involved more job training and childcare, stiffer work requirements, and limits on the amount of time families could receive public assistance benefits—not what Americans typically think of as typical liberal rhetoric from a Democratic president.

These are some of the basic ideas of the political ideologies that frame conflict over social welfare policy in the United States. In subsequent chapters we describe more of these ideas and also consider the welfare models of social democracies in which benefits such as childcare, healthcare, and job training are far more universal in nature than they are in the United States.

SPECIAL INTERESTS   Special interest groups are a staple of the political landscape, and they do their best to influence the political agenda either directly or indirectly. Special interest groups may represent people based on race, ethnicity, gender, sexual orientation, age, income, profession, or other factors.

Many special interest groups are organized as nonprofit 501(c)(3) organizations, which limits their ability to lobby or support political candidates, but they can educate on issues of concern to them. Groups from Mothers Against Drunk Drivers to the Nature Conservancy do just that.

Other special interest groups are organized as political action committees (PACs). Some PACs are operated by corporations or trade, industry, and labor unions. Other PACs are ideological and do not have a corporate or labor sponsor. Virtually all types of social welfare interest groups have PACs, including the American Medical Association, the American Hospital Association, the National Association of Social Workers, and the American Federation of State, and County and Municipal Employees (AFSCME is a labor union affiliated with the AFL-CIO that represents many social welfare professionals).

PACs are not political party or candidate committees per se, but they support candidates that support their views, or oppose those that do not (see Illustration 1.1). Those interested in seeing specific types of legislation passed or defeated naturally support candidates who share their views. Support may come verbally through endorsements, and financially through campaign contributions. For the last 25 years, the number of federally registered PACs in the United States has been fairly constant at about 4,000.[13] Some PACs have existed for a long time; others come and go. Many report no financial contributions to candidates.

ILLUSTRATION 1.1
Women's Empowerment Political Action Committee (WePAC) Criteria for Endorsed Candidates

WePAC believes that actions count more than rhetoric. Our endorsement criteria will therefore concentrate on a candidate's record. What actions has the candidate taken to solve the problems that women face? Below are the issues we will consider.

If the candidate is an incumbent:

What legislation has the candidate introduced, co-sponsored, or voted on relating to women's issues?

For each year in the legislature, the candidate must have introduced, co-sponsored, or at least voted favorably on a bill that advances the interests or status of women.

What is the candidate's voting record on women's issues?

She or he must have a 90 percent positive voting record on women issues.

Does the makeup of the candidate's staff reflect principles of pay equity and gender equality?

The answer to this must be yes.

Has the candidate spoken out publicly in the media or on the campaign trail about women's issues, including when appropriate condemning sexism or other gender discrimination?

The answer to this must be yes.

Has the candidate supported—either by financial help or endorsements—other women candidates who also support women's issues?

The answer to this must be yes.

If the candidate is a challenger:
What activities in the candidate's past indicate that she/he is committed to women's issues?

She or he must have engaged in some activities that indicate she/he is committed to women's issues. For example, is she or he a member of any women's rights group? Has he or she worked for women's issues in state or local arenas?

Does the makeup of the candidate's campaign staff reflect principles of pay equity and gender equality?

The answer to this must be yes.

Has the candidate commented publicly or in the media or on the campaign trail about women's issues, including when appropriate condemning sexism or other gender discrimination? Does the candidate have a position on gender discrimination?

The answer to this must be yes.

(Continued)

ILLUSTRATION 1.1 (Continued)

Note on Incumbency Advantage

WePAC will endorse candidates who have been strong supporters of our issues in the legislature. Therefore, incumbents will have the advantage over challengers if they have been supporters of women's issues while in office.

By the same token, when a challenger is running against an incumbent who has been an opponent of women's issues, the challenger will also have an advantage in regards to WePAC's endorsement and support.

Source: Women's Empowerment Network, retrieved March 14, 2010, from http://www.we-pac.org/candidates/

Table 1.1 shows the top 15 political contributors from 1989 to 2010 and whether their leaning is Democrat or Republican. Note that AT&T, which is fairly well balanced in donations to Democrats and Republicans, is the all-time high political contributor at over $44 million, while AFSCME, which clearly favors Democrats, is second highest at nearly $42 million.

Special interests not only support or oppose candidates, they also want to make sure that legislation is favorable to them or that they are not adversely affected by new legislation, budget cuts, and government regulations. The Center for Responsive Politics reported that in 2009, more

TABLE 1.1 Top 15 Political Donors 1989–2010

LEGEND: Republican Democrat On the fence
= Between 40% and 59% to both parties
= Leans Dem/Repub (60%–69%)
= Strongly Dem/Repub (70%–89%)
= Solidly Dem/Repub (over 90%)

Rank	Organization	Total '89–'09	Dem %	Repub %	Tilt
1	AT&T Inc	$44,228,138	44%	55%	
2	American Fedn of State, County & Municipal Employees	$41,945,511	98%	1%	
3	National Assn of Realtors	$35,643,323	48%	51%	
4	Intl Brotherhood of Electrical Workers	$31,544,407	97%	2%	
5	Goldman Sachs	$31,544,275	64%	35%	
6	American Assn for Justice	$31,465,429	90%	9%	
7	National Education Assn	$30,162,867	92%	6%	
8	Laborers Union	$28,993,900	92%	7%	
9	Teamsters Union	$27,992,624	92%	6%	
10	Service Employees International Union	$27,933,732	95%	3%	
11	Carpenters & Joiners Union	$27,768,183	89%	10%	
12	Citigroup Inc	$27,150,883	50%	49%	
13	Communications Workers of America	$27,047,896	99%	0%	
14	American Medical Assn	$26,307,905	39%	60%	
15	American Federation of Teachers	$26,285,941	98%	0%	

Source: "Top All-Time Donors, 1989–2010," retrieved March 16, 2010, is reprinted by permission of The Center for Responsive Politics, from http://www.opensecrets.org/orgs/list.php?type=A

than 13,700 registered federal lobbyists businesses, labor unions, and other organizations spent nearly $3.5 billion lobbying Congress and federal agencies.[14]

The poor and disadvantaged, who need help the most, are not represented in Washington in the same fashion as other groups in society.[15] They rarely write letters to members of Congress, and they do not make significant campaign contributions. They are rarely found on a representative's home state lecture circuit—service club lunches, civic meetings, and dedications. The poor cannot afford to come to Washington to visit their representatives' offices. Indeed, they do not turn out at the polls to vote as often as the nonpoor.

To the extent that the poor and disadvantaged or disenfranchised are represented at all in Washington, they are usually represented by "proxies"—groups that are not poor, disadvantaged, or disenfranchised themselves but that claim to represent these groups. Among these proxy groups are the Children's Defense Fund, the National Low Income Housing Coalition, the Food Research and Action Center, the National Association of Social Workers, the Gray Panthers, and the Human Rights Campaign. For those who wish to get involved in political action, Illustration 1.2 provides suggestions for doing so.

ILLUSTRATION 1.2
Changing Policy Through Grassroots Action

This illustration provides a view of policy change from the grassroots perspective. Broad-scale political participation is essential to democracy. Money, power, and influence all play a part in the policy process, but we should never become cynical about our own participation and the effects it can have. Here are some suggestions, excerpted and adapted from the Community Tool Box, a service of the Work Group for Community Health and Development at the University of Kansas.

All policy change starts with an assumption on someone's part that current policy, or lack of policy, is not what's needed, and that the current situation is unacceptable. Policy change is difficult and time-consuming, and it may look discouraging. But, with work and dedication, policy change is possible—it happens all the time, usually because ordinary people care enough to keep at it. Here are some general guidelines for changing policies and choosing tactics. We've called them the Eight Ps:

1. Preparation: Prepare well for changing policies. Conduct the necessary research to get to know as much as possible about the issue. Make yourself and your group the acknowledged expert, the one that individuals, groups, and the media contact when they want information on your issue. Know the current policy intimately and know who actually makes and influences the policy. Know who your allies and opponents are, who's open to public pressure, and who is ideologically flexible or inflexible. Be particularly aware of who your most difficult opponents are, their arguments, and whether they are distorting the situation and your point of view, and be ready to counter their arguments and attacks.

2. Planning: Plan carefully for policy change. To ensure that your overall strategy makes sense, and that changing policies is a necessary and appropriate part of it, strategic planning is essential. If you haven't engaged in strategic planning that involves representation from all groups affected by or concerned with the issue, stop, back up, and do so now. It will take time and effort, and may result in changing some of your ideas, but it will pay huge dividends in the long run.

3. Personal contact: Establish or maintain contact with those who influence or make policy. All politics is not only local, as former House Speaker Tip O'Neill said, but all politics, at bottom is personal. Personal relationships,

(Continued)

ILLUSTRATION 1.2 (Continued)

even with opponents, are the key to successful advocacy of all kinds, and changing policy is no exception. Develop *mutual* relationships with legislators and their aides, local elected and appointed officials, key personnel at regulatory and funding agencies, national, state, and local organizations, and the media.

4. Pulse of the community: Take the pulse of the community (however the community of interest is defined) to understand what citizens will support, what they will resist, and how they can be persuaded. You will have a far greater chance of success if you set out to change policies in ways the community will support, or at least tolerate, than if you challenge people's basic beliefs. You may have to put off your final goal and work toward an intermediate one the community can support.

5. Positivism: Where you can, choose tactics that emphasize the positive. Suggesting incentives (tax breaks, for instance) for doing the right thing, rather than punishment (special taxes) for doing the wrong thing, is one way to accentuate the positive elements of a proposed change. On the other hand, research seems to show that people are more likely to take action when they have something to lose. The possibility of *both* incentives and punishment may be one to consider in some circumstances.

6. Participation: Involve as many people as possible in strategic planning and action. Try to engage key people, particularly opinion leaders and trusted community figures, but concentrate on making your effort participatory. That will give it credibility, encourage community ownership of the effort, make sure that a wide range of ideas and information are considered in developing a plan and action steps, and encourage community leadership of the effort.

7. Publicity: Use the media, the Internet, your connections, and your imagination to keep people informed of the effort and the issues, and to keep a high profile. You can use everything from straight news stories to street theater and demonstrations [or tea parties and coffee parties] to get the message out. Publicity will help you gain and maintain support, which will increase your chances of success.

8. Persistence: Policy change can take a long time. Monitor and evaluate your actions to make sure they are having the desired effect, and change them if they are not. You should be prepared to keep at it for as long as it takes if you hope to be successful.

For more information on how to use the Eight Ps to effect policy change, see The Community Tool Box at http://ctb.ku.edu/en/.

Source: Adapted by permission from "Changing Policies: An Overview," by Phil Rabinowitz and edited by Bill Berkowitz, Chapter 25, The Community Tool Box, retrieved March 15, 2010, from http://ctb.ku.edu/en/

Churches (the United States Conference of Catholic Bishops, the National Council of Churches, B'nai Brith, and others) often support programs for the poor out of a sense of moral obligation. Civil rights groups (the National Urban League, the National Association for the Advancement of Colored People, the National Council of La Raza) support programs for the poor and disadvantaged as a part of their general concern for the conditions affecting particular ethnic groups. Liberal organizations (Common Cause, Americans for Democratic Action) often support social programs out of an ideological commitment. Organized labor and social welfare program administrators and lawyers also support programs for disadvantaged groups.

Even though the clout of organized labor has waned in recent years with declining union membership, labor groups like the AFL-CIO do all the things that poor and disadvantaged members of society find difficult to do in politics: political organizing, campaign financing, letter writing, and personal lobbying. Historically, organized labor has tended to support programs for the poor, even though union pay scales have moved a great distance from the poverty line. Among those who comprise organized labor, labor leaders may be more likely to support social programs than the rank-and-file membership. Of course, the first concern of organized labor is labor legislation—labor relations, minimum wages, fair labor standards, and so on—but when labor leaders join other members of the welfare lobby in support of social programs, the result is a stronger political coalition.

AFSCME is prominent among the organizations representing social welfare program administrators. AFSCME includes many public workers whose jobs are directly affected by cutbacks in social programs. Another organization concerned about social welfare services is the Legal Service Corporation (LSC), whose attorneys provide legal assistance to poor and disadvantaged individuals. The LSC is chartered as an independent corporation, but much of its funding comes from the federal government. Conservative Congressmembers have criticized the LSC for what they perceived as lobbying on its own behalf, and Congress limited the LSC's reach by prohibiting its involvement in activities such as class action suits. Of course, there are very few government bureaucracies—from the Defense Department, to the National Aeronautics and Space Administration, to the Department of Agriculture—that do not, directly or indirectly, lobby Congress for their own programs.

Although a law passed in 1907 still makes it illegal for corporations to donate directly to federal candidates, and a 1947 law makes it illegal to use union dues to do so, one would hardly know it. In fact, in January 2010, the U.S. Supreme Court stunned many when it supported First Amendment free speech rights in ruling that corporations can spend as much as they want on political ads to support or oppose political candidates. The ruling does not affect the laws prohibiting direct donations to candidates by corporations and unions.

In 1974, Congress limited the amount of money that individuals and PACs could give to national party committees and candidates running for national offices. Some politicians refuse to accept PAC money, but these contributions remain an important feature of election campaigns. The fear, of course, is that elected officials are beholden to these special interests and this affects public policy. For this reason, many individuals concerned about political ethics advocate campaign finance reform (see Illustration 1.3).

ILLUSTRATION 1.3
Campaign Finance Reform

In an attempt to reduce the influence of special interests, Congress passed the Bipartisan Campaign Reform Act (BCRA) of 2002. BCRA prohibits national party committees from raising or spending "soft" money. Soft money used to refer to the unlimited contributions individuals, groups, and organizations could give to party committees for general purposes (e.g., voter education, ads supporting party platforms but not specific candidates) at the state and local levels. The concern was that these contributions were used to defray federal election expenses, like overhead and computer equipment, thus freeing up other money to support federal candidates.

The BCRA, championed by Republican Senator John McCain and Democratic Senator Russell Feingold, is the most sweeping federal campaign reform since Watergate era reforms were spurred by President Nixon's secret slush funds financed by business. The U.S. Constitution gives Congress the power to regulate federal elections only, but some of its provisions may have implications for state and local parties and elections.

The BCRA also addressed "hard" money, which generally refers to the amount an individual can contribute to a candidate and that can be used for any legitimate campaign purpose. The BCRA raised the amount of "hard" money an individual can contribute to a federal candidate from $1,000 to $2,000 per election (this amount is adjusted each year for inflation) and

(Continued)

ILLUSTRATION 1.3 (Continued)

limited the amount of individual contributions to PACs and national and state party committees.[a] The soft money ban does not seem to be hurting the parties, because political polarization among Americans has apparently caused many more individuals to make at least small contributions to the party of their choice.

The Federal Election Commission (FEC), charged with enforcing federal election laws, has itself been criticized for allowing campaign finance loopholes. FEC rule making is having its own effects on how the BCRA is interpreted. In May 2004, the FEC failed to take action to close the 527 organization loophole. These organizations are considered another form of soft money. During the 2004 presidential campaign, the controversy over 527s intensified following ads by the Swift Boat Veterans for Truth, a 527 organization, claiming that presidential candidate John Kerry's heroic actions during the Vietnam War had been exaggerated.

In the 2008 presidential campaign, John McCain accepted public financing for the general election, which limited him to $84 million dollars in campaign spending. Barack Obama chose not to utilize the public finance system, becoming the first major party candidate to refuse taxpayers' money for the general election. Despite the criticism Obama received for this decision, it allowed him to raise money from many donors (much of it done through the Internet). According to the Center for Responsive Politics, in September 2008 alone, Obama raised $66 million more than the $84 million McCain got for the entire general election.

Campaign finance laws are also issues in many states. Some people see these laws as efforts to limit political expression, and these efforts continue to raise legal challenges. Given the amount it takes to get elected to federal, state, and even local offices, most politicians are unlikely to impose their own caps on what they spend on election campaigns, and individuals and groups may look for ways to circumvent the law.

[a]For more details on campaign contributions, see *Citizens' Guide* (Washington, DC: Federal Election Commission, January 2009), retrieved January 12, 2010, from http://www.fec.gov/pages/brochures/citizens.shtml#how_much

THE MASS MEDIA   Deciding what is "news" and who is "newsworthy" is a powerful political weapon. There are different views of the mass media's role in political agenda setting. One view is that the media exert substantial influence in deciding what problems will be given attention and what problems will be ignored.[16] Television executives and producers and newspaper and magazine editors decide what people, organizations, and events will be given public attention. Without media coverage, the general public would not know about many of the conditions or government programs affecting those who are poor or other groups or about alternative policies or programs. Without media coverage, these topics would not likely become objects of political discussion, nor would government officials likely consider them important, even if they knew about them. Media attention creates issues and personalities. Media inattention can doom issues and personalities to obscurity. The media are key in directing attention to issues, although the consensus is that they do not change people's minds on issues as much as they influence individuals who have not yet formed an opinion.[17]

Others are less enthusiastic about the media's influence. In his classic study of agenda setting at the federal level, Kingdon found that "the media report what is going on in government, by and large, rather than having an independent effect *on* government agendas."[18]

The media, especially the major television networks, are often accused of having a liberal bias.[19] Even if this is true, today, countervailing opinions get their share of coverage from conservative television and radio commentators, talk show hosts, newspaper columnists, and special television channels devoted to their opinions. Cable TV has provided many more networks from which to choose, but corporate mergers and the loss of local, independent radio stations and newspapers also have an effect. Many cities now have just one local, daily newspaper, and newspaper subscriptions have dropped.

Even when journalists' personal views are liberal, the media that employ them are owned by powerful business interests that exert a countervailing conservative influence, and they demand a focus on what produces the most profit.[20] Many important social issues receive little coverage, or little in-depth coverage, because the media are caught up in sensationalizing other events, especially personalities such as movie stars, pop singers, and sports figures.

Public policy theorists also note the importance of policy images in agenda setting, images that combine "empirical information and emotive appeals."[21] The 1936 film *Reefer Madness* depicted lurid images of the supposed consequences of smoking marijuana. The images that the terms *drug addicts* and *crack addicts* conjure up have helped to fuel drug policies that have filled U.S. jails and prisons with unprecedented numbers of inmates. Ultrasound pictures of fetuses broadcast on television and the Internet may play a role in more restrictive abortion policies. The label *socialism* is used to dissuade Americans from supporting social welfare programs that would be more universal in nature such as government-run national health insurance.

Policy images generally work best when they are "connected to core political values and can be communicated simply and directly to the public."[22] Widely accepted policy images contribute to stability in policymaking. Public policy is more likely to undergo significant change when there are competing policy images—nuclear power as a source of economic progress or a source of environmental and human destruction;[23] those addicted to drugs as criminals or individuals in need of treatment; increased immigration as contributing to or taking away from America's vitality; disabled individuals as in need of public assistance or civil rights.

New forms of communication are also rapidly changing the way people obtain information. The Internet has become a popular source of political exchange. Websites of special interest groups and think tanks representing the spectrum of political positions abound. Anyone with an Internet connection can belong to listservs or receive Really Simple Syndication (RSS) feeds that provide continuous information on political issues. Blogging and websites like YouTube are other sources of information that give individuals unprecedented ability to post their own views for the world to read or hear. These sources may prompt interested parties to contact their legislators, attend demonstrations, or donate to groups and politicians that support their causes.

Perhaps the real danger today is that we are overwhelmed with the number of issues that have caught the media's attention and the number of groups and organizations that want us to pay attention to the issues they deem important. The media and interest groups are themselves competing for attention. Government inaction and public indifference may result when people feel that there are too many problems to consider or that problems continue to grow even when they try to intervene. The media may work most effectively to bring light to a cause when there is some consensus about the problems to be addressed. But often, such consensus is elusive.

PUBLIC OPINION   Even in a democracy, public opinion may not determine public policy, but politicians are mindful of what their constituents—particularly their powerful constituents—think. Politicians often send surveys to their constituents asking for their views on policy matters. Relatively few Americans take time to make their views known to their elected officials, but doing so might be more effective than many Americans realize.

The Gallup Poll and other polling organizations keep their finger on the pulse of the country with continuous telephone surveys of scientifically selected samples of adult Americans. Since 1935 Gallup has asked Americans what they think is the country's most important problem.

Economic issues—unemployment, inflation, high living costs—frequently top the list, although wars and international matters also prevail at times. Public opinion polls also consider Americans' views on specific policy issues such as taxes, the budget deficit, or healthcare. The public, like politicians, frequently do not agree on public policy issues, and their own views are often inconsistent. For example, an analysis of public opinion surveys showed that although Americans tend to express resentment for "welfare" programs, they also say that they want to help people in need.[24]

Formulating Policy Proposals

Policy proposals can be formulated through political channels by policy-planning organizations, interest groups, government bureaucracies, state legislatures, and the president and Congress. Since neither Congress nor state legislatures can continuously attend to all policy issues, much policymaking is done in relative obscurity by groups of specialists that may be called *iron triangles, policy subsystems,* or *issue networks,* but some policy issues do "catch fire."[25] "Average citizens" certainly have policy preferences, but in most areas of governments, policy is highly complex and generally requires the efforts of those whose careers are devoted to particular policy subsystems.[26]

Kingdon likens the process of selecting policy alternatives to a process of "biological natural selection":

> Many ideas are possible in principle, and float around in a "policy primeval soup" in which specialists try out their ideas in a variety of ways—bill introductions, speeches, testimony, papers, and conversation. . . . [These] proposals . . . come into contact with one another, are revised and combined . . . , and floated again. But the proposals that survive to that status of serious consideration meet several criteria, including their technical feasibility, their fit with dominant values and the current national mood, their budgetary workability, and the political support or opposition they might experience.[27]

Legitimizing Public Policy

Policy is legitimized as a result of the public statements or actions of government officials, both elected and appointed—the president, Congress, state legislators, agency officials, and the courts. This includes executive orders, budgets, laws and appropriations, rules and regulations, and administrative and court decisions that set policy directions.

Kingdon found that as problems are being identified and certain policy proposals float to the top, the political climate—the current national mood, interest group pressure or lack of pressure, and who is in office—must all converge for a proposal to be adopted.[28] These forces may serendipitously align to produce such a "policy window," but policy entrepreneurs try to seize the opportunity to bring these forces to bear for a new policy or a policy change to occur.

In Congress and in state legislatures, the leaders of each chamber, committee chairmen, and the party that holds the majority of seats in each chamber play critical roles in determining which bills will be given consideration. As bills are assigned to committees, hearings are held and invited experts provide testimony, or members of the public may voice their opinions. Legislators negotiate, compromise, trade votes, filibuster, and engage in other activities that Americans generally think of as "politics." The process may seem chaotic, and often it is, but some legislation does get passed. Other forms of policymaking—court decisions, Executive Orders, rulemaking—occur through bureaucratic processes and often outside the public spotlight, but they are no less political because groups view themselves as winners or losers in these processes, too.

Implementing Public Policy

Policy implementation includes all the activities that result from the official adoption of a policy. Policy implementation is what happens after a law is passed. We should never assume that the passage of a law is the end of the policymaking process. Sometimes laws are passed and nothing happens! Sometimes laws are passed and executive agencies, presuming to act under these laws, do a great deal more than Congress ever intended. Political scientist Robert Lineberry writes,

> The implementation process is not the end of policy-making, but a *continuation of policy-making by other means.* When policy is pronounced, the implementation process begins. What happens in it may, over the long run, have more impact on the ultimate distribution of policy than the intentions of the policy's framers.[29]

Traditionally, public policy implementation was the subject matter of public administration. And traditionally, administration was supposed to be free of politics. Indeed, the separation of "politics" from "administration" was once thought to be the cornerstone of a scientific approach to administration. But today it is clear that politics and administration cannot be separated. Opponents of policies do not end their opposition after a law is passed. They continue their opposition in the implementation phase of the policy process by opposing attempts to organize, fund, staff, regulate, direct, and coordinate the program. If opponents are unsuccessful in delaying or halting programs in implementation, they may seek to delay or halt them in endless court battles (school desegregation and abortion policy are certainly cases in point). In short, conflict is a continuing activity in policy implementation.

In the course of implementing public policy, federal bureaucracies have decided such important questions as the extent to which women and members of particular ethnic groups will benefit from affirmative action programs in education and employment, whether opposition political parties or candidates will be allowed on television to challenge a presidential speech or press conference, and whether welfare agencies will search Social Security Administration files to locate parents that do not support their children. Congress or the courts can overturn decisions of bureaucracies if sufficient opposition develops, but most bureaucratic decisions go unchallenged. There are analogous layers of bureaucracy at the state and local levels.

Evaluating Social Welfare Policy

Over the years, increasing numbers of formal evaluations of social policies have been conducted. Governments, especially the federal government, have spent millions of dollars to determine if the policies and programs they have initiated are having effects. In discussing these studies in the chapters that follow, it is evident that program evaluations can produce their own political fallout. There may be disagreements about study methodology, and people with different views will interpret the same study results differently. Policy evaluations can be helpful to policymakers, but they usually do not solve political controversies or change deeply held values.[30]

FINANCING THE WELFARE STATE

Prior to the Great Depression, local and state governments shouldered the major public responsibility for social welfare programs. Since 1935 there have been important changes in the way most social welfare programs are established and funded. Although federal, state, and local social welfare expenditures have all increased, the federal government now finances the major share of social insurance and public assistance benefits, while states and local governments pay for most public safety and public school education costs.

Federal Taxes

Governments fund their activities, from social welfare to defense, through the taxes they collect. In 2010, if we did not count the major borrowing that occurred due to the country's economic crisis, individual income taxes were the largest single source (45 percent) of federal government revenues (budget receipts) (see Figure 1.1). Until 1913 there was some sporadic but no regular collection of income tax by the federal government.[31] When regular income tax collection began, only one percent of Americans were assessed income taxes. By 1930 income taxes made up 60 percent of the federal government's receipts. Since 1990, income taxes have accounted for 43 to 50 percent of federal budget revenues. Income taxes are channeled to the

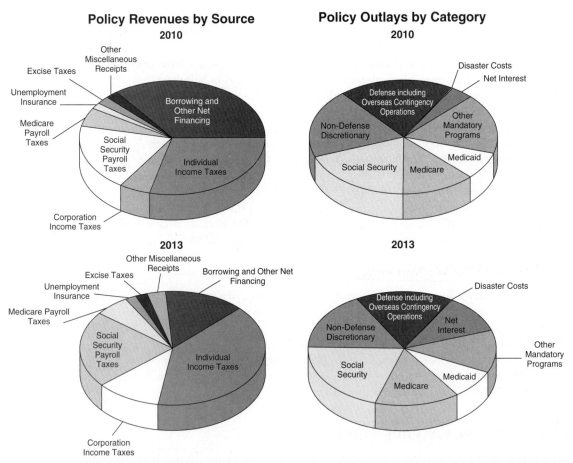

FIGURE 1.1   Budget of the United States Government: Where It Comes From and Where It Goes, 2010 and 2013 (figures are estimates)   *Source: Budget of the United States Government,* Fiscal Year 2010, Updated Summary Tables (Washington, DC: Office of Management and Budget, May 2009), retrieved March 16, 2010, from http://www. gpoaccess.gov/usbudget/fy10/pdf/summary.pdf

federal government's general revenue fund, which is used for many purposes, among them, financing public assistance programs.

The second major source of revenue the federal government collects is the Social Security tax. This special tax is levied against an individual's salary or wages and is used to finance the country's major social insurance programs (also see Chapter 5). Social insurance taxes were enacted in 1935. In 2010 they constituted an estimated 40 percent of the federal government's revenues (excluding borrowing) and have ranged from 32 to 40 percent since 1990.

The federal government also collects revenues through corporate income taxes, excise taxes (taxes on products), and other sources. In 2010 corporate income taxes accounted for an estimated 8 percent of government receipts and have ranged from 8 to 15 percent since 1990. While customs duties and estate taxes were once the federal government's major source of revenues, in 2010, excise taxes were an estimated 3 percent of revenues and customs duties and estate and gift taxes combined were less than 2 percent. Clearly, individual Americans shoulder the major federal tax burden through the personal income taxes and Social Security taxes they pay.

State Taxes

Although their overall financial role is smaller, the states are important players in social welfare, especially with respect to some of the major public assistance and social service programs. The states also collect taxes in several ways. Like the federal government, most states levy a personal income tax. Seven states (Alaska, Florida, Nevada, South Dakota, Texas, Washington, and Wyoming) have no state income tax, and New Hampshire and Tennessee levy income taxes against dividend and interest income only. State income tax rates are lower than federal rates. While federal income taxes range from 10 to 35 percent of income, state income taxes range from less than 1 percent to 9.5 percent.[32] The sales tax is another major mechanism that states use to generate revenue for their functions, including social welfare services.

Local Taxes

At the local level, the property tax is the major source of revenue. Local governments (cities, counties, and municipalities) provide the smallest share of social welfare services. These governments are mainly concerned with providing other services, such as public school education and police and fire protection.

Other Revenue Streams

Other ways governments may raise revenues are license fees, toll roads, park entrance fees, state lotteries, fines for parking and traffic tickets or crimes, and fees charged to probationers to have their cases monitored. Occasionally, a portion of such fees is dedicated for social welfare programs. For example, some marriage license fees may be used to support battered women's shelters or family violence programs, or some state lottery ticket sales may go to support public schools.

Who Pays? Who Benefits?

At each level of government, there is always concern about the types of taxes that should be used to generate revenues, who should pay those taxes and how much they should pay, and who should benefit from them. Some taxes are *progressive* (people with more income or resources are taxed at a higher rate than people with less income or resources), and others are *regressive* (people with less income or resources pay a higher percentage of their income or resources than those with more income or resources). The Social Security tax and sales tax are regressive. Federal and state income taxes are progressive, although they are less progressive than some people think they should be.

Many people believe that there are two distinct groups of citizens in the United States—those who pay taxes and those who receive welfare. Citizens for Tax Justice (CTJ) found that in 2009, when federal (including income and payroll), state, and local taxes are considered, Americans in each income bracket are paying taxes that are basically equal in proportion to the share of income they receive.[33] Thus, CTJ notes that all Americans pay taxes of some sort. It can also be said that "everyone is on welfare" because the government helps all people, some directly through social welfare programs, others through various tax incentives.[34] In fact, these tax breaks, also called tax expenditures, have been called "the equivalent of entitlement programs administered by the Internal Revenue Service."[35]

Government-sponsored social welfare programs (public assistance and social insurance) comprise the bulk of help to the poorest citizens. Low-income workers may benefit from the *earned income tax credit* (EITC; a special tax rebate paid to low-income workers through the Internal Revenue Service). Tax credits are a popular way of helping those in need because they reward work, make use of the existing tax system, and impact a broader segment of the population than public assistance.

Much of the social welfare assistance the middle classes receive comes in the form of tax deductions for the mortgage interest paid on their home and for property taxes. Many middle-class employees also receive fringe benefits from their employers (such as healthcare and retirement plans) offered by employers. Most people don't call these benefits "welfare" since governments don't provide them, but workers generally do not pay taxes on health insurance premiums paid by their employers or on retirement contributions their employer makes. In fact, "fringe" is no longer a good word for these benefits, because they comprise a substantial employment and tax benefit. Those in the middle classes may also receive deductions for things like contributions to individual retirement accounts or interest on student loans.

Workers also benefit from such provisions as the dependent care *tax credit.* The primary example is a deduction for working families who pay for childcare. This credit is available to most workers, but those in low-income tax brackets use it less frequently because the costs of childcare may be beyond their reach. Some have called for eliminating this credit for upper-income workers in order to increase tax revenues and to concentrate more resources on poorer families. There have also been suggestions for expanding the dependent care tax credit to offer more incentives for families to care for their aged and disabled members, rather than rely on public assistance programs like Medicaid that cover the costs of custodial nursing home care for those who are poor.

Some tax loopholes (such as certain deductions for real estate investment losses and business-related entertainment) that were used primarily by wealthier Americans have been narrowed or closed over the years. But the well-to-do also get much of their government assistance from tax deductions. Some of these deductions are for the mortgage interest paid on second (as well as first) homes and for property taxes and charitable contributions. These deductions are also very important for the middle class, but the wealthy generally have more to deduct. Because all Americans pay taxes in proportion to their income, Citizens for Tax Justice notes that the U.S. tax system is not very progressive at all.

Finally, while businesses pay corporate taxes, they also receive government assistance such as federal contracts, farm subsidies, and various tax deductions. This is called *corporate welfare.* Although some of this help goes to small-business owners who might be struggling to get by, much of it goes to more affluent business owners. Government tax deductions also help to offset the cost of fringe benefits that employers pay to workers. Some corporations also take advantage of offshore tax sheltering that reduces their tax liability.

As a percentage of the country's gross domestic product, the United States has among the lowest corporate tax rates of industrialized nations.[36] We have all heard accounts of how some large, wealthy corporations avoid paying taxes, but the government bailouts of financial institutions following the economic crisis that hit in the fall of 2008 are perhaps the prime examples of corporate welfare. Considered in this way, all groups benefit from government assistance. In fact, it can be argued that much of the income redistribution that results from public policy favors the more rather than the less affluent.

In addition, while Americans may complain a lot about paying taxes, the average U.S. worker pays a lower tax rate than do workers in 21 of the 30 countries that are members of the Organization for Economic Cooperation and Development (OECD).[37] Many of these countries have more generous social welfare systems than the United States.

The Budget: A Government's Most Important Policy Statement

The budget is the single most important policy statement of any government. The expenditure or outlay side of the budget tells us who gets what in public money, and the revenue side of the budget tells us who pays the cost. There are few government activities or programs that do not require an expenditure of funds, and no public funds may be spent without legislative authority. The budgetary process provides a mechanism for reviewing government programs, assessing their costs, relating them to financial resources, and making choices among expenditures. Budgets determine what programs and policies are to be increased, decreased, allowed to lapse, initiated, or renewed. The budget lies at the heart of all public policies.

In the federal government, the Office of Management and Budget (OMB), located in the Executive Office of the President, has the key responsibility for budget preparation. OMB begins preparing a budget more than a year before the beginning of the fiscal year for which it is intended (for example, work began in January 2010 on the budget for the fiscal year beginning October 1, 2011 and ending September 30, 2012). Budget materials and general instructions go out from OMB to departments and agencies, which are required to submit their budget requests for increases or decreases in existing programs and for new programs to OMB. With requests for spending from departments and agencies in hand, OMB begins its own budget review. Hearings are held for each agency. Top agency officials support their requests as convincingly as possible. On rare occasions, a dissatisfied department head may ask the OMB director to present the department's case directly to the president. As the following January approaches, the president and the OMB director devote a great deal of time to the budget document, which is nearing its final stages of assembly. Then, by the first Monday in February, the president sends his proposal—*The Budget of the United States Government*—to the Congress. After the budget is in Congress's hands, the president may recommend further amendments as needs dictate.[38]

Congress has established separate House and Senate Budget Committees and a joint Congressional Budget Office (CBO) to review the president's budget after its submission to Congress. The CBO was created "to check OMB's growing power" in the budget process.[39] The House and Senate Budget Committees initially draft a concurrent resolution setting target totals to guide congressional actions on appropriations and revenue bills considered throughout the year. Thus, congressional committees considering specific budget appropriations have the president's recommendations to guide them and the guidelines of the budget committees. If an appropriations bill exceeds the target set by the earlier resolution, it is sent back to the budget committees for reconciliation.

Considering specific appropriations is a function of the Appropriations Committee in each house. Both of these important committees have about ten fairly independent subcommittees to review the budget requests of particular agencies or groups of related functions. These subcommittees hold hearings in which department and agency officials, interest groups, and other witnesses testify about new and existing programs and proposed increases or decreases in spending. The appropriations subcommittees are very important, because neither the full committees nor the Congress has the time or expertise to conduct in depth reviews of programs and funding. Although the full committee reviews the work of the subcommittees, and the full Congress must pass the appropriations acts, in practice, most subcommittee decisions are routinely accepted.

Even after all its work, Congress usually makes no more than small changes in the total budget figure recommended by the president. Of course much of the federal budget is "uncontrollable." Congress has made long-term commitments in programs like Social Security and Medicare, some public assistance programs, and other items like interest on the national debt. About two-thirds of the budget falls into the mandatory spending category, but the other one-third is discretionary, including military spending.[40] Major struggles do ensue over particular programs. On some social welfare spending issues (big ones like Medicare and smaller ones like the volunteer service program called AmeriCorps), budget battles have been especially acrimonious. Political partisanship is contributing to an increasingly contentious budget process, but given the number of appropriations to be made, most are still determined by executive agencies interacting with the OMB. Congress usually makes only minor adjustments in them.

If this description of the federal government's budget process makes it sound as though it were the most rational aspect of policymaking, nothing could be further from the truth. The budget process is no less political than other aspects of policymaking. This is because government spending is very big business. Methods such as "planning, programming, and budgeting systems," "zero-based budgeting," and performance-based budgeting have been introduced over the years to make budgeting more rational, but in the long run,

> if politics is regarded in part as conflict over whose preferences shall prevail in the determination of national policy, then the budget records the outcomes of this struggle . . . . The size and shape of the budget is a matter of serious contention in our political life. Presidents, political parties, administrators, congressmen, interest groups, and interested citizens vie with one another to have their preferences recorded in the budget. The victories and defeats, the compromises and the bargains, the realms of agreement and the spheres of conflict in regard to the role of the national government in our society all appear in the budget. In the most integral sense, budgeting—that is, attempts to allocate scarce financial resources through political processes in order to realize disparate visions of the good life—lies at the heart of the political process.[41]

The pie charts in Figure 1.1 tell us where the federal government's money comes from and where it goes. In fiscal year 2010, the federal government's total estimated receipts (taxes collected) were about $2.3 trillion while its estimated outlays or expenditures were an estimated $3.6 trillion, leaving a deficit of about $1.3 trillion.[42]

Each year's annual federal budget deficit accumulates into the federal debt. The gross federal debt is made up of two parts: the public debt (the amount the government owes the public from whom it borrowed money to pay for past annual budget deficits) and debt held by government accounts (the amount of money the federal government borrowed from itself, largely from government trust funds). Although both are important, it is public debt that takes the most direct toll on the economy.[43] The biggest domestic worries of the federal government are how to manage spending and how to meet the needs of the American people within budgetary constraints, and at the same time keep the economy strong.

When the federal government spends more than it takes in, it must borrow money by selling U.S. Treasury bonds or bills to the public (or by taking money from its trust funds). The interest that must be paid to the public on these debts drains money that could fuel the economy through expenditures on transportation, education, technology, health, nutrition, or other public needs. With less money available for investment and for others to borrow, interest rates, and, in turn, inflation, are subject to increases, thus inhibiting economic growth.

Although some level of federal borrowing may be necessary or even desirable, the gravity of the federal debt can be difficult to appreciate. Most of us cannot really comprehend what trillions of dollars mean. One way to put it is that at the beginning of 2010, the national public debt was more than $12 trillion and was mounting at a rate of about $4 billion a day, and the U.S. government owed about $40,000 per person.[44] At this same time, the federal government was taking in enough to spend $7,775 per person, but was spending nearly $12,000 per person.[45]

Congress's failure to balance the federal budget has led to talk of a balanced budget amendment to the U.S. Constitution to force its hand. Proponents believe it is the only way to ensure that the government reduces its debt. Opponents feel it would hamstring the federal government in times of war or recession when deficit spending might be necessary. In 1996, a balanced budget amendment proved to be a real cliff hanger in Congress, but it and subsequent attempts have failed to be enacted.

Social Security trust funds and mechanisms like "off-budget" items mask much of what the federal government owes. People disagree on the importance of a balanced budget and the federal debt. Balancing the federal budget is not like balancing the household budget. Unlike you and me, the federal government can print money and manipulate the economy. But most people probably agree that the country is better off when the federal government is not constantly operating in the minus column. In good economic times, Congress and the president like to indulge in self-congratulatory behavior and take the credit for the country's prosperity. U.S. budgetary policy and monetary policy (the work of the Federal Reserve Board) are important; however, some of the country's economic state depends on factors like the health of the stock market and international events such as occurred on September 11, 2001, factors over which government has far less control.

Summary

Politics intervenes at every stage of the policymaking process. Many energetic lobbies and political action committees in the United States work to influence elected officials every day. Politicians' work is difficult because the values espoused by competing interest groups can differ widely. When it comes to social welfare policy, Americans represent the political spectrum from conservatives to middle-of-the-road centrists to liberals. This diversity of opinion causes the country to pursue a pluralist approach to social welfare policymaking. Policymakers follow several lines of thinking and arrive at policies and programs that are often contradictory and overlapping because they try to see that there is something there for everyone.

Social welfare policy development and implementation are much more a political "art and craft"[46] than a rational science. It is not enough for human service professionals to know the needs of people and to want to pass policies and provide services to help them. Policy advocates for the disenfranchised must both understand the political process and be adept at working within it if they are to have a voice in shaping social policy.

Discussion Questions and Class Activities

1. Go to the website of PollingReport.com, http://www.pollingreport.com, and select polls on topics of interest to you (e.g., healthcare reform, the Obama administration, U.S. involvement in Iraq). How do the various polls on these topics compare with your opinions of the issues? Why do you think your opinions are similar to or different from those of the majority of Americans? If you have not done so already, you may also wish to compare your views on issues with those of your elected federal, state, and local representatives.
2. This chapter discussed the federal budget. Study the budget of your state government. Look particularly at the sources of revenues and the categories of expenditures. What portion of the budget is allocated to social welfare versus other functions? You may wish to invite a speaker from the state budget office to discuss the state's budget process.
3. Invite representatives of grassroots political organizations that represent various constituencies to talk with your class about their points of view and the strategies they use to effect policy change.
4. Observe or participate in one or more political events in your community—a demonstration, rally, march; city council, county commission, or school board meeting; candidate rally; political party meeting; or other event. Who spoke at the event, who was present, what points of view were presented, what tactic or tactics were used to persuade others toward a particular point of view? Think about how the views presented fit or did not fit with your own. Did your views change as a result of what you observed and heard?
5. Peruse the website of the Center for Responsive Politics, http://www.opensecrets.org, for information on top political donors in federal elections and other information the site provides. Study federal campaign laws and your state's campaign finance laws. Have a class discussion on whether there should be restrictions on individual, PAC, and corporate contributions and how political campaigns should be financed. You may wish to invite people who have run for office in your community to discuss the methods they used to raise campaign contributions and their views on campaign finance.

Websites

Center for Responsive Politics, http://www.opensecrets.org, is a nonpartisan, nonprofit organization that tracks money in U.S. politics to educate voters and make government more transparent and responsive.

Community Toolbox, http://ctb.ku.edu/en, provides many useful tools for those who wish to promote and influence policies and programs.

Federal Election Commission, http://www.fec.gov/about.shtml, is an independent regulatory agency created by Congress to administer and enforce the Federal Election Campaign Act.

Office of Management and Budget (OMB), http://www.whitehouse.gov/omb, assists the president in preparing the federal budget and supervises its administration in Executive Branch agencies.

Notes

1. See Charles O. Jones, *An Introduction to the Study of Public Policy,* 2nd ed. (North Scituate, MA: Duxbury Press, 1978).

2. Paul A. Sabatier, Ed., *Theories of the Policy Process,* 2nd ed. (Westview Press, 2007), p. 7; see also Peter L. Hup and Michael J. Hill, "The Three Action Levels of Governance: Re-framing the Policy Process Beyond the Stages Model," in B. Guy Peters and Jon Pierre, Eds., *Handbook of Public Policy* (Thousand Oaks, CA: Sage, 2006), pp. 13–30.

3. The remainder of this paragraph relies on John W. Kingdon, *Agendas, Alternatives, and Public Policies,* 2nd ed. (New York, Longman, 2003), see chapter 5.

4. Peter Bachrach and Morton S. Baratz, *Power and Poverty* (New York: Oxford University Press, 1979), p. 7.

5. William Safire, *New Political Dictionary* (New York: Random House, 1993).

6. *Ibid.*

7. Jeffrey M. Jones, More Americans See Democratic Party as "Too Liberal," Gallup, June 30, 2009. Retrieved January 11, 2010, from http://www.gallup.com/poll/121307/more-americans-see-democratic-party-too-liberal.aspx

8. H. W. Brands, *The Strange Death of American Liberalism* (New York: Yale University Press, 2001). For other views of liberalism, see John Rawls' *Political Liberalism* (New York: Columbia University Press, 1993).

9. "Unmasking Religious Right Extremism," *American Association of University Women Outlook,* Summer 1994, pp. 20–25.

10. Robert Bork, *Slouching toward Gomorrah: Modern Liberalism and American Decline* (New York: ReganBooks, 1996), p. 337.

11. "Abortion and Birth Control," Washington Post Poll, November 19–23, 2009. Retrieved January 11, 2009, from http://www.pollingreport.com/abortion.htm.

12. "Same-Sex Marriage, Gay Rights," PollingReport.com. Retrieved January 11, 2009, from http://www.pollingreport.com/civil.htm

13. The remainder of this paragraph relies on Federal Election Commission, "Number of PAC's Increases," Washington, DC: August 12, 2008, retrieved February 2, 2009, from http://www.fec.gov/press/press2008/20080812paccount.shtml

14. Center for Responsive Politics, "Lobbying Database," Retrieved March 15, 2010, from http://www.opensecrets.org/lobby/index.php

15. Paragraphs on lobbying on behalf of the poor and disadvantaged rely on Bill Keller, "Special Treatment No Longer Given Advocates for the Poor," *Congressional Quarterly Weekly,* Vol. 39, No. 16, April 18, 1981, pp. 659–664.

16. Thomas R. Dye and Harmon Zeigler, *American Politics in the Media Age,* 3rd ed. (Monterey, CA: Brooks/Cole, 1989).

17. See Thomas R. Dye, *Understanding Public Policy,* 12th ed. (Upper Saddle River, NJ: Pearson Prentice Hall, 2008); Morris P. Fiorina and Paul E. Peterson, *The New American Democracy,* alternate 2nd ed. (New York: Longman, 2002).

18. Kingdon, *Agendas, Alternatives, and Public Policies,* p. 59.

19. Bernard Goldberg, *Bias: A CBS Insider Exposes How the Media Distort the News* (Washington, DC: Regnery Publishing, 2002); Christopher Hewitt, "Estimating the Number of Homeless: Media Misrepresentations of an Urban Problem," *Journal of Urban Affairs,* Vol. 18, No. 3, 1996, pp. 431–447, especially p. 440.

20. Fiorina and Peterson, *The New American Democracy.*

21. James L. True, Bryan D. Jones, and Frank R. Baumgartner, "Punctuated-Equilibrium Theory: Explaining Stability and Change in Public Policymaking," in Sabatier, *Theories of the Policy Process,* 2nd ed., pp. 155–187; quote from p. 161.

22. Frank R. Baumgartner and Bryan D. Jones, *Agendas and Instability in American Politics* (Chicago: University of Chicago Press, 1993) paraphrased in True et al., "Punctuated-Equilibrium Theory: Explaining Stability and Change in Public Policymaking," p. 159.

23. See True et al., "Punctuated-Equilibrium Theory: Explaining Stability and Change in Public Policymaking."

24. R. Kent Weaver, Robert Y. Shapiro, and Lawrence R. Jacobs, "Welfare (The Polls-Trends), *Public Opinion Quarterly,* Vol. 59, No. 4, 1995, pp. 606–627; also see Robert Weissberg, "Why Policymakers Should Ignore Public Opinion Polls," *Policy Analysis,* No. 2 (Washington, DC: Cato Institute, May 29, 2001). Retrieved January 15, 2009, from http://www.cato.org/pubs/pas/pa402.pdf

25. True et al., "Punctuated-Equilibrium Theory: Explaining Stability and Change in Public Policymaking," p. 158.

26. On the issue of policy specialists, also see Paul A. Sabatier and Christopher Weible, "The Advocacy Coalition Framework," in Sabatier, *Theories of the Policy Process,* pp. 189–220.

27. Kingdon, *Agendas, Alernatives, and Public Policies,* pp. 19–20.

28. *Ibid.*

29. Robert L. Lineberry, *American Public Policy* (New York: Harper & Row, 1977), p. 71.

30. On the issue of deeply held beliefs in the policy process, see Sabatier and Weible, "The Advocacy Coalition Framework."

31. This section relies on Budget of the United States Government: Historical Tables, Washington, DC: Executive Office of the President, 2008. Retrieved January 30, 2009, from http://www.gpoaccess.gov /usbudget/fy09/pdf/hist.pdf; also see History of the U.S. Tax System, Washington, DC: U.S. Department of the Treasury, no date, retrieved Janaury 30, 2009, from http://www.treas.gov/education/fact-sheets /taxes/ustax.shtml

32. "State Individual Income Taxes" (Washington, DC: Federation of Tax Administrators, March 2008), retrieved January 12, 2010, from http://www.taxadmin .org/fta/rate/ind_inc.pdf

33. Citizens for Tax Justice, "All Americans Pay Taxes" (Washington, DC: Author, April 15, 2010). Retrieved May 7, 2010, from http://www.ctj.org/pdf /taxday2010.pdf

34. Mimi Abramovitz, "Everyone Is on Welfare: The Role of Redistribution in Social Welfare Revisited," *Social Work,* Vol. 28, No. 6, 1983, pp. 440–445; Richard M. Titmuss, "The Role of Redistribution in Social Policy," *Social Security Bulletin,* Vol. 39, 1965, pp. 14–20.

35. Committee on Ways and Means, U.S. House of Representatives, *Overview of the Federal Tax System, 1993 edition* (Washington, DC: U.S. Government Printing Office, 1993), p. 263.

36. Igor Greenwald, "High Corporate Tax Rate Is Misleading," *The Wall Street Journal,* January 25, 2008, retrieved March 14, 2010, from http: //www.smartmoney.com/investing/economy /high-corporate-tax-rate-is-misleading-22463

37. "Taxes on the Average Worker," *OECD Factbook 2009: Economic, Environmental and Social Statistics* (Paris: Organization for Economic Cooperation and Development), retrieved March 14, 2010, from http: //oberon.sourceoecd.org/vl=3232222/cl=29/nw=1 /rpsv/factbook2009/10/04/02/index.htm

38. Bill Heniff, Jr., "The Role of the President in Budget Development" (Washington, DC: Congressional Research Services, August 28, 2003). Retrieved May 7, 2010, from http://www.rules.house.gov/archives /RS20179.pdf

39. Fiorina and Peterson, *The New American Democracy,* p. 427.

40. "Federal Budget Timeline" (Northampton, MA: National Priorities Project, n.d.). Retrieved May 7, 2010, from http://www.nationalpriorities.org/fed- eral%20budget%20timeline

41. Aaron Wildavsky, *The New Politics of the Budgetary Process* (Glenview, IL: Scott Foresman, 1988), p. 8; see also Kurt M. Thurmaier and Katherine G. Willoughby, *Policy and Politics in State Budgeting* (Armonk, NY: M. E. Sharpe, 2001).

42. Office of Management and Budget, *Budget of the United States Government 2010,* Historical Tables, Table 1.1 (Washington, DC: Office of the President, May 2009). Retrieved January 15, 2009, from http:// www.whitehouse.gov/omb/budget/Historicals

43. Much of the discussion of the federal debt in this section relies on Executive Office of the President, *Budget of the United States Government, Analytical Perspectives, Fiscal Year 1995* (Washington, DC: U.S. Government Printing Office, 1994), p. 186.

44. This information is from the U.S. National Debt Clock, retrieved January 15, 2010, from http://www .brillig.com/debt_clock

45. These figures are based on a U.S. population of 300 million and estimates for 2010 budget receipt and outlay figures from Office of Management and Budget, *Budget of the United States Government, 2010,* Table 1.1 (Washington, DC: Office of the President). Retrieved January 15, 2010, from http: //www.whitehouse.gov/omb/budget/Historicals

46. Aaron Wildavsky, *The Art and Craft of Policy Analysis* (Boston: Little, Brown, 1979).

2 | ANALYZING, IMPLEMENTING, AND EVALUATING SOCIAL WELFARE POLICY

Americans were once confident that if Congress adopted a policy and appropriated money for it, and the executive branch organized a program, hired people, spent money, and carried out the activities designed to implement the policy, then the effects of these policies would be those that Congress intended. Today, Americans are much more skeptical about governments' ability to solve social problems. Given the scrutiny public policy gets, this chapter takes a deeper look at the politics of policy analysis, implementation, and evaluation.

THE POLITICS OF POLICY ANALYSIS

Prudence dictates that before Congress or any other legislative body passes a law, the proposed policy should be carefully studied to determine what its likely effects, including its monetary and social costs, might be. This activity is referred to as policy analysis. Policy analysis is generally defined as a rational activity. Consider these definitions from contemporary texts:

> *Policy analysis* is a process of multidisciplinary inquiry designed to create, critically assess, and communicate information that is useful in understanding and improving policies.[1]

> Policy analysis [is] the *process* through which we identify and evaluate alternative policies or programs that are intended to lessen or resolve social, economic, or physical problems.[2]

Rational policy analysis involves asking good questions about the problem to be solved and the proposals to remedy it. Dozens of techniques or methods can be employed in policy analysis. Some are relatively straightforward. For example "back-of-the-envelope calculations" are "simple ways to estimate numbers that are important to defining the direction and magnitude of a problem."[3] Other techniques are much more complex, such as various forms of theoretical or statistical modeling used to forecast or predict the future. For example, Social Security officials predict the future of the program based on different sets of assumptions about how well the economy will perform, how the demographic composition of the population is expected to change, and other factors.

Analysts often provide side-by-side comparisons of policy alternatives to help decision makers and the public compare and contrast various policy proposals. In totalitarian regimes, such comparisons are not necessary, or if they are used, the analysis is clearly one-sided in favor of the government leader's preferred policy. Even in a country like the United States where scientists and the public have access to vast quantities of information, it has been noted that "in many of the most important cases, analysts simply do not know the relationship between policies, policy outcomes, and the values in terms of which such outcomes should be assessed."[4] Nevertheless, governments, think tanks, and advocacy groups frequently engage in policy analysis. Chapter 1 discussed steps in a rational approach to policymaking. Let's look more closely at the steps in a typical rational model of policy analysis.

1. How is the problem defined?   Before policy analysts can proceed with analyzing proposed policies, a problem must be identified and defined in some way. The introduction to this book noted that defining the problem to be addressed is at the heart of the political process. Some so-called policy analysts are really partisan players seeking to present their point of view. Others work for think tanks that have a particular ideological leaning (liberal, conservative, etc.) on policy issues. Other policy analysts are employed by nonpartisan governmental entities such as the Congressional Budget Office. Theoretically, at least, policy analysts should refrain from imposing their own definition of a policy problem, although they might offer ideas about how to improve on measuring the problem more precisely. Often, however, the task of crafting some kind of workable definition falls to policy analysts, even though political debate often ensues over their choice.

Sometimes analysts consider the possible effects of a policy proposal using different definitions of the problem. In determining, for example, how proposed changes to the Supplemental Nutrition Assistance Program (SNAP or food stamps) might affect the number of people living in poverty, analysts may use several definitions (measures) of poverty since there is substantial disagreement over whether the government's official poverty measure is the best one to use. Some groups are still likely to contend that the definitions used were deficient or do not reflect their views.

Some problem indicators are readily available (e.g., the number of people who had no insurance coverage in the previous year), although most are subject to a certain amount of error (e.g., people may fail to recall whether they had insurance coverage at some point during the year). Other times, information is difficult to acquire because a population is hidden (e.g., people who use IV drugs or are homeless), or a problem is so recently identified that hard data are difficult to obtain. Of course, data can also be manipulated or certain points emphasized to promote a particular point of view. All these factors must be considered in defining a problem.

2. What is the nature or cause of the problem? It is not enough to know how many people are affected by a problem. To effectively connect policy solutions to a problem, it is often necessary to know what social, economic, political, environmental, health, or other conditions spawned the problem. Why, for example, are so many people with disabilities unemployed? Is it because they feel their disabilities are too severe to engage in gainful employment, they fear losing public benefits, or that employers do not see that they can do the job? Social problems often defy simple explanations. Multiple forces often interact to cause a problem, but often problems are portrayed in rather simplistic terms. Policy analysts face challenges in explaining complex situations in ways that most of us can understand.

In providing background or context to aid in understanding social welfare problems, it is also helpful to identify whether the problem has increased, decreased, or remained constant over time, and to identify the causes of any changes. For example, in addition to knowing that the number of uninsured Americans has grown, we want to know what segments of the population are most likely to lack health insurance and why this is so. Here, too, different explanations often vie for political attention.

3. What are the proposed policy alternatives and what do they intend to accomplish? Is the desire to change people's physical or economic condition—for example, to increase the cash income of those who are poor, to provide decent housing for inner-city residents, to reduce child maltreatment, or to improve the health of the elderly? Or is the program designed to change knowledge, attitudes, or behavior—for example, to provide job skills; to improve literacy; to prevent drug use, unwanted pregnancy, or sexually transmitted diseases; or to increase awareness of legal rights? If several different effects are desired, what are the priorities among them?

Policymakers and policy advocates often come to the table with very different ideas about how to solve a policy problem and what the end result should be. For example, in the debate over cash versus "in-kind" services to address the nutritional needs of Americans, in-kind benefits (i.e., food stamps) won out because of the concerns of those who thought cash might be used for other purposes (rent, drugs, or other things). Even today, when electronic benefit transfer is used to deliver nutrition benefits rather than paper food coupons (stamps), the emphasis is on ensuring that recipients obtain food rather than ensuring that participants have income to purchase life's necessities. This may seem like a subtle difference, but it is an important distinction in public assistance policy that analysts must consider.

The form that benefits take is just as important as providing a benefit because issues of control and preference can determine how the benefit will be administered and the extent to which it will be used.[5] A consideration of policy alternatives not only concerns what goods, services, privileges, rights, or other benefits might be received, it may also include how these benefits will be distributed and who will be responsible for seeing that the policy will be carried out.[6] A novice might think that government should make it as easy as possible for people to get benefits for which they legitimately qualify. This book contains examples that show this is often not how social welfare policy and programs are designed. The policy analyst's job is to consider the different effects—pros and cons—each policy alternative might have. Of course, policymakers may already have firmly held beliefs about how things should be done.

Some communities or states are more innovative than others.[7] For example, "housing first" options provide publicly supported residences to people with alcohol problems who are still drinking. When policy ideas are more innovative or creative, it might be more difficult for policy analysts to predict their outcomes. The analyst's work is even more difficult when the policy under consideration is as controversial as "housing first" programs.

In comparing alternatives, policy analysts as well as policymakers and policy advocates often consider how other governments have addressed the problem, including how successful or unsuccessful these efforts have been. For example, after seeing that some states were extending foster care benefits (housing, education, healthcare) to children after they reach age 18, other states decided they might be able to remedy some of the problems that foster care children experience (e.g., unemployment, homelessness) as they move out of the foster care system. In this way, policies often diffuse to other locations.

Some policies translate well from one jurisdiction to another; others do not. For example, a ban on sleeping in public parks might work better in communities that have a substantial number of beds in homeless shelters. It might prove devastating in areas where shelters are in very short supply. The policy analyst may contact experts in the area of concern to get their opinions on factors to consider and their views on what effects, if any, a proposed policy might have. Policy analysts consider many factors that involve critical thinking as much as purely technical skills.

4. To what extent will the proposed policies address the need? Identifying *target groups* means defining the segment of the population for whom the policy is intended. The target group may mean all those in need or a segment of that group. Public programs may help to ameliorate need but they rarely eradicate social welfare problems. In analyzing policy proposals, analysts generally try to determine how many people will benefit from or otherwise be directly affected by the proposed policy. For example, in healthcare reform debates, estimates are usually made of the number of Americans who would be covered under the various policy proposals offered by Democrats and Republicans. Once these numbers are publicized, claims will be made that members of the different political parties are being more (or less) sensitive to the needs of those who currently have no health insurance.

Often analysts with the best intentions don't agree on what the likely effects of proposed policies will be. Try as they might to be neutral, they, too, have their own biases about issues and the analytical techniques that might produce the best estimates of problems and the effects of proposed policies.

5. What will the costs of the proposed policy be? Most policies require funds or other resources to be carried out. As described in Chapter 1, governments raise money for their programs through the various taxes or user fees they levy. Today, there is often a requirement that policies be *cost neutral,* that is, that their costs will be defrayed by savings in other areas or that they contain mechanisms that will produce enough revenue to cover their costs. Bills introduced to legislative bodies must usually contain fiscal notes, and analysts must estimate the price tags of each policy proposal. The Congressional Budget Office has the job of attaching cost estimates to bills considered by the U.S. Congress. State and local government agencies have offices and personnel that do the same.

Rational policymakers must measure benefits and costs in terms of general social well-being. Government agencies have developed various forms of cost-benefit analysis to identify the direct costs and benefits (usually, but not always, in dollars) of providing aid and assistance to the *average* family, worker, or job trainee. "Average," however, is a poor description of many individuals and families. It is also important, but difficult, to identify and measure general units of social well-being in more than dollar terms. For example, how do parenting skills programs affect the quality of children's lives? Do work requirements for parents receiving public assistance affect their children's aspirations? Policy analysts struggle with better ways to estimate health, job skills, employment opportunities, and other social values and their costs.

6. What are the possible unintended effects of the policy?   Unintended effects of policies are also called *spillover effects* or *externalities*. Since these effects are unintended, they can be difficult to identify, but from the perspective of rational policymaking, attempting to predict or anticipate them is crucial. For example, do emergency shelters for homeless people risk forgoing the establishment of permanent housing units for them?

We can also pose questions about unintended consequences for nontarget groups. For example, in communities that welcomed evacuees (the target group) after hurricane Katrina, a positive benefit might accrue to nontarget groups such as the owners of empty rental units. Negative effects might accrue to other nontarget groups if competition for jobs in the area also increased. If the government begins subsidizing health insurance for low-income workers whose employers do not offer health insurance, will this cause other employers to stop providing health insurance for their employees? Policy analysts often face the difficult task of predicting the extent to which these phenomena might occur.

Analyst should also consider effects that might be called unintended but really represent hidden policy agendas. For example, in an effort to control illicit drug use, were policies that require stiffer sentences for drug crimes promoted as a boon to prison industry expansion?

7. What recommendations might be made with regard to the proposed policy?   Finally, analysts may be asked to make recommendations or suggestions for improving a policy. For example, they may be asked how the policy can be better targeted to meet the needs of those in the direst circumstances. Or in the health insurance example above, they might be asked to suggest how the policy might be modified to deter employers from dropping their health insurance benefits for employees.

Any recommendations analysts make are subject to counterclaims or different points of view. Anticipating this, the independent and nonpartisan Government Accountability Office (GAO) offers government agencies that are the subject of its reports the opportunity to respond to its analyses and suggestions. Their responses are included in the GAO's reports.

The extent to which policymakers consider the work of policy analysts as they debate proposed legislation will vary from situation to situation. As policymakers engage in the political process, the proposed legislation the analysts originally studied may look quite different from what legislators agree on in the end, that is, if they agree on anything at all.

THE POLITICS OF POLICY IMPLEMENTATION

Many problems in social welfare policy arise after a law is passed—in the implementation process. Policy implementation includes all the activities designed to carry out the intention of the law: (1) creating, organizing, and staffing agencies to carry out the new policy, or assigning new responsibilities to existing agencies and personnel; (2) issuing directives, rules, regulations, and guidelines to translate policies into specific courses of action; (3) directing and coordinating both personnel and expenditures toward the achievement of policy objectives; and (4) monitoring the activities use to carry out the policy.

There is always a gap—sometimes small, sometimes very large—between a policy decision and its implementation. Over the years scholars of implementation have taken an almost cynical view of the process:

> Our normal expectation should be that new programs will fail to get off the ground and that, at best, they will take considerable time to get started. The cards in this world are stacked against things happening, as so much effort is required to make them move. The remarkable thing is that new programs work at all.[8]

Why isn't implementation a more rational activity? Why can't policies be directly implemented in decisions about organization, staffing, spending, regulation, direction, and coordination? The many obstacles to rational implementation can be categorized in terms of (1) communications, (2) resources, (3) attitudes, and (4) bureaucracy.[9]

Communications

To effectively implement public policy, people running a program must know what they are supposed to do. Directives give meaning to policy. Rather than being clear, directives are often vague, inconsistent, and contradictory. Moreover, directives may not be consistent with the original intention of the law, allowing people who disagree with the policy to read their own biases into programs.

The U.S. Department of Health and Human Services, a major federal government agency, is divided into many offices that are responsible for administering hundreds of social welfare programs (see Figure 2.1). These programs affect every state, community, and individual in the nation. The DHHS constantly struggles with maintaining accurate communications. Many other federal agencies also administer social welfare programs. Every federal, state, and local bureaucracy faces communication problems.

Generally, the more decentralized the administration of a program, and the greater the number of layers of administration through which directives must flow, the less likely it is that policies will be transmitted accurately and consistently. Take the Temporary Assistance for Needy Families (TANF) block grant program. The federal government establishes broad TANF guidelines, and each state sets many of the rules of the program. Whatever their advantages may be, prompt, consistent, and uniform policy implementation is *not* usually found in such decentralized structures.

Frequently, Congress (and state legislatures) is deliberately vague about public policy. Legislative bodies may pass vague and ambiguous laws largely for symbolic reasons—to reassure people that "something" is being done to help with a problem. In these cases, Congress and the president may not really know exactly what to do about the problem. They therefore delegate wide discretion to administrators who act under the "authority" of broad laws to determine what, if anything, actually will be done. Often Congress and the president want to claim credit for the high-sounding principles enacted into law but do not want to accept responsibility for any unpopular actions that administrators must take to implement these principles. It is much easier for political leaders to blame the "bureaucrats" and pretend that government regulations are a product of an "ungovernable" Washington bureaucracy.

Policies and related communications can also conflict with one another. As part of the 2002 Farm Bill, Congress authorized states to increase access to the Food Stamp Program by simplifying application and recertification processes. However, in an effort to keep error rates low and avoid financial penalties the federal government might impose, states often require more documentation from applicants and recipients than federal law requires. Such cumbersome application and recertification processes deter rather than increase program access.[10]

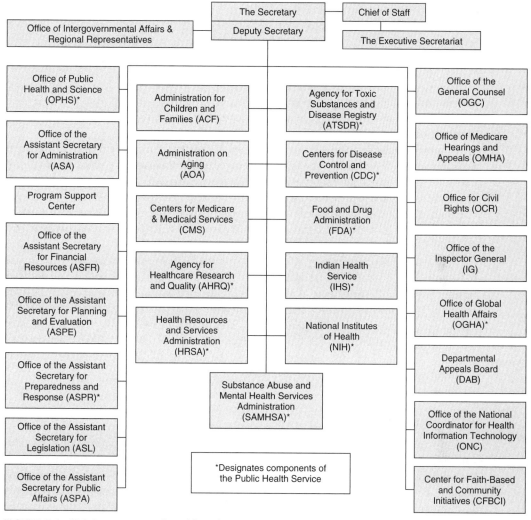

FIGURE 2.1 **U.S. Department of Health and Human Services Organizational Chart** *Source*: U.S. Department of Health and Human Services, retrieved March 16, 2010, from http://www.hhs.gov/about/orgchart/index.html

Resources

Even if policy directives are clear, when administrators lack the resources to carry out these policies, implementation fails. A crucial resource is funds—the money needed to implement new policies. Sometimes new policies require only limited funds to implement, but many new policies and programs seem doomed to fail because insufficient resources are allocated for startup and maintenance functions. An example is the lack of subsidized childcare placements available in some communities to ensure that a substantial number of parents receiving TANF are able to obtain and maintain employment.

Offices and equipment needed to implement policy may be difficult to acquire. Programs must have staff with the proper skills to carry out their assignments and with the authority and facilities necessary to translate a paper proposal into a functioning public service. Government agencies commonly claim that problems with implementation arise from undersized staffs. Often this is true. Personnel must also have the skills necessary for the job. Consider that convicted sex offenders are often required to get treatment. There may not be enough highly skilled therapists available to provide this treatment, even if treatment programs were adequately funded. In highly innovative and experimental programs, there may be no ready-made reserves of people who are trained for the program and who know what to do. Yet there is always pressure to show results as quickly as possible to ensure the continuation of the program the next year.

Sometimes government agencies lack the authority to implement policy. Even agencies with the necessary authority may be reluctant to exercise this authority because of the adverse political repercussions that might ensue. Rather than order local agencies, private corporations, or individual citizens to do something or take them to court for noncompliance, higher-level officials may consult with them, ask for their cooperation, or appeal to their sense of public duty. Agencies or administrators who must continually resort to sanctions will probably be unsuccessful in the long run.

One tactic of opponents, even after they lose the fight over the actual policy in Congress, is to try to reduce the size of the budget and staff that is to implement the policy. The political battle does not end with the passing of a law. It continues each year in fights over resources to implement the law. This has certainly been the case with the Legal Services Corporation (LSC), an agency that provides legal aid in noncriminal cases to low-income people. The Reagan administration wanted to abolish the LSC and appointed members to the LSC's board that shared these sentiments. "When Congress refused to . . . cut the corporation's budget further, . . . the board actually hired lobbyists to press the lawmakers for less . . . money."[11]

Attitudes

Administrators and program personnel who sympathize with a particular policy are likely to carry it out as policymakers intended. When the attitudes of agency administrators and staff personnel differ from those of the policymakers, the implementation process can be anything but smooth. Because administrators always have some discretion (and occasionally a great deal) in implementation, their attitudes toward policies have much to do with how a program is implemented. When people are told to do things with which they do not agree, inevitable slippage will occur between a policy and its implementation.

Generally, social service personnel enter the field because they want to "help people"—especially those who are aged, poor, disabled, or otherwise vulnerable. There is seldom any attitudinal problem in social agencies in implementing policies to expand social services. But highly committed social service personnel may find it very difficult to implement policies to cut back or eliminate social services.

Conservative policymakers are aware of the social service orientation of the "welfare bureaucracy." For example, they do not believe that welfare administrators really try to enforce work provisions of welfare laws. They believe that the welfare bureaucracy itself is directly responsible for much of the growth in caseloads over the years. They see welfare administrators as a major obstacle to policies designed to tighten eligibility, reduce overlapping benefits, and encourage work. School lunch program administrators, for example, have been criticized for lax certification processes that allow ineligible students to receive free lunches.[12]

In government agencies, it is generally impossible to remove staff simply because they disagree with a policy. Direct pressures are generally unavailable. Pay increases are primarily across the board, and promotions are infrequent and often based on seniority. If those who implement policy cannot be convinced that the policy is good for their clients or themselves, perhaps they can be convinced that it is less offensive than other alternatives that policymakers might impose.

Bureaucracy

Despite widespread distaste for the word *bureaucracy*,[13] virtually all public functions are handled by this type of organization. All of us have been frustrated at times when dealing with bureaucracies from public ones like the Internal Revenue Service (IRS) to private ones such as insurance companies. These situations may be even more frustrating to those who are ill, disabled, or have little formal education.

The federal bureaucracy makes major decisions about public policy implementation. There are about 2 million civilian employees of the federal government (not counting the approximately 680,000 civilian employees of the Department of Defense).[14] This huge bureaucracy has become a major base of power in the United States—independent of the Congress, the president, the courts, or the people.

Bureaucracies do more than fill in the details of congressional policies, although this is one power of bureaucratic authority. Bureaucracies also make important policies on their own by proposing legislation for Congress to pass; writing rules, regulations, and guidelines to implement laws passed by Congress; and deciding specific cases in the application of laws or rules.

Standard operating procedures (SOPs) are routines that enable officials to perform numerous tasks every day; SOPs save time. If every worker had to invent a new way of doing things for every case, there would not be enough time to help very many people. SOPs bring consistency in handling cases; rules can be applied more uniformly. Lack of standardization may be at the heart of why services do not work as well as they might. For example, the Social Security Administration (SSA) utilizes offices around the country to decide who qualifies for government disability assistance, but the disability determination process often lacks standardization from office to office. This may be one reason the SSA faces a huge backlog of appeals from applicants who were denied benefits.

SOPs can also obstruct policy implementation because "they tend to remain in force long after the conditions that spawned them have disappeared."[15] Many bureaucrats prefer the stability and familiarity of existing routines. Organizations have spent time, effort, and money in developing these routines. These "sunk costs" commit organizations to limit change as much as possible. This is why advocacy organizations like the Food Research and Action Center closely monitor changes in nutrition policy, publicize them, and encourage their constituents to make sure that state and local agencies implement changes that will be beneficial to those eligible to participate.

Bureaucratic organization also affects workers' abilities to implement policy, especially when responsibility for a policy is dispersed among many governmental units. The number of governments has proliferated. There are more than 89,000 governments in the United States: a national government, 50 state governments, about 3,000 county governments, over 19,000 municipal (city governments), over 16,000 township governments, about 13,000 school districts, and about 37,000 special districts that provide functions such as hospital and utility services.[16] Even within the national government, many departments have responsibility for various types of social welfare programs. For example, a dozen federal agencies from the Department of Defense to the Department of Education share responsibility for administering the nation's illicit drug control strategy.[17]

The more governments and agencies involved with a particular policy, and the more independent their decisions, the greater the problems of implementation. Every government and every agency becomes concerned with its own "turf"—areas each considers its exclusive responsibility. The national government and the states frequently struggle over how states will implement federal regulations. State governments often fight with the national government to hold onto their traditional areas of authority, particularly when the federal government imposes regulations on them but fails to provide sufficient funding for the new mandate, or when the states perceive that federal rules and regulations are unfair. For example, one view is that Congress (at president George W. Bush's urging) overstepped its authority when it passed the No Child Left Behind Act (discussed in Chapters 6 and 9), not only in telling states and schools what and how to teach, but in failing to provide sufficient funds to meet the new standards for students and teachers that the law imposes.

Proponents of particular programs may insist to Congress that their programs be administered by separate agencies that are largely independent of traditional executive departments or other agencies. These proponents believe their projects are special. They fear that consolidating program responsibilities will downgrade the emphasis that a separate department will give to their particular program. For example, advocates of special programs for people with alcohol problems may resist a merger of the National Institute on Alcohol Abuse and Alcoholism and the National Institute on Drug Abuse. They fear that a merger will reduce attention to alcohol problems because the public views illegal drugs as the greater menace to society even though many more people abuse alcohol than abuse other drugs.

Some separation of programs among governments is probably desirable. The argument for federalism—the division of responsibilities between the national government and the fifty state governments—is that it allows each state to deal more directly with the particular conditions confronting its residents. Government "closer to home" is sometimes thought to be more flexible, manageable, and personal than a distant bureaucracy in Washington. But some states are more generous to people in need than others, as noted in programs such as TANF and mental health services. To see that more people receive adequate services, many social welfare advocates press for centralized programs, such as national health insurance.

In 1993, the government-appointed Advisory Committee on Welfare Simplification and Coordination[18] recommended replacing the country's [public assistance] programs with "one, family-focused, client-oriented comprehensive program" that "should be overseen by only one committee in the House and Senate," rather than "the 24 congressional subcommittees [that] oversee the various welfare programs."[19] It also suggested a single application form and the same means tests for programs. Some states have merged their TANF, Medicaid, and SNAP applications, but given that different federal (and sometimes state) agencies are responsible for each of these programs, no serious consideration has been given to merging them into anything like one comprehensive program.

Making bureaucracy more rational is a challenge to every social welfare administrator. In an effort to follow the rules and respond to so many in need, administrators may forget that they are helping consumers or clients. Administrators rarely ask for clients' input, and they may be constrained by limited resources and rigid rules and regulations about what they can do to help people. Illustration 2.1 presents a striking example of the failures of policy and program implementation.

ILLUSTRATION 2.1
Hurricane Katrina and the Failures of Implementation

Hurricane Katrina hit the U.S. Gulf Coast on August 29, 2005. In the wake of this hurricane, Americans were stunned by the lives lost and damaged sustained, largely because the National Weather Service had forecasted that this would be one of the fiercest hurricanes in the nation's history. Criticism was directed at the city government of New Orleans, the state government of Louisiana, and the Federal Emergency Management Agency (FEMA), a part of the U.S. Department of Homeland Security (DHS). Since the size of the disaster clearly outstripped city and state resources, much of the blame was heaped on FEMA. Problems at FEMA, which predated hurricane Katrina, were blamed on its being downgraded from a Cabinet-level agency, budget cuts, loss of staff, and staff with insufficient expertise to respond to problems of this magnitude. The inadequate response to hurricane Katrina resulted in the departure of FEMA's head, a Bush administration political appointee, who was criticized for lacking experience in crisis management.

Of particular concern was the treatment of those who lacked transportation or the funds to evacuate on their own. Pictures of people camped in the New Orleans Superdome and sitting on bridges without food or water, and coverage of the sick and disabled who died in hospitals and nursing homes, were heartbreaking. Thousands of residents were sent to other cities to wait and hear when they would be allowed to return home. Some families were separated in the process, unaware of their loved ones' whereabouts.

The most stinging accusations were that people who were poor and African American had been forsaken. Knight-Rider News Service analyzed available, though incomplete, data on several hundred Katrina-related deaths and found that poor people and African Americans were not disproportionately represented among the dead.[a] Though of little consolation to their loved ones, deaths were proportionate to these groups' representation in the population. The analysis indicated that lack of transportation was not a factor for many of the dead because cars were found in their driveways. Consistent with news coverage of rescues, some people did not heed the belated warning to evacuate, perhaps because it was difficult to do so, or because nothing so bad had happened before. The group that did have higher deaths rates was older people. Nearly three-quarters of the dead were aged 60 or older, and nearly half were aged 75 or older. Many were at nursing homes and hospitals.

Communities such as Houston, Texas, welcomed tens of thousands of evacuees. Remuneration from the federal government fell short of expectations, and state and community resources were stretched thin. The federal government launched a massive initiative to house those displaced by hurricane Katrina, rebuild New Orleans, and assist those in other communities in states affected not only by hurricane Katrina but by hurricanes Rita and Wilma as well. Criticisms of the rebuilding process also mounted. The *New York Times* reported that low-income residents faced difficulty rebuilding because they were being turned down for loans due to low incomes or poor credit.[b] Dealing with insurance companies and what claims they will or will not pay may take years to resolve.

Statements, based on a preliminary study by the Comptroller General of the United States, sounded like an "I told you so." They emphasized that the Government Accountability Office (GAO) had long urged that a senior official in the White House be designated "to oversee federal preparedness for, and response to, major catastrophic disasters."[c] The report also sharply criticized the Secretary of the Department of Homeland Security for leadership failures. The GAO also

(Continued)

ILLUSTRATION 2.1 (Continued)

found that the National Flood Insurance Program is not actuarially sound, that is, the premiums collected are insufficient to meet flood losses expected in the future.[d] Some of the Katrina-related deaths resulted because floodwaters poured over levees, but a greater number of deaths resulted in areas where floodwalls collapsed. Accusations were that the floodwalls were poorly designed, poorly engineered, or poorly maintained.[e]

In addition to leadership failures, a major theme that emerged was communications failures within DHS and FEMA and across agencies and units of government.[f] The lessons to be learned from Katrina are that people will be spurred to evacuate sooner in the face of predictions of natural disasters, and government officials will realize that they will be held to high standards of accountability to prevent the loss of life and property.

[a]John Simerman, Dwight Ott, and Ted Mellnik (Knight Ridder News Service), "Early Data Challenge Assumptions About Katrina Victims," *Austin-American Statesman*, December 30, 2005, pp. A1&8.

[b]"The Poor Need Not Apply," *New York Times*, December 21, 2005. Retrieved March 16, 2010, from http://www.nytimes.com/2005/12/21/opinion/21wed2.html?_r=1&scp=1&sq=poor%20need%20not%20apply&st=cse

[c]"Statement by Comptroller General David M. Walker on GAO's Preliminary Observations Regarding Preparedness and Response to Hurricanes Katrina and Rita," GAO-06-365R, Washington, DC: U.S. Government Accountability Office, February 1, 2006, p. 3. Available at http://www.gao.gov

[d]"Challenges for the National Flood Insurance Program," GAO-06-335T, Washington, DC: U.S. General Accountability Office, January 25, 2006. Available at http://www.gao.gov

[e]John Simerman, Dwight Ott, and Ted Mellnik (Knight Ridder News Service), "Canal Breaches Led to Most New Orleans Deaths," *Austin-American Statesman*, December 30, 2005, p. A8; also see John Simerman, Dwight Ott, and Ted Mellnik (Knight Ridder Newspapers), "Majority of New Orleans Deaths Tied to Floodwalls' Collapse," December 29, 2005. Retrieved March 16, 2010, from http://lawnorder.blogspot.com/2006/01/krt-wire-12312005-majority-of-new.html

[f]"U.S. Senate Homeland Security and Governmental Affairs Committee Hearing on DHS Preparation for and Response to Hurricane Katrina," February 15, 2006. Retrieved March 16, 2010, from http://www.washingtonpost.com/wp-dyn/content/article/2006/02/15/AR2006021501475.html

EVALUATING SOCIAL POLICY

Even if public policies and the programs they spawn are well organized, adequately funded, efficiently operated, appropriately used, and politically popular, the questions still arise "So what?" "Do they make a difference?" "Do these programs have any beneficial effects on society?" "Could we be doing something else of more benefit to society with the money and human resources devoted to these programs?" Can the federal government say, for example, that TANF and Medicaid, family preservation programs, or community mental health services are accomplishing their objectives, that their benefits to society exceed their costs, and that there are no better or less costly means of achieving the same ends? What about other types of policies? For example, does greater use of border enforcement and detention dissuade illegal immigration? What effects do such policies have on family members who are residing legally in the United States?

While policy analysts often try to predict what will happen if policies and programs are adopted, it is also their job to determine what happens *after* policies and programs are put into place. This activity is called policy evaluation.

Does Policy Evaluation Matter?

In 1970, one surprisingly candid report by the liberally oriented think tank, the Urban Institute, argued convincingly that the federal government did *not* know whether most of its social service programs were worthwhile:

> The most impressive finding about the evaluation of social programs in the federal government is that substantial work in this field has been almost nonexistent.
>
> Few significant studies have been undertaken. Most of those carried out have been poorly conceived. Many small studies around the country have been carried out with such lack of uniformity of design and objective that the results rarely are comparable or responsive to the questions facing policy makers . . . .
>
> The impact of activities that cost the public millions, sometimes billions, of dollars has not been measured. One cannot point with confidence to the difference, if any, that most social programs cause in the lives of Americans.[20]

In the 1980s there was still considerable pessimism about social service program evaluation. Take, for example, comments by two social scientists on the state of job creation and training programs:

> Despite nearly twenty years of continuous federal involvement, . . . we still have to do a good deal of guesswork about what will work and for whom. We have had substantial and on-going difficulties in identifying what works, for whom, and why. This has been, in large part, because of an unwillingness on the part of Congress and policy makers to allow for adequate experimentation in the delivery of employment and training services.[21]

In the 1990s some people were more optimistic about the future of program evaluation. According to a *New York Times* story lauding evaluations of job training programs:

> Recent experiments designed and monitored by the Manpower Demonstration Research Corporation, a nonprofit organization spun off from the Ford Foundation in 1974, have had enormous impact on the direction of welfare reform. And with admirers in high places, the experimenters are likely to influence everything from the design of public schools that work to so-called managed competition in health care . . . .[22]

Evaluation science has continued to grow and along with it the number of people prepared to conduct rather sophisticated program evaluations. Still, in 2008, Carol Weiss, who has had a long career in program evaluation, wrote:

> Despite all the exhortations, admonitions, and blue-ribbon reports, there is widespread agreement that social science research has not generally had major influence on policy or practice.[23]

Why is this the case? Why don't policymakers pay more attention to what the "evidence" says about policy evaluation? Weiss attributes the lack of "productive collaboration between research and policy" to various shortcomings. Some shortcomings lie with research and researchers—sufficient data may not be available to produce the kind of evidence that is really needed; programs themselves or other factors in the environment that affect them may have changed substantially by the time findings are reported; findings are often not clear cut, and findings from different program evaluation studies often contradict each other, leaving the directions for social policies and programs less than clear. Policymakers are often anxious for results because the political agenda and re-election are often uppermost in their minds. Researchers, policymakers, and program administrators have different agendas, and each group speaks a different language.

But with people's lives hanging in the balance and with the price tags that accompany programs in the twenty-first century, Americans need far more definitive information about what social policies work, for whom they work, and why they work. The need for improved program evaluation is especially great because of the proliferation of social programs, the size of some of these programs, and competing demands for scarce public dollars.

Large-scale, methodologically rigorous, scientific evaluations of social programs are costly. The National Institute on Alcohol Abuse and Alcoholism spent at least $25 million on Project MATCH, which compared the effectiveness of three psychosocial treatments for alcoholism (the three proved equally effective).[24] NIAAA followed this with another ambitious study to determine whether certain medications in combination with behavioral therapy can increase the effectiveness of alcoholism treatment (no combination outperformed one of the medications alone or the behavioral therapy alone).[25]

The Urban Institute's Assessing the New Federalism (ANF) project has analyzed many of the effects of devolution—the transfer of responsibility for social programs from the federal government to the states that has occurred through legislation, primarily the Personal Responsibility and Work Opportunity Reconciliation Act (PRWORA) or welfare reform of 1996. Among the titles of ANF studies and reports are: "Fewer Welfare Leavers Employed in Weak Economy," "Children's Insurance Coverage and Service Use Improve," and "Gains in Public Health Insurance Offset Reductions in Employer Coverage among Adults." Reports from think tanks and policy planning groups may move policymakers to take action. More often they serve as the basis for the work of scores of advocacy groups that want action on the issues that concern them the most.

Policy Evaluation as a Rational Activity

Evaluation scholars understand that policy and program evaluation takes place in a political environment, but they define evaluation as a rational activity. Take a look at these definitions by leaders in the field:

> Policy evaluation is the objective, systematic, empirical examination of the effects ongoing policies and programs have on their target in terms of the goals they are meant to achieve.[26]
>
> Evaluation research is viewed by its partisans as a way to increase the rationality of policy making. With objective information on the outcomes of programs, wise decisions can be made on budget allocations and program planning. Programs that yield good results will be expanded; those that make poor showings will be abandoned or drastically modified.[27]
>
> Program evaluation is the use of social science research methods to systematically investigate the effectiveness of social intervention programs. It . . . is intended to be useful for improving program and social action aimed at ameliorating social problems.[28]

These definitions of policy evaluation assume that the goals and objectives of programs and policies are clear, that we know how to measure progress toward these goals, that we know how to measure costs, and that we can impartially weigh benefits against costs in evaluating a public program. In short, these definitions view policy evaluation as a rational activity. Contemporary evaluation scholars know that policy and program evaluations must be "adapted to their political and organizational environments,"[29] but they also want evaluation to be a more rational activity.

Ideally, an evaluation would address all the questions about program needs, conceptualization and design, monitoring, impact and utility, and efficiency described in Illustration 2.2, "Rational Evaluation: What Questions to Ask." This illustration notes that there are five steps in a

---

ILLUSTRATION 2.2
Rational Evaluation: What Questions to Ask

Several ideal, rational models of program evaluation have been proposed. Social scientists Peter Rossi, Howard Freeman, and Mark Lipsey suggest that rational evaluation include five types of questions:

1. Questions about the need for program services (**needs assessment**)
   - What are the nature and magnitude of the problem to be addressed?
   - What are the characteristics of the population in need?
   - What are the needs of the population?
   - What services are needed?
   - How much service is needed, over what time period?
   - What service delivery arrangements are needed to provide those services to the population?

2. Questions about the program's conceptualization or design (**assessment of program theory**)
   - What clientele should be served?
   - What services should be provided?
   - What are the best delivery systems for the services?
   - How can the program identify, recruit, and sustain the intended clientele?
   - How should the program be organized?
   - What resources are necessary and appropriate for the program?

3. Questions about program operations and service delivery (**assessment of program process or implementation**)
   - Are administrative and service objectives being met?
   - Are the intended services being delivered to the intended persons?
   - Are there needy but unserved persons the program is not reaching?
   - Once in service, do sufficient numbers of clients complete service?
   - Are the clients satisfied with services?
   - Are administrative, organizational, and personnel functions handled well?

4. Questions about program outcomes (**outcomes assessment**)
   - Are the outcome goals and objectives being achieved?
   - Do the services have beneficial effects on the recipients?
   - Do the services have adverse side effects on the recipients?
   - Are some recipients affected more by the services than others?
   - Is the problem or situation the services are intended to address made better?

5. Questions about program cost and efficiency (**efficiency assessment**)
   - Are resources used efficiently?
   - Is the cost reasonable in relation to the magnitude of the benefits?
   - Would alternative approaches yield equivalent benefits at less cost?

Source: Peter H. Rossi, Howard E. Freeman, and Mark W. Lipsey, *Evaluation: A Systematic Approach,* 7th ed. (Thousand Oaks, CA: Sage Publications, 2004), pp. 87–88, copyright © 2004 by Sage Publications, Inc. Reproduced with permission of Sage Publications, Inc., via Copyright Clearance Center.

comprehensive, rational evaluation. The first two steps are similar to those in the model of the policy analysis described earlier, but often the policy analyst must work very quickly while evaluators sometimes have the luxury of more lengthy periods of study.

In a perfect world, policy evaluators would first conduct a carefully executed *needs assessment* to identify the target group. In other words, how many individuals, families, schools, communities or other entities would need or benefit from a policy, program, or service. In some cases, governments already collect such social indicators. For example, each year the Substance Abuse and Mental Health Services Administration conducts a survey to determine how many people have alcohol and drug problems, how many received treatment, how many did not receive treatment, and the reasons they did not get treatment. When such indicators are not available, analysts might use a proxy measure (e.g., the number of people using soup kitchens as a proxy for the number of homeless people) or collect their own data.

From the rational evaluator's perspective, the second step is *identifying a rational or logical response to the problem.* What do theory and previous research or other evidence indicate about the ways that problems should be resolved? What goods, services, rights, or privileges should be provided and how broadly or narrowly should the target group be specified? Even in cases where there is agreement on a general strategy to solve a problem, specifics are another matter. For example, stakeholders may agree that education should be a major strategy to reduce pregnancies among teenagers. But even in the face of studies that show abstinence-only education programs are ineffective,[30] they may continue to disagree on what the content of that education should contain (e.g., *more* abstinence-only education[31] or education that includes safer sex practices[32]).

Once a policy strategy is developed, it must be implemented. In this phase or step, the evaluator's role is to conduct a *process, implementation,* or *progress* evaluation to determine if the policy or program is being implemented according to plan. If a clear model of treatment or services is being utilized, then *fidelity* (adherence) to the model is important. This is accomplished by monitoring program implementation to prevent *drift* away from the model. If there is too much drift, we really don't know what is being evaluated. In Project MATCH, delivery of the three treatment models selected to assist people with alcohol problems was carefully monitored through methods such as experts' evaluations of tapes of the treatment sessions delivered to participants. One way opponents of policies and programs may try to affect a policy or program is to encourage drift.

Rather than wait until members of the target population have completed a program, process evaluation is also used to determine whether interim or short-term goals are being met and whether the expected number of target group members are participating in the program. Modifications may be needed if the program is not progressing as expected; however, few decent implementation studies are conducted because they are often tedious and time consuming. Illustration 2.3 contains an example of an implementation evaluation.

The fourth step is *outcome* or *product* evaluation. This is what most people really want to know—did the program produce its intended effect? In making these identifications and measurements, policy *outputs* (what governments do) should not be confused with policy *impacts* (what consequences these government actions have). Benefits should not be measured in terms of government activity alone. For example, the number of clients served or the number of units of services provided are not really measures of the impact of government activity. We cannot be content with counting how many times a bird flaps its wings; we must learn how far the bird has flown. In assessing the impact of public policy, we must identify the changes in individuals, groups, and society brought about by public policies. Measuring effects, both positive and negative, on target and nontarget groups is essential, although more effort is usually focused on measuring target group effects.

ILLUSTRATION 2.3
Smaller Learning Communities Implementation Study

The Smaller Learning Communities (SLC) program was established in response to growing national concerns about students too often lost and alienated in large, impersonal high schools, as well as concerns about school safety and low levels of achievement and graduation for many students. Authorized under the Elementary and Secondary Education Act, the SLC program was designed to provide local educational agencies with funds to plan, implement, or expand SLCs in large high schools of 1,000 students or more.

The SLC legislation allows local educational agencies to implement the most suitable structure or combination of structures and strategies to meet their needs. The *Implementation Study of Smaller Learning Communities: Final Report* was designed to study the early implementation of the SLC program. The study based its findings on data from 119 grantees from among those funded in 2000 in the first cohort of grantees and surveyed in the spring of 2002 and fall of 2003. The report also used data from in-depth case studies of 18 grantees that intended to use freshman or career academies to structure a smaller learning community.

Major implementation and outcome findings from the study included:

IMPLEMENTATION FINDINGS

The most prevalent SLC structures were freshman and career academies.

Most participating schools chose to implement one or more SLC strategies, with block scheduling and teacher teams the most popular choices.

Smaller Learning Community-related professional development, although provided by nearly all schools, was not very extensive.

Most schools reported they applied for SLC funds to increase overall student academic achievement, academic achievement of at-risk students and student motivation.

Schools reported a number of factors limiting effective SLC implementation, including scheduling and logistical issues, physical space, lack of teacher SLC professional development, and school staffing needs, especially in terms of core academic teachers and guidance counselors.

While the study was primarily focused on implementation issues, some limited data on outcomes from the first Annual Performance Reports (APRs) are included in the report along with a number of limitations and cautions in interpreting the data. The data were based on school overall statistics observed immediately before and after participation in the federal program, and in no way imply a causal connection.

The data suggest an upward trend in student extracurricular participation before and after program participation.

There was a statistically significant positive trend in the percentage of ninth-grade students being promoted to tenth grade during the post-grant period.

There was also a downward trend in the incidence of violence in SLC schools over time.

The data suggest increases in the percentage of graduating students who reported they planed to attend either two- or four-year colleges.

There were no significant trends observed in academic achievement, as measured by either scores on statewide assessments or college entrance exams over the short period of the study.

Source: U.S. Department of Education, Office of Planning, Evaluation and Policy Development, Policy and Program Studies Service, *Implementation Study of Smaller Learning Communities, Final Report.* Washington, D.C., 2008. Retrieved January 17, 2009, from http://www.ed.gov/news/pressreleases/2008/05/05122008.html

The fifth step in the policy and program evaluation process is *assessing cost-benefit and efficiency.* Such studies are often difficult to conduct because considering all possible effects and obtaining the data is difficult, especially if long-term program effects are being discerned.

Perhaps the most difficult problem confronting evaluators is weighing costs against benefits. Benefits may be measured in terms of bettering human conditions—greater educational attainment, longer life spans, better nutrition, steady employment, and so on. Costs are usually measured in dollars, but many of the values of education, health, or self-esteem cannot be measured in dollars alone. Cost savings are not the only goals that society wants to achieve. It is difficult to pursue rational evaluation when benefits and costs are measured in different ways.

Policy Evaluation as a Political Activity

Policy and program evaluation may resemble rational, scientific inquiry, but it can never really be separated from politics. Let us look further at the political problems that make rational policy evaluation difficult, if not impossible.

UNCLEAR, AMBIGUOUS PROGRAM GOALS   As we have noted, legislative language is often purposely vague—"improve nutrition" or "increase school readiness" are examples. There may be no specific indication of what improvements or how much improvement is intended or when it is expected to occur. Even interviews with the original legislative sponsors (Congressmembers, state legislators, county commissioners, or city council members) may produce ambiguous, or even contradictory, goals.

There is also "confusion between policy ends and policy means."[33] If the goal of welfare reform is to "reduce dependence on welfare," does it mean that researchers should be measuring how many people left the public assistance rolls, how many got jobs, or how many are no longer poor, have health insurance, childcare, or other resources? A rational response might be that we should measure all these indicators, but advocates for reduced welfare spending and smaller government will focus on how many have left the rolls while advocates of expanded social welfare programs will focus on the number who have left the rolls and are still in poverty.

When policy analysts and evaluators must define the goals or outcomes themselves, evaluation itself becomes a political activity. In addition, unless there are clear specifications for when reports will be issued and who will follow up on this, programs may not be well monitored for results.

SYMBOLIC GOALS   Many programs and policies have primarily symbolic value. They are not designed so much to change social conditions as they are to make groups feel that their government "cares." Of course, an agency does not welcome a study that reveals its efforts have no tangible effects. Indeed, such a finding, if widely publicized, is likely to reduce the symbolic impact of the program by telling target groups or other supporters of its uselessness. Drug prevention programs, for example, are popular initiatives, but many have done little to deter drug use. The Defense of Marriage Act might please conservatives, but it is unclear how it will, as some claim, help "save" the institution of marriage.

UNHAPPY FINDINGS   Agencies and administrators usually have a heavy investment—organizational, financial, psychological—in current programs and policies. They are predisposed against findings that these programs do not work, involve excessive costs, or have unexpected negative consequences. If a negative report is issued, the agency may adopt a variety of strategies to offset the findings, as suggested in Illustration 2.4, "What to Do If Your Agency's

ILLUSTRATION 2.4
What to Do If Your Program Receives a Negative Evaluation

What if you are faced with clear evidence that your favorite program is useless, or even counterproductive? Here is a tongue-in-cheek list of last-ditch efforts to save it.

1. Claim that the effects of the program are long range and cannot be adequately measured for many years.
2. Argue that the effects of the program are general and intangible and that these effects cannot be identified with the crude methodology, including statistical measures, used in the evaluation.
3. If the classic experimental research design was used, claim that withholding services or benefits from the control group was unfair; claim that there were no differences between the control and experimental groups because both groups had knowledge of the experiment.
4. If a quasiexperimental design was used, claim that initial differences between the experimental and comparison groups make the results useless.
5. If a time series research design was used, claim that there were no differences between the "before" and "after" observations because of other coinciding variables that hid the program's effects. That is to say, claim that the participants' condition would be even worse without the program.
6. Argue that the lack of differences between the people receiving the program services and those not receiving them only means that the program is not sufficiently intensive and indicates the need to spend more resources on the program.
7. Argue that the failure to identify positive program effects is due to the inadequacy of the evaluation research design or of bias on the part of the evaluators.

Program Receives a Negative Evaluation." Furthermore, a program that promises to meet a recognized national need—for example, to eradicate poverty or cover prescription drug costs—but actually meets only a small percentage of that need, may generate great praise at first but bitterness and frustration later when it becomes known how insufficient the impact really is.

PROGRAM INTERFERENCE   Most serious evaluation studies involve some burdens on ongoing program activities. Accomplishing an agency's day-to-day business is generally a higher priority in the minds of program administrators and frontline workers than making special arrangements for evaluation. High-quality evaluation studies also usually require a substantial expenditure of funds, facilities, time, and personnel, all of which administrators may not want to sacrifice from their programs.

USEFULNESS OF EVALUATIONS   Unless chosen to dismantle a program or change it drastically, program administrators are clearly usually defensive about evaluative studies that conclude, "The program is not achieving the desired results." Not only is such a finding a threat to the agency, but standing alone, it fails to tell administrators why the program is failing. Agency staff may be more receptive to evaluations when they include some action recommendations that might conceivably rescue the program. But even when studies show programs to be failures, the usual reaction is to patch things up and try again. Few programs are ever abolished. Unless a program is very unpopular, any attempt to abolish it is sure to be met with protests.

EVALUATION BY WHOM?   A central political issue is who will do the evaluation. From the agency's perspective, the evaluation should be done by the agency itself. This type of "in-house" evaluation is most likely to produce favorable results. The next best thing, from the agency's perspective, is to allow the agency to contract with a private firm for an "outside" evaluation. A private firm that wants to win future contracts from the agency, or from any other agency, is very hesitant about producing totally negative evaluations. The worst evaluation arrangement, from the agency's perspective, is an outside evaluation conducted by an independent government agency such as the Government Accountability Office (formerly the General Accounting Office), an independent contractor hired by the government, or a state comptroller's office or auditor general's office. Agency staff fear that outsiders do not understand clearly the nature of their work or the problems faced by the clients they serve and that this will hurt the program.

THREATS TO EVERYONE   Political obstacles to evaluation operate at all levels of the social service delivery system. Evaluation is threatening to elected officials because it might imply that they have developed poor policies, passed inadequate laws, provided inadequate funding in relation to need, or funded ineffective programs. Evaluation is threatening to social service administrators because it might suggest that they have done a poor job of implementing the policies and managing the programs that legislators mandated. Evaluation is threatening to social service workers because it might indicate that they are not adequately skilled in delivering and providing social services to clients. Finally, evaluation can be threatening to clients because the process may invade their privacy, place additional pressure on them in times of personal crisis, and make them feel even more conspicuous about receiving social services.

Why Hasn't Head Start "Cured" Poverty?

Head Start is a very popular social welfare program. In some circles, Head Start is known as much for the evaluations that have been conducted of it as it is for the program itself. Let's consider those studies as an example of the politics of policy evaluation.

As part of President Lyndon Baines Johnson's war on poverty of the 1960s, substantial funding was earmarked for the Head Start preschool program. By the late 1960s over one-half million children were enrolled throughout the country. Some communities expanded Head Start to full-time programs and also provided children with health services and improved daily diets.

POLITICS, EVALUATION, AND HEAD START   Head Start programs were very popular, but were they really making a difference? Understandably, Head Start officials within the OEO were discomforted by the thought of a formal evaluation of their program. They argued that educational success was not the program's only goal—child health and nutrition and parental involvement were equally important goals. After much internal debate, Sargent Shriver ordered an evaluative study, and in 1968 a contract was given to Westinghouse Learning Corporation and Ohio University to perform the research.

When Richard Nixon assumed the presidency in January 1969, hints of negative findings had already filtered up to the White House. Nixon alluded to studies showing the long-term effects of Head Start as "extremely weak," prompting the press and Congress to call for the release of the Westinghouse Report. The researchers had randomly selected 104 Head Start projects across the country to participate—70 percent were summer projects, and 30 percent were full-year projects. Children who had gone on from these programs to the first, second, and third grades in local schools (the experimental group) were matched on socioeconomic background with children in the same grades who had not attended Head Start (the control group). The children were given a series of standardized tests covering various aspects of cognitive and affective development. The parents of both groups of children were also matched on achievement and motivation.

The unhappy results can be summarized as follows: summer programs did not produce improvements in cognitive and affective development that could be detected into the early elementary grades, and full-year programs produced only marginally effective gains for certain subgroups, mainly black children in central cities. However, parents of Head Start children strongly approved of the program.[34] Head Start officials reacted predictably in condemning the report. Liberals attacked the report believing that President Nixon would use it to justify major OEO cutbacks. The *New York Times* reported the findings under the headline "Head Start Report Held 'Full of Holes.'" It warned that "Congress or the Administration will seize the report's generally negative conclusions as an excuse to downgrade or discard the Head Start Program"[35] (not unreasonable in light of the findings, but politically unacceptable to the liberal community). Academicians moved to defend the War on Poverty by attacking methodological aspects of the study. In short, scientific assessment of Head Start was drowned in a sea of political controversy.

YEARS LATER   It is difficult for educators and the social welfare establishment to believe that education, especially intensive preschool education, does not have a lasting effect on the lives of children. The prestigious Carnegie Foundation decided to fund research in Ypsilanti, Michigan, at the Perry Preschool, that would follow disadvantaged youngsters from preschool to young adulthood. The study was conducted with a small sample consisting of 123 children whose scores on the well-known Stanford-Binet intelligence test put them at risk of school failure. Fifty-eight of these children (the experimental group) received a special Head Start-type education at ages 3 and 4 and continued to receive weekly visits during later schooling. The others (the control group) received no special educational help. Both groups came from low socioeconomic backgrounds; half their families were headed by a single parent, and half received welfare. Researchers have also reported on the progress of this small, local sample at ages 27 and 40.[36]

Initial results were disappointing. Most gains made by the children with preschool education had disappeared by the time they had completed second grade. As children in the experimental group progressed through grade school, junior high school, and high school, their grades were not better than those of the children in the control group, although they did score slightly higher (by about 8 percent) on reading, mathematics, and language achievement tests. More importantly, only 19 percent of those in the experimental group ended up in special education classes, compared to 39 percent of the control group. The former preschoolers also showed fewer delinquent tendencies and held more after-school jobs. The key to this success appeared to be a better attitude toward school and learning among those with preschool education. At age 27, compared to those who had not received the special preschool program, the female former preschoolers were more likely to have finished high school, less likely to have given birth out of wedlock, and more likely to be married and employed. The male former preschoolers had more years of marriage and earned more money. The former preschoolers also had fewer arrests and were more likely to have avoided welfare and to own their own homes. The researchers reported that the program reaped $7.16 for every dollar spent, four-fifths of it due to potential criminal justice and crime victim savings. When study participants were age 40, the program's positive results were again confirmed.

But even academics and researchers who support early childhood education programs like Head Start are concerned about naive acceptance of this sevenfold benefit because evaluations of model programs like the Perry Preschool Project (which spent far more per child than does the average Head Start program) indicate what *can* be achieved, not necessarily what *is* being achieved.[37] They also note that, since each program is locally managed, there is concern about the quality of some Head Start programs, that long-term benefits are far more modest than the public has been led to believe, and that much more innovation is needed to help current generations.

The Head Start children of today often have only one parent to support them, and they live in environments where substance abuse, poor education, violence, unemployment, and teen pregnancy are common. They also come from diverse cultures with various languages spoken in the home, providing additional challenges to the staff who operate programs.[38] As two people who have studied Head Start over the years stated:

> Head Start is not a panacea for poverty, and attempts to posture it as such will lead to an inevitable fall. Clearly, it will be unwise to strengthen our national investment in Project Head Start if this investment is not accompanied by the continuation, improvement, and expansion of the other services and institutions that affect Head Start children and families.[39]

Much more research than the widely cited Perry Preschool study has been conducted on early childhood education and other early childhood interventions. One meta-analysis of 35 experimental and quasi-experimental early childhood education studies gave these programs high marks in terms of effects on children's intelligence and academic achievement and personal and social problems.[40] Another meta-analysis, this one of 13 state-funded preschool programs, found more modest support for results, calling them "similar to evaluations of other large-scale preschool programs for low-income children, such as Head Start."[41]

Some Faces of Program Evaluation

Most governments make some attempt to assess the utility of their programs. These efforts usually take one or more of the following forms.

PUBLIC HEARINGS   Public hearings are one type of program review. Legislative committees often ask agency heads to give formal or informal testimony regarding the accomplishments of their programs. This usually occurs near budget time. At other times hearings are called due to a crisis or scandal. For example, the head of the Federal Emergency Management Agency (FEMA) and others were called to testify before Congress after the property devastation and loss of life caused by hurricane Katrina in New Orleans and surrounding areas. Senate hearings that are televised and reported in the news allow senators the opportunity to show constituents how concerned or outraged they are by the lack of attention to an issue or insensitive treatment received.

Other government entities also request input from services providers or member of the public. For example, in 2009, the U.S. Sentencing Commission held hearings in several cities on the 25th anniversary of the Sentencing Reform Act of 1984 and invited judges, attorneys, probation officers, academics, and other to testify on how sentencing guidelines are working and how they think the policy should be modified. Citizen input may also be requested at the state and local level at budget time or when important changes might be made to social service allocation and delivery.

Presidents sometimes hold summits or forums on particular issues. Hunger forums and education summits are cases in point. State and local agencies may also hold community forums to obtain input on homelessness, mental health services, or other social concerns. Sometimes changes may be made as a result of citizen input, but these meetings are often little more than symbolic gestures.

Often, testimonials and reports of program administrators and those served by the program are not very objective means of program evaluation. Unless there has been substantial wrongdoing, public hearings frequently magnify the benefits and minimize the costs of programs.

SITE VISITS   Occasionally teams of legislators, high-ranking federal or state officials, or expert consultants (or some combination of them) will descend on agencies to conduct investigations "in the field." These teams can interview workers and clients and directly observe the operation of the agency. They can accumulate impressions about how programs are being run, whether they have competent staffs, whether the programs seem to be having beneficial effects, and perhaps even whether the clients (target groups) are pleased with the services. But site visits can also provide a biased view of the program. Program staff are usually on their best behavior, and clients that meet with the site visit team are usually hand-picked.

PROGRAM MEASURES   Often the evaluation data agencies develop themselves describe program or output measures—the number of people enrolled in work and training programs, the number of hospital beds available, or the number of people treated by mental health programs. Sometimes these measures also indicate the impact these numbers have on society—reductions in poverty figures, decreases in criminal activity by drug addicts, the success of work trainees in later finding and holding useful employment in the nation's workforce, or improvements in parenting skills that reduce the need for intervention by child protective service programs.

Government agencies also provide program reports to legislators as a "public information" activity. Government agencies may be required to produce annual reports. For example, federal agencies must submit annual Performance and Accountability Reports (PARs) each year to the Office of Management and Budget (OMB) that includes significant financial data, performance standards and results, and management control practices. These reports are generally posted on the agencies' websites for public review as well.

COMPARISON WITH PROFESSIONAL STANDARDS   In some areas of social welfare activity, professional associations have developed their own "standards" of benefits and services. These standards may be expressed in terms of the maximum number of cases that a mental health, child welfare, or public assistance worker can handle effectively, or the minimum number of hospital beds required by a population of 100,000 people, or in other ways. Actual governmental outputs can be compared with these "ideal" outputs. Although this kind of study may be helpful, it still focuses on the outputs and not on the impacts that government activities have on the conditions of target and nontarget groups. Although professionals usually develop the standards, these individuals may lack concrete data on which to determine the ideal levels of benefits and services. Having too many cases can obviously result in insufficient attention to each client, and too many hospital beds waste resources, but there is very little hard evidence about what optimal caseload sizes are or that these supposedly ideal levels of government outputs have significant impact.

Formal Research Designs

Another rational approach is to conduct formal evaluation studies employing the techniques of scientific research.

CLASSIC EXPERIMENTAL DESIGN   In many social scientists' opinion,[42] the most highly regarded, although least frequently used, approach is the *classic experimental design.* This design employs two groups—an *experimental group* and a *control group*—that are theoretically equivalent in every way except that the policy has been applied only to the experimental group. In order to ensure that control and experimental groups are comparable, research subjects or participants are assigned randomly to the two groups and the program must be applied only to the experimental group. After the application of the policy for a given length of time, its impact is measured by comparing the status of the experimental group with the status of the control group. The postprogram status of both groups must be carefully measured. Also, every effort must be made to make certain that any observed postprogram differences between the two groups can be attributed to the program and not to some other intervening cause that affected one of the groups as the program was administered. This classic research design (see Figure 2.2) is preferred because it provides the best opportunity for estimating changes that can be directly attributed to policies and programs.

Although revered by many, the classic experimental design presents many challenges in the social sciences. Methodologically, it is difficult to avoid contamination (the introduction of extraneous factors) in social science research. Many studies of new medications use double-blind procedures in which neither the person administering the "medication" nor the research subject taking the "medication" know whether it is the real thing or a placebo. This "double-blind" approach is nearly impossible to use when it comes to studying social interventions. Generally, both those administering the social intervention (for example, a job training program or drug rehabilitation services) and the research subjects or participants know whether they are receiving the intervention or not. As in medication studies, potential participants in social experiments must receive clear explanations of the intervention and an opportunity to decide whether or not they want to participate. If they do enter the study, they usually can withdraw at any time.

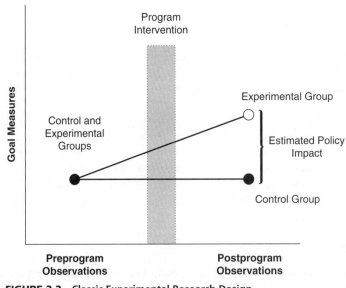

FIGURE 2.2 Classic Experimental Research Design

THEORETICAL EVALUATION   Controlled experiments are sometimes called reductionistic because they focus on narrowly defined interventions and narrowly defined outcomes. As Lisbeth Schorr argues, controlled studies may not be well suited to studying complex interventions offered to individuals who face myriad problems and changing life circumstances.[43] She recognizes the difficulty of "breaking with the dogma of experimental designs," because, as another evaluation expert, Robinson G. Hollister, has said, it is "like the nectar of the gods" when it comes to evaluation. But Schorr believes that some evaluation alternatives, although providing less certainty about cause and effect, can offer "both rigor and relevance." If there is hope for bridging the gap between rational evaluation and politics, maybe the model of "theoretical evaluation" Schorr suggests will help. This approach begins with interested parties, like social service personnel, working *together* with evaluators to develop a "conceptual map" or "logic model" (like the one in Figure 2.3) that links theoretical assumptions about what works to promote change with interventions that flow from these ideas and with interim measures of progress as well as outcome measures.

Schorr offers the example of early childhood education programs. These programs are often based on assumptions that children who are "ready to learn" do better in school than children who are "not ready to learn." Policies and programs would focus on factors that appear to be most useful in helping children become ready to learn, such as good health, proper nutrition,

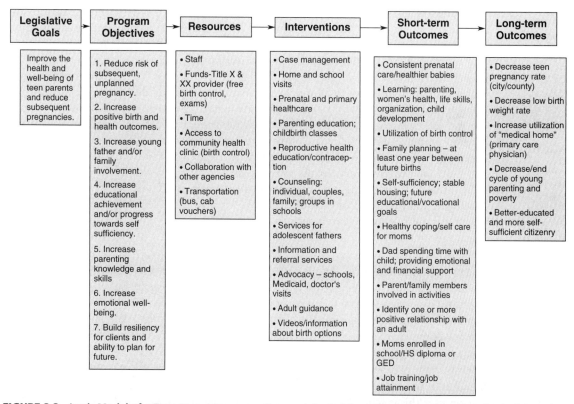

FIGURE 2.3   Logic Model of a Teen Parent Program   *Source:* Adapted from Carol M. Lewis, Center for Social Work Research, The University of Texas at Austin, in collaboration with the Tandem Teen Prenatal and Parenting Program at People's Community Clinic in Austin, Texas.

high-quality preschool education, and supportive families. Interim measures might include more children receiving regular healthcare, more children enrolled in high-quality preschool education programs, and more families receiving supportive services like decent housing, earlier intervention to prevent child abuse or neglect, and education to help them read to their children and encourage learning. As program personnel deliver services and review with evaluators interim and outcome measures, the conceptual map is refined, hopefully leading to more effective services and improved outcomes for children and their families, such as better school performance.

Another reason to consider methods like theoretical evaluation is that even when one wants to conduct controlled experiments in public policy, it is frequently impossible to do so because sometimes the human beings involved cannot be placed arbitrarily in experimental or control groups just for the sake of program evaluation. Indeed, if experimental and control groups are really identical, the application of public policy to one group of citizens and not the other may violate the "equal protection of the laws" clause of the Fourteenth Amendment to the U.S. Constitution. In addition to legal issues, differential treatment of people with the same social problems raises ethical concerns. Social workers and other professionals may find it unacceptable to deny what may be a promising treatment to clients, even if better program evaluation is desired.

QUASIEXPERIMENTAL DESIGN   Frequently, it is only possible to conduct studies that compare individuals and groups that have participated in programs with those that have not, or to compare cities, states, and nations that have programs with those that do not. Comparisons are made of the extent to which the groups that participated in the program achieved the desired goals in relation to those groups that did not participate. Such studies are called *quasiexperimental.* Because subjects are not randomly assigned to experimental and control groups, researchers cannot be certain that the two groups were alike before the experiment began. They must try to eliminate the possibility that any difference between the two groups in goal achievement was caused by some factor other than experience with the program. For example, the employment records of job program participants may be compared with those who did not participate. Following the quasiexperiment, if the job program group did not have higher employment rates and greater earnings than other groups, it may be because the job program participants were less skilled to begin with. If they were more successful, it may be because the job program officials "creamed off" or "cherry picked" the local unemployed and gave services only to those who already possessed skills and job experience. Thus, quasiexperimental research designs (see Figure 2.4), like most social science research, still leave room for discussion and disagreement about the utility of social welfare programs.

PRETEST-POSTTEST DESIGN   Another type of research design involves a comparison of conditions before and after a policy or program has been adopted. Usually only the target group is examined. This design may be the only choice in jurisdictions where no control or comparison group can be identified. The simplest before-after or *pretest-posttest study* involves taking one measure before the program is implemented and one after the program is administered, but this is a very weak design.

TIME SERIES DESIGN   When several observations are made before and several observations are made after, this is generally referred to as a *time series or longitudinal design* (see Figure 2.5). New or innovative programs sometimes have short-term positive effects. The novelty of the program or the target group's knowledge that is being given special treatment and being

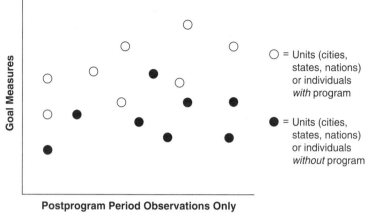

Postprogram Period Observations Only

FIGURE 2.4   Quasiexperimental Research Design

watched closely may create measurable changes (the Hawthorne or "halo" effect). These positive effects may disappear as the program's novelty and enthusiasm for it wear off. In other cases, it may take a long time for policy and program effects to be realized. Due to constraints of time and money, time series designs that involve collecting data from many individual program participants are rarely conducted. Such studies are easier to conduct when available data (e.g., drug arrests, traffic fatalities) can be compared before and after policy implementation.

Unless a time series design includes a control group (many do not), it is very difficult to know whether any changes that might have occurred were due to the program itself or were a

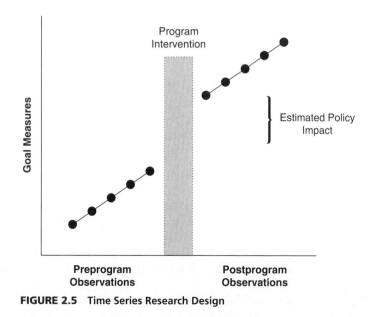

FIGURE 2.5   Time Series Research Design

result of other changes occurring in society at the same time. For example, a program evaluator may be faced with the problem of determining whether increased employment among former TANF recipients was due to stiffer work requirements, improved job services, or improved economic conditions that expanded the number of jobs available.

An Affinity for D.A.R.E.

Even rigorously conducted research does not end controversy over social programs. A recent example of how programs flourish even in the face of negative evaluations concerns the popular Drug Abuse Resistance Education (D.A.R.E.) program.[44] The idea that children may use drugs strikes fear in the hearts of parents. Sources like *Monitoring the Future* and the *National Survey on Drug Use and Health,* both ongoing surveys funded by the federal government, provide data that substantial numbers of youth at least experiment with alcohol, and to a lesser extent with other drugs. For example, 28 percent of students in grades 8, 10, and 12 report they have tried marijuana at least once.[45] This type of information has given rise to a spate of drug prevention programs.

Throughout the 1970s, most drug abuse prevention programs were educational in nature, directed at adolescents, and implemented through the schools. Early programs combined information with scare tactics. These programs were generally so ineffective that the federal government's Special Office for Drug Abuse Prevention (SODAP) denounced them.[46] In fact, SODAP was so disillusioned that it took the bold step of temporarily banning funding for drug information programs. Lacking evidence of effective information approaches, interest grew in *affective* approaches and other alternatives. Affective approaches assume that adolescents will be deterred from using drugs if their self-esteem and interpersonal, decision-making, and problem-solving skills are improved. Recreational activities, community service, and involvement in the arts were stressed as ways of providing meaningful, fulfilling experiences that would deter drug use. These methods also proved ineffective.

Then a new generation of programs began to emerge based on theories of *social and cognitive inoculation* that addressed children's social milieu. These approaches are based on the premise that if adolescents are provided with counterarguments and techniques with which to resist peer pressure to use drugs, as well as factual information about drugs, they are more likely to abstain.

In 1983 D.A.R.E. was established as a joint project of the Los Angeles Police Department and the Los Angeles Unified School District.[47] Combining elements of affective education and social inoculation, it was initially designed to help fifth- and sixth-grade students recognize and resist peer pressure, a major factor in youths' experimenting with alcohol and drugs. Several lessons focused on building self-esteem; others emphasized the consequences of alcohol and drug use and identification of alternative ways to cope with stress, gain peer acceptance, and have fun. Most important, the program teaches students ways to respond to peers who offer drugs, and it helps them practice these techniques (changing the subject, walking away, saying "no" and repeating it as often as necessary). The curriculum contained 17 classroom sessions conducted by a police officer, coupled with other activities taught by the regular classroom teacher. Curricula were also developed for middle and high school students to reinforce the lessons taught during the fifth and sixth grades. D.A.R.E. reports that its program is used in 75 percent of all school districts in the United States and in 43 foreign countries.

A great deal of public funding has gone to support D.A.R.E., and initial reports suggested that the program was effective. But a later evaluation study funded by the U.S. Department of Justice (DOJ) and conducted in 1994 by the widely respected Research Triangle Institute found the program ineffective in preventing or reducing drug use.[48] The DOJ refused to approve the report, and D.A.R.E. tried to prevent others from publishing criticisms of the program.[49] According to Weiss and colleagues, "Whenever evidence suggested that it was not successful" D.A.R.E. "tried to substitute political pressure for empirical evidence."[50]

Subsequent reports of ineffectiveness also did little to dull enthusiasm for D.A.R.E. A ten-year follow-up study by researchers at the University of Kentucky found "no reliable short-term, long-term, early adolescent, or young adult positive outcomes associated with receiving the intervention."[51] The Kentucky researchers also noted that even though most children do not use drugs even when they do not participate in a drug prevention program, "[T]hese 'feel-good' programs are ones that everyone can support, and critical examinations of their effectiveness may not be perceived as necessary."[52]

The Government Accounting Office (GAO) also decided to review the major evaluations of D.A.R.E. In a 2003 report, the GAO stated:

> [T]he six long-term evaluations of the DARE elementary school curriculum that we reviewed found no significant differences in illicit drug use between students who received DARE in the fifth and sixth grade (the intervention group) and students who did not (the control group). . . . All of the evaluations suggested that DARE had no statistically significant long-term effect on preventing youth illicit drug use. Of the six evaluations we reviewed, five also reported on students' attitudes toward illicit drug use and resistance to peer pressure and found no significant differences between the intervention and control groups over the long term. Two of these evaluations found that the DARE students showed stronger negative attitudes about illicit drug use and improved social skills about illicit drug use about 1 year after receiving the program. These positive effects diminished over time.[53]

Thus, the scientific community came to recognize the approach as ineffective.

Some schools dropped D.A.R.E., but because of the program's already extensive, established network, the prestigious Robert Wood Johnson Foundation, which has a history of funding alcohol and drug research, invested nearly $14 million to allow D.A.R.E. to test a new curriculum called Take Charge of Your Life (TCYL). TCYL was designed to help middle-school students develop "life skills such as communication, decision-making, assertiveness and refusal skills" that would help them refrain from alcohol and illicit drugs use and appreciate the risks of tobacco, alcohol, and illicit drug use.[54] University of Akron researchers found that compared to students in schools that did not participate in TCYL, TCYL participants were no less likely to use marijuana and slightly more likely to use alcohol and cigarettes by the eleventh grade.[55] This time, D.A.R.E. decided to replace TCYL with "*keepin' it REAL*," a prevention program on the Substance Abuse and Mental Health Services Administration's National Registry of Evidence-based Programs and Practices.[56] President Barack Obama proclaimed April 8, 2009, National D.A.R.E. Day, recognizing the organization's efforts to prevent drug use, gang involvement, and violence.[57]

Summary

Policy analysis, implementation, and evaluation are important steps in the policy process. They involve more than just technical skills. They are as political as any other steps in the policy process.

Policy analysts face difficult tasks because different groups are vying for the policy proposals they favor. In addition to determining the intent of social policies, which is not always clearly defined in legislation, problems in policy implementation may include obtaining sufficient resources, overcoming negative attitudes toward a program, and seeing that bureaucratic structures do not prevent the program from operating smoothly.

Americans have learned how difficult it can be to remedy social problems, especially in a society where people often differ on the definition of the problem as well as the solutions. A rational, scientific approach to evaluation includes identifying and ranking program goals and objectives, developing ways to measure these goals, identifying target groups and nontarget groups that might be affected, measuring tangible and intangible program effects, and measuring direct and indirect program costs. Conducting rigorous program evaluations is not an easy task. The difficulties are magnified when there is strong political support for or opposition to a program. Programs often continue even in light of negative findings.

Discussion Questions and Class Activities

1. Invite a policy analyst and/or policy evaluation researcher to discuss his or her work focusing on the political as well as rational aspects of policy and program evaluation research.

2. Read one or more policy briefs developed by organizations such as the Urban Institute, Brookings Institution, Hoover Institution, Cato Institute, or other think tank. How does it compare to the description of a policy analysis presented in this chapter? As a course assignment, you may wish to write a policy brief of your own on a topic of special interest to you.

3. In the wake of hurricane Katrina, Americans were stunned by the loss of life and the damage sustained. Criticisms were directed at the city government of New Orleans, the state government of Louisiana, and the Federal Emergency Management Agency (FEMA), a part of the Department of Homeland Security. Since the size of the disaster outstripped city and state resources, FEMA took much of the blame. Problems at FEMA, which predated hurricane Katrina, were blamed on being downgraded from a Cabinet-level agency, budget cuts, loss of staff, and staff with insufficient expertise to respond to problems of the magnitude caused by Katrina. The situation resulted in the resignation of FEMA's director. Read accounts of what happened and discuss whether Katrina was a failure of policy implementation with regard to bureaucracy, communications, leadership, resources, and/or other failures (see, for example, reports by the Government Accountability Office). What policies should have been in place to prevent this type of situation from happening? After reading the section in Chapter 3 on the subprime mortgage crisis, you may wish to engage in a similar exercise.

4. Spend some time observing or volunteering on a policy or program evaluation study being conducted by a researcher at your college or university or interview the researcher about the study. What points raised in this chapter are illustrated by the project? Is the study a controlled or quasiexperiment? Is it a longitudinal study? Are there tensions between what the funders (such as government agencies) want from the evaluation and what the researchers think should be studied? Are clients, program administrators, or others anxious or reluctant to participate?

5. Find a policy or program evaluation study in the literature on a topic of interest to you. What did the study find? Critique the study from a methodological perspective. For example, was a control group used? Was it possible to have a control group? Do the findings suggest a clear direction for policy? Does the article indicate if any policy or program modifications were made following the study?

Websites

American Enterprise Institute for Public Policy Research, http://www.aei.org, is a nonpartisan, not-for-profit organization that conducts research and education on government, politics, economics, and social welfare. It is considered a conservative think tank.

Brookings Institution, http://www.brookings.edu/, is a nonprofit public policy organization that conducts research and provides recommendations to foster democracy, security, and opportunity for Americans and a cooperative international system. It is perhaps the nation's oldest think tank and may be considered centrist in orientation.

Center on Budget and Policy Priorities, http://www.cbpp.org, conducts research and analysis on proposed budget and tax policies and focuses on policies that alleviate poverty and help low-income families and individuals.

Government Accountability Office, http://www.gao.gov, is an independent, nonpartisan government agency charged with providing Congress with timely, objective information on government funded programs, services, and activities.

Notes

1. William Dunn, *Public Policy Analysis: An Introduction, 4th ed.* (Upper Saddle River, NJ: Pearson/Prentice Hall, 2008), p. 1.
2. Carl V. Patton and David S. Sawicki, *Basic Methods of Policy Analysis and Planning, 2nd ed.* (Englewood Cliffs, NJ: Prentice Hall, 1993), p. 21; see pages 21–23 for a discussion of the concept of policy analysis dating back to the 1950s.
3. Patton and Sawicki, *Basic Methods of Policy Analysis and Planning;* also see Dunn, *Public Policy Analysis: An Introduction, 4th ed.*
4. Dunn, *Public Policy Analysis: An Introduction, 4th ed.*, p. 54.
5. See Diana M. DiNitto, *Social Welfare: Politics and Public Policy, 6th ed.* (Boston: Allyn and Bacon, 2005), especially chapter 7, and Neil Gilbert and Paul Terrell, *Dimensions of Social Welfare Policy, 7th ed.* (Boston: Allyn and Bacon, 2010), especially chapter 5.
6. For further discussion of choice in the types of benefits or social provisions that social policy may allocate and how they will be distributed, see Gilbert and Terrell, *Dimensions of Social Welfare Policy, 7th ed.*
7. Frances Stokes Berry and William D. Berry, "Innovation and Diffusion Models in Policy Research," in Sabatier, *Theories of the Policy Process,* pp. 223–260.
8. Jeffrey Pressman and Aaron Wildavsky, *Implementation* (Berkeley: University of California Press, 1973), p. 109.
9. This discussion relies on George C. Edwards, *Implementing Public Policy* (Washington, DC: Congressional Quarterly, 1980).
10. Robert Kornfeld, *Explaining Recent Trends in Food Stamp Program Caseloads, Final Report* (Cambridge, MA: Abt Associaes, March 2002). Retrieved January 16, 2009, from http://www.ers.usda.gov/publications/efan02008/efan02008.pdf
11. Richard Lacayo, "The Sad Fate of Legal Aid," *Time,* June 20, 1988, p. 59.
12. Child Nutrition Program Reauthorization Center, *Overcertification Talking Points* (Washington, DC: Food Research and Action Center, September 30, 2003). Retrieved January 17, 2010, from http://www.frac.org/html/federal_ http://www.frac.org/html/federal_food_programs/cnreauthor/overcerttalkingpoints.htm
13. Larry B. Hill, Ed., *The State of Public Bureaucracy* (Armonk, NY: Sharpe, 1992).
14. *Statistical Abstract of the United States, 2010,* Table 484 (Washington, DC: U.S. Bureau of the Census). Retrieved January 15, 2010, from http://www.census.gov/compendia/statab/2010/tables/10s0484.pdf
15. Herbert Kaufman, *Red Tape* (Washington, DC: Brookings Institution, 1977), p. 13.
16. *Statistical Abstract of the United States, 2010,* Table 416 (Washington, DC: U.S. Bureau of the Census). Retrieved January 16, 2009, from http://www.census.gov/compendia/statab/2010/tables/10s0416.pdf
17. Office of National Drug Control Policy, Table 2: Federal Drug Control Spending by Agency, FY2008-F2010 (Washington, DC: Executive Office of the President, May 2009). Retrieved January 17, 2009,

from http://www.ondcp.gov/publications/policy/10budget/tbl_2.pdf

18. *Federal Register,* Vol. 58, No. 38, March 1, 1993, p. 11830.

19. Richard Whitmire, "Study: Single State Agency Should Direct Welfare," *Gannett News Service,* Tuesday, June 29, 1993.

20. Joseph S. Wholey, John W. Scanlon, Hugh G. Duffy, James S. Fukumoto, and Leona M. Vogt, *Federal Evaluation Policy* (Washington, DC: Urban Institute, 1970), p. 15.

21. Laurie J. Bassi and Orley Ashenfelter, "The Effect of Direct Job Creation and Training Programs on Low-Skilled Workers," in Sheldon H. Danzinger and Daniel H. Weinberg, Eds., *Fighting Poverty: What Works and What Doesn't* (Cambridge, MA: Harvard University Press, 1986), p. 150.

22. Peter Passell, "Like a New Drug, Social Programs Are Put to the Test," *New York Times,* March 9, 1993, pp. C1, 10.

23. Carol H. Weiss, Erin Murphy-Graham, Anthony Petrosino, and Allison G. Gandhi, "The Fairy Godmother—and Her Warts: Making the Dream of Evidence-Based Policy Come True," *American Journal of Evaluation,* Vol. 29, No. 1, 2008, pp. 29–47.

24. Project MATCH Research Group, "Matching Alcoholism Treatments to Client Heterogeneity: Project MATCH Posttreatment Drinking Outcomes," *Journal of Studies on Alcohol,* Vol. 58, 1997, 7–29.

25. Raymond F. Anton et al., for the COMBINE Research Group, "Effect of Combined Pharmacotherapies and Behavioral Intervention (COMBINE Study) for Alcohol Dependence," *Journal of the American Medical Association,* Vol. 295, No. 17, 2006, pp. 2003–2017.

26. David Nachmias, *Policy Evaluation* (New York: St. Martin's, 1979), p. 4.

27. Carol H. Weiss, *Evaluation Research: Methods of Assessing Program Effectiveness* (Englewood Cliffs, NJ: Prentice Hall, 1972).

28. Peter H. Rossi, Howard E. Freeman, and Mark W. Lipsey, *Evaluation: A Systematic Approach,* 7th ed. (Thousand Oaks, CA: Sage Publications, 2004), p. 28.

29. Peter H. Rossi, Howard E. Freeman, and Mark W. Lipsey, *Evaluation: A Systematic Approach,* 6th ed. (Thousand Oaks, CA: Sage Publications, 1999), p. 2.

30. Christopher Trenholm, Barbara Devaney, Kenneth Fortson, Melissa Clark, Lisa Quay, Justin Wheeler, "Impacts of Abstinence Education on Teen Sexual Activity, Risk of Pregnancy, and Risk of Sexually

Transmitted Diseases," *Journal of Policy Analysis and Management,* Vol. 27, No. 2, 2008, pp. 255–276.

31. Maggie Fox, "Abstinence Education Doesn't Work: Report," *Reuters,* April 14, 2007. Retrieved January 17, 2010, from http://www.reuters.com/article/idUSN1423677120070414

32. Laura Sessions Stepp, "Study Casts Doubt on Abstinence-Only Programs," *Washington Post,* April 14, 2007. Retrieved January 17, 2010, from http://www.washingtonpost.com/wp-dyn/content/article/2007/04/13/AR2007041301003.html

33. Robert Morris, *Social Policy of the American Welfare State: An Introduction to Policy Analysis* (New York: Harper & Row, 1979), p. 133.

34. Westinghouse Learning Corporation, Ohio University, *The Impact of Head Start* (Washington, DC: Office of Economic Opportunity, 1969).

35. See James E. Anderson, *Public Policy-Making* (New York: Holt, Rinehart, & Winston, 1975), p. 150.

36. Lawrence J. Schweinhart and David P. Weikart, "High Scope/Perry Preschool Program Effects at Age Twenty-Seven" in Jonathan Crane, Ed., *Social Programs That Work* (New York: Russell Sage Foundation, 1998); Lawrence J. Schweinhart, J. Montie, Z. Xiang, W. S. Barnett, C. R. Belfield, and M. Nores, *Lifetime Effects: The HighScope Perry Preschool Study Through Age 40,* Monographs of the HighScope Educational Research Foundation, 14 (Ypsilanti, MI: HighScope Press, 2005). Retrieved March 16, 2010, from http://www.highscope.org/Content.asp?ContentId=219

37. See Edward Zigler, Sally J. Styfco, and Elizabeth Gilman, "The National Head Start Program for Disadvantaged Preschoolers" in Edward Zeigler and Sally J. Styfco, Eds., *Head Start and Beyond: A National Plan for Extended Childhood Intervention* (New Haven, CT: Yale University Press, 1993), pp. 1–41.

38. Valora Washington and Ura Jean Oyemade Bailey, *Project Head Start: Models and Strategies for the Twenty-First Century* (New York: Garland, 1995).

39. Ibid., p. 141; also see John Hood, "Caveat Emptor: The Head Start Scam," *Policy Analysis,* No. 187, December 18, 1992. Retrieved March, 16, 2010, from http://www.cato.org/pubs/pas/pa-187.html

40. Kevin J. Gorey, "Early Childhood Education: A Meta-Analytic Affirmation of the Short- and Long-term Benefits of Educational Opportunity," *School Psychology Quarterly,* Vol. 16, No. 1, 2001, pp. 9–30.

41. Walter S. Gilliam and Edward F. Zigler, "A Critical Meta-analysis of All Evaluations of State-Funded Preschool from 1977 to 1998: Implications for

Policy, Service Delivery and Program Evaluation," *Early Childhood Research Quarterly,* Vol. 15, No. 4, 2000, pp. 441–473.

42. For further discussion of classic experimental research in the area of public policy, see Bassie and Ashenfelter, "The Effects of Direct Job Creation and Training Programs on Low-Skilled Workers"; Douglas J. Besharov, Peter Germanis, and Peter H. Rossi, *Evaluating Welfare Reform: A Guide for Scholars and Practitioners* (College Park, MD: School of Public Affairs, University of Maryland, 1997). For an interesting account and critique see also William M. Epstein, *Welfare in America: How Social Science Fails the Poor* (Madison: University of Wisconsin Press, 1997).

43. Lisbeth B. Schorr, *Common Purpose: Strengthening Families and Neighborhoods to Rebuild America* (New York: Anchor Books/Doubleday, 1997).

44. Some of this section relies on C. Aaron McNeece and Diana M. DiNitto, *Chemical Dependency: A Systems Approach, 3rd ed.* (Boston: Allyn and Bacon, 2005).

45. Lloyd D. Johnston, Patrick M. O'Malley, Jerald G. Bachman, and John E. Schulenberg, *Monitoring the Future: National Results on Adolescent Drug Use: Overview of Key Findings, 2008* (NIH Publication No. 09-7401) (Bethesda, MD: National Institute on Drug Abuse, 2009). Retrieved March 16, 2010, from http://monitoringthefuture.org/pubs/monographs/overview2008.pdf

46. This paragraph relies on Lawrence Wallack and Kitty Corbett, "Illicit Drug, Tobacco, and Alcohol Use among Youth: Trends and Promising Approaches in Prevention," in Hank Resnick, Ed., *Youth and Drugs: Society's Mixed Messages,* Office of Substance Abuse Prevention Monograph No. 6 (Rockville, MD: U.S. Department of Health and Human Services, Alcohol, Drug Abuse, and Mental Health Administration, 1990).

47. The D.A.R.E. website is http://www.dare.com/home/default.asp

48. Christopher L. Ringwalt, Jody M. Green, Susan T. Ennett, Ronaldo Iachan, Richard Clayton, and Carl G. Leukfeld, *Past and Future Directions of the D.A.R.E. Program: Draft Final Report* (Research Triangle Park, NC: Research Triangle Institute, June 1994).

49. Stephen Glass, "Don't You D.A.R.E.," *New Republic,* March 3, 1997, pp. 18–20, 22–23, 26–28.

50. Weiss et al., "The Fairy Godmother—and Her Warts: Making the Dream of Evidence-Based Policy Come True," p. 42.

51. Donald R. Lynam, Richard Milich, Rick Zimmerman, Scott P. Novak, T. K. Logan, Catherine Martin, Carl Leukefeld, and Richard Clayton, "Project DARE: No Effects at 10-year Follow-up," *Journal of Consulting and Clinical Psychology,* Vol. 67, No. 4, 1999, pp. 590–593.

52. *Ibid.,* p. 592.

53. Marjorie E. Kanof, *Youth Illicit Drug Use Prevention: DARE Long-term Evaluations and Federal Efforts to Identify Effective Programs* (Washington, DC: United States General Accounting Office, 2003), GAO-03-172R, p. 2. Retrieved March 16, 2010, from http://www.gao.gov/docsearch/locate?searched=1&o=0&order_by=date&search_type=publications&keyword=GAO-03-172R&Submit=Search

54. "Evaluation of the D.A.R.E. School-based Substance Abuse Curriculum" (Princeton, NJ: Robert Wood Johnson Foundation, 2009). Retrieved December 22, 2009, from http://www.rwjf.org/pr/product.jsp?id=42049

55. Zili Sloboda et al., "The Adolescent Substance Abuse Prevention Study: A Randomized Field Trial of a Universal Substance Abuse Prevention Program," *Drug and Alcohol Dependence,* Vol. 102, Nos. 1–3, 2009, pp. 1–10.

56. "D.A.R.E. and the Take Charge of Your Life Research Study" (Los Angeles, CA: D.A.R.E. America). Retrieved December 22, 2009, from http://www.dareamerica.net/home/Resources/documents/RevisedLGIwebposting2.pdf

57. "National D.A.R.E. Day, 2009" (Washington, DC: The White House, April 8 2009). Retrieved December 23, 2009, from http://www.dare.com/home/tertiary/default1b34.asp

3

POLITICS AND THE HISTORY OF SOCIAL WELFARE POLICY

Diana M. DiNitto
David H. Johnson

Since the early 1900s, many factors have contributed to the growth of social welfare programs in the United States. They include the rural-to-urban migration, the elimination of residency requirements, the welfare rights movement, cost-of-living adjustments, the aging of America, and increasing numbers of single-parent families. Other factors that have shaped social welfare policy and programs include differing philosophical views of social welfare, different ideas about federalism, privatization of social welfare, and wars and global forces that focus attention away from domestic concerns about social welfare.

THE EARLY HISTORY OF SOCIAL WELFARE POLICY IN AMERICA

If history is a good teacher, we should take time to review, at least briefly, major events in the history of social welfare policy and services in the United States.[1]

The Elizabethan Poor Laws

In the Old World, the first source of welfare assistance was mutual aid. In time of need, the only recourse was reliance on one another. If a family's food crop failed or the breadwinner became ill and unable to work, brothers, sisters, or neighbors pitched in, knowing that they would receive the same assistance should they need it one day. Later, it became the duty of the church and of wealthy feudal lords to help the needy.[2] During much of Europe's Middle Ages, the emphasis was on doing charitable works as a religious duty. Attitudes toward the poor were benevolent. Those destitute through no fault of their own were treated with dignity and respect and were helped through the hard times.

These early systems of aid were informal, but as the structure of society became more complex, so did the system of providing welfare assistance. The first laws designed to curb poverty were passed in England during the fourteenth and fifteenth centuries. In 1349 the Black Death (bubonic plague) drastically reduced the population of the country and caused profound social disorganization. King Edward III responded with the Statute of Laborers to discourage vagrancy and begging. All able-bodied people were ordered to work, and giving alms was forbidden.

Changes in the structure of society eventually pushed the Elizabethan government to develop its own brand of social welfare. The first wave of industrialization in England occurred with a shift from an agrarian economy to an economy based on the wool industry. People left their home communities to seek industrial employment in the cities. The feudal system of life fell apart as this shift was completed. Government was becoming more centralized and played a stronger role in many aspects of society, including social welfare, while the church's role in welfare was diminishing.

The interplay of new social forces, the reduction of the labor force, the breakdown of the feudal system, and the move toward industrialization brought about the Elizabethan Poor Law of 1601, the first major event in the Elizabethan government's role in providing social welfare benefits. The law was passed mostly as a means of "controlling" those poor who were unable to locate employment and who might cause disruption. Taxes were levied to finance the new welfare system. The demands placed on recipients were harsh. Children whose parents were unable to support them faced apprenticeship, and able-bodied men dared not consider remaining idle.

Distinguishing the "deserving" from the "nondeserving" poor was a central part of the Elizabethan Poor Law. More affluent individuals did not want to be burdened with assisting any but the most needy. The deserving poor were orphaned children and adults who were lame, blind, widowed, or unemployed through no fault of their own. The nondeserving poor were vagrants or drunkards—those considered lazy and unwilling to work. "Outdoor relief" was the term used to describe assistance provided to many deserving poor in their own homes. "Indoor relief" was also provided to those unable to care for themselves, but such relief was generally provided in institutions called almshouses. The nondeserving poor were sent to workhouses, where they were forced to do menial work in return for only the barest of life's necessities. Welfare recipients had to meet stringent residency requirements. Local units of government called parishes administered aid. Parishes were instructed to provide aid only to people from their own jurisdictions.

Early Relief in the United States

Social welfare policy as we know it today in the United States dates back to the beginning of the seventeenth century in Elizabethan England. In the American colonies, as in England, the earliest sources of welfare aid for the destitute were families, friends, and churches. English colonists who settled in North America also brought with them many English welfare traditions. For example, residency requirements were strictly enforced through the policies of warning out and passing on.[3] "Warning out" meant that newcomers were urged to move on to other towns if it appeared that they were not financially responsible. More often, "passing on" was used to escort the transient poor back to their home communities.

Life for the colonists was austere. The business of settling America was a tough job, and the colonists were by no means well off. "Many of them were paupers, vagrants, or convicts shipped out by the English government as indentured servants."[4] Although many preferred life in the colonies, sickness or other misfortune could readily place a person in need.

The colonists used four methods to "assist" the needy. The least popular method was "auctioning" the poor to families who were willing to care for them at the lowest cost. A second method was to place the poor and sick under the supervision of a couple who was willing to care for them at as little cost as possible. The third method, outdoor relief, was provided to most of the needy. The fourth method was almshouses. Many claimed that almshouses were the best method of aid because of the medical care they provided to the sick and elderly. Almshouses in the cities provided a higher level of care than rural almshouses, which were often in deplorable condition and little more than rundown houses operated by a farm family. "Overseers of the poor" were appointed to coordinate the community's efforts.

The 1800s brought more ideas about what could be accomplished for the poor.[5] The Society for the Prevention of Pauperism and successor groups emerged to help the poor overcome the personal shortcomings that had supposedly led to their condition. In this tradition, the private Charity Organization Societies (COS) that developed in the United States in the late 1870s adopted a method called "scientific charity" that involved the study of the causes of social problems and methods to address them. These organizations also worked with other community groups and agencies to provide services to the poor in a more coordinated fashion. COS workers became the forerunners of today's social workers, and their methods developed into today's casework services. The philosophies of Calvinism, the work ethic, and social Darwinism prevailed during this period. COS workers preferred to give advice and encourage people to work whenever possible rather than provide material aid. Politicians, welfare administrators, doctors, and charity workers seemed pleased with their progress in assisting the needy during the eighteenth and nineteenth centuries.

The Rural-to-Urban Migration

The United States experienced some of its sharpest growing pains as the Industrial Revolution reached its peak. From 1870 to 1920, rapid industrialization and heavy immigration changed the country from a rural, agrarian society to an urban, industrial society. People migrated from poor rural farming communities hoping to find jobs and brighter futures in the cities. This *rural-to-urban migration* was the first major factor in the growth of social welfare. People from other countries were also immigrating to American cities, seeking a better life. Many people's dreams were shattered. Those who found jobs were often forced to work long hours for low pay under poor working conditions. Housing was often crowded; sanitation and health problems were common. Those who had come to the cities to "make good" were often far from their families who could have provided financial and psychological support. Social welfare became a growing problem for governments.

The Progressive Era

The Progressive Era encompassed the late 1890s and first two decades of the twentieth century. Private groups such as the COS, settlement houses, churches, and big-city political "machines" and "bosses" provided much of the assistance to the needy. Settlement house workers offered many services to those coming to the cities from rural areas and those emigrating from other countries, such as help in finding jobs, counseling, education, and childcare. They also prepared people for their roles as citizens in their new communities, and they actively campaigned for social reforms. The political machines operated by trading baskets of food, bushels of coal, and favors for the votes of the poor. To finance this early welfare system, the machine offered city contracts, protection, and privileges to business interests, which in return paid off in cash. Aid was provided in a personal fashion without red tape or delays. Recipients did not feel embarrassed or ashamed, for, after all, "they were trading something valuable—their votes—for the assistance they received."[6]

As social problems mounted—increased crowding, unemployment, and poverty in the cities—local and state governments began to take a more active role in welfare. States adopted "mothers' aid" and "mothers' pension" laws to help children in families where the father was deceased or absent. Other state pension programs were established to assist poor people who were aged, blind, or disabled. This era was one of progressivism. Progressives went head to head with corrupt governments and businesses and industries that exploited workers. Progressives were successful in achieving many social welfare and labor reforms.[7] Many states adopted workers' compensation programs to assist those injured on the job. The federal Children's Bureau was established to investigate and improve the lives of children. Women won the right to vote, and additional laws were passed to improve the working conditions of women and children. The Progressives were ahead of their time. They urged a program of social insurance rather than charity. Large-scale federal government involvement in social welfare was not far away.

THE GREAT DEPRESSION AND FDR'S NEW DEAL

The Great Depression, one of the bleakest periods in U.S. history, followed the stock market crash in October 1929. Prices dropped dramatically, and unemployment was rampant. By 1932 one of every four people had no job, and one of every six was receiving welfare. Americans who had always worked no longer had jobs, and they depleted their savings or lost them when banks failed. Many had to give up their homes and farms because they could no longer meet the mortgage payments. Economic catastrophe struck deep into the ranks of the middle classes. Many of the unemployed and homeless slept on steps and park benches because they had nowhere else to go.[8] The cities were no longer able to cope with worsening social conditions.

The Great Depression dramatically changed American thought about social welfare. The realization that poverty could strike so many forced Americans to consider large-scale economic reform. Movements formed on the left and right, including those that raised the specter of socialism or communism, and threatened the political establishment. As a response to the country's problems, President Franklin Delano Roosevelt began to elaborate the philosophy of the "New Deal" that would permit the federal government to devote more attention to the public welfare than did the philosophy of "rugged individualism" so popular in the earlier days of the country. The New Deal was not a consistent or unifying plan; instead, it was a series of improvisations that were often adopted suddenly, and some of them were even contradictory. Roosevelt believed that the government should act humanely and compassionately toward those suffering from the Depression. The objectives of the New Deal were "relief, recovery, and reform." Roosevelt called for "full persistent experimentation. If it fails, admit it frankly and try something else. But above all try something. The millions who are in want will not stand by silently forever while the things to satisfy their needs are in easy reach."[9] Americans came to accept the principle that the entire community has a responsibility for welfare.

The New Deal contained emergency aid, such as food assistance, and temporary work programs, such as the Works Progress Administration and the Civilian Conservation Corps that provided a living for many Americans. But the New Deal's most enduring provision was the Social Security Act of 1935, which remains the cornerstone of social welfare legislation today. The act included social insurance programs (benefits for retired workers administered by the federal government and a federal-state unemployment insurance program) and federal grant-in-aid programs to states to provide public assistance payments for dependent children as well as people who were elderly or blind. It included social services—child welfare and vocational rehabilitation programs, and maternal and child health and public health programs. The Fair Labor Standards Act of 1938 established a minimum wage and overtime pay and restricted the work of children. Additional legislation protected workers' rights to organize and engage in collective bargaining. The federal government had established its role in social welfare.

LBJ AND THE WAR ON POVERTY

From the time of the New Deal until the 1950s, a few notable amendments were made to the Social Security Act. Dependents of retired workers and survivors of deceased workers became eligible for social insurance benefits, eligibility requirements were loosened in some social welfare programs, and payments were increased, but there were few other changes in the system. Then, beginning in the 1950s, the number of workers covered under Social Security expanded substantially, disabled workers became eligible for social insurance benefits, and the states were able to obtain federal funds to provide public assistance payments to poor people with severe disabilities. Some medical care was also made available to public assistance recipients, but more changes in social welfare were in store.

The 1950s and 1960s were unusual times for Americans. Although this was a period of increased prosperity for many, the dichotomy between the "haves" and "have nots" became more apparent. As the decade of the 1960s began, the nearly 40 million people still living in poverty, many of them members of racial and ethnic minority groups, overshadowed the relative affluence of the times. The writings of economist John Kenneth Galbraith directed attention to the existence of poverty in the midst of this affluent culture and influenced President John F. Kennedy to begin acting on the problem. Kennedy initiated a pilot food stamp program and aid to Appalachia and other severely depressed areas.

Domestic turmoil raged on several fronts. The civil rights movement was reaching a crescendo. On August 28, 1963, The Reverend Dr. Martin Luther King, Jr. delivered his famous "I have a dream" speech at the Lincoln Memorial in Washington, DC. Civil rights demonstrations and marches were held across the country. King, head of the Southern Christian Leadership Conference, preached a message of nonviolence, but from 1964 to 1968, race riots rocked major U.S. cities. President Kennedy's assassination in 1963, Reverend King's in 1968, and Robert Kennedy's in 1968, during his run for the Democratic nomination for president, also marked the period.

The Welfare Rights Movement

Americans were bitterly divided over the Vietnam War, and college campuses were the sites of many anti-war protests, including the 1970 Kent State University massacre in which Ohio National Guardsmen killed four people. In addition to the anti-war movement and the civil rights movement, a "welfare rights movement" also arose to help people obtain benefits to which they were entitled. Members of the newly formed National Welfare Rights Organization (NWRO) organized and aided many people in this process. The welfare rights movement helped people organize to demand the aid due them (especially Aid to Families with Dependent Children) and better treatment of applicants and recipients. Among the strategies used were demonstrations, threats of legal action, and education about social welfare benefits. The movement brought changes in the behavior and attitudes of public aid recipients. Frances Fox Piven and Richard Cloward note, "The mood of applicants in welfare waiting rooms had changed. They were no longer as humble, as self-effacing, as pleading; they were more indignant, angrier, more demanding."[10] The mood of welfare administrators and caseworkers also changed. Many practices that had been part of lengthy background investigations ceased. The process of obtaining aid was speeded up, and welfare agencies were not so quick to terminate benefits when recipients did not comply with the rules. "For all practical purposes, welfare operating procedures collapsed; regulations were simply ignored in order to process the hundreds of thousands of families who jammed the welfare waiting rooms."[11]

Economic Opportunity Act

Following John F. Kennedy's assassination, President Lyndon Baines Johnson took the lead of his predecessor in addressing the needs of the poor. In fact, his enthusiasm for what the country could accomplish was so great that in 1964 he was moved to state that "this administration today, here and now, declares unconditional war on poverty." Later that year, in signing the Economic Opportunity Act of 1964, the president also declared the country's "commitment to eradicate poverty among its people." The New Deal of the 1930s, the first major war on poverty in the United States, was waged by moderates with its centerpiece of social insurance (designed to *prevent* poverty) and dabs of public assistance (designed to *alleviate* poverty). The war on poverty of the 1960s, waged by liberals, was an attempt to apply a *curative* strategy to the problem of poverty in order to break the cycle of poverty and allow economically disadvantaged Americans to move into the country's working classes and eventually its middle classes. The strategy was "rehabilitation and not relief." The Economic Opportunity Act of 1964, the centerpiece of the War on Poverty, was to "strike at the causes, not just the consequences, of poverty." The goals of the "war" were to allow ghetto and poor communities to develop their own programs to arrest poverty and to root out inequality in the lives of Americans.

When Lyndon B. Johnson assumed the presidency, he saw an opportunity to distinguish his administration and to carry forward the traditions of Franklin D. Roosevelt. Johnson, a former public school teacher, believed that government work and training efforts, particularly those directed at youth, could break the cycle of poverty by giving people the basic skills to improve their employability and make them self-sufficient adults. In order to do this, he championed the Economic Opportunity Act.

The Economic Opportunity Act created a multitude of programs that were to be coordinated in Washington by a new, independent federal bureaucracy—the Office of Economic Opportunity (OEO). OEO was given money and authority to support varied and highly experimental techniques for combating poverty in both urban and rural communities. As evidence of its priority, OEO's first director was Sargent Shriver, brother-in-law of the late President Kennedy and later Democratic vice-presidential candidate with George McGovern in 1972. OEO was encouraged to bypass local and state governments and to establish new programs throughout the nation, with the poor participating in their governance. OEO was generally not given authority to make direct, cash grants to the poor as relief or public assistance. Most OEO programs were aimed, whether accurately or inaccurately, at curing the causes of poverty rather than alleviating its symptoms.

The core of the Economic Opportunity Act was grassroots *community action programs* to be carried on at the local level by public or private nonprofit agencies, with federal financial assistance. Model cities programs, community action agencies, and other strategies, such as the Head Start preschool program, were tried as part of the Economic Opportunity Act. Communities were urged to form community action agencies composed of representatives of government, private organizations, and, most importantly, the poor themselves. OEO was originally intended to support antipoverty programs devised by the local community action agency. Projects could include literacy training, health services, legal aid, neighborhood service centers, vocational training, childhood development activities, or other innovative ideas. The act also envisioned that the community action agencies would help organize poor people so that they could become participating members of the community and could avail themselves of the many programs designed to serve them. In addition, the act attempted to coordinate federal and state programs for the poor in each community.

Community action programs were to be "developed, conducted, and administered with the maximum feasible participation of the residents of the areas and members of the groups served." This was perhaps the most controversial language in the act, and there was more than a little consternation among local officials when community members took seriously the phrase "maximum feasible participation" of local residents. In some communities this meant organizing to fight city hall. The more militant members of the OEO administration frequently cited this phrase as authority to "mobilize" the poor "to have immediate and irreversible impact on their communities." This language implied that the poor were to be organized as a political force by government antipoverty warriors using federal funds. Needless to say, neither Congress nor the Johnson administration really intended to create rival political organizations that would compete for power with local governments.

The typical community action agency was governed by a board consisting of public officials (perhaps the mayor, a county commissioner, a school board member, and a public health officer), prominent public citizens (from business, labor, civil rights, religious, and civic affairs organizations), and representatives of the poor (in some cases selected in agency-sponsored elections, but more often hand-picked by ministers, social workers, civil rights leaders, and other prominent community figures). A staff was hired, including a full-time director, paid from an OEO grant. A target area was defined—a low-income area of the county or the ghetto of a city. Neighborhood centers were established in the target area, perhaps with counselors, employment assistance, a recreation hall, a childcare center, and a health clinic. Staff also assisted the poor in their contacts with the school system, the welfare department, employment agencies, the public housing authority, and so on. Frequently, the centers and the antipoverty workers who staffed them acted as advocates for the poor and as intermediaries between the poor and public agencies.

Among the War on Poverty programs were the Job Corps (for youth), the Neighborhood Youth Core, Legal Services, Head Start, family planning programs (advice and devices to facilitate family planning by the poor), homemaker services (advice and services on how to stretch low family budgets), and additional job training programs (such as special outreach to bring the hard-core unemployed into established workforce programs). There were also programs to help small businesses and to provide direct economic assistance to residents of rural areas. Finally, Volunteers in Service to America (VISTA), which continues today, was modeled after the popular Peace Corps. VISTA volunteers work in domestic, poverty-impacted areas rather than in foreign countries. Many of the volunteers are young people who want to serve their country.

The Great Society

Today, programs such as the Head Start preschool program continue to enjoy strong support, but most enduring programs of the "Great Society" of the 1960s were enacted separately from the Economic Opportunity Act. President Johnson's plan included a number of other programs. Among the most important are:

- ***The Elementary and Secondary Education Act of 1965:*** This was the first major, general federal aid-to-education program. It included federal funds to "poverty-impacted" school districts and became the largest source of federal aid to education. The act continues today under its current version, the No Child Left Behind Act.
- ***The Food Stamp Program:*** This nutrition program was an important step in the development of major in-kind benefit programs. Today it is called the Supplemental Nutrition Assistance Program (SNAP). It remains a major source of relief to a broad cross-section of those who are poor or low income (see Chapter 4).

- *Medicare:* This health insurance program was created as an amendment to the Social Security Act. It covers virtually all older people in the United States, as well as many younger former workers with long-term disabilities (see Chapter 8).
- *Medicaid:* This amendment to the Social Security Act is still the major federal healthcare program for certain groups of poor people (see Chapter 8).
- *Job Training:* This array of programs expanded the Manpower Development and Training Act and has evolved into other job and training programs. Its current version is the Workforce Investment Act.
- ***The Public Works and Economic Development Act of 1965 and the Appalachian Regional Development Act of 1965:*** These efforts continue to encourage economic development in distressed areas.

With all these policies and programs, a revolution in U.S. spending priorities was taking place (see Illustration 3.1 and Figure 3.1).

Politics Overtakes the War on Poverty

The reasons for the OEO's demise are complex. OEO programs were often the scene of great confusion. Personnel were young, middle-class, inexperienced, and idealistic, and there was a high turnover among administrators. Aside from Head Start, most community action agencies lacked clear direction. Many of the poor believed that the program was going to provide them with money; they never really understood or accepted that community action agencies provided other

ILLUSTRATION 3.1
The Revolution No One Noticed

While Americans were preoccupied with the turmoil of the 1960s, the civil rights movement, and the war in Vietnam, a revolution no one noticed was taking place.[a] For many years, the argument for increased attention to social welfare in America had followed clear lines: The United States was spending the largest portion of its budget for defense; programs for people who were poor, sick, or aged and for minorities were underfinanced. Social welfare proponents contended that in order to be more responsive to the needs of its citizens, the nation should "change its priorities" and spend more for social programs to reduce poverty and less on wars like that in Vietnam. The argument ended with a call for a change in national priorities.

In a single decade, U.S. national priorities were reversed. In 1965, national defense expenditures accounted for 43 percent of the federal government's budget; social welfare expenditures (social insurance, health, and public assistance) accounted for 24 percent. While the mass media focused on the war in Vietnam and Watergate, a revolution in national policy from "guns to butter" was occurring. By 1975, defense accounted for only 26 percent of the federal budget, and social welfare expenditures had grown to 42 percent of the budget. In fiscal year 2010, social welfare expenditures are expected to total 60 percent of the budget compared to 19 percent for defense. Health programs alone (primarily Medicaid and Medicare) will comprise about 25 percent of the total budget. Social welfare is clearly the major function and major expenditure of the federal government.[b]

Figure 3.1 shows the changing trends in spending for social welfare and defense. Note that defense spending jumped up at the beginnings of the Korean War (1950–1952) and the Vietnam War (1964–1968) and later in

(Continued)

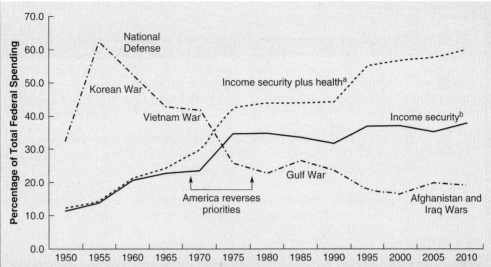

FIGURE 3.1 **Social Welfare and Defense Priorities (Percentage of Total Federal Spending)** *Source:*
Data are from Office of Management and Budget, *The President's Budget, Fiscal Year 2011, Table 3.1—
Outlays by Superfunction and Function* (Washington, DC: Executive Office of the President). Retrieved
March 3, 2010, http://www.whitehouse.gov/omb/budget/Historicals/. Data for 2010 is an estimate.

[a] Income security plus health values are sum of Income Security, Medicare, Medicaid, and
Healthcare annual spending.

[b] Income security values are sum of total Income Security and Social Security annual spending.

the military buildup begun under President Carter and continued under President Reagan. In contrast, social welfare spending rose slowly for many years and then "exploded" in the 1970s after the Great Society programs of the War on Poverty were in place. Social welfare and health spending remained at high levels despite a significant increase in defense spending. This reversal of national priorities occurred during both Democratic and Republican administrations and during the Vietnam War—the nation's longest war. "The mid to late 1960s were quite prosperous years. The unemployment rate fell under 4 percent, real income rose briskly. In the flush of affluence, new programs could be introduced with minimal fiscal strain, even as the Vietnam War expenditures were swelling."[c] In short, ideas that welfare expenditures are not likely to increase during Republican administrations or during times of war turned out to be wrong. The U.S. commitment to social welfare was growing.

Not everyone was comfortable with this change in public spending priorities. There was fear that the nation was sacrificing national defense in order to spend money on social welfare programs that might not work. As the 1980s emerged, a more cautious attitude toward social welfare had developed. Far too many people remained poor in spite of increased welfare spending, and there were some successful attempts to curb these social programs.

Today, addressing poverty does not rank where it once did on the public policy agenda.[d] However, the portion of the total federal budget devoted to social welfare continues to grow, largely due to growing demands on the major social insurance (Social Security) and health (Medicare and Medicaid) programs, along with prescription drug coverage for Medicare recipients. These programs will balloon in the coming years as the baby boomers retire.

Through the 1990s the United States experienced reductions in military spending as

(Continued)

ILLUSTRATION 3.1 (Continued)

a result of amazing political changes in various parts of the world—greater democratization in Russia and the other communist bloc countries, the fall of the Berlin Wall between East and West Germany, and the demise of the Cold War. The trend in military spending shifted upward slightly in 2000 and grew in response to terrorists' attacks on the World Trade Center and the Pentagon in 2001, and the subsequent ongoing war efforts in Afghanistan and Iraq.

Social welfare problems remain significant, from child poverty and child abuse to alcohol and drug abuse, unemployment, and the large proportion of the population with no health insurance. The U.S. population continues to live longer, necessitating even more and more varied social services. With the astronomical growth in the federal deficit during the early years of the new millennium, the growing social welfare demands of the U.S. population, the continued threat of terrorist attacks and the growth in the number of rogue states with nuclear capabilities, it will take even greater resolve and ingenuity in the years ahead to meet the country's social welfare needs.

[a]See Aaron Wildavsky, *Speaking Truth to Power: The Art and Craft of Policy Analysis* (Boston: Little, Brown, 1979), especially pp. 86–89, for elaboration on this discussion of "the revolution no one noticed."
[b]Office of Management and Budget, *The President's Budget, Fiscal Year 2011, Table 3.1—Outlays by Superfunction and Function* (Washington, DC: Executive Office of the President). Retrieved March 3, 2010, http://www.whitehouse.gov/omb/budget/Historicals
[c]Robert D. Plotnick, "Social Welfare Expenditures: How Much Help for the Poor?" *Policy Analysis*, Vol. 5, No. 2, 1979, p. 278.
[d]"More than Half of Americans say Dealing with the Problems of Poor and Needy People Should Be a Top Priority for Congress, But Many Issues Rank Higher," data from the Pew Research Center, January 2006 (New York: Public Agenda). Retrieved March 3, 2010, from http:// http://www.publicagenda.org/charts/more-half-americans-say-dealing-problems-poor-and-needy-people-should-be-top-priority-congress

services—community organization, outreach, counseling, training, and similar assistance. Many community action agencies duplicated, and even competed with, existing welfare and social service agencies, and some organized the poor to challenge local government agencies. As a result, more than a few local governments called on the Johnson administration and Congress to curb community action agencies that were using federal funds to "undermine" existing programs and organizations. There were frequent charges of mismanagement and corruption, particularly at the local level. Some community action agencies became entangled in the politics of race; some big-city agencies were charged with excluding whites; and in some rural areas, whites believed that poverty agencies were "for blacks only."

Perhaps the failures of the War on Poverty can be explained by lack of knowledge about how to *cure* poverty. In retrospect, it seems naive to believe that local agencies could have found their own cures for eliminating or even reducing poverty. OEO became an unpopular stepchild of the Johnson administration even before LBJ left office, so the demise of the OEO programs cannot be attributed to political partisanship—that is, to the election of a Republican administration under Richard Nixon. Nor can the demise of the poverty program be attributed to the Vietnam War since both "wars" were escalated and later de-escalated at the same time. The Nixon administration reorganized the OEO in 1973, transferring most of its programs to other government agencies. The Ford administration abolished the OEO in 1974, turning its remaining programs over to other agencies. Today, community action agencies around the country receive assistance through the Community Services Block Grant (CSBG), established in 1981 and currently administered by the Administration for Children and Families of the Department of Health and Human Services. Community action agencies continue to offer a variety of antipoverty, social, health, and related services.

Some have argued that the War on Poverty itself was never funded at a level that would make a substantial impact. OEO funds were spread over hundreds of communities. Such relatively small amounts could never offset the numerous, deep-seated causes of deprivation. The War on Poverty raised the expectations of the poor, but it never tried to cope with poverty on a scale comparable to the size of the problem. Often the outcome was only to increase frustration.

In an obvious reference to public policies affecting the poor and blacks in America, in 1968, Aaron Wildavsky wrote:

> A recipe for violence: Promise a lot; deliver a little. Lead people to believe they will be much better off, but let there be no dramatic improvement. Try a variety of small programs, each interesting but marginal in impact and severely underfinanced. Avoid any attempted solution remotely comparable in size to the dimensions of the problem you are trying to solve. Have middle-class civil servants hire upper-class student radicals to use lower-class Negroes as a battering ram against the existing local political systems; then complain that people are going around disrupting things and chastise local politicians for not cooperating with those out to do them in. Get some poor people involved in local decision-making, only to discover that there is not enough at stake to be worth bothering about. Feel guilty about what has happened to black people; tell them you are surprised they have not revolted before; express shock and dismay when they follow your advice. Go in for a little force, just enough to anger, not enough to discourage. Feel guilty again; say you are surprised that worse has not happened. Alternate with a little suppression. Mix well, apply a match, and run.[12]

Whether one believes that the War on Poverty was more of a defeat or more of a victory, many other programs borne of the Great Society era, like Medicaid, Food Stamps (now SNAP), and Head Start, continue to serve millions of poor and low-income Americans.

MORE EXPANSION OF SOCIAL WELFARE

During the twentieth century, the United States developed its own unique system of social welfare.[13] Congressional actions, court decisions, and demographic forces were all contributing to the growth of the welfare state.

Residency Requirements Eliminated

Another important event that occurred during the 1960s was an end to *residency requirements.* As society became more mobile and people moved more frequently to seek jobs and other opportunities, the argument for residency requirements no longer seemed to hold up. Yet states and communities continued to impose these restrictions. Requiring that potential recipients had resided in the city or state for six months or a year, or even requiring that they intended to reside in the city or state, were ways to keep public assistance caseloads small. Following a number of court challenges, in 1969, in the case of *Shapiro v. Thompson,* the U.S. Supreme Court declared residency requirements in federally supported welfare programs unconstitutional.[14] As a result, it became easier to qualify for aid, and public assistance caseloads grew.

Shapiro v. Thompson was not the last case the U.S. Supreme Court heard on residency requirements. The 1996 welfare reform law allowed states to impose a 12-month residency requirement before paying full TANF benefits, if a state's benefits were higher than in the recipient's previous state of residence. States quickly implemented the residency requirement, and welfare advocacy organizations, poverty law centers, and civil rights organizations filed lawsuits in protest. California's Supreme Court and other courts soon found these residency rules discriminatory and a violation of individuals' rights to travel and equal protection under the law. In May 1999, the U.S. Supreme Court, in *Saenz v. Roe,* confirmed its earlier decision that residency requirements are unconstitutional.[15]

As the 1970s approached, the new presidential administration of Richard M. Nixon began dismantling the agencies of the War on Poverty. The "welfare rights movement" of the 1960s had raised the nation's consciousness about social welfare needs. Many more people were receiving public assistance. But with so many added to the rolls, a perception developed that the public assistance system now needed reform. President Nixon, determined to clean up the "welfare mess," proposed another type of reform in the early 1970s—a guaranteed annual income for all poor people. Parts of the plan were adopted, notably the Supplemental Security Income (SSI) program, which provides cash assistance to those who are aged, blind, or disabled and living in poverty (see Chapter 6). For the most part, however, Congress rejected the idea of a guaranteed annual income. Some thought it was too much welfare, and others were concerned that the guarantees were too low.

Cost-of-Living Adjustments

Much of the increase in federal social welfare spending since the 1970s has resulted from congressional approval of *cost-of-living adjustments* (COLAs), also known as indexing, designed to keep federal social welfare programs—Social Security, SSI, and food stamp benefits—in line with inflation. COLAs were enacted in 1973 and became effective in 1975. Prior to this, Congress had to approve any increase in Social Security payments and SSI payments. Political scientist Aaron Wildavsky noted, "Such action was not intended to provide greater benefits to recipients, but only to automatically assure them of constant purchasing power."[16]

Since 1975, annual COLAs have varied considerably.[17] In 1980, the COLA was 14.3 percent, the highest ever. During the high-inflation years of the early 1980s, COLAs came under attack. Although social welfare payments were being adjusted for cost-of-living increases, the wages of many workers in the sluggish economy had not kept pace with inflation. Some modifications were made to control COLAs. In 2010, for the first time since their enactment, the COLA was zero due to the country's worst economic recession since the Great Depression.

The Graying of America

In the wake of World War II (1941–1945), as soldiers returned from the European and Pacific Theaters of the War, they were anxious to start their families. Post-war prosperity and the return of factories to domestic production activities, combined with more efforts at wage and benefit increases, largely by organized labor, led to a growing and prosperous middle class. This ushered in the era of the "baby boom." Baby boomers are those who were born between 1946 and 1964. There are an estimated 78 million baby boomers in the population today.[18] As these citizens approach their middle 60s, they will begin to access Social Security, Medicare, and other social welfare programs for older Americans, placing increased demands on the social welfare system. Today those over age 65 comprise nearly 13 percent of the U.S. population, compared to 4 percent at the turn of the twentieth century. By the year 2030, this figure will approach 20 percent.[19] Improved living conditions and advances in medicine have helped Americans look forward to longer lives than ever before, but in advanced age people may become increasingly vulnerable and unable to meet all their own needs.

The tripling of the proportion of the older population over the past century has meant the need for greater planning and more services to ensure that they receive proper treatment. The largest social welfare programs in the United States are Social Security and Medicare (see Chapters 5 and 8). The vast majority of recipients of these programs are older Americans, who are well represented at the polls, and who receive a higher level of social welfare support than any other segment of the population. Although there is general agreement that the older population deserves publicly supported assistance, there is also a growing feeling that those who are wealthier should carry more of the costs of their own care.

Increase in Single-Parent Families

The changing patterns of U.S. family life are among the most controversial factors explaining increased social welfare expenditures. The divorce rate has continued to decline since it peaked in 1980, but family breakup remains common.[20] The number of children born to unmarried women continues to increase, reaching a historic high of nearly 40 percent of all births in 2007, and the increase in pregnancies among teenagers who are unmarried and ill equipped to care for children has also begun to climb again after a decade of decline.[21] These social and demographic trends mean that single parents, primarily women, head many families today.

Families headed by single women have an exceptionally high poverty rate that is still more than double that of families headed by single men. Women head 85 percent of all single-parent families living in poverty.[22] Public assistance programs (primarily TANF, Medicaid, and food stamps) and the earned income credit, a special tax credit for low-income workers, are crucial resources for making ends meet, especially for the large number of female-headed families living in poverty or laboring at low-wage jobs. Young families' use of Medicaid, SCHIP, SNAP, and other programs is on the rise.

Social Services

The federal government's Title XX Social Services Block Grant initiated in 1975 as well as the Community Services Block Grant provide a wide range of social services, often directed at low-income individuals and families. Another type of social welfare movement also arose as services designed to address problems in addition to poverty grew increasingly popular in the 1960s and 1970s. Consequently, new legislation was passed to assist abused children, to provide mental health services, and to develop social service programs for older Americans. During the 1960s every state passed child abuse reporting legislation, and child welfare services grew. Legislation such as the Community Mental Health Centers Construction Act of 1963 was instrumental in increasing mental health services in the light of court decisions and laws limiting authorities' ability to use involuntary hospitalization. However, mental health and housing services lagged well behind need for those with serious mental illnesses contributing to the homeless population. In 1965 the Older Americans Act provided services like nutrition programs that helped older adults remain in their own homes.

Medicare, Medicaid, and other health insurance coverage expanded access to mental health, home health, nursing homes, and other social services. Given the demand for social services by those in the middle and upper classes, the private sector began offering and expanding these services.

THE REAGAN AND BUSH YEARS

In contrast to the New Deal and the Great Society, during the 1980s, a decidedly different response to hardship in the United States emerged. Concerned with growing costs and disillusioned with the perceived failure of many public assistance programs, the administration of President Ronald

Reagan attempted to limit the federal government's role in social welfare and to increase reliance on state governments and the private sector in providing services. A major step toward achieving these goals was the passage of the Family Support Act (FSA) of 1988, which weakened poor families' entitlement to Aid to Families with Dependent Children (AFDC) and shifted the program toward a mandatory work and training program. The George H. W. Bush administration followed a similar path.

There was consternation with social welfare programs—particularly growing public assistance rolls—and the amount spent on these programs. The most severe criticisms were that these programs encourage dependency and were directly to blame for the large number of people who turn to governments for help. The 1988 Family Support Act (FSA) was intended to (1) reduce spending on public assistance programs, (2) minimize the government's role in public assistance, (3) provide assistance only to the "truly needy," and (4) provide assistance on a short-term basis only. FSA was the most sweeping reform to the public assistance system since the New Deal. Spending was cut in the AFDC program, and work and training mandates increased. Eligibility requirements for other public assistance programs, such as the Food Stamp Program, were tightened. As a result, significant numbers of recipients were removed from the rolls. Homelessness became more evident in the context of these welfare reforms.

The Supply Side

When Ronald Reagan entered office, the nation faced major economic problems: unemployment, inflation, low productivity, and low investment. Reagan saw this as an outcome of "big government." He believed, "The federal government through taxes, spending, regulatory, and monetary policies, [had] sacrificed long-term growth and price stability for ephemeral, short-term goals."[23] In addressing the economic troubles of the country, Reagan moved away from the more liberal Keynesian economic policies and embraced conservative supply-side economics, dubbed "Reaganomics," during his tenure in office. The neoconservative movement had been born.

Keynesian economics is based on the notion that government can boost employment or cut inflation by manipulating the demand side of the economy—increasing government spending and expanding the money supply to boost employment, and doing just the opposite to hold down inflation. It also holds that unemployment and inflation should not occur together—unemployment should reduce income, which in turn would force down prices. But according to government figures, both unemployment and inflation remained high during the 1970s. Government efforts to reduce unemployment simply added to inflation, and government efforts to cut inflation simply added to unemployment. Reagan combined the unemployment rate with the inflation rate and called it the *misery index*.

To reduce the misery index and boost the economy, Reagan implemented a series of changes that were the "most ambitious economic reform in the United States since the New Deal."[24] These reforms were concentrated on the supply side of the economy and included (1) cuts in the rate of growth in federal spending, (2) tax cuts for individuals and businesses, (3) deregulation of industry to reduce the cost of doing business, and (4) slowing the growth of the nation's money supply. During his first term, Reagan successfully encouraged Congress to cut personal income taxes by 25 percent, and to "index" tax rates to eliminate "bracket creep," which occurs when inflation carries taxpayers into higher brackets. Today, taxes are "adjusted" or indexed, so that taxpayers will not carry a heavier burden as inflation rises.

Under Reagan's tax reform, the number of individual tax brackets was reduced from 15 to two primary categories—a 15 and a 28 percent bracket (actually, due to a complicated set of rules, some earners incurred a 33 percent rate). Corporate tax brackets were also reduced, and other reforms included increasing the personal income tax exemption, eliminating some real estate tax shelters used primarily by the wealthy, and taxing capital gains (taxes paid on profits from the sale of assets such as real estate and stocks) as ordinary income instead of using lower rates (a move that Reagan did not support). President Reagan, known as the Great Communicator, called it "the best anti-poverty bill, the best pro-family measure, and the best job-creation program ever to come out of the Congress."[25]

Reagan's policies were designed to encourage Americans to work, save, and invest. Taxes and regulations on businesses and affluent Americans were reduced in the hope that they would reinvest their profits and expand job opportunities for the poor and working classes. In other words, incentives were provided for the wealthy in the hope that benefits would "trickle down" to the poor in the form of new jobs.[26]

As George H. W. Bush campaigned for the presidency and assumed the office after two very popular terms of the Reagan administration, his favorite phrase was "Read my lips—no new taxes." But a growing budget deficit and the inability to balance the federal budget caused him to eat his words. The budget battle that ensued resulted in a series of measures enacted in 1990 that raised taxes on alcohol, gasoline, and luxury items such as expensive cars and boats. The highest personal income tax rate was raised to 31 percent for individuals with annual taxable incomes of more than $125,000 and couples with incomes of more than $200,000. The payroll tax that supports Medicare was increased for higher-income earners. On the other side of the ledger, the earned income credit for low-income families was increased, and new credits for healthcare and parents with newborn children were included. In exchange for his tax compromise, George H. W. Bush got new measures to strengthen spending ceilings to bring the budget into line. However, rescinding his promise of "no new taxes" was probably a major factor in President George H. W. Bush's defeat in the 1992 presidential race. By the end of the Reagan–Bush era, the federal budget deficit had grown to $290 billion.[27]

The New Federalism

President Reagan was anxious to restructure federal–state relations—specifically to turn over to the states many of the domestic programs of the national government. He believed that this would "end cumbersome administration" and make the programs "more responsive to both the people they are meant to help and the people who pay for them."[28] Critics contended that this would be a step backward in social welfare policy. The federal government assumed many social welfare functions *because* the states failed to respond to the needs of the poor. Even when state governments are well motivated to care for their poor, differences in states' economic resources can result in unequal treatment from state to state. Liberals soundly criticized the Reagan administration's policy of devolution. Illustration 3.2 provides a brief overview of federalism and social welfare programs.

The Reagan administration instituted block grant funding as a means to cut federal spending, restructure state and federal relations, and establish a "new federalism."[29] Block grants are federal payments to state or local governments for general functions, such as health, welfare, education, law enforcement, and community development. The money must be spent for the general function of the block grant, but states and communities have a great deal of freedom to decide specific uses for the funds. Block grants were intended to reduce

ILLUSTRATION 3.2
Federalism and Social Welfare

At the country's inception, the founding fathers laid out the federal government's powers in the Constitution and retained many powers for the states.[a] They did not want too much power vested in a single government. Originally, the federal government concentrated on national defense, foreign affairs, and issues that cut across state lines, like interstate commerce and postal service. The states were the major government entities, and social welfare, like most domestic issues, was the states' concern. Martin Grodzins referred to the separate functions of federal and state governments as "layer cake" federalism, also known as "dual federalism."[b] Much has changed in regard to federalism since the U.S. Constitution was signed in 1787.

Several events began to transform the conception of federalism, such as economic changes brought about by the Industrial Revolution, the country's involvement in World War I, and the institution of the federal income tax, which greatly increased the federal government's coffers. The Great Depression and the New Deal were defining moments for federalism in the social welfare arena. As the twentieth century progressed, the United States engaged more and more in "cooperative federalism" ("marble cake" federalism, as Grodzins called it) in which the federal and state governments share functions like social welfare. With the inception of the Great Society programs—like Food Stamps, Medicare, and Medicaid—during the 1960s, the federal government's role in social welfare grew even larger, resulting in a more centralized federalism.

For many years following the New Deal, the trend was toward greater centralization or federalization of social welfare programs. During the Reagan presidency, debate over the appropriate approach to federalism in social welfare took on new vigor. Reagan had some successes in turning more responsibility for social welfare services and other services back to the states, primarily by collapsing a number of small programs into several block grants.

His successor, George H. W. Bush, continued this new federalism by allowing some states to experiment with reforms in AFDC and other programs, a practice expanded during the Clinton administration. Clinton did want to institute national health insurance (see Chapter 8), but even his plan called for a certain amount of state discretion in administering the program.

People feel differently about which brand of federalism best serves social welfare interests. Some people (generally liberals) believe that only greater federal involvement can assure fair treatment of those in need and that the federal government can muster more resources to provide a higher standard of payments or care. Others (generally conservatives) believe that public assistance and social service programs should be the responsibility of state (or local) governments—government closer to home. They feel that the fifty state governments can be more responsive to their residents and that they create more innovation. But at the state and local levels, politics over social welfare programs and other programs is more contentious because the costs are spread over fewer people than when Congress takes action and institutes a program directed at needy individuals across the nation.

This diversity of opinion has led to very different arrangements in the social welfare programs. Social Security and Medicare, the largest social welfare programs, are the sole responsibility of the U.S. government. Unemployment insurance is largely a state program, although the federal government does help to extend benefits when unemployment rates remain high. Workers' compensation is almost entirely the purview of the states.

The major public assistance programs are also administered and funded in different ways. The Supplemental Nutrition Assistance Program (SNAP) and the Supplemental Security Income (SSI) program are primarily programs of the federal government. The federal government assumes responsibility for eligibility

(Continued)

requirements and benefit levels in SNAP. In the SSI program, the federal government finances a basic benefit and establishes basic eligibility requirements, but most states make some effort to supplement federal SSI benefits for at least some categories of recipients.

The Temporary Assistance for Needy Families (TANF) and Medicaid programs are joint ventures of the federal and state governments, which share in funding the programs. The federal government sets administrative guidelines, but the states play a major role in determining eligibility requirements and benefits. There are, however, important differences in the intergovernmental arrangements in these two programs. Medicaid remains an open-ended entitlement program available to all who qualify. As part of the new federalism or devolution, TANF (formerly AFDC) is now structured as a block grant program with capped federal funding, regardless of how many families meet eligibility requirements. Under TANF, states have considerably more discretion over program rules than they did under the AFDC entitlement program (see Chapter 7). There are continued calls to turn over Medicaid and other social welfare programs entirely to the states—and just as much effort to resist these kinds of actions by supporters of a more federalized approach. General Assistance is a highly discretionary type of program and is the major public assistance program funded and administered by state

and/or local governments with no federal participation.

The federal and state governments jointly fund most social service programs such as mental health, child welfare, and vocational rehabilitation. The federal and state governments' involvement in funding and administration vary substantially depending on the specific program.

Clashes over federalism in the social welfare arena occur not only in the cash and in-kind benefit programs, but in other areas as well. State and local governments become frustrated when they feel the federal government issues mandates without providing sufficient resources to meet them. Such is the case with achieving new educational standards under the No Child Left Behind Act. Even if states believe in the spirit of the law, they argue that funding is inadequate to do the job. Some states also argue that that the federal government has exceeded its authority by making them the subject of lawsuits under certain provisions of the Americans with Disabilities Act. We continue to debate the appropriate roles of the federal, state, and local governments in social welfare (and other domains), but the states have become dependent on the federal government for monies to meet social welfare needs. There is really no turning back, even if more responsibility for public assistance decisions has been returned to the states.

[a]Some of this material relies on Thomas R. Dye, *Understanding Public Policy*, 9th ed. (Upper Saddle River, NJ): Prentice Hall, 1998).
[b]Morton Grodzins, *The American System: A New View of Government in the United States*, Edited by Daniel Elazar (Chicago: Rand McNally, 1966).

the power of "the Washington bureaucrats," to return decision making to state and local governments, and to make federal money available for various purposes with few "strings attached."

Block grants may have sounded like a good deal for the states, but when President Reagan consolidated many of the smaller social welfare programs into state block grants, the funds allocated were less than the sum previously spent on the individual social welfare programs. The block grants also shifted decision making about specific uses of federal social welfare dollars to state political arenas, where support for social welfare programs is not always as great as it is in Washington. As these changes occurred, much of the politicking and competition over funds also shifted from Washington to state and local levels.

The States as Laboratories

President George H. W. Bush also encouraged state responsibility for public assistance, but he called for a "kinder and gentler America," perhaps to distance his administration from Reagan's harsh stance toward social welfare. George H. W. Bush referred to the "states as laboratories" and encouraged experimentation by providing federal funds to help support state demonstration projects and by granting waivers that allowed states to deviate from federal rules. State initiatives have been used to test ideas for program designs and service delivery that may have been too controversial to gain nationwide support. For example, Wisconsin's "Learnfare" program allowed the state to reduce a family's public assistance benefit if a teenage child dropped out of school. According to President George H. W. Bush, "some of these experiments are controversial, some may not work, others may prove to cost too much for the benefits produced. That is the nature of 'states as laboratories.' As any scientist knows, the road to success is marked by numerous laboratory failures."[30]

Privatizing Public Services

Another theme emphasized during the Reagan–Bush years was *privatization* of government services. Privatization means that federal, state, and local governments give nongovernmental organizations more responsibility for providing public services—from postal delivery and space exploration to mass transportation and even prisons, public assistance, and child protective services. "Generally, privatization can be defined as the transfer of government services, assets, and/or enterprises to private sector owners and suppliers, when [they] have the capability of providing better services at lower costs."[31] How often they provide better services at lower cost is a subject of debate.

The private sector has long provided social welfare services (see also Chapter 10). For example, most childcare centers are owned by private for-profit and private nonprofit organizations. Most healthcare services come from private physicians and other private providers, private hospitals, and other privately owned facilities.

Many social welfare organizations today are really quasi-public or semiprivate.[32] The line between the private and public sectors continues to blur. Many so-called private enterprises rely heavily on government funds. The housing industry, for example, benefits from construction projects funded through the federal government's Department of Housing and Urban Development. Many of the country's community mental health centers (CMHCs) are actually nonprofit corporations originally established with federal funds along with help from state and local governments. Charter schools are private entities that receive public funds to educate children. When it comes to social welfare, the United States has truly become a public/private or "mixed economy."

Privatization of public services, or "spinning the poor into gold" as Barbara Ehrenreich calls it, has raised important questions. For example, does this practice result in federal, state, and local governments abrogating responsibility for social welfare services? Sometimes this abrogation has occurred through deregulation.[33] For example, it has been increasingly difficult to assess the impacts of childcare services[34] and services for the elderly,[35] because the government has reduced its efforts to collect data and monitor these programs. In other cases, privatization can result in governments spending less for services and subsequent reductions in services.[36] Many concerns about adequacy and accountability are raised when private companies provide public social services. There have been some whopping examples of privatization failures in areas such as public assistance eligibility.

The Reagan–Bush Finale

So what actually happened after twelve years of Reagan and Bush policies? Although everyone was supposed to benefit from supply-side economics, evidence mounted that the rich got richer and the poor got poorer. The effects of the tax cuts were widely debated, but the Congressional Budget Office estimated that the lower and middle classes paid a higher net federal tax rate for 1990 than they paid in 1980 prior to tax reform.[37] Personal income taxes had dropped, but other taxes, primarily social insurance taxes, had increased. Poor Americans saw their income drop during the Reagan and Bush years, and their combined federal tax rate increased 16 percent. At the same time, the Americans enjoyed substantial increases in income, because their income tax rates dropped by 5.5 percent. The nonpartisan Citizens for Tax Justice found that only the very poor and the very rich saw tax decreases.[38]

Unemployment and inflation rates had once again abated, but the word "recession" was still being used, and the budget deficit had grown tremendously. Poverty rates were higher than before the Reagan years. Severe cuts in social welfare programs had hurt the poorest Americans, and the *underclass* (the most marginalized Americans) had fallen further behind. An assessment of the Reagan–Bush years may depend on one's own political perspectives, but after twelve consecutive years of Republican presidencies, many Americans were ready for a change.

THE PRESIDENTIAL YEARS OF BILL CLINTON

The 1992 presidential campaign turned out to be a three-way race between Republican President George H. W. Bush, Democratic candidate and governor of Arkansas William Jefferson "Bill" Clinton, and an independent candidate—Texas billionaire businessman H. Ross Perot. Independent presidential candidates are rarely considered viable opponents. Perot, however, garnered substantial support (19 percent of the popular vote, more than any third-party presidential candidate since Theodore Roosevelt ran on the progressive Bull Moose Party ticket in 1912), although not nearly enough to win the election. President George H. W. Bush failed to make strong showings in the presidential debates, and disillusionment among Americans with the state of the economy and other domestic matters gave way to the election of Bill Clinton. Clinton was the first "baby boomer" and the third-youngest president ever elected. Clinton chose Albert "Al" Gore, former senator from Tennessee, also a "boomer," as his vice president. The two set out to accomplish an ambitious set of goals. Among the most important were economic recovery, healthcare reform, welfare reform, and crime control.

Managing the Federal Debt

The budget deficit was a major issue in the 1992 presidential campaign. Upon taking office, President Clinton faced a $290 billion budget deficit, and the gross federal debt had grown from $909 billion in 1980 to $4 trillion in 1992. The gross federal debt equaled 64 percent of the gross national product (GNP).

Congress had tried to grapple with the deficit. It took a major step in 1985 with the Balanced Budget and Emergency Deficit Reduction Act, also known as Gramm-Rudman-Hollings after its sponsors, Senators Phil Gramm (R-TX), Warren Rudman (R-NH), and Ernest Hollings (D-SC). The act called for across-the-board spending cuts in defense and many domestic programs if Congress failed to meet specific deficit-cutting measures. More stringent deficit-cutting measures were enacted in the 1990 Budget Enforcement Act (BEA). But all this proved insufficient because some of the provisions were emasculated. Presidents Reagan and George

H. W. Bush both were criticized for never proposing something that resembled a balanced budget, and Congress could not bring itself to enact a balanced budget. President Clinton revived the deficit-reduction measures contained in the BEA.

During his campaign, Bill Clinton promised to cut the federal budget deficit in half. In fiscal year 1994, President Clinton and Congress achieved a substantial deficit reduction. There are only three ways to reduce the deficit—increase tax revenue, decrease spending, or do both. A compromise was finally reached that included $241 billion in tax increases and $255 billion in spending cuts.

The booming economy of the 1990s, helped by Clinton's economic policies, did much to reduce the federal deficit. Economic prosperity during this period boosted tax receipts and lowered borrowing and interest rates, which in turn reduced government's interest expenses. In addition, Medicare and Medicaid spending was restrained during this period by slower than normal growth in medical costs. Fiscal policy changes under the Budget Enforcement Act (BEA) tightened Medicare reimbursements to providers and increased income and excise taxes. For fiscal years 1991–1995, the BEA imposed two budget restrictions: (1) It capped defense and other discretionary spending at $550 billion during this period, and (2) it tied entitlement spending (such as Social Security) to tax increases and/or decreases. Tax reductions were prohibited unless entitlement spending was also reduced, and any increase in entitlement spending required an increase in taxes. A 1993 amendment to the BEA extended the life of the law to 1998.[39]

Although two things in life are certain—death and taxes—tax policy is not. To further reduce the federal deficit, taxes were raised. Two higher tax brackets were added, bringing the total to five brackets of 15, 28, 31, 36, and 39.6 percent. Other important changes were subjecting all the wages workers earn to the Medicare payroll tax and taxing more of the Social Security benefits of higher-income recipients. The highest corporate tax bracket was raised by one percent for corporations earning over $10 million (making the highest corporate bracket 35 percent). The earned income tax credit (EITC) was increased for working families with children, a smaller EITC was initiated for low-income workers without children, and deductions for certain equipment purchased by small businesses were increased. The Congressional Budget Office determined that the president would remain true to his pledge not to raise taxes on middle-income Americans—90 percent of the new taxes were estimated to fall on those earning $100,000 or more.[40]

The 1993 Budget Reconciliation Act squeaked by Congress without a single Republican vote for it. Vice President Al Gore broke the tie vote in the Senate. The economic reforms contained in the bill relied on investments in education, healthcare, science and technology, and opening foreign markets. The bill's passage helped to reverse 12 years of trickle-down economics and turned the largest deficit in history into the largest surplus in history, created 22 million jobs, increased wages, and brought homeownership to its highest rate on record. Under the Clinton economic plan, the country was predicted to be debt free by 2012.[41] According to Federal Reserve Chairman Alan Greenspan, the 1993 legislation was "an unquestioned factor in contributing to the improvement in economic activity that occurred thereafter."[42] The 1993 plan also contained the Empowerment Zones and Enterprise Communities initiative that provided $3.5 billion in job and wage credits and other incentives to build and revitalize economically depressed areas. By the end of the Clinton presidency, $10 billion had been invested in 135 communities.[43]

The next major budgetary event of great importance was the Balanced Budget Act (BBA) of 1997. Medicare cost containment was central in the BBA. There were additions to some programs, notably an effort to insure more low-income children through state Medicaid programs, restoration of some public assistance benefits that had been taken away from immigrants during the 1996 welfare reform, and more money for states to use in helping people go from welfare to work. The budget deficit for fiscal year 1997 was $22 billion, the lowest in three decades.

The fiscal year 1998 budget reflected many provisions passed in the Taxpayer Relief Act of 1997.[44] Although there were some tax hikes (e.g., a 15 cent increase in the federal cigarette tax), there were many tax cuts, making it the biggest cut since the Reagan years. New child tax credits and education tax credits gave many families relief. This budgetary package did not increase federal revenues by much, but when all these budget measures were combined with the effects of a strong economy, in 1999, the federal budget was back in black ink. For the first time since 1948, the country was living within its means. When President Clinton left office, the budget surplus was $236 billion. The gross federal debt was $5.6 trillion, or 58 percent of GNP—down from 64 percent when he took office, and interest payments were reduced to 12.5 percent of the budget (down from 14.4 percent).[45]

As Republicans took congressional control from the Democrats in 1994, the next years resulted in serious budget battles for President Clinton. In 1996, a bill that raised the minimum wage also ended up including tax provisions. It lowered some business taxes, gave homemakers the right to shelter money in tax-deferred individual retirement accounts, provided new options for people to save for retirement, and gave tax credits to many people who adopt children.

Many federal workers got unexpected vacations when lack of agreement over the 1996 budget led to two shutdowns of many federal government operations. Welfare reform was at the heart of the differences.

Ending Welfare as We Knew It

Bill Clinton pledged to end "welfare as we know it" by turning the welfare office into an employment office and by limiting the time families could remain on welfare. The president vetoed two major welfare reform bills before an agreement was reached on an overhaul of the public assistance programs (see especially Chapter 7 of this book). After a long and often bitter debate, in 1996, Congress reached a bipartisan compromise on "welfare reform" called the Personal Responsibility and Work Opportunities Reconciliation Act (PRWORA). This legislation ended the entitlement status of the Aid to Families with Dependent Children program, made work mandatory, and put time limits on the length of time families can receive cash assistance.

The president finally signed the PRWORA of 1996—even though some of its provisions disturbed him. Among them was cutting most aid to immigrants residing legally in the United States. Some of these provisions were later modified, but the president lost a number of allies as a result of signing the bill. Many thought the approach was an affront to the nation's children. Public assistance caseloads had begun to drop before the PRWORA due to the healthy economy. In the years following welfare reform, the rapid fall of caseloads was seen as a sign of success, but many people leaving the welfare rolls had not achieved self-sufficiency.

Assessing the Clinton Years

During Clinton's presidency, the country enjoyed near full employment, low inflation, and the lowest misery index in three decades, owing largely to a strong economy that seemed to keep the president's popularity high despite the scandals that led to his impeachment trial. Like most other presidencies, the Clinton administration saw its share of failures and successes in promoting its social welfare agenda. In addition to economic reform and welfare reform, the president's domestic agenda included healthcare reform and crime control.

Probably most disappointing to President Clinton was the rejection of his proposed Health Security Act, a plan that would have entitled all Americans to healthcare coverage (see Chapter 8). The plan failed in large part because many thought it was too much government interference in healthcare. President Clinton did get a major crime bill passed with provisions for more community police, bans on assault weapons, life sentences for three-time felony offenders, more prison funding, more crime prevention funds, and more attention to crimes against women under the Violence Against Women Act of 1994. Following the implementation of the crime bill, violent crime rates dropped 55 percent from 1994 to 2002.[46]

As the federal budget surplus grew and the bullish economy continued, Republicans insisted on returning the money to the American people through tax cuts, while Democrats demanded that the surplus be allowed to grow to ensure the stability of Social Security for the soon-to-be-retiring baby boom generation. As part of the fiscal year 1999 budget, Republicans tried unsuccessfully to pass more tax cuts that would have primarily benefited the upper classes. Tax cuts were a high priority for President George W. Bush as he took office in January 2001.

THE GEORGE W. BUSH PRESIDENCY

The 2000 presidential election between Republican candidate Governor George W. Bush of Texas and Democratic candidate U.S. Vice President Al Gore proved to be a dead-heat contest that came down to counting and recounting the last few votes in the state of Florida. Recounts in certain Florida counties raised serious questions about how votes were being interpreted (and whether many states' recount laws would be considered constitutional). It took five weeks and U.S. Supreme Court intervention to decide the outcome. In the case of *Bush v. Gore,* the 5–4 Supreme Court decision gave the Florida election to Bush with a 537 vote margin.[47] This allowed Bush to win the electoral votes in Florida, and thus the Electoral College election nationally, even though Gore had won the popular vote by 540,000. In October 2002, the Senate passed election reform legislation, the Help America Vote Act (HAVA). The bill provided about $3.9 billion over four years for upgrades to voting equipment, improvement of voting and voter registration procedures, and training for poll workers.

The United States at War

The election results may have been more than questionable, but as the 43rd president of the United States, George W. Bush won the confidence of substantial numbers of Americans. His overall approval ratings were generally high, soaring to 90 percent in response to his handling of the September 11, 2001, terrorist attacks on the United States.

During his campaign, President Bush promised to cut taxes, reform schools, and build the nation's defense. Soon after taking office, the president's domestic agenda took a backseat to the war on terrorism, retaliation for the attacks on the World Trade Center and Pentagon, and the war in Iraq.

9/11 AND THE WAR ON TERRORISM   This book is about social welfare, but it can hardly ignore sweeping events that have consumed much of the country's energy and resources and made it more difficult to concentrate on domestic concerns. Damage from the September 11, 2001, terrorist attacks was massive. Nearly 3,000 airline passengers and crew members, workers in the World Trade Center and the offices of the Pentagon, firefighters and rescue workers, and others perished.[48] The World Trade Center's twin towers collapsed, and surrounding buildings were damaged or had to be destroyed. The Pentagon was also severely damaged. Human service workers' primary concerns for the marginalized in society shifted to caring for victims of the attack, helping families cope with losses, and stabilizing communities. They joined with the rest of the country in trying to process the attack on American values, the U.S. Constitution, and the country's way of life. The country was in mourning, and it responded with tremendous outpourings of cash aid and volunteer services to those in New York City (although it diverted charitable giving from local communities).

President Bush called the attacks "The Pearl Harbor of the 21st century,"[49] and declared that we would "win the war against terrorism."[50] Intelligence officials concluded that the Al-Qaeda terrorist organization was attempting to destroy the U.S. government.[51] On the evening of September 11, 2001, President Bush addressed the country and announced, "We will make no distinction between those who planned these acts and those who harbor them."[52] This message was intended for the Taliban regime in Afghanistan, comprising extreme Islamic fundamentalist militias, who were harboring Al-Qaeda terrorists in exchange for substantial sums of money from Osama bin Laden.[53] Over the next few days, what appeared to be authentic threats on the White House continued. On September 14, 2001, Congress, with only one dissenting vote, authorized President Bush to use any necessary force in retaliation against the terrorists responsible for the attacks. When the Taliban refused to surrender bin Laden and his Al-Qaeda terrorists, President Bush ordered the capture and removal of the Taliban and Al-Qaeda terrorists from Afghanistan with military force.[54]

Between September 11, 2001, and October 30, 2002, Congress passed 19 pieces of legislation in direct response to the terrorist attacks. Legislation provided funds for victims and their families and money to help communities' recovery. Security was a primary focus, as was economic support for airlines to get the nation flying again. To expedite the fight against terrorism, multiple pieces of legislation provided funds for intelligence gathering, law enforcement, and new rules for preventing terrorism. Appropriations made for the use of military force paved the way for rooting out the Al-Qaeda terrorist camps in Afghanistan. Funds for food, medical supplies, educational assistance, and other humanitarian aid were appropriated for Afghanistan's citizens.

Perhaps the most controversial piece of post-September 11, 2001, legislation is the U.S.A. Patriot Act. It has been criticized for infringing on the civil liberties of Americans by expanding surveillance abilities (e.g., use of wiretaps and access to personal computers and library records) and reducing the checks and balances previously given to courts to guard against abuse of power. The expanded definition of "domestic terrorism" called into question the right of U.S. citizens to legitimately stage public protests.[55] The original act was set to "sunset" in 2005, but it was reauthorized in early 2006, with some provisions set to expire on December 31, 2009. Congress passed a 60-day extension of the act in late 2009, set to expire in February, 2010,[56] and on February 27, 2010, President Obama signed a one-year extension of several provisions in the act.[57]

Some communities condemned parts of the U.S.A. Patriot Act, such as denial of legal rights to those who are not U.S. citizens. Many groups, including the American Library Association, also opposed provisions of the act. Americans certainly saw the need to institute new policies such as airport screenings in the wake of the terrorist attacks, but granting the government powers to detain U.S. citizens and others without access to legal counsel and providing broad powers to survey patrons' library use are other matters. Civil liberties are the core of democracy, and attempts to erode them shake the foundation of virtually every aspect of American life.

THE DEPARTMENT OF HOMELAND SECURITY As part of the response to terrorism, President Bush created the U.S. Department of Homeland Security (DHS) by consolidating 22 previously distinct domestic agencies for the primary purpose of protecting the nation against future terrorist attacks. A major function of the DHS is to assist states and cities in developing first-response teams in the event of attack. State and local governments received funding to help meet the needs of first responders and to offset costs associated with extra security measures.

DHS has been involved in many activities, such as working with the Centers for Disease Control to develop strategies against biological warfare, developing safeguards for the nation's financial system, working with scientists to implement new technologies for improved safety, and providing an advocate on immigration issues. One thing has become abundantly clear: Sealing the U.S. borders is nearly impossible, even with heightened security. Americans remain concerned that more attacks may occur.

WAR IN IRAQ During his 2002 State of the Union address, President George W. Bush declared Iraq, Iran, and North Korea "an axis of evil." He altered U.S. war policy when he said, "I will not wait on events," suggesting that he would act preemptively against perceived threats to the United States.[58] By April 2002, the president was openly advocating for a regime change in Iraq. Objections to the war were raised around the world. Bush called Iraq's leader Saddam Hussein a threat to national security because he and others believed that Hussein had stockpiled weapons of mass destruction (chemical, biological, and nuclear). Hard evidence supporting this position was limited and unconvincing to the international community.[59] The threat of an imminent attack on Iraq by the U.S. spawned antiwar and anti-Bush protests by millions of people around the world, and by the tens of thousands at home.

The talk of war with Iraq put world leaders on edge, especially those in the Middle East. Some feared that such a war could destabilize the whole region and have staggering economic implications given the oil-rich countries in the region. Others believed that it could prompt more terrorist attacks and escalate the rising resentment toward the United States worldwide.[60] President Bush made the decision to invade Iraq in March 2003 with military support from Britain, Spain, and Australia. Other allies (e.g., Germany, France, and Russia) objected, and there were massive antiwar demonstrations across Europe. Bush's intention was "to disarm Iraq of its weapons of mass destruction, and enforce 17 United Nations Security Council resolutions" and to "liberate the Iraqi people from one of the worst tyrants and most brutal regimes on earth."[61]

U.S. and coalition forces declared victory three weeks later when the major military resistance in Baghdad fell, symbolized by U.S. Marines and Iraqi citizens toppling a statue of Saddam Hussein.[62] In December 2003, U.S. soldiers captured Hussein, but the hostilities in Iraq persisted. The continued U.S. presence in Iraq prompted Muslim militants to reenter Iraq and launch attacks against the occupying forces amid rumors that fundamentalist Islamic terrorist groups see Iraq as the battleground for *jihad,* the Holy War against the Americans. Attacks continued, killing 40 to 80 military personnel each month and hundreds of civilians.[63] As the hostilities continued, President Bush faced growing criticism of his decision to invade Iraq, the prolonged U.S. military occupation of the country, and concerns that no weapons of mass destruction were found. Particularly disturbing were the intelligence failures upon which the war decision was made as detailed in a report by the U.S. Senate's Select Committee on Intelligence.[64]

The United States has spent billions to wage the war in Iraq. It is spending billions more to stabilize Iraq, rebuild the country, and engage in the difficult task of instituting democracy. Some Americans supported the president's decision to invade Iraq; others opposed the war, but there is no question that the financial burdens of the invasion and the attention it has demanded from the executive, legislative, and judicial branches of the U.S. government are tremendous, draining time and resources from many aspects of the country's domestic agenda.

Economic Troubles at Home

At home, a precipitous drop in the stock market, the onset of a recession, the loss of millions of jobs, unprecedented exposure of corporate crime, and a rising unemployment rate called for President George W. Bush's attention. Government's reaction to these events set the stage for the even deeper recession that began in December 2007.

THE STOCK MARKET BUBBLE BURSTS   The rapid growth of the stock market during the 1990s produced what has become known as the "stock market bubble." Such "bubbles" occur when favorable events (such as the invention of the World Wide Web, or the end of the Cold War) occur suddenly and unexpectedly, producing "irrational exuberance" about the stock market's future performance. A "bubble" such as occurred during the mid- and late-1990s makes the economy vulnerable to uncertainty. As economies around the world have grown increasingly interdependent, economic crises in one region of the world also impact other regions.[65]

Two events in the late 1990s negatively affected the U.S. economy. First was the Asian financial crisis in 1997,[66] followed by the Russian default on foreign loans in 1998.[67] These economic events shook investor confidence in the global market. The technology market went from an after-tax profit of nearly $22 billion in 1996 to an after-tax loss of $28 billion in 2000. From January 2000 to January 2001, the NASDAQ stock market dropped by 45 percent. The stock market bubble had burst.[68]

Then, in October 2001, Enron Corporation ushered in an era of corporate scandals when it unexpectedly announced a big quarterly loss and a huge write-down in shareholder equity. Indictments at Enron and of its accounting firm, Arthur Andersen LLP, on fraudulent practices ensued. Other corporate scandals (including Adelphia Communications, ImClone Systems, Tyco International, and WorldCom Inc.) swept the business world. The illegal accounting practices, earning shortfalls, bankruptcies, and criminal indictments severely shook investor confidence in the stock market.[69]

Many workers lost their jobs, and many individual investors found themselves postponing retirement or other plans after their stock portfolios and investment accounts nosedived. Stock market investing, once reserved for the rich, is now used by many middle-class Americans, who were affected by these events. Escalating federal defense and homeland security spending combined with a poor economy and joblessness was fast turning the federal budget surplus into a serious deficit. Even as the stock market improved, unemployment was slow to budge, perhaps due to practices like offshoring, which can boost corporate profits without much effect on employment at home.

BOOSTING THE SLUGGISH ECONOMY   Economic policymakers used two major strategies to address the national recession and resistant economy from 2001 to 2003. First, the Federal Reserve progressively lowered interest rates, which boosted consumer spending for big-ticket items like homes and automobiles. Second, President George W. Bush convinced Congress to pass a series of tax relief measures. Relying on the principles of supply-side economics embraced by the Reagan administration, President Bush believed that (1) tax cuts for individuals would return money to Americans to stimulate consumption and thus put a demand on production (although the biggest tax cuts were enjoyed by the top 1 percent of earners) and (2) tax relief for businesses would stimulate investments and job creation.[70]

The Economic Growth and Tax Relief Reconciliation Act of 2001 (EGTR) provided some of those tax cuts, giving U.S. households money to stimulate consumer buying. Many Americans were probably surprised to see a special tax refund check in their mailboxes ($300 for an individual, and $600 for a couple). Some thought the government should have used the money to pay down the federal debt instead. EGTR also increased the child tax credit. The Job Creation and Worker Assistance Act of 2002 extended unemployment benefits for unemployed workers, provided tax credits to businesses affected by the September 11th attacks, and continued tax credits that expired in 2001 to employers who hired workers from "underprivileged groups" or participated in welfare-to-work programs.[71] EGTR was followed by the Jobs and Growth Tax Relief Reconciliation Act of 2003 (JGTR), which aimed to increase consumer buying through tax cuts, produce jobs using business incentives, and accelerate many EGTR provisions.[72] JGTR provided temporary tax relief from 2003 to 2008.

The combined tax cuts provided in the EGTR, the Job Creation and Worker Assistance Act, and the JGTR all seemed to favor the very wealthiest of earners. Given the tax cuts on dividends, interest, capital gains, and inheritance, more of the tax burden shifted to *earned* income such as wages, benefitting the rich at the expense of lower-income wage earners. Over the 10-year period from 2001 to 2010, the average cumulative tax cut to the lowest-income earners was expected to be about $800; the estimated benefit to the top 1 percent averaged more than $500,000.[73]

After the tax cuts, some economic indicators—the Gross Domestic Product (GDP), unemployment, the stock market—began to rebound; however, job growth remained stagnant and the number of discouraged workers (those who have given up looking for work) continued to increase. With almost no job growth, this economic recovery earned the name of the "jobless recovery." Many blamed the North American Free Trade Agreement and other legislation for encouraging job loss and allowing corporations to export jobs to countries where they can hire workers at a pittance. Others point out that many, if not most, of the jobs that moved overseas went to places like India, China, and Pacific Rim nations with whom the United States does not have free trade agreements.

STATES STRUGGLE TO BALANCE BUDGETS   Like the federal government, state budgets suffered under the declining economy, but unlike the federal government, all states except Vermont are required to balance their budget every year. States also experienced a fiscal insult from the tax cuts passed by Congress in 2001, 2002, and 2003. Some states' taxes (like state income taxes) are tied to federal tax rates, so as federal rates decline, state taxes often do the same. Other fiscal hardships for states included the rising cost of Medicaid and federal spending mandates to states for homeland security, education, and election reform. Almost every state experienced a budget crisis from 2001 to 2003.[74]

THE FEDERAL BUDGET—FROM SURPLUS TO DEFICIT   Not surprisingly, the major pubic opinion polls indicated that Americans' biggest concerns as they considered their vote in the November 2004 presidential election were the economy and jobs. Prior economic forecasts and American optimism that budget surpluses would continue to melt away the federal debt could not have been more erroneous. The federal balance sheet went from a surplus of $236 billion in

2000 to an estimated $475 billion deficit for 2004.[75] Nevertheless, President George W. Bush pledged to cut the deficit in half over the next five years, while at the same time requesting that the temporary tax cuts enacted over the previous three years be made permanent.

Compassionate Conservatism

President George W. Bush campaigned for president on the concept of "compassionate conservatism" to help the needy and underserved in the nation. As part of this approach, he launched his faith-based initiative during his first year in office, which included leveling the playing field for faith-based groups to receive federal funds to provide social welfare services.[76] But funding priorities quickly shifted after September 11, 2001, and relatively little attention was given to his faith-based initiative. With TANF reauthorization in the offing, the president called for increased work requirements (40 hours per week for many parents receiving aid) but no increase in childcare funding.[77] Believing that marriage is a key to addressing poverty and ending welfare dependency, the president also promoted controversial incentives for states to encourage couples to marry (see Chapter 7).

Even with so much attention focused on the U.S. military presence in Afghanistan and Iraq, President Bush was able to push his domestic agenda forward on several fronts. On his first day in office, Bush pleased antiabortion groups by reinstating a policy prohibiting any federal funding of family-planning groups that offer abortion services or abortion counseling overseas. This policy, originally instated by President Ronald Reagan, had been rescinded by President Clinton in 1993.[78]

During his first year as president, President Bush successfully garnered support for the passage of the No Child Left Behind Act of 2001 (also see Chapters 6 and 9). This act provides some of the most sweeping school reforms since 1965, and redefines the federal role in K-12 education by targeting the achievement gap in reading and math between disadvantaged students and their peers. The act is intended to increase standards and accountability for schools across the country.[79]

A major victory for George W. Bush was the passage of the Medicare Prescription Drug Improvement and Modernization Act of 2003, which allows Medicare beneficiaries to purchase their drugs through privately managed prescription drug plans. Critics of the legislation contended that the biggest benefit of the $400 billion (over 10 years) healthcare plan would go to drug companies and private prescription drug plans. Just weeks after the landmark legislation, the Office of Management and Budget announced that the new estimated cost of the drug program was $534 billion. Legislators who voted for the bill under assurances that the cost would not exceed $400 billion were outraged.[80]

The Great Recession—The Housing Bubble Bursts

Sometimes the start of an economic recession can only be identified in retrospect. Reports of economic indicators can lag by weeks or even months and are frequently revised after their initial publication. The Census Bureau reported in early 2009 that today's Great Recession, as some have called it, actually began about December 2007, during President George W. Bush's second term.

In the wake of the economic prosperity of the late 1990s, and with the support of the government-sponsored enterprises (GSEs) Fannie Mae (Federal National Mortgage Association) and Freddie Mac (Federal Home Mortgage Corporation), banks took off on a home-mortgage lending spree. Traditionally, banks financed mortgages with their depositors' money. Banks carefully scrutinized mortgage applications to make sure borrowers were good risks for making their monthly payments throughout the life of the loan. But mortgage practices changed.[81] Using derivative instruments like mortgage-backed securities, banks sold the mortgages in the bond markets, causing the liquidity in the mortgage markets to soar. Banks and other mortgage lenders began making increasingly risky loans to the subprime market—borrowers whose credit histories, incomes, or other factors would not qualify them for a standard (regular) mortgage rate. In some cases, borrowers were encouraged to lie about their incomes in order to qualify for these subprime mortgages. These were called "liar's loans." In many cases, borrowers with no cash or insufficient cash for a down payment were given second mortgages to cover the down payment on the first mortgages. These mortgages typically enjoyed very favorable repayment terms in the early years, sometimes with lower interest rates and sometimes with negative amortization, which means that the payments were set at a level so low that they did not even cover all of the interest on the loan. The remaining interest is added to the mortgage principal amount.

Banks had significant financial incentives to make these riskier loans. Typically, the riskier the mortgage, the higher the fee the bank earned because the interest rate charged to the borrower was higher due to his or her poor credit rating. Providing mortgages at high interest rates to people who could not afford them may sound foolhardy, but this is what happened. Some people who took out these mortgages knew the risk they were taking, but others were duped. If you have ever bought a house, you know how many papers you must sign. Many people never read all this paperwork, and many probably couldn't understand all the "legalese" even if they read them.

So, how does this result in a "bubble"? As with the stock market bubble, irrational exuberance began to occur in the real estate market as interest rates declined early in the George W. Bush administration. In response to the bursting of the stock market bubble, the Federal Reserve lowered interest rates. This led to a rash of refinancing, which caused banks to ramp up the numbers of mortgage originators and related staff. When the rates were slowly adjusted upwards from about 2004 to 2006, banks found other ways to utilize these employees by creating secondary markets for "mortgage paper," thus increasing liquidity in the market. Too much money chasing too few goods led to massive price increases; in this case, the price of houses began to rise dramatically.

Banks and other mortgage lenders then predicated lending practices on the idea that housing prices would never fall. This proved to be a near-fatal error. Most of the subprime mortgages had a "reset" point—usually around the fifth year—when the interest rate and the payments would automatically reset to a higher rate. As long as housing prices continued to rise, people who could not afford their new payment could simply sell the house (at a projected large profit), pocket the cash equity from the home, and purchase a more modestly priced home or start the process again with a new subprime mortgage at a lower rate. That strategy continued to work—until 2007 when the mortgage rates started resetting in large numbers. Suddenly, banks and mortgage investors who had been "irrationally exuberant"[82] about the market began to worry that they might not be repaid. They stopped lending, especially to subprime borrowers. No longer able to refinance, and now *under water*—owing more on their houses in many cases than they were worth, borrowers began defaulting and mortgage holders began foreclosing.

In Cleveland, for example, by late 2007, one in ten homes was vacant.[83] Banks and mortgage companies were now the owners of most of those vacant homes. When large blocks of homes become vacant, property values are further depressed—partly because supply exceeds demand, but also because vacant houses begin to deteriorate, which affects values across the neighborhood. A spiral of downward pressure forced more and more people from the homes they could no longer afford. The foreclosure rate began to take on epic proportions. Banks around the world had been financing these high-risk mortgages, mostly through purchasing mortgage-backed securities, i.e., pools of subprime mortgages packaged by lenders and sold to other banks and investors to raise additional capital for lending expansion.[84]

The Securities and Exchange Commission (SEC) is supposed to regulate the securities markets in the United States. As part of their regulations, assets held by certain entities, including banks, must be carried on the books at their market value, an accounting practice called "mark to market." As the market for these mortgage-backed securities dried up, banks were required to write down the value of these securities on their balance sheets to essentially a value of "zero." Banking laws determine how much capital the bank has to maintain for loans it makes. In other words, banks can loan ten dollars for every one dollar of capital that they have on their books. When the value of these massive assets were reduced to zero, many banks could not meet their capital reserves requirements and, therefore, had to cease lending activities or, at the very least, radically contract them. Whether the "mark-to-market" problem actually led to the credit/financial crisis of 2008 has been a matter of some debate, with former Federal Deposit Insurance Corporation (FDIC) chairman William Isaac leading the criticism of the SEC for its rules "destroy[ing] $500 billion of bank capital by its senseless marking to market of these assets for which there is no marking to market, and that has destroyed $5 trillion of bank lending."[85]

In late summer of 2008, as the country prepared to elect its 44th President, the financial crisis came to a head. On September 19, 2008, President George W. Bush's Treasury Secretary Henry Paulson proposed the Troubled Asset Relief Program (TARP) as a way "to remove these illiquid assets that are weighing down our financial institutions and threatening our economy."[86] This is a fancy way of saying that the federal government bailed out many banks and other financial institutions that were in financial difficulty at taxpayers' expense. In his statement, Paulson referred to "lax lending practices" and "irresponsible borrowing," an apparent attempt to blame both lenders and borrowers. At that time, Paulson also reported that more than 5 million homeowners were either delinquent or in foreclosure proceedings. Paulson asked Congress for $700 billion for the TARP purchase fund. Paulson's proposed legislation included a provision that decisions made by the [Treasury] Secretary "may not be reviewed by any court of law or any administrative agency."[87] Congress authorized Paulson's $700 billion request, with $350 billion to be spent prior to the new president's taking office and the remaining half reserved for action by the Treasury Secretary to be appointed by the new president.

By Election Day of 2008, President George W. Bush's approval ratings had dropped to 20 percent, the lowest ever recorded for any sitting president, as the economy remained sluggish and in response to the situation in Iraq.[88] His 90 percent approval ratings following the 9/11 attacks had vanished.

On November 4, 2008, Senator Barack Obama (D-IL) was elected the 44th President of the United States. On January 20, 2009, he was inaugurated and took the reins of a country in financial and economic upheaval and fighting two wars on foreign soil.

BARACK OBAMA'S PRESIDENCY: YEAR ONE

The 2008 election was unusual in many ways. It was the first time an African American was elected U.S. president. It was the first time a Roman Catholic was elected vice president. It was the first time a sitting president or vice president was not in the running for president since 1952. It was the first time a woman (Senator Hillary Clinton of New York) was a major presidential contender in the primary of the Democratic or Republican party. It was the first time that a woman (Governor Sarah Palin of Alaska) was the Republican candidate for vice president.

The 2008 election campaigns began almost immediately following the 2006 mid-term elections in which Democrats regained control of both the House and the Senate. Early attention was focused on former First Lady Senator Hillary Clinton (D-NY), with former vice president and failed 2000 Democratic candidate for president Al Gore seen as her major competition for the nomination early on. Senator Barack Obama (D-IL) was being mentioned, but many speculated that the freshman senator was not experienced enough to assume the Oval Office.[89] The pundits proved to be wrong, although Obama's nomination was not firmly clinched until after all the primaries were over in early June, partly a result of the way Democrats apportion their convention delegates, and partly due to the support Obama received from super-delegates to the convention. Super-delegates are either selected by state parties as "unpledged add-on delegates" or seated at the convention automatically because of positions they hold.[90] Hillary Clinton refused to concede the nomination to Obama until several days after the last primary. After his election as president, Obama named Senator Clinton to be his Secretary of State, a post to which she won a relatively easy Senate confirmation.

The Republican nomination was equally poorly predicted. Early in the process, pundits favored former New York mayor Rudolph Giuliani with Senator John McCain (R-AZ) and former Senator Fred Thompson (R-TN) battling for second place. Governor Mike Huckabee (R-AR) and former Governor Mitt Romney (R-MA) were also considered contenders for the nomination. By March 2008, McCain clinched the Republican nomination sweeping primaries in Texas, Vermont, Ohio, and Rhode Island.[91]

Obama emerged from a field of 10 candidates. Many speculated that he would choose Hillary Clinton as his running mate, but she denied any interest in the job. Obama selected Senator Joe Biden (D-DE), who had also sought the presidential nomination, as his running mate. McCain had emerged from a field of 12 candidates. He went outside the primary contender pool and tapped little-known Alaska Governor Sarah Palin to be his running mate. McCain and Obama went head to head in the first presidential election ever to pit two sitting Senators against each other for the presidency.[92] It was also the most expensive presidential election in the nation's history. The presidential race alone cost about $1.6 billion, and the combined costs of the races for the White House and Congress topped $5.3 billion.[93]

On September 15, 2008, investment bank Lehman Brothers filed for bankruptcy protection, a sign that the financial crisis was continuing to deteriorate rapidly. On September 24, McCain suspended his campaign to return to Washington to work on the $700 billion TARP bailout bill, calling on Obama and the Presidential Debate Commission to delay the debates until the Congress passed the bailout bill. Obama refused to delay the debate.[94] Two days later, on September 26, McCain decided to attend the presidential debate at The University of Mississippi in Oxford.

As the economy and the incumbent Republican president's approval ratings continued to worsen, so did the prospects of the McCain/Palin ticket. On Election Day, Obama won 53 percent of the popular vote[95] and 365 of the 538 electoral votes to become President of the United States.[96] Obama invigorated many young people to participate in the election process. For example, his margin of victory in the Iowa caucuses—the first state to select convention delegates—was largely due to record numbers of first-time voters in the under-25 age group.[97] Many Americans thought they would never see the election of an African American president in their lifetimes. It was a historic moment for the United States, and a deeply moving event for many people.

Whether one is a supporter or an opponent of President Obama, all must concede that his first year in the White House was historic. The first piece of legislation he signed into law was the Lilly Ledbetter Fair Pay Act of 2009, which extended the statute of limitations for pay discrimination cases.[98] Beyond that, Obama's first year was consumed by four major themes: improving America's image abroad, the economy, the nation at war, and reforming the American healthcare system.

Improving America's Image Abroad

Social welfare policy is usually considered *domestic* policy, but many U.S. policy decisions have global implications. Americans are compelled to think globally and to act globally as well. For example, the nation's economic well-being is affected by its ability to obtain from other countries resources like oil that the United States consumes in great quantities. Obtaining these resources is contingent not only on U.S. purchasing power but also on its relationship with other countries.

With respect to improving the U.S. image abroad, Obama enjoyed a successful first year by most measures. His calm demeanor and demonstrated respect for Muslims, combined with his call for the worldwide elimination of nuclear weapons, has earned him respect in many foreign countries. Evidence of this can be found in his being awarded the Nobel Peace Prize. Obama accepted the award in Oslo on December 10, 2009.

Improving the Economy

The economy continued to spiral downward during the early months of the Obama presidency. The steps his administration and Congress have taken to stabilize the situation have been met with broad resistance from Republicans and mixed results in political terms. The first major step was the American Recovery and Reinvestment Act (ARRA), passed by Congress in February 2009. The Act appropriated an estimated $787 billion for recovery programs, including aid to states and localities, an extension of unemployment assistance, assistance in paying insurance premiums for unemployed persons, and energy and infrastructure programs.[99] Not a single Republican in the House of Representatives voted for the ARRA; only three Republican senators voted for it.

Conservatives have railed against the spending that occurred in the first year of the Obama administration and the rise of government debt to what might be considered gargantuan proportions (about $12 trillion dollars by the beginning of 2010). They also continued to point to the failure of the ARRA, as unemployment climbed into double digits. However, by the end of August 2009, the Council of Economic Advisers reported that only a little more than 19 percent of the funds had actually been spent.[100] In its first year in office, the Obama administration was credited with stabilizing the economy, in part by using vast sums of *borrowed* money to prevent the collapse of the financial system, and to rescue two American carmakers (General Motors and Chrysler), in addition to banks and insurers. Despite these successes, Obama's approval rating dropped from nearly 70 percent at the time of his inauguration to less than 50 percent a year later, while unemployment climbed from just below 8 percent to 10 percent over the same period.[101]

A Nation Still at War

Prior to his election, Barack Obama promised to close the military prison holding alleged terrorists at the U.S. Naval Base in Guantanamo Bay, Cuba, in his first year in office, a promise he has not yet fulfilled. Some of the prisoners there have been held for years without being afforded trials. On November 13, 2009, Attorney General Eric H. Holder, Jr., announced that five of the prisoners suspected of playing a role in the 9/11 attacks would be brought to trial in the United States. Holder's announcement was met with opposition from many Americans who believe that bringing these alleged terrorists into the United States for trial is dangerous. Many who oppose this idea also believe that such prisoners should not be afforded the same civil rights and protections as U.S. citizens enjoy under the law and the Constitution.

President Obama also promised to begin bringing home troops from Iraq, a promise he has kept as the Iraqi military has gained strength in controlling the country. It now appears that most troops will be out of Iraq by the end of 2011. Obama also promised to prosecute the war in

Afghanistan more vigorously. Although he delayed a decision on increasing troop levels in Afghanistan until late 2009, he announced an increase of 30,000 additional troops for that war.[102]

Healthcare

Finally, the president saw that healthcare reform legislation that will insure many more Americans was passed, a feat that eluded the last Democratic president, Bill Clinton. Both the House and the Senate passed versions of healthcare reform, strictly on partisan lines with Democrats voting for and Republicans voting against. For most of his first year in office, the president's party had 60 votes in the Senate, giving them a supermajority to break filibusters. In early January 2010, Republican Scott Brown won the special election for the Senate seat left vacant by the death of Democratic Senator Edward "Ted" Kennedy of Massachusetts, a seat Kennedy had held since 1962. Brown's surprise election gave Republicans 41 seats in the Senate, enough to sustain a filibuster. The irony of Brown's election was, of course, that in Congress there had been no stronger or longer supporter of universal health insurance than Senator Kennedy.

The president invited legislative leaders from both parties to a seven-hour televised meeting on February 25, 2010, at Blair House in the hopes of breaking the partisan deadlock over the healthcare bills. The Republican leadership largely rebuffed the president's attempt but efforts persisted to reach a compromise (see Chapter 8). On March 21, 2010, the House of Representatives passed the Senate bill along with a separate reconciliation bill to address changes to the Senate bill to reflect compromises reached between Democratic leaders of the two houses. Four days later, again along strict party lines, Senate Democrats passed the reconciliation bill.

Issues Ahead

Congress and the president continue to grapple with the massive Wall Street failures and near-failures that led to unprecedented bailouts of the financial system. Their task now is to decide what safeguards must be put in place to ensure that no such crisis occurs again.

Climate change is another topic that President Obama is anxious to tackle. The President has been vocal in his support of "cap-and-trade" legislation that would set limits for carbon dioxide emissions. According to the Environmental Protection Agency (EPA), "Cap and trade is an environmental policy tool that delivers results with a mandatory cap on emissions while providing sources flexibility in how they comply."[103] Companies that emit less than the maximum allowed are permitted to sell part of their allotted emission quota to other companies, offering a market-based approach to emissions reductions. The House passed a weakened version of the original proposed legislation. The Senate is likely to have a much tougher time passing it with a fractured Democratic majority facing certain filibuster from the Republicans.[104]

Another issue topping President Obama's agenda is immigration policy. Like climate change, it has taken a back seat to the economy and healthcare. The number of individuals who wish to immigrate to the United States is strongly affected by their countries' standards of living and political conditions such as war and civil rights, which the United States often has a hand in shaping. Immigration policy is closely intertwined with social welfare policy. Congress not only determines the number of people who will be allowed to emigrate from various countries, it also determines how, or whether, social welfare policy and programs will be used to assist immigrants (see Chapter 12). A major issue in immigration reform will be whether those currently residing in the United States illegally will be allowed to remain in the country legally under "amnesty" provisions.

Summary

The roots of the U.S. welfare system can be traced back to Elizabethan times, but the United States has also developed its own unique brand of social welfare. Responsibility for social welfare, once the purview of neighbors, private charities, and local governments, filtered up to the states and then to the federal government, largely in the form of the Social Security Act of 1935. The act was a response to the Great Depression. President Franklin Delano Roosevelt's New Deal of the 1930s and President Lyndon B. Johnson's Great Society programs of the 1960s have been the country's major responses to the needs of those who are poor.

By the time Ronald Reagan assumed the presidency in the early 1980s, much more conservative philosophies of social welfare prevailed. President Reagan's approach was to limit public assistance, turn as much of it back to the states as possible, and focus on tax cuts (trickle down economics) that would boost the economy and provide jobs for the poor. The presidencies of George H. W. Bush, and George W. Bush were similar to President Reagan's in their tenor towards social welfare. Even Democratic president Bill Clinton gave in to major conservative modifications of public assistance programs. Clinton was unsuccessful in getting Congress to pass national healthcare legislation, but his economic policies helped move the country out of deficit spending that had occurred under Republican administrations and into a budget surplus.

The country's most recent presidents have faced crises of major proportions—one international and one domestic. President George W. Bush's two terms were consumed with addressing the terrorist attacks of September 11, 2001, and the wars he supported in Afghanistan and Iraq. President Barack Obama's historic election came on the heels of a collapse of financial institutions and a subprime mortgage crisis that resulted in an economic recession second only to the Great Depression. In his first year in office, President Obama was successful in getting Congress to pass legislation that will give many more Americans access to health insurance. However, the measures Congress has taken to help Americans, especially those to shore up financial institutions to avoid utter economic collapse, have left the United States with a federal debt of gargantuan proportions. What this means for the future of U.S. social welfare policy remains to be seen.

Discussion Questions and Class Activities

1. Have a class discussion on how methods to help those who are poor have changed since colonial times, and how have they remained the same.

2. Discuss how effective President Obama's administration has been in the domestic policy arena with regard to problems such as unemployment, healthcare, and other matters. Check newspapers, journals, and other media for updated accounts.

3. Divide the class into groups and have each investigate a period in the history of social welfare. Bring materials to class such as documents, videos, and pictures that illustrate the mood of the era and social welfare concerns.

4. Look at ProPublica's website on the bailout at http://bailout.propublica.org/main/list/index to see which financial institutions have received money from the Troubled Asset Relief Program. Invite a financial expert from your university or the local business community to discuss the subprime mortgage crisis and its effects on the local community and state.

5. Hold a class debate on federalism and social welfare programs. Have one team take the position that public assistance and social service programs should be the responsibility of state governments and the other team take the position that the responsibility should be the federal government's.

Websites

Cornell University Library's Social Welfare Digital Collection, http://dlxs.library.cornell.edu/s/social/index.html, contains a variety of materials on the history of social welfare in the United States.

400 Years of Welfare, http://www.wpt.org/welfare/timeline/, presents information on social welfare history by time period.

Social Security History, http://www.ssa.gov/history/, contains a collection of materials on the history of the Social Security Administration and the Social Security program.

Notes

1. For more detailed descriptions of the history of social welfare in the United States, see June Axinn and Mark J. Stern, *Social Welfare: A History of the American Response to Need,* 7th ed. (Boston: Pearson, 2008); Phyllis J. Day, *A New History of Social Welfare,* 6th ed. (Boston: Pearson, 2009).

2. This section relies on Blanche D. Coll, *Perspectives in Public Welfare: A History* (Washington, DC: U.S. Department of Health, Education, and Welfare, 1973); Ronald C. Federico, *The Social Welfare Institution: An Introduction,* 3rd ed. (Lexington, MA: Heath, 1980).

3. Much of this section relies on Coll, *Perspectives in Public Welfare: A History.*

4. *Ibid.,* p. 17.

5. P. Nelson Reid, "Social Welfare History," in Richard L. Edwards, ed., *Encyclopedia of Social Work,* 19th ed. (Washington, DC: NASW Press, 1995), pp. 2206–2225.

6. Thomas R. Dye, *Understanding Public Policy,* 4th ed. (Englewood Cliffs, NJ: Prentice Hall, 1981), pp. 116–117.

7. Reid, "Social Welfare History."

8. Paragraphs describing the Great Depression rely on Thomas R. Dye and L. Harmon Zeigler, *The Irony of Democracy,* 5th ed. (Monterey, CA: Duxbury Press, 1981), pp. 100–101.

9. Cited in Richard Hofstadter, *The American Political Tradition* (New York: Knopf, 1948), p. 316.

10. This paragraph relies on Frances Fox Piven and Richard A. Cloward, *Poor People's Movements: Why They Succeed, How They Fail* (New York: Vintage Books, 1977); quote is from p. 275.

11. *Ibid.*

12. Aaron Wildavsky, "The Empty Headed Blues: Black Rebellion and White Reactions," *Public Interest,* Spring No. 11, Spring 1968, pp. 3–4.

13. Reid, "Social Welfare History."

14. *Shapiro v. Thompson,* 394 U.S. 618; see Frances Fox Piven and Richard A. Cloward, *Regulating the Poor: The Functions of Public Welfare* (New York: Random House, 1971) for an elaboration on residency requirements, especially pp. 306–308.

15. *Saenz, Director, California Department of Social Services, et al. v. Roe et al., on behalf of themselves and all others similarly situated,* Supreme Court of the United States 526 U.S. 489. Retrieved January 17, 2010, from http://supreme.justia.com/us/526/489/index.html

16. Aaron Wildavsky, *Speaking Truth to Power: The Art and Craft of Policy Analysis* (Boston: Little, Brown, 1979), p. 98.

17. "Cost of Living Adjustments" (Washington, DC: Social Security Administration, October 15, 2009). Retrieved January 2, 2009, from http://www.ssa.gov/OACT/COLA/colaseries.html

18. U.S. Census Bureau, Facts for Features, "Oldest Baby Boomers Turn 60!," January 3, 2006. Retrieved January 10, 2010, from http://www.census.gov/Press-Release/www/releases/archives/facts_for_features_special_editions/006105.html

19. U.S. Census Bureau, *2009 National Population Estimates* (Washington, DC, December 2009). Retrieved January 10, 2010, from http://www.census.gov/popest/national/national.html; see also population estimates from U.S. Department of Commerce, *Population Projections of the United States by*

Age, Sex, Race and Hispanic Origin: 2010–2050 (Washington, DC). Retrieved January 10, 2010, from http://www.census.gov/population/www/projections/files/nation/summary/np2008-t2.xls

20. U.S. Census Bureau, *Statistical Abstracts of the United States: 2010* (Washington, DC), Table 1302. Retrieved January 10, 2010, from http://www.census.gov/compendia/statab/2010/tables/10s1302.pdf

21. Centers for Disease Control, "Births: Preliminary Data for 2007," *National Vital Statistics Report,* Vol. 57, Number 12, March 18, 2009. Retrieved January 10, 2010, from http://www.cdc.gov/nchs/data/nvsr/nvsr57/nvsr57_12.pdf

22. Figures in this section rely on U.S. Census Bureau, *Income, Poverty, and Health Insurance Coverage in the United States: 2008* (Washington, DC, September, 2009). Retrieved January 10,2010, from http://www.census.gov/prod/2009pubs/

23. President of the United States, *A Program for Economic Recovery* (Washington, DC: U.S. Government Printing Office, February 18, 1981), p. 4.

24. Murray Weidenbaum, "A Participant Looks at the Pros and Cons of Reaganomics," *Christian Science Monitor,* October 8, 1991. Retrieved January 2, 2009, from http://www.csmonitor.com/1991/1008/08082.html

25. Quoted in Eileen Shanahan, "President Signs Sweeping Overhaul of Tax Law," *Congressional Quarterly,* October 25, 1986, p. 2668.

26. See William Greider, "The Education of David Stockman," *Atlantic Monthly,* December 1981, pp. 27–54.

27. Office of Management of the Budget, *Budget of the United States Government, Fiscal Year 2004, Summary of Receipts, Outlays, and Surpluses or Deficits: 1789-2008,* Historical Table 1.1 (Washington, DC: Executive Office of the President). Retrieved March 3, 2010, from http://www.whitehouse.gov/omb/rewrite/budget/fy2004/index.html

28. President Ronald Reagan, *State of the Union Address* (Washington, DC: U.S. Government Printing Office, January 26, 1982).

29. For a concise review and bibliography on the issue of federalism, see Kenneth Jost, "The States and Federalism," *Congressional Quarterly Researcher,* September 13, 1996, pp. 795–815.

30. This section relies on Executive Office of the President, Office of Management and Budget, *Budget of the United States Government, Fiscal Year 1991* (Washington, DC: U.S. Government Printing Office, 1990), section IV; quotes are from p. 176.

31. Executive Office of the President, Office of Management and Budget, *Management of the United States Government, Fiscal Year 1990* (Washington, DC: U.S. Government Printing Office, 1989), p. 3-105.

32. Martin Rein, "The Social Structure of Institutions: Neither Public nor Private," in Sheila B. Kamerman and Alfred J. Kahn, Eds., *Privatization and the Welfare State* (Princeton, NJ: Princeton University Press, 1989), pp. 49–71.

33. Marc Bendick, Jr., "Privatizing the Delivery of Social Welfare Services: An Idea to Be Taken Seriously," in Kamerman and Kahn, *Privatization and the Welfare State,* pp. 97–120.

34. Kamerman and Kahn, *Privatization and the Welfare State,* p. 10.

35. Andrew W. Dobelstein with Ann B. Johnson, *Serving Older Adults: Policy, Programs, and Professional Activities* (Englewood Cliffs, NJ: Prentice Hall, 1985), pp. 125–128.

36. Bendick, "Privatizing the Delivery of Social Welfare Services"; for some interesting accounts of the problems raised by privatization, see Michael B. Katz, *The Price of Citizenship: Redefining the American Welfare State* (New York: Metropolitan Books, 2001).

37. "Study: Poor Get Poorer as Rich Find Wealth Less Taxing," *Champaign-Urbana News Gazette,* February 17, 1990, p. 5.

38. As reported in Tom Kenworthy, "15 Years of Cuts Said to Enrich the Rich," *Wall Street Journal,* September 13, 1991, p. A23.

39. Alan D. Viard, "The New Budget Outlook: Policymakers Respond to the Surplus," *Economic and Financial Review,* 2nd Quarter, 1999, Federal Reserve Bank of Dallas.

40. Gilbert A. Lewthwaite, "1994 Brings Higher Taxes for Wealthy, Break for Poor," *Austin American-Statesman,* January 1, 1994, pp. A1, 8; Office of Management and Budget, *Budget of the United States Government, Fiscal Year 1995* (Washington, DC: Executive Office of the President), p. 58.

41. White House Office of the Press Secretary, "President Clinton and Vice President Gore's Economic Plan: Building the Path to Prosperity for America's Families" (Washington, DC, August 5, 2000). Retrieved January 31, 2004, from http://www2.ed.gov/PressReleases/08-2000/wh-0805.html

42. Alan Greenspan, Housing Committee Testimony (Washington, DC, February 20, 1996), as cited in *ibid.*

43. *Ibid.*

44. Executive Office of the President, *Budget of the United States Government, Fiscal Year 1998* (Washington, DC: U.S. Government Printing Office, 1997).

45. Executive Office of the President, *Budget of the United States Government,* Historical Tables, Fiscal Year 2005 (Washington, DC, U.S. Government Printing Office, 2004).

46. U.S. Department of Justice, *Violent Crime Rates Have Declined Since 1994, Reaching the Lowest Level Ever Recorded in 2002* (Washington, DC: Office of Justice Programs, Bureau of Justice Statistics, 2002).

47. *Bush v. Gore* (00-949), Supreme Court of the United States (Washington, DC, December 12, 2000). Retrieved January 10, 2010, from http://supct.law.cornell.edu/supct/html/00-949.ZPC.html

48. "Official 9/11 death toll climbs by one: Missing NYC Doctor the 2,751st Victim of World Trade Center Attacks," *CBS News,* July 10, 2008. Retrieved January 10, 2010, from http://www.cbsnews.com/stories/2008/07/10/national/main4250100.shtml

49. See Bob Woodward, *Bush at War* (New York: Simon & Schuster, 2002), p. 37.

50. President George W. Bush, "Address to the Nation in Light of the Terrorist Attacks of September 11" (Washington, DC, September 11, 2001). Retrieved January 10, 2010, from http://www.nationalcenter.org/BushGW91101Address.html

51. President George W. Bush, "Address to a Joint Session of Congress and the American People" (Washington, DC, September 20, 2001). Retrieved May 6, 2010, from http://www.dhs.gov/xnews/speeches/speech_0016.shtm

52. President George W. Bush, "Address to the Nation in Light of the Terrorist Attacks of September 11."

53. Woodward, *Bush at War,* p. 32.

54. Library of Congress, 107th Congress, Joint Resolution to Authorize the Use of United States Armed Forces Against Those Responsible for Recent Attacks Launched Against the United States, P.L. 107-40 (Washington, DC, September 18, 2001), [S. J. Res. 23]. Retrieved January 10, 2010, from http://frwebgate.access.gpo.gov/cgi-bin/getdoc.cgi?dbname=107_cong_bills&docid=f:sj23enr.txt.pdf

55. Electronic Frontier Foundation *Analysis of the Provisions of the USA PATRIOT Act* (San Francisco, October 27,2003). Retrieved January 10, 2010, from http://w2.eff.org/Privacy/Surveillance/Terrorism/20011031_eff_usa_patriot_analysis.php

56. John Bresnahan, "Patriot Act Renewal Delayed," *Politico,* December 16, 2009. Retrieved January 10, 2010, from http://www.politico.com/news/stories/1209/30649.html

57. "Obama Signs One-year Extension of Patriot Act," *Associated Press,* February 27, 2010. Retrieved May 6, 2010 from http://www.usatoday.com/news/washington/2010-02-27-Patriot-Act_N.htm

58. President George W. Bush, *State of the Union Address* (Washington, DC, January 29, 2002). Retrieved January 10, 2010, from http://frwebgate.access.gpo.gov/cgi-bin/getdoc.cgi?dbname=2002_presidential_documents&docid=pd04fe02_txt-11.pdf

59. See Jennie Green, Barbara Olshansky, and Michael Ratner, *Against War with Iraq: An Antiwar Primer* (New York: Seven Stories Press, 2003).

60. Woodward, *Bush at War,* p. 44.

61. See "White House Releases List of Coalition Members (Alexandria, VA: GlobalSecurity.org, March 20, 2003). Retrieved May 7, 2010, from http://www.globalsecurity.org/wmd/library/news/iraq/2003/iraq-030320-usia01.htm

62. Woodward, *Bush at War,* p. 357.

63. "The Human Toll," *Air Force Times,* September 20, 2004; also see U.S. Casualties in Iraq, Alexandria, VA: GlobalSecurity.org. Retrieved May 6, 2010, from http://www.globalsecurity.org/military/ops/iraq_casualties.htm

64. Select Committee on Intelligence, "Report on the U.S. Intelligence Community's Prewar Intelligence Assessments of Iraq" (Washington, DC: United States Senate, July 7, 2004).

65. United States Congress, Joint Economic Committee, Vice Chairman Jim Saxton (R-NJ), *Economic Repercussions of the Stock Market Bubble: A Joint Economic Committee Study* (Washington, DC, July 2003). Retrieved January 11, 2010, from http://www.house.gov/jec/growth/07-14-03.pdf

66. *Ibid.*

67. Commentary: Russian Default: Four Years Later," *On-line Pravda,* August 16, 2002. Retrieved January 12, 2010, from http://english.pravda.ru/economics/2002/08/16/34706.html

68. U.S. Congress, *Economic Repercussions of the Stock Market Bubble.*

69. Kenneth Jost, "Corporate Crime," *Congressional Quarterly Researcher,* October 11, 2002, Vol. 12, No. 35, pp. 1–33.

70. Kenneth Jost, "Stimulating the Economy," *Congressional Quarterly Researcher,* January 10, 2003, Vol. 13, No. 1, pp. 1–34.

71. Library of Congress, *Bill Summary and Status for the 107th and 108th Congress,* P.L. 107-16, "The Economic Growth and Tax Relief Reconciliation Act of 2001." Retrieved May 6, 2010, from http://thomas.loc.gov/cgi-bin/bdquery/z?d107:HR01836:\|TOM:/bss/d107query .html

72. Library of Congress, *Bill Summary and Status for the 107th and 108th Congress,* P.L. 107-16, "The Jobs Growth and Tax Relief Reconciliation Act of 2003." Retrieved May 6, 2010, from http://thomas.loc.gov/cgi-bin/bdquery/z?d108:HR00002:\|TOM:/bss/d108query .html

73. Citizens for Tax Justice, *The Bush Tax Cuts: The Latest CTJ Data,* March, 2007. Retrieved January 13, 2010 from http://www.ctj.org/pdf/gwbdata.pdf

74. Kenneth Jost, "Stimulating the Economy."

75. Congressional Budget Office, *An Analysis of the President's Budgetary Proposals for Fiscal Year 2004* (Washington, DC, March 2003). Retrieved March 30, 2010, from http://www.cbo.gov/doc.cfm?index=4129

76. Kenneth Jost, "The Bush Presidency," *Congressional Quarterly Researcher,* February 2, 2001, Vol. 11, No. 4.

77. Office of the Press Secretary, *President Discusses Welfare Reform and Job Training* (Washington, DC, February 27, 2002). Retrieved January 13, 2010, from http://georgewbush-whitehouse.archives.gov/news/releases/2002/02/20020227-5.html; *Fact Sheet: President Announces Welfare Reform Agenda,* February 26, 2002. Retrieved January 13, 2010, from http://georgewbush-whitehouse.archives.gov/news/releases/2002/02/20020226-11.html

78. Kenneth Jost, "The Bush Presidency."

79. Paul E. Peterson and Martin R. West, Eds., *No Child Left Behind? The Politics and Practice of School Accountability* (Washington, DC: Brookings Institution Press, 2003).

80. Amy Goldstein and Juliet Eilperin, "Medicare Drug Cost Estimate Increases," *Washington Post,* January 30, 2004, p. A01. Retrieved January 17, 2010, from http://www.highbeam.com/doc/1P2-150038.html

81. For more information on the subprime crisis, see BBC World News America, "The Downturn in Facts and Figures," November 21, 2007. Retrieved May 16, 2009, from http://news.bbc.co.uk/2/hi/business/7073131.stm

82. "Remarks by Chairman Alan Greenspan at the annual dinner and Francis Boyer Lecture of The American Enterprise Institute for Public Policy Research, Washington, D.C., December 5, 1996." Retrieved May 7, 2010 from http://www.federalreserve.gov/boarddocs/speeches/1996/19961205.htm.

83. Steve Schifferes, "Foreclosure Wave Sweeps America," *BBC News Online,* November 5, 2007. Retrieved January 13, 2010 from http://news.bbc.co.uk/2/hi/business/7070935.stm.

84. *Ibid.*

85. Brooke Sopelsa, "Former FDIC Chair Blames SEC for Credit Crunch," CNBC.com, October 9, 2008. Retrieved January 13, 2010, from http://www.cnbc.com/id/27100454

86. Statement of Treasury Secretary Henry Paulson on September 19, 2008, as reported by Politico.com. Retrieved January 13, 2010, from http://www.politico.com/news/stories/0908/13609.html

87. "Treasury's Financial-bailout Proposal to Congress," *Wall Street Journal,* September 20, 2008. Retrieved January 13, 2010, from http://blogs.wsj.com/economics/2008/09/20/treasurys-financial-bailout-proposal-to-congress

88. "As Voters Go to Polls to Pick His Successor, George W. Bush Hits New Low in Approval Rating," *Los Angeles Times,* November 4, 2008. Retrieved January 10, 2010, from http://latimesblogs.latimes.com/presidentbush/2008/11/unpopular.html

89. Julian Borger, "Now the Real Race Begins," *The Guardian,* November 11, 2006. Retrieved January 15, 2010 from http://www.guardian.co.uk/world/2006/nov/11/midterms2006.usa2. Also see John Hughes, "With Midterms Over, All Eyes Turn to the 2008 Presidential Race," *The Christian Science Monitor,* November 15, 2008. Retrieved January 15, 2010, from http://www.csmonitor.com/2006/1115/p09s01-cojh.html?s=widep

90. Democratic National Committee, *Delegate Selection Rules for the 2008 Democratic National Convention,* Democratic Party of the United States, Governor Howard Dean, Chairman. Retrieved January 17, 2010, from http://s3.amazonaws.com/apache.3cdn.net/3e5b3bfa1c1718d07f_6rm6bhyc4.pdf

91. "Clinton Wins Key Primaries, CNN Projects; McCain Clinches Nod," *CNN.com,* March 5, 2008. Retrieved January 15, 2010, from http://www.cnn.com/2008/POLITICS/03/04/march.4.contests

92. Brian Wingfield, "The Senator President," *Forbes.com,* February 8, 2008. Retrieved January 15, 2010, from http://www.forbes.com/2008/02/08/obama-clinton-mccain-biz-beltway-cx_bw_0208senate.html

93. Brody Mullins, "Cost of 2008 Election Cycle: $5.3 Billion," *Washington Wire, The Wall Street Journal Online,* October 23, 2008. Retrieved January 15, 2010, from http://blogs.wsj.com/washwire/2008/10/23/cost-of-2008-election-cycle-53-billion

94. John Ibbitson, "McCain Suspends Campaign—But Over What Crisis?", *The Globe and Mail,* September 24, 2008. Retrieved January 15, 2010, from http://www.theglobeandmail.com/archives/mccain-suspends-campaign—-but-over-what-crisis/article712366

95. 2008 Official Presidential General Election Results, January 22, 2009, Federal Election Commission. Retrieved January 15, 2010, from http://www.fec.gov/pubrec/fe2008/2008presgeresults.pdf

96. Legislative Day of January 8, 2009, 111th Congress – First Session, Office of the Clerk, U.S. House of Representatives. Retrieved January 15, 2010, from http://clerk.house.gov/floorsummary/floor.html?day=20090108

97. David von Drehle, "Obama's Youth Vote Triumph," *Time,* January 4, 2008. Retrieved January 17, 2010, from http://www.time.com/time/politics/article/0,8599,1700525,00.html

98. Joanna L. Grossman, "The Lilly Ledbetter Fair Pay Act of 2009: President Obama's First Signed Bill Restores Essential Protection Against Pay Discrimination," *FindLaw,* February 13, 2009. Retrieved January 15, 2010, from http://writ.news.findlaw.com/grossman/20090213.html

99. Public Law 111-5, 111th Congress, February 17, 2009. Retrieved January 15, 2010, from http://www.gpo.gov/fdsys/pkg/PLAW-111publ5/pdf/PLAW-111publ5.pdf

100. "The Economic Impact of the American Recovery and Reinvestment Act of 2009 First Quarterly Report," Executive Office of the President of the United States: Council of Economic Advisers, September 10, 2009. Retrieved January 15, 2010, from http://www.whitehouse.gov/assets/documents/CEA_ARRA_Report_Final.pdf

101. "Reality Bites," *The Economist,* January 14, 2009. Retrieved January 15, 2010, from http://www.economist.com/displayStory.cfm?story_id=15268930

102. Darlene Superville and Steven R. Hurst, "Obama West Point Speech on Afghanistan: Full Details," *The Huffington Post,* December 1, 2009. Retrieved January 15, 2010, from http://www.huffingtonpost.com/2009/11/25/obama-west-point-speech-o_n_370582.html

103. "Cap and Trade," United States Environmental Protection Agency website. Retrieved January 17, 2010 from http://www.epa.gov/captrade/

104. "Reality Bites," *The Economist.*

4 | ENDING POVERTY: IS IT AN ISSUE ANYMORE?

In the 1930s and again in the 1960s, reducing poverty topped the nation's domestic agenda. Despite the efforts of many nonprofit organizations and liberal think tanks to maintain this focus, in the 1980s and 1990s attention shifted to how to limit public assistance rather than how to reduce poverty. In his failed bid for the 2008 presidential nomination, former Senator and vice presidential nominee John Edwards (D-NC) tried to revive the issue by making poverty a center-piece of his campaign. Today, we might ask whether Americans have come to view a certain level of poverty as inevitable and even acceptable. The country's current economic crisis may serve to reinforce this view with attention focused on providing economic supports for broader segments of the population.

WHAT IS POVERTY?

A major obstacle the United States faces in developing a rational approach to reducing poverty is conflict over the very definition of the problem. Defining poverty is a *political* activity. Proponents of increased governmental support for social welfare programs frequently make high estimates of the number of the population that is poor. They view the problem of poverty as a persistent one, even in a generally affluent society. They argue that many millions of Americans suffer from hunger, inadequate housing, remediable illness, hopelessness, and despair. Given the magnitude of the problem, their definition of poverty practically mandates the continuation and expansion of a wide variety of public welfare programs.

In contrast, others minimize the number of poor in the United States. They see poverty as diminishing over time. They view the poor in the United States today as considerably better off than the middle class of fifty years ago and even wealthy by the standards of most societies in the world. They deny that people need to suffer from hunger or remediable illness if they make use of the public services already available. They believe that there are many opportunities for upward mobility in the United States and that no one need succumb to hopelessness or despair. This definition of the problem minimizes the need for public welfare programs and encourages policymakers to limit the number and size of these programs.

Political conflict over poverty, then, begins with contending definitions of the problem. In an attempt to influence policymaking, various political interests try to win acceptance for their own definitions of the problem. Political scientist E. E. Schattschneider explained:

> Political conflict is not like an intercollegiate debate in which the opponents agree in advance on a definition of the issues. As a matter of fact, *the definition of the alternatives is the supreme instrument of power*; the antagonists can rarely agree on what the issues are because power is involved in the definition.[1]

Poverty has always been with us, but in the United States, poverty emerged as a *political issue* about 50 years ago. Prior to the 1960s, the problems of the poor were almost always segmented. According to James Sundquist, not until the Kennedy and Johnson administrations did the nation begin to see that these problems were tied together in a single "bedrock" problem—poverty:

> The measures enacted, and those proposed, were dealing separately with such problems as slum housing, juvenile delinquency, dependency, unemployment, illiteracy, but they were separately inadequate because they were striking only at surface aspects of what seemed to be some kind of bedrock problem, and it was the bedrock problem that had to be identified so that it could be attacked in a concerted, unified, and innovative

way . . . . The bedrock problem, in a word, was "poverty." Words and concepts determine programs; once the target was reduced to a single word, the timing became right for a unified program.[2]

But even if there was political consensus that poverty was a problem, this does not mean that everyone defined poverty in the same fashion. This chapter discusses six different approaches to conceptualizing poverty—as deprivation, inequality, lack of human capital, culture, exploitation, and structure. It also discusses the approaches to reducing poverty that arise from each of these definitions.

Poverty as Deprivation

One way to define poverty is as *deprivation*—insufficiency in food, housing, clothing, medical care, and other items required to maintain a decent standard of living. The World Bank uses the equivalent of $1.25 or less per day in U.S. currency to define deprivation or poverty in the world's poorest countries like those in Sub-Saharan Africa.[3] In developing countries in Latin America or Eastern Europe, it uses $2.00 per day. Poverty in these countries is substantially different from poverty in the United States, but the U.S. government also uses a measure of deprivation as its official poverty measure.

The U.S. Government's Official Poverty Definition

The U.S. government's poverty definition assumes that there is a standard of living below which Americans can be considered "deprived." This standard is admittedly arbitrary; no one knows for certain what level of material well-being is necessary to avoid deprivation. But each year the federal government calculates the cash income Americans need to satisfy minimum living needs and uses it to determine how many people are poor. This measure is called the *poverty thresholds.* The federal government calls simplified versions of the poverty thresholds *poverty guidelines.* The guidelines are used to determine who qualifies for certain federally supported public assistance programs. The poverty thresholds are the same for all 50 states. The guidelines are the same for the 48 contiguous states and higher for Alaska and Hawaii. Many people also use the terms "poverty line" or "poverty level," although these are not official federal government terms.

The Social Security Administration (SSA) first developed official poverty threshold calculations in 1964. Economist Mollie Orshansky was the key figure in devising the measure, and there was much debate over whether her conceptualization was too high or too low.[4] Originally, the poverty thresholds were derived by estimating a low-cost but nutritious food budget for households (similar to today's U.S. Department of Agriculture Thrifty Food Plan). These figures were then multiplied by 3, since surveys indicated that about one-third of the average household budget was spent on food. Orshansky said her formula was intended only for the aged; nevertheless, it became the government's official definition.[5]

Some revisions have been made in the poverty threshold formula over the years. Since 1963, the previous year's poverty thresholds are simply adjusted to reflect changes in the Consumer Price Index (CPI).[6] There are several variations of the CPI. The measure currently used to update poverty thresholds is the CPI for All Urban Consumers (CPI-U). It includes the living costs of more segments of the population than the measure previously used. Since 1981, lower poverty-level figures are no longer used to calculate poverty rates of female-headed households and farm families. Some distinctions based on whether a household is headed by an individual aged 65 or older are still made. Despite revisions, the poverty thresholds remain a crude measure of poverty.

Table 4.1 provides the U.S. government's poverty thresholds for families of varying sizes and compositions in 2008. For example, in 2008, the poverty threshold for a family of four composed of two adults and two children was $21,834, up from poverty thresholds of $16,530 in 1998, $11,997 in 1988, and $6,610 in 1978.[7] Based on these thresholds, of all the *families* in the United States, 8.1 million, or 10.3 percent, of them were poor in 2008.[8] In 2007, it would have taken an average of $9,102 to bring each family up to the poverty threshold. This figure is called the *income deficit* or, more informally, the "poverty gap."

In addition to poverty rates for families, the federal government publishes poverty rates for individuals. In 2008, an estimated 39.8 million Americans or 13.2 percent of the total population lived in poverty (see Figure 4.1). Nearly 6 percent of individuals had incomes that were less than half of poverty thresholds.

What's Wrong with the Government's Definition?

The poverty thresholds are an *absolute* measure of poverty because they provide one figure for the number of poor in the country, and individuals and families fall either above or below. Even if we were to agree that poverty should be defined as deprivation, there are still many problems in determining who is poor based on the federal government's official poverty definition. This definition includes only cash income (such as wages, Social Security and public assistance checks, and interest from bank accounts, all *before* taxes) and excludes *in-kind* benefits such as medical care, food stamps, school lunches, and public housing. If these government benefits were "costed out" (calculated as cash income), there would be fewer poor people in the United States than shown in official statistics. Also, many people (poor and nonpoor)

TABLE 4.1   Poverty Thresholds in 2008 by Size of Family and Number of Related Children Under 18 Years (Dollars)

Size of family unit	Related children under 18 years								
	None	One	Two	Three	Four	Five	Six	Seven	Eight or more
One person (unrelated individual):									
Under 65 years	11,201								
65 years and older	10,326								
Two people:									
Householder under 65 years	14,417	14,840							
Householder 65 years and older	13,014	14,784							
Three people	16,841	17,330	17,346						
Four people	22,207	22,570	21,834	21,910					
Five people	26,781	27,170	26,338	25,694	25,301				
Six people	30,803	30,925	30,288	29,677	28,769	28,230			
Seven people	35,442	35,664	34,901	34,369	33,379	32,223	30,955		
Eight people	39,640	39,990	39,270	38,639	37,744	36,608	35,426	35,125	
Nine people or more	47,684	47,915	47,278	46,743	45,864	44,656	43,563	43,292	41,624

Source: U.S. Census Bureau. Retrieved March 9, 2010, from http://www.census.gov/prod/2009pubs/p60-236.pdf

Numbers in millions, rates in percent

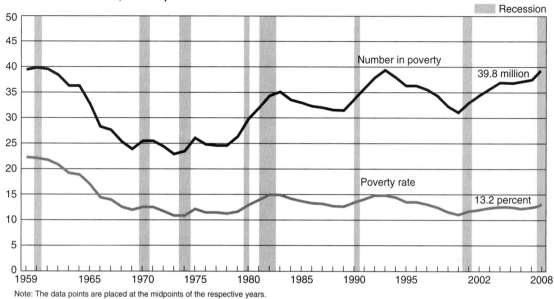

Note: The data points are placed at the midpoints of the respective years.

FIGURE 4.1 Number in Poverty and Poverty Rate: 1959 to 2008 *Source:* U.S. Census Bureau, Current Population Survey, 1960 to 2009 Annual Social and Economic Supplements. Retrieved March 9, 2010, from http://www.census.gov /prod/2009pubs/p60-236.pdf

apparently underreport their incomes.[9] Taking this into account might further reduce the number of people counted as poor.

There are other problems with the federal government's official poverty definition. It does not consider regional differences in the cost of living, including climate differences that affect energy consumption. It is unlikely that a family of four could live at the government's current poverty threshold in New York City, even if it might be possible in Carroll County, Mississippi. The official poverty definition also does not account for family assets. An older family that has paid off its mortgage does not usually devote as much to housing as a young family that rents or has recently purchased a home. It does not recognize other differences in the status of individuals or families—for example, whether family members are students or retirees. Some of these people are counted as poor in official government statistics, but they may not consider themselves "poor." This official definition also does not consider work-related expenses such as childcare or commuting costs. Nor does it recognize the needs of families that have incomes above the poverty level but have special circumstances or hardships—chronic illnesses, large debts, or other problems— that drain away income and leave them without enough to cover necessities.

In addition, the estimate that one-third of family income is spent on food is outdated. The high cost of housing, in particular, has changed the composition of the family budget. Estimates today are that low-income families spend roughly one-sixth of their budget on food.[10] In 2008, the maximum Supplemental Nutrition Assistance Program (formerly called the Food Stamp Program) benefit for a family of four was $542 per month or $6,504 for the year. This is the amount the federal government believed a family of four needed to maintain an adequate but eco- nomical diet. Multiplying this figure by six rather than three would have yielded a poverty thresh- old for a family of four of $39,024, a figure 79 percent higher than the 2008 poverty threshold for a family of this size (see Table 4.1). Economist Patricia Ruggles long ago noted that the official poverty measure would have to be increased by at least 50 percent to bring it in line with current consumer spending patterns.[11]

The Self-Sufficiency Standard is an approach to determining how much individuals and families need to cover basic living expenses without government assistance. Unlike the government's poverty thresholds, the Self-Sufficiency Standard is calculated for individual cities or counties to take into account geographic differences in the cost of living, and it includes childcare, healthcare, and transportation costs. Illustration 4.1 contains the Self-Sufficiency Standards for Osage County, Oklahoma, and Seattle, Washington. In Osage County, each parent in a two-parent family with two children, one preschool age and one school age, would need to work full-time and earn at least $8.59 an hour to cover major expenses. In Seattle, each parent would have to earn at least $12.88. The annual standard for each area—$36,296 in Osage County and $54,425 in Seattle—is well above the federal government's poverty thresholds or guidelines.

Since liberals, conservatives, and government officials realize that poverty thresholds are outdated, why hasn't the definition changed? One reason may be the administrative practicality of the current measure since it has long been used to determine how many people live in poverty and who qualifies for federal, and often state, assistance programs.[12] Another reason may be the measure's relative simplicity.

> Why is the poverty rate still the statistic of choice . . . despite its defects? One important reason may be the perception that better measures are too complex to be communicated to a wider audience. If the whole point of measuring poverty is to affect the policies that might affect poverty, then a poverty index that cannot be understood by the public and by policy makers is pointless.[13]

Economist Rebecca Blank of the Brookings Institution also blames "politics [for] getting in the way of good statistics."

> Back in the 1960s, the poverty measure was placed under the control of the White House. This is in contrast to all of our other national statistics, which are defined and updated by agencies with a long history of nonpolitical decision making. Unfortunately, no president (Democrat or Republican) has wanted to touch this political hot potato. If a new measure shows higher poverty, the president looks bad, but if a new measure shows lower poverty, he'll be accused of dismissing the problem.[14]

Actually, the U.S. government has studied numerous ways to alter its official poverty definition over the past four decades, and bills have been introduced into Congress to change the way poverty is measured. So far, none has succeeded. In fact, multiple measures of poverty may be needed depending on our purposes.[15] Even if other definitions are adopted, one good reason to continue to include the current definition is that it will allow the government to continue to track how far we have come, or how far we still have to go, in reducing poverty.[16]

Measuring Poverty: Let Me Count the Ways

In 1992, the U.S. Congress commissioned a major study of the poverty measure by the National Academy of Sciences (NAS).[17] The study panel recommended changes to address long-noted problems with the current measure such as the need to adjust for costs across geographic regions, counting in-kind benefits such as food stamps, and taking into account work-related expenses

ILLUSTRATION 4.1
Examples of the Self-Sufficiency Standard[a]

The Self-Sufficiency Standard is a calculation of how much money working adults need to meet their basic needs without subsidies of any kind. Unlike the federal poverty standard, the Self-Sufficiency Standard accounts for the costs of living and working as they vary by family size, composition, and geographic location.

Two Adults, One Preschool Child, and One School-age Child

Monthly Costs, 2009	Osage County, Oklahoma	City of Seattle, Washington
Housing	$556	$963
Child Care	$640	$1438
Food	$652	$860
Transportation	$481	$144
Health Care	$452	$414
Miscellaneous	$278	$382
Taxes	$450	$667
Earned Income Tax Credit (−)	−$166	$0
Child Care Tax Credit (−)	−$86	−$100
Child Tax Credit (−)	−$167	−$167
Making Work Pay Tax Credit	−$67	−$67
Self-Sufficiency Wage[b]		
Hourly	$8.59 per adult	$12.88 per adult
Monthly	$3,025 combined	$4,535 combined
Annual	$36,296 combined	$54,425 combined

[a]The Standard is calculated by adding expenses and taxes and subtracting tax credits. Taxes include federal and state income tax (including state tax credits except state earned income tax credit and child tax credit) and payroll taxes.

[b]The hourly wage is calculated by dividing the monthly wage by 176 hours (8 hours per day times 22 days per month). The hourly wage for families with two adults represents the hourly wage that each adult would need to earn, working full time, while the monthly and annual wages represent both parents' wage combined.

Note: Totals may not add exactly due to rounding.

Sources: Adapted with permission from Diana M. Pearce, *The Self-Sufficiency Standard for Oklahoma* (© 2009 Diana Pearce and Wider Opportunities for Women); Diana Pearce, *The Self-Sufficiency Standard for Washington State 2009* (© 2009 Diana Pearce, Workforce Development Council of Seattle-King County, and Wider Opportunities for Women); The Self-Sufficiency Standard for all participating states can be found at the website of the Center for Women's Welfare: http://www.selfsufficiencystandard.org/pubs.html

and out-of-pocket medical costs. The lone dissenter, John F. Cogan of the conservative Hoover Institution, called the suggested measure "value judgments made by scientists—with a particular point of view."[18]

The federal government publishes poverty estimates using definitions that include various combinations of factors such as cash income (including government benefits), many in-kind government benefits, taxes and tax credits, work expenses, and capital gains. In 2006, of the 13 different measures reported, poverty ranged from 9 percent to 18.5 percent, while the government's official poverty figure was 12.2 percent.[19]

One reason noncash or in-kind benefits have not been included in official government calculations is the difficulty in deciding how much these benefits are worth. Much attention has been paid to how to calculate the value of in-kind benefits, and most serious students of social welfare think they should be included. Calculating the value of SNAP (food stamp) benefits is relatively straightforward. The cash value of these benefits can be used, although it has been estimated that recipients would trade $1,500 of inkind food benefits for $1,400 in cash.[20]

Calculating the value of medical or healthcare benefits is more difficult. Without these benefits, people might have to use money that they would ordinarily spend on other things to cover medical expenses. But since in-kind medical benefits cannot be spent for other items in the household budget, most experts agree that these benefits do not raise household income. If healthcare benefits and costs were included in calculating poverty rates, should we use the cash value of medical services received, or the value of employer- or government-provided healthcare benefits (premiums), or should only out-of-pocket medical costs be considered? Each of these methods produces very different estimates, and there has been little agreement about whether to include them at all in calculating income and poverty or how to do so if they were included.

Calculating government housing benefits presents another set of headaches. The Census Bureau does have a way of valuing housing subsidies.[21] It uses figures from the 1985 American Housing Survey and assigns values based on region and family size and income and adjusts for inflation using a rental price index. This method seems to underestimate the value of housing subsidies. One experimental method uses fair market rents. Since this method produces higher subsidy figures, it produces lower estimates of the poverty rate.

Even though in-kind benefit programs have grown much faster than cash public assistance programs,[22] in-kind (and cash) benefits have only a modest effect on reducing poverty figures because "the reductions from any single program are generally quite small."[23] For example, in 2002, the poverty rate for children was 19.7 percent based on cash income before government transfers (social welfare benefits). After social insurance programs were considered, this rate fell to 17.4; after cash means-tested (public assistance) program transfers, it dropped by less than 1 percent to 16.7 percent, and after considering a number of means-tested noncash (in-kind) benefits, it dropped by almost two points to 14.8 percent. After subtracting federal payroll and income taxes and adding benefits from the earned income tax credit (EITC), the poverty rate dropped to 12.6 percent. Therefore, social insurance and tax benefits were the most effective in helping children out of poverty, followed by in-kind public assistance benefits; least effective were cash public assistance benefits.[24] In 2002, before any government transfers, the poverty gap for children was $37.4 billion; after government transfers it was $17.2 billion, a 54 percent reduction.

For those aged 65 and older, the effect of government transfers is much more dramatic. Poverty was an amazing 49.9 percent before any government transfers and fell to 11.5 percent after social insurance (primarily Social Security) was factored in; means-tested cash transfers reduced poverty to 10.4 percent, and means-tested noncash benefits reduced poverty to 9 percent; poverty remained at 9 percent after factoring in the EITC and federal payroll and income taxes.[25] In 2002, the poverty gap for older people was $89.7 billion before any of these transfers and $7 billion after, a reduction of 92 percent! Obviously, Social Security made the biggest difference. Means-tested benefits had only a modest effect. Public assistance programs, both cash and in-kind, may not reduce *national* poverty rates dramatically, but they can substantially increase the quality of life of those who are poor.

Who Is Poor?

The incidence of poverty varies among subgroups of the population and areas of the country (see Figures 4.2 and 4.3). In absolute figures, more whites are poor than blacks. Of the 39.8 million people counted as poor by government definition in 2008, approximately 17 million were white (non-Hispanic) while 9.4 million were black. However, the likelihood of blacks experiencing poverty is about three times that for whites: *The 2008 poverty rate for the nation's black population was 24.7 percent compared to 8.6 percent for the white (non-Hispanic) population.* In other words, whites outnumber blacks among the poor, but a much larger percentage of the nation's black population is poor. In 2008, there were 11.0 million poor people of Hispanic origin in the United States (they may be of any race). Their poverty rate was 23.2 percent. Among people of Asian origin in the United States, 1.6 million or 11.8 percent were in poverty.

   The very highest poverty rates occur in families headed by women where no husband is present. In 2008, the poverty rate for these female-headed households was 28.7 percent compared to 13.8 percent for families headed by men with no wife present and 5.5 percent for families headed by married couples. *For families headed by non-Hispanic white women, the rate was 21.5 percent; the rates for families headed by black women and women of Hispanic origin were much higher—each had a rate of 40.5.* Families headed by women of Asian origin had the lowest poverty rate—16.0 percent.

   In 1959 poverty among children (under age 18) was 27.4 percent. By 1969 it had reached a low of 14 percent, much better than we can report for 2008. In 2008, approximately 19 percent (14.1 million) children in the United States lived in poverty. For children of Hispanic origin and black children, the situation was much worse; *30.6 percent of all children of Hispanic origin and 34.7 percent of all black children lived in poverty, compared to 14.6 percent of Asian children and 10.6 percent of white children.*

   Poverty rates for Americans aged 65 and older have dropped substantially over the years—from 35.2 percent in 1959 to 24.6 percent in 1970 and 9.7 percent in 2008. Among these older Americans, poverty is 20.0 percent for blacks, 19.3 percent for those of Hispanic origin, 12.1 percent for those of Asian origin, and 7.6 percent for whites. Older women have higher poverty rates compared to older men. Although poverty rates for older people have dropped substantially over the years, compared to the overall population, their incomes are concentrated more at the near-poor level (defined as income that is 25 percent higher than poverty thresholds), and remember that official poverty thresholds for households headed by those aged 65 or older are lower than for younger people.

   As Figure 4.2 also illustrates, education figures prominently in poverty rates. In 2008, the poverty rate for those with less than a high school diploma was 23.5 percent. Poverty drops as education increases.[26] Poverty among those with a bachelor's degree or more was 4.1 percent. As one might expect, work is also a substantial factor. The poverty rate for those who did not work at all was 22.0 percent compared to 2.6 percent for those who worked full time.

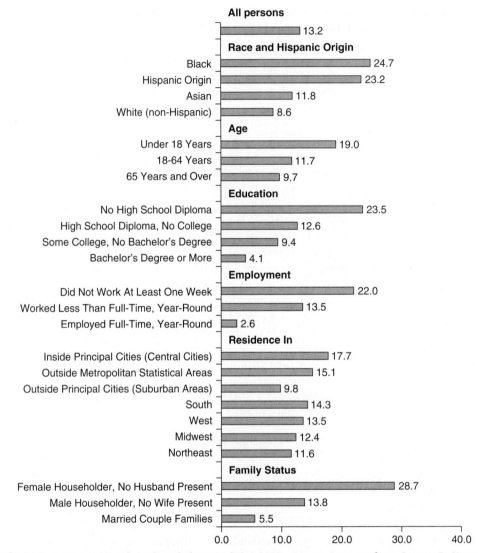

FIGURE 4.2 Poverty Rate by Selected Characteristics: 2008   *Source:* Data are from Carmen DeNavas-Walt, Bernadette D. Proctor, and Jessica C. Smith, *Income, Poverty and Health Insurance Coverage in the United States: 2008,* Current Population Reports, P60-236(RV) (Washington, DC: U.S. Census Bureau, September 2009). Retrieved March 9, 2010, from http://www.census.gov/prod/2009pubs/p60-236.pdf

Poverty occurs in large, urban areas and in rural communities (outside metropolitan statistical areas) as well. In 2008 about 17.7 percent of central city residents were poor, and about 15.1 percent of rural residents were poor. Suburban areas have less poverty (a rate of 9.8 percent) because those with low incomes are less likely to find affordable housing there. Poverty rates are always higher in the South than in other regions of the country. In 2008, 14.3 percent of residents of southern states are poor compared to 13.5 percent in the West, 12.4 percent in the Midwest, and 11.6 percent in the Northeast.

Percent

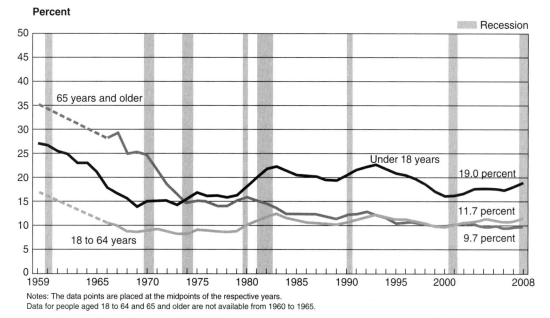

Notes: The data points are placed at the midpoints of the respective years.
Data for people aged 18 to 64 and 65 and older are not available from 1960 to 1965.

FIGURE 4.3   Poverty Rates by Age: 1959–2008. *Source:* U.S. Census Bureau, Current Population Survey, 1960 to 2009 Annual Social and Economic Supplements. Retrieved March 9, 2010, from http://www.census.gov/prod/2009pubs/p60-236.pdf

How Persistent Is Poverty?

An important question we must ask is whether poverty is a temporary or transient rather than a persistent, long-lasting problem. Information on this issue is largely derived from the University of Michigan's Panel Study of Income Dynamics (PSID), which has tracked nearly 8,000 U.S. families and individuals since 1968.[27] The U.S. Census Bureau's Survey of Income and Program Participation (SIPP) is also used to estimate transitions in and out of poverty.

Few longitudinal studies of transitions in and out of poverty have been conducted since the welfare reform initiated in 1996, but a review of studies indicates that in the early 1990s, about 4 percent of Americans entered poverty each year, about half of those who entered poverty exited poverty in about one year, and 75 percent in less than four years.[28] Although there is some consolation in knowing that many people escape poverty, there is apparently a group of people who experience persistent poverty. Methodologically sensitive studies of "spells of poverty" indicate that this persistent poverty is more serious than once thought. One study conducted in the 1980s found that although the majority still experienced poverty for a short time (one or two years), 60 percent of those classified as poor at any given time experienced poverty for seven years or longer.[29]

Other analyses also indicate that the chances of escaping poverty diminish over time. One estimate based on a study conducted in the early 1990s indicated that the probability of leaving poverty was .53 in the first year of a spell, dropping to .36 the second year, and .20 or less by the fifth year.[30] Another study of poverty dynamics from January 1996 to December 1999 (following welfare reform of 1996) includes those who were poor for at least two months during these years. The study found that 34 percent were poor for at least two months during the four-year period; only 2 percent were poor for all 48 months.[31] In total, 51 percent were in poverty two to four months, 28 percent were poor for five to 12 months, 11 percent for 13 to 24 months, 4 percent for 25 to 36 months, and 6 percent were poor for 36 to 48 months.

Poverty can also be viewed across the life cycle and in terms of consecutive years and total years (indicating that some people cycle in and out of poverty). For example, researchers found that at age 20, 11 percent of Americans were poor; by age 40, 36 percent had spent at least one year in poverty, and by age 65, this figure had increased to 51 percent.[32] In addition, between ages 20 to 40, nearly 4 percent had experienced a spell of poverty lasting five consecutive years or more, and nearly 13 percent had spent a total of five or more years in poverty. [33] The occurrence of poverty spells was lower in the 40 to 60 and 60 to 80 age groups.

It is also important to know what factors promote poverty entry and exit. [34] Employment changes (job loss or reduced earnings) are by far the *most frequent* explanations of poverty entry, and getting a job or increased earning are the most frequent factors in poverty exits. Some individuals have emphasized the effects of family composition on poverty. While becoming a female-headed household results in the *highest probability* of poverty entry, and becoming a household headed by two adults results in the highest probability of exiting poverty, these events occur *much less* frequently than employment changes. Becoming disabled or recovering from a disabling condition are also important but relatively infrequent events in poverty entry and exits, respectively. Adding a child to the household is another important but less frequent event in poverty entry, while education gains promote poverty exit. From 1996 to 1999, in the years following welfare reform when the economy was in a robust period, employment factors became more frequent events in poverty entry and exit and changes in household composition less frequent.

Demographic characteristics also play a role in poverty dynamics. The strongest and most consistent evidence is that blacks, young adults, and female-headed households are substantially more likely to enter poverty, less likely to exit, and more likely to have longer spells of poverty.[35]

Has the percentage of poor in this country changed substantially? Franklin D. Roosevelt said in his second inaugural address in 1937, "I see one-third of a nation ill-housed, ill-clad, ill-nourished." He was probably underestimating poverty; economic historians think that over 50 percent of the nation would have been classified as poor during the Great Depression. Since poverty levels account for the effects of inflation, there is no question that the proportion of the population that is poor (as defined in official government statistics) has declined. Poverty declined dramatically during the 1960s and reached lows of 11 to 12 percent during the 1970s (see Figure 4.3). But in 1983 and again in 1993, the poverty rate exceeded 15 percent. Although good economic times brought a near record low poverty rate in 2000 (11.3 percent), poverty began to increase in the new millennium as the economy soured. As the economic recession that hit so hard in 2008 began to unfold, poverty increased. The country's official poverty rate for 2008 jumped to 13.2 percent. Among all the statistics we have presented, one thing remains clear: Millions of Americans are still poor by government definition.

Poverty as Inequality (or Who Shrank the Middle Class?)

Poverty can also be defined as *inequality* in the distribution of income. Unlike the federal government's official definition of poverty, which is tied to an absolute level of deprivation, inequality refers to *relative deprivation*—some people perceive that they have less income or material possessions than most Americans, and they believe they are entitled to more.[36] Even with a fairly substantial income, one may feel a sense of relative deprivation in a very affluent society where commercial advertising portrays the "average American" as having a high level of material well-being. According to economist Victor Fuchs,

By the standards that have prevailed over most of history, and still prevail over large areas of the world, there are very few poor in the United States today. Nevertheless, there are millions of American families who, both in their own eyes and in those of others, are poor. As our nation prospers, our judgment as to what constitutes poverty will inevitably change. When we talk about poverty in America, we are talking about families and individuals who have much less income than most of us. When we talk about reducing or eliminating poverty, we are really talking about changing the distribution of income.[37]

How can we measure poverty as inequality? One method, used often in cross-national comparisons of poverty, is to calculate poverty as a percentage (e.g., one-half) of each country's median income. In the United States, economists frequently measure the distribution of total personal income across various classes of families. Since relative deprivation is a psychological as well as a social and economic concept, these classes or groups are difficult to establish, but a common method is to divide all U.S. families into five groups—from the lowest one-fifth in personal income to the highest one-fifth. Table 4.2 shows the percentage of total personal income received by each of these groups for selected years since 1950. If perfect income equality existed, then each fifth of U.S. families would receive 20 percent of all family personal income, and it would not even be possible to rank fifths from highest to lowest. But clearly, personal income in the United States is distributed unequally.

The poorest one-fifth of U.S. families now receive only 4 percent of all family personal income. This group's share of income rose slowly for many years but has declined in recent decades. The second and third quintiles have also lost ground. The fourth quintile is just about where it was in 1950, garnering roughly 23 percent of the nation's income. The wealthy, defined in Table 4.2 as the highest one-fifth of all Americans in personal income, saw its share of income decline for many years, but in recent decades this group's share has increased and is nearly half of the nation's income. Those in the top 5 percent of income also lost ground for many years, but they, too, have captured more of the country's wealth in recent decades. Meanwhile, the lowest,

TABLE 4.2 Share of Aggregate Income Received by Each Fifth and Top 5 Percent of Families, Selected Years

Quintiles	1950	1970	1990	2008
Lowest	4.5%	5.4%	4.6%	4.0%
Second	12.0	12.2	10.8	9.6
Third	17.4	17.6	16.6	15.5
Fourth	23.4	23.8	23.8	23.1
Highest	42.7	40.9	44.3	47.8
Total	100.0	100.0	100.0	100.0
Top 5 Percent	17.3	15.6	17.4	20.5

Source: U.S. Census Bureau, *Historical Income Tables-Families,* "Table F-2, Share of Aggregate Income Received by Each Fifth and Top 5 Percent of Families, All Races: 1947–2008." Retrieved June 14, 2010, from http://www.census.gov/hhes/www/income/data/historical/inequality/index.html

second, and third quintiles have fallen behind. To demonstrate just how much inequality has grown, between 1970 and 2008, the income share of the poorest Americans (those in the lowest quintile) declined by 26 percent. The income share of the lower-middle class (the second-lowest quintile) dropped by 20 percent since 1970 and that of the third (middle) quintile by 11 percent. Meanwhile, the income share of the wealthiest one-fifth of the population increased by nearly 17 percent and of the top five percent by 31 percent.

Another measure of income distribution is the *Gini index,* with zero indicating perfect income equality and one indicating total inequality. The *Gini index* also shows that income inequality in the United States has grown. In 1950 the Gini index was .379. By 1968 it had reached a low of .348. Since then the Gini has grown. In 2008 it was .438.[38]

Although the hardships of some of the poor are still mitigated by in-kind benefits (nutrition programs, public housing, Medicaid, and similar programs) that are not counted as income, even small reductions in their cash incomes can have serious consequences. Those who study income dynamics describe the shrinking middle class and increasing economic polarization in the United States as a "tidal wave of inequality."[39] The Organization for Economic Cooperation and Development (OECD) reports that the gap between rich and poor has increased in most of its member countries in the last two decades, "but nowhere has this trend been so stark as in the United States." Those who think that "redistribution of income" is blasphemy might be less concerned if they knew that of all 30 OECD member countries, only in Korea does such redistribution play a smaller role than in the United States. In the United States,

> the level of spending on social benefits like unemployment benefits and family benefits is low—equivalent to just 9% of household incomes, while the OECD average is 22%. The effectiveness of taxes and transfers in reducing inequality has fallen still further in the past 10 years.[40]

Poverty is relative to a country's standard of living, but as Figure 4.4 also shows, of the 30 OECD countries, only Mexico and Turkey have higher poverty rates than the United States. Of course, some take exception to the calculations of poverty that show that the United States has a higher rate than in other developed countries.[41]

WHY ARE THE POOR, POOR?

Poverty can be defined in terms of deprivation and as inequality, but what are the underlying causes of poverty? We consider explanations of human capital, culture, exploitation, and structure.

Poverty as Lack of Human Capital

Economists often explain poverty in terms of the *human capital theory.* This theory explains income variations in a free market economy as a result of differences in productivity. The poor are poor because their economic productivity is low. They do not have the human capital—knowledge, skills, training, education—to sell to employers in a free market. As partial evidence for this theory, we observe that poverty ranges from a low of 4.1 percent for those with at least a bachelor's degree to a high of 23.5 percent for those with less than a high school education (see Figure 4.2 on page 116).

Poverty may also result from inadequate demand in the economy as a whole, in a particular segment of the economy, or in a particular region of the nation. A serious recession and widespread unemployment raise the proportion of the population living in poverty. Full

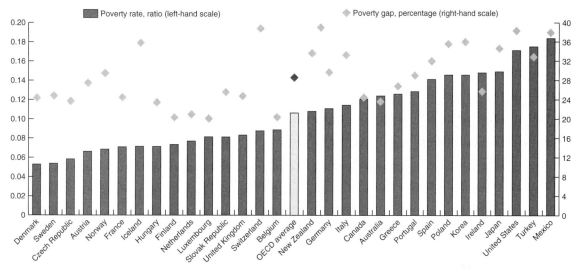

FIGURE 4.4   Poverty Rate and Poverty Gap for OECD Countries, mid-2000s

Relative income poverty is measured here by the poverty rate and the poverty gap. The poverty rate is the ratio of the number of people who fall below the poverty line and the total population; the poverty line here is taken as half the median household income. However, two countries with the same poverty rates may differ in terms of the income-level of the poor. To measure this dimension of poverty, the poverty gap, *i.e.* the percentage by which the mean income of the poor falls below the poverty line, is also presented.   *Source:* Organization for Economic Cooperation and Development, *OECD 2009 Factbook* (Paris). Retrieved March 9, 2010, from http://oberon.sourceoecd.org/ vl=10909638/cl=51/nw=1/rpsv/factbook2009/12/02/01/12-02-01-g1.htm

employment and a healthy economy improve opportunities for marginal workers, but these factors do not directly reduce poverty among people who have no marketable skills or are unable to work.

As Figure 4.2 also demonstrates, absence from the labor force is a major source of poverty—22 percent of unemployed individuals were poor compared to 2.6 percent who worked full time. No improvement in the national economy is likely to affect those who are unable to work due to advanced age or severe disabilities. They are outside the labor market and, therefore, are largely the concern of government rather than of the private economy. Many of the poor are children. There is hope of helping them out of poverty by improving opportunities for them and their parents.

Finally, we must consider poverty that is the direct effect of discrimination against women and people of particular racial or ethnic groups. It is true that some differences in incomes are a product of educational differences between groups. However, even if we control for education among year-round, full time workers, we can see, for example, that at every educational level, black men and men of Hispanic origin earn less than white men (see Table 4.3). If the human capital theory operated freely—without interference in the form of discrimination—then we would not expect to see such differences between blacks and whites at the same educational levels (or between men and women as discussed in Chapter 11). But unfortunately this is not the case.

When in 1776 Thomas Jefferson wrote on behalf of the Second Continental Congress that "all men are created equal," he was expressing the widespread dislike for hereditary aristocracy—lords and ladies, dukes and duchesses, and queens and kings. The Founding Fathers wrote their belief in equality of law into the U.S. Constitution. But their concern was *equality of opportunity,*

TABLE 4.3 Mean Income of Men 25 Years and Older Who Worked Year-Round, Full-Time by Race or Ethnicity and Education, 2007

Education	White (non-Hispanic)	Black	Hispanic	Asian
Less than 9th grade	$40,704	$27,239	$26,084	$25,942
9th to 12th grade (no diploma)	38,479	28,735	30,127	31,273
High school graduate	47,500	36,043	36,235	38,007
Associate degree	55,179	46,812	49,917	51,046
Bachelor's degree	84,166	55,881	56,793	65,778
Master's degree	98,932	65,146	88,983	88,230

Source: U.S. Census Bureau, "Table PINC-03, Educational Attainment—People 25 Years Old and Over, by Total Money Earnings in 2007, Work Experience in 2007, Age, Race, Hispanic Origin, and Sex." Retrieved March 9, 2010, from http://www.census.gov/hhes/www/macro/032008/perinc/new03_000.htm

not absolute equality. Indeed, the Founding Fathers referred to efforts to equalize income as "leveling," and they were strongly opposed to this notion. Jefferson wrote,

> To take from one, because it is thought his own industry and that of his fathers has acquired too much, in order to spare to others, who, or whose fathers have not, exercised equal industry and skill, is to violate arbitrarily the first principle of association, the guarantee to everyone the free exercise of his industry and the fruits acquired by it.[42]

Equality of opportunity requires that artificial obstacles to upward mobility be removed. There is no place for distinctions based on race, ethnicity, gender, birth, and religion in a free society. But this is not to say that all people's incomes should be equalized. Andrew Jackson, one of the nation's first democrats, explained,

> Distinctions in every society will always exist under every just government. Equality of talents, education or wealth cannot be produced by human institutions. In the full enjoyment of the gifts of heaven and the fruits of superior industry, economy, and virtue, every man is entitled to protection by law; but when the laws undertake to add to these national distinctions, to grant titles, gratuities, and exclusive privileges, to make the rich richer . . . then the humble members of society have a right to complain of the injustice of their government.[43]

Just how much equality should we try to achieve? Utopian socialists have argued for a rule of distribution: "From each according to his ability, to each according to his needs." In other words, everyone produces whatever he or she can, and wealth and income are distributed according to each person's needs. There is no monetary reward for hard work, skills and talent, or education and training. Since most people's needs are roughly the same, they will each receive roughly the same income. Collective ownership replaces private property. If such a Utopian society ever existed, then near-perfect income equality would be achieved.

But all societies—capitalist and socialist, democratic and authoritarian, traditional and modern—distribute wealth unequally. It is not likely that income differences will ever disappear. Societies reward hard work, skill, talent, education, training, risk taking, and ingenuity. Distributing income equally throughout society threatens the work ethic. The real questions we must confront are how much inequality is necessary or even desirable for a society, and conversely, how much inequality can society afford to tolerate? Americans argue about the fairness of the current distribution of income (as shown in Table 4.2 on page 119), but virtually everyone recognizes that a country in which nearly one-fifth of children are growing up in poverty cannot lead to positive outcomes for them or for society.

Of course, when defined as *inequality,* the problem of poverty is not capable of a total solution. Regardless of how well off poor individuals and families may be in absolute standards of living, there will always be a lowest one-fifth of the population receiving something less than 20 percent of all income. We can reduce income inequalities through less drastic political changes than communism or socialism (greater educational opportunities, a more progressive personal income tax, or more generous social welfare benefits, for example), but some differences will remain, and to the extent they do, someone will see them as a problem.

Poverty as Culture

Some argue that poverty is a "way of life" passed on from generation to generation in a self-perpetuating cycle. This notion of a *culture of poverty* involves not just a low income but also attitudes of indifference, alienation, and apathy, along with lack of incentives and of self-respect. These attitudes make it difficult for people who are poor to use the opportunities for upward mobility that may be available to them. According to this perspective, increasing the income of poor people may not affect their joblessness, lack of incentives and educational opportunities, unstable family life, incidence of crime, and other social problems.

There are sharp differences between scholars and policymakers over whether a culture of poverty exists. The argument resembles the classic exchange between F. Scott Fitzgerald and Ernest Hemingway. When Fitzgerald observed, "The rich are different from you and me," Hemingway retorted, "Yes, they have more money." Observers who believe that they see a distinctive culture among the poor may say, "The poor are different from you and me." Opponents of the culture-of-poverty notion may reply, "Yes, they have less money." But are the poor undereducated, unskilled, poorly motivated, and "delinquent" because they are poor? Or are they poor because they are undereducated, unskilled, poorly motivated, and "delinquent"? This distinction has important policy implications.

Former Harvard University government professor Edward C. Banfield set forth one especially controversial view of the culture of poverty by contending that poverty is really a product of "present-orientedness."[44] According to Banfield, individuals caught up in the culture of poverty are unable to plan for the future, to sacrifice immediate gratifications in favor of future ones, or to exercise the discipline required to get ahead. Banfield admitted that some people experience poverty because of involuntary unemployment, prolonged illness, death of the family breadwinner, or some other misfortune. But even with severe misfortune, he claimed, this kind of poverty is not squalid, degrading, or self-perpetuating; it ends once the external cause of it no longer exists. According to Banfield, other people will be poor no matter what their "external" circumstances are. They live in a culture of poverty that continues for generations because they are psychologically unable to plan for the future. Improvements in their circumstances may affect their poverty only superficially. Even increased income is unlikely to change their way of life, for the additional money will be spent quickly on nonessential or frivolous items.

There are other controversial views of the culture of poverty. Nicolas Lemann attributed hard-core poverty in inner-city communities comprised largely of black residents to an anthropological cause—the rural southern heritage of many of its residents.[45] As sharecroppers, blacks were unable to own property, save money, maintain stable family relationships, or obtain an education.

Lemann contends these patterns have carried over to the present day. Opponents of the culture of poverty idea argue that this notion diverts attention from the conditions of poverty that currently foster family instability, present orientedness, and other ways of life of the poor.

Social reformers are likely to focus on the condition of poverty itself as the fundamental cause of the social pathologies that afflict the poor. They note that the idea of a culture of poverty can be applied only to groups who have lived in poverty for several generations. It is not relevant to those who have become poor during their lifetimes because of sickness, accident, or old age. The cultural explanation of poverty basically involves parental transmission of values and beliefs, which in turn determines the behavior of future generations. In contrast, the situational explanation shows how present social conditions and differences in opportunities and financial resources operate directly to cause poverty and determine behavior. Perhaps the greatest danger in the idea of a culture of poverty is that it may cast poverty as an unbreakable, puncture-proof cycle. This outlook may lead to inaction or at least a relaxation of efforts to ameliorate the conditions of poverty.

If one assumes that the poor are no different from other Americans, then one is led toward policies that emphasize opportunity for individuals as well as changes in their environment. If poor Americans are like other Americans, it is necessary only to provide them with the ordinary means to achieve—for example, job-training programs, good schools, and counseling to make them aware of opportunities that are available to them. The intervention that is required to change their lives, therefore, is one of supplying a means to achieve a level of income that most Americans enjoy.

In contrast, if one believes in the notion of a culture of poverty, it is necessary to devise a strategy to interrupt the transmission of self-defeating cultural values from generation to generation. The strategy must try to prevent the socialization of young children into an environment of family instability, lack of motivation, crime and delinquency, and so forth. One drastic means to accomplish this would be to remove children at a very early age from homes dominated by these values and to raise them in a controlled environment that transmits the values of the conventional culture. This was done to some extent in the early part of the twentieth century (see Chapter 10). Such a solution is no longer realistic (although certain conservatives have suggested a return to the use of orphanages for children whose parents are unable to provide an adequate upbringing). More acceptable solutions today are special daycare centers and preschool programs to remedy cultural deprivation and disadvantage such as Head Start (see Chapters 3 and 9). These programs are intended to bring about change in young children through "cultural enrichment."

Poverty as Exploitation

Both Marxist and non-Marxist writers have defined poverty as a form of *exploitation* by the ruling class. Sociologist Herbert Gans contended that poverty serves many functions for the middle and upper classes in the United States such as providing a cheap source of labor.[46] In fact, a substantial number of people who are poor work at least part-time (see Figure 4.2 on page 116), yet they did not earn enough to escape financial hardship. Gans's implication is that the ruling classes maintain poverty in order to make their own lives more pleasant. Poverty does not have to exist; it could be eliminated with the cooperation of the middle and upper classes. But it is unlikely that these classes will ever give up anything they believe they have earned through their own hard work, useful skills, or business enterprise. Even if many middle- and upper-class Americans recognize that they are not fully insulated from financial disaster and poverty, most probably do not think they have much in common with those who are poor.

Two authors who have also written about the class-based nature of poverty call the United States the "upside-down welfare state" since it "is a complicated system in which those who need help the most get the least, and those who need it least get the most."[47] They say that all Americans, rich or poor, benefit from government welfare programs. The poor and near-poor receive government assistance through programs called Temporary Assistance for Needy Families, the Supplemental Nutrition Assistance Program (food stamps), Medicaid, and the earned income tax credit. The middle classes receive government assistance primarily in the form of home mortgage loans and associated tax deductions and educational grants. The rich receive government assistance through favorable tax laws, government contracts, and subsidies to business and industry. The difference is that government assistance to the poor is called "welfare," while government assistance to the rich is called "good business"—an investment in the economy and in the nation. In the final analysis, the poor often remain poor while the middle and upper classes improve their position with government aid.

Social scientists Frances Fox Piven and Richard A. Cloward have also commented on the economic, political, and social utility that the upper classes see in maintaining poverty. In 1971 their book *Regulating the Poor: The Functions of Public Welfare* claimed that "the key to an understanding of relief-giving is in the functions it serves for the larger economic and political order, for relief is a secondary and supportive institution."[48] Piven and Cloward saw welfare, especially the former Aid to Families with Dependent Children (AFDC) program, as a device to control the poor in order to maintain social stability. According to this view, welfare programs were expanded in times of political unrest as a means of appeasing the poor, and welfare rules and regulations were used as a means of "forcing" the poor into the labor market during times of political stability, especially when there was a need to increase the number of people in the workforce. Piven and Cloward later updated their original ideas when they saw that this cyclical pattern of contraction and expansion of welfare had been replaced by a more permanent set of welfare programs, making people less dependent for their survival on business and industry and fluctuations in the labor market.[49] Piven and Cloward espoused the right to welfare, and they encouraged Americans to resist cuts in social welfare programs. The 1996 federal welfare reforms again put social welfare programs on more shaky footing in another attempt to modify the behavior of the poor[50] (also see Chapter 7).

If poverty is defined as the exploitation of the poor by a ruling class, then it might be that only a radical restructuring of society to eliminate class differences would solve the problem of poverty. Marxists call for the revolutionary overthrow of capitalist society by workers and farmers and the emergence of a new "classless" society. Presumably, in such a society there would be no ruling class with an interest in exploiting the poor. Of course, in practice, Communist-ruled societies have produced one-party governments that dominate and exploit nearly the entire population. Most of these governments have now given way to more democratic governance.

Civil rights legislation is one example of a less radical means than communism for achieving a more egalitarian society. Substantial numbers of people have benefited from civil rights laws, but many people view the remaining class differences as still far too wide. Others reject this class-based notion of poverty, believing that many people who are poor simply fail to work hard and do not avail themselves of the many opportunities a capitalist society like the United States provides.

These perspectives help us to understand that there are indeed class differences in views on poverty. If the upper classes do not deliberately exploit those who are poor, they sometimes express paternalistic attitudes toward them. Although the upper classes generally have little understanding of the lives of poor people, they believe they "know what's best" for them.

Moreover, the upper classes frequently engage in charitable activities and support liberal welfare programs to demonstrate their idealism and "do-goodism," regardless of whether the poor are actually helped.

Poverty as Structure

Poverty can also be considered by studying the *institutional* and *structural* components of society that foster its continuation. As already mentioned, some poverty can be attributed to the effects of discrimination. The term *institutional discrimination* refers to practices that are deeply embedded in schools, the criminal justice system, and other organizations that serve gatekeeper functions in society. For example, poor school districts generally receive fewer resources that can be used to promote educational opportunities for their young citizens than schools in wealthier districts. Such differences have become the bases for court challenges to the ways in which public school education is funded in a number of states. Healthcare and other services are generally not well organized in poorer communities. Lack of access to healthcare and other resources also contributes to circumstances that make it more difficult to avoid poverty. Another example of institutional discrimination occurs in the criminal justice system, since jails and prisons are overpopulated with those who are black or of Hispanic origin and poor. The only way to ameliorate problems of this nature is to change the deep-seated values of the societal institutions that perpetuate them.

Deep-seated poverty not only arises from institutional discrimination but also from changes in the country's economic structure such as inadequate demand in a particular sector of the economy or in a particular region of the nation. Industrialization and technological development have bypassed large segments of Appalachia, one of the country's poorest areas. The closing of steel mills in large eastern cities and auto plants in midwestern cities forced some workers into poverty and others into lower-paying jobs. "Offshoring," a euphemism for exporting jobs to countries where labor is much cheaper, has been made increasingly possible by various trade agreements the United States has entered into with other countries. Whether it is Brach's Confections, Inc., leaving Chicago, Levi Strauss & Co. leaving El Paso, or FotJoy (the last shoe manufacturing plant left in Brockton, Massachusetts) closing its doors, working communities are deeply affected as more jobs make their way to Mexico, Asia, and other countries. More highly paid workers have also felt the effects as jobs in the high-tech sector, for example, are "offshored" to countries like India. Many workers are able to locate new jobs, but those with few marketable skills are least likely to secure jobs in other segments of the economy. Neither are they able to relocate to find employment. The structure of work is also changing. Contract work is becoming more common, and it lacks benefits like health insurance and retirement plans, thus increasing poverty risks. Some former highly paid professionals are beginning to wonder if they will ever see the kinds of jobs, salaries, and benefits they once had. But this does not mean that these individuals with good educations and community status have increased empathy for the poor or feel they have much in common with them.

Karl Marx used the term *lumpenproletariat* (the proletariat in rags) more than a hundred years ago to describe those who had, in essence, dropped out of society.[51] In the 1960s this concept reemerged to refer to those most severely affected by changes in community and economic structure. Nobel Prize winner Gunnar Myrdal coined the term *underclass* to describe those who had been unable to weather changes in the country's economic structure and who were not able to obtain jobs in a market that relies increasingly on more highly skilled and educated workers. Today, the term underclass is used with particular reference to residents of poor, black, ghetto communities that are characterized by long-term unemployment, long-term welfare dependency, and overall social disorganization, including high levels of street crime.[52] The term is controversial because of its derogatory sound and because it fails to distinguish the diversity among those who are poor. Members of this so-called "underclass," also called the "ghetto poor," are of considerable concern because they are outside the mainstream of the social, economic, and political institutions that are part of the lives of most citizens.

Prior to the 1960s these inner-city communities were not as severely depressed as they are today.[53] In the 1940s and 1950s they were home to blacks of all social classes who utilized the schools, businesses, and other social institutions in these neighborhoods. Fair housing and other antidiscrimination laws had not yet evolved that would allow many middle- and upper-class blacks to move to more affluent city and suburban neighborhoods. The economic exchange in these communities provided jobs for many residents, including those with marginal job skills. But as professional and blue-collar workers were able to find better housing in the suburbs, the most disadvantaged were left behind. According to several authors, community leaders were no longer present to bring stability to these neighborhoods. Their departure also caused a severe decline in economic enterprises. At the same time, the job market in the cities underwent considerable change. Industrial and manufacturing jobs were replaced by jobs in the financial, technical, and administrative fields. Most poor inner-city residents were not prepared for these kinds of jobs. Jobs in the food and retail industries, which inner-city residents might have been able to fill more readily, were increasing in numbers in the suburbs, but those who needed these jobs the most could not find housing there. It has been said that these structural changes left open a path for social disorganization. As a result, inner-city neighborhoods deteriorated and problems such as unemployment, teen pregnancy, and drug dealing increased.

To remedy this type of severe or persistent poverty, recommendations are that multiple approaches be used; for example, that job training, relocation, and other types of services be coupled with efforts to bring the poor in closer touch with mainstream society. These solutions sound similar to those suggested to interrupt the culture of poverty. The important distinction is that the notion of a culture of poverty is concerned with changing *personal* characteristics of the poor that prevent them from functioning in the mainstream. Some refer to this as a "blame the victim" mentality. Poverty viewed as a *structural* issue is quite different. It implies that the solutions to the problem lie in developing new social institutions or modifying existing ones to be more responsive to disadvantaged members of society. This is also an important distinction in developing social policies. For example, rather than provide housing for the poor in ghetto communities, a structural approach would be to offer housing in middle-class communities to allow disadvantaged individuals to avail themselves of greater societal opportunities. Another suggestion to bring young people into the mainstream is a national service requirement for *all* youth. This type of universal program differs substantially from job programs that target only youth from disadvantaged backgrounds. The concept behind such a universal program is that it would provide for better integration of all members of society, but clearly such a requirement would meet with opposition from those who are already better off and feel that they would not gain by it.

THE POLITICS OF HUNGER

The most basic subsistence need the government meets is for food. The federal government's main food program for low-income individuals and families is the Supplemental Nutrition Assistance Program (SNAP).

From Food Stamps to SNAP

SNAP was formerly called the Food Stamp Program. Electronic benefit transfer (EBT), the same technology utilized in ATM and debit and credit card transfers, made paper food stamp coupons and the cumbersome process of distributing, collecting, and redeeming them obsolete. The United States Department of Agriculture (USDA) Food and Nutrition Service says that the program's new name better reflects its focus on nutrition. It may still be more accurate to call SNAP a food program since participants can buy just about any food product they want through the program regardless of whether the food is nutritious. SNAP benefits can be used to purchase food but not soap and paper, cleaning, and hygiene products many people include in their grocery shopping. Although fraud is always possible, EBT has helped to quell criticisms that food stamps were being sold for cash or traded for all kinds of non-food products.[54] SNAP is available to a broader cross section of the population that is poor than any other public assistance program.

Particularly important is whether a substantial number of Americans can really be considered hungry. According to the USDA, in 2007, 13 million households (11.1 percent of the population) were "food insecure," meaning that "at some time during the year, they had difficulty providing enough food for all their members due to a lack of resources." About one-third of these households had very low food security; that is, at least some household members' food consumption was reduced and their normal eating patterns were disrupted because they were unable to obtain sufficient food. The other two-thirds of food-insecure households avoided disruptions in food consumption by eating less varied diets, participating in government food programs, or utilizing community food pantries or emergency kitchens.[55] When rent, utility, or medical bills strain household budgets, individuals or families may skimp on food. This food insecurity is different from the severe undernutrition experienced by inhabitants of the world's poorest regions. Nevertheless, according to government definition, some U.S. households lack the resources necessary to feed themselves.

By 1994, Food Stamp Program participation had grown to approximately 27.5 million individuals. Given better economic times and welfare reform, participation dropped to approximately 17 million individuals in 2000. By the end of 2009 with the economy again in trouble, SNAP participation grew to 33.7 million individuals and the cost of benefits rose to more than $50 billion (see Figure 4.5).

Discovering and Rediscovering Hunger

The U.S. government's initial foray into food assistance began in 1930 when farmers were able to persuade Congress to stabilize farm prices by buying their surplus agricultural commodities. The added benefit was that the food was made available to those stricken by the Great Depression. From 1939 to 1943 the government utilized a type of food coupon or food stamp program in some parts of the country. The program provided more food choices and solved the problem of keeping quantities of perishable commodity foods fresh, but it was abandoned when demand for agricultural products increased after World War II. The government returned to commodity food distribution.

In the 1960s, a study called Hunger U.S.A., supported by the Field Foundation of Chicago's Marshall Field department store, and a CBS television documentary helped the country "discover" hunger. Particularly poignant was Nick Kotz's book describing Senators Robert F. Kennedy and Joseph Clark's 1967 visit to Cleveland, Mississippi, where Annie White and her six children lived.[56] The trip was made at the request of Marian Wright Edelman, who later became head of

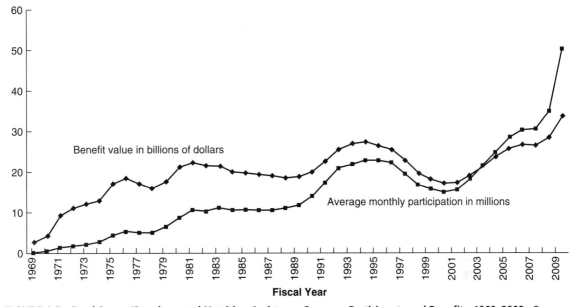

FIGURE 4.5 **Food Stamp/Supplemental Nutrition Assistance Program Participants and Benefits: 1969–2009.** *Source:* Data are from Food and Nutrition Service, Supplemental Nutrition Assistance Program Participation and Costs (Washington, DC: U.S. Department of Agriculture, March 3, 2010). Fiscal Year 2009 data are preliminary. Retrieved March 9, 2010, from http://www.fns.usda.gov/pd/SNAPsummary.htm

the Children's Defense Fund. The senators were stunned at what they saw. One of the children, a girl about 2 years old, had a swollen stomach and was so listless that Senator Kennedy was unable to get her to respond to his cajoling. At that time, families had to contribute to the cost of their food stamps, and White said she could not afford to purchase them. All the family had left to eat was the last rice and biscuits from its surplus commodity allotment.

In 1977, during the Carter administration, the food stamp purchase requirement was finally eliminated. At the same time other income and eligibility requirements were tightened. The 1980s began with more tightening of eligibility requirements and disagreement about the extent of hunger in the United States. President Reagan felt the Food Stamp Program had grown too large because families with incomes above poverty thresholds were allowed to participate, "divert[ing] the Food Stamp Program away from its original purpose toward a generalized income transfer program, regardless of nutritional need."[57] New claims emerged that hunger was on the rise due to Reagan's social program cuts and rising unemployment. Concerned that reports of hunger in the United States were exaggerated,[58] Reagan appointed a task force to study the issue. The task force's general conclusion, published in 1984, was that undernutrition was not a serious problem. Social action groups lambasted the report, and leading nutrition experts charged, "Despite their almost total lack of qualifications, the task force members did manage to find that hunger has reappeared in America. But because of their ineptitude, they were unable to qualify its extent, or to discern the presence of chronic malnutrition."[59]

Meanwhile, the Food Research and Action Center publicized results of its own work indicating that infant mortality had increased in some areas of the country due to nutritional deficiencies. The Citizens' Commission on Hunger in New England also concluded that malnutrition and hunger again confronted the United States, and the Physician Task Force on Hunger in America identified 150 "hunger counties" in which substantial numbers of poor people were not receiving food stamps.[60] The Reagan task force recommended replacing the Food Stamp Program with a block grant, monitoring spending more closely, and beefing up efforts to detect fraud and abuse. The other groups encouraged increased food stamp spending, making it easier to obtain and use benefits, and forming a bipartisan commission to put an end to the nation's hunger.

During the mid- and late-1980s food stamp legislation became kinder to recipients. Public assistance (AFDC and Supplemental Security Income program) recipients were declared automatically eligible for food stamps. States that charged a sales tax on food could no longer tax food stamp purchases. Homeless people could apply for food stamps even though they had no fixed address, and they could use their stamps to purchase low-cost meals in participating restaurants. Food stamp allotments were increased. States could use federal funds for outreach to increase program participation (although outreach was optional). On the other side of the ledger, states were also required to establish an Employment and Training (E&T) program in order to reduce Food Stamp Program participation among those able to work.

In 1990, the Mickey Leland Memorial Domestic Hunger Relief Act, named after the late representative from Texas, reauthorized the Food Stamp Program through 1995. Leland's efforts to bring attention to the problem of world hunger were well known, and he chaired the House Select Committee on Hunger. The committee's efforts were highly respected, but it had only an advisory role, and the House abolished it in 1993 despite strong outcries. A USDA-sponsored hunger forum was held in 1993 to help the Clinton administration set its nutrition agenda. People with various interests in food programs, including food stamp participants, testified at the forum. During this period, Congress made it easier to qualify by increasing income deductions and disregards. The 1996 farm bill reauthorized the Food Stamp Program through 1997, but bigger changes were in store.

The Food Stamp Program or SNAP has a history of expansion and contraction. In keeping with the country's mood to reform welfare, the Personal Responsibility and Work Opportunity Reconciliation Act (PRWORA) of 1996 reauthorized the Food Stamp Program through 2002 along with substantial program changes. The program was saved from being converted into a block grant, which might have resulted in a cap on the number of eligible people who could be assisted, but many eligibility rules were made more stringent. For example, in determining household eligibility, some income deductions were frozen rather than adjusted annually.

The PRWORA made it easier for states to operate Food Stamp E&T programs but increased work requirements for recipients. This law also "delete[d] lack of adequate childcare as an explicit good cause exemption for refusal to meet work requirements" and established minimum disqualification periods for those who fail to meet work requirements. Able-bodied adults (aged 18 to 50) without dependents who did not meet work requirements could receive food stamps for only three months in a three-year period. In the response to the country's latest economic recession, the American Recovery and Reinvestment Act (ARRA) of 2009 extended the time limit for these recipients unless a state chose to offer a qualifying work activity.

Each year SNAP benefits are adjusted for inflation. As part of the ARRA, benefits got an additional increase. A family of four receiving the maximum monthly benefit would have received $588 in 2009. Their benefit was raised to $668 ($1.85 per person per meal). Benefits will stay at that level until the normal adjustments that would have occurred exceed $668. One economist called increased SNAP benefits the best economic stimulus with unemployment insurance second, because people who get these benefits are usually in dire straits and spend them quickly.[61]

To qualify for SNAP, participants' net income cannot exceed poverty guidelines. Illustration 4.2 describes SNAP eligibility requirements. SNAP benefits are entirely funded by

ILLUSTRATION 4.2
Qualifying for the Supplemental Nutrition Assistance Program in the Continental United States

Here are many of the eligibility requirements that individuals and families must meet if they are to receive benefits from the Supplemental Nutrition Assistance Program (SNAP).

Countable Assets

- Most households are limited to $2,000 in countable assets (e.g., bank accounts).
- Those aged 60 or older or disabled may have countable assets totaling $3,000.
- A home, personal effects, and some other items are not counted.
- In many cases, the value of a vehicle that exceeds $4,650 is counted.
- Some vehicles are not counted (e.g., if it is primarily used to earn income, as a home, or to transport a disabled household member).

Gross and Net Income Tests

- Households in which all members receive TANF, SSI, or in some places General Assistance, are exempt from gross and net income tests.
- Households with at least one person who is aged 60 or older or disabled must meet the net but not the gross income test.
- For most households, gross income (which includes most cash received, e.g., earnings, cash public assistance, social insurance) cannot exceed 130 percent of federal poverty guidelines (in fiscal year 2010, $2,389 a month for a family of four).[a]

- Generally, net household income cannot exceed 100 percent of poverty guidelines ($1,838 a month for a family of four in fiscal year 2010).[a]

Deductions from Net Income

In determining net income, certain amounts of money are deducted to cover some household expenses. These include:

- A standard deduction of $141 a month for households of one to three members, $153 for four members, and more for larger households.
- 20 percent of all income earned from work.
- Legally owed child support payments.
- Costs of child or other dependent care while household members work or participate in training or education. (Few SNAP households use this deduction because they cannot afford this type of care.)
- Many households use the income deduction for excess shelter costs, calculated by determining the amount of the household's housing costs (mortgage or rent, utilities, and property taxes) that exceeds 50 percent of their remaining income after all other deductions are made. Some states use a standard utility cost rather than actual utility costs. The shelter deduction cannot exceed $459 unless a household member is elderly or disabled.[a]
- Individuals who are elderly or disabled may deduct all but $35 of the medical expenses that they pay themselves.

[a]Gross and net income limits are slightly higher for Hawaii and Alaska. The shelter deduction is higher in Alaska, Hawaii, and Guam. Due to higher food prices, SNAP benefits are higher in Alaska, Hawaii, Guam, and the Virgin Islands than in the continental United States.

Source: Adapted from U.S. Department of Agriculture, "Supplemental Nutrition Assistance Program, Eligibility," September 22, 2009. Retrieved March 9, 2010, from http://www.fns.usda.gov/fsp/applicant_recipients/eligibility.htm#income

the federal government. The states share administrative costs of the program. The USDA also operates a number of other programs to provide food and promote nutrition among low-income groups. The Women, Infants, and Children (WIC) program is highly regarded in promoting the health of pregnant and postpartum women and young children. The school breakfast, lunch, and milk programs are important sources of nutrition for many children.

THE POLITICS OF AFFORDABLE HOUSING

Shelter is another subsistence need that the federal and local governments help people meet. The largest item in most household budgets is housing. Whether it is the monthly rent or mortgage payment, housing has consumed an increasingly greater larger portion of the personal budget. As far back as the Housing Act of 1949, Congress acknowledged the need for a "decent home and a suitable living environment for every American family."

Since 1989, the National Low Income Housing Coalition (NLIHC) has conducted studies of affordable *rental* housing. The NLIHC's 2009 report indicates that in no U.S. county can someone working full-time at his or her *state's* prevailing minimum wage afford a one-bedroom dwelling at fair market rent (FMR), and in 30 states it takes more than two full-time minimum wage jobs to afford a two-bedroom dwelling (in many states the prevailing minimum wage is considerably higher than the federal minimum wage).[62] The U.S. Census Bureau found that in 2006, "in 15 states and the District of Columbia, about 55 percent or more of renters in the *lowest* income quartile spent 50% or more of their income on housing costs."[63] (The situation was worse for those with mortgages. "In 31 states and the District of Columbia, 70 percent or more of mortgaged owners in the lowest income quartile spent 50% or more of their income on housing costs.") Residents of publicly supported housing are generally expected to contribute 30 percent of their income for rent. Thus, many Americans are considered "shelter poor" because they have difficulty meeting other expenses after paying rent,[64] but housing expenses must be paid because of the threat of eviction. Decent housing in a decent neighborhood is central to safety and security.

Government and Rental Housing

The U.S. Department of Housing and Urban Development (HUD) is the federal government's main agency for helping low-income Americans find housing. Today, approximately 1.2 million families reside in the nation's 14,000 public housing developments located in 3,300 communities.[65] Many residents are elderly or disabled.

When Americans think of government-sponsored housing, their image may be of the large, high-rise public housing projects that gained notoriety in the past for being rodent-, drug-, and crime-infested. Many of these units have been demolished. Today's public housing does include high rises, but much of it is also of the lower-density type, including single-family dwellings scattered throughout neighborhoods.

The nation's public housing supply has dwindled. The federal government has not funded new public housing developments since 1994.[66] Neither has it required public housing authorities (PHAs) to replace demolished units, and it has prohibited them from increasing the supply of public housing.[67] Much of the remaining public housing is falling into disrepair because housing authorities lack funds for upkeep.[68]

Today, HUD's major approach for assisting very low-income families and individuals who are disabled or elderly is the Housing Choice Voucher Program, commonly called Section 8,[69] initiated in 1974 during the Nixon administration. HUD provides funds to local public PHAs that administer the program. Vouchers generally go to those whose incomes are not more than half of the area's median income, and three-quarters of vouchers must go to those whose income is not more than 30 percent of the median. A small number of participants use their subsidies to purchase homes, but the vast majority use them to defray rent costs. PHAs may give preference to certain types of applicants, for example, low-income families who are homeless, living in substandard housing, displaced, or paying an inordinate amount for rent. PHAs use fair market rent (FMR) calculations to determine the size of subsidies under the voucher program. Illustration 4.3 defines FMRs and contains FMRs

ILLUSTRATION 4.3
Fair Market Rents for Selected Cities in 2010

Each year the U.S. Department of Housing and Urban Development (HUD) publishes the Fair Market Rents (FMRs) it uses to determine standard payments for the Section 8 Housing Choice Voucher program and other HUD purposes. FMRs are currently available for 530 metropolitan areas and 2,045 nonmetropolitan areas. FMRs are gross rent estimates. They include rent and basic utilities (but not telephone, cable TV, or Internet service). HUD's objective is to set FMRs to assure that a sufficient supply of rental housing is available to program participants. To accomplish this objective, FMRs must be high enough to permit a selection of units and neighborhoods and low enough to serve as many low-income families as possible. The level at which FMRs are set is expressed as a percentile point within the rent distribution of standard-quality rental housing units. HUD currently sets FMRs at the 40th percentile rent (the dollar amount below which 40 percent of the standard-quality housing units are rented). These percentiles are drawn from the distribution of rents of all units occupied by recent movers (renter households that moved to their present residence within the last 15 months). Public housing units and units less than two years old are excluded.

City	FMR for One-Bedroom Apartment
Atlanta, GA	$820
Baltimore, MD	$1002
Bloomington, IN	$555
Boston, MA	$1,156
Colorado Springs, CO	$630
Lawrence, KS	$576
Los Angeles, CA	$1,137
Madison, WI	$761
Mobile, AL	$620
Omaha, NE	$614
Orlando, FL	$921
Seattle, WA	$878

Source: Adapted from "Fair Market Rents" (Washington, DC: U.S Department of Housing and Urban Development, April 20, 2009). Retrieved May 13, 2010, from http://www.huduser.org/portal/datasets/fmr.html

for selected cities. Families or individuals generally pay 30 to 40 percent of their monthly, adjusted gross income (certain deductions are allowed) for rent and utilities, and the PHA pays the difference between this amount and fair market rent. Families or individuals must find their own housing and the housing must meet minimum health and safety standards. If the family or individual selects housing that exceeds the amount established by the PHA, the family must pay the difference.

About 2 million families participate in the voucher program, but it is not an entitlement program. In most places demand is high and there are long waiting lists. For example, in March 2009, the Housing Authority of the city of Austin (Texas) was not accepting new applications; about 5,000 families were on its waiting list, with about 30 to 40 families added to the voucher program each month. At this rate, it could take 10 years to reach the top of the list. Families that do obtain a voucher may have a hard time finding an affordable housing unit or a landlord who will accept a voucher. As costs of the Housing Choice Voucher program grew rapidly, the George W. Bush administration wanted to take steps to stem costs. About 150,000 families were eliminated from the program between 2004 and 2006 due to "deep and persistent funding shortfalls."[70]

The federal government also operates a Section 8 Project-Based Rental Assistance program, a public–private partnership serving about 1.3 million families. HUD contracts with owners of rental properties who provide this housing. But no new contracts have been awarded since the mid-1980s,[71] and property owners have been dropping out of the program due to long delays in obtaining payment.[72]

The picture has been bleak for many seeking assistance to secure affordable rental housing. According to a report by the Center for Budget and Policy Priorities:

> Since 1995, federal spending on low-income housing assistance has fallen by well over 20 percent both as a share of all non-defense discretionary spending and as a share of the Gross Domestic Product. Even when combined with the Low-Income Housing Tax Credit, the federal government's total commitment to low-income housing assistance is less than one-third the size of the three largest tax breaks provided to homeowners (such as the mortgage interest deduction).[73]

In fact, it has been said that in the zeal to promote homeownership, attention to increasing the nation's supply of affordable rental housing has suffered.[74] Now, in the wake of the country's economic recession, the Obama administration has proposed plans to increase the supply of rental housing for low-income Americans through efforts such as increased funding for rental vouchers and for the National Housing Trust Fund (NHTF) and tax credits for those who build affordable housing.[75] President Bush signed NHTF legislation in the fall of 2008 to boost the affordable housing supply with an emphasis on help for very low-income families.[76]

Since housing is so integral to health and general well-being, it may seem surprising that it has not been the focus of more government attention. The relatively modest amount of assistance the Department of Housing and Urban Development has provided may be a result of the many difficulties the agency has faced. Republican Jack Kemp, HUD secretary during the George H. W. Bush administration, was charged with changing the image of an agency tarnished by scandals. There were accusations that prominent Republicans and former HUD officials had raked in millions of dollars in consulting fees in order to steer HUD contracts to particular firms and that private escrow agents siphoned off millions from the sale of foreclosed homes. Kemp worked hard to instill pride in public housing projects, and he even managed to turn ownership of a few projects over to their residents.[77]

President Clinton appointed former San Antonio mayor Henry Cisneros HUD secretary. Cisneros worked to assist the homeless, to demolish decayed public housing and rehabilitate other units under a program called HOPE VI, and to use the voucher program to integrate poor people into decent neighborhoods. HUD's budget shrank, however, amid calls to get rid of the financially troubled agency entirely. Eventually, faced with personal problems, Cisneros left the agency. Poor management at some local public housing authorities further compounded HUD's problems. In 1999, the agency faced criticisms that it had left unspent more than $14 billion dollars that could have gone to assist poor renters.[78] HUD's problems did not end there. During the George W. Bush administration, HUD secretary Alphonso Jackson resigned (during the 2008 mortgage crisis) amid accusation of favoritism involving HUD contractors and FBI and Justice Department investigations about whether he steered business to cronies.[79] Three years later, the investigation was apparently dropped.[80] The embattled HUD has been called a relatively small agency with little political power.[81]

Home Ownership: Chasing the American Dream

Nothing typifies the American dream more than home ownership. Nonprofit groups and government programs help low-income individuals and families achieve this goal. The nonprofit group Habitat for Humanity International is well known for constructing or "rehabilitating" homes for low-income and poor individuals and families. Among the organization's most prominent volunteers are former president and first lady Jimmy and Rosalyn Carter. Many Habitat beneficiaries contribute "sweat equity"—their own labor—to help build these homes. Most also make modest mortgage payments. Community development corporations are also nonprofit organizations formed by community stakeholders that often raise funds and support projects to help increase home ownership.

Federal and local governments also design programs to make home ownership affordable to lower-income individuals and families. Communities often raise money through bond initiatives in order to offer low-interest mortgages to low- and moderate-income first-time home buyers. Bonds are loans to the municipality. Investors purchase the bonds, which the municipality pays back to them with interest. Also credited with increasing home ownership are many pieces of federal legislation such as the Community Reinvestment Act of 1977, which put more pressure on banks to make loans in low-income communities, and the Cranston-Gonzalez National Affordable Housing Act of 1990, which provides block grants to state and local governments for housing assistance such as home ownership programs.

Home ownership is not distributed equally among the population. At the end of 2008, homeownership rates were about 47 percent for African Americans, 49 percent for Hispanic Americans, and 75 percent for non-Hispanic whites. The George W. Bush administration adopted the term "ownership society." As part of this concept, it wanted to help an additional 5.5 million minority families become homeowners with legislation such as the American Dream Downpayment Act of 2003, a formula grant program dedicated to increasing homeownership rates, particularly among lower income (defined as income not less than 80 percent of the area's median income) and minority households.[82] The act helped first-time homebuyers and those who had not owned a home in the last three years by helping with downpayment and closing costs and with home rehabilitation. Purchasers could receive up to $10,000 or 6 percent of the purchase price of the home, whichever was greater. The Obama administration is helping individuals and families buy homes using similar approaches.

Home ownership is especially important in reducing *asset poverty*. Assets like savings, investments, and home ownership provide a cushion when resources are needed due to unemployment, illness, or other hardships. Asset inequality is even greater than income inequality. Adding assets to income provides a clearer picture of how wealth is distributed in the United States. Home equity is generally the largest component of a household's net worth, especially for those in lower-income groups. Using the definition that "a household is asset poor if it has insufficient net worth to stay above the federal poverty level for three months if all income was cut off," the Corporation for Enterprise Development found that 22 percent of all U.S. households and nearly 40 percent of minority households were asset poor in 2004.[83]

For many years, home ownership rates were on the rise. In 1950, 55 percent of Americans owned their own homes. In 2004, home ownership rates peaked at 69.2 percent of the population. Unemployment, inflation, and home mortgage interest rates were low, helping more Americans purchase homes despite rising home prices. Since then, the subprime mortgage debacle and failing economy (see Chapter 3) have caused home ownership rates to fall. By the end of 2009, the home ownership rate was 67.2.[84]

In response, Congress and the Obama administration devised two types of programs so that fewer people will face foreclosure. One allows some homeowners to modify their existing loans. Another allows homeowners to refinance their current loans. The federal government has made billions of dollars available for these programs, but mortgage company participation is voluntary. One stipulation is that only loans owned by Fannie Mae and Freddie Mac qualify for the refinancing program. Fannie and Freddie as they are called are private corporations the government established to increase home ownership. In addition, the borrower cannot owe more than 105 percent of what the home is currently worth. For the loan modification program, lenders must agree to reduce the monthly mortgage payment and split some costs with the government to bring the payment to 31 percent of the homeowner's income. The intent was to help 4 million people modify their home loans and another 5 million refinance. To help more people, in 2010, the administration made some changes in the programs, but they remain largely focused on those who can still make their mortgage payments, not the many homeowners who do not meet the criteria because they are in more dire straits.[85] Many of these individuals will need to seek rental housing, but they may have trouble qualifying because their credit ratings have dropped, and demand for the supply of affordable housing has increased. More Americans are facing the affordable housing crisis.

POOR AND HOMELESS: NOT INVISIBLE ANY MORE

In an influential book of the 1960s, *The Other America,* Michael Harrington argued that most Americans were blind to the poverty of millions in their own country.[86] Harrington wrote of two nations within the United States—one a nation of comfortable and affluent Americans, the other a nation of the poor—those who suffer deprivation and humiliation because they are without access to adequate education, housing, employment, and healthcare. Harrington believed that most Americans were blind to poverty because the poor were "invisible"—they did not live near, go to school, work, or socialize with the more affluent. Even today, a beautiful rural countryside masks the extent of poverty in rural areas. With mass production of clothing and many discount clothing stores, poor and low-income individuals may be relatively well dressed but unable to afford decent housing or healthcare. The elderly poor remain invisible because they rarely venture far from home. And finally, most poor people are invisible because they have no political power; in fact, they are often the victims of political action.

Most of the poor have some permanent residence. Although the quality of this housing may vary, they do have an address to call home. But some Americans have no address of their own at all. Since the 1980s, poverty has become more visible, primarily because of increased homelessness. Just how many people are homeless? There are a number of interesting accounts of how figures on homelessness have been derived. [87] Early estimates ranged from 250,000 in a 1984 HUD study[88] to suggestions of 3 million in a 1983 report published by the Community for Creative Non-Violence (CCNV).[89] Mitch Snyder was the controversial activist who led the CCNV. Snyder sued HUD over estimates he considered lowball.[90]

Of course, it is difficult to get an accurate count of homeless people when some are sleeping in alleys and under bridges and might be reluctant to be counted. The process has been likened to "fly-fishing with a blindfold."[91] Furthermore, just what constitutes homelessness? Should the definition be reserved for those sleeping on the street? Should it include those in shelters, or should it be broadened to include those "doubled up" with family and friends because they cannot afford their own living quarters?[92] In conjunction with the 1990 national census, the Census Bureau conducted the S (street and shelter)-Night Enumeration using an innovative method of decoys and observers to determine the study's comprehensiveness.[93] The figure derived was 228,000 homeless individuals, an estimate that even conservative Rush Limbaugh thought was too low.[94] Among the flaws were serious deficiencies in counting people living on the streets. The Census Bureau declared that this was not an official count. The 2000 U.S. census did include people in emergency and transitional shelters, although the Bureau again emphasized that it was not an official count of homeless Americans. Determining the extent of homeless in rural areas is especially difficult since many areas lack shelters or easily accessible locations where people who are homeless congregate.

Even so, recent, serious attempts to count the number of people who experience homelessness have produced fairly similar estimates. These estimates from various sources indicate that during a year, the number of homeless people is much greater than previously thought, perhaps 2 to 3 million.[95] For example, in a report published by the Urban Institute, Burt and Aron found that "even in a booming economy, at least 2.3 million adults and children are likely to experience a spell of homelessness at least once during a year,"[96] and the National Law Center on Homelessness and Poverty estimates that generally speaking, one percent of the population or 2.3 to 3.5 million people (including 1.35 million children) are homeless at some time during the year.[97] A study conducted for HUD found approximately 672,000 sheltered and unsheltered homeless persons on a single night in January 2007.[98]

The studies mentioned above address the *incidence* of homeless, i.e., those who have been homeless recently. In a study published in 1995, another team of researchers wanted to determine the *prevalence* of homelessness, i.e., how many people had been homeless over their lifetime. They used a telephone survey of a representative sample of U.S. households.[99] Since these individuals currently have phones, the study obviously underestimated homelessness. Findings were that 12 million people had been literally homeless (e.g., living in an abandoned building or shelter) at some point during their lifetime because they could not afford another arrangement. The figure rose to 28 million when people who had moved in with family or others were included. Those literally homeless often reported deprivation (e.g., lack of food) and victimization (e.g., being robbed or even raped), and they spent considerable time with no place to live. In other words, "being unhoused is highly disruptive of nearly all other aspects of life and the pathway from homeless to becoming housed once again is a difficult one."[100]

Who Is Homeless?

Two groups comprise most of the homeless population. One is people who have alcohol or drug problems. Men who have alcohol problems have long been a significant portion of the homeless population. An increase in other types of drug abuse has added to the homeless population.[101]

The second group is those with severe mental illness.[102] Deinstitutionalization of people with mental illness, beginning in the 1960s, combined with the lack of community-based mental health services and housing, increased the homeless population (see also Chapter 10). Some have both mental illness and substance-use disorders. Today homelessness has a third face—one- and even two-parent families with young children. Given the current economic recession, homelessness, especially among families, seems to be on the rise.[103] High housing costs, combined with unemployment and low-paying jobs, contribute to families' inability to locate permanent housing. Domestic violence also adds to the number seeking shelter, and some children are homeless because they have run away as a result of abuse, neglect, or other family problems.[104] Another group of homeless young people have been released from foster care on reaching adulthood without an appropriate transition to independent living.[105]

Among HUD's most recent estimates are that 63 percent of the homeless are unaccompanied individuals (2 percent are unaccompanied youth) and that families comprise about 37 percent of the homeless population.[106] Homeless adults are most likely to be middle-aged. Of homeless individuals in shelters, about two-thirds are men, 39 percent have chronic substance abuse problems, 28 percent have severe mental illness, and 13 percent are domestic violence victims. About 14 percent are military veterans. Blacks or African Americans are overrepresented among the sheltered homeless population.

One couple that has ministered to homeless people suggests that the nation must overcome its "politics of denial" and recognize that alcoholism, drug addiction, and serious mental illness, accompanied by disaffiliation and alienation from family and friends, are the major causes of homelessness today.[107] They say the population bulge created by the baby boomers and the growth of the underclass has added to the problem. Others contend that the increase in homelessness is caused by social factors (loosening of family and community ties), economic and structural conditions (unemployment, a more competitive work environment, low wages), and politics (cutbacks in public assistance and social services).[108] Many advocates for homeless individuals and families believe that the root of homelessness is the lack of affordable housing, not alcohol or drug addiction or mental illness. One point on which everyone seems to agree is that people who are homeless need good, affordable housing, and that those with mental health and alcohol or drug problems also need treatment.[109] Martha Burt summed it up this way:

> It is clear that personal conditions such as poverty, mental illness, alcoholism, physical handicap, and drug addiction increase a person's vulnerability to homelessness; hence a large proportion of homeless people exhibit these characteristics. But many people have had these vulnerabilities in past decades. Only the changes in structural factors can explain why the vulnerabilities [have] led to a much larger homeless population.[110]

Governments' Response to Homelessness

The Salvation Army and church missions have long provided shelter to people with alcohol problems and others on "skid row." Municipal governments also use various approaches to address homelessness, often because business owners and residents do not want to deal with homelessness people on downtown streets or in parks or other public areas. Municipalities often resort to ordinances that restrict panhandling or "camping" (sleeping in public places). Today, most communities of any size also have shelters for a broad cross-section of the homeless population. Some operate with government assistance, others with private support, or a combination of the two.

Although this humanitarian aid is welcome, temporary shelters are not substitutes for permanent homes. The addition of families to the ranks of the homeless is perhaps the straw that motivated Congress to pass the Stewart B. McKinney Homeless Assistance Act in 1987, now reauthorized as the McKinney-Vento Homeless Assistance Act.

The states receive some of the McKinney-Vento funding in the form of a block grant from the U.S. Department of Housing and Urban Development (HUD), and they provide matching funds for most program components.[111] The noncompetitive formula grant program (based on factors such as population size and poverty rate) primarily covers emergency shelter services. Communities also compete for much of the funding for homeless services rather than receive it on a formula basis. The competitive HUD programs are supportive housing, which includes additional services to alleviate homelessness; the Shelter Plus Care Program for homeless persons who have disabilities; and the Single Room Occupancy (SRO) Program, which provides rental assistance to individuals along with funds for "moderate" rehabilitation of SROs (often residential-type hotels operated by groups like the YMCA). HUD promotes a continuum of care approach, requiring that each community submitting a funding application show how it will coordinate services to those in need.

During his presidency, George W. Bush pledged to end chronic homelessness, defining this population as about 150,000 individuals who suffer from addiction, mental illness, or a physical disability and experience multiple periods of homelessness.[112] The Bush administration indicated that this group may be only 10 percent of the homeless population, but they use a large number of services because their needs are not addressed in a holistic way.

A HUD commissioned study highlights the efforts that some cities have made in addressing homelessness among groups considered most difficult to assist.[113] The city of Philadelphia uses an Outreach Coordination Center (OCC) to address street homelessness. The OCC relies on daytime outreach efforts using teams from several agencies who work together. There is a comprehensive database of information, and services are available from health, mental health, and substance abuse agencies. San Diego's approach is based on two strategies that involve the police department (and may be considered more coercive)—the Homeless Outreach Team (HOT) and the Serial Inebriate Program (SIP). HOT teams are composed of a police officer, a mental health worker, and a benefits eligibility technician. Homeless individuals are encouraged to accept services, but the officer is there as an authority figure who can involuntarily move the individual from the street if necessary. SIP is for those with chronic substance abuse problems, primarily alcoholism, who do not accept services. These individuals are often arrested for public drunkenness. Once they traverse the court system, they are offered treatment and transitional housing as an alternative to jail.

Cities like Columbus, Ohio; San Diego, California; Seattle, Washington; and Los Angeles, California, are using various "housing first" approaches that may include access to "safe havens" and other "low demand" housing.[114] In the lingo of service providers, these approaches generally do not require that residents be "housing ready," that is, they do not have to be abstinent (although HUD regulations forbid using illegal drugs on premises) or receiving mental health or substance abuse services to move in, but these services are available and encouraged. By providing decent shelter first, service providers hope that homeless people with alcohol, drug, and mental health problems will be more likely to accept services. In addition to resolving substance use problems and mental health crises, the approach aims to help these individuals maintain stable housing. Needless to say, opposition to "housing first" approaches comes from those who question the merit of providing housing to those who do not comply with societal norms.

A FUNDAMENTAL SHIFT

Our discussion of poverty, hunger, and homelessness has considered contending definitions and different ideas about what causes these problems. In the 1920s poverty was attributed to the dominance of business interests and worker exploitation; in the 1930s national economic collapse was the cause, and in the 1960s discrimination (racism and sexism) and lack of opportunity were the prevailing explanations. During each of these eras, the solutions were generally agreed upon. Respectively, they were minimum wages and other fair labor standards; economic recovery, work programs, and a safety net of social insurance and public assistance programs; and greater equality of opportunity through civil rights and gender rights legislation and access to nutrition, job training, healthcare, and early education programs. In the past three decades there have been sharp differences of opinions about the causes of poverty in the United States. Our discussion turns to the contemporary view of conservatives or neoconservatives that public assistance programs promote poverty and that a philosophy of mandatory work will root out all but some small unavoidable vestige of the problem.

Doesn't Welfare Cause Poverty?

The belief that welfare programs can actually *increase* the number of poor people is certainly not new. Since Elizabethan times, welfare payments have been kept minimal (the principle of *less eligibility*) to discourage potential recipients from choosing welfare over work. The large numbers of people from all social classes who became poor during the Great Depression of the late 1920s and early 1930s made the country realize that poverty could befall almost anyone. Yet many people still believe that "welfare" (public assistance) should be made an unattractive alternative to earnings. A good deal of attention has been given to the argument that much of today's poverty is a *direct* result of the social policies and programs of the 1960s and 1970s. The argument is presented this way: From 1947 to 1965 the poverty rate dropped by more than half without massive government social welfare intervention; by the mid-1960s many believed that the poverty that remained was due to lack of opportunities and bad luck.[115] The solution was government intervention to reduce poverty and create more opportunities for the disadvantaged. Welfare spending and the number of welfare programs increased, but the number of poor did not decrease. During the 1970s the poverty rate remained at about 12 percent.

The first book to receive widespread attention that claimed public assistance was to blame for welfare dependency was George Gilder's *Wealth and Poverty,* published in 1981. Gilder made no bones about what he called "the devastating impact of the programs of liberalism on the poor":[116]

> What actually happened since 1964 was a vast expansion of the welfare rolls that halted in its tracks an ongoing improvement in the lives of the poor, particularly blacks, and left behind—and here I choose my words as carefully as I can—a wreckage of broken lives and families worse than the aftermath of slavery.[117]

Gilder argued that the expansion of the public assistance system led to an erosion of the work ethic and self-reliance. He contended that as these welfare benefits increase, the value of a *man's* labor to his family decreases, especially if he earns low wages at his job. The welfare system saps his dignity by making him less necessary to his family, leading to family breakup and to further reliance on welfare. Gilder also criticized antidiscrimination policies, which he says favor credentials over the drive to succeed, and he invoked the ire of many women because he focused on the importance on jobs for men over those for women. Using many Horatio Alger-type success stories, Gilder pointed to examples of how poor Americans and immigrants to the United States were able to achieve prosperity through their hard work (the "bootstrap" approach). He praised capitalism for the advantages it affords to those who are willing to "sacrifice to succeed."

In 1984 Charles Murray made much the same argument in his book *Losing Ground: American Social Policy, 1950-1980*.[118] Using statistical presentations, Murray concluded that more people were poor following the social programs of the Great Society; the underclass had fallen further behind, and social welfare policy was responsible. To make his point, Murray compared three measures of poverty. "Official poverty," as discussed earlier, is the amount of poverty as measured by the U.S. government each year. "Net poverty" is official poverty minus the value of in-kind benefits. "Latent poverty" is the number of people who would be poor if they did not receive social insurance and public assistance payments. Murray claimed that in-kind benefits (e.g., food stamps and Medicaid) have reduced official poverty figures—but not as much as they should considering the amounts of money spent on these programs. Even worse, he argued, was that latent poverty is so much higher than official poverty. In 1980 official poverty was 13 percent. Latent poverty increased after 1968, reaching 22 percent of the population by 1980. The War on Poverty was supposed to make people economically self-sufficient and get them off welfare. The unfortunate situation is that these programs failed to reduce the need for public aid.

Critics of Murray's work called his analyses misleading, because poverty is a complex issue, and many factors must be presented in any discussion of the rising numbers of poor people.[119] For example, bad economic times result in higher unemployment (the lesson of the Great Depression and of the country's current economic crisis). Lack of preparation for good jobs—not the desire to be on the dole—adds to the ranks of the poor. In hard times it is not surprising that more people will be unemployed and require social welfare assistance. Murray's arguments focused mostly on public assistance programs like Aid to Families with Dependent Children (now Temporary Assistance for Needy Families), a program that is a small part of the social welfare system (see Chapter 7). He blamed "the system" for enticing low-income individuals to abandon work and family values and use social welfare programs instead. He used a fictitious couple to illustrate his points. Perhaps most damning was that he had little faith this couple would ever obtain more education or seek a better life. Murray ignored many of the approaches to understanding the root causes of poverty suggested in this chapter—structure, exploitation, and discrimination. But Murray's arguments should not be taken lightly. They resonate not only with conservative intellectuals and political pundits but also with many Americans who do not get the kind of governmental benefits known as welfare, but who work hard and still struggle to make ends meet.

Whither Public Assistance?

Murray's view led him to advocate an end to all existing federally supported public assistance programs for working-age people (AFDC, food stamps, Medicaid, and so on), and leaving the rest of welfare to private charities and state and local governments. This is a provocative position to take since federal intervention came about as a result of the inability of the local approach to respond to social welfare needs. Turning all public assistance programs back to the states would certainly mean severe cuts in these programs, thereby making welfare even less desirable and more degrading than it is now. But the approaches Gilder and Murray suggested have had a significant impact on public assistance programs, to an extent that may have surprised even these conservatives. Most of us agree that being a productive member of society is important, but there are some public assistance costs to be paid in a highly competitive, technological society, and we continue to struggle with what should be done.

Some thought that Gilder and Murray did not go far enough. Libertarian Michael Tanner calls the solutions proposed by most neoconservatives insufficiently radical to bring about change. Most conservatives, he believes, think that they can alter the government's approach to achieve their ends. Tanner believes there is no hope at all for government welfare: "Welfare has failed and cannot be reformed. It is time to end it. In its place, the civil society would rely on a reinvigorated network of private charity."[120] Like journalism professor Marvin Olasky,[121] who inspired Newt Gingrich and the Republican Contract with America in 1994, Tanner writes about "the bond" or the personal relationship that develops between those in need and those who wish to help—a relationship that the welfare bureaucracy finds difficult to emulate. Private charities can pick and choose whom they want to help, and they can hold those helped accountable for the assistance they receive. Sounding very much like Ronald Reagan and his supply side economic approach (see Chapter 3), Tanner says that high taxes and excessive regulatory policies stand in the way of job creation and economic growth that provide opportunities for people to rise out of poverty.

Olasky, an evangelical Christian, emphasizes "abstinence and adoption" as keys in reducing welfare. Olasky calls governmental programs "too stingy in what only individuals can give: time, love, and compassion."[122] He makes three suggestions to increase "effective compassion": (1) allow states, rather than the federal government, to levy most of the taxes, and have states give citizens generous tax breaks for philanthropy and volunteerism; (2) allow religious groups to utilize government funding without restricting their religious activity, since change from within, including spiritual change, can help people transcend poverty; (3) allow organizations that help the poor redeem vouchers for the services they provide—but only if they show that the situation of the individual being helped has improved. Olasky's views are deeply akin to those of former President George W. Bush, who promoted the use of religious or faith-based organizations to deliver social welfare services as well as initiatives to promote marriage as a solution to social problems.

These ideas have varying degrees of appeal to Americans, but is it realistic to think that private citizens and organizations can accomplish so much? Many people who are well entrenched in serving the poor through the nonprofit and religious sectors do not believe their organizations, let alone individuals of good will, can do it all, even with the government's support. Rather than decreased dependency, they see increased misery without federal government involvement in helping the poor.

According to Julian Wolpert, the idea that charitable giving, even coupled with state and local government expenditures for welfare, can substitute for federal funding is highly implausible. Many charitable organizations are locally based, and they spend their monies within their own communities. Many people give to churches, YMCAs, museums, and public television and radio—services they use themselves rather than those used by the needy.[123] Some communities are also much more generous than others. In 2008, charitable giving in the United States was nearly $308 billion with $47.5 billion directed to health and human services.[124] By comparison, the cost of the Medicaid program alone for 2008 was projected to be nearly $340 billion.[125]

Americans have not rejected government intervention to reduce poverty. Instead, through their elected officials, they placed their hopes on "welfare reform," and in particular, the views represented by those like political scientist Lawrence Mead. Mead contends that the welfare state has been too permissive by failing to "set behavioral standards for the poor."[126] He rejects notions that low wages, lack of jobs, discrimination, and lack of access to childcare and healthcare are what cause people to reject work and, consequently, to fall into hard core poverty. He believes that liberals have failed the country because they do not give poor people "credit to advance their own interests." With increased public assistance benefits, poor people simply were no longer motivated to work, and poverty became personal, not structural. Complacency developed by thinking of the poor as "victims" rather than "workers." Calling the poor "dutiful but defeated," Mead says:

> To a great extent, nonwork occurs simply because work is not enforced. Overall, I think conservatives have the better of the barriers debate—the chance to get ahead is widely available. But liberals have the more realistic view of the psychology of poverty—the poor do not *believe* they have the opportunity, and this still keeps them from working.[127]

Espousing a "new paternalism," Mead's analysis is that the poor respond well to structure, including the structure imposed by work programs. For Mead and those like him, poverty has become a problem of too much dependency, which requires that the poor become motivated to be like most Americans who toil at jobs to try to better themselves and their families. "Work, not welfare," has become the order of the day. Individuals such as Robert Rector[128] and others at conservative think tanks continue to expound on these views. Others, of course, contend that most poor people are motivated to work when work can be found and that explanations of poverty such as structure and exploitation are as relevant as ever. They point to explanations of changes in the economy (e.g., offshoring) and the work environment (e.g., part-time and contract labor) and slow job growth, even when the economy is doing well. Jobs that fail to pay a living wage, lack healthcare benefits, and do not allow people to amass assets like retirement accounts, leave even working people in jeopardy.

Mead points to a reality that is all too clear to anyone who watches the political pundits on TV or reads the print or electronic media—in the ongoing discourse about the causes and solutions to poverty, communication between liberals and conservatives has broken down.[129] For many who have devoted themselves to theorizing about poverty, advocating for those who are poor, or helping the poor directly, the welfare reform of 1996 was a bitter pill to swallow. Conservatives clearly won the last round in the poverty debates, but the websites of liberal, conservative, libertarian, religious, and nonprofit organizations indicate that the debate continues. Illustration 4.4 presents a more experiential consideration of the debate focusing on the works of Barbara Ehrenreich and Adam Shepard. Today, in the midst of deep economic recession, the emphasis seems to be more on saving the middle classes than on eradicting poverty.

ILLUSTRATION 4.4
Can Everyone Make It in America?

Young Author's Nickel and Dimed: Rebuttal Revisits Life in the Low-Wage Lane by Katherine Kersten, Minneapolis *Star-Tribune*, December 8, 2008, is reprinted by permission of the publisher.

I wish I had a nickel for every college student I know who's been assigned to read *Nickel and Dimed*, by journalist Barbara Ehrenreich. The book recounts Ehrenreich's two years working undercover at low-wage jobs such as waitress, hotel maid, and Wal-Mart salesperson.

Her dire conclusion: The United States condemns its unskilled workers to a life of poverty and hopelessness.

This view is orthodoxy on college campuses, where many professors spoon-feed it to wide-eyed students. But now a young man named Adam Shepard has stepped forward to challenge Ehrenreich's tale of woe.

Shepard, 26, hails from North Carolina, where *Nickel and Dimed* was a required freshman text at the state's flagship public university at Chapel Hill. At age 19, he read the book after a woman for whom he did yard work handed him a copy. "I know what you're going through," she assured him. "You'll love this book."

Shepard was dubious. "I decided to find out for myself if the American Dream is dead," he said at a speech last week sponsored by the Freedom Foundation of Minnesota. He launched his own undercover investigation, and chronicled it in a new book, *Scratch Beginnings*.

Shepard began his experiment in 2006, after graduating from Merrimack College in Massachusetts. He chose a random city—Charleston, SC—and got off the train there with $25 and the goal of reentering mainstream society in a year with a car, an apartment, and a $2,500 bank account. He would do it all without using a credit card or disclosing his college education.

Initially, Shepard bedded down in a homeless shelter and scrounged for day labor. Soon, he landed a back-breaking job as a furniture mover, making $9 an hour.

He set a tight budget, sought out free entertainment and shopped at Goodwill. Within six months, he had socked away enough money to buy a rattletrap car and move to a small apartment.

Along the way, Shepard met others who were trying to scramble up the ladder of success. One was Derrick, a high school dropout who became Shepard's hero. Derrick—a fellow mover—had a profound work ethic, a house, a wife and daughter, and a growing bank account. "In just three years, he had catapulted himself to the top of the list as the guy that everyone wanted to work with," wrote Shepard.

But Shepard also met many folks who were going nowhere. They included BG, Derrick's cousin, who routinely blew his money on beer, cigarettes, and lottery tickets.

"I expected to find a lot of old, bearded men with whiskey on their breath in the shelter," said Shepard in an interview. "I was amazed at the number of young, healthy guys who just couldn't keep their hands on a dollar."

Why did Derrick succeed while BG didn't?

"Guys like Derrick took their jobs seriously. They wanted to excel, and they took pride in what they accomplished. But you could tell that other guys just came to work to make a few bucks to party or get their landlords off their back."

Ehrenreich portrays low-wage workers as exploited and frequently depressed. But Shepard says he found that those who took responsibility for their own ups and downs tended to be happy, while those who viewed themselves as victims did not.

"Take the bus driver who drove my 6 a.m. bus every day. He could have been grouchy and bored. Instead, he lifted everyone's spirits with a smile as wide as his bus, and a friendly comment or witty remark. Everyone who got off his bus had his demeanor changed for the better."

Shepard ended his project after 10 months, when his mother had a recurrence of cancer. He had met all his goals and had piled up a whopping $5,200 in the bank.

And Ehrenreich?

"It's clear from her book that she wanted to fail, and then write a book about it," Shepard said.

Shepard's objective now is to share what he's learned with his own generation. "Too many of those on the bottom see themselves as victims," he explained. "Too many of those on the top are hampered by a sense of entitlement."

"I'm frustrated with hearing 'I don't have,' rather than "'Let's see what I can do with what I do have,'" he adds.

Summary

Defining poverty is more of a political activity rather than a rational exercise. This chapter discussed poverty as deprivation, as inequality, as a lack of human capital, as culture, as exploitation, and as structure. The way in which poverty is defined has important implications for strategies to alleviate the problem. Americans have not agreed on a best approach for defining poverty or reducing it. Poverty, according to the official government definition, has declined substantially since the 1960s, but the lows of 11 percent achieved in the 1970s have yet to be achieved again. Poverty rates are highest for blacks, Hispanics, and households headed by women. Child poverty rates are higher than adult poverty rates.

There is also controversy over the extent of hunger or food insecurity in the United States. The federal government's main food or nutrition program is the Supplemental Nutrition Assistance Program. Poverty has become more visible in the United States due to an increase in homelessness. The federal government continues to implement programs to assist those who are homelessness or need affordable housing, but the stock of affordable housing has decreased, and the subprime mortgage crisis and subsequent financial recession have made the housing situation more acute.

Conservative or neoconservative authors believe that public assistance programs have destroyed incentives to self-sufficiency and undermined the spirit of the poor, making welfare a more attractive alternative than low-paying jobs. Congress and the Clinton administration moved to "end welfare as we know it," and the George W. Bush administration supported this approach. Fluctuations in poverty rates that have occurred in recent years seem to be related to the state of the economy as much as they are to changes in the welfare system. The topics of poverty and dependency, their causes, and their solutions remain one of the great debates of the American people.

Discussion Questions and Class Activities

1. Check the latest Census Bureau reports on national poverty figures at www.census.gov. How have poverty rates changed for the nation as a whole and for subgroups of the population by gender, age, race/ethnicity, marital status, and so forth? Discuss possible reasons for any changes.

2. Investigate the extent of poverty in your state or community and compare it to national poverty rates or rates for other areas of the country. Utilize the Census Bureau website and its tools for obtaining poverty data and also check state and local websites. Discuss factors that contribute to higher or lower poverty rates in your state and/or community.

3. Devise a poverty threshold or guideline for your community (consider how much it costs to rent an apartment, buy food, and cover other essential expenses). How do your calculations compare with the federal government's thresholds or guidelines, the Self Sufficiency Standard if one is available for your community, and your own living standard?

4. Visit or volunteer at a community food bank or pantry, a homeless shelter, or an organization like Habitat for Humanity International. Interview staff and other volunteers. Under what auspices does the organization operate (nonprofit, church, etc.)? In the last few months, have requests for assistance increased, remained constant, or decreased? How does the organization obtain operating resources? Are donations currently increasing or decreasing? Discuss what you learned in class.

5. Learn more about the Supplemental Nutrition Assistance Program at the website of the Food and Nutrition Service of the U.S. Department of Agriculture. Would you be able to eat on the current SNAP maximum benefit? Determine what you would eat during a week if you did, or actually eat on this budget. Discuss what you learned in class.

6. Learn more about policies and programs related to homelessness and homeless persons in your community. Are there one or more homeless shelters? Who can stay at the shelter? What are the rules about staying in the shelter (check in time, length of stay, etc.)? What other programs aid people who are homeless? Are there "housing first" programs for those with mental illness or alcohol or drug problems? What municipal ordinances are directed at homeless persons? Can people solicit money on the streets? Are there "camping bans" that prevent people from sleeping on the streets, in parks, or other public places? How would you rate your community's response to individuals and families who are homeless?

7. Read Barbara Ehrenreich's book *Nickel and Dimed: On (Not) Getting By in America* (New York: Metropolitan Books, 2001) and Adam Shepard's book *Scratch Beginnings: Me, $25, and the Search for the American Dream* (New York: Collins, 2008). Have a class discussion to compare and contrast the books and the lessons learned about "making it" in the United States. What circumstances might have changed the outcomes for those discussed in the books? Go to scratchbeginnings.com for more information, including a reading and discussion guide for Shepard's book. A reader's guide is included in the back of Ehrenreich's book. Search YouTube for videos of and about Ehrenreich and Shepard.

Websites

Bureau of the Census, poverty page, http://www.census.gov/hhes/www/poverty/poverty.html, contains information on poverty measures and data on poverty in the United States and links to other websites about poverty.

Feeding America, related links page, http://feedingamerica.org/our-network/related-links.aspx, contains a list of organizations that address hunger in the United States and other parts of the world.

The following programs are supported by the U.S. Department of Health and Human Services, Office of the Assistant Secretary for Planning and Evaluation, and focus on interdisciplinary research into the causes and consequences of poverty and social inequality in the United States:

Institute for Research on Poverty (IRP) at the University of Wisconsin-Madison, http://www.irp.wisc.edu

National Poverty Center at the University of Michigan, http://npc.umich.edu/about_us

Center for Poverty Research at the University of Kentucky, http://www.ukcpr.org/History.aspx

West Coast Poverty Center at the University of Washington, http://wcpc.washington.edu/about/overview.shtml

Notes

1. E. E. Schattschneider, *The Semi-Sovereign People* (New York: Holt, Rinehart, & Winston, 1961), p. 68.
2. James L. Sundquist, *Politics and Policy* (Washington, DC: Brookings Institution, 1968), pp. 111–112.
3. The World Bank, "Poverty" (Washington, DC: Author, 2010). Retrieved May 12, 2010, from http://web.worldbank.org/WBSITE/EXTERNAL/TOPICS/EXTPOVERTY/0,,contentMDK:20040961~menuPK:373757~pagePK:148956~piPK:216618~theSitePK:336992~isCURL:Y,00.html
4. Patricia Ruggles, *Drawing the Line: Alternative Poverty Measures and Their Implications for Public Policy* (Washington, DC: Urban Institute Press, 1990), p. 36.
5. Dana Milbank, "Old Flaws Undermine New Poverty-Level Data," *Wall Street Journal,* October 5, 1995, pp. B1, 8.
6. Assistant Secretary for Planning and Evaluation, "Frequently Asked Questions Related to the Poverty Guidelines and Poverty" (Washington, DC: U.S. Department of Health and Human Services, January

25, 2010). Retrieved May 10, 2010, from http://aspe.hhs.gov/poverty/faq.shtml#CPI

7. U.S. Census Bureau, "Poverty Thresholds" (Washington, DC: Author, February 25, 2010). Retrieved March 9, 2010, from http://www.census.gov/hhes/www/poverty/threshld.html

8. Unless otherwise noted, poverty figures for 2008 are from Carmen DeNavas-Walt, Bernadette D. Proctor, and Jessica C. Smith, *Income, Poverty and Health Insurance Coverage in the United States: 2008,* Current Population Reports, P60-236(RV) (Washington, DC: U.S. Census Bureau, September 2009). Retrieved March 9, 2010, from http://www.census.gov/prod/2009pubs/p60-236.pdf

9. U.S. Bureau of the Census, *Measuring the Effect of Benefits and Taxes on Income and Poverty: 1992,* Current Population Reports, Series P60-186RD (Washington, DC: U.S. Government Printing Office, 1993), Appendix F; U.S. Department of Commerce, *U.S. Census 2000,* "C. Income and Employment" (Washington, DC: U.S. Census Bureau). Retrieved May 12, 2010 from http://www.census.gov/dmd/www/pdf/04c_in.pdf; "IRS Updates Tax Gap Estimates" (Washington, DC: Internal Revenue Service, February 14, 2006). Retrieved March 7, 2010, from http://www.irs.gov/newsroom/article/0,,id=154496,00.html

10. Bureau of Labor Statistics, "Table 1. Quintiles of income before taxes: Average annual expenditures and characteristics, Consumer Expenditure Survey, 2007." Retrieved May 9, 2009, from http://www.bls.gov/cex/2007/Standard/quintile.pdf; Nicholas Eberstadt, "Why Poverty Doesn't Rate," AEI Outlooks & On the Issues (Washington, DC: American Enterprise Institute, September 15, 2006). Retrieved May 9, 2009, from http://www.aei.org/issue/24900; Jesse Willis, *How We Measure Poverty: A History and Brief Overview* (Silverton, OR: Oregon Center for Public Policy, February 2000). Retrieved May 9, 2009, from http://www.ocpp.org/poverty/how.htm

11. Ruggles, *Drawing the Line: Alternative Poverty Measures and Their Implications for Public Policy,* pp. xiii–xiv, 2, 167.

12. See Ibid.

13. Lars Osberg, "Trends in Poverty: The UK in International Perspective: How Rates Mislead and Intensity Matters," Working Papers of the Institute for Social and Economic Research, Paper 2002-10 (Colchester, England: University of Essex, June 2002). Retrieved March 5, 2004, from http://www.iser.essex.ac.uk/pubs/workpaps/pdf/2002-10.pdf

14. Rebecca M. Blank, "How We Measure Poverty," *Los Angeles Times,* September 15, 2008. Retrieved March 1, 2009, from http://www.brookings.edu/opinions/2008/0915_measure_poverty_blank.aspx

15. Ruggles, *Drawing the Line: Alternative Poverty Measures and Their Implications for Public Policy,* p. 36.

16. *Ibid.,* p. xiii; Stephanie Riegg Cellini, Signe-Mary McKernan, and Caroline Ratcliffe, "The Dynamics of Poverty in the United States: A Review of Data, Methods, and Findings," *Journal of Policy Analysis and Management,* Vol. 27, No., 3, 2008, pp. 577–605.

17. Constance F. Ciro and Robert T. Michael, Eds., *Measuring Poverty: A New Approach* (Washington, DC: National Academy Press, 1995).

18. *Ibid.,* p. 386.

19. U.S. Census Bureau, "Percent and Number of People in Poverty Under Alternative Income Definitions and Using Three-Parameter Thresholds: 2006—All Races" (Washington, DC, December 31, 2007). Retrieved May 12, 2010, from http://pubdb3.census.gov/macro/032007/altpov/newpov01_001.htm

20. U.S. Census Bureau, *Estimates of Poverty Including the Value of Noncash Benefits: 1987,* Technical Paper 58 (Washington, DC: U.S. Government Printing Office, August 1988).

21. Kathleen Short, *Experimental Poverty Measures: 1999* (Washington, DC: U.S. Census Bureau, October, 2001). Retrieved May 20, 2009, from http://www.census.gov/prod/2001pubs/p60-216.pdf

22. Committee on Ways and Means, *Overview of Entitlement Programs: 1993 Green Book* (Washington, DC: U.S. Government Printing Office, 1993).

23. Short, *Experimental Poverty Measures: 1999,* p. 1.

24. Committee on Ways and Means, *2004 Green Book* (Washington, DC: U.S. House of Representatives, 2004), Appendix H—Data on Poverty, Table H-20, p. H-39. Retrieved March 9, 2010, from http://www.gpoaccess.gov/wmprints/green/2004.html

25. *Ibid.,* Table H-19, p. H-36.

26. U.S. Census Bureau, POV29: Years of School Completed by Poverty Status, Sex, Age, Nativity and Citizenship: 2008, *Current Population Survey,* 2009 Annual Social and Economic Supplement. Retrieved March 9, 2010, from http://www.census.gov/hhes/www/cpstables/032009/pov/new29_100_01.htm

27. The Website of the Panel Study of Income Dynamics at the University of Michigan, Institute for Social Research is http://psidonline.isr.umich.edu/

28. Cellini et al., "The Dynamics of Poverty in the United States: A Review of Data, Methods, and Findings."

29. Mary Jo Bane and David T. Elwood, "Slipping into and out of Poverty: The Dynamics of Spells," *The Journal of Human Resources,* Vol. 21, No. 1, 1986, pp. 1–23, especially pp. 11–13. Also see Martha S. Hill, "Some Dynamic Aspects of Poverty," in M. S. Hill, D. H. Hill, and J. N. Morgan, Eds., *Five Thousand American Families: Patterns of Economic Progress,* Vol. 9 (Ann Arbor, MI: Institute for Social Research, University of Michigan Press, 1981); Mary Jo Bane, "Household Composition and Poverty," in Sheldon H. Danzinger and Daniel H. Weinberg, Eds., *Fighting Poverty: What Works and What Doesn't* (Cambridge, MA: Harvard University Press, 1986), pp. 209–231 and p. 398, note 3; William Julius Wilson and Kathryn Neckerman, "Poverty and Family Structure: The Widening Gap between Evidence and Public Policy Issues," in Danzinger and Weinberg, *Fighting Poverty: What Works and What Doesn't,* especially p. 241; William Julius Wilson, *The Truly Disadvantaged: The Inner City, the Underclass, and Public Policy* (Chicago: University of Chicago Press, 1987), pp. 9–10.

30. Ann Huff Stevens, "The Dynamics of Poverty Spells: Updating Bane and Ellwood," *American Economic Review,* Vol. 84, No. 2, 1994, pp. 34–37; see also T. J. Eller, "Who Stays Poor? Who Doesn't?," *Dynamics of Economic Well-Being: Poverty, 1992–1993,* Current Population Reports, Household Economic Studies, P70–55 (Washington, DC: U.S. Bureau of the Census, June 1996).

31. John Iceland, *Dynamics of Economic Well-Being, Poverty 1996-1999.* Current Population Reports, P70-91 (Washington, DC: U.S. Census Bureau, 2003).

32. Mark R. Rank, *One Nation Underprivileged: Why American Poverty Affects Us All* (New York: Columbia University Press, 2004); Mark R. Rank and Thomas A. Hirschl, "The Likelihood of Poverty Across the American Life Span," *Social Work,* Vol. 4, pp. 201–216.

33. Mark R. Rank and Thomas A. Hirschl, "The Occurrence of Poverty Over the Life Cycle: Evidence from the PSID," *Journal of Policy Analysis and Management,* Vol. 20, No. 4, 2001, pp. 737–755.

34. This paragraph relies on Cellini et al., "The Dynamics of Poverty in the United States: A Review of Data, Methods, and Findings"; Signe-Mary McKernan and Caroline Ratcliffe, "Events That Trigger Poverty Entries and Exits," *Social Science*

Quarterly, supplement to Vol. 86, 2005, pp. 1146–1169; Signe-Mary McKernan and Caroline Ratcliffe, *Transition Events in the Dynamics of Poverty* (Washington, DC: Urban Institute, 2002).

35. Cellini et al., "The Dynamics of Poverty in the United States: A Review of Data, Methods, and Findings."

36. On the subject of relative deprivation, see Edward C. Banfield, *The Unheavenly City Revisited* (Boston: Little, Brown, 1974), especially chapter 6.

37. Victor R. Fuchs, "Redefining Poverty and Redistributing Income," *Public Interest,* No. 8, Summer 1967, p. 91.

38. U.S. Census Bureau, Income, Historical Income Tables-Families, Table F-4. Gini Ratios for Families, by Race and Hispanic Origin of Householder: 1947-2008. Retrieved March 7, 2010, from http://www.census.gov/hhes/www/income/histinc/incfamdet.html

39. Testimony of Greg Duncan Before the House Select Committee on Children, Youth and Families, February 1992, based on Greg J. Duncan, Timothy Smeeding, and Willard Rodgers, "W(h)ither the Middle Class: A Dynamic View?" University of Michigan, Survey Research Center, 1991, cited in Committee on Ways and Means, *Overview of Entitlement Programs: 1993 Green Book,* pp. 1447–1448; also see Greg J. Duncan, Timothy Smeeding, and Willard Rodgers, "Why the Middle Class Is Shrinking," December 1992, cited in Committee on Ways and Means, *Overview of Entitlement Programs: 1993 Green Book,* pp. 1448–1450.

40. Organization for Economic Cooperation and Development, "Growing Unequal: Income Distribution and Poverty in OECD Countries," Country Note: United States (Paris Author, October 21, 2008). Retrieved March 9, 2009, from http://www.oecd.org/dataoecd/47/2/41528678.pdf

41. See Robert Rector, "Understanding and Reducing Poverty in America," Testimony before the Joint Economic Committee, United States Senate, delivered September 25, 2008. Retrieved March 8, 2010, from http://www.heritage.org/Research/Welfare/tst040209b.cfm

42. Cited in Richard Hofstadter, *The American Political Tradition* (New York: Knopf, 1948), p. 42.

43. *Ibid.,* p. 45.

44. Edward C. Banfield, *The Unheavenly City* (Boston: Little, Brown, 1968); Banfield, *The Unheavenly City Revisited;* also see William A. Kiskanen, "Welfare and the Culture of Poverty," *Cato Journal,* Vol. 16, No. 1, 1996, pp. 1–15.

45. Nicolas Lemann, "The Origins of the Underclass," *Atlantic Monthly,* June 1986, pp. 31–55, and July 1986, pp. 54–68.

46. Herbert J. Gans, "The Uses of Poverty: The Poor Pay All," *Social Policy,* Vol. 2, No. 2, July–August 1971, pp. 20–24.

47. Thomas H. Walz and Gary Askerooth, *The Upside Down Welfare State* (Minneapolis, MN: Elwood Printing, 1973), p. 5.

48. Frances Fox Piven and Richard A. Cloward, *Regulating the Poor: The Functions of Public Welfare* (New York: Random House, 1971), quote from p. xiii.

49. Frances Fox Piven and Richard A. Cloward, *The New Class War* (New York: Pantheon Books, 1982); on the relationship between social welfare and labor force participation see also John Myles and Jill Quadagno, Eds., *States, Labor Markets, and the Future of Old-Age Policy* (Philadelphia: Temple University Press, 1991).

50. Frances Fox Piven and Richard A. Cloward, *The Breaking of the American Social Compact* (New York: The New Press, 1997); also see Frances Fox Piven and Richard A. Cloward, *Regulating the Poor: The Functions of Public Welfare,* updated ed. (New York: Vintage Books, 1993).

51. The first part of this paragraph relies on Michael Harrington, *The New American Poverty* (New York: Penguin Books, 1984).

52. This discussion of the term underclass relies on Wilson, *The Truly Disadvantaged,* especially p. 7.

53. Much of the remainder of this section relies on Wilson, *The Truly Disadvantaged,* and Lemann, "The Origins of the Underclass."

54. See previous editions of this textbook for a discussion of this issue.

55. Mark Nord, Margaret Andrews, and Steven Carlson, Household Food Security in the United States, 2007 (Washington, DC: Economic Research Service, U.S. Department of Agriculture, November 2008). Retrieved May 18, 2009, from http://www.ers.usda .gov/Publications/ERR66/ERR66.pdf; also see Food Research Action Center, "Hunger and Food Insecurity in the United States" (Washington, DC: Author, November 24, 2008). Retrieved May 18, 2009, from http://www.frac.org/html/hunger_in_ the_us/hunger_index.html

56. The remainder of this paragraph relies on Nick Kotz, *Let Them Eat Promises: The Politics of Hunger in America* (Englewood Cliffs, NJ: Prentice Hall, 1969).

57. President of the United States, *America's New Beginning: A Program for Economic Recovery* (Washington, DC: U.S. Government Printing Office, February 18, 1981), p. 1.

58. Mary Cohn, Ed., "Hunger Reports Prompt Food Aid Expansion," *1983 Congressional Quarterly Almanac* (Washington, DC: Congressional Quarterly, 1983).

59. Jean Mayer and Jeanne Goldberg, "New Report Documents Hunger in America," *Tallahassee Democrat,* March 29, 1984, p. 16E.

60. Physician Task Force on Hunger in America, *Hunger in America: The Growing Epidemic* (Middletown, CT: Wesleyan University Press, 1985), Chapter 7.

61. Written testimony of Mark Zandi before the Senate Budget Committee, "The Economic Stimulus Outlook and Beyond," November 19, 2009. Retrieved May 18, 2009, from http://www.dismal.com/mark-zandi/ documents/Senate_Budget_Committee_11_19_08.pdf

62. Keith E. Wardrip, Danilo Pelletiere, and Sheila Crowley, *Out of Reach 2009: Persistent Problems, New Challenges for Renters* (Washington, DC: National Low Income Housing Coalition, April 2009). Retrieved March 8, 2010, from http://www.nlihc. org/oor/oor2009

63. Mary Schwartz and Ellen Wilson, *Who Can Afford to Live in a Home?: A Look at Data from the 2006 American Community Survey* (Washington, DC: U.S. Census Bureau, no date). Retrieved May 11, 2009, from http://www.census.gov/hhes/www/housing/ special-topics/files/who-can-afford.pdf

64. Michael E. Stone, *Shelter Poverty: New Ideas on Housing Affordability* (Philadelphia: Temple University Press, 1993).

65. U.S. Department of Housing and Urban Development, "HUD's Public Housing Program" (Washington, DC: Author, November 2007). Retrieved March 21, 2009, from http://www.hud .gov/renting/phprog.cfm; Douglas Rice and Barbara Sard, "Decade of Neglect Has Weakened Federal Low-Income Housing Programs" (Washington, DC: Center for Budget and Policy Priorities, February 25, 2009). Retrieved May 12, 2009, from http://www .cbpp.org/files/2-24-09hous.pdf

66. "HUD Public Housing Development Program" (Washington, DC: U.S. Department of Housing and Urban Development, May 17, 2008). Retrieved May 11, 2009, from http://www.communityinvestment-network.org/nc/single-news-item-states/article/ hud-public-housing-development-program/?tx _ttnews%5BbackPid%5D=1077&cHash=8df1846dbb

67. Committee on Ways and Means, "Federal Housing Assistance," *Background Material and Data on the*

Programs within the Jurisdiction of the Committee on Ways and Means, 2008 edition (Washington, DC: U.S. House of Representatives, 2008). Retrieved May 10, 2010, from http://waysandmeans.house.gov/media/pdf/110/hap.pdf

68. Rice and Sard, "Decade of Neglect Has Weakened Federal Low-Income Housing Programs."
69. For information on the Housing Choice Voucher Program, see "Housing Choice Vouchers Fact Sheet" (Washington, DC: U.S. Department of Housing and Urban Development, n.d.). Retrieved May 10, 2010, from http://www.fhasecure.gov/offices/pih/programs/hcv/about/fact_sheet.cfm; Committee on Ways and Means, "Federal Housing Assistance."
70. Rice and Sard, "Decade of Neglect Has Weakened Federal Low-Income Housing Programs."
71. Committee on Ways and Means, "Federal Housing Assistance."
72. Rice and Sard, "Decade of Neglect Has Weakened Federal Low-Income Housing Programs."
73. *Ibid.*
74. Clea Benson, "Rentals Out of Reach," *Congressional Quarterly Weekly,* October 15, 2007. Retrieved May 16, 2009, from http://www.housingpolicy.org/assets/preservation%20resources/RentalsOutOfReach—CQWeekly.pdf
75. Jennifer Lin, "A New Focus on Rental Housing for the Poor," *The Philadelphia Inquirer,* May 19, 2009. Retrieved May 22, 2009, from http://www.philly.com/inquirer/local/philadelphia/20090519_A_new_focus_on_rental_housing_for_poor.html
76. "National Housing Trust Fund" (Washington, DC: National Low Income Housing Coalition). Retrieved May 22, 2009, from http://www.nlihc.org/template/page.cfm?id=40
77. Jeffery L. Katz, "Rooms for Improvement: Can Cisneros Fix HUD?" *Congressional Quarterly,* April 10, 1993, pp. 914–920.
78. Stephen Koff (Newhouse News Service), "Billions Intended for Poor Go Unspent," *Austin American-Statesman,* November 11, 1999, pp. A1, A13; "HUD Needs to Get Own House in Order," *Austin American-Statesman,* November 15, 1999, p. A10.
79. Dan Eggen and Carol D. Leonnig, "Jackson Resigns as HUD Secretary," *Washington Post,* April 1, 2008, p. A1. Retrieved May 16, 2009 from http://www.washingtonpost.com/wp-dyn/content/article/2008/03/31/AR2008033102672.html
80. Ed O'Keefe, "Probe of Former HUD Secretary Alphonse Jackson Said to Be Closed," *Washington Post,* May 4, 2010. Retrieved May 10, 2010, from http://www.washingtonpost.com/wp-dyn/content/article/2010/05/03/AR2010050304420.html
81. Jonathan Chait, "HUD Sucker Proxy," *The New Republic,* June 23, 1997, p. 11–13.
82. "American Dream Downpayment Initiative" (Department of Housing and Urban Development, April 29, 2009). Retrieved May 16, 2009, from http://www.hud.gov/offices/cpd/affordablehousing/programs/home/addi
83. This paragraph relies on Corporation for Enterprise Development, *Guide to the 2007-2008 Assets and Opportunity Scorecard* (Washington, DC: Author, September 2008). Retrieved May 15, 2009, from http://www.cfed.org/imageManager/scorecard/2007/scorecard_guide_web.pdf
84. U.S. Census Bureau, "Housing Vacancies and Home Ownership—Historical Tables," Table 14: Home-ownership Rates for the U.S. and Regions: 1965 to Present. Retrieved March 8, 2010, from http://www.census.gov/hhes/www/housing/hvs/historic/
85. "Housing Program Enhancements Offer Additional Options for Struggling Homeowners" (Washington, DC: Making Home Affordable.gov, March 26, 2010). Retrieved May 10, 2010, from http://makinghomeaffordable.gov/pr_03262010.html
86. This paragraph relies on Michael Harrington, *The Other America: Poverty in the United States* (New York: Macmillan, 1962).
87. See Christopher Hewitt, "Estimating the Number of Homeless: Media Misrepresentation of an Urban Problem," *Journal of Urban Affairs,* Vol. 18, No. 3, 1996, pp. 431–447; Anna Kondratas, "Estimates and Public Policy: The Politics of Numbers," *Housing Policy Debate,* Vol. 2, Issue 3, 1991, pp. 631–647.
88. Office of Policy Development and Research, *Report to the Secretary on the Homeless and Emergency Shelters* (Washington, DC: U.S. Department of Housing and Urban Development, 1984).
89. Mary Ellen Hombs and Mitch Snyder, *Homelessness in America: A Forced March to Nowhere* (Washington, DC: Community for Creative Non-Violence, 1983), p. xvi.
90. James D. Wright and Joel A. Devine, "Housing Dynamics of the Homeless: Implications for a Count," *American Journal of Orthopsychiatry,* Vol. 65, No. 3, 1995, pp. 330–329, especially p. 320.
91. Kim Hopper, "Definitional Quandaries and Other Hazards," *American Journal of Orthopsychiatry,* Vol. 65, No. 3, 1995, pp. 340–346, especially p. 340.
92. Robert C. Ellickson, "The Homeless Muddle," *The Public Interest,* No. 99, Spring 1990, pp. 45–60.

93. See James D. Wright, Ed., *Evaluation Review,* Vol. 16, No. 4, August 1992, which is devoted to S-Night surveys; and Wright and Devine, "Housing Dynamics of the Homeless: Implications for a Count."

94. Rush Limbaugh, *The Way Things Ought to Be* (New York: Pocket Star Books, 1992).

95. See Martha Burt, "Critical Factors in Counting the Homeless: An Invited Commentary," *American Journal of Orthopsychiatry,* Vol. 65, No. 3, 1995, pp. 334–339.

96. Martha K. Burt and Laudan Y. Aron, "America's Homeless II: Population and Services" (Washington, DC: Urban Institute, January 1, 2000). Retrieved May 12, 2010, from http://www.urban.org/publications/900344.html

97. National Coalition for the Homeless, *Fact Sheet #2: How Many People Experience Homelessness?* (Washington, DC: Author, June 2008). Retrieved March 21, 2009, from http://www.nationalhomeless.org/publications/facts/How_Many.html

98. Office of Community Planning and Development, *The Third Annual Homeless Assessment Report to Congress* (Washington, DC: U.S. Department of Housing and Urban Development, July 2008). Retrieved May 20, 2009, from htp://www.hudhre.info/documents/3rdHomelessAssessmentReport.pdf

99. Bruce Link, Jo Phelan, Michaeline Bresnahan, Ann Stueve, Robert Moore, and Ezra Susser, "Lifetime and Five-Year Prevalence of Homelessness in the United States: New Evidence on an Old Debate," *American Journal of Orthopsychiatry,* Vol. 65, No. 3, 1995, pp. 347–354.

100. "Shelter Poverty: A Real-Life Way to Measure Inadequate Incomes," Utah Issues Information Program, Poverty Paper Series. Retrieved December 30, 1997, from http://www.xmission.com/~ui/shelter.html

101. Gordon Berlin and William McAllister, "Homelessness," in Henry J. Aaron and Charles L. Schultze, Eds., *Setting Domestic Priorities: What Can Government Do?* (Washington, DC: Brookings Institution, 1992), p. 64.

102. See, for example, *Outcasts on Main Street* (ADM) 92-1904 (Washington, DC: U.S. Department of Health and Human Services, Interagency Council on the Homeless, and Federal Task Force on Homelessness and Severe Mental Illness, 1992).

103. Center on Budget and Policy Priorities, "Number of Homeless Families Climbing Due to Recession" (Washington, DC: Author, January 8, 2009).

104. *A Report on the 1988 National Survey of Shelters for the Homeless* (Washington, DC: U.S. Department of Housing and Urban Development, 1989).

105. "Programs and Resources for Youth Aging Out of Foster Care" (Washington, DC: Child Welfare League of America, no date). Retrieved May 10, 2009, from http://www.cwla.org/programs/foster-care/agingoutresources.htm; *Youth Aging Out of Foster Care* (Washington, DC: National Association of Counties, February 2008). Retrieved May 10, 2009, from http://www.naco.org/Content/ContentGroups/Issue_Briefs/IB-YouthAgingoutofFoster-2008.pdf; Kathleen Myers, Tammy White, Mary Whalen, and Paul DiLorenzo, *Aged-Out and Homeless in Philadelphia* (Philadelphia: Greater Philadelphia Urban Affairs Coalition, 2007). Retrieved May 10, 2009, from http://www.gpuac.org/documents/Aged-OutandHomelessinPhiladelphia_000.pdf

106. Office of Community Planning and Development, *The Third Annual Homeless Assessment Report to Congress.*

107. Alice S. Baum and Donald W. Burnes, *A Nation in Denial: The Truth about Homelessness* (Boulder, CO: Westview Press, 1993).

108. See Joel Blau, *The Visible Poor: Homelessness in the United States* (New York: Oxford University Press, 1992); Paul Koegel, "Mental Illness among the Inner City Homeless," *Journal of the California Alliance for the Mentally Ill,* Vol. 1, No. 1, 1989, rev. 1992, pp. 16–17.

109. Koegel, "Mental Illness Among the Inner City Homeless"; Berlin and McAllister, "Homelessness," p. 67; Martha R. Burt, *Over the Edge: The Growth of Homelessness in the 1980s* (New York: Russell Sage, 1992), chapter 2.

110. Burt, *Over the Edge,* p. 226.

111. "Homeless Assistance Programs" (Washington, DC: U.S. Department of Housing and Urban Development, March 21, 2008). Retrieved March 21, 2009, from http://www.hud.gov/offices/cpd/homeless/programs/index.cfm

112. See, for example, Jeffrey M. Jones, "Bush's War on Poverty Part I," *Hoover Digest,* No. 1, 2005. Retrieved May 10, 2009, from http://www.hoover.org/publications/digest/3001826.html

113. This paragraph relies on Martha R. Burt, John Hedderson, Janine Zweig, Mary Jo Ortiz, Laudan Aron-Turnham, and Sabrina M. Johnson, *Strategies for Reducing Chronic Street Homelessness: Final Report* (Washington, DC: U.S. Department of Housing and Urban Development, 2004).

114. *Ibid.;* also see Shawn Zeller, "'Housing First' Champion Touts Success of Program," *CQ Weekly Online,* September 29, 2008, pp. 2561–2563. Retrieved May 21, 2009, from http://library.cqpress.com

ezproxy.lib.utexas.edu/cqweekly/weeklyreport110-000002963723

115. James Gwartney and Thomas S. McCaleb, "Have Antipoverty Programs Increased Poverty?", *Cato Journal,* Vol. 5, No. 1, 1985. Retrieved May 20, 2009, from http://www.cato.org/pubs/journal/cj5n1/cj5n1-1.pdf

116. George Gilder, *"Wealth and Poverty* (New York: Bantam Books, 1981), p. ix.

117. *Ibid.,* p. 13.

118. Charles Murray, *Losing Ground: American Social Policy, 1950–1980* (New York: Basic Books, 1984).

119. Robert Kuttner, "Declaring War on the War on Poverty," *Washington Post,* November 25, 1984, pp. 4, 11; see also Daniel Patrick Moynihan, "Family and Nation," Godkin Lectures (Cambridge, MA: Harvard University, April 8–9, 1985).

120. Michael Tanner, *The End of Welfare* (Washington, DC: Cato Institute, 1996), quote from p. 148.

121. Marvin Olasky, *The Tragedy of American Compassion* (Washington, DC: Regnery Gateway, 1992); Marvin Olasky, *Renewing American Compassion* (New York: Free Press, 1996); Marvin Olasky, *Compassionate Conservatism: What It Is, What It Does, and How It Can Transform America* (New York: Free Press, 2000); see also Myron Magnet, *The Dream and the Nightmare: The Sixties' Legacy to the Underclass* (San Francisco: Encounter Books, 2000, reprint).

122. Olasky, *Renewing American Compassion,* p. 152.

123. Much of this paragraph relies on Julian Wolpert, "We Can Take Care of Our Own . . . Or Can We?", Washington Post, June 29, 1995; Julian Wolpert, Testimony Before the Subcommittee on Oversight of the House Committee on Ways and Means, *Hearing to Examine Whether Charitable Organizations Serve the Needs of Diverse Communities,* 110 Cong., 1 sess., September 25, 2007.

124. Overview of *Giving USA 2009* Key Findings (South Barrington, IL: American City Bureau). Retrieved May 10, 2010, from http://www.acb-inc.com/wp-content/uploads/Giving-USA-2009-Key-Findings.pdf http://www.acb-inc.com/wp-content/uploads/Giving-USA-2009-Key-Findings.pdf

125. Centers for Medicare and Medicaid Services, "Medicaid Spending Projected to Rise Faster Than the Economy" (Washington, DC: U.S. Department of Health and Human Services, October 17, 2008). Retrieved May 10, 2010, from http://www.hhs.gov/news/press/2008pres/10/20081017a.html

126. Quotes in this paragraph rely on Lawrence M. Mead, *The New Politics of Poverty* (New York: Basic Books, 1992); also see Lawrence M. Mead, *Beyond Entitlement* (New York: Free Press, 1986); Lawrence M. Mead, *The New Paternalism* (Washington, DC: Brookings, 1997).

127. Mead, *The New Politics of Poverty,* p. 134.

128. Kiki Bradley and Robert Rector, "Stronger Welfare Work Requirements Can Help Ailing State Budgets" (Heritage Foundation, June 19, 2009). Retrieved May 10, 2010, from http://www.heritage.org/Research/Reports/2009/06/Stronger-Welfare-Work-Requirements-Can-Help-Ailing-State-Budgets

129. Lawrence M. Mead, "Conflicting Worlds of Welfare Reform," *First Things,* August/September 1997, pp. 15–17. Retrieved May 12, 2010, from http://www.leaderu.com/ftissues/ft9708/opinion/mead.html

5 PREVENTING POVERTY: SOCIAL INSURANCE AND PERSONAL RESPONSIBILITY

One way to address poverty is to have people insure themselves against its occurrence, much as they insure themselves in the event of death, accident, or property loss. In the social welfare arena, this preventive strategy is called *social insurance*. Social insurance programs compel individuals or their employers to purchase insurance against the possibility of their own indigency, which might result from forces over which they have no control—loss of job, death of a family bread-winner, advanced age, or disability. As statesman Thomas Paine said in 1795, "Were a workman to receive an increase of wages daily he would not save it against old age. . . . Make, then, society the treasurer to guard it for him in a common fund."[1] The United States eventually adopted this strategy.

PREVENTING POVERTY THROUGH COMPULSORY SAVINGS

If you have ever held a job, you have probably paid Social Security taxes, and someday you may wish to retire. You, therefore, already have a direct financial interest in the topics covered in this chapter. And, undoubtedly, you have heard concerns that the country's largest social insurance program, known as Social Security, is in trouble.

Social insurance is based on many of the same principles as private insurance—the sharing of risks and the setting aside of money for a "rainy day." Workers and employers pay "premiums" in the form of Social Security taxes, which the government records under each worker's name and Social Security number. When age, death, disability, or unemployment prevents workers from continuing on the job, they or their dependents are paid from Social Security trust funds. Social insurance offers one relatively simple and rational approach for addressing poverty.

Social insurance differs from another government approach for addressing poverty called *public assistance.* If (1) the beneficiaries of a government program are required to make contributions to it before claiming any of its benefits (or if employers must pay into the program on behalf of their workers) and if (2) the benefits are paid out as legal entitlements regardless of the beneficiaries' personal wealth, then the program is called social insurance. However, if (1) the program is financed out of general tax revenues and if (2) the recipients are required to show that they are poor in order to claim benefits, then the program is called public assistance. Although the history of public responsibility for helping people in need in the United States began with public assistance approaches, social insurance programs became the more viable political strategy.[2]

Because workers pay taxes into a Social Security trust fund, and the U.S. government records these contributions under each worker's name, Americans feel entitled to receive Social Security. This is different from public assistance programs, which are financed from the general tax revenues. There is no "public assistance" trust fund earmarked for each American. Although most Americans pay taxes into the general revenue fund during their lifetimes, this is not a requirement for receiving public assistance benefits. Despite any taxes poor or low-income individuals have paid, there is much less of a perception that they have a right to public assistance. Moreover, while the vast majority of Americans probably expect to live long enough to receive Social Security benefits, they probably do not expect to become public assistance recipients.[3]

The concept of government-sponsored social insurance originally appealed to conservatives because it represented a form of thrift. Social insurance programs also appeal to liberals because they can be used to redistribute income to former workers who are aged or disabled and their dependents, to survivors of deceased workers, and to unemployed workers.

Government old-age insurance, the first social insurance program, was introduced in Germany in 1889 by the conservative regime of Chancellor Otto von Bismarck. The idea spread quickly, and most European nations had old-age insurance pension programs before the beginning of World War I in 1914. In the United States, many railroads, utilities, and large manufacturers instituted private old-age pensions at the beginning of the twentieth century. The U.S. government began its own Federal Employees Retirement program in 1920. By 1931 seventeen states had adopted some form of compulsory old-age insurance for workers, although eligibility requirements were strict and payments were small.[4]

During the Great Depression, Francis E. Townsend, a California dentist, began a national crusade for very generous old-age pensions of $200 a month to be paid by the government from a national sales tax. Government and business leaders perceived the politically popular and very expensive "Townsend Plan" as totally unfeasible, even radical, but the combination of economic depression and larger numbers of older people in the general population and in the workforce helped to develop pressure for some type of old-age insurance.[5] Despite fears that social insurance would foreshadow a socialist state, during the presidential campaign of 1932, Franklin D. Roosevelt advocated a government insurance plan to protect the unemployed and the aged. This campaign promise and party platform plank was embodied in the Social Security Act, signed by President Roosevelt on August 14, 1935.

One might attribute the Roosevelt administration's political success in gaining acceptance for the Social Security Act to several factors:

1. The weakening of ties among family members and the increasing inability of urban families to care for their aged members.
2. The economic insecurities generated by the Great Depression of the 1930s, including the increasing fear of impoverishment, even among the middle class.
3. Political movements of different ilks, from the Townsend Plan to socialism and communism, that threatened the established order.

Roosevelt's skills as a national leader should also be added to these factors. Social Security was presented to the Congress as a conservative program that would eventually eliminate the need for public assistance. For the first time, Americans would be required to protect themselves against poverty.

The Social Security Act of 1935 established the country's basic social welfare policy framework. Although Americans tend to think of Social Security mostly as retirement benefits, the original act contained social insurance, public assistance, social service, and public health programs. Social Security Act programs have expanded over the years.[6] Today, the social insurance programs it includes are:

- Old-age and survivors insurance (OASI)
- Disability insurance (DI)
- Health insurance (HI) for older and long-term disabled individuals, called Medicare
- Unemployment insurance (also called unemployment compensation)

This chapter examines these major social insurance programs (Medicare is also discussed in greater length in Chapter 8). We also consider one's own personal responsibility to prepare for old age or untoward circumstances. Even when we think about personal responsibility, public policy is important. Some Americans whose private pension funds and other investments have evaporated or been severely reduced might have benefited from stricter government regulations and oversight of the investment industry.

SOCIAL SECURITY: THE WORLD'S LARGEST SOCIAL WELFARE PROGRAM

Today, 94 percent of the workforce (slightly less than the 96 percent reported in previous years) plus their employers pay Social Security taxes.[7] At its beginning, the Social Security program covered retirement benefits for only about half of the labor force. Many farm and domestic workers, self-employed people, and state and local government employees were exempt. The program was financed by employer-employee contributions of 1 percent each on a wage base of $3,000, or a maximum contribution by workers of $30 per year plus a $30 contribution by their employers. It paid for retirement benefits at age 65 at a rate of about $22 per month for a single worker, or $36 per month for a married couple. Benefits were paid as a matter of right, regardless of income, as long as a worker was retired. This spared retired workers the humiliation often associated with public charity. Actually, no taxes were collected until 1937, and no benefits were paid until 1940, to allow the trust fund to accumulate reserves.

There have been scores of amendments to the Social Security Act. The first major amendments came in 1939 when Congress made dependents and survivors of retired workers and survivors of insured workers who died before age 65 eligible for benefits. In the early 1950s, farmers, domestic workers, and self-employed people were added to the program, bringing the total number of covered workers to over 90 percent of the labor force. In 1954 the "earnings test" for retired workers was liberalized so that those engaged in some employment could earn more without losing Social Security benefits. In 1956 women in the labor force were permitted to retire with Social Security benefits at age 62 rather than 65 on the condition that they accept 80 percent of the monthly benefit otherwise available at 65; beginning in 1961, men were also allowed to retire with 80 percent of benefits at age 62. In 1956 disability insurance was approved for totally and permanently disabled workers aged 50 and older; benefits for their dependents were added in 1958. Disabled workers younger than age 50 were added to the disability program in 1960. In 1965 Medicare was adopted, and in 1972 Congress

TABLE 5.1 Social Security (OASDI) Growth: 1950–2009

	1950[a]	1970	1990	2000	2009
Number of OASDI beneficiaries (in millions)[b]	3.5	25.7	39.8	45.4	52.5
Annual OASDI benefits (in billions)[b]	$10	$32	$248	$408	$675
Average monthly benefit for retired workers (in dollars)[c]	$44	$118	$603	$844	$1,159
Social insurance taxes (OASDI) as percentage of all federal revenue [d]	5.3	17.4	27.3	23.7	30.4

[a]Data for 1950 pertain to OASI only; disability insurance was added in 1956.

[b]Data are from the Social Security Administration, Office of the Chief Actuary. Retrieved May 13, 2010 from http://www.ssa.gov/OACT/ProgData/benefits.html

[c]Data for 1950 to 2000 are from *Social Security Bulletin, Annual Statistical Supplement, 2009* (Washington, DC: Social Security Administration, February 2010), Table 5.C2. Retrieved May 13, 2010, from http://www.socialsecurity.gov/pressoffice/basicfact.htm http://www.ssa.gov/policy/docs/statcomps/supplement/2009/5c.pdf; data for 2009 are for June and are from "Social Security Basic Facts" (Washington, DC: Social Security Administration, August 5, 2009). Retrieved May 13, 2010, from http://www.socialsecurity.gov/pressoffice/basicfact.htm

[d]Data are from Office of Management and Budget, Budget of the U.S. Government FY 2009, Historical Tables, Tables 1.1 and 2.4. Data for 2009 is based on estimates. Retrieved May 13, 2010 from http://www.gpoaccess.gov/usbudget/fy10/pdf/hist.pdf

enacted COLAs—automatic cost-of-living adjustments (measured by rises in the Consumer Price Index)—to help Social Security payments keep pace with inflation.

Social Security soon became the nation's largest social welfare program. Today, the U.S. Social Security system may rightfully be called the world's largest government program. In 2009, 159 million workers plus their employers paid Social Security taxes,[8] and more than 52 million Americans collected benefits totaling about $675 billion (see Table 5.1). The public assistance programs pale in comparison to the scope and effects of Social Security.

Social Security, more specifically, old age, survivors, and disability insurance (OASDI), is administered by the federal government's Social Security Administration (formerly part of the U.S. Department of Health and Human Services and now an independent federal agency). When Medicare (health insurance) is included, the total package is called OASDHI. Medicare is administered by the Centers for Medicare and Medicaid Services, part of the U.S. Department of Health and Human Services.

By compelling people to insure themselves against the possibility of their own poverty, Social Security and Medicare have reduced the problems that state and local governments might otherwise face in helping their residents. But as we shall see in this chapter, today's social insurance programs present a new set of challenges that concern virtually all Americans.

Figure 5.1 shows the categories of Social Security (OASDI) beneficiaries, and Table 5.1 shows Social Security growth in numbers of beneficiaries, total benefits, average monthly benefits, and as a percentage of the federal government's total budget. The tax paid to support these programs is marked on most workers' monthly earnings statement with the words Social Security or the abbreviation FICA, which stands for the Federal Insurance Contributions Act. Self-employed people pay under SECA, the Self-Employment Contributions Act. By 2009, the *combined maximum* annual Social Security contribution for each employee and his or her employer had grown to $13,243, not including the Medicare tax, which is now assessed on *all* earnings. Social Security taxes are the federal government's second largest source of income; these tax revenues are exceeded only by the federal personal income tax.

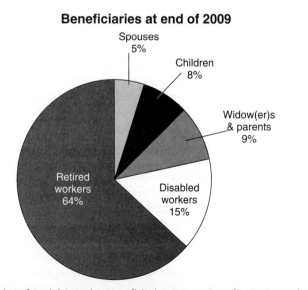

Beneficiaries at end of 2009

FIGURE 5.1 **Categories of Social Security Beneficiaries** *Source:* Benefits By Type of Beneficiary (Washington, DC: Social Security Administration). Retrieved February 9, 2010, from http://www .socialsecurity.gov/OACT/ProgData/icp.html

The Social Security tax takes a chunk out of workers' paychecks, but it is especially controversial because the tax is regressive—it takes a larger share of the income of middle and lower-income workers than of the affluent. That is because:

1. Social Security taxes are levied only against wages and not against other types of income such as dividends, interest, and rents, which are more frequently sources of income for wealthier Americans.
2. OASDI taxes are levied on a fixed amount of wages; wages in excess of that amount are not subjected to these taxes.
3. Unlike the federal personal income tax, Social Security taxes make no allowance for individual situations such as number of dependents or high medical expenses.

The regressive nature of the Social Security tax on current workers is offset at retirement, because benefits are figured more generously for those who earned less, and because retirees in higher income brackets must now pay taxes on part of their Social Security benefits. For many Americans the Social Security tax is a double-edge sword—it takes a major bite out of their paychecks during their working years, but it is a major source of their income when they retire.

Social Security taxes were not a concern when they amounted to very little, but what began as a very modest "insurance premium" is now a major expense for both employers and employees. Today, the size of OASDI alone—more than one-fourth of the federal government's income and about one-fifth of its expenditures—has an important impact on the overall equity of the country's revenue structure. These amounts are even greater if Medicare is included.

Even the Best-Laid Plans

The original strategy of the Social Security program was to create a trust fund with a reserve that would be built from the insurance premiums (Social Security taxes) of working people. This trust fund reserve would earn interest, and both the interest and principal would be used in later years to pay benefits. Benefits would be in proportion to contributions made during the individual's working years. General tax revenues would not be used at all. The Social Security system was intended to resemble private, self-financing insurance. But it did not turn out that way.

President Roosevelt's planners quickly realized that building the reserve was taking money from the depressed economy and slowing recovery. The plan to build a large, self-financing reserve was soon abandoned (in 1939) under political pressure to pump more money into the economy. And over the years, Congress encountered pressure to increase benefit levels to retirees, even though these retirees never paid enough into their accounts to cover these benefits. Moreover, Social Security benefits were no longer proportionate to contributions; they were figured more generously for those whose wages were low than for those whose wages were high. Political pressure to raise benefits while keeping taxes relatively low reduced the trust fund reserve to a minor role in Social Security financing. Social Security taxes were lumped together with all other tax revenue in the federal government's budget. The accounts of workers were simply IOUs—promises to pay—not money specifically set aside in separate accounts for each contributor. Automatic COLAs, adopted in 1972 legislation and effective since 1975, proved to be another very popular program feature because of their hedge against inflation, but Social Security ran into trouble. It could no longer cover these regular increases, especially in times of high inflation.

Social Security mushroomed into such a large program because Americans came to view ever-increasing benefits as a right. Even as the number of workers grew and their wages increased during the affluence of the 1950s and 1960s, there was still little worry about the program. But during the 1970s and 1980s, the growth in Social Security rolls and payments was accompanied by economic recession. Income from the "pay-as-you-go" Social Security system (about $200 billion per year) matched the outgo in Social Security benefits. The program was on the verge of bankruptcy. Something had to be done to fix the ailing retirement system.

In 1977, taxes were increased again, and for the first time in the program's history, benefits were cut. In 1981, the Reagan administration took further measures to reduce program spending. The floor on benefit minimums was removed; benefits for children ages 18 to 22 of deceased, retired, and disabled workers were eliminated; and a national commission chaired by Alan Greenspan (Federal Reserve Board chairman from 1987 to 2006) was established to study the problems of the Social Security system and recommend reforms.

The 1983 Reforms and Beyond

The commission's work was called "a remarkable achievement in political statesmanship," as were Congress's actions.[9] The report was issued with bipartisan support, and in 1983 Congress enacted many of the commission's recommendations. It took just a little more than ten weeks for the bill to clear both the House and the Senate. Among the most important reforms was a delay of the popular cost-of-living adjustment (COLA) and a stabilizer that was placed on future COLAs should Social Security trust funds drop below certain levels.* Since inflation has varied considerably over the years, so have COLAs. (The COLA was 14.3 percent in 1980 and zero in 2010 due to the country's economic recession.[10])

The 1983 amendments also raised the full retirement age (FRA), the age at which full retirement benefits can be received. Originally set at age 65, the FRA is gradually increasing to age 67. This change began in 2003 and affects those born in 1938 (who were 65 in 2003) and later. Those born in 1938 had to be 65 years and 2 months old to receive full benefits, and the FRA is continuing to rise in two-month increments until it reaches a full 67 years in 2027. (Those born in 1960 will be 67 in 2027 and the first Social Security beneficiaries required to be 67 years old before receiving full retirement benefits.) Beneficiaries can still retire earlier, at age 62, but the amount of benefits is gradually falling from 80 percent to 70 percent of full retirement benefits by 2027. These changes may be affecting workers' behavior. The Center for Retirement Research found that Americans are staying in the workforce longer and fewer workers, especially women, are claiming Social Security as soon as they turn 62.[11] In 1985, 62 percent of women and 51 percent of men claimed benefits at age 62 compared to 48 percent of women and 43 percent of men, respectively, in 2006. But as the FRA rises, so is the number retiring before they reach their FRA.[12] As of 2008, those who retire after the full retirement age will receive 5 percent more in benefits than they would have previously (Medicare benefits continue to be available at age 65).

Another measure enacted in 1983 to shore up Social Security was to reduce "windfall" benefits or "double dipping." This means that those who receive Social Security and other government pensions (such as military retirement), but who paid into the Social Security system for only a short time, may receive lower Social Security benefits under a revised formula.

More workers were also included under the Social Security system as a result of the 1983 amendments. All new federal employees must participate as well as all members of Congress, the president and the vice president, federal judges, and all employees of nonprofit organizations, among others. Many of these people were formerly included under other systems. For example, federal employees were covered under a separate, more generous retirement system.

*COLAs are now provided if there is at least a 0.1 percent increase in the Consumer Price Index for Urban Wage Earners and Clerical Workers (CPI-W); however, if Social Security trust funds fall below certain levels, benefits are indexed according to the CPI-W or the average increase in wages, whichever is lower.

The commission made a few changes that primarily benefitted women. For example, many divorced spouses may begin collecting Social Security benefits at age 62 if their former spouses are eligible even if the former spouse has not yet claimed benefits. In addition, payments to disabled widows and widowers aged 50 to 59 were increased.

Under former provisions, Social Security benefits were not counted as taxable income, but in 1983 this change was instituted. In 1993 as part of the Clinton administration's deficit reduction plan, more benefits were subject to taxation.* Approximately one-third of retirees now pay income tax on a portion of their Social Security benefits.[13] It is really quite remarkable that changes such as taxing Social Security benefits are no longer considered the "third rail" of U.S. politics (touch it and one's political career is over). These taxes on benefits are returned to the Social Security trust funds but cover only a small amount of all OASDI benefits paid.

In 1983 and again in 1996, amendments increased the amount retirees could earn from employment without incurring a reduction in their Social Security benefits. Then, in 2000, the Senior Citizens' Freedom to Work Act eliminated the Social Security retirement earnings test for beneficiaries after they reach the full retirement age (FRA). In 2010, early retirees could earn $14,160 before their Social Security benefits were "taxed" or reduced by 50 percent (one dollar was withheld from Social Security benefits for every two dollars earned) until the retiree attained the FRA. During the year the FRA was attained, and for the months prior to reaching the FRA, one dollar of benefits was withheld for every three dollars earned above the annual limit of $37,680 or $3,140 month. Beginning in the month the FRA is attained, Social Security benefits are no longer reduced no matter how much is earned. This change benefits older Americans who need or want to work. It also helps the Social Security program because older workers and their employers continue to pay Social Security taxes. These older workers may also earn enough to pay federal and state income taxes on their wages, which benefits government. They also have more money to spend, benefiting the overall economy.

Especially important among the 1983 amendments were increases in the Social Security and Medicare tax rate and taxable wage base. The tax rate was increased gradually until it reached 7.65 percent for both employers and employees in 1990, a combined rate of 15.3 percent—where it remains today. The 7.65 percent tax is distributed as follows: 5.35 percent goes to the OASI trust fund that pays retirement and survivors' benefits; .85 percent goes to the DI trust fund that pays disability benefits; and 1.45 percent goes to the HI trust fund that supports Medicare. Today, of every dollar OASDI pays out, about 85 cents goes to retirement and survivors benefits, and about 15 cents goes to pay disability benefits.[14] All HI taxes go to the Medicare program.

Because Medicare was in dire need of additional funding due to rapidly escalating health-care costs, the taxable wage base for the HI part of the program was increased a few times in the early 1990s. Since 1994, the HI tax has been applied to all earnings, which has helped shore up Medicare funding and supports the contentions of those who believe that Social Security taxes should be more progressive (or less regressive).

In 2009 the taxable wage base for OASDI was $106,800. Each year the OASDI taxable wage base is adjusted for inflation, and it usually increases each year along with increases in the cost of living. Given the economic recession that was occurring, the taxable wage base for 2010 remained unchanged from 2009.

In addition to the rules that govern how workers pay into the Social Security system during their working years, a complex set of rules govern how one qualifies for benefits and how benefits are determined as described in Illustration 5.1.

---

*Half of Social Security benefits are now subject to regular federal income tax rates if combined income (taxable income plus nontaxable interest) plus one-half of Social Security benefits is between $25,000 and $34,000 for a single person and $32,000 to $44,000 for a couple. For singles whose combined income plus one-half of their Social Security benefits exceeds $34,000 and for couples exceeding $44,000, 85 percent of their benefits are taxed at regular rates.

ILLUSTRATION 5.1
Social Security—Who Qualifies, and How Much Do Beneficiaries Receive?

Approximately 94 percent of workers participate in the Social Security system. Employees and employers continue to pay equal amounts toward the employee's OASDHI insurance, and on retirement, workers receive benefits if they have enough *credits* (formerly called *quarters*) to qualify. For example, those born in 1929 or later need 40 credits (generally equivalent to 10 years of work). In 2009, workers accrued one credit if they earned $1,090 regardless of how much or how long they worked during the year. The maximum number of credits that can be earned in one year is four (equal to $4,360 in 2009). The amount needed to earn each credit rises gradually each year. At retirement, most workers have far more than the number of credits needed to qualify.

Once it is determined that the worker qualifies to receive Social Security benefits, his or her average indexed monthly earnings (AIME) are calculated. This figure is usually the total of the 35 highest years of earnings adjusted (indexed) for inflation and divided by 420 (the number of months in 35 years). Then the worker's primary insurance amount (PIA) is usually calculated based on the AIME. The AIME is the amount that retirees receive if they wait until the full retirement age to collect benefits. Workers may retire as early as age 62, but benefits are reduced and calculated as a percent of the PIA. For a person who had *low* earnings, Social Security replaces about 57 percent of earnings; for a person with *average* earnings, the replacement rate is about 42 percent of earnings; and for high earners, it is about 35 percent. Because of the progressive nature of Social Security benefits, replacement rates are higher for low-income earners and lower for high-income earners. In any case, payments to retirees are relatively modest—an average of about $1,153 a month in 2009; many retirees received less, although some received the maximum—about $2,323 a month.

Insured workers may also be eligible for benefits if they become physically or mentally disabled prior to retirement. The disability must prevent work for at least one year or be expected to result in death. The average monthly payment to disabled workers in 2009 was about $1,064.

Although the rules can be complex, benefits (calculated as a percentage of the worker's PIA) are often also payable to the dependents of retired and disabled workers and to the survivors of deceased workers. The terms *survivors* and *dependents* refer to spouses and minor children, disabled adult children, and occasionally parents of covered workers. Survivors and dependents must meet certain qualifications, such as age requirements and definitions of disability. For example, a woman aged 62 or older who never worked in covered employment, or who worked but earned less than her spouse, is generally entitled to receive an amount that is 50 percent of her retired spouse's benefits. Widows or widowers are also entitled to benefits, generally beginning at age 60 or at age 50 if they are disabled. Widows or widowers caring for children under age 16 can receive benefits at any age, and their children are also entitled to benefits. A lump sum benefit of $255 is also payable on the death of an insured worker to an eligible child or spouse.

Some additional types of benefits are also available. For example, a *special minimum benefit* may be paid to people who had many years of covered employment but earned low wages. And virtually *all* people 65 years of age and over, regardless of whether they have ever paid into Social Security, are allowed to participate in Medicare.

Source: Based on "Benefit Calculation Examples for Workers Retiring in 2009" (Washington, DC: Social Security Administration). Retrieved December 24, 2009, from http://www.socialsecurity.gov/OACT/ProgData/retirebenefit1.html

State of the Trust Funds

The 1983 reforms put Social Security on much more stable footing.[15] Now, more than a quarter of a century later, the combined OASDI trust funds are taking in much more than is being paid out. For instance, in 2008, the OASDI trust funds paid out $625 billion, took in $805 billion, and had assets of $2.4 trillion.[16] The HI trust fund is not in as good a shape. In 2008, the HI trust fund took in $231 billion and paid out $236 billion, although it had assets of $321 billion.

Each year the six-member Social Security Board of Trustees (the Secretary of the Treasury, the Secretary of Labor, the Secretary of Health and Human Services, the Commissioner of Social Security, and two members of the public appointed by the President with Senate confirmation) determines the health of the trust funds by using low cost (optimistic), intermediate cost (moderate or most likely scenario), and high cost (pessimistic) assumptions about the country's economic situation and figuring in demographic changes like life expectancy, fertility, and immigration rates. Forecasting is always risky because even the most savvy economists cannot predict with certainty what will happen in the future. Even small differences in assumptions can have major impacts on long-range predictions, and not everyone agrees on the economic assumptions or other factors that make up the model used to project Social Security's future state. But these are the best "guesstimates" we have to help in planning rationally for the future.

Using intermediate assumptions, the Social Security trustees' 2009 report shows that in the short run (the next 10 years), the OASI Trust Fund is adequately financed, but DI Trust Fund assets will begin to fall short of 100 percent of annual expenditures before the end of 2014. However, OASI funds are used to keep the DI fund, which takes in much less money, solvent. Although the country's economic recession is reducing the amount of Social Security payroll taxes that would otherwise have been collected, the combined OASI and DI Trust Funds are still adequately financed in the short run.

The long-run picture is gloomy. The number of retired workers is expected to grow rapidly from 2010 to 2030 as the "baby boom" generation (the approximately 79 million individuals born from 1946 to 1964) enters retirement, putting an enormous strain on the Social Security system. After 2030, strain will continue due to increased life expectancy and lower fertility rates (the boomers forgot to have enough children to support Social Security). In 2016, as annual OASDI costs begin to exceed the amount collected in Social Security taxes, interest income from the trust fund's assets will be needed to pay some OASDI benefits. By 2037, the OASDI trust funds will be exhausted—they will not have enough to pay all the benefits due in that year.

The HI fund is in the worse shape because healthcare costs are projected to rise much faster than wages. HI benefits already exceed the taxes collected. If current projections hold, the HI trust fund will be exhausted by 2017.

Is Social Security in Crisis?

Given current combined OASDI trust fund assets, it may be overstating the case to say that these Social Security programs are in imminent danger. Some blame the alarm on "those who are hostile to government and therefore favor replacing all or part of one of this nation's most successful and essential programs with private investment accounts."[17] But many people who support the Social Security system are also concerned about ensuring the solvency of nation's main retirement program. Most prudent people would likely agree that long-range planning is warranted. The funds need to remain in good actuarial balance for the country to breathe easy. The following pages consider issues facing Social Security and how the country might go about ensuring the economic security of retired and disabled workers and their dependents and survivors in the years ahead.

SOCIAL SECURITY'S GOALS: ADEQUACY, EQUITY, AND EFFICIENCY

Many Americans, young and old, support the concept of Social Security, but confidence in the program has waned, especially among younger people. Social Security officials have probably grown tired of hearing that young people are more likely to believe in UFOs than think they will collect Social Security.[18] A 2005 random digit dial survey with a nationally representative sample of Americans found that nearly 60 percent lacked confidence in Social Security's future, but 86 percent thought the program should continue.[19] A 2008 survey also found declining confidence among retirees and workers that Social Security "will continue to provide benefits of at least equal value to the benefits received by retirees today."[20] As we think about Social Security for the years ahead, let's appraise how well the program has maintained its goals of adequacy, equity, and efficiency.

Intergenerational Adequacy and Equity

Social Security has been praised for achieving "a unique blend of adequacy and individual equity," two principles on which the program was founded.[21] It is adequate because it helps many older people escape poverty. It is equitable because those who contributed more get higher benefits, while at the same time lower-income workers (who paid Social Security taxes as the same rate as higher income workers) receive benefits that are proportionally more generous than higher income workers receive.

Social Security is the major source of income for most retired Americans.[22] Social Security comprises at least 90 percent of the income of 20 percent of older married couple beneficiaries and 41 percent for single beneficiaries. It comprises at least 50 percent of the income of 52 percent of older married couples and 72 percent of single beneficiaries. In 1959, the overall poverty rate among those aged 65 and older in the United States was 35 percent. By 1984, it was down to about 12 percent, and in 2008, it was under 10 percent (although the poverty rate for elderly women and people of color is much higher). Experts agree that Social Security is the single most important factor in lifting the elderly out of poverty.[23] The word "social" in Social Security is important because unlike private pension and retirement programs, Social Security also redistributes income to those less fortunate (those who earned less during their working years, retired early due to disability, or suffered the death of the family breadwinner).

Participation in Social Security is, however, a different experience for younger generations than for older ones. Current workers realize that they are paying a substantial tax to participate. The current system might not be viewed so pessimistically if (1) today's workers and employers did not view the Social Security tax as overly burdensome (lower-income workers today pay more in Social Security taxes than income taxes) and (2) the number of aged people supported by the working population were not increasing so fast. These factors give pause to many younger people who are paying in but unsure of what they might get in return. The fact is that Social Security was never intended to support people fully during their "golden" years.

The analogy of a three-legged stool has been used to describe what workers need to retire comfortably: One leg is Social Security, the second is pension income, and the third is personal savings and investments. Many beneficiaries have at least a small income from sources other than Social Security. Most also receive Social Security retirement benefits that greatly exceed their original investment, and more if Medicare is considered. No wonder the program is so popular among its more than 52 million current beneficiaries, most of them older people who comprise a very large bloc of the most active voters in the United States. With such strong support, it is generally difficult to consider major changes like benefit cuts.

As members of each succeeding generation pay Social Security taxes to support current retirees, they also want to get a fair return on their investment. Will today's workers get their "money's worth"? It is taking longer for younger generations to recoup their investment. A single worker born in 1910 who retired at age 65 in 1975 after earning average wages and contributing a total of $5,857 to Social Security recouped the OASI taxes he or she paid plus interest just before age 67.[24] A single worker born in 1930 who retired in 1995 at the age of 65 after earning average wages and contributing $67,564 to Social Security recouped his or her OASI taxes plus interest just before age 73, while a single worker born in 1949 who retires at age 66 (remember, the full retirement age is rising slowly) in 2015 after earning average wages and contributing $258,824, would not recoup his or her investment until just after age 78. If the taxes their employers paid plus interest are added in, then payments for these workers are recouped at ages 68 years and 7 months, 83 years and 6 months, and 95 years, respectively. Clearly, it is taking longer to recover one's investment, and many retirees will not live to age 95.

What if you are a young person today? What will it take for you to be able to retire? Illustration 5.2 provides a rough idea of what you might get in Social Security benefits and how much more you might need to live comfortably in retirement.

ILLUSTRATION 5.2
Will You Have Enough to Retire?

You might be thinking ahead to your own retirement and wondering how much money you will get from Social Security and how close it will come to allowing you to live comfortably. The Social Security Administration (SSA) helps people estimate their Social Security retirement benefits if they take early retirement at age 62, wait until the full retirement age (which is gradually rising to age 67), or retire at age 70 or later. You can estimate your own Social Security retirement benefits at http://www.ssa.gov/OACT/anypia/index.html.

These figures are only estimates since it is difficult to predict one's future income or what the Social Security system will look like in the years ahead. The younger one is now, the less certain the calculations for retirement years are, but let's take an example. We used the SSA's Quick Calculator and entered wages of $30,000 for Joe, who was born on January 1, 1984 and was age 25 in 2009. Looking at Table A, the SSA must have assumed that Joe was in college in the years from 2001 through 2004, or otherwise earned little, and assigned him small amounts of earnings. It also must have assumed that Joe took his first regular job in 2005 and earned $23,400 that year. The SSA estimated Joe's future earnings based on projected national average earnings' growth. In 2045 just before turning age 62, Joe would be earning $115,300 annually based on 2009 earnings of $30,000. As Table B shows, if Joe retired early, at age 62, his monthly Social Security benefit would be an estimated $3,369 (Joe may also have a spouse whose benefits are not shown here). If Joe kept working until he reached the full retirement age of 67 to retire, his benefit would be $5,391 a month, and if he retired at age 70, his monthly benefit would be $7,358.

This might sound like a substantial amount of money today, but let's look at the figures more closely. Let's say Joe retires at his full retirement age of 67 on January 1, 2051. In 2050 his projected annual earnings are $132,900. At age 67, Joe's monthly Social Security benefit of $5,391 or $64,692 annually will replace slightly less than half of what he earned in 2050. Joe might not need as much to live in retirement as he did when he was working. He might have paid for his home by then, and he might not need as much money to cover clothing or automobile or other commuter expenses that he needed when he was working, but a 50 percent reduction in income may be more than Joe had planned. If Joe retires early at age 62, his annual Social Security benefits will be less than one-third of his annual earnings of $115,300 in 2045, just before he turns age 62. Perhaps Joe will have a retirement plan through his employer (or

(Continued)

employers) that will help make up the differ-ence. If Joe becomes disabled before retire-ment age, his Social Security benefits will be lower because he will not have worked as long.

To make up the difference in any addi-tional money needed during retirement, saving at a younger age is better than saving at an older age because interest (returns on your money) compound over time. For example, if Joe invested $5,000 at an interest rate of 5 percent, compounded once annually, in 10 years he would have $8,144 (1.63 times the original value, or a 63 percent increase); if he kept the same investment for 30 years, the total value would be $21,610 (4.32 times its original value, or a 332 percent increase). An old saying goes something like, "life is short; enjoy it now," but Joe may live well into old age, and he may also want to be able to enjoy life then.

TABLE A Joe's Annual Earnings (selected years)

Past Earnings		Future Earnings[a]	
2001	$2,400	2025	$55,200
2004	$2,800	2045	$115,300
2005	$23,400	2046	$118,600
2007	$26,600	2049	$129,200
2008	$28,200	2050	$132,900
2009	$30,000	2052	$140,600

[a]Adjusted for estimated national average wage growth (inflation)

TABLE B Joe's Estimated Monthly and Annual Social Security Benefits

Retirement Age[a] and Year	Monthly Benefit	Annual Benefit[b]
62 and one month in 2046	$3,369	$40,428
67 in 2050	$5,391	$64,692
70 in 2053	$7,358	$88,296

[a]The last year of earnings used in estimating the retirement benefit is the year before the year in which retirement begins.

[b]Assumes future increases in prices or earnings.

Since there is no individual interest-accruing account for each worker who contributes to Social Security, the program's adequacy and equity are directly affected by the *dependency ratio*—the ratio of beneficiaries to workers. In 1950 there were 16 workers for each beneficiary. As the U.S. population grows increasingly older due to lower birthrates and longer life spans, the dependency ratio is decreasing. Today it takes about 3.2 workers to pay for every one person receiving benefits. By 2034, the number of workers supporting each beneficiary will decline to 2.1.[25] This is a heavy responsibility to place on younger generations of workers.

Social Security has been described as an "intergenerational compact" in which one generation of workers agrees to help current retirees with the promise of being helped themselves in retirement.[26] This was less of a problem when younger generations were much larger than older ones. Today, a key to making everyone feel better about the program may be to promote "intergenerational equity," that is, to be as fair as possible to both the old and the young.[27]

Largely due to OASDHI, older people's financial status has improved over the years. Some argue that older Americans are now living a better life at the expense of the young. Others bristle at this thought. They note that the baby boomers made it possible for many younger individuals to enjoy a very nice standard of living as they were growing up. They also note that many older people are not terribly well off (in 2008, 23 percent lived at 150 percent of the poverty or less and 36 percent lived at 200 percent of poverty or less[28]). Others suggest that cuts in Social Security would not necessarily mean that more would be done to help younger people. The more salient issue is to consider what can be done to ensure a decent standard of living for members of all generations, but as we will see in Chapter 7, helping younger people is a different political issue than helping older Americans.

Will Generations X and Y see the boomers' retirement as a source of consternation? Economist Henry Aaron believes that the fuss about the boomers putting a strain on younger generations is ill founded.[29] After all, the boomers have paid a substantial tax for their retirement while supporting retirees who are getting back more than their share. The boomers will not get the same rate of return as older generations. The problem of too few workers in the future is not confined to the Social Security system. There will also be fewer workers to support all government (and private sector) activities.[30]

Another crucial intergenerational aspect of Social Security is that it protects younger people from having to support their own elderly or disabled parents. Most workers would find it difficult to provide much financial support to their parents (although they may help in other ways), and older people generally do not want to burden their children with this responsibility. Historically, Social Security benefits and costs have been "distributed widely across the generations."[31]

Adequacy and Equity Across Racial and Ethnic Groups

Another point of contention is whether the Social Security program is operating at unfair expense to members of certain racial and ethnic groups. This issue has received increased attention as the country has become more ethnically diverse. Organizations such as the Libertarian Cato Institute and the conservative Heritage Foundation have long argued that Social Security disadvantages people of color.[32] For example, they claim that since the average life span of African Americans is shorter than whites, they will collect less in Social Security retirement benefits even though they paid into the system at the same rate during their working years.

Conservatives and Libertarians also argue that the regressive Social Security tax contributes to the wealth gap between people of color and whites. They see Social Security taxes as draining money away that African Americans (and others) could put toward building assets or wealth (e.g., owning a home, saving for children's college education, building private retirement savings) during their younger years.

In addition, because African Americans and Hispanics often work at jobs that take a physical toll and cause them to retire earlier, Social Security reforms such as raising the retirement age put them in an even more untenable position. The Hispanic population is also considerably younger than the white population, which places a substantial burden on them to support the growing retirement population that is disproportionately white and more affluent.[33]

Many liberal organizations as well as groups that represent older Americans and people of color reject the idea that the Social Security program is unfair to people of color. They point to the many reasons that Social Security is a good deal for African Americans and Hispanics.[34] Among their arguments is that people of color rely more heavily than whites on Social Security at retirement. This is because they more often work in lower wage jobs that prevent them from acquiring personal savings, and their employers often do not contribute to private retirement accounts that would provide them a retirement pension (of course, Libertarians and many conservatives argue that this is exactly why Social Security is *not* a good deal for African Americans and Hispanics).

While acknowledging that African Americans' average lifespan is shorter than whites, organizations like the National Committee to Preserve Social Security and Medicare make another point. They note that while African American men often die at dramatically younger ages than white men, for those who reach age 65, their life expectancy is only about two years shorter than white men. In addition, because African American men tend to retire earlier, on average, the difference in the number of years they collect Social Security compared to white men is smaller than one might imagine (less than two years).[35]

A number of organizations also believe that Social Security is fair to African Americans because they receive disability benefits and their dependents receive survivors' benefits more frequently than whites.[36] Although receiving disability and survivors' benefits at higher rates may not be much consolation to African Americans, the Center on Budget and Policy Priorities' review of studies shows that African Americans' *overall* rate of return on their Social Security contributions is modestly higher than for whites (the same or slightly higher in the retirement and survivors programs and higher in the disability portion).[37]

Paradoxically, Hispanics have higher morbidity (disability) rates but longer life expectancies than the general population; thus, they rely more on the disability portion of the Social Security and spend more years receiving retirement benefits.[38] Without Social Security, many younger people of all racial and ethnic groups might be left with little or no income, since they may not have private disability insurance or large life insurance policies that would guarantee them or their family adequate income in the event of misfortune.

Immigration is another point of discussion. Pro-immigrant groups emphasize that immigrants help Social Security because they are often employed and pay Social Security taxes. Even undocumented immigrants may pay these taxes although they are not eligible to receive Social Security benefits.[39] In general, immigrant groups' fertility rates tend to be slightly higher than that of non-immigrants, which helps ease the dependency ratio.[40] However, since analyses suggest that additional immigration will likely have only a modest (but favorable) effect on Social Security finances, the Center on Budget and Policy Priorities suggests that this "should not be a significant consideration in setting either immigration or Social Security policy."[41]

Changing immigration policy could produce a more positive impact on Social Security. According to Georgetown University immigration scholar Susan Martin, since it often takes 15 to 20 years for an immigration application to be approved, and the primary applicant's median age is 55, those admitted are often nearing retirement.[42] If applicants, especially higher income earners, were admitted during their most productive working years, more might be done to improve Social Security's financial status (and perhaps decrease illegal immigration).

Adequacy, Equity, and Gender

In general, both men and women rely heavily on Social Security during retirement, but the situation is more acute for women. Women on average live longer than men and they are less likely to have pensions or other retirement income, which increases their reliance on Social Security. In 2007, among those aged 65 and older, women's average annual Social Security income was $10,685 compared to $14,055 for men.[43] Among unmarried individuals, including widows and widowers, Social Security comprised an average of 48 percent of women's income compared to 37 percent for men (the figure for couples was 30 percent). In addition, of all unmarried female Social Security recipients aged 65 and older, 47 percent relied on Social Security for 90 percent or more of their income.

When the Social Security system was first adopted, men's and women's roles were different than they are today. Women were less likely to work outside the home, and divorce was less common. The Social Security system reflected the social conditions of the 1930s when most women were considered "dependents" of their working husbands. Most efforts to reduce gender inequities in the Social Security programs have had minimal impact. One measure allows divorced husbands to claim benefits based on their former wife's earnings records. Another allows divorced spouses to qualify for benefits at age 62 based on a former spouse's earnings, even if the ex-spouse has not claimed benefits. Congress has not addressed many of the gender inequities that continue to exist in the program. Gender inequities persist for many reasons:[44]

1. Women's wages are generally lower than men's, resulting in lower Social Security benefits paid to women at retirement or disability.
2. Women may spend less time in the paid workforce because they continue to carry the major unpaid responsibilities for the home and family care. This also results in lower Social Security paid to women.
3. Divorced individuals who were married for at least ten years are entitled to a Social Security payment equal to half of their former spouse's retirement benefits. Women use this provision more than men since it more often affords them a higher benefit than they would get on their own work record. If this is a woman's only income, it may be inadequate to support her during retirement.
4. Homemakers are not covered on their own under Social Security unless they have held jobs in the paid labor force.
5. Widowed spouses generally do not qualify for Social Security benefits until they are 60 years old unless they are disabled or have children under age 18. This provision can also disadvantage women who have remained at home.
6. Social Security retirement benefits are often based on the earnings of the primary worker, generally the husband. The wages of a second earner, usually the wife, may not raise the couple's combined Social Security benefits.
7. Couples in which one worker (generally the husband) earned most of the wages may receive higher retirement benefits than those in which the husband and wife earned equal wages even if both couples' incomes were identical.
8. Increasing numbers of women have never married. Married workers benefit from Social Security more than single workers because married people who have never worked can obtain Social Security benefits based on their spouse's work. Single workers do not receive additional benefits although they have made Social Security payments at the same rate as married workers.

Women's workforce participation has increased, which increases their Social Security benefits at retirement. Increasing numbers of women are also earning more than their spouses.[45] However, many women still earn less than their husbands and continue to receive higher Social Security payments based on their husbands' earnings rather than their own. Several options have been suggested for remedying gender inequities in the Social Security system and bringing the program in line with the times:

> The *earnings-sharing* option would divide a couple's earnings equally between the husband and wife for each year of marriage, allowing Social Security benefits to be calculated separately for the husband and the wife regardless of whether they remained married.[46] This option eliminates the idea of the "primary wage earner" and the "dependent spouse" and recognizes that a spouse with primary responsibility for care of the home and/or children is an equal partner in the marriage. However, depending on total annual earnings, the amount credited to each spouse for each year married could be quite low and substantially reduce the Social Security

benefits to which each is entitled upon retirement or disability. Crediting the entire amount of annual earnings to each spouse would increase the program's adequacy, but it would reduce the equity aspects for never-married workers who would not be able to "double-dip" in this way. It would also be considerably more costly to the Social Security system than the current arrangement.

Under the *double-decker plan*, every American would be eligible for a basic benefit, regardless of whether they had ever worked for pay.[47] Those with paid work experience would receive a payment in addition to the basic benefit.

Dependent care proposals focus on the caregiving role, which the wife usually assumes.[48] One such proposal is a *dependent care credit*. It would give at least a minimal Social Security earnings credit for each year an individual stays at home to raise children or earned little. Another is a *specified earnings credit*. For a fixed number of years, caregivers would be credited with one-half of their prior average earnings for each year they had a child in care *and* they had no earnings or earned less than in prior years. Another option is to *subtract the number of caregiving years* from earning averages. Today, Social Security benefits are based on an average of the worker's 35 highest years of earnings. A specified number of years in which no income was earned could be excluded. Because low-income parents might not be able to take entire years off from work, this approach might not help them as much as dependent care credit proposals.

Other ideas have been offered for providing Social Security benefits to women and others with low incomes at retirement. They include increasing minimum benefits and survivors' benefits and reducing the requirement that divorced spouses must have been married 10 years to collect on their former spouse's earnings record. Others might say that the decision to stay out of the workforce is a choice and that the government has no responsibility for subsidizing the retirement incomes of those who have not paid into the Social Security system.

Efficiency of the Social Security System

In addition to adequacy and equity, efficiency is a Social Security program goal. Slightly less than one cent per dollar collected is used to administer the program. However, the number of Social Security Administration (SSA) staff has dropped so low compared to the number of individuals using the system that it can be difficult to get help with questions or concerns. As described in Chapter 6 of this book, the SSA is also struggling with a tremendous backlog of disability case hearings.

SAVING SOCIAL SECURITY

In the near future, the president and Congress are clearly going to have to decide whether to fix the current Social Security system or whether to take a new course of action.

Fix the Current System

Many reform proposals call for modifying the current Social Security system. Illustration 5.3 presents several of these proposals and how far they might go in closing Social Security's projected funding gap. Options 1, 2, and 3 place the burden on current workers. Option 1, raising the taxable wage base, could close the gap substantially. In fact, if all wages were currently taxed *and* benefits were *not* raised for higher earners, there would be no shortfall. Although this would

ILLUSTRATION 5.3
Closing the Projected Social Security Funding Gap

	1	2	3	4
	Collect Social Security taxes on at least 90% of earnings	**Raise the payroll tax rate**	**Gradually raise the full retirement age from 67 to 70**	**Adjust the COLA to reflect the true inflation rate**
Cuts Gap:	35%–50%	50%–100%	20%–35%	20%–75%
Description:	Social Security retirement and disability benefits are funded by a tax on a set amount of wages. In 2009, this taxable wage base was $106,800. The goal has been to tax 90% of all wages but this has not happened. A small percent of Americans earn above the cap. One option is to raise the cap to 90% of earnings or remove the cap entirely.	Workers and employers each pay a 6.2% tax to fund retirement, disability, and survivors' benefits (a combined rate of 12.4%). Raising the cap to 13.4% would reduce the projected gap by half. Raising it to 14.4% could close it.	This option is founded on Americans' increasing life expectancy.	Each year, Social Security payments are adjusted for inflation, but some say the current consumer price index (CPI) overstates inflation.
Pros:	Raising the cap to 90% of wages would reduce the gap 35-50%. If all wages were taxed today, there would be no projected shortfall.	The payroll tax rate has not been raised since 1990. Some think this is a straightforward approach to close the funding gap.	Because Americans are living longer, they should expect to work longer in order to fund longer retirement periods.	Cost-of-living adjustments (COLAs) should accurately reflect inflation.
Cons:	Political support for Social Security might weaken because higher-wage earners would not get much more in benefits even though they paid more.	This would make the payroll tax even more regressive. Employers would object to paying more, and it might cause them to layoff workers.	The full retirement age (FRA) is already increasing from age 65 to 67, but most people begin collecting Social Security benefits before their FRA. Those who work at physically taxing jobs may be most disadvantaged as would those caring for elderly spouses or parents.	A lower COLA might not adjust appropriately for rising healthcare costs. Any downward adjustment would hurt poor recipients the most.
Outlook:	Broad public support for raising the cap improves the odds for bipartisan action.	AARP reports substantial public support for this option, but lawmakers would be skittish.	This option is likely to trigger strong opposition.	The outlook is mixed, but the Bureau of Labor Statistics is testing a new CPI.

Source: Adapted from AARP, "Keeping Social Security Afloat: How We Can Do It," AARP Bulletin, May 2007, pp. 12–13. Based on estimates by the Office of the Actuary, Social Security Administration, www.ssa.gov/OACT. Reprinted by permission of the author, Thomas N. Bethell.

5	6	7	8
Increase the tax on Social Security benefits	**Reduce future retirees' benefits**	**Invest part of the Social Security trust funds in securities**	**Preserve a limited estate tax and dedicate it to Social Security**
10%–15%	25%–70%	15%–45%	25%–30%
Higher-income retirees already pay a tax on their benefits. The tax could be further increased for those in higher income brackets.	This could be done in many ways, such as using different formulas to calculate retirement benefits so that lower-income earners would not face a cut or as much of a cut as higher-income earners.	Today, Social Security revenues that are not needed to pay current benefits are invested in safe, low-interest government bonds. Investing some of this money in indexed funds could earn higher interest and help close the long-term funding gap.	The estate tax has been declining. In 2009 it was collected only on estates worth $7 million or more for a couple. Freezing the tax at this level and dedicating it to Social Security would substantially reduce the long-term funding gap.
Those in higher income brackets may well be able to absorb a higher tax on their benefits without harming their lifestyle.	Rather than put the burden solely on current workers, retirees should also assume some of the burden for reducing the projected funding gap.	Low-risk, higher earning investments could help close at least part of the projected gap without putting more burden on workers or retirees. Almost all other public and private pension funds do this. Social Security could ride out market downturns.	Preserving some tax on the nation's most wealthy families is justifiable.
It is unfair to further tax those who have paid Social Security taxes and also managed to obtain a comfortable standard of living in retirement. Depending on how the tax is structured, middle-income earners could be hurt.	With private pensions in decline, 401(k) plans and other investments at risk, and individual savings at dangerously low levels, more older people might end up needing public assistance or help from their children.	Government should not be involved in the stock market.	If a limited estate tax is retained, it should be dedicated to more urgent needs like Medicare.
This option is a possibility, but it will depend on whether Congress and the president are willing to consider tax increases of any kind.	Congress would be politically wary of this approach.	Because of current stock market volatility, policymakers are skittish about promoting this option.	The estate tax is unpopular, but public opinion may be shifting.

make Social Security look more like public assistance and might erode support for the program, an AARP poll found a good deal of public support for this option.

Option 2 is raising the payroll tax. AARP reports more public support for this option than one might imagine, and (based on this 2007 analysis) if raised to 14.4 percent from the current 12.4 percent OASDI tax, it could fully cover the gap. However, it would make the Social Security tax more regressive and place an even greater burden on low-income workers. Employers are also likely to balk at paying more taxes, and it might result in job layoffs. President Obama has suggested a combination of Options of 1 and 2 by increasing the Social Security tax for those who make $250,000 or more (not by the current full 12.4 percent OASDI tax rate, but in the range of 2 to 4 percent more in total combined employer and employee contributions).

Option 3 is to gradually raise the full retirement age (FRA) to age 70. Although it could reduce the gap by as much as a third, it is likely to trigger substantial opposition. Americans are living and working longer, but most begin drawing Social Security earlier than their FRA, and this would most disadvantage those who work at physically demanding jobs.

Options 4, 5, and 6, put the onus on retirees. Option 4 would reduce cost of living adjustments, hurting the poorest Social Security recipients the most. Few politicians would probably want to go on record supporting it, even though it has the potential to close three-fourths of the gap. Option 5, increasing taxes on Social Security benefits, would make the system more progressive by placing the responsibility to shore up Social Security on retirees with higher incomes. It would make less of a dent in the Social Security funding gap than other options (10-15 percent).

Option 6 would cut future retirees' benefits, but to be viable, benefits of lower-income retirees would need to be protected to keep them out of poverty. Although this option might cut the gap by more than two-thirds, it is worrisome because so many Americans rely heavily on Social Security at retirement. One example of this option is called *progressive price indexing*.[49] Low-income workers (those currently earning about $20,000 or less annually) would be treated as they are today by Social Security. Their benefits would continue to be indexed (adjusted) according to the average increase in wages, and their benefits would not be reduced. The benefits of higher-income earners (those earning $90,000 or more today) would be indexed according to prices (increases in the costs of good and services). Their benefits would be lower than they are today because prices grow more slowly than wages. Middle-income earners' Social Security benefits would be indexed using a combination of wage and price indexing.

The Center on Budget and Public Policy Priorities is highly critical of progressive price indexing, primarily because of cuts in retirement benefits for future retirees. For example, projections are that an average-income earner retiring at age 65 in 2045 would see a 16 percent benefit cut, and an average-income earner retiring at age 65 in 2075 would see a 28 percent cut. Furthermore, despite differences in what workers pay into the system, they would end up getting about equal retirement benefits. Although this approach preserves retirement benefits for the lowest-wage earners, it would also move Social Security away from its social insurance mission and closer to public assistance. Proponents are not worried about this. They see progressive price indexing as a solid centrist solution to Social Security's future problems because costs would be borne by those best able to afford them, while keeping program finances in check and preserving the Social Security safety net.[50]

If the current Social Security system is modified, it is probably more politically viable to think about combining some of the options described above so that current workers and retirees share the costs of fixing Social Security. Another option is to look outside the Social Security system for funding. Option 8 would do this by using estate taxes to keep Social Security afloat. The estate tax is levied on the affluent, and although it is unpopular among them, this option does not harm less affluent individuals and could close at least a quarter of the gap.

Create a New System

The United States could also take a substantially different direction in reforming Social Security. Among the major suggestions in this category are privatization and prefunded systems.

PRIVATIZATION   As presented in Illustration 5.3, option 7 is to invest some of the Social Security taxes not needed to pay current benefits in conservative stock market investments. This is a more modest proposal than many other ideas for privatizing Social Security.

Privatization of Social Security received a good deal of attention during the George W. Bush administration. Social security privatization plans in the country of Chile and the city of Galveston, Texas, are often hailed as examples of privatization's success. Detractors point out the downside of these systems, particularly increased risk, less program oversight, and loss of the longstanding social insurance, or collective mission, of the U.S. Social Security system.

Privatization can take many forms. At one extreme, workers could simply be left to save and invest as they wish for their retirement. This is the riskiest of the all the strategies for obvious reasons. Workers might not save or invest at all, leaving them penniless at retirement and dependent on family, friends, public assistance, or private charities. Workers might invest, but they may pick investments that perform poorly, leaving them with little retirement income, or they might pick investments that fail completely due to poor investment strategies or even fraud, again causing them to rely on others in retirement. Many ideas for privatizing Social Security are safer than this and rely on the government to invest the funds. The 13-member Advisory Council on Social Security was formed in 1969 and met every four years until 1994. Because the council could not agree on a single plan for Social Security reform, its final report offered three plans for averting OASDHI trust fund exhaustion. All involved some degree of privatization of Social Security through stock market investments.[51]

When the Advisory Council issued its report, the stock market was performing remarkably well. Many thought (or hoped) this upward trend would continue. The council's report generated much discussion among economists, Congress, other policymaking bodies and individuals, and the public at large. President George W. Bush toured the country to drum up support for privatization. While Congress was in recess, he appointed an ardent supporter of privatization as deputy commissioner of Social Security, but sufficient momentum to make such changes to what is arguably the most successful U.S. social welfare program never materialized. Since then, the economy and the stock market have undergone major upheavals. Stock market losses of billions of dollars in 2000 and 2001 and even more stunning losses in 2008 have put the brakes on consideration of privatizing Social Security. As many Americans try to comprehend the losses in their private pensions and private investment accounts, and as many think about whether they will have to work longer before retiring, they know that Social Security is still there for them.

Did Congress's incremental approach to policymaking save the day, or are groups like the Cato Institute right?[52] Cato, perhaps the country's most zealous supporter of privatization, contends that despite tremendous stock market losses, over the long haul, privatization is still the best way to generate retirement income. For example, Michael Tanner reports that a hypothetical $100 invested in 1965 would have resulted in about $255 at Social Security's annual return rate of about 2.2 percent for an individual retiring today compared to about $4,136 if invested in the market, even with the 2008 economic downturn.[53]

A PREFUNDED SYSTEM   Another alternative for making Social Security more structurally sound is to convert it to a prefunded system.[54] In the current pay-as-you-go system, one generation (current workers) pay taxes that are used to pay benefits for another (retired) generation. In a prefunded system, each generation funds its own retirement by investing today's Social Security taxes for tomorrow's retirement. Theoretically, at least, the retirement fund never runs out of money. However, depending on how it is structured, a prefunded system could eliminate the more favorable treatment of low-income workers that exists under the current system.

Prefunded systems can be created through the private market, but as mentioned earlier, this approach has inherent risks because the market is unpredictable and even volatile. Under this scenario, *individuals* would bear the risks of their personal circumstances, personal investment choices, and general economic conditions. Alternatively, a prefunded system could be government-based rather than market-based. Because the government could control the amounts that workers pay in and the amounts paid to beneficiaries, the adequacy and equity of the current system could be retained while simultaneously ensuring the trust funds' long-term solvency.

The switch to a prefunded system would come with sticker shock—in 2008 the figure approached $14 trillion (the amount of Social Security's current unfunded liabilities[55]). While this is a hefty upfront price tag, it is a one-time fee to fix a very large problem that touches virtually all Americans. The cost could be phased in over time and across generations to ease the burden.

Avoiding Exhaustion

As Congress, advisory boards, think tanks, and advocacy groups continue the debate about how to fix Social Security, the problem grows, and the resources needed to avert insolvency become greater. In 1996, the Social Security Advisory Board replaced the Advisory Council on Social Security. Congress established this bipartisan board and the president and Congress appoint the members. Much like the old Advisory Council, the Advisory Board is charged with monitoring the health of the OASDHI programs and trust funds and making recommendations to improve the system. The Advisory Board has provided a convincing list of reasons why action should be taken *now:*

• More choices are available.
• Phasing in changes gradually will be less burdensome for workers and/or beneficiaries.
• Costs can be spread more evenly over more generations of workers and beneficiaries.
• There will be more advanced notice for retirement planning.
• Confidence in Social Security's ability to pay benefits to future generations will be strengthened.
• Individuals and families will have more time to make decisions about consumption and savings.
• There will be less labor market disruption. For example, advanced notice about payroll tax increases can help employers plan for the size of their workforce.[56]

The Social Security trustees also recommend taking action soon.

Congress has amended the Social Security Act many times to address financial and other important concerns of the Social Security system. It has never allowed the system to break its promises to the public, and it is unthinkable that it would ever do so. The Advisory Board recommended that any reforms to the Social Security system be integrated with measures to strengthen other parts of individuals' retirement plans, such as private pensions and private investments.

To resolve political impasses over fixing Social Security, former U.S. Treasury Secretary Robert Rubin suggests a bipartisan process like that used to pass the 1983 Social Security amendments: The president and Democratic and Republican heads of the Senate and House of Representatives would work together to develop a plan and send their recommendations to Congress as a package that is not subject to amendments.[57] The *Christian Science Monitor* reported that President Obama tried to form a bipartisan commission early in his presidency but some Democrats opposed it.[58] With problems like a major recession and health insurance reform on the table, addressing Social Security has not been the focus of attention, but it will return to the forefront. Younger Americans in particular should be thinking about the kind of Social Security program they want for their future.

PUBLIC POLICY AND PRIVATE PENSIONS

This chapter has focused on Social Security—the social insurance or publicly sponsored leg of the three-legged retirement savings stool. We now turn to the second leg—pension income—and the third leg—personal savings and investments, because public policy (or its absence) is also important to them.

Many employers, especially governments and large corporations, provide employees with pension plans. Employers contribute to these plans on the employee's behalf. Usually the employee can contribute, too. One type of employer-sponsored pension is *defined benefit plans.*[59] At retirement, the employer guarantees the employee a fixed (prescribed) amount for life based on a formula outlined in the plan. The contributions are invested, but regardless of how well the investments perform, the employer is required to pay employees at the prescribed rate.

To protect employees should an employer go bankrupt and does not have sufficient defined benefit plan funds, or if the employer would have to shut down if its defined benefit plan was not terminated, Congress established the federal Pension Benefit Guaranty Corporation (PBGC) under the Employee Retirement Income and Security Act of 1974. The PBGC is funded entirely by insurance premiums paid by employers who have defined benefit plans for their employees. To participate in the PBGC, the defined benefit plan must meet the requirements of Section 401 of the Internal Revenue Code. The guarantee applies only to benefits employees earned *before* bankruptcy or plan termination. The amount the PBGC guarantees is limited by law and likely will be only part of the benefits due employees.

Many employers have moved away from defined benefit plans because they are so costly. The 2006 Pension Protection Act (PPA) was designed to strengthen defined benefit plans, but rather than encouraging companies to offer these plans, its stringent rules are causing more employers to choose *defined contribution plans* in which the employer contributes, but the employee bears all the risks of the investment. The PBGC does not insure defined contribution plans. If you have heard people talk about their 401(k) plan, they are probably referring to their employer's defined contribution plan. Employees can often take their investment in these plans with them if they change jobs, unlike defined benefit plans. But many people do not enroll in these voluntary 401(k) plans. One suggestion to shore up retirement funds is to automatically enroll employees in these plans; they can then opt out if they wish.

The vast majority of people with defined contribution plans are still reeling from the effects of the country's 2008 investment market collapse. They wonder why there was not better oversight of public and private mortgage companies and of the Securities and Exchange Commission to prevent the losses investors suffered.

About half of U.S. workers have no private pension plan through their employer,[60] but they may be able to save for retirement with an individual retirement account (IRA). Generally, workers are permitted to contribute monies tax-free during their working years up to specified amounts. When monies are withdrawn at retirement, they are subject to taxes as they are in most other types of retirement accounts. IRAs are particularly important for those who do not have employer-sponsored pension programs.

What about the third leg of the stool—other personal savings and investments? Apparently, many Americans are not saving what they need for retirement, and they grossly underestimate what they will need to retire. By some measures, Americans are saving less than those in other major industrialized countries, and the U.S. personal saving rate has fallen to Great Depression era levels (less than one percent of disposable personal income in 2005 and 2006).[61] Nearly one-third of workers have no money set aside for retirement.[62] If projections are correct, Generation Xers will be less prepared financially for retirement than the baby boomers. Without saving more or working longer, the "retirement savings crisis" will worsen due to factors we have already discussed such as decreases in the number of workers covered by defined benefit plans and increases in life expectancy and retirement periods.[63] Public policies that help boost private retirement savings among lower- and middle-income Americans, such as substantial tax breaks and even savings matching programs, might put Americans in better fiscal shape at retirement.

UNEMPLOYMENT INSURANCE

Another major social insurance program—unemployment insurance (sometimes called unemployment compensation)—provides a temporary income to many individuals recently unemployed through no fault of their own and helps stabilize the economy during recessions. To accomplish this, the federal government requires employers to pay into state-administered unemployment insurance programs that meet federal standards, but the states have considerable flexibility in shaping their own programs.

Until unemployment insurance was first adopted in 1935 as part of the original Social Security Act, losing one's job could have meant sheer destitution. Most families depended on the support of one worker—usually the father. If he lost his job, the family's income was immediately reduced to zero. Today many U.S. families benefit from the earnings of more than one worker. Unemployment is still serious, but a second income can provide a buffer against economic disaster. Unemployment insurance (and public assistance programs like the Supplemental Nutrition Assistance Program) can reduce hardship when unemployment lasts for more than a short time. These changes have had an important effect on the motivations and expectations of unemployed Americans. Unemployment insurance is not a protection against long-term or "hard-core" unemployment, but it is can keep Americans afloat between jobs, especially during bad economic times. Unemployed workers may now decide to pass up, at least for a while, low-paying or undesirable jobs in the hope of finding jobs that pay more and make better use of their skills.[64] But unemployment spells are getting longer, and workers are concerned that it is harder to find good jobs.

To receive unemployment insurance benefits, unemployed workers must complete the application process and show that they are willing, able, and ready to work. In practice, this means that unemployed workers must register with the U.S. Employment Service (usually located in the same building as the state's unemployment insurance office), actively seek work, and accept a "suitable" job if found. Suitability is generally defined in terms of risks to health, safety, and morals, as well as the individual's physical capabilities; prior education, work experience, and earnings; the likelihood of obtaining employment in one's customary line of work; and distance to the job. As the unemployment period grows, the unemployment insurance program may expect workers to consider to a wider range of job options. One's own dwindling financial reserves may have the same affect.

States cannot deny benefits to unemployed workers for refusing to work as strikebreakers or refusing to work at jobs where the pay or other conditions are substantially less favorable than similar jobs in the area. They also cannot deny benefits for refusing to take jobs that require union membership, and they cannot deny benefits solely because a woman is pregnant (however, attempts to allow workers to obtain unemployment insurance while taking leave from work under the Family and Medical Leave Act have been unsuccessful).

Most decisions about eligibility requirements, benefit amounts, and how long benefits are paid are left to the states, but, in all states, unemployment insurance is temporary, usually a maximum of 26 weeks of regular coverage financed by the states, and sometimes 13 weeks of extended coverage financed by both the federal and state governments. When unemployment is high, Congress generally extends benefits. For example, in 2002 and 2003, Congress extended unemployment benefits an additional 13 weeks (for a total of 39 weeks). And again, in 2008, when the country's economic situation had worsened, benefits were extended twice. The first extension was for an additional 13 weeks. The second extension was for either seven more weeks or 13 more weeks in states with the highest unemployment rates, bringing the total to either 46 or 59 weeks of coverage. This occurred as unemployment claims hit a 16-year high, and some states unemployment insurance coffers faced exhaustion. A similar extension of either 14 or 20 weeks was passed in 2009 as the national unemployment rate reached 10.2 percent, and again in 2010, Congress made more provisions to extend benefits. Some states also made their own provisions for extended benefits.

Under the Federal Unemployment Tax Act (FUTA), employers' taxes are placed in a federal unemployment trust fund that contains an account for each state plus accounts for groups such as federal employees. Currently, the federal government requires that employers pay 6.2 percent of the first $7,000 that each employee earns ($434 a year per employee).[65] States with no delinquent federal loans get back 5.4 percent. The funds the federal government keeps cover federal program administration costs, pay for half the federal-state extended benefit program, and fund a loan account states can use if their trust funds become exhausted.

The states pay regular state unemployment claims and half of the claims for the federal-state extended benefits program. The states vary in both the taxable wage base and the tax rate they use to fund their programs. Forty-four states use a wage base higher than that mandated by the federal government. Three states also tax employees' wages.[66] The states determine their tax rates based on an employer's unemployment (layoff) history; these rates range from zero to 10.96 percent. The states also determine the weekly benefit amounts to be paid to unemployed workers. In 2008, maximum allowable weekly benefits ranged from $230 in Mississippi to $600 to $900 in Massachusetts (where benefits are also based on the employees' number of dependents). Unemployment insurance benefits have risen, but, on average, they replace slightly less than half of national average earnings.[67] In 2007, approximately 7.5 million workers received a total of $32.2 billion in benefits,[68] and an average weekly benefit of about $288.[69]

Gaps in Unemployment Insurance Programs

Although nearly all wage and salary workers have unemployment insurance protection, an estimated 60 percent of unemployed people do *not* receive unemployment benefits.[70] Many of them are "exhaustees"—not a bad name since most people feel exhausted after pounding the pavement or the Internet looking for work for 26 weeks or more. Exhaustees are actually individuals who have used all the benefits to which they were entitled and still have not found work. Others did not earn enough or did not work at their last job long enough to qualify, or they utilized the weeks of benefits to which they were entitled during an earlier spell of unemployment. Still others are unemployed for relatively short periods and do not bother to apply for benefits. States have also tightened eligibility rules, making more people ineligible for unemployment benefits.[71] Workers who were fired for poor job performance or misconduct or who leave their jobs voluntarily, including strikers, are not eligible for unemployment insurance.

Unemployment insurance covers a higher proportion of lower earners' wages than higher earners' wages, but lower-wage workers do not qualify for unemployment insurance as often as higher-wage workers, even though their unemployment rates are higher (and they may need financial assistance the most). Urban Institute researchers found that among the unemployed in 2006, 22 percent of low-wage working families reported receiving unemployment insurance compared to 33 of middle-income earners and 39 percent of high-income earners.[72]

Lower-wage workers change jobs more often and are more often employed part-time, which may not give them the work time or earnings needed to qualify for unemployment insurance benefits.[73] The Government Accountability Office (GAO) also found that low-wage workers were 2.5 times more likely than higher-wage workers to be unemployed, but that low-wage workers were half as likely to get unemployment insurance even when they had worked as long and had been employed full-time.[74] The retail and service sectors where many low wage workers are employed have the lowest rate of unemployment insurance receipt. Part-time workers who generally earn lower wages, have less employment skills, and less job security, are also far less likely to get unemployment benefits. In addition, although employers pay into the system on behalf of part-time workers, most states require that those receiving unemployment benefits be willing to accept full-time work.

Modernizing Unemployment Insurance

Unemployment insurance programs have not kept pace with changes in the structure of employment such as temporary and contingent work and the introduction of large numbers of women in the workforce.[75] Unemployment insurance could better help unemployed Americans by counting more months of higher earnings in calculating benefits. Benefits could also be provided to those who became unemployed and must resort to part-time work when they want full-time work or only desire or can only take part-time work, and to those who leave jobs due to pregnancy, domestic violence, disability, care of a family member, or because they are training for new work.[76]

Some states have taken steps to improve their response to unemployed workers by covering groups such as these. The federal government could provide incentives to states to spur such reforms, or it could mandate that states enact such reforms. The idea of federal mandates generally draws strong opposition. Objections arise when the federal government tells the states what to do, especially when the states are largely responsible for the program and believe that the required reforms are too costly. States also point out that programs through the Supplemental Nutrition Assistance Program (SNAP), Temporary Assistance for Needy Families program, and the state's workforce commission are also available to help people secure work. In addition, states differ considerably in their employment and unemployment pictures, requiring different approaches, and some states have already moved ahead with reforms that fit the specifics of their economic situation and workforce.

The federal government has not mandated that states modernize their unemployment insurance programs. Instead, as part of the American Recovery and Reinvestment Act of 2009, the states have been offered millions of dollars in additional, temporary funding as incentives for expanding their unemployment insurance programs. Whether to accept the additional funding has caused controversies in some states. Some individuals believe that once states change the laws that govern eligibility to help more people during the recession, it will be difficult to revert back to the old rules. States will then be required to increase payroll taxes on employers or take other steps to support the enhanced unemployment insurance programs. Employers usually balk at increased taxes, claiming that this will prevent them from creating new jobs or cause them to lay-off workers.

To boost funding for their unemployment insurance programs, states could also utilize more levels of taxation based on an employer's layoff history (which may further discourage workers from laying off employees).[77] The taxable wage base could also be increased, which would make the tax less regressive, and in combination with lower tax rates may encourage employers to hire more less-skilled workers.

The federal government could also make its own changes. Technically, federal law includes an automatic extended benefits program when unemployment is high, but it is so difficult for states to meet the unemployment rates to qualify that the program has, for all intents and purposes, become defunct. In addition, extensions are primarily a response to national unemployment rates. They are not very sensitive to differences in unemployment in particular locales that may be economically depressed even when their state's or the nation's overall unemployment rate is low. Rather than take action each time the economy wanes, Congress could make it easier for states, or even smaller jurisdictions, to qualify for the automatic extended benefits program.

Three Types of Unemployment

U.S. unemployment rates have fluctuated considerably during the past century. The worst of times occurred during the Great Depression of the 1930s when unemployment was estimated to be between 20 and 30 percent and in the early 1980s when unemployment rates exceeded 10 percent in some months. The best of times occurred during the 1950s when unemployment reached lows of 2.5 to 3.5 percent and in the late 1960s and early in the new century when unemployment dipped below 4 percent in some months. Figure 5.2 shows recent fluctuations in the unemployment rate. The economic crisis that struck in the later part of the century's first decade took a severe toll. By October 2009, 15.6 million Americans were unemployed, constituting a U.S. unemployment rate of 10.2 percent, the highest rate since 1983.[78] Nine states had unemployment rates of at least 10 percent with Michigan leading at 15.1 percent.

There is some unavoidable minimum unemployment. In a large, free economy, hundreds of thousands of people move and change jobs and temporarily find themselves unemployed. This

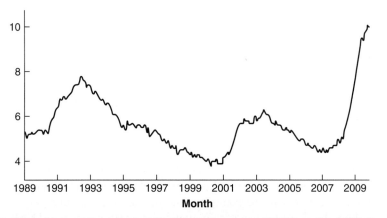

FIGURE 5.2 Unemployment Rate: Seasonally Adjusted, January 1989-December 2009 *Source:* Labor Force Statistics from the Current Population Survey (Washington, DC: Bureau of Labor Statistics). Retrieved February 9, 2010, from http://www.bls.gov/data/#unemployment

is called *frictional* unemployment. A second type is *cyclical* unemployment, which increases when the economy is doing poorly and more people lose their jobs and can't find work. Many of these individuals return to work when the economy improves. But others are unemployed for long periods due to poor job skills, ill health, or limited intellectual capacities, or because they live in areas with few job opportunities. This third type is called *structural* unemployment and is the most difficult to address. During nonrecession periods, frictional unemployment was estimated to be about half of the total unemployment. Structural unemployment was estimated to be less than 20 percent. Today, given technological and other labor market changes, structural factors have outpaced cyclical factors as causes of unemployment.[79]

Who Gets Counted as Unemployed?

Each month the U.S. Department of Labor estimates the percentage of the workforce that is out of work and actively seeking jobs (state and local unemployment figures are calculated differently). This official unemployment rate is based on a survey of about 60,000 households and includes those 16 years of age and older.[80] The Labor Department is often criticized because many of the downtrodden are never counted as unemployed. "Marginally attached" workers want to work, are available for work, and have looked for a job some time in the prior 12 months, but only those who have actively looked for a job in the four weeks prior to the unemployment survey are included in the official unemployment rate. In December 2009, there were approximately 2.5 million marginally attached workers; 929,000 of them were "discouraged workers."[81] These discouraged workers believe there are no jobs available for them and have given up looking for work. Including all marginally attached workers would increase the official unemployment rate.

The Labor Department used to be criticized because it counted part-time workers as fully employed. Those who worked 35 hours a week or more were counted as full-time workers even if they worked at more than one job and even if they wanted a full-time job. In 1994, the household survey was modified to address this and other issues. Part-time jobs often pay lower (hourly) wages and workers often do not receive fringe benefits. An excess of part-time employment is an indicator that the economy is not performing as well as the country would like.

At any given time, the number of individuals working part-time (fewer than 35 hours per week) rather than full-time and who are working for noneconomic reasons (in school, family obligations, etc.) outpaces the number who are working part-time for economic reasons (slack work or business conditions). In hard economic times, the proportion working part-time for economic reasons increases. If those working part-time for economic reasons were combined with marginally attached workers and included in official figures, the unemployment rate would also be higher.

A figure that remains totally unaccounted for is the number of people who are *underemployed.* Underemployment occurs when people work at jobs for which they are overqualified, but have taken due to need rather than preference. These jobs also tend to pay less than workers may be capable of earning.

How much unemployment is too much? There is an old saying: "When your neighbor is unemployed, it's a recession. When *you* are unemployed, it's a depression." Most controversy over measuring unemployment centers on underestimates of unemployment, although some believe the estimates are too high. For example, some people receiving unemployment insurance may not be looking that hard for work.[82] To qualify for programs such as SNAP, able-bodied individuals must sign up with the state employment office in their area. It has been argued that this artificially inflates unemployment, because some public assistance beneficiaries do not really intend to seek work.[83] Welfare reform has probably mitigated this effect, since many public assistance recipients must now meet more stringent work requirements in exchange for their checks.

It is also important to examine unemployment among subgroups of the population. In good economic times or bad, African Americans' unemployment rate is usually at least double that for whites. In 2008, the unemployment rate averaged 4.0 percent for Asians, 5.2 percent for whites, 7.6 percent for Hispanics, and 10.1 percent for blacks.[84] (All these figures increased in 2009 as the economic recession worsened.) The teenage (16 to 19 years old) unemployment rate is often three times higher than the rate for the general population. The highest unemployment rate of all is for African American teens. Since the 1990s, women's unemployment rates have been at least slightly lower than men's (prior to that women's unemployment was higher), but women are concentrated in lower-paying jobs.

The unemployment picture would improve considerably if jobs and unemployed workers were better matched. This could be done in at least two ways. First, more high quality and intensive job training and retraining programs could be offered to help workers with limited or outdated skills learn skills that employers are seeking (also see Chapter 9). Second, those unable to find employment near their homes could be encouraged or assisted to relocate to areas where jobs are available. Employers often provide relocation assistance to higher-paid workers but not to low-wage earners, who may need this assistance the most. As U.S. companies have increasingly located operations in other countries, a vigorous debate has ensued about the effects of this "offshoring" and the strategies needed to ensure sufficient jobs for Americans in the increasingly global economic environment.

Once the economic recession that began in the late 2000s abates and the economy stabilizes again, future demographic trends may help to ease unemployment. During the 1970s and 1980s, the large population of baby boomers entered the labor market, contributing to unemployment. But as the boomers retire, there will be more room for younger people in the workforce, particularly blacks, Hispanics, and immigrants, who will contribute substantially to new labor force additions. The preparation of future workers is crucial, because the bulk of new jobs with good salaries and fringe benefits will require a highly skilled workforce. Those without solid qualifications will continue to comprise the ranks of the poor and the unemployed.

WORKERS' COMPENSATION

Workers' compensation (not to be confused with unemployment insurance) is a social insurance program that provides medical benefits and often cash payments to workers who are injured on the job or develop job-related diseases. Benefits are also provided to survivors of workers killed in job-related accidents. Although workers' compensation does not get the same kind of public attention as the much larger Social Security program, it is a critical safety net component for those seriously hurt at work, and it faces similar policy challenges.

Each state is entirely responsible for the laws governing workers' compensation program in its jurisdiction, and each state's labor department administers the program. The federal government is responsible for programs that cover federal employees and certain categories of workers (coal miners permanently disabled by black lung disease, longshore and harbor workers, and those involved in producing and testing nuclear weapons).[85] The U.S. Department of Labor's Office of Workers' Compensation administers these federal programs. The U.S. Department of Veterans Affairs administers a separate program for disabled veterans. Self-employed workers are not covered by workers' compensation.

Following Germany's lead and then England's, the United States adopted a program to provide workers' compensation to some federal employees in 1908.[86] The first state "workers' comp" programs were initiated in Wisconsin and New Jersey in 1911; all states had programs by 1948.[87] Workers' compensation programs emerged as state efforts because businesses wanted control closer to home.

Workers' compensation programs are considered a major achievement of business and labor.[88] Before their enactment, most workers' only recourse when injured or disabled at work was to sue on the basis of employer negligence. The process was often lengthy and expensive. Employers' generally claimed that the injury resulted from an ordinary employment hazard or employee negligence. Employers usually won in litigation, but they were still subject to cases in which an employee could win a large settlement. Today, unemployment compensation programs provide employees a way to obtain compensation quickly and employers a way to limit their liability.

Workers' compensation is intended to provide wages lost to injury or disease and to make the worker "whole" rather than to compensate for "pain and suffering" or achieve a broader concept of justice.[89] There are appeals processes, but except in unusual circumstances, employees or their survivors are prevented from suing the employer. Who is at fault is generally not an issue, but employees are usually not entitled to benefits if they were injured due to their own intoxication or willful misconduct.

Issues in Workers' Compensation

Workers' compensation is intended to limit litigation, but in recent years, litigation has increased.[90] Workers and their employers may disagree on the severity of an injury or illness and the treatment and recuperation period needed. Claims make take years to settle. Compared to traumatic injury cases that occur on the job, disease-related cases can be difficult to prove because the disease may have developed over a long time, the employee may have had multiple employers, or the cause of the disease may not be clear. Medical problems that take time to manifest are also problematic because workers' compensation programs may include time limits on filing claims. New classes of injuries or disabilities that arise (e.g., repetitive motion disorders like carpal tunnel syndrome), must also be addressed.

Although there are many common aspects of workers' compensation programs, they do vary considerably across states with regard to factors such as how disabilities are evaluated and compensated. There is currently no federally mandated reporting of workers' compensation program data. The National Academy of Social Insurance (NASI) uses various sources to estimate program characteristics and trends.[91] The vast majority of workers have unemployment compensation coverage. Most workers are also protected against short-term illness and disability through sick time paid by their employers, but 30 percent of workers have no protection from temporary illness or disability other than workers' compensation. In all states except Texas, most private employers must participate in the workers' compensation program. In Texas, 77 percent of workers are covered because their employers do participate, and injured employees can sue employers who do not participate.

Administrative and legal expediency has resulted in the development of aids such as schedules that equate particular injuries with a given number of weeks of compensation. Workers' compensation payments are usually calculated as two-thirds of the worker's weekly wages at the time of illness or injury, although the maximum weekly amount is capped. These maximum payments vary widely by jurisdiction and are usually more generous in federal programs than in state programs. Differences in factors such as workforce composition and average wages make it difficult to compare programs across states, but in 2006, weekly payments to permanently and totally disabled former workers ranged from a high of $1,173 in Illinois and Iowa to a low of $351 in Mississippi.[92]

Descriptions of workers' compensation programs suggest that benefits are supposed to be adequate, but wages are replaced at less than their full value in order to encourage workers to return to work and to discourage workers from filing fraudulent claims. The Insurance Information Institute calls some states' benefits "inadequate" and others "overly generous," and notes an imbalance in some states that overcompensate in permanent partial disability cases and undercompensate in permanent total disability cases.[93]

Like Social Security Disability Insurance and Medicare, workers' compensation can help when disabilities are long-term or permanent and total (as long as they are work-related). Workers' compensation is especially important, because unlike Social Security, it also helps with short-term disabilities and long-term partial disabilities. Most injured employees recuperate quickly and receive only medical benefits. They constitute 77 percent of workers' compensation cases but account for only 6 percent of all benefits paid. The other 23 percent of cases involve cash and medical benefits and account for 94 percent of costs.[94] Workers who die or sustain permanent and total disabilities are one percent of cases. Totally and permanently disabled workers may receive both workers' compensation and Social Security benefits. Benefits are adjusted to keep them in line with the worker's past earnings.

Employers bear the costs of unemployment compensation programs. Most employers insure their workers through a private insurance company; others self-insure; and, in some cases, the state insures employers. Employers' premiums are based on the hazardousness of the work involved and their safety record. Due to the risks involved in some industries, employers may not be able to obtain private coverage and must resort to state-operated "high-risk pools."

Averaged nationally, in 2008, employers paid 1.7 percent of their payroll to fund workers' compensation programs.[95] In 2006, employers paid nearly $88 billion into workers' compensation programs.[96] Benefits paid to workers or their survivors totaled about $55 billion with about half going to cash payments to workers and half going to their medical care. Nationally, the total cost of cash and medical benefits declined 1.5 percent from 2004 to 2005. This was largely due to declines in cash and medical payments in the populous state of California. Many states have seen increases in unemployment compensation costs.

The number of work-related fatalities has increased in recent years, while the Bureau of Labor Statistics' survey of private-sector employees indicates substantial reductions over time in the much larger number of nonfatal accidents.[97] Technology (e.g., robots, power-assisted devices, and cordless tools) has helped to reduce workplace accidents.[98] There is also greater emphasis on workplace safety with employers and insurers often required to undertake specific safety activities such as accident prevention programs or safety committees. Eligibility standards for obtaining benefits have also become stricter. In addition, a substantial number of injured workers never file for benefits. Among the reasons cited are that employees may not know they are covered; fear retaliation from their employer; believe that obtaining benefits is difficult, stressful, or not worth the risks; or may not realize that an injury or illness is work-related (especially those that take time to develop).[99]

Along with the number of workplace accidents, the number of claims has dropped, but the dollar amount of claims has increased, with medical costs rising faster in workers' compensation cases than in general healthcare.[100] In recent years, some states workers' compensation programs have faced increased costs of claims, rapidly rising insurance rates, and large program deficits in addition to other concerns. One columnist summarized the problems this way:

> Organized labor says too many injured workers are denied adequate compensation and face too much resistance from insurance companies on claims. Business complains that too many doctors and chiropractors play the system for maximum profit rather than focus on getting an injured worker back on the job. Doctors face so much hassle justifying treatment that many of them have simply quit accepting workers' compensation patients. The cost of health care itself—as it has for everyone—continues to climb rapidly.[101]

Modernizing Workers' Compensation

States have used a variety of means to control medical costs in their workers' compensation cases such as fee schedules that limit what will be paid for medical care, utilization reviews and treatment plan coordination, evidence-based medical treatment guidelines, and limiting physician choice.[102] These types of reforms have been credited with substantial reductions in program costs in California. Another idea for modernizing workers' compensation is to coordinate or integrate it with the group healthcare and disability insurance plans that employers offer.[103]

In addition to efforts to evaluate cases fairly and reduce fraudulent claims, more attention has been paid to encouraging workers to return to employment as quickly as possible using the vocational rehabilitation system (see Chapter 6) when needed. A quick return to work is seen as beneficial to the employee as well as to the employer. The longer an employee is out of work, the greater the costs to the employer and the lower the likelihood that the employee will return to work.[104] Emphasis is on initiating treatment and rehabilitation early, making the system easy to navigate, reducing emotional stress, and keeping the employee attached to and integrated in the workplace, all of which can also limit attorney involvement and litigation.[105]

As with other social welfare concerns, greater consistency could be achieved through a federal program,[106] but there is no indication of a movement in this direction. In 1972 the National Commission on State Workmen's Compensation Laws issued 19 recommendations considered essential to improve programs.[107] Although many states improved their programs,[108] many have not adopted all the recommendations. Some states still exempt employers that employ only a few workers, and benefit levels often fall below standards the commission recommended.

A primary reason that states are concerned about their programs is that businesses may consider the workers' compensation environment in deciding where to locate. Programs are faced with balancing the interests of injured workers (and in some cases their attorneys), employers, insurers, medical providers, and states trying to keep their systems afloat. When policy changes result in escalating worker' compensation costs, there is a call to make additional changes so that the state's economy will not be adversely affected.[109] Technically, the employer bears the cost of participating in the workers' compensation program, but any cost of doing business is thought to take away from wages that employers might potentially pay their workers. Therefore, there are many incentives to operate unemployment compensation efficiently and to treat employees fairly.

Summary

Social insurance programs are a primary strategy for preventing poverty among workers and retirees and their dependents or survivors. Rather than build large reserves in the Social Security retirement and disability trust funds as originally intended, Social Security developed into a pay-as-you-go program as funds were used to invigorate the economy, life expectancy increased, and payments were continually raised to keep pace with the cost of living. Many changes have been made to keep the program solvent, but deeper structural changes may be needed to maintain the system for the decades ahead given the large numbers of retirees who will start drawing benefits. The challenge is how to do this while maintaining the adequacy and equity of the current social insurance system. Social Security needs fixing, but it is the nation's most effective antipoverty effort, and it will remain the country's most important social welfare program for years to come.

Unemployment insurance, another important social insurance program that is funded by a tax paid by employers, helps workers with short-term unemployment. Unemployment insurance programs have not kept pace with the changing composition of the workforce, and extended benefits are often not available to unemployed workers in locales with high unemployment because state and national unemployment rates may be much lower and do not trigger the needed benefits. The state workers' compensation programs are also social insurance programs funded by a tax on employers. Workers' compensation assists workers who are injured or become ill in work-related situations. The program is especially important because it provides medical and cash benefits in cases of temporary and partial disabilities as well as total and permanent disabilities. In addition to preventing injury or illness in the first place, these programs also need modernizing to see that injured or ill workers get the services they need to return to work as quickly as possible. The social insurance programs remain the bedrock of the U.S. social welfare system.

Discussion Questions and Class Activities

1. Discuss the many options for reform of the Social Security system (see Illustration 5.3 in this chapter). Read articles on the subject and talk with people of various age groups to get their views on the current Social Security program and how they think it should be changed for the future. Which options do you think are most feasible?
2. Read Illustration 5.2: Will You Have Enough to Retire? Think about how much you might earn over your lifetime. Go to the Social Security website and calculate your potential Social Security retirement benefits. How much do you think you will need in pension or personal savings to live comfortably in retirement?
3. Go to the Bureau of Labor Statistics website and compare your state's unemployment rate with other states. Why is it higher or lower than other states? Learn about your state's unemployment insurance or unemployment compensation program. How does it compare with other states' programs with regard to benefits and coverage? For example, are part-time workers covered? Has the program changed recently in response to economic stimulus funds the federal government has offered to encourage states to modernize their unemployment insurance programs? Do you think your state's program should be modified? If so, how?
4. Learn about your state's workers' compensation program. How does it compare with other states' programs with regard to methods for determining disability, payment levels, and other features? Do you think the program should be modified in any ways?

Websites

The Bureau of Labor Statistics (a division of the U.S. Department of Labor), http://www.bls.gov, provides a wealth of data on employment, the labor force, unemployment, and related topics.

The National Academy of Social Insurance, http://www.nasi.org, is a nonpartisan, nonprofit organization comprised of social insurance experts dedicated to increasing understanding of how the broad range of social insurance and related programs

"contribute to economic security and a vibrant economy."

Social Security Online, http://www.ssa.gov, is the official website of the Social Security Administration. It provides a wealth of information on the Old Age, Survivors, and Disability Insurance programs and the Supplemental Security Income program, including program data and tools for program participants.

Notes

1. Thomas Paine, "Agrarian Justice," 1797. Retrieved January 14, 2009 from Social Security Administration, "Social Security History Page," http://www.ssa.gov/history/tpaine3.html
2. Eric R. Kingson and Edward D. Berkowitz, *Social Security and Medicare: A Policy Primer* (Westport, CT: Auburn House, 1993), pp. 29–37.
3. Although most Americans may not expect to become public assistance recipients, analyses indicate that by age 65, 65 percent of Americans will have received some form of public assistance. See Mark R. Rank, *One Nation Underprivileged: Why Poverty in America Affects Us All* (New York: Columbia University Press, 2004).
4. Kingson and Berkowitz, *Social Security and Medicare: A Policy Primer,* p. 33.
5. Joseph A. Pechman, Henry J. Aaron, and Michael K. Taussig, *Social Security: Perspectives for Reform* (Washington, DC: Brookings Institution, 1968).
6. See Andrew W. Dobelstein, *Understanding the Social Security Act:* The Foundation of Social Welfare for America in the Twenty-first Century (New York: Oxford University Press, 2009).
7. *Social Security Basic Facts* (Washington, DC: Social Security Administration, August 5, 2009). Retrieved January 25, 2010, from http://www.socialsecurity.gov/pressoffice/basicfact.htm
8. *Ibid.*
9. Wilbur J. Cohen, *Social Security: The Compromise and Beyond* (Washington, DC: Save Our Security Education Fund, 1983), pp. 4-5.
10. *Cost-of-Living Adjustments* (Washington, DC: Social Security Administration, October 15, 2009).

Retrieved January 25, 2010, from http://www.ssa.gov/OACT/COLA/colaseries.html
11. Dan Muldoon and Richard W. Kopcke, *Are People Claiming Social Security Later?*" (Boston: Trustees of Boston College, Center for Retirement Research, June 2008). Retrieved January 14, 2009 from http://crr.bc.edu/images/stories/ib_8-7.pdf
12. Jeanne Sahadi, "A Retirement Mistake Boomers Should Avoid," CNNMoney.com, June 6 2007. Retrieved July 24, 2008, from http://money.cnn.com/2007/06/06/pf/retirement/social_security_early/index.htm; also see Carrie Schwab-Pomerantz, "Social Security Benefits: Timing Can Make A Difference" (Charles Schwab & Co., Inc., 2009). Retrieved May 13, 2010, from http://www.creators.com/lifestylefeatures/business-and-finance/money-and-you/social-security-benefits-timing-can-make-a-difference.html
13. Scott S. Burns, "Tax on Social Security Benefits Snares More Retirees Each Year," *Austin American-Statesman,* August 12, 2008, p. D2; "Changing the Income Tax Treatment of Social Security Benefits" (Washington, DC: Urban Institute, 2010). Retrieved February 8, 2010, from http://www.urban.org/retirement_policy/ssincometax.cfm
14. *Social Security: Understanding the Benefits, 2009* (Washington, DC: Social Security Administration, January 2009), SSA Publication No. 05-10024. Retrieved January 14, 2009, from http://www.socialsecurity.gov/pubs/10024.pdf
15. For a more detailed description of the 1983 reforms, see "Report of the National Commission on Social Security Reform," *Social Security Bulletin,* Vol. 46, No. 2, 1983, pp. 3–38. For more on House and Senate

action, see "Social Security Rescue Plan Swiftly Approved," *1983 Congressional Quarterly Almanac* (Washington, DC: Congressional Quarterly, 1984), pp. 219–226. For a concise consideration of the changes adopted, see Wilbur J. Cohen, "The Future Impact of the Social Security Amendments of 1983," *The Journal/The Institute of Socioeconomic Studies,* Vol. 8, No. 2, 1983, pp. 1–16.

16. OASDHI trust fund figures reported in this section are from *The 2009 Annual Report of the Board of Trustees of the Federal Old-Age and Survivors Insurance and the Federal Disability Insurance Trust Funds* (Washington, DC: Social Security Administration, March 15, 2009). Retrieved May 26, 2009, from http://www.ssa.gov/OACT/TR/2009/index.html; Social Security Administration, *Status of the Social Security and Medicare Programs,* May 12, 2009. Retrieved May 26, 2009, from http://www.ssa.gov/OACT/TRSUM/index.html.

17. Matt Homer, Elah Lanis, and Bernard Wasow, *Why Social Security Is Not In Crisis* (New York: The Century Foundation, 2008). Retrieved January 14, 2009, from http://www.tcf.org/Publications/RetirementSecurity/ScareTactics6-25-2008.pdf

18. See Marshall N. Carter and Williams G. Shipman, *Promises to Keep: Saving Social Security's Dream* (Washington, DC: Regnery Publishing, 1996), based on a Third Millennium Survey by Frank Lutz and Mark Siegel; Sam Beard, "Minimum-Wage Millionaires: The Capitalist Way to Save Social Security," *Policy Review,* No. 73, Summer 1995. Retrieved January 14, 2009, from http://www.hoover.org/publications/policyreview/3565567.html

19. *Social Security 70th Anniversary Survey Report: Trends Over Time* (Washington DC: American Association of Retired Persons, August 11, 2005). Retrieved January 14, 2009, from http://assets.aarp.org/rgcenter/econ/ss_70_anniv.pdf

20. Ruth Helman, Mathew Greenwald & Associates, Jack VanDerhei, and Craig Copeland, *The 2008 Retirement Confidence Survey: Americans Much More Worried About Retirement, Health Costs a Big Concern,* EBRI Issue Brief #316 (Washington, DC: Employee Benefit Research Institute, April 2008). Retrieved January 14, 2009, from http://ebri.matrixgroup.net/publications/ib/index.cfm?fa=ibDisp&content_id=3903

21. Eric R. Kingson, "Misconceptions Distort Social Security Policy Discussions," *Social Work,* Vol. 34, No. 4, 1989, pp. 357-362; also see Kingson and Berkowitz, *Social Security and Medicare: A Policy Primer;* Gordon Sherman, "Social Security: The Real Story," *National Forum, The Phi Kappa Phi Journal,* Vol. 78, No. 2, 1998, pp. 26–29.

22. *Social Security Basic Facts.*

23. Committee on Ways and Means, *2004 Green Book,* Appendix H: Data on Poverty (Washington, DC: U.S. House of Representatives, August 4, 2004), p. H-38. Retrieved January 14, 2009, from http://www.gpoaccess.gov/wmprints/green/2004.html

24. Data from the Social Security Administration as reported in Patterson Clark, "Will You Get Your Money's Worth?", *The Miami Herald,* August 13, 1995, p. 45.

25. *Social Security Basic Facts.*

26. Kingson and Berkowitz, *Social Security and Medicare: A Policy Primer,* p. 23; J. Douglas Brown, *Essays on Social Security* (Princeton, NJ: Princeton University Press, 1977), pp. 31–32.

27. Martha N. Ozawa, "Benefits and Taxes under Social Security: An Issue of Intergenerational Equity," *Social Work,* Vol. 29, No. 2, 1984, pp. 131–137.

28. U.S. Census Bureau, *POV01: Age and Sex of All People, Family Members and Unrelated Individuals Iterated by Income-to-Poverty Ratio and Race.* Retrieved January 25, 2010, from http://www.census.gov/hhes/www/cpstables/032009/pov/new01_000.htm

29. Henry J. Aaron, "Costs of the Aging Population: Real and Imagined Burdens," in Henry J. Aaron, Ed., *Social Security and the Budget: Proceedings of the First Conference of the National Academy of Social Insurance* (Lanham, MD: National Academy of Social Insurance and University Press of America, 1990), pp. 51–61. Also see Ellen M. McGee and Gloria M. Gutman, Eds., *The Overselling of Population Aging: Apocalyptic Demography, Intergenerational Challenges, and Social Policy* (Canada: Oxford University Press, 2000).

30. Philip J. Longman, "Costs of the Aging Population: Financing the Future," in Aaron, *Social Security and the Budget: Proceedings of the First Conference of the National Academy of Social Insurance,* p. 67.

31. Eric R. Kingson, Barbara A. Hirshorn, and John M. Cornman, *Ties That Bind: The Interdependency of Generations* (Washington, DC: Seven Locks Press, 1986).

32. Michael Tanner, "Disparate Impact: Social Security and African Americans," Briefing Paper No. 61, (Washington, DC: Cato Institute, February 5, 2001). Retrieved January 15, 2009, from http://www.cato.org/pubs/briefs/bp-061es.html; William W. Beach and Gareth E. Davis, Social Security's Rate of Return, *Center for Data Analysis Report #98-01* (Washington, DC: The Heritage Foundation January

15, 1998). Retrieved December 22, 2008, from http://www.heritage.org/Research/socialsecurity/CDA98-01.cfm; William W. Beach and Gareth G. Davis, Social Security's Rate of Return For Hispanic Americans, *Center for Data Analysis Report #98-02* (Washington, DC: The Heritage Foundation, March 27, 1998). Retrieved December 22, 2008, from http://www.heritage.org/Research/SocialSecurity/CDA98-02.cfm

33. For a discussion of these issues, see Bernard Wasow, *Setting the Record Straight: Social Security Works for Latinos* (New York: Century Foundation, May 2002). Retrieved January 15, 2009, from http://www.socsec.org/facts/Record_Straight/Latinos.pdf

34. William Spriggs and Jason Furman, *African Americans and Social Security: The Implications of Reform Proposals* (Washington, DC: Center on Budget and Policy Priorities, January 19, 2008). Retrieved July 28, 2008, from http://www.cbpp.org/1-18-06socsec.htm

35. National Committee to Preserve Social Security and Medicare, *Why Social Security Is Important to African Americans* (Washington, DC: Author, May 2008). Retrieved July 28, 2008, from http://www.ncpssm.org/news/archive/vp_africanamericans

36. Eric Kingson, "Misconceptions Distort Social Security Policy Discussions," *Social Work,* Vol. 34, No. 4, 1989, pp. 357–362; Bernard Wasow, *Setting the Record Straight: Two False Claims about African Americans and Social Security* (New York: Century Foundation, March 2002). Retrieved January 15, 2009, from http://www.socsec.org/facts/Record_Straight/African_Americans.pdf

37. Spriggs and Furman, *African Americans and Social Security: The Implications of Reform Proposals.*

38. National Committee to Preserve Social Security and Medicare, *Why Social Security Is Important to Hispanic and Latino Americans* (Washington, DC: Author, August 2008). Retrieved December 23, 2008 from http://www.ncpssm.org/news/archive/vp_hispanics/; National Education Association, *Social Security Privatization: A Bad Deal for Hispanic Communities* (Washington, DC: Author, February 2005). Retrieved May 6, 2009, from http://www.nea.org/home/16499.htm

39. League of United Latin American Citizens, *The Truth About Undocumented Immigration* (Washington, DC: Author, no date). Retrieved January 15, 2009, from http://www.lulac.org/advocacy/issues/immigration/truth.html; also see Paul N. Van de Water, *Immigration and Social Security* (Washington, DC: Center on Budget and Policy Priorities, November 20, 2008). Retrieved January 15, 2009, from http://www.cbpp.org/11-20-08socsec.htm

40. Joel Feinleib and David Warner, *The Impact of Immigration on Social Security and the National Economy,* Social Security Advisory Board Issue Brief #1 (Washington, DC: Social Security Advisory Board, December 2005). Retrieved January 15, 2009, from http://www.ssab.gov/documents/IMMIG_Issue_Brief_Final_Version_000.pdf

41. Van de Water, *Immigration and Social Security.*

42. Reported in Feinleib and Warner, *The Impact of Immigration on Social Security and the National Economy,* Social Security Advisory Board Issue Brief #1.

43. This paragraph relies on Social Security Administration, *Social Security Is Important to Women,* October 2008. Retrieved December 22, 2008, from http://www.socialsecurity.gov/pressoffice/factsheets/women.htm

44. U.S. Department of Health, Education and Welfare, *Social Security and the Changing Roles of Men and Women* (Washington, DC: U.S. Government Printing Office, February 1979), Chapters 1 & 2; also see Ekaterina Shirley and Peter Spiegler, *The Benefits of Social Security Privatization for Women,* SSP No. 12 (Washington, DC: Cato Institute, July 20, 1998). Retrieved January 15, 2009, from http://www.cato.org/pubs/ssps/ssp12.html

45. Richard Fry and D'Vera Cohn, *New Economics of Marriage: The Rise of Wives* (Washington, DC: Pew Research Center, January 19, 2010). Retrieved January 24, 2010 from http://pewresearch.org/pubs/1466/economics-marriage-rise-of-wives

46. U.S. Department of Health, Education and Welfare, *Social Security and the Changing Roles of Men and Women.*

47. *Ibid.*

48. Government Accountability Office, *Retirement Security: Women Face Challenges in Ensuring Financial Security in Retirement* (Washington, DC: Author, October 2007). Retrieved December 22, 2008, from http://www.gao.gov/new.items/d08105.pdf

49. Information on progressive price indexing relies on Jason Furman, *An Analysis of Using "Progressive Price Indexing" to Set Social Security Benefits* (Washington, DC: Center for Budget and Policy Priorities, May 2, 2005). Retrieved January 16, 2009, from http://www.cbpp.org/3-21-05socsec.htm

50. Ed Lorenzen, *Progressive Approaches to Benefit Changes in Social Security Reform* (Washington, DC: Centrists.Org, January 26, 2005). Retrieved January

16, 2009, from http://www.centrists.org/pages/2005/01/26_lorenzen_wealth.html

51. Advisory Council on Social Security, *Report of the 1994-1996 Advisory Council on Social Security* (Washington, DC: Social Security Administration, January, 1997). Retrieved January 17, 2009, from http://www.ssa.gov/history/reports/adcouncil/report/toc.htm

52. Michael Tanner, "The 6.2 Percent Solution: A Plan for Reforming Social Security" (Washington, DC: Cato Institute, February 17, 2004). Retrieved January 17, 2009, from http://www.socialsecurity.org/pubs/ssps/ssp-32es.html

53. Michael D. Tanner, *Personal Accounts for Social Security: Still the Best Deal* (Washington, DC: Cato Institute, October 31, 2008). Retrieved December 22, 2008, from http://www.cato-at-liberty.org/2008/10/31/personal-accounts-for-social-security-still-best-deal/

54. Social Security Advisory Board, *Social Security: Why Action Should Be Taken Soon (revised edition)* (Washington, DC: Author, July 2001), pp. 18–19. Retrieved January 17, 2009, from http://www.ssab.gov/Publications/Financing/actionshouldbetaken.pdf; Alan D. Viard, "Pay-as-you-go Social Security and the Aging of America: An Economic Analysis," *Economic and Financial Policy Review* (Dallas: Federal Reserve Bank of Dallas, 2002), Vol. 1, No. 4. Retrieved January 17, 2009, from http://www.dallasfed.org/research/efpr/pdfs/v01_n04_a01.pdf

55. See Richard W. Fischer, "Storms on the Horizon," Remarks before the Commonwealth Club of California, San Francisco, California, May 28, 2008. Retrieved January 17, 2009 from http://www.dallasfed.org/news/speeches/fisher/2008/fs080528.cfm

56. Social Security Advisory Board, *Social Security: Why Action Should Be Taken Soon (revised edition)*, pp. 14–15.

57. "Legacy Politics Could Save Social Security," *AARP Bulletin,* May 2007, p. 3.

58. David R. Francis, "Obama Faces Larger Problems than Social Security Shortfalls," *CSMonitor.com*, March 2, 2009. Retrieved May 8, 2009, from http://www.csmonitor.com/2009/0302/p15s01-wmgn.html

59. Much of this section relies on Pension Benefit Guarantee Corporation, "FAQs About PBGC." Retrieved January 2, 2009, from http://www.pbgc.gov/about/wrfaqs.html; Committee on Ways and Means, Section 14—"The Pension Benefit Guarantee Corporation," *2008 Green Book* (Washington, DC: U.S. House of Representatives, 2008). Retrieved January 2, 2009, from http://waysandmeans.house.gov/Documents.asp?section=2168

60. General Accountability Office, *Retirement Security: Women Face Challenges in Ensuring Financial Security in Retirement* (Washington, DC: Author, October 2007), p. 9. Retrieved January 17, 2009, from http://www.gao.gov/new.items/d08105.pdf

61. *Ibid.,* p. 10.

62. *Social Security Basic Facts.*

63. Alicia H. Munnell, Anthony Webb, and Francesca Golub-Sass, "Is There Really a Retirement Savings Crisis? An NRRI Analysis," August 2007, Number 7-11 (Boston: Trustees of Boston College, Center for Retirement Research). Retrieved June 16, 2010, from http://crr.bc.edu/index.php?option=com_content&task=view&id=466&Itemid=3

64. The remainder of this paragraph relies on Alan Krueger, "Insuring Against Recession," *Pathways,* Summer 2008 (Stanford, CA: Stanford University, The Center for the Study of Poverty and Inequality). Retrieved January 7, 2009, from http://www.stanford.edu/group/scspi/pdfs/pathways/summer_2008/Krueger.pdf

65. Employment and Training Administration, "Unemployment Insurance Tax Topic" (Washington, DC: U.S. Department of Labor, October 1, 2008). Retrieved January 5, 2009, from http://www.workforcesecurity.doleta.gov./unemploy/uitaxtopic.asp

66. Employment and Training Administration, "Significant Provisions of State Unemployment Insurance Laws" (Washington, DC: U.S. Department of Labor, October 22, 2008). Retrieved January 5, 2009, from http://www.workforcesecurity.doleta.gov./unemploy/content/sigpros/2000-present/July2008.asp; also see Margaret C. Simms and Daniel Kuehn, "Unemployment Insurance During a Recession" (Washington, DC: The Urban Institute, December 2008). Retrieved January 5, 2009 from http://www.urban.org/UploadedPDF/411808_unemployment_insurance.pdf

67. Simms and Kuehn, "Unemployment Insurance During a Recession."

68. *Ibid.*

69. Howard Rosen, "Unemployment Insurance Is in Desperate Need of Modernization" (Washington, DC: Urban Institute, July 16, 2008). Retrieved January 19, 2009, from http://www.urban.org/publications/411731.html

70. Simms and Kuehn, "Unemployment Insurance During a Recession."

71. *Ibid.*

72. *Ibid.*

73. *Ibid.* and Rosen, "Unemployment Insurance Is in Desperate Need of Modernization."

74. Government Accountability Office, "Unemployment Insurance: Low-Wage and Part-Time Workers Continue to Experience Low Rates of Receipt," GAO-07-1147 (Washington, DC: Author, September 7, 2007). Retrieved January 19, 2009, from http://www.gao.gov/products/GAO-07-1147

75. *Ibid.*

76. Krueger, "Insuring Against Recession"; Simms and Kuehn, "Unemployment Insurance During a Recession."

77. This paragraph relies on Krueger, "Insuring Against Recession."

78. "Regional and State Employment and Unemployment Summary" (Washington, DC: Bureau of Labor Statistics, November 20, 2009). Retrieved January 25, 2010, from http://www.bls.gov/news.release/archives/laus_11202009.pdf

79. Rosen, "Unemployment Insurance Is in Desperate Need of Modernization."

80. Bureau of Labor Statistics, *Handbook of Methods,* Chapter 1, "Labor Force Data Derived from the Current Population Survey" (Washington, DC: U.S. Department of Labor, April 17, 2003). Retrieved January 21, 2009, from http://www.bls.gov/opub/hom/homch1_b.htm

81. Bureau of Labor Statistics, "The Employment Situation: December 2009" (Washington, DC: U.S. Department of Labor, January 8, 2010). Retrieved January 25, 2010, from http://www.bls.gov/news.release/empsit.nr0.htm

82. Amity Shlaes, "Job Hunters Slack Off When Given a Helping Hand," Bloomberg.com, April 12, 2010. Retrieved May 13, 2010, from http://www.bloomberg.com/apps/news?pid=20601039&sid=aC1feyaZB9zU

83. Kenneth W. Clarkson and Roger E. Meiners, "Government Statistics As a Guide to Economic Policy: Food Stamps and the Spurious Rise in the Unemployment Rates," *Policy Review,* Vol. 1, 1977, pp. 27–51.

84. Economic News Release, Table A-2 and Table A-3, Bureau of Labor Statistics. Retrieved January 25, 2010 from http://www.bls.gov/news.release/empsit.t02.htm; http://www.bls.gov/news.release/empsit.t03.htm

85. For more information about federal workers' compensation programs, see Office of Workers' Compensation Programs, "About OWCP" (Washington, DC: U.S. Department of Labor). Retrieved January 16, 2009, from http://www.dol.gov/esa/owcp/index.htm

86. Ishita Sengupta, Virginia Reno, and John F. Burton, Jr., "Workers' Compensation: Benefits, Coverage, and Costs, 2006" (Washington, DC: National Academy of Social Insurance, August 2008). Retrieved January 15 2009, from http://www.nasi.org/publications2763/publications_show.htm?doc_id=702308

87. The remainder of this paragraph relies on Edward D. Berkowitz, *Disabled Policy: America's Programs for the Handicapped* (Cambridge, England: Cambridge University Press, 1987), pp. 15–16.

88. Much of this paragraph relies on Sengupta et al., "Workers' Compensation: Benefits, Coverage, and Costs, 2006"; also see Committee on Ways and Means, Section 15—"Workers' Compensation," *2008 Green Book* (Washington, DC: U.S. House of Representatives, 2008). Retrieved May 13, 2010, from http://waysandmeans.house.gov/singlepages.aspx?NewsID=10490

89. Most of this paragraph relies on Committee on Ways and Means, Section 15—"Workers' Compensation.

90. Much of this paragraph relies on Committee on Ways and Means, "Workers' Compensation."

91. The remainder of this paragraph relies on Sengupta et al., "Workers' Compensation: Benefits, Coverage, and Costs, 2006."

92. See U.S. Department of Labor data reported in Committee on Ways and Means, "Workers' Compensation."

93. Insurance Information Institute, "Workers' Compensation" (New York: Author, June 2010). Retrieved June 18, 2010, from http://www.iii.org/media/hottopics/insurance/workerscomp/

94. Sengupta et al., "Workers' Compensation: Benefits, Coverage, and Costs, 2006."

95. See Insurance Information Institute, "Workers' Compensation."

96. The remainder of this paragraph relies on Sengupta et al., "Workers' Compensation: Benefits, Coverage, and Costs, 2006."

97. *Ibid.*

98. Insurance Information Institute, "Workers' Compensation."

99. For a summary of studies on this topic, see Sengupta et al., "Workers' Compensation: Benefits, Coverage, and Costs, 2006."

100. Insurance Information Institute, "Workers' Compensation."

101. Bruce Hight, "Who Can Clean Up Workers' Compensation?" *Austin American-Statesman,* July 8, 2004, p. A11.

102. See, for example, Committee on Ways and Means, "Workers' Compensation."

103. See, for example, Insurance Information Institute, "Workers' Compensation."

104. *Ibid.*

105. Sengupta et al., "Workers' Compensation: Benefits, Coverage, and Costs, 2006."

106. Berkowitz, *Disabled Policy: America's Programs for the Handicapped.*

107. See Committee on Ways and Means, "Workers' Compensation"; Insurance Information Institute, "Workers' Compensation."

108. See Insurance Information Institute, "Workers' Compensation" for a list of recent changes in state workers' compensation programs.

109. *Ibid.*

6

DISABILITY POLICY: FROM PUBLIC ASSISTANCE TO CIVIL RIGHTS

There are many conditions that may result in disabilities—amputations, arthritis, blindness, brain injuries, cerebral palsy, deafness, diabetes, mental illness, epilepsy, heart disease, learning difficulties, multiple sclerosis, respiratory disorders, stroke, and stuttering among them. Each may present unique challenges for those that have these conditions. Some individuals have disabilities so severe that they can perform few activities of daily living. Others function quite well even with significant disabilities. This chapter considers public policy responses to disability.

A FAIR DEFINITION, A FAIR POLICY

Although we might think of disability on a continuum or in terms of degree of impairment from no disability to severe disability, public policy often categorizes people as being disabled or not. Rarely is the individual's view of himself or herself considered. Some people adopt the concept of disability embodied in various public policies; others reject it. The definition of disability has evolved from health-related problems that prevent an individual from working to limitations on any role or task a person usually performs in society, especially if these limitations persist.[1] It has also evolved from one focused almost entirely on medical factors to one that has also begun to consider the social, economic, and political environment.[2] No definition written on paper can really capture the abilities or the limitations of an individual with a disability, but in order to craft policies that address disability, definitions must be written and guidelines developed to carry out the policy.

In addition to disagreements about the definition of disability, the country's disability policies and programs are beset by controversies over the process of determining who is disabled and who qualifies for assistance. More importantly, scholars have raised important questions about the fundamental goals of disability policy: Is it the right of individuals with disabilities to receive social welfare benefits, or is it their obligation to make whatever contributions they can? Does society prefer to pay benefits to individuals with disabilities rather than do what is necessary to include individuals with disabilities in the mainstream of U.S. life? Is our goal to make individuals with disabilities fit the workplace and other social institutions, or is it to make society accommodate individuals with disabilities?[3] To what extent should Americans pursue measures that would more fully integrate people with disabilities in the workforce and other aspects of community life? These topics are at the crux of discussions about disability policy in the United States today.

Chapter 5 addressed two important social insurance programs for people with disabilities—Social Security Disability Insurance and Workers' Compensation. The federal government's response to disability also includes a public assistance program that pays cash benefits, social service and rehabilitation programs, civil rights legislation, and programs specifically for disabled veterans. Americans can also purchase private policies to insure themselves in case of disability.

PUBLIC ASSISTANCE FOR THE "DESERVING POOR"

Prior to the Social Security Act of 1935, many states had public assistance programs to aid the elderly poor who were unable to work. Massachusetts was among the first to appoint a commission to study the problems of the elderly.[4] In 1914 Arizona passed a law establishing a pension program for the aged, and in 1915 the territory of Alaska did the same. By 1935, 30 states had old-age assistance programs. Eligibility requirements for these state programs were stringent. In addition to financial destitution, recipients generally had to be at least 65 years old, be U.S. citizens, and meet residency requirements in the location where they applied for benefits. In cases where relatives were capable of supporting an elderly family member, benefits were often denied. Elderly participants usually had to agree that any assets they had left at the time of their death would be assigned to the state.

Individuals who were blind were also considered deserving. Eligibility requirements were often more lenient in state pension laws for these individuals than they were for the elderly. By 1935, 27 states had pension programs for people who were blind.[5] Individuals with other disabling conditions were also of concern, but early in the 1900s, policies to assist them varied considerably among states, and many states had no program at all. It was not until 1956 that disabled workers were included in the Social Security program, since many officials apparently preferred to aid them using public assistance programs.[6]

Following the precedent that many states established, the Social Security Act of 1935 included three public assistance programs: Aid to Dependent Children (ADC), Old Age Assistance (OAA), and Aid to the Blind (AB). Public assistance programs for people with disabilities continued to lag behind, but in 1950, Aid to the Permanently and Totally Disabled (APTD) was added to the Social Security Act.

OAA, AB, and APTD were called the "adult categorical public assistance programs." Although these programs were federally authorized, each state could decide whether to participate. All states eventually adopted OAA and AB, but several states chose not to participate in APTD. The federal government shared costs for these public assistance programs with the states and set some basic requirements for participation. Elderly individuals had to be at least 65 years old to receive federal aid. Those who were blind or had other disabilities had to be at least 18 years old. The states retained primary responsibility for program administration and for determining eligibility requirements and monthly benefits.

State administration of the OAA, AB, and APTD was problematic for some beneficiaries. Those who moved to another state might have been denied benefits because they did not meet eligibility requirements in their new state of residence or because they were required to re-establish residency. Benefits were often meager, and beneficiaries in poorer states generally received less because their states had less money to operate the program. Other states had a history of limited public assistance benefits.

The Federal Government Steps In

When President Nixon took office in 1972, he proposed to clean up the "welfare mess" and bring an end to the uneven treatment of public assistance recipients from state to state. To accomplish this, he wanted to replace the Aid to Families with Dependent Children (AFDC, formerly ADC), OAA, AB, and APTD programs with a *guaranteed annual income* program for those in economic need. This proposal, known as the Family Assistance Plan, was the target of controversy in Congress. Liberals considered it too stingy. Conservatives thought it provided too much in welfare benefits and would reduce the incentive to work. Debate focused mostly on the AFDC program, which was not reformed.[7] In the midst of this controversy, substantial revisions were made to the OAA, AB, and APTD programs that went almost unnoticed.[8]

The major change Congress enacted in 1972 was to "federalize" the adult categorical public assistance programs under a new program called Supplemental Security Income (SSI), which became Title XVI of the Social Security Act. Federalizing meant that Congress largely took these programs out of the states' hands, including most policy and administrative aspects. These changes, which became effective in 1974, were the most sweeping reform of the adult categorical assistance programs since APTD was added in 1950. SSI replaced the OAA, AB, and APTD programs by establishing a minimum income for participants and by standardizing eligibility requirements across all states, but no state could pay participants less than they had previously received. Today, all but five states (Arkansas, Kansas, Mississippi, Tennessee, and West Virginia) supplement the minimum SSI payment to at least some participants.[9]

The Social Security Administration (SSA) administers both the Social Security Disability Insurance (SSDI) and SSI programs, but it is important to keep the distinction between the two programs in mind. SSDI is a social insurance program for workers who become disabled. As discussed in Chapter 5, participation requires prior contributions through payroll chapters. SSI remains a means-tested public assistance program. No prior contributions are required for participation. SSA administration, rather than administration by state welfare departments, is supposed to make receiving SSI less stigmatizing for program participants.

Elderly and disabled individuals may receive SSI benefits in addition to Social Security retirement or disability benefits if their income from Social Security and other sources and their assets do not exceed SSI eligibility criteria. Despite its reputation as a guaranteed income for those who cannot earn it themselves, SSI is a "program of last resort"; that is, applicants must claim all other benefits to which they are entitled before they can qualify for SSI. As its name also implies, SSI is intended to supplement other income, but because people must be poor to qualify, they cannot have much in other income or assets. It is impossible to describe SSI's many eligibility rules in a few pages, but Illustration 6.1 provides the basics.

ILLUSTRATION 6.1
How the Supplemental Security Income (SSI) Program Works

WHO CAN QUALIFY

- U.S. citizens and some immigrants who are legal U.S. residents.
- Those who are blind, otherwise disabled, or at least 65 years old.
- Residents of many public institutions do not qualify, but there are exceptions.

WHO IS DISABLED

- Adults (18 years or older) who cannot work because of a medically determined physical or mental impairment.
- Children (under age 18 or under age 22 if a full-time student) with a medically determined physical or mental impairment that causes marked and severe functional limitations.
- Individuals who have 20/200 vision or less in the better eye with a correcting lens or tunnel vision of 20 degrees or less.
- Individuals whose disabilities are expected to result in death or have lasted or are expected to last for at least 12 continuous months.

RESOURCES AND INCOME

- Resources (e.g., savings accounts, some real estate, some personal belongings) cannot exceed $2,000 for an individual and $3,000 for a couple. Some resources are not counted

(e.g., one's home and normal household goods). Allowances are made for a car.

- In determining *eligibility,* "countable" income cannot exceed the maximum monthly federal SSI payment. Countable income can be "earned" (e.g., income from work) or "unearned" (e.g., Social Security and other cash benefits, interest income).
- In determining *payments,* countable income cannot exceed the maximum federal payment plus any state supplementation.
- The value of scholarships and grants for educational expenses, Supplemental Nutrition Assistance Program benefits, and most food, clothing, and shelter provided by nonprofit organizations is not counted as income, but some in-kind (noncash) assistance does count.
- Part of the income of a spouse, child's parents, or sponsor of an immigrant is generally counted (called "deeming").
- Income that is *not* counted (disregarded) in calculating benefits includes:
  - Usually, the first $20 a month from any source.
  - The first $65 of income from work and half of all additional earnings until countable income exceeds eligibility limits.
  - Certain disability-related work expenses for individuals who are disabled and additional work-related expenses for those who are blind.

(Continued)

ILLUSTRATION 6.1 (Continued)

OTHER FACTORS AFFECTING SSI ELIGIBILITY AND PAYMENTS

- Since income disregards differ by SSI program component, an individual who qualifies under more than one component (e.g., aged and disabled), should consider which will provide the higher benefit.
- An individual cannot receive SSI and Temporary Assistance for Needy Families benefits simultaneously; if an individual qualifies for both programs, a determination should be made as to which provides the greatest benefits.
- SSI payments are reduced by one-third if an SSI participant lives in the home of someone who contributes to his or her support.
- Monthly payments are adjusted each year to keep pace with inflation.

Source: Background Material and Data on the Programs within the Jurisdiction of the Committee on Ways and Means (Washington, DC: U.S. House of Representatives, 2008). Retrieved August 14, 2009, from http:// waysandmeans.house.gov/media/pdf/110/ssi.pdf

Supplemental Security Income in Figures

In December 2008, more than 7.5 million people received SSI.[10] Approximately 1.2 million received SSI on the basis of age, 70,000 due to blindness, and 6.2 million due to other disabilities (see Table 6.1). Of the 7.5 million recipients, approximately 1.2 million were children, 2 million were aged, and more than 4.3 million were age 18 to 64.

When SSI began, the standard definition of disability that was adopted helped many more people join the rolls. Over the years, laws, regulations, and court decisions also expanded eligibility. Increases in the number of adults aged 18 to 64 receiving SSI was a concern, especially during the early 1990s when their numbers increased by 50 percent. In recent years, growth has leveled off with about 2.3 percent of the total U.S. population receiving SSI.[11]

Roughly one-fifth of both children and adults (aged 18 to 64) receiving SSI have intellectual disability (mental retardation). Nearly 40 percent of adult and nearly 50 percent of child beneficiaries have other mental disabilities.[12] The number of blind individuals receiving SSI is at an all-time low due to improvements in preventing blindness and increases in the number of blind individuals who are self-supporting.

Kentucky and West Virginia have the highest SSI participation rate—4.3 percent of each state's population. This rate is four times higher than the states with the lowest rates—Utah, New

TABLE 6.1 Supplemental Security Income: Participants, Payments, and Costs, 2008

	Aged	Blind	Disabled
Number of participants receiving federally administered payments	1.2 million	70,000	6.2 million
Average monthly benefit (including federally administered state supplementation)	$393	$508	$494
Total annual federal payments and federally administered state supplementation payments	$5.4 billion	$416 million	$37.2 billion

Source: Social Security Bulletin, Annual Statistical Supplement, 2009, Tables 7.A1 and 7.A4. Retrieved February 27, 2010, from http://www.ssa.gov/policy/docs/statcomps/supplement/2009/7a.pdf

Hampshire, and Wyoming. Differences in state participation rates may be attributed to a variety of factors such as state poverty levels and residents' occupational characteristics (for example, coal mining versus white-collar jobs).

In 2008, the total cost of federal SSI payments was $38.7 billion, and federally administered state supplements were $4.4 billion. In that year, the federal SSI payment constituted about 74 percent of the poverty threshold for an individual and about 82 percent for a couple.[13] This is less than in 2002 when SSI payments constituted 76 percent of the poverty threshold for an individual and 90 percent for a couple.[14] These figures do not include the value of state SSI supplements, nutrition program benefits, or other aid SSI participants might receive. Still, it may be fair to say that the federal SSI benefit is modest at best. In 2010, the maximum monthly federal SSI payment was $674 for an individual and $1,011 for a couple when both members received SSI. Average monthly SSI payments (see Table 6.1) are lower than the federal maximum payment because some people have other income that counts against their SSI payment. Most people who receive SSI also qualify for Medicaid, the joint federal-state health insurance program for many low-income individuals.

Determining Who Is Disabled

Deciding whether an individual is disabled may seem like a relatively straightforward process, but often it is not. Once SSI's income and assets tests are met, the more difficult part may be deciding whether the applicant meets the federal government's definition of disabled noted in Illustration 6.1. This definition of disability rests on whether a physical or mental impairment prevents the individual from engaging in any "substantial gainful activity" (SGA), that is, paid employment available in sufficient numbers in the workforce.[15] From 1980 to 1989, most individuals who earned the substantial gainful activity amount of $300 or more a month, not counting certain expenses, such as special equipment to perform their job, were not eligible for SSI or SSDI. This amount has increased over the years. In 2010, the SGA amount for disabled individuals was $1,000 a month in the SSDI and SSI programs. For individuals who are blind, no SGA is specified in the SSI program; in the SSDI program the amount was $1,640.[16]

The process of "disability determination" is the same in the SSDI and the SSI programs.[17] It includes five sequential steps:

Step 1: Adult applicants who earn more than the amount considered substantial gainful activity (SGA) are generally disqualified. Applicants who are not employed or are earning less than the SGA proceed to step 2.

Step 2: A determination is made as to whether the individual's condition interferes with basic work-related activities. If the condition does not interfere, the individual is denied benefits; if it does interfere, the applicant moves to step 3.

Step 3: The SSA maintains lists of impairments organized by 14 major body systems (e.g., musculoskeletal, respiratory, neurological) that are so severe an individual with them is automatically considered disabled (the list for adults and the list for children are available at the Social Security Administration website). If the individual's condition is not on the list, the SSA determines if it is as severe as conditions on the list. Cases that meet this criterion are awarded benefits; those that do not proceed to step 4.

Step 4: A determination is made as to whether the applicant can perform the work he or she did previously. If the determination is that the individual can, the case is denied. If the individual cannot, the case proceeds to step 5.

Step 5: A determination is made as to whether the applicant can adjust to other work. The applicant's disability, age, education, work history, and skills are considered. Those deemed unable to adjust are awarded SSI; those that can adjust are denied SSI.

SSI applications are processed through (1) Social Security field offices, which verify non-medical eligibility criteria such as citizenship, legal residency, income, and resources, and (2) federally funded state agencies called Disability Determination Services (DDS), which evaluate disability. Applications can be made in person or by mail, telephone, or online. The DDS usually uses information from the applicant's own medical providers but can request information from independent sources. A two-person "adjudicative" team composed of a disability examiner and a medical or psychological consultant makes the initial decision on an application.

SSI and SSDI payments generally do not start until a person has been disabled for at least five months. In cases referred to as "compassionate allowances," a disability application is processed rapidly because the individual clearly has a severe condition (e.g., acute leukemia, Lou Gehrig's disease [ALS], pancreatic cancer). In other cases a "quick disability determination" is done using computer screening that identifies cases where the probability of being awarded SSI or SSDI is high. But the disability determination process often takes a few months or more, not only because medical evidence must be obtained and reviewed, but because the Social Security Administration processes so many cases.

Appealing SSI Decisions

Many people who apply for disability benefits do not get them. For example, during the past 45 years in the SSDI program, the percent of applicants approved for disability benefits has vacillated from about one-third to about one-half.[18] In 2008, about 38 percent of applications were approved, but the total number of applications continues to grow.

Since most initial applications for SSDI and SSI are denied, many applicants appeal the decision. Applicants can also appeal other decisions such as the amount of their "award" (benefit). There are four levels of appeals.[19]

- The first level of appeal, "reconsideration," is much like the initial application process, but a different adjudicative team reviews the case. If the applicant is not successful, he or she may ask for a "hearing."
- At the second appeal level, an administrative law judge usually conducts a hearing and considers any additional evidence presented or may request additional information. The applicant may attend the hearing and the judge may ask the applicant and any "witnesses" questions. The applicant and an attorney or other person representing the applicant may also ask questions.
- A third appeal level allows applicants who are unsuccessful at the hearing level to request an Appeals Council review. The council may deny or dismiss the case or return it to the judge for further action.
- An applicant dissatisfied with the Appeals Council's action may proceed to the fourth and final appeal level and file a civil suit with the U.S. District Court in his or her area.

SSI participants with disabilities may be required to accept vocational rehabilitation services since the federal and state governments have a financial interest in seeing that people who can work do so rather than receive public assistance. Cases are reviewed periodically to ensure that the individual continues to qualify for benefits. Reviews are more frequent when the individual's condition is expected to improve: every 18 months if improvement is expected; about every three years if improvement is possible; and every five to seven years if improvement is not expected.[20] Following the outcry that arose after efforts to trim the welfare rolls during the Reagan administration years, criteria were established to help ensure that participants would not be cut from the SSI program unless their medical condition improved or they were able to engage in substantial gainful activity.

As a result, or perhaps a cause, of the appeals and litigation that are often involved in obtaining SSI and SSDI, many lawyers specialize and advertise their services in this area. Since many decisions are reversed on appeal, those who believe they are disabled and want benefits may have to be persistent and patient, but people with disabilities may lack the mental, physical, and financial resources to do so.

SSI Hot Spots

Since SSI's inception, many issues have arisen in the program. During the 1980s, for example, there were controversies over how HIV status fit into the definition of disability. Court decisions supported that HIV and AIDS were disabling conditions included under federal law. Definitional issues persist. Social workers and disability policy theorists Gilson and DePoy note:

> Explanations such as alcohol dependence, obesity, and chemical sensitivity, which in other policy arenas are explained as medical but often considered to be under one's personal control, personally excessive or even hypochondriacal, are not acceptable explanations for legitimate disability status under SSDI [or SSI] policy even though these explanatory conditions may be consistent with the descriptive outcome of long term or permanent impairment advanced under the policy guidelines.[21]

Let's look more specifically at some of the population groups and processes that are sources of concern and controversy in the SSI program.

PEOPLE WITH ALCOHOL AND DRUG PROBLEMS   When SSI began in 1974, individuals disabled due to alcohol or drug problems were eligible for benefits. They were required to use a third party (called a "representative payee") to receive their benefits since they were generally considered unable to manage their own money. They were also supposed to participate in a substance abuse treatment program. Apparently the treatment provision was not well monitored, and resentments toward this group of recipients grew. In addition to the feeling that most could work if they would stop using alcohol or drugs, some believed "that SSI checks were fueling addiction."[22] In 1994, benefits to those with alcohol or drug disabilities were limited to three years. Then, in 1996 as part of welfare reform, individuals disabled solely due to alcohol or drug use were no longer eligible for SSI and SSDI.

Following the 1996 welfare reform, of the more than 200,000 SSI or SSDI recipients identified as having alcohol or drug disabilities, 60 percent lost their benefits. The other 40 percent were continued based on another disability or because of old age.[23] Studies of these SSI participants indicate that after two years, those who lost their benefits had higher rates of substance abuse and were more likely to commit drug-related crimes than those who requalified for benefits.[24] In one study, the number participating in substance abuse treatment dwindled from 41 percent to 15 percent.[25] In another study, nearly half who lost SSI did not have access to healthcare because they also lost their Medicaid benefits.[26]

IMMIGRANTS   Another group of SSI recipients that came under scrutiny were immigrants legally admitted to the United States but who were not U.S. citizens (illegal immigrants are not eligible for SSI or other public assistance benefits). The number of noncitizens receiving SSI was growing, and their SSI benefits were often higher than those of citizens because many had not worked in the United States or had not worked long enough to qualify for Social Security benefits.[27] As part of the package of welfare reforms that Congress passed in 1996, most noncitizen immigrants legally residing in the country were declared ineligible for benefits even if they were already receiving SSI. Exceptions were made for some immigrants such as refugees and asylees who had fled their countries of origin for political reasons and those who had worked in the United States and paid Social Security taxes for 10 years or more.

The battle over immigrants and SSI was fought again in 1997. The *Congressional Quarterly* called it "the most protracted struggle" in the debates over what should be changed in the 1996 welfare overhaul.[28] Perhaps better economic times helped to quell some of the backlash. This time, the decision was to allow those who were in the United States as of August 22, 1996 (the day the welfare reform bill was signed) to receive benefits in the future should they became disabled (House Republicans had urged that benefits be available only to those already disabled as of that date).

The specifics of applicants' immigration status are carefully considered to make sure they qualify for SSI. A refugee's or asylee's eligibility may be limited to seven years unless the individual becomes a citizen. In 2008, some immigrants were granted temporary extensions. Legally admitted immigrants who were not U.S. citizens were a little more than 3 percent of all SSI recipients in 1982, 12 percent in 1995, and just under 9 percent in 2008.[29] They are more than 5 percent of blind and disabled recipients and nearly 28 percent of aged recipients.

CHILDREN   Another group that drew the scrutiny of welfare reformers was a less likely target—children. In 1990 the U.S. Supreme Court issued its decision in *Sullivan v. Zebley*.[30] Prior to this decision, children who did not meet the criteria in the Listing of Impairments were disqualified, and some serious childhood conditions were missing from the list. The *Zebley* decision required that children be afforded the additional functional tests given to adult applicants. According to this ruling, a child was considered impaired if he or she was substantially unable to function as children of the same age are expected to do (i.e., unable to engage in "age-appropriate" activities). Following the ruling, the Social Security Administration had to try locating and reassessing 452,000 children denied benefits as far back as 1980.[31]

Shortly after the *Zebley* decision, the number of children enrolled in SSI more than doubled.[32] The major increase was due to an expanded category of mental disorders, including intellectual disability (mental retardation) and attention deficit hyperactivity disorder. Concern was that these children might remain on the rolls throughout their lifetimes. Reports emerged of parents coaching children to seem more impaired than they were in an effort to get benefits. It was difficult to prove this, but in response, some government-sponsored studies recommended "strengthened" definitions of disability and eligibility criteria.

As part of the 1996 welfare reform, Congress again changed the definition of disability for children, saying that children must have "marked and severe functional limitations" to qualify. The functional test for children was eliminated, and children must again meet criteria in the Listing of Impairments or have disabilities equal to them. The current Listing of Impairments reflects the new definition of disability for children.

In 1996 about one million children were receiving SSI benefits, a 14-fold increase from 1974. Following the 1996 welfare reform law, 288,000 children were slated for eligibility redetermination.

Benefits to 101,000 of these children were terminated because they did not meet the more stringent eligibility definition included in the new law. Children receiving SSI prior to passage of the new law on August 22, 1996, remained eligible for Medicaid even if they lost their SSI benefits as a result of the new disability definition.

By December 2000, the SSI child caseload had fallen to about 847,000.[33] Although the total number of child cases has since increased, the percentage of children receiving SSI has stabilized at about 1.4 percent of the country's population under age 18.[34] About two-thirds of child SSI recipients are males.

When children reach age 18, they are re-evaluated for SSI based on adult disability criteria. About one-third lose SSI eligibility at this point. There is special concern about those with "behavioral disorders and mental disorders other than mental retardation" because they "may not have been sufficiently prepared for life without SSI."[35] School dropout rates among SSI child recipients are high. Services they received may no longer be available when they reach adulthood. Losing SSI may also mean loss of Medicaid.

To better prepare children receiving SSI to enter the workforce when they reach adulthood, the Social Security Administration is studying programs that allow them to keep more of their earnings and provide them with additional employment and planning services.[36] A project in New York is helping youth who receive SSI with self-determination skills and includes parent-peer mentoring workshops and summer work experiences. Project Maryland is targeting youth with severe emotional problems and offers mentoring and counseling and includes job development, work experiences, links with community agencies, and life skill education. The program also incorporates parents and counselors, and follow-up services are considered vital.[37]

OLDER ADULTS   SSI participation among adults aged 65 and older has dropped substantially over the years both in total numbers and as a percentage of the older adult population as more have qualified for Social Security benefits or have other sources of income. In 1974, nearly 9 percent of the older adult population in the United States received SSI; today, that number is about 3 percent.[38] Given that the baby boomers are reaching the age at which disabilities are more likely to occur, SSI and SSDI participation is also like to increase, but studies suggest that 40 to 55 percent of older Americans who qualify don't participate in SSI.[39] For some, their cash SSI benefit would be minimal; others may not participate due to the lengthy eligibility process, difficulty accessing Social Security offices, the time involved, reluctance to share personal information, and the stigma associated with receiving welfare. Those who qualify but do not participate are better off than those who participate; for example, they are more likely to have private health insurance and own their own home. Raising SSI benefits even moderately might significantly increase older adults' participation. Researchers estimate that a $100 increase in monthly benefits would increase participation by 15 percent. Eligibility and benefits would also increase if the amount of income that is automatically disregarded in determining eligibility ($20, a figure that has not changed since 1972) and the asset limit ($2,000 for an individual and $3,000 for a couple, figures that have not changed since 1984) were raised.[40] Such measures would also lift more older adults out of poverty and be especially helpful to older women.

PEOPLE WHO ARE HOMELESS   Estimates are that less than one percent of the homeless population receives SSI benefits compared to 2.3 percent of the housed population.[41] Individuals who are homeless face many barriers to program participation: confusion about eligibility criteria, missing personal or contact information on the SSI application, lack of required documentation, and difficulty completing enrollment following application.

Once they apply for SSI, applicants who are homeless are disproportionately denied benefits,[42] and they are often terminated from public benefit programs because they do not receive their redetermination notices.[43] In some states, 95 percent of their SSI claims are denied.[44] Even in states that do comparatively well in enrolling individuals who are homeless, such as Massachusetts, the denial rate is nearly twice the rate of the housed population. One reason that Massachusetts does better is that it has created homeless claims units staffed by representatives who are sensitive to the needs of those who are homeless and knowledgeable about procedures for processing their claims.

In response to former President George W. Bush's Samaritan Initiative to end chronic homelessness, Congress appropriated funds for outreach demonstration projects to enroll eligible homeless individuals in the SSI program. The National Care for the Homeless Project has encouraged the Social Security Administration to adopt lessons learned from these projects and to make other improvements to SSI. These include increasing SSI payments so that people who are homeless do not remain "nearly destitute," reducing the time it takes to hear an appeal, and resuming SSI for people who have alcohol or drug addiction to reflect medical knowledge about these conditions, "including needed access to medical services and treatment for these progressive and often fatal disorders."[45]

RACE AND OTHER FACTORS There are also concerns that race or other factors may affect disability determination. The General Accounting Office (GAO) found that in cases that go to an administrative law judge, African Americans who were not represented by an attorney were less likely to be approved for benefits than whites who were not represented.[46] Members of other racial or ethnic groups were approved as often as whites. In cases where an attorney represented the applicant, blacks and whites were approved at equal rates. The study did not address whether these different approval rates are due to racial bias or other factors not accounted for in the study. SSA's response has been to educate employees to limit the possibility of racial bias, but whether racial bias exists remains a question. Other groups less likely to receive benefits were males, those with lower incomes, and non-English speakers who *had* a translator at the hearing.

IMPROVING DISABILITY DETERMINATION The need for better methods to determine who cannot engage in substantial gainful activity caused the Social Security Administration to ask the Institute of Medicine (IOM) to consider the challenges and recommend ways to improve the process.[47] One concern is that the 54 Disability Determination Services offices across the United States vary in their decision-making processes. A state's resources can also affect disability claims processing because some offices lack access to the full range of medical specialists who can help decide cases. Quality assurance procedures also differ across offices. Health insurance or other personal resources that can give the applicant access to clinical or laboratory tests may also affect case decisions. Standardization, such as requiring the 54-state Disability Determination Services (DDS) to use the same processing system is considered long overdue, although instituting a uniform system would be a massive, expensive, and lengthy undertaking. In the long run, however, it would likely provide a higher quality of service to consumers as well as improvements in areas such as tracking case trends and identifying issues in case processing.

Other challenges involve the current Listing of Impairments. The list allows for approving cases that clearly meet the Social Security Security's disability definition. However, the listing, which once covered 90 percent of approvals, now covers about half of them. In part, this is because the listing relies on a medical model to define disability that fails to consider advancements in technologies and treatments that help people with disabilities engage in work in other activities.

The IOM recommends using a broader and more comprehensive functional assessment that focuses on what the individual can do rather than medical diagnoses alone, but developing such functional criteria would be a major undertaking. In the meantime, the listing is important since no better tool currently exists. Because some of the listings have not been updated in decades, the SSA intends to update each listing every five years.[48] SSA's databases could also be better utilized to identify the types of cases where approval is likely, and expert knowledge could be better utilized to update listings and processes.

Many groups have a vested interest in monitoring the SSA's attempts to update disability criteria and disability determination processes. For example, when new rules were being considered for determining psychiatric and intellectual disabilities for children and adults, the Social Security Administration solicited comments on the proposals by posting a notice in the *Federal Register*. Among the responders was the Depression and Bipolar Support Alliance.[49] The Alliance's opinion was that the current listings were working well. One reason it cautioned against some of the rule changes is that some individuals with disabilities may lack access to new medications that can improve functioning and help people maintain employment. These medications can be costly and Medicare and Medicaid may not cover them.

REDUCING CASE BACKLOGS   The Social Security Administration's workload is daunting. Currently, it handles about 2.5 million disability applications each year. Perhaps the most serious issue the SSA is facing is the backlog of disability case hearings in the SSI and SSDI programs.[50] In 1997, the average processing time for disability claims appeals was 398 days. President Clinton promised to reduce the time to 284 days and implemented changes to reduce processing time for initial claims, hearings, and appeals.[51] In 2003 the appeals processing time was down to 294 days.[52] Today, the SSA admits that some people die before they get an appeals hearing before an administrative law judge. The average wait for a decision is now 500 days, perhaps not so surprising given that in 2008, 750,000 applicants were waiting for a hearing.[53] The Social Security Administration calls eliminating the hearings backlog a moral imperative and the agency's "highest priority."[54] By 2013, the SSA hopes to reduce the backlog to 466,000 cases and to reduce the waiting time by nearly half, to 270 days, but three-quarters of a year is still a very long time to wait for those who cannot work and lack the income needed to support themselves and their families. To improve the situation, one suggestion has been to eliminate the "reconsideration" step in the appeals process.

Factors contributing to the backlog include increased disability applications as the baby boomers age, insufficient SSA resources, and SSA's admission of inertia in embracing more effective technology. From 2000 to 2006, the number of individuals filing for disability benefits increased 60 percent. People in their mid-fifties today are apparently in worse health than their counterparts in the past. To keep up with demand, the SSA could utilize online applications, video hearings, and improved databases. High quality research is also needed to improve the disability determination process.

VETERANS ADMINISTRATION DISABILITY SYSTEM

Since America's inception, public aid has been provided to disabled military veterans. These benefits are often more generous than what many civilians might receive. Today, with so many U.S. military troops stationed in dangerous areas like Iraq and Afghanistan, there are continuous reports of those who have sustained serious injuries that result in permanent disabilities. Veterans can also receive benefits (compensation) if their disability is incurred or aggravated while in the military even if the disability is not caused by military service.

The compensation system for veterans differs from SSDI and SSI because it covers partial, permanent disability as well as total, permanent disability. But like the Social Security Administration (SSA), the Veteran's Affairs (VA) disability determination system has been criticized for case backlogs and deficiencies in case processing.[55] There have also been reports of deplorable conditions at Walter Reed Army Medical Center where many injured soldiers receive treatment and rehabilitation. One report indicated that 630,000 disability claims were pending with some sitting for more than six months. On appeal, 60 percent of case decisions were found "deficient or erroneous." Like the SSA, the VA is a federal agency, but payments for veterans with similar injuries vary widely across states where disability claims are processed. The Department of Defense (DOD) and the VA are working to correct problems. They face challenges such as inadequate staffing, processing complex cases, and changing regulations. Given the incidence of posttraumatic stress disorder and traumatic brain injuries, another suggestion is that the VA and DOD ensure that "service members . . . have continuous access to mental health services both before and after they separate from the military."[56] The Veterans' Benefits Improvement Act of 2008 attempts to correct many of the problems in the current disability system.

DISABILITY AND WORK

The first institutions for people with disabilities in the United States were established in the early nineteenth century. Training and education programs to assist those living in the community with potential for employment emerged in the twentieth century.[57] One of the first of these educational programs began in Massachusetts in 1916. The U.S. Congress soon followed with its own rehabilitation legislation.[58]

Vocational Rehabilitation and Employment Services

In 1920 Congress passed the Vocational Rehabilitation Act (also called the Smith-Fess Act) to assist vocationally ("industrially") disabled civilians by providing funds through a federal-state matching formula.[59] The federal and state governments shared costs of the Vocational Rehabilitation (VR) program on a 50-50 basis. The program was appealing from conservative and economic viewpoints because rehabilitation is generally less costly than long-term care and income maintenance payments. In fact, it was said:

> [P]eople do not regard vocational rehabilitation as a welfare program . . . . Where welfare fosters dependence, rehabilitation promotes independence. Welfare represents a net cost to society; vocational rehabilitation is an investment in society's future.[60]

Although originally intended for individuals with physical disabilities, in 1943 individuals with mental illness and intellectual disability were included in the VR program; in the 1960s, those with "socially handicapping" conditions, including adult and juvenile offenders, were added.[61]

The Rehabilitation Services Administration (RSA) of the U.S. Department of Education is responsible for administering formula grant funding for state-operated vocational rehabilitation agencies. There are 80 state VR agencies (many states have a separate VR agency for those who are blind). VR agencies "help individuals with physical or mental disabilities obtain employment and live more independently through the provision of supports such as counseling, medical and psychological services, job training and other individualized services."[62] The states have latitude to operate their programs as long as they follow federal guidelines. Today, the federal government pays for the majority of VR program costs using a formula based on a state's population and per capita income. Federal and state VR program funding was $1.1 billion in 1980, $1.9 billion in 1990, $3.1 billion in 1999, and $3.4 billion in 2005 with $2.6 billion in federal funds and $772 million in state funds.[63] These are relatively small amounts compared to the amount spent on public assistance programs like SSI.

In the earlier days of the program, VR was accused of "creaming"—focusing on applicants who could achieve rehabilitation most easily. Critics claimed that most of the program's clients were young white males whose disabilities were neither chronic nor severe.[64] This did not sit well with many potential consumers (clients) and rehabilitation advocates. Pressure developed to serve those with more severe disabilities, today called "significant" disabilities. The 1973 amendments to the Vocational Rehabilitation Act helped accomplish this change.

Doctors or other experts evaluate applicants for VR services to determine whether they have a *bona fide* disability. Those who have a reasonable chance of becoming employed or reemployed and remaining so qualify for services. Each client or "consumer" accepted for services is assigned a VR counselor, and each develops an individualized plan for employment, which includes the consumer's employment goal and the services needed to reach the goal. Although this sounds like a rational way to optimize services, VR is not an entitlement program. It may be difficult to stretch available funds to meet all the needs of those who qualify for services. As is often the case with state-administered programs, individuals with the same or similar circumstances may receive different types and amounts of VR services depending on where they live.

VR programs place about 200,000 individuals in competitive employment each year.[65] The figure has "never made a noticeable impact on the employment rate nationwide,"[66] perhaps because of the limited funds directed to these programs. The number of new applications processed by state VR agencies has generally declined over the years from 800,000 in 1975 to 590,000 in 2005.[67] In 1975, VR agencies served a total of 1.4 million clients. This number declined over time but again reached nearly 1.4 million in 2005. Ninety-one percent of clients had significant disabilities. Clients are considered successfully rehabilitated if they receive VR services that result in nine months of continuous employment.[68]

The federal government uses various performance indicators to determine if state VR agencies are meeting their goals.[69] For example, the agencies are supposed to increase the number of individuals who meet their employment outcome compared to the previous year. In fiscal year 2005, 64 percent of the 80 state VR agencies met this goal. Another performance indicator is that each of the 24 agencies serving only individuals who are blind is expected to help at least 69 percent of consumers meet an employment goal. In 2005, 13 (54 percent) of these agencies did so. The other 56 agencies were expected to help at least 56 percent of consumers leaving VR services achieve an employment outcome. Forty (71 percent) did so. The RSA's annual performance report also provides some information about clients' earnings, but it leaves us wanting to know more about how well clients are faring with regard to income and other aspects of their work.

In addition to state VR agencies, state employment offices have a legal responsibility to assist those with disabilities find jobs, and people with disabilities may also qualify under the Workforce Investment Act or other programs (see Chapter 9). The programs described below are also intended to encourage more people with disabilities to work.

Eliminating Work Disincentives, Supporting Work

Over the years, much of the effort to contain SSI growth has centered on disability determination and review processes. The Government Accountability Office warned that "if SSA is to decrease long-term reliance on these [SSI and SSDI] programs . . . it will need to rely less on assessing medical improvement and more on return-to-work programs."[70] Despite advances in medicine and assistive technology, in 2008, less than 6 percent of SSI recipients aged 18 to 64 had any earned income.[71] Perhaps this should not be surprising since individuals receiving SSI have been declared unable to participate in substantial gainful activity.[72]

A perverse feature of public policy is that individuals with disabilities who receive SSDI and/or SSI risk losing all government-sponsored benefits if they work. Thus, it has long been noted that these programs are more likely to promote dependency than self-sufficieny.[73] (The same is true for the pension program for disabled military veterans and in the private insurance programs that some people purchase to protect themselves against loss of income in the case of disability.) The strong link between the state and federal cash disability assistance programs and vocational rehabilitation originally intended never materialized.

Although only a small percentage of those who receive disability payments work, and previous attempts to boost work participation have met with modest success at best, efforts persist to encourage SSI and SSDI recipients to work. One reason is that given the size of the SSI and SSDI programs, even modest increases in the number of recipients who return to work could result in substantial cost savings.[74]

Keeping More Cash Benefits and Health Benefits

To at least partially address concerns about losing social insurance benefits, SSDI recipients who wish to work are offered a trial work period. From 1990 to 2000 the trial period worked this way: once SSDI recipients earned more than $200 a month for nine months over a 60-month period after deducting work-related expenses, they generally lost all SSDI benefits and Medicare health-care coverage. Today, the amount is adjusted annually. In 2010 it was $720 a month.[75]

Congress has also attempted to encourage more SSI recipients to work by amending the Social Security Act in 1980 and again in subsequent years with a provision known as section 1619. It allows SSI participants who are blind or disabled to keep more earnings from work as long as their disability persists and their earnings do not exceed the total SSI benefit amount to which they would be entitled if they did not work. In December 2006, over 17,000 SSI recipients worked and continued to receive SSI under the section 1619 provision. This was just 0.4% of all SSI recipients aged 18 to 64.[76] In December 2006, their average earnings were about $500 more than the SGA. In 2009, SSI recipients could earn $1,433 a month under section 1619 before they reached the point at which their SSI check was reduced to zero.

Another section 1619 benefit is that SSI participants who no longer receive cash SSI payments because of increased earnings can continue to receive Medicaid if they remain disabled, continue to meet the SSI asset test, and need Medicaid to maintain employment. Medicaid continues if the participants' earnings do not exceed their state's "SSI threshold," which includes any SSI supplement the state pays in addition to the federal SSI payment plus the state's per capita Medicaid expenditure.[77] In 2009 these thresholds ranged from nearly $24,000 in Alabama to nearly $55,000 in Connecticut.[78] A few states have higher thresholds for people who are blind. Other factors can also be considered in determining the threshold for an individual such as high medical or work-related expenses. Considering the high costs of private health insurance, and considering that individuals with disabilities may have substantial medical expenses, expanded provisions for keeping Medicaid are welcome, but in December 2006, only 2.2 percent of SSI beneficiaries aged 18 to 64 received Medicaid under this provision. Under similar provisions, Medicare benefits for disabled individuals receiving them may also continue for extended periods.

Plan to Achieve Self-Support (PASS)

Another effort to help individuals with disabilities is Plan to Achieve Self-Support (PASS), which allows people receiving SSI to save money for a specific work goal, such as attending school or starting a business. The money saved must be from income, such as pay from a job, and not from SSI. The PASS is a formal agreement with the government. The money saved is disregarded in calculating a participant's SSI benefit. If the individual violates the PASS agreement, the money saved can be counted as income or assets and may result in the individual having to reimburse the government for any SSI benefit overpayments.

An example of what happens to SSI benefits when an individual works and uses a PASS is described in Illustration 6.2. Few SSI recipients use the PASS provision. In December 2006, slightly less than 1,600 or .04 percent of all SSI beneficiaries aged 18 to 64 had a PASS account.[79]

ILLUSTRATION 6.2
Working and Using a Plan to Achieve Self-Support (PASS) Under the Supplemental Security Income (SSI) Program

Denni Hunt is disabled and lives in a state that does not supplement Supplemental Security Income (SSI) payments. She was receiving the federal maximum SSI payment of $674 each month (she also has Medicaid coverage). She has no other income. She was offered a job in a local fast food restaurant. Denni decided to take the job. The Social Security Administration does not count the first $85 of her earnings against her SSI payment ($20 is automatically disregarded and another $65 is disregarded because she is working). Half of her earnings over $85 are also not counted against her SSI payment. Here is how her SSI payment was affected:

Gross monthly earnings	$275
Less automatic and initial work disregards	−$85
	$190
Divide by 2 to get earnings counted	$190/2 = $95
Subtract earnings counted from maximum allowable SSI payment	$674[1] − $95
New SSI payment	$579
Add monthly earnings	+$275
Total Income	$854

Note that before Denni started working, her total income was her SSI check of $674. Once she began working, she had that income in addition to her SSI check, so her total income increased to $854, even though her SSI payment was less.

After several months, Denni's pay increased to $375 a month. To help her move better at work, she purchased an electric wheelchair, which cost $60 a month. She can deduct the monthly payment from her countable earnings, which also increases her income:

[1] In 2010, the maximum federal SSI payment for an individual was $674.

(Continued)

ILLUSTRATION 6.2 (Continued)

Gross monthly earnings	$375
Less automatic and initial work disregards	−$85
	$290
Subtract work expense	−$60
	$230
Divide by 2 to get earnings counted	$230/2 = $115
Subtract earnings counted from maximum allowable SSI payment	$674 − $115
New SSI payment	$559
Add monthly earnings	+$375
Total Income	$934

So, even though Denni's earnings increased by $100 (from $275 to $375), her SSI payment was reduced by only $20 (from $579 to $559) because of the work expense deduction for her new wheelchair. Her total income increased to $934, substantially more than the $674 she received before she started working.

Denni decided that she wants to get a college degree. Her sister helped her write a Plan to Achieve Self-Support (PASS), which described her plans to work and save money for school. She is saving $100 each month for school. Here's how the PASS is helping her:

Gross monthly earnings	$375
Less automatic and initial work disregards	−$85
	$290
Subtract work expense	−$60
	$230
Divide by 2 to get earnings counted	$230/2 = $115
Subtract PASS amount to get new amount of counted earnings	$115 − $100
	$15
Subtract new amount of counted earnings from maximum allowable SSI payment	$674 − $15
New SSI payment	$659
Add monthly earnings	+$375
Total Income	$1034

Even though Denni's earnings remain the same, her SSI checks are increased because the Social Security Administration does not count the income she is setting aside to go to school in determining her SSI payment. Her total income is now $1,034 a month ($375 in earnings plus $659 in SSI).

Source: Adapted from Social Security Administration, *Social Security: Working While Disabled . . . How We Can Help,* SSA Publication No. 05-10095, January 1997.

Ticket to Work

In 1999, Congress enacted the Ticket to Work and Work Incentives Improvement Act to revamp the traditional VR service system for many SSI and SSDI recipients and service providers. The vision was to make Ticket to Work a voluntary, comprehensive, "wraparound" program to help individuals with disabilities make the transition to work and sustain work and earnings over the long run. It was intended to decrease SSI and SSDI program use and improve participants' quality of life. Because the program was underutilized, changes were made in 2005, but it took three years of negotiations before new programs rules were issued in 2008. Under these new rules, all adults aged 18 to 64 who receive cash SSI and/or SSDI benefits are eligible for the program.

Ticket to Work allows SSI and SSDI recipients to obtain vocational rehabilitation, employment services, and other support services from the state VR agency or an approved private Employment Network (EN) selected through a competitive bidding process.[80] Ticket to Work has attempted to attract more private rehabilitation providers to give SSI and SSDI recipients more choices. Providers can be community-based rehabilitation service providers, state labor departments' one-stop service centers, educational institutions, and businesses-oriented entities such as Chambers of Commerce. SSI and SSDI participants receive a Ticket to Work voucher (see Illustration 6.3) they can present to

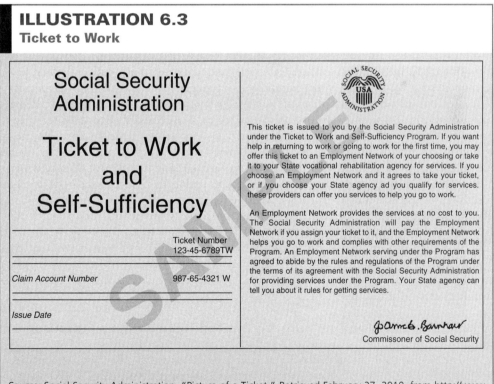

ILLUSTRATION 6.3
Ticket to Work

Social Security Administration

Ticket to Work and Self-Sufficiency

Ticket Number
123-45-6789TW

Claim Account Number   987-65-4321 W

Issue Date

This ticket is issued to you by the Social Security Administration under the Ticket to Work and Self-Sufficiency Program. If you want help in returning to work or going to work for the first time, you may offer this ticket to an Employment Network of your choosing or take it to your State vocational rehabilitation agency for services. If you choose an Employment Network and it agrees to take your ticket, or if you choose your State agency ad you qualify for services. these providers can offer you services to help you go to work.

An Employment Network provides the services at no cost to you. The Social Security Administration will pay the Employment Network if you assign your ticket to it, and the Employment Network helps you go to work and complies with other requirements of the Program. An Employment Network serving under the Program has agreed to abide by the rules and regulations of the Program under the terms of its agreement with the Social Security Administration for providing services under the Program. Your State agency can tell you about it rules for getting services.

Joanne B. Barnhart
Commissoner of Social Security

Source: Social Security Administration, "Picture of a Ticket." Retrieved February 27, 2010, from http://www.yourtickettowork.com/ttw_ticket

an EN or the state VR program. Participants can also request services through the traditional state VR program rather than Ticket to Work.

From the beginning, concerns were raised about the program. One concern is that as a form of privatization, Ticket to Work could result in creaming, more euphemistically called "favorable risk selection."[81] For example, EN providers may be reluctant to accept clients who have more severe disabilities because these individuals may face major obstacles to earning amounts (such as the full SGA) sufficient for EN providers to obtain reimbursement for their services. The Ticket program was criticized for failing to recognize the benefits of helping people with disabilities who are able to earn only more modest amounts.[82] In fact, Ticket to Work has attracted only a small number of participants and private providers.[83]

As of April 2008, only 1.8 percent of tickets issued had been used with state VR agencies, and only .1 percent with private ENs.[84] Although 40 percent of SSDI beneficiaries express an interest in working, and 16 percent say they plan to earn enough in five years to leave SSDI,[85] few have attempted to use their ticket, perhaps because they do not see fulltime work as feasible for them.[86] Other reasons may be that they fear jeopardizing their cash and Medicaid benefits, or perhaps their disabilities are too severe, services do not match their needs, or the incentives offered are insufficient to encourage work participation. Individual factors may also be involved that have little to do with public policy and the incentives it may provide.

Despite cheery publications and testimonials from EN providers,[87] many ENs had never accepted a ticket and were dropping out of the program. Evidence indicates that because ENs cannot afford to take on cases that will require them to make a substantial upfront financial investment, they have taken on cases where their financial outlays will be small, and they refer higher cost cases to the state VR programs.[88] People might disagree about whether this should be called a rational economic choice or favorable risk selection.

ENs have been discouraged by the way they are reimbursed. In addition to lag times in getting reimbursed, under Ticket to Work, providers are reimbursed much differently than in the traditional state VR program. In the traditional VR program, state agencies must demonstrate outcomes, but once certain outcomes are achieved, services are paid on a cost reimbursement basis. Originally, ENs were reimbursed only if the SSI or SSDI recipient successfully returned to work. Providers could choose to be paid in one of two ways. Under the "outcome payment" option, for any month the client received *no* SSI or SSDI check because of work earnings, the EN got a percentage of what would have been the client's average monthly SSI or SSDI benefit for up to 60 months. Under the "milestone-outcome payment" option, the EN received partial payments based on progress (milestones) the participant achieved in terms of specified numbers of months of work over a 15-month period if the participant earned at least the amount considered substantial gainful activity. Providers who selected the milestone method began collecting payments for services earlier than under the outcome option, but they also received less in total than they would have under the outcome option. Private providers had to choose one option or the other for all clients they served. State VR agencies could opt for cost reimbursement for a client rather than the outcome or milestone option. Today, ENs can earn payments earlier and more often in the employment process as participants meet intermediate goals, and payments under both option plans have increased. Nevertheless, Ticket to Work is governed by a complicated array of rules and regulations that may make participation for consumers and providers difficult.

The SSA has used various methods to encourage more people with disabilities to participate in Ticket to Work. A major effort is its Work Incentives Planning and Assistance (WIPA) program. WIPA staff conduct outreach to identify potential program participants, inform them of their work incentives choices, educate them on issues such as how work will effect their benefits, and connect them with appropriate ENs. If Ticket participants are making "timely progress" toward their employment goals, their continuing SSI medical disability reviews are postponed.

Ticket to Work participants who are unable to continue working because of a medical condition can have their SSI benefits reinstated without filing a new application if their benefits were terminated due to increased earnings, and if they file the request within 60 months of their benefit termination date. States can also raise their Medicaid income and asset eligibility limits for participants. States may require that participants "buy in" to the Medicaid program on a sliding scale basis depending on their income. Medicare can continue for 8.5 years after returning to work.[89] Even with these sweeteners, it seems that participants must have a strong desire to participate in gainful employment, and EN providers must have a strong commitment to help them do so. While it is important to explore new methods to help people with disabilities pursue their employment goals and to offer choices in service providers, Ticket to Work's limited success may raise questions as to whether funds should be channeled to traditional VR services program that already have decades of experience assisting people with disabilities return to work.

THE ERA OF CIVIL RIGHTS FOR INDIVIDUALS WITH DISABILITIES

In the course of history, people with disabilities have been subjected to shame, degradation, isolation, and worse.[90] In the United States, during the early twentieth century, a eugenics movement emerged prompted by the concept of Social Darwinism or survival of the fittest. Using flawed "scientific evidence," advocates sought to perfect the gene pool through methods such as segregation, sterilization, and laws restricting immigration and marriage.[91] In Nazi Germany, thousands of people with disabilities were the victims of genocide. Today, individuals concerned that a baby may be born with a disability can choose to abort the fetus. Some people believe the decision to abort a fetus or end life due to severe disability is a personal one. Others are adamant that such decisions devalue human life.

Among the first responses of modern society to people with severe physical and mental disabilities was "indoor relief"—"warehousing" them in large institutions. Treatment in these places was frequently deplorable. Even with efforts to see that patients or residents had some decent level of care, beliefs mounted that one should not be subjected to a life in an institution.

Vocational rehabilitation constituted one wave of a more enlightened public response to disability and income maintenance through public assistance and social insurance programs a second. The third and most recent wave is civil rights reform.[92]

> The disability rights perspective views people with disabilities as a minority group that has been subject to discrimination and unfair treatment—in legal terms, a protected class of people. It stands in contrast to a charitable perspective which views people with disabilities as unfortunate and deserving of pity and care. Likewise, it stands in contrast to a medical model, which views people with disabilities as needing to be "cured." It also stands in contrast to a rehabilitation perspective, which views people with disabilities as needing experts and professionals who can provide services to enhance the functioning of the individual.[93]

The disability rights or social model views disability as an aspect of human diversity since humans vary in many ways, including their abilities.[94] Disability is considered "a natural and normal part of the human experience"; rather than "fixing" the individual, this paradigm focuses "on eliminating the attitudinal and institutional barriers that preclude individuals with disabilities from fully participating in society's mainstream."[95]

From Deinstitutionalization to Normalization and Inclusion

The movement toward "deinstitutionalization" eventually gained judicial backing when, in 1972, the U.S. Supreme Court ruled in the case of *Wyatt v. Stickney* that "No persons shall be admitted to the institution unless prior determination shall have been made that residence in the institution is the least restrictive habilitation setting."[96] Subsequent court decisions, such as the 1985 decision in *City of Cleburne, Texas v. Cleburne Living Center*, and the 1999 decision in *Olmstead v. E. C. and L. W.*, affirmed the rights of people with intellectual and mental health disabilities to live in the community. In its 6 to 3 *Olmstead* ruling, Justice Ruth Bader Ginsburg delivered the court's majority opinion stating that:

> States are required to place persons with mental disabilities in community settings rather than in institutions when the State's treatment professionals have determined that community placement is appropriate, the transfer from institutional care to a less restrictive setting is not opposed by the affected individual, and the placement can be reasonably accommodated, taking into account the resources available to the State and the needs of others with mental disabilities.[97]

But the goals of the disability rights movement go much further than simply deinstitutionalizing people with mental disabilities and other disabilities "if the placement can be reasonably accommodated." The goals include "normalization" and "independent living."

The concept of normalization apparently emerged in Scandinavia, particularly in Denmark as part of its 1959 Mental Retardation Act.[98] Other countries adopted the concept, which was broadened to include those with other disabilities. Normalization means that regardless of the severity of an individual's disability, he or she should have the opportunity to live like other citizens, including opportunities for shopping, recreation, and other everyday activities and living in homes located in residential communities that resemble other neighborhood homes.[99] Normalization also means that individuals with disabilities should have the right to occupy the same social roles—spouses, parents, workers, etc.—as others.[100]

The concept of normalization or inclusion has been promoted for over 50 years, but individuals with disabilities continue to face negative attitudes from the general public, employers, and even human service professionals who underestimate their abilities. Too often, architectural and other barriers continue to prohibit or restrict the use of buildings. Public transportation and other facilities and programs still provide minimal assistance and foster dependence rather than promote integration.[101] Furthermore, while deinstitutionalization is generally considered a humane concept, the educational, vocational, financial, and social resources that many people with disabilities need to live adequately in the community never followed.

Almost every policy has some opposition. Some parents reject deinstitutionalization. They feel the transition to the community would be traumatizing for their child after years of life in an institution or that it would be difficult to replicate the quality of care outside the institution.[102] Employees of institutions and unions representing them, elected officials, and community residents may oppose deinstitutionalization because it would mean job loss for many people who have dedicated themselves to caring for people with disabilities, or they feel it will compromise patients' or residents' care.[103]

The Independent Living Movement

Along with deinstitutionalization and normalization has come the independent living movement. *Independent living centers* (ILCs) are "private non-profit self-help organization[s] that offer a range of basic services that help individuals with disabilities live independently in the community."[104] Advancements in educational techniques, technology, and medicine have made it possible for many more individuals to live independently. Equally important is that individuals with disabilities began to force the issue of their civil rights. ILCs developed through local efforts to empower individuals with disabilities via their own self-help movement. A prototype is the Center for Independent Living in Berkeley, California. The centers break with the professional model of care because individuals with disabilities are in charge. They teach others with disabilities how to get all the services to which they are entitled such as social insurance, public assistance, rehabilitation, education, attendant care (also called personal assistance services), and other services that will allow them to live as independently as they can and wish. The national grassroots advocacy group American Disabled for Attendant Programs Today (ADAPT) focuses on obtaining these services. ADAPT's slogan is "free our people." ADAPT's home page on the World Wide Web proclaims, "There's no place like home, and we mean real homes, not nursing homes."[105] In addition to activities that most grassroots organizations pursue, ADAPT members sometimes engage in nonviolent civil disobedience to promote the civil and human rights of people with disabilities, thus risking arrest.

People with disabilities want the same choices and control over where they live, work, and spend leisure time as others. Disability rights advocates have protested attempts to reduce funding for the Section 8 Housing Choice Voucher program (see Chapter 4) because it would have serious repercussions for individuals with disabilities who need affordable housing to live independently. The federal government's Money Follows the Person (MFP) demonstration grants, initiated under the George W. Bush administration, allowed many states to experiment by utilizing funds that usually go to nursing homes to help people live in the community. Among the challenges MFP programs face is lack of affordable housing, including affordable housing that is accessible to people with disabilities.[106] In addition, many state Medicaid plans do not include personal attendant care services or do not cover the number of hours an individual may need to transition to community living or live independently. A comprehensive report on the outcomes of the federally funded MFP demonstration grants is due in 2012. Congress is also considering a Community Choice Act that would extend the MFP program. ADAPT has called for a meaningful act as described in Illustration 6.4.

A New Bill of Rights for Individuals with Disabilities

Persistent political efforts by individuals with disabilities, their families, and other advocates have resulted in legislation requiring increased access for individuals with disabilities. For example, The 1986 Air Carrier Access Act (ACAA) prohibits airlines from discriminating against travelers with disabilities. Initial ACCA rules were promulgated in 1990. New rules became effective in May 2009. Among the ACAA's provisions are that many planes are required to have movable armrests, and wide-body planes must have an accessible lavatory. In addition, individuals with disabilities must be allowed to select any seat, except where this might be a safety hazard. An air carrier may insist that a "safety assistant" travel with the passenger, but if the passenger believes he or she can travel independently, the traveler cannot be charged for the assistant's fare.[107]

The Architectural Barriers Act of 1968 was aimed at making buildings accessible and safe for individuals who are blind, deaf, using wheelchairs, or who have other disabilities. It "requires

ILLUSTRATION 6.4
Talking Points on the Community Choice Act

The **demographics of our country are changing.** More and more people with disabilities are living, and could be thriving! Reasons for these changes include: a) the **aging** process, the graying of America, b) **children born** with disabilities are living, c) **young adults,** who previously would have died from accidents or illnesses, are **living**—thanks to **medical technology and other advances.**

Our **long-term service system must change.** Created over 40 years ago, it is funded mainly by Medicare and Medicaid dollars, medical dollars not originally meant to meet people's long-term care needs. We must think out of the box to empower people and allow REAL choices.

The money should follow the individual, not the facility or provider. A national long-term service policy should not favor any one setting over the other. It should let the users choose where services should be delivered. **Our current system is not neutral, and it doesn't reflect people's choices.**

The **current system is needlessly expensive.** We must explore cost-effective ways to meet people's needs. **Community services have been shown to be less expensive on average than institutional services, and better liked by individuals.** In **FY 2005, 63 percent of our total $94.5 billion long term care Medicaid dollars** ($59.34 billion) were spent on nursing homes and other **institutional** services, leaving only 37 percent ($35.16 billion) for all community services (waivers, personal care, home health, etc.).

People with disabilities—both old and young—even those with severe mental and/or physical disabilities **want services** in the most integrated setting possible. Overwhelmingly, people prefer **community services** so they can stay in their own home.

People with disabilities and their families want REAL choice, which means: a) **equitable funding** opportunities, b) **no programmatic or rule disincentives to community services,** and c) **options** for services delivery that include agency-based services, vouchers, and fiscal intermediaries. Empower people with disabilities and families.

Family values **keep families together** a) **children** belong in families b) grandparents at home c) **mom and dad** together with the kids d) **communities** take care of their own.

Money following the individual can eliminate overburdening government rules and regulations.

A **functional system based on need instead of medical diagnosis** could end FRAGMENTATION of the service delivery system.

Keeping people in the community allows the possibility for individuals with disabilities to train for work so they can become **TAXPAYERS instead of TAX USERS.**

The federal government needs to **work in partnership with the states to create flexible delivery systems** that give people REAL choice.

Change can cause fear of the unknown. Some long-time providers of services and families believe REAL choice would threaten what they have. **We cannot continue the system as it is today;** it is expensive, fragmented, overly medical, and disliked by almost everyone.

Source: American Disabled for Attendant Programs Today, 2009. Retrieved November 21, 2009, from http://www.adapt.org/cca-talkingpts.php. Reprinted by permission of ADAPT.

that buildings and facilities that are designed, constructed, or altered with federal funds, or leased by a federal agency, comply with federal standards for physical accessibility"[108] such as ramps, elevators, and other barrier-free access. Many buildings today continue to fall short of the standards for restrooms, parking lots, doors, and warning signals.

Houses or apartments that everyone can navigate because they meet standards for *universal access* are particularly scarce. For example, individuals using wheelchairs find that few apartments or houses have accessible entrances, sufficiently wide doorways, or appliances that can be easily reached. The *visitability* movement works to ensure that "virtually all new homes—not merely those custom-built for occupants who currently have disabilities—offer a few specific features that make the home easier for people who develop mobility impairments to live in and visit."[109] The specifics of what makes an apartment or house "visitable" vary, but some states and communities have passed visitability legislation, and visitability bills have introduced to the U.S. Congress. Legislation generally refers only to new home construction.

Making a home or other building visitable or accessible at time of construction is less costly than many people may realize and much less costly than modifying it later. According to the organization Concrete Change:

> In new construction, total added cost is typically less than $100 when building on a concrete slab and less than $600 when building with a basement. No added square footage is required. Wider doors can be obtained for, at most, only a few dollars more per door . . . .Only interior passage doors on the main level are covered by most ordinances (not closets, nor second floor doors). Only one of the entrances is mandated to be zero-step, and that can be accomplished at little or not cost on the great majority of lots.[110]

Universal design and access include more than the "built environment." The concept also includes communications such as printing documents in fonts large enough to be easily read, the use of closed captioning, and audio signals that alert people to the possibility of danger.

THE REHABILITATION ACT Among the most important pieces of civil rights legislation for individuals with disabilities is Title V of the Rehabilitation Act of 1973.[111] The act:

1. Requires federal agencies and businesses, organizations, and institutions holding contracts with the U.S. government to have affirmative action programs to hire and promote qualified individuals with disabilities.
2. Prohibits all public and private institutions receiving federal assistance from discriminating against qualified individuals with disabilities—employees, students, and consumers of healthcare and other services.
3. Established a board to enforce the 1968 Architectural Barriers Act. Today, it is called the Access Board, and in addition to the built environment and transit vehicles, it also covers telecommunications and electronic and information technology access.

The Rehabilitation Act was the first to provide specific protections for individuals with disabilities in programs receiving federal funding. The Department of Justice and many other U.S. government agencies such as the Department of Education and the Department of Health and Human Services have responsibility for enforcing federal laws that prohibit discrimination against individuals with disabilities.

THE AMERICANS WITH DISABILITIES ACT   Perhaps no other recent legislation, court decision, or administrative ruling holds more significance for individuals with disabilities than the Americans with Disabilities Act (ADA). The ADA passed with overwhelming Congressional support in 1990 and was substantially amended in 2008. Title I of the ADA covers employment, Title II covers public services, and Title III covers public accommodations. Representative Steny Hoyer (D-MD), the ADA's chief sponsor in the House, called the bill an "Emancipation Proclamation" for those with disabilities.

The ADA's "three-prong" definition identifies an individual with a disability as one who has "a physical or mental impairment that substantially limits one or more major life activities, a record of such an impairment, or being regarded as having such an impairment." This definition is consistent with those contained in the Rehabilitation Act and the Fair Housing Act. The ADA's goals are "equality of opportunity, full participation, independent living, and economic self-sufficiency."

The ADA goes much farther than any previous legislation in requiring private sector compliance. For example, retail establishments such as restaurants, hotels, and theaters must be accessible. In debates over the bill, businesses argued that not only were the costs to adopt the new measures unrealistic and outrageously expensive, but that they were also unclear and potentially unsafe. In testimony to the Senate, a representative of the National Association of Theater Owners argued against allowing patrons in wheelchairs to sit where they want, because "it is not only reasonable, but it is essential from a safety standpoint that wheelchair patrons be seated near an exit."[112]

The ADA's telecommunications provisions require that telephone companies provide relay services for customers with hearing and speech impairments. In the area of transportation, all new buses and trains must be made accessible to wheelchair users (airlines are covered under the Air Carrier Access Act).

The ADA broadened prohibitions on employment discrimination for businesses with 15 or more employees. It includes bans against discrimination in the hiring, firing, compensation, advancement, and training of people with disabilities, and also requires employers to make "reasonable accommodations" for individuals with disabilities unless this would case "undue hardship." Reasonable accommodations may include providing readers or interpreters, modifying buildings, adjusting work schedules, and purchasing needed assistive devices. Undue hardship to employers is defined as "requiring significant difficulty or expense." One perspective was that the ADA "was legislation on the cheap, mandating new responsibilities for private employers without offering any new financial assistance either to the employers or to the disabled people themselves."[113] The Equal Employment Opportunity Commission helps employers comply with the ADA and determines just how far they must go to make "reasonable" efforts and what would be considered a "significant" expense. At the time of its passage in 1990, the U.S. Chamber of Commerce called ADA language "an invitation to litigation."[114]

Many lawsuits have indeed been filed since the ADA was passed. In the prevailing conservative political environment, rulings were more likely to favor business (defendants) rather than employees (plaintiffs who brought the suits). In a number of cases, the court concluded that individuals whose impairment could be corrected, for example, with medication or eyeglasses, are not truly disabled and therefore are not entitled to disability employments protections. The outcome was that some people were considered not "disabled enough" to receive protection under the ADA, but they were considered "disabled enough" to be refused a job or fired because an employer felt their physical or mental limitations kept them from safely or effectively fulfilling job requirements. In various cases, courts ruled against individuals who claimed they were disabled due to vision impairments, high blood pressure, carpal tunnel syndrome, liver disease, and stroke. The U.S. Supreme Court supported a strict definition, indicating that a disability must interfere with essential tasks such as brushing one's teeth or washing one's face (see, for example, *Sutton v. United Airlines; Toyota Motor Manufacturing, Kentucky, Inc. v. Williams*). The definition of disability was interpreted so strictly "that hardly anyone could meet it."[115]

State employees also lost employment discrimination cases based on the notion of "sovereign immunity" provided under the Eleventh Amendment to the U.S. Constitution. Sovereign immunity holds that it is unlawful to sue a state without the state's permission. For example, Patricia Garrett was denied damages when she tried to sue her employer, a state hospital, for demoting her after being diagnosed and treated for breast cancer, and Milton Ash was denied damages he sought from his state employer for not providing reasonable workplace accommodations for his severe asthma.[116] In its *Garrett* case ruling, the U.S. Supreme Court agreed that sovereign immunity protects states from suits filed by individuals under Title I of the ADA. Court cases can be long and arduous for plaintiffs. They set important precedents, though often not the one the plaintiff hoped to see.

Some argue that the ADA transcends sovereign immunity. Others argue that the ADA and the Rehabilitation Act are unconstitutional because Congress overstepped its authority in telling states what to do. Though the U.S. Supreme Court ruled that a private individual could not sue a state under the ADA's Title I employment provisions, the federal government can sue states under Title I and "private individuals may sue state officials in their official capacities as long as the plaintiffs do not seek money damages."[117] Subsequent court decisions indicate that under Title II of the ADA, individuals may be entitled to sue states to make public services, in these cases, courts and prisons, accessible. In one of these cases, a wheelchair user contended that he had to crawl up two flights of stairs to be present for a legal proceeding.

Major changes were made to the ADA in 2008.[118] To return the act to what Congress originally intended, the definition of disability is supposed to be interpreted more broadly than the narrower definition or higher standard that was being used. Except for "ordinary eyeglasses and contact lenses," other "mitigating measures" like hearing aids, medications, and prosthetic devices are no longer to be included in determining whether an individual is disabled. The definition of "major life activity" has also been broadened so that more people may now be able to make claims for ADA protection. In addition to self-care, examples of major life activities are "manual tasks, seeing, hearing, eating, sleeping, walking, standing, lifting, bending, speaking, breathing, learning, reading, concentrating, thinking, and communicating" and "major bodily functions" such as "functions of the immune system, normal cell growth, digestive, bowel, bladder, neurological, brain, respiratory, circulatory, endocrine, and reproductive functions."

The ADA act amendments should make it easier for employees to take action under the third prong of the ADA's definition of disability. Previously, employees had to prove that the employer "regarded" them as having a disability that substantially limited a major life activity. Under the new, broader standard, the language is that the employer "perceived" the individual to have a disability even if a perceived (or actual) disability does not limit a major life activity.

The amended act also clarifies that the Equal Employment Opportunity Commission (EEOC) has the authority to issue regulations and interpretative guidance to carry out the intent of the ADA. The 2008 amendments are likely to throw the door open to many more disability discrimination claims that will be much more difficult for employers and other defendants to deflect.[119]

The ADA act amendments became effective on January 1, 2009, but it was not until the fall of 2009 that public hearings were held and the deadline for comments on rulemaking ended. As 2010 approached, no final rules had yet been issued. Part of the ADA's importance is that it is applicable across the United States, but some states already have more stringent legislation or include provisions not found in the ADA. For example, California's Fair Employment and Housing Act provides for damages that the ADA does not.[120]

THE U.N. CONVENTION ON THE RIGHTS OF PERSONS WITH DISABILITIES   In December 2006, the United Nations General Assembly adopted the Convention on the Rights of Persons with Disabilities. It is the first United Nations' convention of the new century.[121] This comprehensive document outlines the rights to which the United Nations believes all people with disabilities should be entitled. The U.S. House of Representatives passed a resolution encouraging adoption of the convention, and the Obama administration signed the document in July 2009. The U.S. Senate will consider the convention for approval, which is necessary for ratification. Ratification indicates that a country will comply with all provisions of the convention. In its history, the United States has ratified only three U.N. conventions (these conventions concerned torture, civil and political rights, and racial discrimination).

The National Council on Disability (NCD), an independent federal agency that provides advice to the president, Congress, and federal agencies to improve the lives of people with disabilities, compared the Americans with Disabilities Act to the Convention on the Rights of Persons with Disabilities and found that the ADA is consistent with the spirit of the convention and inspired many aspects of it. It also indicated a number of areas in which it believes the United States falls short of the measures contained in the convention. For example, regarding accessibility, the NCD calls federal laws underenforced, and in the area of independent living and community inclusion, U.S. law "limits the right to live in the community to services that do not cause fundamental alterations."[122] The NCD recommends stronger implementation and enforcement actions to bring the United States closer to meeting the goals of the convention. Illustration 6.5 provides more information on the U.N. Disability Convention.

ILLUSTRATION 6.5
The United States and the UN Disability Convention
Nancy Langer

July 30, 2009

Today Ambassador Susan Rice will sign, on behalf of the United States, an international human rights treaty at the UN. The United States has ratified only 3 of 26 international human rights treaties, with some in Congress still clinging to the idea that the United States should forever view itself as an exception. It's not a sensible policy, and President Obama is right to move in another direction.

For decades there has been growing dissonance between U.S. leadership on human rights and institutional U.S. resistance to international instruments. History on the Disability Convention exemplifies the point.

Americans created the Americans with Disabilities Act (ADA) and the Rehabilitation Act, giving governments an education in how to include people with disabilities in their social and economic architecture. When the AIDS epidemic hit, U.S. law ultimately viewed the disease through the prism of the ADA, leading policymakers around the world away from reprisal policies like quarantine and job discrimination. Yet this same state resisted joining the global community in most verbal commitments to human rights principles. The approach puzzled allies and advocates alike.

During the last U.S. Administration, as the UN General Assembly formally considered a specialized disability human rights treaty in 2001, U.S. diplomats said disability was a domestic issue, of no international importance. The United States insisted it would never sign or ratify an international agreement relating to disability rights. Why?

650 million people worldwide live with disability. Eighty percent live in developing nations. People with disabilities in poor countries face ostracism and worse. Women and girls are particularly vulnerable. A 2004 survey in India found that virtually all of the women and the girls with disabilities were beaten at home; 25 percent of women with intellectual disabilities had been raped. Conflict creates human insecurity, including more people with disabilities.

Secretary Clinton is promoting broad development goals as pillars of U.S. foreign policy. Clearly, the UN Convention on the Rights of Persons with Disabilities is in line with what the United States is trying to achieve in post-conflict countries. Rule of law and participatory democracy all require access for people with disabilities; societies that respect the rights of disabled people are more likely to respect the rights of women and other minorities.

U.S. humanitarian assistance and disaster relief must incorporate a disability dimension into emergency preparedness and relief programs, in line with Article 11 of the Disability Convention that addresses the rights of persons with disabilities in situations of risk. Disability rights are not merely "domestic" as the Bush Administration insisted. Disability rights—like the rights of girls and women—represent a cross-cutting issue that transcends the individual and has domestic, regional, and international policy outcomes.

By making good on his promise to support the UN Disability Convention, President Obama has set sail toward more sensible U.S. policy, a course correction long overdue. The Senate should support the President and people with disabilities around the world and ratify the Convention.

Source: "The US and the UN Disability Convention" by Nancy Langer, July 30, 2009, copyright © 2009 by The Henry L. Stimson Center. Retrieved November 21, 2009, from http://www.stimson.org/pub.cfm?ID=841. Reprinted by permission.

DISABILITY POLICY FOR CHILDREN

Efforts in the 1960s promoted many advances for individuals with developmental disabilities (DD). Advocates for improved policies gained a valuable ally in President John F. Kennedy who had a sister with intellectual disability.

Developmental Disabilities Assistance and Bill of Rights Act

The original, federal definition of developmental disabilities appeared in the Developmental Disabilities and Facilities Construction Act of 1970 and was expanded in the Developmental Disabilities Assistance and Bill of Rights Act of 1975. In 1987, the Rehabilitation Comprehensive Services and Developmental Disabilities Amendments eliminated specific diagnostic categories such as mental retardation, cerebral palsy, epilepsy, and autism in favor of a broader definition of developmental disability. The current federal definition of developmental disabilities is found in the Developmental Disabilities Assistance and Bill of Rights Act Amendments of 2000. According to this act:

> Developmental disabilities are severe, life-long disabilities attributable to mental and/or physical impairments that manifest themselves before the age of 22 years and are likely to continue indefinitely. They result in substantial limitations in three or more of the following areas:
>
> self-care
>
> comprehension and language
>
> skills (receptive and expressive language)
>
> learning
>
> mobility
>
> self-direction
>
> capacity for independent living
>
> economic self-sufficiency
>
> ability to function independently without coordinated services.
>
> Persons with developmental disabilities require continuous individually planned and coordinated services and supports (e.g., housing, employment, education, civil and human rights protection, health care) from many providers in order to live in the community.[123]

On the positive side, this definition is more functionally oriented, is considered less stigmatizing, and does not restrict services to only those with specific diagnoses. On the negative side, the definition may leave too much room for interpretation and prevent individuals with less severe disabilities from receiving services that could substantially improve the quality of their lives.[124]

In addition to state vocational rehabilitation agencies that serve people who are blind, a number of schools throughout the United States provide education and training specifically to children who are blind and/or deaf. At the federal level, the Rehabilitation Services Administration (RSA) provides consultation to the states in developing services for individuals who are deaf or have other communication disorders. RSA also works on developing technological devices to assist individuals with disabilities. Since 1972 the Economic Opportunity Act has included a goal that 10 percent of Head Start enrollees be children with disabilities.

Education Policy for Children with Disabilities

Many children with disabilities were once relegated to "special education" classes where they spent most, if not all, of the school day separated from other students. Today, mainstreaming in the school environment (also called inclusion) is now an accepted right of children with disabilities and their families thanks to the Education for All Handicapped Children Act of 1975, signed by President Gerald Ford, and renamed the Individuals with Disabilities Education Act (IDEA) in 1990.

INDIVIDUALS WITH DISABILITIES EDUCATION ACT   IDEA states that every child with a disability is entitled to an "appropriate elementary and secondary education." Most children are served in regular public schools. If a child must be placed in a private school by the local education authority in order to obtain an appropriate education, this service must be provided at no cost to the child's family. Other services, including transportation and special devices, must also be provided. In 1997, IDEA was reauthorized with various amendments, including provisions to expand mediation services when parents and schools disagree on what a child needs and will get. In 2004, President George W. Bush signed the Individuals with Disabilities Education Improvement Act, reauthorizing IDEA.

Inclusion has been hailed as a sensible and effective way to ensure that children with physical and mental disabilities are afforded full opportunities to learn and to interact with other children. It allows for the integration of children with disabilities into the mainstream of society and prepares them to be part of the community. In the 2006–2007 school year, nearly 6.7 million or 14 percent of public school students aged 3 to 21 received services related to a disability.[125] About 40 percent had specific learning disabilities, 22 percent had speech or language impairments, 8 percent had intellectual disability, 7 percent had emotional disturbances, and the remaining had other types of disabilities. Students with disabilities are spending increasing amounts of time in regular school classrooms.[126]

Despite the appeal of the concept, early efforts at mainstreaming met with resistance as the number of children requiring services grew and states had to bear the majority of the cost of their education. Small school systems and those in poor areas were particularly hard pressed to meet the demands of the law. Advocates have long contended that Congress has never come close to providing the 40 percent of funding it promised in the 1975 act for the additional costs of educating children with disabilities. Current estimates are that the federal government now provides about 18 percent of what it costs to serve students with disabilities.[127] Some consider this an unfunded federal mandate. The U.S. Department of Education claims there are no unfunded mandates because states can decide not to participate in a particular federal program.[128] Many states would, however, be hard pressed to do without the federal funds that are provided to serve children with disabilities.

NO CHILD LEFT BEHIND ACT Another piece of legislation that affects students with disabilities and their schools is the No Child Left Behind (NCLB) Act of 2001, championed by the George W. Bush administration. President Bush called the law an attempt to address the "soft bigotry of low expectations."[129] In fact, special education has also been criticized on other grounds—as a dumping ground for students with behavioral problems and as a category in which far too many children of color, especially black boys, have been placed because schools fail to meet their needs.[130]

NCLB reauthorized the Elementary and Secondary Education Act, originally enacted in 1965 (and discussed at greater length in Chapter 9). NCLB requires that all students—including students with disabilities—perform proficiently on reading, math, and science tests. States must report data for various groups of students, including students with disabilities, who had largely been excluded from state testing in the past. These tests are often referred to as "high stakes" because states may use them to determine if students move to the next grade level or graduate.[131]

On one hand, many teachers and parents welcome increased expectations given that schools would be expected to provide an education that would better prepare children with disabilities for life. On the other hand, they were concerned that these new expectations might invite unintended and harsh consequences. Since this is the first time federal law required public schools to demonstrate how well they are serving children with disabilities, making this assessment in a fair and appropriate manner is a concern. Many students with disabilities are not impaired in their ability to learn, especially given appropriate accommodations, but others have severe learning disabilities. Students with disabilities who need accommodations to take the same assessment tests as other students are supposed to receive them, such as having a test read aloud or having more time to take the test. In the first year of testing under NCLB, in 30 of 39 states with complete data, students in special education scored 30 percentage points lower on fourth-grade reading tests than other students; in six states the gap exceeded 50 percentage points.[132]

In December 2003, the U.S. Department of Education responded to concerns about testing procedures for students with the most significant cognitive disabilities. States may now use "alternative forms" of assessment geared to grade level or "alternate standards," i.e., the student's learning level rather than the student's grade level. For example, a student may be given a test for a lower grade level or be assessed using examples or a portfolio of his or her work. However, in assessing "adequate yearly progress," states can count such assessments for no more than one percent of students (states can, however, appeal this figure).[133] Given the new rules, there was some concern that schools might change the way they assess disability or determine how many students have disabilities.[134]

In 2005, states were given more flexibility for testing students whose disabilities may not be as significant as those in the one percent group but who are not ready to take the usual achievement tests. These tests are described as using "alternate means" and "modified standards." In reporting yearly progress, states may utilize this method for up to two percent of students.

Assessing remaining achievement gaps and comparing how well states are doing is difficult because of "fuzzy data"—states use different testing methods and the validity of alternate tests has often not been established.[135] Alternate tests are expensive to design and administer, and no single assessment can do the job because students vary widely in tests that will meet their needs.[136] States may report similar percentages of students meeting proficiency levels, but achieve them in different ways. For example, in 2007, Kansas reported that 73 percent of fourth graders with disabilities scored proficient in reading; Nebraska's figure was 78 percent.[137] Kansas's figure was comprised of 50 percent of students who took the regular test, 6 percent who took the alternate standards test, and 19 percent who took the modified standards test. In Nebraska, which has not adopted a modified standards test, 74 percent of students with disabilities who were proficient took the regular test and 4 percent took the alternate standards test.

Students with disabilities have made gains, but substantial gaps still exist. For example, among fourth graders, estimated gaps of at least 30 to 40 percent in reading and math are still not uncommon.[138] Significant challenges lie ahead. By 2014, all students, including students with disabilities, are expected to perform at the proficient level on state tests. When it comes to testing, there is indeed a lot at stake for students, their families, school districts, and state education departments.

Another issue of concern is the interface between IDEA, which focuses on *individualized* learning plans and goals for students, and NCLB, which requires that all students meet the *same* levels of proficiency.[139] One purpose of IDEA's 2004 reauthorization was to increase consistency between IDEA and NCLB. One way to do this is to better align students' individual education plans (IEPs) required under IDEA with NCLB's proficiency standards.

DISABILITY POLICY FOR THE FUTURE

Americans may disagree on the definition of disability, but they now take for granted many aspects of disability policy—a financial safety net for people whose disability prevents them from working, rehabilitation services for those who can become employed or return to work, features that make the environment accessible (e.g., wheelchair-accessible curbs, lifts on public transportation, ramps to buildings, sign language interpreters for public speeches and events), and civil rights protections such as nondiscrimination in employment when qualified for a job. However, the financial safety net is not particularly generous because policymakers worry about malingering, leaving poverty rates among people with disabilities higher than they are in the general population. Unemployment rates are also higher, perhaps due to continued discrimination against people with disabilities or because of the costs of accommodations. The owners of some facilities and establishments must still be prodded to make them fully accessible.

Many other civil rights issues for people with disabilities remain unresolved such as the right to obtain as well as to refuse treatment and to informed consent, guardianship, fair treatment if accused of a crime, voting rights, and zoning restrictions on community residences. Additional issues confront advocates of the rights of individuals with intellectual disability. Institutionalization has been a particularly vexing issue because individuals with intellectual disability are often denied the same rights as individuals who are mentally ill to have their cases reviewed for discharge. In addition, they may be unable to express their wishes or inform others if they have been abused. In 2002 the U.S. Supreme Court finally ruled that execution of death row inmates who are mentally retarded constituted cruel and unusual punishment, but it left the states to determine what constitutes mental retardation (intellectual disability).

We could discuss many other questions about disability policy. For example, would people with disabilities and the country-at-large benefit from one disability system rather than the multiple systems that now exist—SSDI for people with sufficient work histories, SSI for those who do not have sufficient work histories, VA programs for veterans? Should benefits and services be based entirely on need rather than work history? Another important question that has been raised is whether policy designed exclusively for people with disabilities promotes their separation from the rest of society, rather than policies like universal access, which are designed to promote integration.[140]

Disability rights activists and advocates agree that monitoring and enforcement are keys to assuring that the rights of individuals with disabilities are upheld.[141] Each year the EEOC reports on the number of cases it has addressed and the amount of payments it has collected on behalf of those who have faced employment discrimination. Federal enforcement agencies are often criticized for not pursuing more cases more aggressively.

To improve disability policy, historian and disability policy expert Edward Berkowitz recommends a congressional oversight committee and a federal agency dedicated to bringing together stakeholders to address disability in a holistic way.[142] The committee would address the national budget for disability policy and programs and serve as the conduit for disability policy. In addition, Berkowitz recommends expanding the scope of the National Council on Disability (NCD). The NCD itself has encouraged President Obama to issue an Executive Order to establish an Interagency Disability Coordinating Council and require the participation of all federal agencies serving people with disabilities.[143] Berkowitz also recommends flexible policies that provide the supports needed by those who can and want to remain in the labor force and that help others retire with dignity. He advocates the creation of "independence initiatives" that individuals could use to purchase attendant care or to make environmental modifications, and "independent living block grants" to localities to establish ILCs along with the guarantee of healthcare and the "vigorous enforcement" of civil rights protections.

Summary

Americans have responded to disability with public assistance, social insurance, social service, and civil rights legislation. The approach to disability policy is moving away from medically or expert-centered to one in which the locus of control is with people who have disabilities. Some disability policies, such as many aspects of the Rehabilitation Act and the Americans with Disabilities Act (ADA), are intended to cover all people with disabilities. Others, like the Vocational Rehabilitation Act, focus more on those who wish to obtain or maintain employment. Still other policies, such as sections of the ADA and other policies that promote universal access, may make life easier for the population in general. Although disability policy has improved in many ways, people with disabilities continue to have higher poverty rates and unemployment rates than the population. Those who want to work may face obstacles because employers are protected from incurring unreasonable costs in making workplace accommodations. Many people with disabilities have limited choices with regard to housing or face barriers to participation in other aspects of community life such as voting. Advocacy is an important tool for people with disabilities. Those who are unable to participate directly in the political process must rely on others to see that their rights are protected. The United Nations Convention is an attempt to make additional improvements for people with disabilities in the United States and other countries.

Discussion Questions and Class Activities

1. Invite a speaker from the nearest Social Security office to discuss the Social Security Disability Insurance (SSDI) program and the Supplemental Security Income (SSI) program in your state. Be prepared to ask the speaker questions about the Disability Determination (DD) process, the appeals process, and supplemental SSI payments the state may make. You may also to wish to invite individuals receiving SSDI or SSI to discuss their experience with the program and an attorney or other advocate who assists people in navigating the DD process about their experiences with these programs.

2. Invite speakers from ADAPT, Advocacy, Inc., the Arc, or other disability rights organizations to discuss the current issues on which they are working and the strategies they are using to advance disability policy and the rights of people with disabilities.

3. Study a disability rights issue such as the proposed Community Choice Act or ratification of the U.N. Convention in more depth and write a letter to a member of Congress supporting the measure, suggesting improvements, or taking another position.

4. Tour your campus (or other public or private facilities in your community) and make note of barriers to access for people with various types of disabilities. Invite a staff member or members on your campus in charge of architectural compliance and other forms of accessibility (or government officials who enforce compliance) to discuss the law and challenges or issues that hinder compliance with accessibility.

5. Invite a staff member from your campus to discuss services for students with disabilities and the challenges that the college or university faces in serving students with disabilities. Invite students with disabilities to provide their perspectives.

6. Read a biography or autobiography of an individual who has/had a disability. Report on points raised in the biography or autobiography that were surprising to you or increased your knowledge about disability and disability policy.

7. Invite a member of the armed forces who sustained a physical and/or mental disability as a result of combat to speak to the class about the experience, how the disability has changed him or her, the rehabilitation process, and other information the individual is willing to share. Ask the individual what policy changes he or she feels are needed to better assist veterans and others with disabilities.

8. Debate whether alcohol and drug dependence, obesity, or other illnesses that are often considered to be under the individual's control should be covered under disability policy, and if so, should there be any special stipulations or conditions on receiving benefits?

9. Invite a school social worker, teacher, school administrator, or other individual who works with children who have disabilities and their families to discuss his or

her work as it relates to the Developmental Disabilities Assistance and Bill of Rights Act, the Individuals with Disabilities Education Act (IDEA), and/or the No Child Left Behind Act. Also invite parents and children with disabilities to discuss the ways in which these pieces of legislation affect them. What does each see as the strengths and weaknesses of this legislation? You may wish to organize this as a panel presentation.

Websites

ADAPT, www.adapt.org/, is "a national grass-roots community that organizes disability rights activists to engage in nonviolent direct action, including civil disobedience, to assure the civil and human rights of people with disabilities to live in freedom."

The Arc, http://www.thearc.org/NetCommunity/Page .aspx?pid=183, is a "community based organization of and for people with intellectual and developmental disabilities." The Arc and its state and local chapters provide services and support for individuals and families.

The National Council on Disability, http://www.ncd. gov, is an independent federal agency that provides information on publications and other resources that promote equal opportunity for all individuals with disabilities and that empower individuals with disabilities to achieve economic self-sufficiency, independent living, and inclusion and integration in all aspects of society.

The Office of Special Education and Rehabilitation Services, http://www.ed.gov/about/offices/list/osers/ programs.html, is a federal government agency that is part of the U.S. Department of Education. Its mission is to "guide and support a comprehensive array of programs and projects that support individuals with disabilities." It has three components: the National Institute on Disability and Rehabilitation Research, Office of Special Education Programs, and the Rehabilitation Services Administration.

Social Security Administration (SSA), www.ssa.gov, is the federal government agency that administers the Social Security Disability Insurance (SSDI) program and the Supplemental Security Income (SSI) program. SSA's website contains information about these and related programs such as Medicare, Medicaid, and provisions that encourage employment among SSDI and SSI recipients.

Notes

1. For information on how the definition of disability has evolved, see Monroe Berkowitz, William G. Johnson, and Edward H. Murphy, *Public Policy Toward Disability* (New York, Holt, Reinhart, & Winston, 1976), especially p. 7; Edward D. Berkowitz, ""The American Disability System in Historical Perspective," in Edward D. Berkowitz, ed., *Disability Policies and Government Programs* (New York: Holt, Rinehart, & Winston, 1979), especially p. 43; Gary L. Albrecht, Katherine D. Seelman, and Michael Bury, eds., *Handbook of Disability Studies* (Thousand Oaks, CA: Sage Publications, 2001); Stephanie L. Bernell, "Theoretical and Applied Issues in Defining Disability in Labor Market Research," *Journal of Disability Policy Studies,* Vol. 14, No. 1, 2003, pp. 36–45.

2. Stephen French Gilson and Elizabeth DePoy, "Explanatory Legitimacy: A Model for Disability Policy Development and Analysis," in Karen M. Sowers and Catherine N. Dulmus, eds.-in-chief, Comprehensive *Handbook of Social Work and Social Welfare,* Ira Colby (Ed.), *Social Policy and Policy Practice, Vol. 4,* (Hoboken, NJ: John Wiley & Sons, 2008, pp. 203–218).

3. Edward D. Berkowitz, *Disabled Policy: America's Programs for the Handicapped* (Cambridge, England:

Cambridge University Press, 1987); Eric Kingson and Edward D. Berkowitz, *Social Security and Medicare: A Policy Primer* (Westport, CT: Auburn House, 1993).

4. This paragraph relies on Robert J. Myers, *Social Security* (Bryn Mawr, PA: McCahan Foundation, 1975), pp. 400–401; John G. Turnbull, C. Arthur Williams, Jr., and Earl F. Cheit, *Economic and Social Security* (New York: Ronald Press, 1967), p. 83.

5. Much of this paragraph relies on Ibid.

6. Berkowitz, *Disabled Policy: America's Programs for the Handicapped,* p. 58.

7. Daniel P. Moynihan, *The Politics of a Guaranteed Income* (New York: Random House, 1973).

8. Robert A. Diamond (Ed.), *Future of Social Programs* (Washington, DC: Congressional Quarterly, August 1973), p. 15.

9. For additional information on state supplements, see "SSI Benefits," in *Understanding Supplemental Security Income* (Washington, DC: Social Security Administration, 2009 Edition). Retrieved August 14, 2009, from http://www.ssa.gov/ssi/text-benefits-ussi.htm; Committee on Ways and Means, "Supplemental Security Income," *2008 Green Book* (Washington, DC: U.S. House of Representatives, 2008), pp. 3-14–3-16. Retrieved February 27, 2010, from http://waysandmeans.house.gov/singlepages .aspx?NewsID=10490

10. Figures in this paragraph are from the *Social Security Bulletin, Annual Statistical Supplement, 2009,* "Supplemental Security Income." Retrieved February 27, 2010, from http://www.ssa.gov/policy/ docs/statcomps/supplement/2009

11. Committee on Ways and Means, "Supplemental Security Income," *2008 Green Book,* pp. 3–29, 3–30.

12. *Ibid.,* pp. 3-24–3-25.

13. *Ibid.,* p. 3–17.

14. Committee on Ways and Means, "Supplemental Security Income," *2004 Green Book* (Washington, DC: U.S. House of Representatives), p. 3–6. Retrieved May 16, 2010, from http://waysandmeans .house.gov/singlepages.aspx?NewsID=10489

15. Committee on Ways and Means, "Supplemental Security Income," *2008 Green Book,* p. 3–4.

16. For information on the history of these amounts, see "Substantial Gainful Activity" (Washington, DC: Social Security Administration, October 15, 2009). Retrieved November 16, 2009 from http://www.ssa. gov/OACT/COLA/sga.html

17. This section relies on *Disability Evaluation Under Social Security* (also known as the "Blue Book") (Washington, DC: Social Security Administration, September 2008). Retrieved August 7, 2009, from http://www.ssa.gov/disability/professionals/bluebook/ general-info.htm

18. "Applications for Disability Benefits and Disability Awards" (Washington, DC: Social Security Administration, June 1, 2009). Retrieved August 10, 2009, from http://www.ssa.gov/OACT/STATS/ table6c7.html

19. "Appeals Process," in *Understanding Supplemental Security Income* (Washington, DC: Social Security Administration, 2009 Edition). Retrieved August 14, 2009, from http://www.ssa.gov/ssi/text-appeals-ussi.htm

20. *What You Need To Know When You Get Social Security Disability Benefits* (Washington, DC: Social Security Administration, November 2008), SSA Publication No. 05-10153. Retrieved August 7, 2009, from http://www.ssa.gov/pubs/10153.pdf

21. Stephen French Gilson and Elizabeth Depoy, "Policy Legitimacy: A Model for Disability Policy Analysis and Change," *Review of Disability Studies,* Vol. 5, No. 4, 2009.

22. Melanie Conklin, "Out in the Cold: Washington Shows Drug Addicts the Door," *The Progressive,* Vol. 61, No. 3, March 1997, pp. 25–27.

23. Committee on Ways and Means, U "Supplemental Security Income" *2004 Green Book,* pp. 3-45–3-47.

24. "Report Highlights Impact of Welfare Reform on Addicted Population," *Alcoholism and Drug Abuse Weekly,* Vol. 15, No. 31, August 18, 2003. For an in-depth look at the "Multi-Site Study of the Termination of Supplemental Security Income Benefits for Drug Addicts and Alcoholics," see the complete issue of *Contemporary Drug Problems,* Vol. 30, Issue 1/2, 2003.

25. James A. Swartz, Kevin Campbell, Jim Baumohl, and Peggy Tonkin, "Drug Treatment Participation and Retention Rates among Former Recipients of Supplemental Security Income for Drug Addiction and Alcoholism," *Contemporary Drug Problems,* Vol. 30, Nos. 1/2, 2003, pp. 335–364.

26. Patricia Hanrahan, Daniel J. Luchins, Lea Cloninger, and James Swartz, "Medicaid Eligibility of Former Supplemental Security Income Recipients with Drug Abuse or Alcoholism Disability," *American Journal of Public Health,* Vol. 94, No. 1, 2004, pp. 46–47.

27. Committee on Ways and Means, "Welfare Benefits for Noncitizens," Section J, *2004 Green Book,* pp. J-1–J-11.

28. "Issue: Welfare," *Congressional Quarterly,* December 6, 1997, p. 3013.

29. The remainder of this paragraph relies on *Social Security Bulletin, Annual Statistical* Supplement, 2009, Table 7.E6. Retrieved February 27, 2010, from http://www.ssa.gov/policy/docs/statcomps/supplement/2009/7e.pdf

30. For a further description of the Zebley decision, see Committee on Ways and Means, U.S. House of Representatives, *Overview of Entitlement Programs, 1996 Green Book* (Washington, DC: U.S. Government Printing Office, 1996), pp. 262–263.

31. Committee on Ways and Means, U.S. House of Representatives, *Overview of Entitlement Programs, 1993 Green Book* (Washington, DC: U.S. Government Printing Office, 1993), pp. 852–853.

32. Committee on Ways and Means, U.S. House of Representatives, *1996 Green Book,* pp. 297–298; Committee on Ways and Means, U.S. House of Representatives, *Overview of Entitlement Programs, 1998 Green Book* (Washington, DC: U.S. Government Printing Office, 1998), pp. 301–302.

33. Committee on Ways and Means, "Supplemental Security Income," *2004 Green Book,* pp. 3-42–3-44.

34. The remainder of this paragraph relies on U.S. House of Representatives, "Supplemental Security Income," *2008 Green Book,* Table 3-8, p. 3-25 and Table 3-11, pp. 3-27–3-28.

35. Jeffrey Hemmetera, Jacqueline Kauff, and David Wittenburgb, "Changing Circumstances: Experiences of Child SSI Recipients Before and After Their Age-18 Redetermination for Adult Benefits," *Journal of Vocational Rehabilitation,* Vol. 30, 2009, pp. 201–221. Retrieved November 2, 2009, from http://www.mathematica-mpr.com/publications/PDFs/Disability/changingcircumstances.pdf

36. Several articles in the *Journal of Vocational Rehabilitation,* Vol. 30, No. 3, discuss the Youth Transition Demonstration Projects.

37. For more information on specific projects, see "Youth Transition Demonstration (YTD) Project Descriptions" (Washington, DC: Social Security Administration, November 9, 2009). Retrieved November 27, 2009, from http://www.ssa.gov/disabilityresearch/ytdprojects.htm

38. Committee on Ways and Means, "Supplemental Security Income," *2008 Green Book,* pp. 3-29–3-30.

39. Most of the remainder of this paragraph relies on Paul Davies, "SSI Eligibility and Participation Among the Oldest Old: Evidence from the AHEAD," *Social Security Bulletin,* Vol. 64, No. 3, 2001/2002, pp. 38–63.

40. Kilolo Kijakazi and Wendell Primus, "Options for Reducing Poverty Among Elderly Women by Improving Supplemental Security Income" (Washington, DC: Center for Budget and Policy Priorities, 2000), paper presented at the National Academy of Social Insurance 12th Annual Conference, January 27, 2000. Retrieved May 16, 2010, from http://www.cbpp.org/cms/index.cfm?fa=view&id=1522

41. Social Security Administration, *U.S. Interagency Council on Homelessness 2005 Annual Report* (Washington, DC: Author, 2005); "Social Security Online: Services to the Homeless." Retrieved January 4, 2010, from http://www.socialsecurity.gov/homelessness/SSA_Homelessness_Report_2005.htm

42. See "Reducing SSI Enrollment Barriers for Homeless Claimants" (Washington, DC: National Health Care for the Homeless Council). Retrieved November 2, 2009, from http://www.hrsa.gov/homeless/pdf/pa4_post_handout_3.pdf

43. Patricia A. Post, *Casualties of Complexity: Why Eligible Homeless People are not Enrolled in Medicaid* (Washington, DC: National Health Care for the Homeless Council, May 2001), pp. 1–73. Retrieved November 2, 2009, from http://www.nhchc.org/Publications/CasualtiesofComplexity.pdf

44. See "Reducing SSI Enrollment Barriers for Homeless Claimants."

45. "Disability Benefits and Homelessness," *2009 Policy Statements* (Nashville, TN: National Health Care for the Homeless Council, 2009). Retrieved November 2, 2009, from http://www.nhchc.org/Advocacy/PolicyPapers/2009/DisabilityBenefits2009.pdf

46. This paragraph relies on General Accounting Office, *SSA Disability Decision Making: Additional Steps Needed to Ensure Accuracy and Fairness of Decision at the Hearings Level,* GAO-04-14 (Washington, DC: Author, November 12, 2003). Retrieved December 29, 2009, from http://www.gao.gov; General Accounting Office, *SSA Disability Decision Making: Additional Measures Would Enhance Agency's Ability to Determine Whether Racial Bias Exists,* GAO-02-831 (Washington, DC: Author, September 9, 2002). Retrieved December 29, 2009, from http://www.gao.gov

47. This paragraph and the next rely on John D. Stobo, Michael McGeary, and David K. Barnes, Eds., *Improving the Social Security Disability Determination*

Process (Washington, DC: National Academies Press, 2007).

48. Social Security Administration, *Strategic Plan: Fiscal Years 2008–2013* (Washington, DC: Author, September 2008), SSA Pub. No. 04-002. Retrieved August 9, 2009, from http://www.ssa.gov/asp/index.htm

49. Depression and Bipolar Support Alliance, "Advance Notice of Proposed Rulemaking on Criteria for Evaluating Mental Disorders," June 16, 2003. Retrieved November 27, 2009, from http://www.dbsalliance.org/site/PageServer?pagename=advocacy_ssaremarks

50. This paragraph and the next rely on Social Security Administration, *Strategic Plan: Fiscal Years 2008–2013.*

51. Executive Office of the President, *Budget of the United States Government, Fiscal Year 1999* (Washington, DC: U.S. Government Printing Office, 1998), p. 232.

52. Social Security Administration, *Performance and Accountability Report: Fiscal Year 2003* (Washington, DC: Author, 2003), p. 67. Retrieved December 29, 2009, from http://www.ssa.gov/finance/2003/FY03_PAR.pdf

53. Social Security Administration, *Strategic Plan: Fiscal Years 2008–2013,* p. 7.

54. *Ibid.*

55. The remainder of this paragraph relies on Government Accountability Office, *Military Disability System: Increased Supports for Servicemembers and Better Pilot Planning Could Improve the Disability Evaluation Process* (GAO-08-1137) (Washington, DC: Author, September 24, 2008). Retrieved December 20, 2009, from http://www.gao.gov/products/GAO-08-1137; Government Accountability Office, *Military and Veterans' Benefits: Analysis of VA Compensation Levels for Survivors of Veterans and Servicemembers* (GAO-10-62) (Washington, DC: Author, November 13, 2009). Retrieved December 20, 2009, from http://www.gao.gov/products/GAO-10-62; Mary Sneyd, A Call to Duty: Fixing the VA's Disability Benefits System, *Cleveland Live, Inc.,* April 28, 2009. Retrieved December 20, 2009, from http://www.cleveland.com/opinion/index.ssf/2009/04/a_call_to_duty_fixing_the_vas.html

56. National Council on Disability, "National Disability Policy: A Progress Report" (Washington, DC: Author, March 31, 2009). Retrieved December 20, 2009, from http://www.ncd.gov/newsroom/publications/2009/Progress_Report_HTML/NCD_Progress_Report.html

57. For a history of programs and policies addressing disability, see Richard K. Scotch, *From Good Will to Civil Rights: Transforming Federal Disability Policy* (Philadelphia: Temple University Press, 1984);

Berkowitz, *Disabled Policy*; E. Davis Martin, Jr., *Significant Disability: Issues Affecting People with Significant Disabilities from a Historical, Policy, Leadership, and Systems Perspective* (Springfield, IL: Charles C. Thomas, 2001).

58. See Berkowitz, "The American Disability System in Historical Perspective," p. 43.

59. Office of Special Education and Rehabilitative Services, Rehabilitation Services Administration, *Annual Report, Fiscal Year 2005, Report on Federal Activities Under the Rehabilitation Act* (Washington, D.C.: U.S. Department of Education, 2009). Retrieved December 19, 2009 from http://www.ed.gov/about/reports/annual/rsa/2005/index.html

60. Berkowitz, *Disabled Policy,* p. 164.

61. Richard K. Skotch, *From Good Will to Civil Rights: Transforming Federal Disability Policy.*

62. Office of Special Education and Rehabilitation Services, "About RSA" (Washington, DC: U.S. Department of Education). Retrieved November, 2007, from http://www.ed.gov/about/offices/list/osers/rsa/index.html

63. Office of Special Education and Rehabilitative Services, Rehabilitation Services Administration, *Annual Report, Fiscal Year 2005, Report on Federal Activities Under the Rehabilitation Act.*

64. Berkowitz, "The American Disability System in Historical Perspective," p. 45.

65. Office of Special Education and Rehabilitation Services, "About RSA."

66. National Council on Disability, *Achieving Independence: The Challenge for the 21st Century* (Washington, DC: The Council, July 26, 1996), p. 63; on the effects of the vocational rehabilitation approach, also see Berkowitz, *Disabled Policy*; Kingson and Berkowitz, *Social Security and Medicare: A Policy Primer,* especially pp. 144–146.

67. Office of Special Education and Rehabilitative Services, Rehabilitation Services Administration, *Annual Report, Fiscal Year 2005, Report on Federal Activities Under the Rehabilitation Act.*

68. Committee on Ways and Means, "Supplemental Security Income," *2008 Green Book,* p. 3–20.

69. Office of Special Education and Rehabilitative Services, Rehabilitation Services Administration, *Annual Report, Fiscal Year 2005, Report on Federal Activities Under the Rehabilitation Act.*

70. General Accounting Office, "Social Security Disability: Improvements Needed to Continuing Disability Review Process," HEHS-97-1 (Washington, DC: Author, October 1996). Retrieved November 27, 2009,

from http://www.gao.gov/archive/1997/he97001.pdf; see also U.S. General Accounting Office, *Supplemental Security Income: SSA Is Taking Steps to Review Recipients' Disability Status,* HEHS-97-17 (Washington, DC: Author, October 1996). Retrieved November 27, 2009, from http://www.gao.gov/archive/1997/he97017.pdf

71. *Social Security Bulletin, Annual Statistical Supplement,* 2009, Table 7.D1.

72. See *Evaluation of the Ticket to Work Program: Initial Evaluation Report* (Washington, DC: Mathematica Policy Research, February 2004). Retrieved November 16, 2009, from http://www.socialsecurity.gov/disabilityresearch/ttw/ttw_report.htm

73. See, for example, Gilson and Depoy, "Policy Legitimacy: A Model for Disability Policy Analysis and Change."

74. Government Accountability Administration, *Better Planning Could Make the Ticket Program More Effective* (GAO-05-248) (Washington, DC: Author, March 2, 2008). Retrieved December 21, 2009, from http://www.gao.gov/docsearch/locate?searched=1&o=0&order_by=date&search_type=publications&keyword=GAO-05-248&Submit=Search

75. For a history of trial work period trigger amounts see Social Security Administration, "Trial Work Period" (Washington, DC: Social Security Administration, October 15, 2009). Retrieved December 19, 2009, from http://www.socialsecurity.gov/OACT/COLA/twp.html

76. Committee on Ways and Means, "Supplemental Security Income," *2008 Green Book,* p. 3–37.

77. "SSI Only Employment Supports," *2009 Red Book* (Washington, DC: Social Security Administration). Retrieved November 12, 2009, from http://www.socialsecurity.gov/redbook/eng/ssi-only-employment-supports.htm#7

78. "Continued Medicaid Eligibility (Section 1619(B))" (Washington, DC: Social Security Administration, November 12, 2009). Retrieved November 15, 2009, from http://www.ssa.gov/disabilityresearch/wi/1619b.htm

79. Committee on Ways and Means, "Supplemental Security Income," *2008 Green Book,* p. 3–37.

80. See Committee on Ways and Means, "Supplemental Security Income," *2004 Green Book,* pp. 3-49–3-50; Kalman Rupp and Stephen H. Bell, *Paying for Results in Vocational Rehabilitation: Will Provider Incentives Work for Ticket to Work?* (Washington, DC: Urban Institute, 2003). Retrieved June 17, 2010, from http://www.urban.org/publications/310603.html

81. Rupp and Bell, *Paying for Results in Vocational Rehabilitation.*

82. David Salkever, "Tickets Without Takers? Potential Economic Barriers to the Supply of Rehabilitation Services to Beneficiaries with Mental Disorders," in Rupp and Bell, *Paying for Results in Vocational Rehabilitation;* Paul Wehman and Grant Revell, "Lessons Learned from the Provision and Funding of Employment Services for the MR/DD Population: Implications for Assessing the Adequacy of the SSA Ticket to Work," in Rupp and Bell, *Paying for Results in Vocational Rehabilitation.*

83. David Stapleton, Gina Livermore, Craig Thornton, Bonnie O'Day, Robert Weathers, Krista Harrison, So O'Neil, Emily Sama Martin, David Wittenburg, and Debra Wright, *Evaluation of the Ticket to Work Program, Ticket to Work at the Crossroads: A Solid Foundation with an Uncertain Future* (Washington, DC: Mathematic Policy Research, September 2008). Retrieved November 7, 2009, from http://www.ssa.gov/disabilityresearch/ttw4/rollout_vol1_title.html

84. Committee on Ways and Means, "Supplemental Security Income," *2008 Green Book,* pp. 3-20–3-21.

85. Stapleton et al., *Evaluation of the Ticket to Work Program, Ticket to Work at the Crossroads: A Solid Foundation with an Uncertain Future.*

86. Tim Silva, "The Involvement of Employment Networks in Ticket to Work," *Journal of Vocational Rehabilitation,* Vol. 27, 2007, pp. 117–127.

87. *Ticket to Work: Inside Employment Networks,* Vol. 3 (Victor, NY: MAXIMUS Federal Services, October 2006). Retrieved November 27, 2009, from http://www.yourtickettowork.com/selftraining/Inside_Employment_Networks_Volume_3_October_2006.pdf?style=blind

88. Silva, "The Involvement of Employment Networks in Ticket to Work."

89. "Ticket to Work-Work Incentives Improvement Act (TWWIIA), Overview" (Washington, DC: Centers for Medicare and Medicaid Services, November 4, 2009). Retrieved November 16, 2009, from http://www.cms.hhs.gov/TWWIIA/01_Overview.asp

90. Romel W. Mackelprang, "Disability: Overview," in Terry Mizrahi and Larry E. Davis, Eds.-in-chief, *Encyclopedia of Social Work,* 20th ed., pp. 36–43 (Washington, DC: NASW Press, 2008).

91. *Image Archive on the American Eugenics Movement* (Cold Spring Harbor, NY: Dolan DNA Learning Center). Retrieved February 28, 2010, from http://www.eugenicsarchive.org/eugenics/list3.pl

92. Berkowitz, *Disabled Policy,* p. 186.

93. National Council on Disability, *Achieving Independence: The Challenge for the 21st Century,* pp. 19–20.

94. Mackelprang, "Disability: Overview"; Gilson and DePoy, "Explanatory Legitimacy: A Model for Disability Policy Development and Analysis."

95. Robert Silverstein, "An Overview of the Emerging Disability Policy Framework: A Guidepost for Analyzing Public Policy," *Iowa Law Review,* Vol. 85, No. 5, 2000, pp. 1757–1802; quote from p. 1761.

96. *Wyatt v. Stickney,* 3195 U.S.3 (1972).

97. *Olmstead V.L.C.,* 527 U.S. 581 (1999).

98. Eric Emerson, "What Is Normalisation?" in Hilary Brown and Helen Smith, Eds., *Normalisation: A Reader for the Nineties* (London: Tavistock/ Routledge, 1992), pp. 1–18; Steven J. Taylor and Stanford J. Searl, "Disability in America: A History of Policies and Trends," in Martin, *Significant Disability,* pp. 16–63.

99. Bengt Nirje, "The Normalization Principle," in R. Kugel and A. Shearer, Eds., *Changing Patterns in Residential Services for the Mentally Retarded,* rev. ed. (Washington, DC: President's Commission on Mental Retardation, 1976), p. 231; Wolf Wolfensberger, Ed., *The Principle of Normalization in Human Services* (Toronto: National Institute on Mental Retardation, 1972).

100. For a discussion of the various conceptions of normalization, see Brown and Smith, *Normalisation,* especially Emerson's chapter, "What Is Normalisation?"

101. This paragraph relies on Roberta Nelson, *Creating Community Acceptance for Handicapped People* (Springfield, IL: Charles C. Thomas, 1978), pp. 12–22. See also Silverstein, "An Overview of the Emerging Disability Policy Framework; Stephanie L. Bernelly, "Theoretical and Applied Issues in Defining Disability in Labor Market Research," *Journal of Disability Policy Studies,* Vol. 14, No. 1, 2003, pp. 36–45.

102. See, for example, E.G. Enbar, Morris A. Fred, Laura Miller, and Zena Naiditch, "A Nationwide Study of Deinstitutionalization & Community Integration" (Chicago: Equip for Equality, 2004). Retrieved November 29, 2009, from http://www .equipforequality.org/publications/cippreport.php; Emily Sweeney, "Test of Wills at Fernald," *Boston Globe,* January 12, 2006. Retrieved November 29, 2009, from http://www.boston.com/news/local/ massachusetts/articles/2006/01/12/test_of_wills_at_ fernald/

103. Enbar et al., "A Nationwide Study of Deinstitution-alization & Community Integration."

104. World Institute on Disability, *Just Like Everyone Else* (Oakland, CA: World Institute on Disability, 1992), p. 9.

105. ADAPT's website address is http://www.adapt.org.

106. Mathematica Policy Research, Inc. and Centers for Medicare and Medicaid Services, "The National Evaluation of the Money Follows the Person (MFP) Demonstration Grant Program," *Reports from the Field,* No. 2, June 2009. Retrieved November 21, 2009, from http://www.cms.hhs.gov/DeficitReductionAct/ Downloads/MFPfieldrpt2.pdf

107. For an explanation of the latest provision of the Air Carrier Access Act, see United Spinal Association, "Accessible Air Travel: A Guide for People with Disabilities" (Jackson Heights, NY: Author, 2009). Retrieved November 29, 2009, from http://www .unitedspinal.org/pdf/accessible_air_travel.pdf

108. U.S. Department of Justice, "A Guide to Disability Rights" (Washington, DC: Author, September 2005). Retrieved November 29, 2009, from http://www.ada. gov/cguide.htm#anchor66055

109. Concrete Change, "Visitability" (Decatur, GA: Author, 2008). Retrieved November 29, 2009, from http://www.concretechange.org/visitability_defined .aspx

110. Concrete Change, "Myths and Objections" (Decatur, GA: Author, 2008). Retrieved November 29, 2009, from http://www.concretechange.org/policy_responses.aspx

111. U.S. Department of Justice, "A Guide to Disability Rights."

112. Testimony of Malcolm C. Green, Chairman, National Association of Theater Owners, presented on May 10, 1989, before the Senate Subcommittee on the Handicapped on S.933, the "Americans with Disabilities Act," *Congressional Digest,* December 1989, Vol. 68, p. 309.

113. Kingson and Berkowitz, *Social Security and Medicare: A Policy Primer,* p. 148.

114. Testimony of Zachary Fasman, U.S. Chamber of Commerce, presented on May 9, 1989, before the Senate Committee on Labor and Human Resources on S.933, the "Americans with Disabilities Act," *Congressional Digest,* December 1989, Vol. 68, p. 299.

115. Office of Disability Employment Policy, "Accommodation and Compliance Series: The ADA Amendments Act of 2008" (Morgantown, WV: Author). Retrieved December 6, 2009, from http: //www.jan.wvu.edu/bulletins/adaaa1.htm

116. Brian Holohan, "Disability & ADA: State Sovereign Immunity to Title I of ADA Under Review-*University of Alabama v. Garrett*," *American Journal of Law and Medicine,* January 1 2001. Retrieved December 20, 2009, from http://www.allbusiness.com/legal/3587395-1.html; "The Plaintiffs in the Garrett Case" (Washington, DC: Bazelon Center for Mental Health Law). Retrieved December 20, 2009, from http://www.bazelon.org/issues/disabilityrights/incourt/garrett/plaintiffs.htm

117. The remainder of this paragraph relies on Civil Rights Division, *Access for All: Five Years of Progress: A Report from the Department of Justice on Enforcement of the Americans with Disabilities Act* (Washington, DC: U.S. Department of Justice, October 12, 2006). Retrieved December 6, 2009, from http://www.ada.gov/5yearadarpt/fiveyearada.pdf

118. In addition to the text of ADA Amendments of 2008, see, for example, Peter N. Hillman, David Gallai, Maryone M. Glover, and Edward P. Smith, "ADA Amendments: New Protections for Employees and Key Obligations for Employers" (New York: Chadbourne and Clark LLP: September, 2008). Retrieved December 19, 2009, from http://www.chadbourne.com/clientalerts/2008/adaamendsnew-protections

119. Fisher & Phillips LLP, "Meet the New ADA: Massive Changes Ahead for Nation's Employers" (Atlanta: Author, September 18, 2008). Retrieved December 6, 2009, from http://www.laborlawyers.com/shownews.aspx?Show=10879&Type=1122

120. World Institute on Disability, "Just Like Everyone Else."

121. Some of this paragraph relies on European Disability Forum, "Historical Step Ahead for the Rights of Persons with Disabilities" (Brussels: Author, July 31, 2009). Retrieved November 21, 2009, from http://www.edf-feph.org/Page_Generale.asp?DocID=13854&thebloc=22154

122. National Council on Disability, *Finding the Gaps: A Comparative Analysis of Disability Laws in the United States to the United Nations Convention on the Rights of Persons with Disabilities (CRPD)* (Washington, DC: Author, May 12, 2008). Retrieved November 21, 2009, from http://www.disabilityfunders.org/un_convention#compare.

123. See Administration on Developmental Disabilities (Washington, DC: U.S. Department of Health and Human Services, January 28, 2009). Quote slightly edited. Retrieved December 14, 2009, from http://www.acf.hhs.gov/opa/fact_sheets/add_factsheet.html

124. See, for example, Kevin DeWeaver, "Disabilities: The Fight for Inclusion Continues," in Diana M. DiNitto and C. Aaron McNeece, *Social Work: Issues and Opportunities in a Challenging Profession,* 3rd ed. (Chicago: Lyceum Books, 2008), pp. 217–237.

125. National Center for Education Statistics, *Digest of Education Statistics 2008* (Washington, DC: U.S. Department of Education, 2009), Chapter 2, Tables 50 and 52. Retrieved December 14, 2009, from http://nces.ed.gov/pubs2009/2009020_2a.pdf

126. *Ibid.,* Table 51.

127. National Education Association, "IDEA Funding Coalition Offers Proposal" (Washington, DC: Author, 2002-2009). Retrieved December 14, 2009, from http://www.nea.org/home/18750.htm

128. U.S. Department of Education, *10 Facts About K-12 Education Funding* (Washington, DC: Author, 2005). Retrieved December 14, 2009, from http://www.ed.gov/about/overview/fed/10facts/index.html

129. U.S. Department of Education "Raising the Achievement of Students with Disabilities: New Ideas for IDEA" (Washington, DC: Author, August 2006). Retrieved December 24, 2009 from http://www.ed.gov/admins/lead/speced/ideafactsheet.html

130. See, for example, Jawanza Kunjufu, "Black Boys and Special Education—Change Is Needed," *Teachers of Color Magazine,* 2009. Retrieved February 28, 2010, from http://www.teachersofcolor.com/2009/04/black-boys-and-special-education-change-is-needed/; also see Martha J. Coutinho and Donald P. Oswald, *Disproportionate Representation of Culturally and Linguistically Diverse Students in Special Education: Measuring the Problem* (Tempe, AZ: National Center for Culturally Responsive Educational Systems, 2006). Retrieved February 28, 2010, from http://www.nccrest.org/Briefs/students_in_SPED_Brief.pdf

131. Candace Cortiella. "Implications of High-Stakes Testing for Students with Learning Disabilities," *GreatSchools,* January 2010. Retrieved February 28, 2010 from http://www.greatschools.org/LD/school-learning/high-stakes-testing-learning-disabilities.gs?content=886

132. "Quality Counts 2004: Count Me In, Special Education in an Era of Standards," *Education Week,* Vol. XXIII, No. 17, January 8, 2004. Retrieved December 15, 2009, from http://www.edweek.org/media/ew/qc/archives/QC04full.pdf

133. *Federal Register,* Vol. 68, No. 236, December 9, 2003, pp. 68697-68708. Retrieved December 15, 2009, from http://frwebgate.access.gpo.gov/cgi-bin/getpage.cgi?position=all&page=68699&dbname=2003_register

134. See, for example, Candace Cortiella. "No Child Left Behind and Students With Learning Disabilities: Opportunities and Obstacles," *GreatSchools,* January 2010. Retrieved February 28, 2010 from http://www.greatschools.org/LD/school-learning/NCLB-learning-disabilities-opportunities-and-obstacles.gs?content=856&page=all

135. Center for Education Policy, *Has Progress Been Made in Raising Achievement for Students with Disabilities?* (Washington, DC: Author, November 2009). Retrieved December 15, 2009, from http://www.edweek.org/media/ew/qc/archives/QC04full.pdf

136. Government Accountability Office, *No Child Left Behind: Enhancements in the Department of Education's Review Process Could Improve State Academic Assessments* (GAO 09-911) (Washington, DC: Government Accountability Office, 2009). Retrieved December 15, 2009, from www.gao.gov/new.items/d09911.pdf

137. The remainder of this paragraph relies on Center for Education Policy, *Has Progress Been Made in Raising Achievement for Students with Disabilities?*

138. *Ibid.*

139. This paragraph relies on *ibid.*

140. Gilson and DePoy, "Explanatory Legitimacy: A Model for Disability Policy Development and Analysis"; Gilson and DePoy, "Explanatory Legitimacy: A Model for Disability Policy Analysis and Change."

141. Robert Silverstein, "An Overview of the Emerging Disability Policy Framework: A Guidepost for Analyzing Public Policy," *Iowa Law Review,* Vol. 85, No. 5, 2000, pp. 1757–1802.

142. Much of this paragraph relies on Berkowitz, *Disabled Policy;* Kingson and Berkowitz, Social Security and Medicare: *A Policy Primer.*

143. National Council on Disability, "National Disability Policy: A Progress Report" (Washington, DC: March 31, 2009). Retrieved December 29, 2009, from http://www.ncd.gov/newsroom/publications/2009/Progress_Report_HTML/NCD_Progress_Report.html.

7 HELPING NEEDY FAMILIES: AN END TO WELFARE AS WE KNEW IT

Melissa Radey
Diana M. DiNitto

The family is the primary social unit, yet the United States has no comprehensive policy to meet families' economic, health, social, and psychological needs. Instead, a variety of approaches—public assistance, child support, and work programs—are used to assist families, especially those with young children, facing dire economic circumstances. If there is any segment of society for whom people have compassion, it is children, who are completely dependent on others to meet their needs. Why then have these public assistance programs been mired in a sea of controversy? As we shall see, the conflict centers on the parents of these children and whether they participate in the labor force and support their children financially.

FROM MOTHERS' AID TO AFDC

Early in the twentieth century, local and state governments began to provide cash aid called *mothers' aid* or *mothers' pensions* to help children remain in their own homes when their mothers faced economic hardship.[1] These programs were primarily intended for children whose father was deceased or sometimes when fathers were absent due to desertion or divorce.

In 1935, as Title IV of the original Social Security Act, the federal government began to assist states with these efforts under the Aid to Dependent Children (ADC) program. ADC was conceived of as a short-term device to assist financially needy children. The program was intended to diminish and eventually become outmoded as more and more families came to qualify for assistance under the social insurance programs of the Social Security Act.[2] According to Senator Daniel P. Moynihan (D-New York), the "typical beneficiary" was supposed to be "a West Virginia mother whose husband had been killed in a mine accident."[3] But the emphasis of the early ADC program was not on providing aid for widows; it was on providing help to mothers on behalf of their children.

Man-in-the-House Rules

The morality of public aid recipients has been a concern throughout the country's history. In the ADC program, this belief was reflected in "man-in-the-house rules." The thought that mothers receiving public assistance might allow able-bodied men to spend time in their homes incensed those who wanted to ensure that payments were directed only to meeting the needs of children in ADC households. It was considered immoral and illegal for the mother to allow anyone else to benefit from the welfare check. "Midnight raids"—home visits to welfare mothers late at night—were sometimes conducted to ensure that no able-bodied adult males resided in

ADC households. This was done on the premise that these men could be considered "substitute fathers" responsible for the family's financial support.

In 1968 the U.S. Supreme Court determined that man-in-the house rules could not be used as a method for "flatly denying" children public assistance. Today, more sophisticated means, such as electronic checks of state and federal records, are used when noncompliance with program rules is suspected.

Trying to Keep Families Together

The ADC program grew slowly for many years with only minor changes made in some aspects of the program. Not until 1950 were mothers' (and in a few cases disabled fathers') needs considered, and they too became eligible for aid. Other improvements were also made. Medical services, paid in part by the federal government, became available to recipients. In 1958 a formula was developed so that states with lower per capita incomes received more federal assistance for their ADC programs than wealthier states.

But other parts of the program were becoming sore spots. One of the most stinging accusations leveled against ADC was that it contributed to fathers deserting their families. Although this argument was difficult to prove,[4] we can see how it arose. Under ADC, families with an able-bodied father residing at home were not eligible for benefits. In some cases, unemployed fathers qualified for other assistance—unemployment compensation, workers' compensation, Social Security Disability Insurance, or Aid to the Permanently and Totally Disabled. But it was quite likely that the father did not qualify for any of these programs or had exhausted his benefits. Consequently, an unemployed, able-bodied father who could not find work did not qualify for ADC and could not support his family. However, if he deserted, the family could become eligible for ADC assistance. It is not known how many fathers left so their families could receive aid. Parents may be absent for many reasons. They may be separated from their spouses because of incompatibility, or they may be in mental hospitals, nursing homes, or prisons. But the fact remained that when an able-bodied but unemployed father was at home, the family could not receive ADC.

To address this problem, two changes were made in ADC. First, in 1961 a new component called the ADC-Unemployed Parent (UP) program was enacted. This antirecession measure made it possible for children to receive aid because of a parent's unemployment.[5] Second, in 1962, the program's name was changed to Aid to Families with Dependent Children (AFDC) to emphasize the family unit. More importantly, a second adult was considered eligible for aid in states with AFDC-UP programs and in cases where one of the child's parents was incapacitated.

In 1967 the AFDC-UP program was changed to the AFDC-Unemployed Father program, but in 1979 the U.S. Supreme Court ruled that it was unconstitutional to provide benefits to unemployed fathers but not to unemployed mothers. The program's name was changed back to AFDC-UP. Only half of the states voluntarily enacted AFDC-UP programs, and the number of fathers who received aid remained small. In 1988, the Family Support Act required all states to have an AFDC-UP program. Despite the commotion over it, relatively few families were added to the rolls.[6] This was probably because many states' eligibility requirements remained quite strict, and AFDC-UP programs had to favor parents who were recently unemployed, while excluding the "hard core" unemployed.

In retrospect, it may seem unfair to have excluded families with able-bodied unemployed parents from the ADC and AFDC programs. In addition, for all the concern about welfare causing family breakup, a 1977 review of studies failed to show that AFDC-UP programs were associated with increased marital stability; in fact, evidence pointed in the opposite direction.[7] Some data did show greater marital instability in states with higher AFDC payments, but there was "little support" for higher payments "being a powerful destabilizer."[8]

A decade later, researchers also concluded that "the impacts of welfare on family structure are very modest. Comparisons of changes in family structure over time with changes in the welfare system and of differences in family structures across states both suggest that welfare has minimal effects on family structure."[9] Changes in family dynamics and family composition had occurred among all segments of the population and seemed to be a more reasonable explanation for increased caseloads and the composition of families receiving AFDC. In the 1990s the evidence remained the same: "While it is true that the system does provide adverse incentives for the formation of two-parent families, the empirical studies show conclusively that the magnitude of these disincentive effects is very small, such that our welfare system cannot explain the high rates of [female] headship and illegitimacy."[10] Nevertheless, the belief that welfare is responsible for family demise persists. In fact, an explicit goal of the country's 1996 welfare reform law was to end welfare dependency by encouraging marriage.[11]

MAKING PARENTS PAY: A HISTORY OF CHILD SUPPORT ENFORCEMENT

Congress's first attempt to see that absent or noncustodial parents provided financial support for their children came in 1950. Subsequent and also largely futile efforts to improve child support collections followed in the 1960s.[12] From 1950 to 1975, the federal government limited its child support efforts to children receiving public assistance. As the 1970s emerged, it became clear that the growing number of single-parent families was due to divorce or separation, or because the parents had never married, not because one parent was deceased. In 1975, Congress created part D of Title IV of the Social Security Act (called the IV-D program) to provide federal matching funds that states could use to collect child support and establish paternity when needed. The rationale was that by putting greater pressure on noncustodial parents to support their children, single-parent families would use fewer welfare benefits. In fact, before poor parents could receive cash welfare benefits, they had to sign over their child support rights to the state. The state kept any child support collected on behalf of AFDC families in order to defray the cost of welfare benefits. To prevent near-poor families from ever receiving cash welfare, the Title IV-D program also authorized state Child Support Enforcement (CSE) agencies to help families that were not receiving public assistance, when they requested it.[13]

Because states were still not collecting much of what was owed in child support, and because their efforts were still considered too lax, the Child Support Enforcement (CSE) Amendments of 1984 toughened the methods states could use to collect overdue support payments. Parents whose payments were in arrears (usually 30 days late or more) could be subjected to warning notices, reports to credit agencies, wage garnishment, civil and criminal charges, interception of federal and state income tax refunds, property liens, seizure and sale of property, and requirements that they post a bond. Unemployment checks could also be tapped. Even so, these measures prompted only a small amount of arrearage collections.[14] The 1984 amendments also required states to pursue medical support awards (in addition to cash awards) to ensure that children of single parents have access to healthcare.[15]

To further strengthen child support laws, the 1996 Personal Responsibility and Work Opportunity Reconciliation Act (PRWORA) made 50 changes to CSE laws. To receive funds for public assistance, a state must operate a CSE program that meets federal standards. PRWORA gave states funds to create automated databases for locating parents and tracking and monitoring cases (attempts to require that all states operate such databases through the 1988 Family Support

Act had failed). In addition, state CSE programs must give families leaving TANF top priority for collecting arrearages to help them stay off welfare.[16]

Every state was also required to adopt procedures for increasing establishment and enforcement of child support orders for noncustodial parents living in a different state than their children. The 1996 law established a National Directory of New Hires. Employers submit the names of newly employed workers, and government officials use the directory to determine if these individuals are in arrears on child support. In addition, Social Security Numbers (SSNs) are required on applications for professional licenses, court records, and death certificates to make tracking noncustodial parents easier. CSE personnel now have authority to order genetic testing to establish paternity without seeking a court order. In 1996, 1998, and again in 2008, the federal government offered states more help to increase the effectiveness and efficiency of their CSE programs.

Making noncustodial parents pay is difficult, in part, because payments for children on public assistance go to the state to repay the family's cash assistance rather than to the child. To encourage parents to pay through the formal CSE system, federal welfare reauthorization legislation in 2008 provides financial incentives for states to allow families receiving public assistance to keep the first $100 or $200 collected each month from the noncustodial parent.[17] Looking back on the last few decades, two things about child support enforcement are clear: (1) More child support is being collected, and (2) collections still fall far short of what is owed.

BENEFITS OF CHILD SUPPORT

The benefits of establishing child support orders and collecting child support payments go beyond improving children's financial well-being. They also provide fathers opportunities to participate in their children's lives. Historically, child support and child visitation have been treated as separate legal issues. However, research shows that fathers are more likely to make child support payments if they have visitation rights or joint custody.[18] In addition to financial benefits, father involvement also provides children social and psychological benefits. Research indicates that children who have a positive relationship with their fathers do better in school, develop better social skills, have fewer behavior problems, and use alcohol and drugs less.[19] The opportunity to know the absent parent's medical history may also be beneficial for the child's health.

Recent Democratic and Republican presidential administrations have supported initiatives to increase fathers' involvement in their children's lives. These initiatives provide incentives for establishing paternity, promoting work opportunities for fathers, supporting non-resident parents' visitation rights with their children, and offering educational programs to prepare fathers for responsible parenthood. In Florida, for example, Equipping Parents to Strengthen Families, a partnership between Florida's Commission on Responsible Fatherhood and Workforce Florida, Inc., helps noncustodial parents find and maintain stable employment, make their child support payments, and improve their relationships with their children. An initial evaluation of the program showed that 50 percent of participants were placed in employment and 25 percent of those placed in employment had increased job retention. Attitudes regarding parenting and child-rearing responsibilities also improved; however, there was no evidence that the level of parent-child interactions increased.[20]

CHILD SUPPORT ENFORCEMENT AGENCY'S SERVICES

Clearly, fathers' social and financial involvement in their children's lives is of fundamental importance. To increase fathers' involvement, CSE agencies provide seven basic services: (1) establishing paternity, (2) establishing child support orders, (3) collecting and distributing child support payments, (4) enforcing child support across state lines, (5) establishing and enforcing medical support orders, (6) locating parents, and (7) reviewing and modifying support orders. In 2006, approximately 70 percent of eligible families received some form of government-funded child support service. CSE assisted in establishing 1.7 million paternities, establishing 1.2 million support orders, and collecting and distributing payments in 8.5 million cases.[21]

Establishing Paternity

In 2007, nearly 40 percent of all births were to unmarried women,[22] and never-married women headed 45 percent of all female-headed families with children under age 18.[23] Children in these female-headed households are far more likely to live in poverty than other children and, therefore, have much to gain financially from child support.

Before child support payments can be awarded, paternity must be established if it is not already acknowledged. Unmarried mothers must cooperate in establishing paternity in order to receive child support awards and welfare assistance, unless doing so is not in their child's best interest or puts the mother at risk of domestic violence. Those who do not cooperate can lose part or all of their cash welfare assistance.

In 2008, paternity was established for 89 percent of children who needed this service.[24] Changes in federal and state laws have promoted increased paternity establishment. For instance, the Family Support Act (FSA) of 1988 required states to adopt "a simple civil process for voluntarily acknowledging paternity," including efforts to have fathers acknowledge paternity at the hospital when their child is born. Research suggests that the highest rates of paternity determinations are made in counties where fathers have more than one opportunity to acknowledge paternity voluntarily, rather than in counties that handle all cases through the courts.[25] Using Social Security numbers to locate missing fathers has also helped, as has granting CSE personnel more authority to conduct genetic testing and streamline paternity determination processes.

Establishing Child Support Orders

A court-established child support order legally obligates the noncustodial parent to provide his or her child a specified amount of financial support. To improve the consistency of the child support award process in each state, states must adopt child support guidelines and make the guidelines available to all judges. States generally use one of three basic approaches to award child support: the income shares method, the percentage of income method, or the Melson-Delaware method.[26]

Thirty-seven states use the income shares method, which is intended to help maintain the child's standard of living as if the parents lived together. The percentage of income parents must pay declines as their income rises, but the total dollar amount of the award rises as income rises. Under this method, the parents' combined income is determined. Each parent's contribution is based on his or her proportionate share of total income. The contribution the noncustodial parent must pay is the child support award.

Nine states use the percentage of income approach. Under this approach, the noncustodial parent must pay a flat rate based on his or her income and the number of children. States differ in the percent assessed. Wisconsin, for example, assesses 17 percent for one child, rising to 34 percent for five or more children. Although this approach is relatively easy to use and understand, some believe it is inequitable because it disregards what the custodial parent can afford to contribute.

Only three states use the Melson-Delaware approach. Under this approach, the state decides the amount parents require to meet their basic needs. An appropriate amount is also determined for each child and is divided between the parents. If the parents have additional income, a percentage of it is also allocated to the children.

Although most states use the income shares approach, agreement is lacking as to which approach best achieves goals such as compliance and administrative efficiency. There is evidence that the income shares model produces the highest awards for low-income families, Melson-Delaware produces the highest awards for middle-income families, and the percentage of income model produces the highest awards for upper-income families.[27] Perhaps most striking is the large differences in award amounts across states, especially for lower-income families.[28]

The fairness of child support laws has been argued on constitutional grounds (e.g., due process, taking property).[29] While lawyers and legal scholars may argue over issues of constitutionality, and such issues are important, families and politicians are more interested in the basic concept of fairness. Among the principles suggested for ensuring fairness is that child support guidelines be based on the children's needs, on what the parent can afford to pay, and recognize that both parents have a duty to support the child based on their financial resources.[30] Needless to say, child support is a contentious issue among many parents. When families include stepparents and blended families, the issues of fairness in child support payments can mount.

Strict child support legislation and increased state enforcement of these laws have helped increase the number of custodial parents receiving child support orders.[31] In 2008, 79 percent of custodial parents had awards, a slight increase from earlier years, yet still below the number of children who presumably could benefit from them.[32]

Several reasons explain why parents do not have a child support order. A detailed analysis indicated that in 2005, approximately 30 percent of custodial mothers without awards did not pursue an award; 14 percent could not locate the child's father; 34 percent had a non-legal arrangement with the noncustodial father, and 24 percent felt that the noncustodial father did not have the money to pay.[33]

Demographic characteristics are also associated with child support awards. Custodial mothers are more likely to have a child support award than custodial fathers (in 2005, 61 vs. 36 percent), and more custodial parents who had been married had awards than those who had not (65 vs. 38 percent). Roughly 63 percent of non-Hispanic whites had child support awards compared to 50 percent of non-Hispanic blacks and 50 percent of Hispanics.[34] In addition, mothers in poverty, whose children may need the support the most, were somewhat less likely to have child support orders (54 vs. 61 percent for all mothers).[35]

Collecting and Distributing Child Support Payments

Obtaining child support involves more than establishing a child support order. In 1998, there were collections in only 23 percent of cases, increasing to 62 percent of cases in 2008. Recent analyses show that most of the improvement in custodial parents' receiving ordered payments is due to states' increased child support enforcement efforts.[36]

Even when there are collections, most children do not receive full payments. In 2005, only 41 percent of mothers receiving payments received full payments. Poor mothers with awards were slightly less to likely to receive payment (73 vs. 78 percent for all mothers with orders), and when they succeeded in receiving a child support payment, poor mothers received less money per year average ($3,369 vs. $4,719 for all mothers).[37] Although there is much room for improvement, especially for mothers in poverty, child support can improve children's standard of living. It increased the custodial mother's (and by default their children's) income by 17 percent, on average, and increased the income of mothers and children living in poverty by 30 percent, on average.[38]

Some parents pay child support directly to the custodial parent, although today, payments are commonly made through a local government office. To further ensure that payments are made, the norm today is to require employers to withhold money directly from the noncustodial parent's paycheck. Since 1994, all states must use this method when a new support order is initiated (although there are exceptions), regardless of whether the state's CSE agency is involved. In 2008, 68 percent of collections were made through wage withholding.[39]

CSE offices have increasingly used the techniques available to them to collect arrearages, such as intercepting federal and state tax refunds and unemployment insurance checks. States are also required to establish procedures for reporting child support debt to credit bureaus. Some communities conduct stings or roundups of "deadbeat" parents, as they are often called, and some judges don't hesitate to send parents to jail when they repeatedly fail to pay. Some communities have resorted to printing the names or pictures of nonsupporting parents in local newspapers or using Internet websites for this purpose. In 1998, things got tougher when Congress passed the Deadbeat Parents Punishment Act, making failure to pay child support in the amount of $5,000 or more a felony with a two-year maximum jail sentence.[40]

Other laws have also helped in criminal non-support cases. Some noncustodial parents pay the money on threat of jail, but many fathers, especially younger fathers, are poor themselves. In some cases, fathers have begun new families, further straining their ability to support all their dependents. Needless to say, this also raises the debate about responsible sexual behavior. The Urban Institute found that fathers in poverty who do not reside with their children and do not pay child support face substantial employment barriers (lack of education, little recent work experience, health problems) and they lacked access to programs to improve their employment potential.[41] Rather than punish them, more efforts are being made to help them prepare for work or obtain employment that will allow them to support their children.

Enforcing Child Support Across Jurisdictions

Following divorce or separation, the likelihood that a parent will move to another state increases.[42] In 2007, in an estimated 25 to 30 percent of cases, parents lived in different states.[43] To make it easier to enforce a child support order when parents do not live in the same state, all states were required to adopt the Uniform Interstate Family Support Act (UIFSA) by 1998. UIFSA's most important feature is that it places control of a noncustodial parent's child support under the jurisdiction of a single state (usually the child's home state). Amendments to improve UIFSA were made in 2001, but states are not required to adopt them. In addition, states do not have to follow UIFSA in all cases. In some instances, using other interstate procedures may be more effective.[44]

Securing child support is especially difficult when a noncustodial parent lives outside the United States. While UIFSA recognizes international claims, it does not necessarily assist parents in establishing child support orders or collecting support payments from parents living abroad because countries lack agreement on noncustodial parents' responsibility, including financial responsibility, in their children's lives.[45]

Establishing and Enforcing Medical Support Orders

Under federal law, all states must require that child support orders include a provision for medical support through a parent's employer-based health insurance or other means. The states can enforce medical support orders for both custodial and noncustodial parents.[46] In addition to giving children access to healthcare, medical support orders are an important federal and state cost-saving mechanism because they free governments from providing health insurance (Medicaid or other coverage) to poor children. In 2008, however, only 28 percent of parents with orders to provide medical support to their children actually did so.[47]

Locating Parents

When an absent, nonsupporting parent cannot be located with information from the custodial parent, states use their own parent locator services (required of all states) with information from tax, motor vehicle registration, and unemployment compensation records, and similar sources. The Federal Parent Locator Service (FPLS), which provides access to Social Security, IRS, veterans, and other national databases, is also used. The Social Security numbers now required on various state applications are a big help in locating parents.[48] In 2006 the FPLS provided information on five million noncustodial parents.[49]

Reviewing and Modifying Support Orders

Initially, child support orders were reviewed and modified only at a parent's request, and the burden of the process was on the parent making the request. The process could be subject to the court's whim. Today, states must establish guidelines for reviewing and modifying child support orders. Prior to the 1996 welfare reform law, states were required to review support orders of families receiving public assistance (e.g., AFDC) every three years. In 1996, this mandate was relaxed, and 32 states discontinued or planned to discontinue the practice.[50] However, welfare reauthorization in 2005 reinstated mandatory child support reviews every three years for families receiving public assistance.[51] In non-public assistance cases, a parent must request a review.

EFFECTIVENESS OF CHILD SUPPORT ENFORCEMENT

The effectiveness of child support enforcement can be measured in three important ways: (1) its ability to meet program goals, such as establishing paternity, establishing child support orders, and collecting payments, (2) its cost effectiveness, and (3) satisfaction levels of parents using the system and of taxpayers who finance the system.

Reaching CSE Program Goals

Given CSE's multiple services and the multiple mechanisms it uses to enforce payments, coupled with the rise of single parenthood and the financial barriers that many noncustodial parents face, just how successful is the government in collecting child support for custodial parents and their children? The greatest gains in child support enforcement over the past 25 years have been in locating parents and establishing paternities. From 1994 to 2008, the number of paternities established increased dramatically, from 676,000 to 1.8 million.[52]

CSE's efforts to encourage custodial parents to establish child support orders have also paid off. The number of parents with orders established increased from 70 percent in 2002 to 79 percent in 2008.[53] In addition, the latest data detailing child enforcement trends show that poor mothers have made significantly more progress than mothers who are not poor. Between 1978 and 2005, the percentage of poor mothers with a child support order rose dramatically, compared to a slight decline among non-poor mothers. Although the neediest mothers and children have gained the most, many still go without a child support order.[54]

How has child support enforcement fared with regard to collections? In 2008, federal and state governments collected approximately $32 billion, a 45 percent increase over 1998.[55] But remember that only 62 percent of all OCSE cases had collections. An estimated $12 billion in child support went unpaid in 2008.[56] In 2005, the last year for which detailed data are available, only 25 percent of all custodial mothers received full payment, a figure that has remained constant over the last decade (of those receiving payments, only 41 percent received the full payment, *down* from 46 percent in 1991).[57] No wonder the child support enforcement system has come under intense criticism.

While poor mothers have made gains in getting support orders, those who received full payment increased merely one percentage point over the past 25 years (from 24 percent to 25 percent).[58] Although 75 percent of poor mothers remain without full child support payments, the money that they do receive has at least a modest impact on poverty. In 2005, child support payments lifted about one-half million children out of poverty.[59] Urban Institute researchers found that child support collections make poor mothers less reliant on government programs and provide significant savings in government programs including TANF, food stamps (now called the Supplemental Nutrition Assistance Program), Medicaid, Supplemental Security Income (SSI), and federal housing programs.[60] In 2004, for example, 331,000 families (16 percent of the welfare caseload) became ineligible for public assistance benefits as a result of child support collections.[61]

There have also been improvements in establishing medical support orders but compliance remains problematic. In 2008, 77 percent of OCSE cases included an order for health insurance coverage (up from 49 percent in 2001) but as noted, the order was complied with in only 28 percent of cases.[62] In addition, detailed 2005 data show that child support orders of never-married mothers and those with low education levels (two indicators of disadvantage) were less likely to include a medical support order.[63] In sum, child support enforcement programs have made progress, yet many children do not receive the support that has been ordered.

CSE's Cost-Effectiveness

Whether child support enforcement programs are cost effective depends on how cost effectiveness is calculated. If only administrative costs are considered, CSE is very effective. Nationally, in 2008, $4.79 was collected for every dollar spent to collect child support payments, although this number varies a great deal by state.[64] This figure may overstate CSE's effectiveness because many noncustodial parents would have made their child support payments without CSE involvement.

In 1998, states collected $11.7 billion in child support for families that were not receiving welfare; in 2008, these collections increased to nearly $25.6 billion. During the same period, as the number of families receiving welfare declined dramatically as a result of welfare reform, the total amount collected for families receiving welfare also declined from nearly $2.6 billion to under 1 billion.[65] Figure 7.1 shows the amount of child support distributed to families receiving TANF and Medicaid assistance and those that did not receive assistance. In total, the cases CSE handles present a net cost to the public. In 2006, the federal and state governments spent $3.1 billion more on CSE cases than they recouped in child support.[66] Of course, we should consider any amount of child support collected for TANF families a gain because it generally reduces public assistance costs to at least some degree.

Satisfaction with CSE

Given this mixed picture of CSE's successes, what is the public perception of child support enforcement? Some program critics complain that too many mothers do not have awards, too many awards are not collected, and the size of awards is often too small. Nonetheless, in the past 25 years, these programs have had important impacts on public attitudes and expectations. The

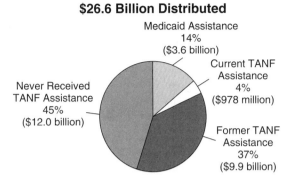

$26.6 Billion Distributed

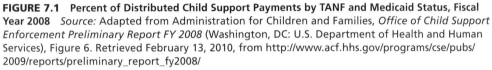

FIGURE 7.1   Percent of Distributed Child Support Payments by TANF and Medicaid Status, Fiscal Year 2008   *Source:* Adapted from Administration for Children and Families, *Office of Child Support Enforcement Preliminary Report FY 2008* (Washington, DC: U.S. Department of Health and Human Services), Figure 6. Retrieved February 13, 2010, from http://www.acf.hhs.gov/programs/cse/pubs/2009/reports/preliminary_report_fy2008/

intent of the original CSE legislation was to collect child support in order to offset public assistance costs. Later, Congress and the public-at-large recognized its importance in reducing poverty and ensuring that noncustodial parents take responsibility for their children. A strong CSE program sends the message to noncustodial parents who would try to avoid paying child support that the system will hold them accountable. The U.S. public has come to believe that paying child support is both a legal and a moral responsibility. Fathers have learned to pay, and mothers have learned to expect to receive financial support from their children's fathers.

Just as some of the U.S. public is unhappy with the child support enforcement system, custodial and noncustodial parents have also had many complaints about the performance of CSE agencies. Mothers complain that CSE agencies do not try hard enough to get fathers to pay and that too often CSE agencies lose the checks. Fathers and mothers complain that they don't see the money because the state takes it to repay the welfare system, and this may cause fathers to pay "under the table" instead.[67]

Hope remains that the programs will continue to improve. Waiver programs and grants encourage states to create and test interventions in child support enforcement. Welfare reauthorization in 2005 demonstrates some further level of commitment to responsible fatherhood initiatives by allocating up to $50 million annually for such programs.[68] Most states have had grants or waivers for implementing new CSE models, collaborating with existing agencies, developing new measures for performance outcomes, or testing new ways to review and modify existing orders. Other state initiatives funded by federal grants are exploring ways to better serve Native Americans, improve parenting, enhance fatherhood, and improve visitation rights.

STATE COMPLIANCE AND CSE PRIVATIZATION

Each year states must report to the U.S. Secretary of Health and Human Services on how well their CSE programs are meeting federal requirements and performance standards. Compliance failures can cost states in welfare funds. The first time a state is not in compliance, its TANF grant is reduced by 1 percent. The second time goals are not met, the penalty is 2 to 3 percent, and, on the third, 3 to 5 percent.[69] With the threat of stiff penalties, states give priority to federal compliance. As in other areas of human services, private firms are being engaged to collect child support payments in the hope that they can meet federal mandates in more cost-effective ways than government agencies themselves.

States' child support enforcement offices have turned to the private sector for reasons such as burgeoning caseloads. In 2005, private collection agencies handled less than 40 percent of all child support cases.[70] An early report indicated that fully privatized local offices generally did as well and sometimes better than public offices in collecting child support payments, locating parents, establishing orders, and establishing payments, perhaps because they often have more personnel flexibility and access to better technology.[71] As of March 2002, 16 states were using 38 private firms to deliver some or all of their child support enforcement services. A subsequent GAO report looked at private firms that take cases independently.[72] These firms performed comparably to state agencies, with collections in about 60 percent of cases. In addition to accepting cases selectively and generally not taking public assistance clients, these independent firms had much smaller caseloads and charged substantial fees that state agencies do not charge. Additional complaints about independent firms include their attempts to appear to be official government agencies in written and oral communication with parents; harassment of employers, family members, and neighbors of noncustodial parents; and refusal to terminate services upon request of the custodial parent.[73]

THE REINCARNATIONS OF WELFARE AND WORK

The original ADC program was designed when mothers were expected to stay home to care for their children. Requiring mothers to work or forcing fathers to pay child support had not yet entered the equation. Demographic, social, and economic changes caused the program to evolve in ways that no one had anticipated. As the 1960s emerged, the focus was no longer on providing financial support alone as a means of alleviating poverty. "Rehabilitating" people to help them escape poverty through greater opportunities became the new focus. But as AFDC rolls continued to climb, Americans became increasingly unhappy about providing public assistance to those who seemed capable of working. The focus shifted again, this time to decreasing welfare dependency through more work incentives and tougher work requirements.

Rehabilitation for Work

The first large-scale approach at rehabilitating people in order to break their ties with public assistance came in the 1962 social service amendments to the Social Security Act. This approach was designed to reduce poverty by treating personal and social problems that stood in the way of financial independence.[74] Services included counseling, vocational training, child management training, family-planning services, and legal services. States received a bonus for providing social services to public assistance recipients—for every dollar they spent, the federal government matched it with three more dollars, far more lucrative than the reimbursement formula for AFDC cash payments. To ensure the success of the social service amendments, worker caseloads were to be small—no more than 60 clients. But states were criticized for claiming federal matching funds for many services they were already providing to clients.[75] It was also difficult to find enough qualified social workers to provide services.[76] What had sounded good in theory could often not be put into practice.

Job Training and WIN

When social services were introduced as a way to help welfare recipients achieve financial independence, the AFDC caseworker was responsible for seeing that the family got its benefit check and its social services. In fact, AFDC mothers may have feared that if they did not accept social services, their cash benefits might have been terminated. At the same time, social workers complained that the time spent determining eligibility left little time to provide social services.[77]

In 1967 Congress separated payments from social services. A payments worker became responsible for matters related to the welfare check, while another worker was responsible for providing social services. This was the era of welfare rights, and this new approach recognized that poverty may result purely from economic conditions. Not all poor families needed rehabilitation through social services. Families who wished to receive social services were still entitled and encouraged to do so. Social workers could devote more time to these cases.

Enthusiasm for the rehabilitation approach faded rapidly as welfare rolls continued to grow. A new strategy was needed, and the one chosen was tougher. Amendments passed in 1967 also emphasized work, and both "carrot" and "stick" measures were employed to achieve this purpose.[78] The "stick" included work requirements for unemployed fathers on AFDC, as well as for mothers and some teenagers. The "carrot" was the Work Incentive Now (WIN) program, established by Congress to train recipients for work and to help them locate employment. (The original name was the Work Incentive Program but the acronym WIP obviously could not be used.) The federal government threatened to deny AFDC matching funds to states that paid benefits to able-bodied recipients who refused to work or receive job training.

Other measures taken to encourage recipients to work included the "thirty plus one-third rule." Welfare payments were not reduced for the first $30 of earned income, and one-third of all additional income was disregarded in determining eligibility until countable earnings reached the amount of AFDC benefits to which the family was entitled. Children of WIN participants were supposed to receive daycare services, but shortages of licensed facilities often prevented placing children while their mothers worked or trained for jobs.

AFDC rolls were still climbing. Strategies aimed at encouraging welfare recipients to work once again failed to produce the results that rational planners had intended. Perhaps these failures had to do with the fact that participants did not earn enough in marginal, low-wage jobs to make work a rational alternative.[79] Short-term training programs generally do not enable recipients to substantially increase their earnings. To survive, it seemed that some recipients were relying on a combination of "some work and some welfare." In fact, researchers found that 40 percent of AFDC mothers had rather substantial work effort over a two-year period, and that these women either combined paid work and welfare benefits or cycled between work and welfare.[80]

Workfare

As more women with young children joined the labor force, the argument was that mothers receiving public assistance should do the same. Thus, the next reincarnation of welfare and work was referred to as "workfare"—mandatory employment in return for welfare payments. This concept is actually as old as the hills. In its most punitive forms, the workhouses of the Elizabethan period and similar institutions in the United States fit under the rubric of workfare.[81]

One author summed up workfare this way: After nearly four hundred years of various forms of these programs, both experience and empirical evidence indicate they have failed to improve the job skills of participants; they have failed to reduce the costs of welfare; they do not discourage malingering because the number of malingerers is already negligible; and welfare recipients who can would gladly take jobs if decent ones were available.[82] Nevertheless, work requirements received increased public and political support.

There was some evidence that work programs could work. For example, in the 1980s Massachusetts' voluntary employment and training program, called ET, got good reviews (albeit at a time when the state's unemployment rate was quite low and recipients could be more easily placed in jobs). Participants could choose between career counseling, education and training, on-the-job training, and job placement. Those in training got daycare services for a year and Medicaid benefits for 15 months. Would a mandatory approach to work programs produce the same success? Early controlled studies funded primarily by the Ford Foundation and conducted by the nonprofit Manpower Demonstration Research Corporation (MDRC) suggested that it was possible, but participants generally worked at entry-level jobs and did not substantially increase their work skills.[83]

MDRC also conducted studies of intensive long-term workfare programs that showed similar results. For example, the Saturation Work Initiative Model (SWIM) in San Diego found higher employment rates and earnings for experimental group participants, and there were also welfare cost savings. But again, net income for the experimental group did not change much—"gains in earnings were largely offset by reductions in government transfer payments."[84]

In a five-year MDRC study of the SWIM program (created under WIN) implemented in Virginia, Arkansas, Baltimore, and San Diego, researchers found that the programs made cost-efficient use of their limited resources; employment among AFDC recipients increased and short-term AFDC receipt was reduced; the portion of AFDC participants' incomes from earnings increased; and two of the four programs also resulted in public savings (San Diego and Arkansas) and one likely broke even (Virginia). Less positive was that participants in two of the programs had little or no net gain in income and only one site (Baltimore) showed clear indication of increased job pay; long-term AFDC receipt was not affected in two programs and in the other two reductions were "modest at best." The MDRC concluded that "The effectiveness of such services may hinge on the proper combination of program structure, rewards and sanctions, and support services and work incentives."[85]

The JOBS Program

The evidence to support traditional work programs may have been weak, but Congress did not give up on work requirements. Instead, Congress enacted what it hoped would be a better approach—the Job Opportunities and Basic Skills (JOBS) program. As part of the Family Support Act of 1988, JOBS was intended to be "a new social contract between government and welfare recipients," changing the AFDC program from a cash assistance program to a jobs and independence program.[86] It replaced WIN and was to be coordinated with the programs of the Job Training Partnership Act (discussed further in Chapter 9). JOBS offered basic education; job skills and readiness training; job development, search, and placement; supportive services; on-the-job training; and community work experience.[87] Most states assigned "case managers" to determine what services AFDC recipients needed to make the transition from welfare to work, and to enroll them in the JOBS program.

In AFDC-UP households, at least one parent was required to work a minimum of 16 hours a week, and single parents whose children were 3 years old or older were required to participate in JOBS, *if* state resources were available. States could draw a 90 percent match for many employment-related services, but many did not draw their full allotment, claiming that state budgets were too tight.

The percentage of AFDC recipients eligible for JOBS averaged 15 percent nationally but varied widely by state with Kansas placing its figure at 6 percent and Nebraska at 73 percent. The federal expectation was that 20 percent of single AFDC parents would participate. Nationally, this expectation was exceeded with 27 percent participating. The participation rate for AFDC-UP families was 38 percent, short of the expectation that 50 percent would participate. Instead of work, teen parents without high school educations receiving AFDC were required to attend school.

The 1988 act also required states to provide childcare to working AFDC families, increase earning disregards, and extend Medicaid healthcare coverage when families left AFDC. Unlimited federal matching funds for childcare were available to states for AFDC parents who were working or in training, and also for working families not receiving AFDC, but at risk of doing so without childcare.

The JOBS program redefined the "welfare problem" from poverty—being poor and lacking opportunity—to dependency—the need for greater incentives to work and self-sufficiency.[88] But did JOBS produce better results than previous efforts? The MDRC studied two JOBS program approaches over a two-year period.[89] One approach was called labor force attachment (short-term approaches to get participants to work quickly); the other was the human capital development approach (which focused on delaying work entry in favor of building job skills over a longer time period). The attachment approach produced a 24 percent increase in the number working, increased by 16 percent the number leaving AFDC, and raised earnings 26 percent. Still, 57 percent of the experimental group remained on AFDC and the group's *average* earnings were just $285 a month. The control group earned $226 a month on average and 66 percent stayed on AFDC. Perhaps because the two-year follow-up period was relatively short, the human capital approach did not produce consistent increases in earnings or employment. There was, however, a 14 percent AFDC cost savings. A survey of 453 JOBS administrators conducted by the General Accounting Office found that less than half of the "job-ready" participants were employed, and that the JOBS programs lacked a strong employment focus.[90]

An extensive MDRC study of a model JOBS program, California's Greater Avenues for Independence (GAIN) program, also showed only modest improvements among participants.[91] The GAIN program emphasized basic education, and AFDC recipients were required to participate. After three years, single parents in the experimental group earned 22 percent ($1,414) more than the control group, and they received 8 percent less in AFDC benefits than controls. A similar percentage of experimental (53 percent) and control (56 percent) subjects continued to receive AFDC. Riverside County (one of six counties included in the study) had the most impressive results. Experimental group participants there earned 49 percent more than controls, and AFDC payments made to experimental group participants were 15 percent less than for controls. Overall, Riverside participants produced $2.84 (in earnings, reduced AFDC payments, and taxes) for every $1 invested in the program. After reviewing results of many MDRC studies, it is not surprising that Senator Daniel Patrick Moynihan dubbed Judith Gueron, head of the MDRC, "Our Lady of Modest but Positive Results."[92]

WHY THE FUSS ABOUT WELFARE?

Public assistance, better known as welfare, is a "hot button" topic even though many people are not well informed about the characteristics of people who receive TANF (see Illustration 7.1). Let's review the facts, figures, and points of view that spawned the major welfare reform of 1996.

ILLUSTRATION 7.1
No One is Driving a Welfare Cadillac

Most people today probably realize that it is a myth that welfare recipients drive new Cadillacs, but what are the characteristics of TANF recipients?

Most families receiving TANF are composed of one parent and one or two children. In 45 percent of TANF cases, payments go only to children and no adult.[a] This may be because the child is being cared for by a relative or other adult who does not qualify for TANF. Slightly more than half of all TANF families and two-thirds of families without an employed adult have a child under age 6 in the home.[b] Urban Institute researchers report that one-third of TANF adults have disabilities and one-fourth have a child with a disability.[c] Despite rules that allow two-parent families to receive TANF, the number of two-parent families receiving aid has declined. Less than 6 percent of cases now include households with more than one adult.[d]

Since TANF families generally lack the traditional nuclear family structure, adults face increased pressures as both economic provider and nurturer. Ninety percent of adult recipients are women, and only 11 percent of adult recipients are married and living together.[e]

Approximately 75 percent of adult TANF recipients are in their twenties or thirties. Teen parents are just 7 percent of those who receive TANF. About 40 percent of adults receiving TANF do not have a high school education. Although the majority of adults receiving TANF are not employed, nearly 22 percent were employed in 2006, up from less than 7 percent in 1988. Blacks are 36 percent of TANF recipients, non-Hispanic Whites are 38 percent, and Hispanics (of any race) are 21 percent.[f]

Under the former AFDC program, and under today's TANF program, most families' stay in these programs has been relatively short. Prior to welfare reform, in 1994, the median length of stay on AFDC was 23 months. In 1995, 34 percent had received AFDC for one year or less, and the majority (51%) received AFDC for two years or less. Only 20 percent of the caseload received benefits for more than five years.[g] As part of welfare reform, the TANF program places limits on the amount of time families can receive benefits. Relatively few families have lost their benefits due to time limits because most families do not stay in the program that long. Between 2002 and 2006, 222,000 families nationwide were reported to have lost their benefits due to time limits.[h]

[a]U.S. House of Representatives, "Temporary Assistance for Needy Families," *2008 Green Book* (Washington, DC: Committee on Ways and Means). Retrieved February 11, 2010, from http://waysandmeans.house.gov/singlepages.aspx?NewsID=10490, p. 7-32.

[b]*Ibid.,* p. 7-43.

[c]Sheila R. Zedlewski and Donald Alderson, *Do Families on Welfare in the Post-TANF Era Differ from Their pre-TANF Counterparts?* (Washington, DC: The Urban Institute, February 1, 2001). Retrieved February 11, 2010, from http://www.urban.org/publications/310298.html

[d]U.S. House of Representatives, "Temporary Assistance for Needy Families," *2008 Green Book,* Table 7-12.

[e]Administration for Children and Families, "Characteristics and Financial Circumstances of TANF Recipients," *TANF Eighth Annual Report to Congress* (Washington, DC: Department of Health and Human Services), p. 75. Retrieved February 15, 2010, from http://www.acf.hhs.gov/programs/ofa/data-reports/annualreport8/TANF_8th_Report_111908.pdf

[f]*Ibid.*

[g]Administration for Children and Families, "Characteristics and Financial Circumstances of AFDC Recipients, FY 1995" (Washington, DC: U.S. Department of Health and Human Services, December 31, 1996). Retrieved February 15, 2010, from http://www.acf.hhs.gov/programs/ofa/character/FY95/t12.htm

[h]U.S. House of Representatives, "Temporary Assistance for Needy Families," *2008 Green Book,* p. 7-83.

Recipients and Costs

The number of ADC recipients grew from 1.2 million individuals (349,000 families and 840,000 children) in 1940 to 8.5 million individuals (2.2 million families and 6.2 million children) receiving AFDC in 1970, and 11.5 million individuals (4 million families and 7.9 million children) in 1990.[93] In part, this growth can be attributed to the increase in child poverty (see Figure 7.2). Population growth also explains some of the increase. We can also view the number of AFDC recipients as a percentage of the population. In 1950 recipients were 1.5 percent of the population; by 1970 they were over 4 percent.[94] At the peak number of 14.2 million individuals in 1994, recipients were 5.5 percent of the population. Perhaps this was a smaller percentage of the population than some people realized, yet the perception was that too many people were "on welfare."

Program costs had also grown. In 1940, ADC benefits totaled $134 million; in 1970 they were $4.9 billion.[95] In 1990 AFDC benefits totaled $18.5 billion.[96] Even after controlling for inflation, costs seemed to spiral. But AFDC was only a very small part of governments' budgets. At its peak enrollment in 1994, less than 1 (.9) percent of all federal, state, and local expenditures went to the program.[97] Still, many people thought that a substantial number of adult recipients could work and did not deserve benefits.

Although total program costs were rising, payments dropped by 51 percent in purchasing power from 1970 to 1995.[98] Just prior to "welfare reform" in 1996, maximum benefits for a three-person family ranged from $120 per month in Mississippi to $703 in Suffolk County, New York.[99] The difference between the two areas is substantial even considering variations in the cost of living, and the payment in each area might be considered modest at best for a family to survive.

States decide what to offer in benefits. They generally started out in a rational manner by calculating a standard of need that considered what it would cost families of various sizes to meet

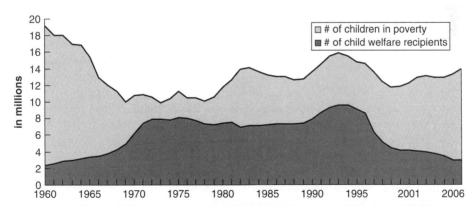

FIGURE 7.2   Number of Children Receiving Cash Welfare Assistance and Number of Children Living in Poverty (in millions), 1960–2008   *Sources:* Compiled from data in U.S. House of Representatives, *2008 Green Book* (Washington, DC: Committee on Ways and Means), Table 7-8. Retrieved February 15, 2010, from http://waysandmeans.house.gov/singlepages.aspx?NewsID=10490; Administration for Children and Families, TANF Data (Washington, DC: U.S. Department of Health and Human Services). Retrieved February 15, 2010, from http://www.acf.hhs.gov/programs/ofa/data-reports/caseload/caseload_current.htm; Carmen DeNavas-Walt, Bernadette D. Proctor, and Jessica C. Smith, *Income, Poverty, Health Insurance Coverage in the United States, 2008,* P60-236(RV), (Washington, DC: U.S. Census Bureau, September 2009). Retrieved February 15, 2010, from http://www.census.gov/prod/2009pubs/p60-236.pdf

basic food, shelter, clothing, and other needs. The most common methods for determining benefit levels were adopting the federal government's poverty guidelines or calculating living expenses for the area using the Bureau of Labor Statistics' figures for a modest standard of living.[100] Other methods were also used, but in some states need was not really determined. For example, in a few states, the legislature determined the standard based on available funding, and another handful had used the same standard for so long that the method used to determine it could not be recalled!

After deciding how much to provide families, each state was supposed to follow guidelines to determine which families were eligible for benefits. To be eligible, a family's gross income could not exceed 185 percent of the standard of need and its net income (after allowable deductions) could not exceed the standard of need. However, states could set their payment standards below the standard of need. Indeed, in 1996, most jurisdictions paid less than the need standard.[101] For example, in Alabama, the need standard for a parent and two children was $673 a month, but its maximum benefit was $164.

Providing cash benefits below the standard of need seems more rational when considering that families usually get food assistance that also help to meet their survival needs. Families in states with lower AFDC payments received more in food stamp benefits than families in states with higher AFDC payments. This is because AFDC benefits were considered in calculating food stamp benefits (but food stamps did not count against AFDC benefits). The same practice is used to calculate benefits to families today.

In 1996, under welfare reform, the Temporary Assistance for Needy Families (TANF) program replaced AFDC. Most states maintained the same payment levels under the new program, but all states reduced or excluded benefits for some groups of recipients.[102] Figure 7.3 shows TANF benefit levels in 2008. After accounting for inflation, the value of welfare benefits in most states has declined substantially since 1994.

Rethinking AFDC

Substantive changes in the public assistance programs began during the Reagan administration. President Reagan wanted "to determine welfare needs more accurately, improve program administration, reduce fraud and abuse, and decrease federal and state costs."[103] Accordingly, various changes were made in the AFDC program, such as counting stepparents' income in determining eligibility, capping deductions for work-related expenses such as childcare, and limiting the "thirty plus one-third" rule to four months. About 500,000 families were removed from the program,[104] with researchers suggesting that many children had been plunged deeper into poverty as a result.[105]

Perhaps President George H. W. Bush's most notable contribution to welfare reform was to encourage more state innovation in the AFDC program. But what some considered a positive innovation, others called punitive. For instance, under Wisconsin's Learnfare program, working families could keep more of their pay without losing AFDC benefits, but if a teenage child dropped out of school, "defined as missing three days of school in a month without a valid excuse," the family's benefits could be reduced.[106] In Wisconsin and New Jersey, women who had another child while receiving AFDC were denied additional payments. In Michigan, AFDC recipients who did not go to work or school or contribute volunteer service faced being docked $100 in benefits a month. A Wisconsin initiative, referred to as "Bridefare," encouraged young women to marry by allowing them to keep some benefits despite their new husband's income. Right-wing conservatives called for more drastic changes, such as ending all government involvement in public assistance and placing poor children whose parents could not afford to care for them in orphanages.

Maximum Monthly Allowance for Family of Three

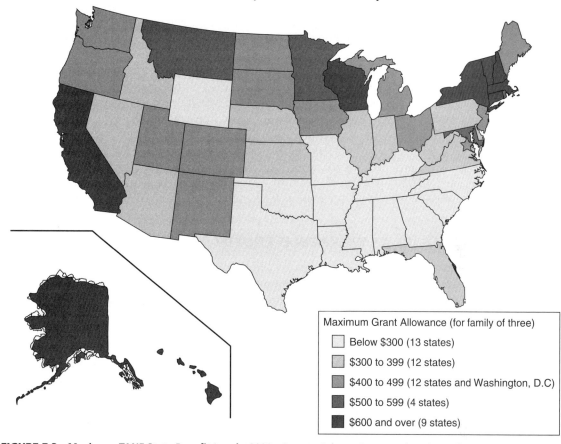

FIGURE 7.3 Maximum TANF State Benefit Levels, 2008 *Source:* Athens County Job and Family Services, *TANF: Failing America's Poorest Children* (Athens, OH: Department of Job and Family Services, October 2009). Retrieved February 20, 2010, from http://jfs.athenscountygovernment.com/documents/AmericasPoorestChildren.updated10-09. pdf. Numbers drawn from individual state TANF policies.

By the time President Bill Clinton took office armed with the campaign pledge to "end welfare as we know it," the stage was set for dismantling the AFDC entitlement program and replacing it, predominantly with a work program. Clinton also wanted to increase incentives to self-sufficiency through education and training, raise the earned income credit, provide "seamless" childcare and healthcare benefits, and "make work pay" by increasing asset limitations and earnings disregards and permitting individual development accounts. Other parts of his proposal included improving paternity establishment and child support collections and promoting contacts between children and their noncustodial parents. The president also wanted to launch a national campaign to curb teen pregnancy. Clinton agreed with many conservatives that welfare payments should be limited to two years and that "welfare should not be a way of life."[107]

There was considerable concern about whether there would be enough jobs for all those who would have to work in lieu of receiving assistance and what would happen to those who did not find employment. Since JOBS had put only a portion of recipients to work, the assumption was that multiple employment strategies would be needed to end welfare. Suggestions included subsidizing private employment, paying groups to place recipients in private-sector jobs, establishing federal public works programs like those used during the Great Depression, and placing recipients in public-sector jobs in the community. Unions were concerned that any large-scale job efforts would displace those already working in low-wage employment. Predictions were that it would be difficult to do better than JOBS unless substantial amounts were allocated for training and education.

While Congress hammered out its plan, the states were moving ahead with welfare reform. The Wisconsin legislature declared that it wanted to withdraw completely from the AFDC program by the end of the decade. It had already begun implementing a two-year moratorium on AFDC payments through its experiment called "Work, Not Welfare." Florida began a demonstration to hire welfare recipients and provide a minimum-wage job to those who did not locate work after two years on AFDC. By the time Congress and the president agreed on a welfare reform plan, about 40 states had already obtained waivers from the federal government so they could make changes to their AFDC programs that fell outside the current rules.

HAS WELFARE AS WE KNEW IT ENDED?

By 1994 the AFDC rolls had already started to drop, but conservatives and many others thought that the program still needed radical restructuring. Congress twice delivered comprehensive welfare reform bills to President Clinton, which he vetoed, believing they were too punitive. Then, on the third try, the president relented and signed the Personal Responsibility and Work Opportunity Reconciliation Act of 1996 even though he disliked some of its components. Some of the nation's best-known welfare experts and the president's closest welfare advisers, Mary Jo Bane, David Ellwood, and Peter Edelman, quit in protest when Clinton signed the bill. Advocates for the poor criticized the president for "selling out." As David Ellwood noted, the Republican takeover of Congress led welfare reform on a "remarkable political journey."[108] One columnist called the president's decision to sign the sweeping welfare reform bill "the biggest social accomplishment of his presidency, even though the Republican Congress wrote it and liberal Democrats hate[d] it."[109] The bill's most dramatic change was the end of the 61-year-old entitlement program known as AFDC and the birth of a block grant program called Temporary Assistance for Needy Families (TANF).

TANF was originally authorized through 2002 and continued through stop-gap measures until the Deficit Reduction Act of 2006 reauthorized the program through 2010. Although reauthorization tightened work requirements for cash welfare and provided additional funding for basic TANF assistance and healthy marriage and responsible fatherhood initiatives, the TANF program remains similar to its inception in 1996.[110] The emphasis is still on providing *temporary* assistance to families.

TANF Goals

Under PRWORA, public assistance for families with children shifted even further from a system historically focused on income supports to one that emphasizes work and economic self-sufficiency.[111] TANF's four main goals are to:

- Provide assistance to needy families so children can be cared for by their parents or other relatives.
- End parents' welfare dependency through job readiness, work, and marriage.
- Reduce out-of-wedlock pregnancies.
- Encourage the formation of two-parent families.[112]

TANF Block Grants

TANF replaced the AFDC and JOBS programs. While AFDC guaranteed cash aid to all eligible families until their youngest child turned age 18, the TANF block grant offers time-limited services to help participants achieve self-sufficiency. TANF program funding is capped. Should a state spend its entire TANF allotment before the end of the fiscal year, additional federal funds may not be made available to serve those in need.

TANF is actually composed of two block grants: one for family assistance and the other for childcare. The family assistance block grant is used to provide cash aid to families, to help families go to work, and to avert out-of-wedlock pregnancies. The money can also be used to encourage parents to establish or maintain two-parent families. The family assistance block grant was capped at $16.5 billion per year through 2010 (slightly more than what was spent for AFDC and JOBS in fiscal year 1995). Since funding has remained constant since 1996, the block grant's value has declined due to inflation, amounting to a 25 percent reduction by 2008.[113]

The childcare block grant is intended to help families reduce their use of public assistance, leave the public assistance rolls, or avoid receiving public assistance by providing childcare while parents work, look for work, or prepare for work. This block grant consolidated several government-supported childcare programs with $20 billion allocated over six years. In 2006, TANF childcare spending totaled $5.4 billion, although after adjusting for inflation this was 22 percent less than in 2000.[114]

Federal Funding for TANF

To receive its entire federal TANF allotment, a state must spend at least 75 percent of what it expended on AFDC in 1994. This is called the state's "maintenance of effort" or MOE. States' MOE includes money spent on TANF cash assistance and support services to help alleviate poverty such as childcare, preschool education programs, after-school programs for youth, postsecondary education for parents, job supports, job retention and advancement programs, supportive services to noncustodial parents, and administrative costs of its TANF program.[115]

States that fail to meet federally established work participation rates for TANF families must spend at least 80 (rather than 75) percent of their 1994 expenditures the following year. In 1997, 25 percent of single-parents were expected to work. By 2010, this figure had increased to 70 percent of single parents. The work participation rate for two-parent families is set higher. Since 1999, 90 percent of two-parent families must have at least one worker. States can reduce these work participation rate requirements. For each percentage point decrease in its TANF rolls, a state's work participation rate is also reduced by one percent.

States that experience more than average population growth or receive less than the national average amount of federal welfare funds for each poor resident are eligible for supplemental TANF funds. Since 1998, 17 states have qualified for these supplemental grants. About half are poorer, southern states.[116]

Until TANF's reauthorization in 2006, states with "high-performing" TANF programs (defined as gains in recipients' job entry, job retention, and earnings) were eligible for bonuses. In addition, from 1999 to 2002, up to 25 states with the greatest reductions in nonmarital births *and* greatest reductions in abortions could get a bonus payment. Six states, the District of Columbia, and the Virgin Islands received these bonuses in amounts that ranged from nearly $1 million to $85 million. Despite these efforts, the national nonmarital birth rate increased slightly during this period.[117]

TANF's 2006 reauthorization eliminated bonus funds and established competitive grants for healthy marriage and responsible fatherhood initiatives. From 2006 to 2010, up to $98 million per year was available for healthy marriage promotion including campaigns to promote marriage in the general population, "social skills" education for couples considering marriage, and reducing financial disincentives to marry (e.g., excluding some of a stepparent's income in determining TANF eligibility). Up to $50 million per year was available for responsible fatherhood initiatives including initiatives to promote marriage and healthy parenting skills, provide employment and job training skills, and create a national clearinghouse of information on responsible fathering.[118]

TANF's Federalism

The brand of federalism exemplified by the TANF program is devolution—returning more responsibility to the states. Under TANF, states can provide many services in addition to cash assistance, especially those most relevant to their populations in economic need. States exercise considerable discretion in the following areas of the TANF program:[119]

- Setting eligibility limits and cash benefit levels
- Determining income supplements for working families
- Providing additional incentives and sanctions to families
- Spending TANF funds on noncash programs and services aimed at meeting TANF goals
- Saving TANF block grant funds for economic downturns
- Extending transitional Medicaid benefits beyond 12 months
- Designing work and education programs

In the area of program eligibility rules, states can opt to provide cash benefits for less than the five-year lifetime limit established by the federal government, or they can provide benefits for a longer period by using state rather than federal funds. States can choose whether to provide unmarried teen mothers with services in addition to cash payments, such as comprehensive case management, and whether to enforce a "family cap" by denying additional payments for a child born while a family is receiving TANF. Flexibility does not stop at the state level. If states wish, they can allow localities to decide how to allocate funds to meet community-specific needs. The wide latitude states have under PRWORA means that programs and program eligibility vary from state to state and, sometimes, from locale to locale.

States must generally use TANF funds to support at least one of TANF's four main goals, but as long as states link services to these goals, they have tremendous flexibility in delivering services. In addition, states may contract with religious and private organizations to deliver public assistance services. This provision is controversial among those who believe that religion and public service functions do not mix well, and among those who believe that governments should not transfer their public responsibilities to enterprises motivated by profit. Each state also has almost free rein in defining groups that will be included or excluded from the TANF program. Federal funds, however, cannot be used to pay TANF benefits to most immigrants legally residing in the United States during their first five years in the country. Most unmarried teen parents must live with an adult and attend school in order to receive TANF benefits.

TANF Work Requirements

As defined in TANF's 2006 reauthorization, a "work-eligible" adult is generally any adult in a TANF family who is a U.S. citizen, does not receive SSI or SSDI, and is not needed at home to care for a disabled family member.[120] Under federal rules, "work-eligible" adults may receive cash assistance for no more than five years (eight states have time limits less than five years, and a few limit benefits to about two or three years[121]), and they are expected to go to work and work toward self-sufficiency *no later than* two years after they begin receiving aid (43 states require that recipients work sooner than two years). There are exceptions to stringent time limits. States may exempt 20 percent of their caseload from work requirements to accommodate situations where family violence or disabilities may make it difficult for the adult head to care for the family without assistance.

States cannot use federal funds to exempt a greater proportion of adults from work requirements, nor can they use federal funds to assist those who have reached their time limits. However, states can apply more lenient requirements by using their own funds. Nine states have, in effect, suspended the federal time limits by paying benefits to "timed-out" families using state funds only. Some states also stop the federal time limit clock by using state funds to pay benefits to families in which an adult is working. Most states, however, enforce the strict federal work requirements or create even stricter state work requirements resulting in case closures when clients do not find work. The Department of Health and Human Services reported that between 2002 and 2006, 142,000 TANF families had reached their time limits and were dropped from TANF.[122]

Under TANF, the current definition of work includes 12 types of activities. In most cases, education and training can count as a work activity for one year only, and no more than 30 percent of a state's participating caseload can be engaged in education and training at any given time.[123] Job search and rehabilitation activities can be counted for a maximum of 12 weeks.[124] To meet work requirements, work-eligible adults with school-age children must work 30 hours weekly, and those with children under the age of 6 must work 20 hours weekly. Those who fail to work all the expected hours can be docked at least a portion of their benefits.

Compared to the former JOBS program, fewer TANF adults are engaged in educational activities. In 1995, under the JOBS program, 47 percent of participants were involved in educational activities such as high school, GED classes, remedial education, English as a second language, vocational training, or higher education. In contrast, in 2006, only 7 percent of TANF work participants were involved in educational activities.[125] More than one observer has questioned the logic of trying to move poor people off TANF and into livable wage jobs when so little is committed to developing marketable skills through education and training and low-skill jobs often pay little (see Illustration 7.2).

Although few participants find living wage jobs that lift them out of poverty,[126] the number of TANF families with a parent involved in work or work-related activities has seen some growth. In 1997, about 28 percent of TANF families nationwide had a working adult. This percentage peaked at just over 38 percent in 1999 but declined to 32 percent in 2006. The rate was higher for two-parent families (nearly 46 percent). About half of all parents participated in unsubsidized work activities (which cost states the least) with the remaining half engaged in job preparation activities, including job search, vocational education, and work experience.[127]

Despite progress, the 2006 national average TANF work participation rate of 32 percent fell far short of federal participation requirements of 50 percent for single-parent families and 90 percent for two-parent families, but the numbers vary widely by state. Work participation rates for single-parent families ranged from nearly 14 percent in Massachusetts to just over 79 percent in Montana with similar variation among two-parent families: 15 percent in Oregon to 94 percent in Rhode Island. Federal rules continue to allow for exempting up to 20 percent of caseloads from work due to hardship, and until 2007, many states had waivers allowing them to use different rules to calculate work participation rates. With these adjustments for caseload reductions and waivers, most states met federal work participation requirements.[128] This

ILLUSTRATION 7.2
How Do Pay Raises Translate for the Working Poor?

A critical component of welfare reform is promoting self-sufficiency, or independence from government support. The Personal Responsibility and Work Opportunity Reconciliation Act (PRWORA) allocates more funding for work supports, such as childcare and transportation vouchers, than AFDC did in hopes that families will work their way off all government support including cash support, food assistance programs, Medicaid, and childcare vouchers. In efforts to lead TANF recipients into the workforce, when recipients gain employment, some states are more generous than others in the amount of earnings recipients can keep without losing benefits—at least at first. However, as recipients' wages increase, their cash benefits and food stamp values decline along with their eligibility for various programs designed to promote work. In theory, PRWORA provides supports to get families engaged in work and takes them away once families can support themselves.

Research suggests, however, that families may lose cash assistance and program eligibility too early in their efforts toward self-sufficiency. When recipients lose government benefits due to increased earnings, this phenomenon is termed "implicit taxation"—recipients do not keep 100 percent of their increased earnings because they lose one or more means-tested benefits. Recipient wage increases are "taxed" at varying percentage rates, and in some cases the tax can be more than 100 percent. In other words, recipients lose more in benefits than they gain in increased earnings. The following two case examples illustrate how implicit taxation can be detrimental to recipients' economic livelihood.

Karen is a single mother with three children who works as a home health aide. Initially, she received Supplemental Nutrition Assistance Program (food stamps), subsidized housing, and Medicaid benefits. When her hourly wage increased from $6.25 to $9.25 an hour, she lost her rent subsidy, and her monthly food benefits were reduced by more than 50 percent. Her raise provided her with $462 more in monthly earnings after payroll taxes, but she lost $177 in rent subsidy, $81 in food stamps, and $154 in the Earned Income Tax Credit for low-income earners. Karen's implicit tax rate was 89 percent (($177+$81+154)/$462), leaving a monthly net gain from her pay raise of $50. This minimal amount of increased earnings led Karen to reduce her work hours in order to re-qualify for additional benefits.

Edith's situation is another example of how pay raises and implicit taxation hurt low-income single mother families. Edith is 31 years old with three children ages 6 years and younger. She worked as a low-wage receptionist and qualified for subsidized childcare and Medicaid. Due to her strong work skills, she was promoted to office manager and earned a monthly take-home pay increase of $554. As a result of her pay increase, Edith was no longer eligible for subsidized childcare. The loss of her subsidy meant her childcare costs increased by $600. Edith's implicit tax rate was 108 percent ($600/$554) leaving her worse off than before her promotion. Edith's loss of childcare subsidies led her to use a relative to watch her children even though she knew that her relative could not provide her children the same educational benefits they received in subsidized care.

These examples highlight how implicit taxation can offset wage gains among the working poor. Although the government saves money (at least in the short term) by taking benefits away from working families, setting appropriate gradients and thresholds for program benefits and eligibility is critical if families are to reach PRWORA's goal of self-sufficiency.

Source: This box draws heavily from Jennifer L. Romich, Jennifer Simmelink, and Stephen D. Holt, "When Working Harder Does Not Pay: Low-Income Working Families, Tax Liabilities, and Benefit Reductions," *Families in Society: The Journal of Contemporary Social Services,* Vol. 88, No. 3, July–Sept., 2007, pp. 418–426. DOI: 10.1606/1044-3894.3651. Used by permission of the publisher. www.FamiliesInSociety.org

may change in the future as states face stricter work requirements and are no longer eligible for waivers. Hard economic times are also causing rising unemployment and place more families in economic straits.

Additional TANF Funding

In addition to the TANF block grants, states have had opportunities to compete for additional TANF funding. Congress appropriated $3 billion through September 2004 for the Welfare-to-Work (W-t-W) grant program specifically for TANF recipients with multiple barriers to employment, noncustodial parents, and TANF recipients facing the end of their five-year time limits within 12 months.[129] The "core" services most often provided to W-t-W participants were intake, assessment, job readiness, pre-employment case management, job development and placement, and post-placement follow-up. An evaluation of these work-focused W-t-W programs found that at least 60 percent of participants were employed at some point during two years of service receipt. The figure dropped to 40 percent employed after two years at most program sites. Average hourly wages were relatively low at $8.00 (but higher than the federal minimum wage), and only 20 percent received employer-sponsored healthcare.[130] Especially concerning, but perhaps not surprising, is that 60 percent of W-t-W enrollees lived below poverty two years following program entry. W-t-W grant programs did not receive an additional round of funding and were discontinued.

TANF reauthorization, however, encouraged states to use innovative programs to help TANF clients. Instead of W-t-W's focus on work, from 2006 through 2010, $250 million was allocated for responsible fatherhood initiatives and $490 million for healthy marriage initiatives.[131] Fatherhood initiatives include programs directed at noncustodial fathers that focus on marriage, parenting skills, job and employment training, media campaigns, and research. Healthy marriage initiatives include programs that promote marriage in the general population, enrich social skills and communication among married couples and those considering marriage, and minimize disincentives for marriage (e.g., some tax laws). Low-income couples show interest in the services, and studies of the programs' effectiveness are being conducted.[132] During the George W. Bush presidency, efforts to promote healthy marriages received a good deal of criticism with critics contending they diverted money away from cash assistance and education and employment programs.[133] These critics suggested that rather than promote marriage as a route to financial security, TANF should focus on making families more financially secure as a route to healthier marriages.

TANF Benefit Levels

Most states have maintained cash benefits at the 1996 level. Some have increased TANF benefits, but six states and the District of Columbia actually reduced benefits below their 1996 level. In most states, the real value of cash TANF benefits has continued to decline. The greatest decline (nearly 35 percent) was in Hawaii. In 2008, the maximum benefit for a family of three ranged from a low of $170 per month (12 percent of the federal government's official poverty threshold) in Mississippi to a high of $923 (50 percent of the poverty threshold) in Alaska (see Figure 7.3 for a comparison of benefit levels by state).[134] In 2006, 81 percent of TANF recipients also received food stamps ($322 per month on average), raising the monthly benefit package (cash plus food stamps) for a family of three to $558 (38 percent of the poverty threshold) in Mississippi to $1,191 (65 percent of the poverty threshold) in Alaska.

With TANF's emphasis on work and self-sufficiency, how do earnings affect a family's access to cash and non-cash benefits? States differ in how they treat earnings. For example, four states (Alabama, Mississippi, Nevada, and North Carolina) ignore all earnings for the first three months of employment, and Connecticut disregards all earnings for as long as earnings fall below federal poverty guidelines. For the first 12 months of employment, earning limits ranged from $269 a month in Alabama to $1,897 in Alaska.[135] Once these earnings levels are reached, the family no longer qualifies for TANF cash assistance.

Nearly every TANF family is also eligible for Medicaid (or the state's medical assistance program).[136] To further help families achieve self-sufficiency, states must offer transitional Medicaid benefits for 12 months after families leave TANF (regardless of whether families leave due to employment). Some states extend transitional Medicaid eligibility beyond 12 months. Although there is wide state variation, it is still safe to say that many states provide minimal cash payments to TANF recipients as they move from government assistance to self-sufficiency, and they also face losing Medicaid.

Traditional monthly cash assistance and work activities are not the only option states use to help needy families reach self-sufficiency. To keep caseloads down, 47 states have implemented "diversion" programs to help individuals who need minimal assistance in securing employment and self-sufficiency. Lump-sum payment programs, available in 35 states in 2008, are the most common diversion programs. Specific guidelines for lump sum programs differ greatly by state (diversion amount, diversion's influence on future TANF eligibility, frequency of eligibility for diversion payments), but the underlying concept is the same. In lieu of regular TANF cash assistance, these programs provide TANF-eligible families with short-term or lump sum assistance in cash or in-kind benefits on a case-by-case basis. Most often the lump sum equals three times the monthly TANF benefit.[137] Because these lump sum payments usually have a negative effect on future TANF eligibility, potential recipients must make the choice to opt for a larger one-time payment carefully. For this reason, states generally target families where an adult is employed or has a job offer because they may be less likely to need ongoing assistance.

TANF Spending Levels

Total AFDC spending (state and federal) peaked in 1995 at just over $30 billion, and dropped sharply following the start of TANF under welfare reform. In 1998, total spending was nearly $24 billion, its lowest level since 1991. In 2006 the federal and state governments spent more than $28 billion on TANF. Spending levels have been constant since 2000, but after adjusting for inflation, spending was 31 percent lower in 2006 compared to its peak in 1995. The federal share of AFDC/TANF spending increased from 54 percent in 1995 to 58 percent in 2006.[138]

As TANF cash assistance caseloads fell by about 50 percent between 1996 and 2000, this dramatic decline freed up TANF funds. In 2006, states spent only 41 percent or about $10 billion of TANF funds on basic assistance (primarily cash) down from 73 percent or about $14 billion in 1997 (see Figure 7.4).[139]

What did states do with the money they once spent on cash welfare benefits? In addition to saving money for a future rainy day, states have spent more on work supports, first referred to as "nonassistance" and now called "non-welfare" spending. Non-welfare spending is spending for noncash or in-kind assistance that helps TANF recipients work and increase their earnings, such as earned income tax credits and child credits, and work supports, such as childcare, transportation, and work subsidies. These "non-welfare" expenditures grew from less one-fifth of TANF expenditures in 1997 to half of expenditures in 2006 (see Figure 7.4).[140] The distinction between "welfare" and "non-welfare" expenditures is important because many TANF regulations, especially time limits, apply to cash welfare assistance but not to non-welfare assistance.[141]

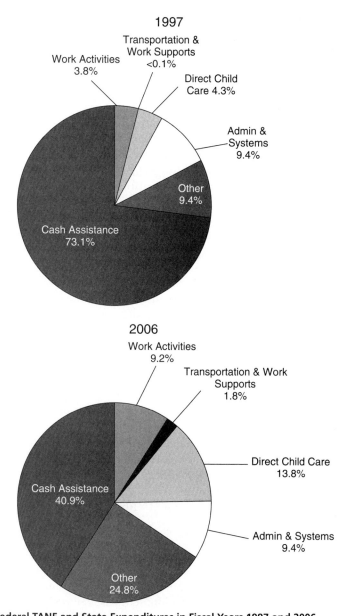

FIGURE 7.4   Federal TANF and State Expenditures in Fiscal Years 1997 and 2006
Source: Administration for Children and Families, "Characteristics and Financial Circumstances
of TANF Recipients," *TANF Eighth Annual Report to Congress* (Washington, DC: Department of Health
and Human Services), Figure A, p. II-15. Retrieved February 15, 2010, from http://www.acf.hhs.gov/
programs/ofa/data-reports/annualreport8/TANF_8th_Report_111908.pdf

Additional Services for TANF and Working Poor Families

Given welfare reform's emphasis on work and self-sufficiency, and given that nearly half of TANF funds go to services other than basic cash assistance, let's take a closer look at some of the benefits available to TANF families and other poor families. TANF's emphasis on work corresponds with an increase in work supports, at least in theory.

THE EARNED INCOME TAX CREDIT (EITC) This federal tax credit was created in 1975 as part of an economic stimulus package based on economist Milton Freedman's idea of a negative income tax. The basic idea is that rather than provide benefits to those who are not working (cash welfare), the government should reward work by supplementing low-wage earners. The Internal Revenue Service (IRS) distributes the EITC as a refundable federal income tax credit. It is available primarily to low-income families (since 1993, single individuals can also receive a small credit). Unlike other tax benefits such as the tax credit for childcare expenditures, eligible recipients do not need to pay taxes in order to receive the EITC. However, they must file a tax return to receive it. In addition, unlike other work supports, the EITC is guaranteed to all those who qualify and apply for it.

The EITC has three ranges based on annual earnings: phase-in range (benefit increases as income increases), plateau range (benefit stays constant as income increases), and phase-out range (benefit decreases as income increases). This design intends to encourage work, provide maximum benefit to those who work for low wages, and decrease benefits as families earn enough income to reach self-sufficiency. In 2009, the EITC's value was 40 percent of earnings for the first $12,570 of earned income for a single parent with two children ($5,028 maximum benefit). Single parents earning more than $16,420 reached the phase-out range, and their EITC benefit declined as earnings rose. Once they earned $40,295, they no longer qualified for the credit.

The EITC is currently the United States' largest antipoverty program for families. EITC spending surpassed cash welfare spending in the mid-1990s and continues to rise. In tax year 2005, approximately 24 million families received more than $41 billion in EITC refunds.[142] Estimates are that approximately 15 to 25 percent of eligible families do not claim the credit, resulting in billions of unclaimed money annually. Very low-income families, Hispanics, immigrants, food stamp recipients, TANF recipients, and those without a high school diploma are less likely to know about or apply for the EITC than other groups.[143] About half the states also have their own, smaller EITC.[144]

CHILDCARE Childcare is another support that is at least theoretically available to TANF and other low-income families. Under AFDC, states were required to provide childcare for recipients who worked or participated in work-related activities. Although childcare funding increased under the 1996 welfare reform legislation, states are not obligated to provide childcare under TANF. However, states can use TANF funds to provide childcare subsidies that allow parents to choose appropriate childcare such as center care, informal home care, or relative care. States have shifted spending from cash assistance to childcare subsidies. Childcare spending grew dramatically between 1997 and 2000 from $249 million to $4 billion, but it dropped to $3.2 billion by 2007.[145] Even with substantial childcare spending, only one of every seven eligible children received childcare assistance through TANF in 2000. This proportion remained relatively constant through 2007. Only 6 percent of all children under age 6 and 15 percent of those under age 6 living in poverty received TANF childcare subsidies in 2003.[146] The United States provides much less childcare assistance than other industrialized nations (see Illustration 7.3).

ILLUSTRATION 7.3
How Does U.S. Child Care Assistance Compare to Other Countries?

People generally classify infants and toddlers living in poverty as part of the "worthy poor." Who can blame infants arriving home from the hospital for their living conditions? Clearly, they are dependent on others to meet their needs. Given that society does not blame young children for their economic condition, how much does the government contribute to a "safety net" for children?

Infants and toddlers get less than their fair share of government spending. In 2007, the nation's 12.5 million infants and toddlers were approximately 4 percent of the population yet they received only 2 percent of federal domestic spending ($44.1 billion). The general public commonly believes that education is the answer to the nation's social ills. However, the federal government spent only 7 percent of its budget for infants and toddlers on early care and education programs such as Head Start and childcare assistance. The biggest federal expenditure for young children was Medicaid, constituting 38 percent of the budget for this population. Although people often complain that single mothers with young children live off cash from the system, only 2 percent of federal spending on families with infants and toddlers came from programs providing cash assistance, such as cash welfare.[1]

The U.S. government provides little in the way of a safety net for children. Instead, welfare reform requires parents of young children to work. Given the stiff work requirements, is childcare available? PRWORA designated $5.4 billion in 2006 for childcare, yet only 12 percent of eligible families received TANF childcare subsidies.[2] Some of these families were receiving TANF, others had left TANF, and some were working poor families who used this aid to avoid becoming TANF recipients.

There is a gap in the United States between what poor families with young children need and the government benefits that they receive. Thinking globally, how does the United States fare in childcare provision compared to other countries? In short, the United States provides much less to poor and non-poor families than other countries do. As Figure 7.5 indicates, U.S. spending on childcare for children under age 3 was only .09 percent of the gross domestic product (GDP), much less than most comparison countries. The United States is more generous to children aged 3 to 5 (.31 percent of GDP), with the majority of this support provided via tax credits or publicly funded preschool or kindergarten programs.

What percent of childcare costs does the U.S. government generally cover? Of developed countries with available data, the United States ranks the lowest at only 25 to 30 percent, while these other countries cover at least two-thirds of child care costs ranging from 68 to 100 percent depending on the child's age and the country.[3]

In summary, the United States views childcare as a private decision and provides little public support for childcare, especially for infants and toddlers, compared to other economically developed countries. If the United States wants a more family-friendly environment, childcare policies that provide families with government-subsidized, quality childcare or with additional money to offset childcare costs could alleviate families' financial strain while also promoting healthy child development.

[1]This paragraph draws heavily from Jennifer Ehrle Macomber, Julia Isaacs, Tracy Vericker, Adam Kent, and Paul Johnson, *Federal Expenditures on Infants and Toddlers in 2007: Key Facts* (Washington DC: The Brookings Institution and the Urban Institute, May 2009). Retrieved February 11, 2009, from http://www.urban.org/publications/411878.html

[2]Committee on Ways and Means, "Temporary Assistance for Needy Families," *2008 Green Book*, (Washington, DC: U.S. House of Representatives), pp. 7-64–7-65. Retrieved February 11, 2010, from http://waysandmeans.house.gov/singlepages.aspx?NewsID=10490

[3]Jane Waldfogel, "International Policies Toward Parental Leave and Child Care," *The Future of Children*, Vol. 11, No. 1, Spring-Summer 2001, pp. 99–111.

(Continued)

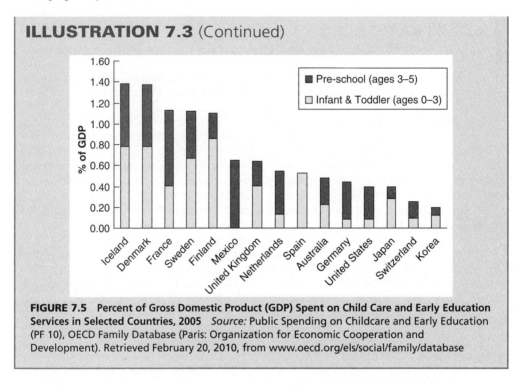

ILLUSTRATION 7.3 (Continued)

FIGURE 7.5 **Percent of Gross Domestic Product (GDP) Spent on Child Care and Early Education Services in Selected Countries, 2005** *Source:* Public Spending on Childcare and Early Education (PF 10), OECD Family Database (Paris: Organization for Economic Cooperation and Development). Retrieved February 20, 2010, from www.oecd.org/els/social/family/database

Federal law allows states to use TANF funds for childcare in two ways: (1) States may directly spend TANF funds on childcare; and (2) states may transfer up to 30 percent of TANF funds to their Childcare and Development Block Grant (CCDBG). Similar to direct TANF funds, states have much discretion in using CCDBG funds to meet TANF families' childcare needs. States can also use CCDBG funds to assist low-income working families not receiving TANF. States transferred $2.6 billion in TANF funds to CCBDG in 1999 and $2 billion in 2007.[147] Reductions in childcare spending since the early 2000s have been linked to downturns in the economy and subsequent state budget crises, but politicians generally support childcare funding. Despite few funding increases in TANF's reauthorization, an additional $2 billion was allocated for childcare funding from 2006 to 2010.[148]

OTHER SUPPORTS As noted, TANF offers states the opportunity to provide a unique smorgasbord of non-cash services to meet the needs of families in poverty. There is always fine print or stipulations, and the federal government may challenge some uses, but as long as states directly tie their services to a TANF goal, they have considerable flexibility. In theory, the sky may be the limit for innovative services; however, states have spent relatively small amounts on supportive services other than the EITC and childcare. Less than 2 percent ($407 million) was used to "enhance skills" in 2006. Similar amounts ($472 million) were spent on transportation and supportive services. Spending on pregnancy prevention programs grew from $102 million in 2000 to $723 million in 2006, constituting 2.5 percent of total TANF funds. Some states have started two-parent family formation programs, but nationwide, little funding ($217 million in 2006) has been used in this effort,[149] perhaps because such programs are controversial or because evidence-based models for doing so are lacking.

States can also help families save money toward their goal of self-sufficiency. Individual Development Accounts (IDAs) are an assets and investment approach designed to complement welfare programs and help families save money for future needs. IDAs allow families to accumulate "wealth" through government matching funds. For example, a state may match every dollar a family saves with a dollar. States' investment in IDAs grew from just $7.7 million in 2002 to $900 million in 2006.[150] Under the former AFDC program, recipients who accumulated even small amounts of cash or other assets were generally disqualified from assistance, but without assets, they may never be able to leave welfare behind. Depending on the specific program, IDAs may be used to buy a home, pay for education, or start a business.[151]

Other ways states can use the savings from TANF caseload declines is to support poor families not receiving traditional basic (cash) TANF assistance by transferring up to 10 percent of TANF funds to their Social Service Block Grant (SSBG). Like other TANF spending trends, the amount of funds transferred to SSBG increased each year until 1999, when it peaked at $1.3 billion. In 2006, $974 million were transferred to SSBG.[152]

Spending Forecast

When caseloads dropped dramatically shortly after PRWORA's passage, states began accumulating savings for a rainy day. In the early 2000s, the economy worsened, but caseloads (total number of recipients) continued to decline, although more slowly than they had immediately after TANF's passage (by 6 percent nationally from 2005 to 2006, with Virginia and South Dakota reporting caseload increases).[153] The rainy day did arrive, causing states to draw from their previous TANF savings. These reserve funds dropped from $3.2 billion in 2000 to less than $2.2 billion in 2006.[154]

In difficult economic times, public assistance advocates and states become increasingly concerned about the ability to maintain cash benefits and work supports, which is complicated by eroding tax bases, rising Medicaid costs, and other concerns.[155] In October 2008, 4.1 million individuals received TANF. In December 2009, the number was 4.6 million.[156] A number of "theories" have been advanced to explain why TANF caseloads did not rise even more during this time of high unemployment. They include changes that have taken place in the TANF program, such as time limits; eroding benefit levels; increased pressure to work, even when jobs may not be available; and other "hassles," including the stigma of receiving public assistance benefits.[157] Another theory is that states have much more incentive to keep people off the rolls under the current TANF block grant program.

How Effective Has TANF Been?

TANF's effectiveness depends on how one measures success. The most publicized measure has been the numbers who have left the welfare rolls. The number of families receiving cash welfare dropped dramatically from a peak of 5 million in 1994[158] to 1.7 million in 2009.[159] The drop is a result of fewer families entering the TANF system and more families exiting.

Did PRWORA cause this decline in AFDC/TANF caseloads? Welfare reform began during the economic boom times of the late 1990s when the economy added 21 million jobs. Much of the decline in caseloads was likely a response not only to welfare reform policies, but also because more jobs were available. That having been said, it is also important to note that, before welfare reform, economic boom times did not result in substantial decreases in caseloads.[160] The Committee on Ways and Means said that factors that shrunk caseloads were "the new 'work first' culture, a rapidly growing economy, tougher work sanctions, . . . a lifetime limit for Federally funded benefits, and widespread adoption of diversion practices."[161] The Council

of Economic Advisers attributed one-third of the drop to welfare policy changes, 8 to 10 percent
to an improved economy, 10 percent to the increase in the minimum wage, and as much as 5
percent to the decrease in the value of cash welfare benefits.[162] Others agree that the strong
economy, changes in welfare policies, and changes in policies affecting low-wage earners, all
contributed to the increase in work among low-income single mothers and the decline in TANF
caseloads.[163]

We can also ask whether families leave TANF voluntarily or for other reasons such as
noncompliance with program rules. In 2006, 95,000 families (5.3 percent of the TANF
caseload), on average, were sanctioned each month, and of them, 16,000 families were cut from
the TANF program each month. From 2002 through 2006, over 222,000 families reached their
time limits and their cases were closed.[164] In sum, approximately 10 percent of those who left
welfare in 2006 were forced to do so.

Another way to examine TANF's effectiveness is to examine how families have fared after
leaving TANF. Studies of recipients who left TANF shortly after its passage show that about 75
percent worked at some point during the year after leaving, and between 30 and 40 percent
worked in all four quarters the year following exit.[165] About one-half to two-thirds of "welfare
leavers" were still working one to two years after exiting TANF, while approximately 25 percent
had returned to TANF. Although employment is critical to many welfare exits, employment was
nearly seven percentage points lower among those who left welfare between 2000 and 2005 compared to those who left in the late 1990s.[166] In 2002, welfare leavers earned $8 an hour on average,
a relatively low wage, although well-above the federal minimum hourly wage of $5.15 at that
time. About one-third of employed former TANF recipients worked part-time (less than 35 hours
a week).[167] The typical mother leaving welfare earned about $10,000 a year.[168]

These studies do not reflect the economic crisis that hit especially hard beginning in the
fall of 2008. The real indictment of welfare reform is that even in better economic times, many
families who left TANF remained poor and experienced hardships because of low earnings.
Most TANF leavers work in the low-wage service sector.[169] About 41 percent of TANF leavers
had incomes below the poverty threshold even when the value of the EITC and food stamps was
added to earnings.[170] In a U.S. Department of Health and Human Services (DHHS) study of
TANF leavers in 15 states in 2001, workers' average monthly earnings exceeded the poverty level
in only two states.[171]

Another DHHS study examined a variety of experimental programs throughout the United
States, including those providing education, job training, or earning supplements (government
transfers to supplement low-wage earners). The conclusion was that neither post-secondary education nor job training programs showed consistently positive results for participants' economic
circumstances or their children's well-being. Job-focused services increased employment and
decreased TANF receipt, yet clients remained poor. Participants who got earning supplements had
short-term gains in income, and their children's academic performance improved, but the positive
effects waned over the five-year follow-up period.[172]

The Urban Institute's initiative called Assessing the New Federalism has tracked the effects
of devolution as welfare moved from federal to state control. It reported that the number of welfare leavers who were employed fell from 50 percent in 1999 to 42 percent in 2002.[173] When compared to welfare recipients before 2000, current welfare recipients were more likely to have health
conditions that limited work and were less likely to have completed high school. Some were
becoming disconnected from both the workforce and the welfare system. These individuals had
no reported source of income—they were not working, did not have a working spouse, and were
not receiving TANF or disability benefits. The Urban Institute also reported that the percentage

of these "disconnected welfare leavers" doubled from 1999 to 2002. Most faced multiple barriers to employment, and thus experienced more material hardship than other TANF leavers. Sixty-three percent reported that they had run out of money to purchase food.[174] Less than half of all TANF leavers (43 percent) were receiving food stamps; only 15 percent were using childcare supports, although 50 to 85 percent received earned income tax credits.[175]

The problems that led families to welfare remain as barriers to work for TANF recipients. Healthcare problems; lack of education and skills; mental illness, substance abuse, and other disabilities; and childcare and transportation problems are the prominent barriers to obtaining and retaining a job. The Joyce Foundation found that the more problems people faced, the less likely they were to work, and that those with the most severe problems often left welfare involuntarily due to sanctions for not meeting program demands.[176] Assessing the successes and failures of TANF policies and programs is challenging because it can be difficult to track families after they leave the program.

If the less than optimistic results of TANF evaluations sound familiar, they should. They mirror the findings of earlier work programs including WIN, workfare, and the JOBS program. Much time and attention has been directed at developing, implementing, and evaluating work-focused welfare, yet net gains for participants and their children are often few or inconsistent. Questions arise as to the point of work-focused welfare given little empirical support for its effectiveness. In a society that places so much emphasis on work, is it important for welfare recipients to be employed no matter how small the monetary gain? The stiffer work requirements of the 2006 welfare reauthorization suggest that it is.

We can also ask what the attention to work says about the value the nation places on mothers (or fathers) who stay at home to raise their children. The rise in dual-earner families among middle-class Americans suggests that the ideal of a parent staying at home to raise children has all but been rejected. Even if work does not seem to be helping very low-income families, the emphasis on work has remained in good and bad economic times.

The Future of TANF

Politicians lack agreement on TANF's effectiveness in part because they focus on different measures of success. Those who believe in more work and less public assistance have been getting their way, but the lack of consensus over what constitutes effectiveness has led to disagreement on the next steps for TANF legislation.

Given the battles that ensued over initial passage of the PRWORA, it is no surprise that Congress had trouble agreeing on reauthorization legislation. State TANF programs were kept running through a series of stop-gap bills from 2002 until 2005 when the Deficit Reduction Act (DRA) of 2006 reauthorized TANF through 2010. The DRA increased work requirements while keeping funding at current levels with no adjustment for inflation. Work requirements are tougher than ever: States must improve work participation rates from 2005 rather than 1995, more single-parent families must be working (70 percent by 2010), and states must follow strict guidelines regarding what constitutes "work."[177]

Although TANF reauthorization did not provide additional funds in light of the worsening economy, President Obama's American Recovery and Reinvestment Act (ARRA) passed in 2009 did. The ARRA provided up to $5 billion in additional TANF funds for 2009–2010. States were eligible for these "emergency" funds if they increased their spending in at least one of three areas: basic assistance; short-term, lump sum diversion payments; or subsidized employment. Furthermore, states could use the emergency funds at their discretion as long as the money was directed towards at least one TANF goal.[178] States with increased TANF caseloads did not incur higher work participation *rates,* but the *number* of participants required to work increased if caseloads increased.[179]

Much of the $5 billion in emergency federal TANF funds has gone unused. This is because states must put up $1 in state funds to draw down $4 in federal funding, and some states say they cannot afford to do this in the recession.[180] Philanthropist George Soros gave millions so the state of New York could draw down funding. In California, the prospect of eliminating the state's welfare program has been discussed as a result of the state's budget crisis.[181]

As preparation for TANF reauthorization debates begins again, the following issues will likely get attention:

- Responding to increased needs of families during the recession
- Helping families with significant employment barriers achieve more employment successes
- Whether TANF programs should provide more education and training to help parents secure better jobs
- How much TANF funding states should receive.[182]

Concerns also arise about setting realistic expectations for work participation during times of high local, state, and national unemployment. It has been suggested that with a Democratic president and Democrats in control of Congress, there might be attempts at "emasculating the work requirements or converting TANF funding back to an entitlement."[183]

Summary

Parents are obligated to support their children, but many children in the United States do not receive this financial support. Some parents cannot afford to pay. Others shirk their responsibilities. Federal and state laws have increased penalties for failure to pay legally owed child support, but much child support is still not collected.

Some countries provide universal children allowances and childcare to ensure all children a decent standard of living, regardless of their family's circumstances. In the United States, only the very poor are entitled to public aid, which comes in the form of means-tested public assistance benefits. For much of the twentieth century, this assistance was called Aid to Families with Dependent Children (AFDC). No social welfare program has been as controversial as AFDC. As AFDC caseloads rose due to divorce, desertion, and especially out-of-wedlock births and the lack of non-custodial fathers paying child support, concerns mounted that AFDC needed a major overhaul. This was accomplished in 1996 with the Temporary Assistance for Needy Families (TANF) program, a major provision of the Personal Responsibility and Work Opportunity Reconciliation Act, also called welfare reform.

Most families can receive TANF for a limited period of time, and the parent or parents must work or participate in work-related activities such as job search or education. Many conservatives have hailed sharp declines in TANF caseloads as evidence of the program's success. Some parents have found jobs. Others have been terminated from TANF for reaching time limits, not complying with program rules, or experiencing barriers to participating in the program. Regardless of the reason, many families that leave the rolls are not doing well financially. The various versions of welfare to work programs have met with limited success, and work participation rates have not met expected standards.

Many more Americans get the Earned Income Tax Credit for working families than get TANF, but many families who qualify never claim the credit. Americans generally agree that policies that encourage work are preferable to public assistance. While Americans once thought that a mother's place was in the home when her children were very young, today, the expectation is that every parent will work when necessary to make ends meet. Americans do realize that some families need public assistance, but that public aid has become much more difficult to get.

Discussion Questions and Class Activities

1. Learn more about the child support enforcement (CSE) program in your state and community and how it compares with other states and communities. How many families does the program serve? How many families receive partial and full payments? How much is collected compared to how much is due? What methods are used to pursue parents who are in arrears? Is there any privatization of child support enforcement activities? What challenges does the program face? Invite a speaker from the state CSE program and one from a private program if there is an office in the area.

2. Invite current or former participants (custodial and non-custodial parents) to discuss their experience with the child support enforcement program (or invite representatives of groups or organizations working to improve child support). What are their thoughts about the quality and responsiveness of CSE services? How effective has the program been for them (or those they represent)? What changes would they like to see in the program?

3. Learn more about the TANF program in your state and community and how it compares with other states and communities. Have payment levels changed in recent years? What are program time limits and other rules? What work programs and other services are in place? How many families are receiving aid and how have these figures changed since 1996? Invite TANF program staff to discuss their views and perspectives on the TANF program.

4. Obtain your state's TANF application form and review it carefully. Discuss how you would feel if you were answering these questions. Note the types and amount of information requested and statements about prosecution for answering falsely or other warnings. Do you have suggestions for improving the application form?

5. Invite current (or former) participants to discuss their experiences with the TANF program. Ask them to discuss the application process and various aspects of program participation. What other assistance (e.g., Supplemental Nutrition Assistance Program benefits [food stamps] and Medicaid) are they also receiving? Are they working, searching for work, participating in education programs, or involved in other work-related activities? What suggestions do they have to make the TANF program more helpful to those in need?

6. Explore the methods other developed countries use to assist families with children such as child allowances and universal day care. The class might divide in pairs or small groups and each can select a different country to study. Discuss reasons the United States has not adopted these approaches. What methods do you think the United States should use to aid low-income families with children?

Websites

Children's Defense Fund, http://www.childrensdefense.org/, is a nonprofit organization founded by civil rights leader Marian Wright Edelman. CDF is dedicated to providing "a strong, effective and independent voice for *all* the children of America who cannot vote, lobby or speak for themselves." CDF focuses on areas such as ending child poverty, seeing that families have sufficient resources, including health and mental health insurance, preventing incarceration, and developing youth leaders.

Office of Child Support Enforcement (OCSE), http://www.acf.hhs.gov/programs/cse/, is part of the Administration for Children and Families, U.S. Department of Health and Human Services. OSCE's mission is to provide assistance that helps children obtain financial and medical support by locating parents, establishing paternity and support obligations, and enforcing those obligations.

Office of Family Assistance (OFA), http://www.acf
.hhs.gov/programs/ofa/, is part of the Administration
for Children and Families, U.S. Department of
Health and Human Services. OFA's TANF Bureau
administers the Temporary Assistance for Needy
Families (TANF) program to help low-income families achieve self-sufficiency, and the Child Care

Bureau administers the Child Care and Development
Fund (CCDF) programs to help low-income families
obtain affordable, quality childcare. OFA works
closely with the states, territories, and tribes, which
have a major role in developing and administering
these programs.

Notes

1. For a history of mothers' aid, see Linda Gordon, *Women, the State, and Welfare* (Madison, WI: University of Wisconsin Press, 1990); Linda Gordon, *Pitied But Not Entitled: Single Mothers and the History of Welfare* (New York: Free Press, 1994).
2. Laurence E. Lynn, Jr., "A Decade of Policy Developments in the Income-Maintenance System," in Robert H. Haveman, Ed., *A Decade of Federal Antipoverty Programs: Achievements, Failures, and Lessons* (New York: Academic Press, 1977), p. 60; Martin Rein, *Social Policy: Issues of Choice and Change* (New York: Random House, 1970), p. 311.
3. Quoted in Lynn, "A Decade of Policy Developments in the Income-Maintenance System," p. 73.
4. Gilbert Y. Steiner, *The State of Welfare* (Washington, DC: Brookings Institution, 1971), p. 81.
5. See Committee on Ways and Means, U.S. House of Representatives, *Overview of Entitlement Programs, 1993 Green Book* (Washington, DC: U.S. Government Printing Office, 1993), p. 623.
6. *Ibid.*, p. 733.
7. John Bishop, "Jobs, Cash Transfers, and Marital Instability: A Review of the Evidence," Institute for Research on Poverty, University of Wisconsin, Madison, written testimony to the Welfare Reform Subcommittee of the Committees on Agriculture, Education and Labor, and Ways and Means of the U.S. House of Representatives, October 14, 1977, p. 9.
8. *Ibid.*, p. 8.
9. David T. Elwood and Lawrence H. Summers, "Poverty in America: Is Welfare the Answer or the Problem?" in Sheldon H. Danzinger and Daniel H. Weinberg, Eds., *Fighting Poverty: What Works and What Doesn't* (Cambridge, MA: Harvard University Press, 1986), pp. 92–93.
10. Hilary Williamson Hoynes, "Work, Welfare, and Family Structure: What Have We Learned?" Working Paper 5644 (Cambridge, MA: National Bureau of Economic Research, July 1996), p. 36.
11. Library of Congress, Personal Responsibility and Work Opportunity Reconciliation Act of 1996 (Washington, DC: Thomas: Legislative Information on the Internet, August 22, 1996). Retrieved September 15, 2009, from http://thomas.loc.gov/cgi-bin/query/z?c104:H.R.3734.ENR:htm
12. Alfred J. Kahn and Sheila B. Kamerman, *Child Support: From Debt Collection to Social Policy* (Newbury Park, CA: Sage, 1988).
13. Committee on Ways and Means, "Child Support Enforcement Program," *2004 Green Book* (Washington, DC: U.S. House of Representatives, December 30, 2003). Retrieved February 2010, from http://waysandmeans.house.gov/media/pdf/greenbook2003/108Transmittal.pdf
14. Committee on Ways and Means, "Child Support Enforcement Program," *1993 Green Book,* p. 776.
15. Committee on Ways and Means, "Child Support Enforcement Program," *2008 Green Book* (Washington, DC: U.S. House of Representatives), p. 8-2. Retrieved September 18, 2009, from http://waysandmeans.house.gov/media/pdf/110/cse.pdf
16. *Ibid.*, pp. 8-77–8-81.
17. This section relies on Committee on Ways and Means, "Child Support Enforcement Program," *2008 Green Book.*
18. Julien O. Teitier, "Father Involvement, Child Health and Maternal Health Behavior," *Children and Youth Services Review,* Vol. 23, No. 4/5, April/May, 2001; U.S. Department of Health and Human Services, "Fatherhood Initiative." Retrieved September 18, 2009, from http://www.cfw.tufts.edu/?/category/family-parenting/2/topic/fathers/36/site/

us-department-of-health-and-human-services-fatherhood-initiative/565/

19. M. Robin Dion and Barbara DeVaney, *Strengthening Relationships and Supporting Healthy Marriage among Unwed Parents* (Princeton, NY: Mathematica, April 2003); Sara S. McLanahan and Marcia J. Carlson, "Welfare Reform, Fertility, and Father Involvement," *The Future of Children*, Vol. 12, No. 1, Winter/Spring 2002, pp. 147–165.

20. Florida Commission on Responsible Fatherhood, "Program Evaluation of Five TANF-Funded Responsible Fatherhood Programs in Florida," February 28, 2003. Retrieved September 29, 2009, from http://web.archive.org/web/20061109200525/http://www.ounce.org/pdf/fathereval.pdf

21. Committee on Ways and Means, "Child Support Enforcement Program," *2008 Green Book*, p. 8-5.

22. Stephanie J. Ventura, "Changing Patterns of Nonmarital Childbearing in the United States," NCHS Data Brief No. 18 (Hyattsville, MD: National Center for Health Statistics, May 2009). Retrieved February 14, 2010, from http://www.cdc.gov/nchs/data/databriefs/db18.pdf

23. Committee on Ways and Means, "Child Support Enforcement Program," *2008 Green Book*, p. 8-4.

24. Administration for Children and Families, *Office of Child Support Enforcement Preliminary Report FY 2008* (Washington, DC: U.S. Department of Health and Human Services), Table 9. Retrieved February 13, 2010, from http://www.acf.hhs.gov/programs/cse/pubs/2009/reports/preliminary_report_fy2008/

25. Freya L. Sonenstein, Pamela A. Holcomb, and Kristen S. Seefeldt, *Promising Approaches to Improving Paternity Establishment at the Local Level* in Irwin Garfinkel, Sara McLanahan, and Philip Robins, Eds., *Child Support and Child-Well Being* (Washington, DC: Urban Institute, February 1994), cited in Committee on Ways and Means, *1993 Green Book*, pp. 756–757.

26. This discussion of methods used to award child support relies on Committee on Ways and Means, "Child Support Enforcement Program," *2008 Green Book*, pp. 8-23–8-25; see also Support Guidelines.com, "Child Support Guidelines on the Web." Retrieved July 22, 2009, from http://www.support-guidelines.com/links.html

27. Lauren W. Morgan, "Child Support Models" in *Child Support Guidelines: Interpretation and Application* (Aspen Law & Business, 1996 & Supps.). Retrieved March 13, 2004, from http://www.supportguidelines.com/book/chap1a.html;

also cited in Committee on Ways and Means, "Child Support Enforcement Program," *2008 Green Book*, p. 8-26.

28. Maureen A. Pirog, Marilyn E. Klotz, M., and Katherine V. Byers, "Interstate Comparisons of Child Support Awards Using State Guidelines," *Family Relations*, Vol. 47, No. 3, 1998, pp. 289–295.

29. Laura W. Morgan, "The Constitutionality of Child Support Guidelines, Part I," Support Guidelines.com, May 16, 2002. Retrieved May 24, 2009, from http://www.supportguidelines.com/articles/art200204.html; Laura W. Morgan, "The Constitutionality of Child Support Guidelines, Part II, An Analysis of Georgia's *Sweat v. Sweat*," May 2002, June 5, 2002, Support Guidelines.com. Retrieved May 24, 2009, from http://www.supportguidelines.com/articles/art200205.html; Roger F. Gay, "The Constitutionality of Child Support Guidelines Debate, Part II," May 20, 2002. Retrieved May 24, 2009, from http://www.geocities.com/capitolhill/5910/FatherMag/ResponseToMorgan_2.htm

30. R. Mark Rogers, "The Economics of Child Support Determination" (Peachtree City, GA: Economic Consulting, June 17, 2005). Retrieved May 24, 2009, from http://www.guidelineeconomics.com/files/faf_presentation.pdf

31. Chien-Chung Huang and Richard L. Edwards, "The Relationship Between State Efforts and Child Support Performance, *Children & Youth Services Review*, Vol. 31, 2009, pp. 243–248.

32. Administration for Children and Families, *Office of Child Support Enforcement Preliminary Report FY 2008*, Table 2.

33. Committee on Ways and Means, "Child Support Enforcement Program," *2008 Green Book*, p. 8-26.

34. *Ibid.*, p. 8-26.

35. *Ibid.*, Table 8-6.

36. Huang and Edwards, "The Relationship Between State Efforts and Child Support Performance"; Administration for Children and Families, *Office of Child Support Enforcement Preliminary Report FY 2008*, Table 9.

37. Committee on Ways and Means, "Child Support Enforcement Program," *2008 Green Book*, p. 8-80.

38. Elaine Sorensen, "Child Support Gains Some Ground" (Washington: DC. Urban Institute, October 6, 2003). Retrieved February 18. 2010, from http://www.urban.org/uploadedpdf/310860_snapshots3_no11.pdf

39. Committee on Ways and Means, "Child Support Enforcement Program," *2008 Green Book*, p. 8-38;

Administration for Children and Families, *Office of Child Support Enforcement Preliminary Report FY 2008,* Figure 7.

40. Committee on Ways and Means, "Child Support Enforcement Program," *2008 Green Book,* p. 8-55.

41. Elaine Sorensen and Chava Zibman, "Poor Dads Who Don't Pay Child Support: Deadbeats or Disadvantaged?" (Washington, DC: Urban Institute, April 1, 2001). Retrieved May 24, 2009, from http://www.urban.org/Publications/310334.html

42. Mary S. Hill, "The Role of Economic Resources and Dual-Family Status in Child Support Payments" (Ann Arbor, MI: Institute for Social Research, University of Michigan, May 1988), cited in Committee on Ways and Means, U.S. House of Representatives, "Child Support Enforcement Program," *2004 Green Book,* p. 8-43.

43. Committee on Ways and Means, "Child Support Enforcement Program," *2008 Green Book,* p. 8-49.

44. *Ibid.,* pp. 8-50–8-51.

45. David S. Rosettenstein, "Choice of Law in International Child Support Obligations: Hague or Vague, and Does It Matter? An American Perspective," *International Journal of Law, Policy, and the Family,* Vol. 22, 2008, pp. 122–134.

46. Committee on Ways and Means, "Child Support Enforcement Program," *2008 Green Book,* p. 8-31.

47. Administration for Children and Families, *Office of Child Support Enforcement Preliminary Report FY 2008,* Table 11.

48. Committee on Ways and Means, "Child Support Enforcement Program," *2008 Green Book.,* p. 8-15.

49. *Ibid.*

50. Office of Child Support Enforcement, *Automated Cost-of-Living Adjustments of Child Support Orders in Three States* (Washington, DC: U.S. Department of Health and Human Services, April 16, 2001). Retrieved May 24, 2009, from http://www.acf.hhs.gov/programs/cse/pubs/reports/cola

51. Committee on Ways and Means, "Child Support Enforcement Program," *2008 Green Book,* p. 8-87.

52. *Ibid.,* p. 8-17; Administration for Children and Families, *Office of Child Support Enforcement Preliminary Report FY 2008.*

53. Administration for Children and Families, *Office of Child Support Enforcement Preliminary Report FY 2005* (Washington, DC: U.S. Department of Health and Human Services), Table 2. Retrieved February 14, 2010 from http://www.acf.hhs.gov/programs/cse/pubs/2005/reports/annual_report/table_2.html; Administration for Children and Families, *Office of Child Support Enforcement Preliminary Report FY 2008,* Table 2.

54. Committee on Ways and Means, "Child Support Enforcement Program," *2008 Green Book,* pp. 8-5–8-6, 8-81–8-82.

55. *Ibid.,* p. 8-5; Administration for Children and Families, *Office of Child Support Enforcement Preliminary Report FY 2008.*

56. Administration for Children and Families, *Office of Child Support Enforcement Preliminary Report FY 2008.*

57. Committee on Ways and Means, "Child Support Enforcement Program," *2008 Green Book,* pp. 8-82, 8-83, 8-92.

58. *Ibid.,* pp. 8-5–8-6, 8-81–8-82.

59. Elaine Sorensen, "Child Support Gains Some Ground."

60. Laura Wheaton, "Child Support Cost Avoidance in 1999, Final Report" (Washington, DC: Urban Institute, 2003). Prepared for HHS, Administration for Children and Families, OCSE. Retrieved February 18, 2010, from http://www.acf.hhs.gov/programs/cse/pubs/2003/reports/cost_avoidance/, cited in Committee on Ways and Means, "Child Support Enforcement Program," *2008 Green Book,* p. 8-78.

61. Committee on Ways and Means, "Child Support Enforcement Program," *2008 Green Book,* p. 8-79.

62. Administration for Children and Families, *Office of Child Support Enforcement Preliminary Report FY 2008.*

63. Committee on Ways and Means, "Child Support Enforcement Program," *2008 Green Book,* p. 8-84.

64. Administration for Children and Families, *Office of Child Support Enforcement Preliminary Report FY 2008.*

65. *Ibid.,* Table 1.

66. Committee on Ways and Means, "Child Support Enforcement Program," *2008 Green Book,* pp. 8-77–8-78.

67. This paragraph relies on Frank F. Furstenberg, Jr., "Daddies and Fathers: Men Who Do For Their Children and Men Who Don't" in Frank F. Furstenberg, Jr., Kay E. Sherwood, and Mercer L. Sullivan, Parents' Fair Share Demonstration, *Caring and Paying: What Fathers and Mothers Say About Child Support* (New York: Manpower Demonstration Research Corporation, July 1992). Retrieved February 18, 2010, from http://fatherhood.hhs.gov/pfs92/index.htm

68. Committee on Ways and Means, "Child Support Enforcement Program," *2008 Green Book,* pp. 8-9–8-10.

69. *Ibid.,* p. 8-8.

70. *Ibid.,* p. 8-57.

71. U.S. General Accounting Office, *Early Results on Comparability of Privatized and Public Offices,* GAO/HEHS-97-4 (Washington, DC: Author, December 1996). Retrieved June 29, 2009, from http://www.gao.gov/archive/1997/he97004.pdf

72. U.S. General Accounting Office, *Child Support Enforcement: Clear Guidance Would Help Ensure Proper Access to Information and Use of Wage Withholding by Private Firms,* GAO-02-349 (Washington, DC: Author, March 2002). Retrieved February 18, 2010, from http://www.gao.gov/new.items/d02349.pdf

73. National Conference of State Legislatures, Regulation of Private Child Support Collection Companies (Washington, DC: Author, 2008), cited in Committee on Ways and Means, "Child Support Enforcement Program," *2008 Green Book,* pp. 8-57–8-58.

74. Steiner, *The State of Welfare,* p. 36; Lynn, "A Decade of Policy Developments in the Income-Maintenance Programs," pp. 62–63.

75. Donald Brieland, Lela B. Costin, Charles R. Atherton, and contributors, *Contemporary Social Work: An Introduction to Social Work and Social Welfare* (New York: McGraw-Hill, 1975), p. 100; Steiner, *The State of Welfare,* p. 37.

76. Steiner, *The State of Welfare,* p. 37.

77. Andrew W. Dobelstein with Ann B. Johnson, *Serving Older Adults: Policy, Programs, and Professional Activities* (Englewood Cliffs, NJ: Prentice Hall, 1985), p. 126.

78. Lynn, "A Decade of Developments in the Income-Maintenance System," p. 74.

79. For further discussion of this point, see Sheldon H. Danzinger, Robert H. Haveman, and Robert D. Plotnick, "Antipoverty Policy: Effects on the Poor and the Nonpoor," in Danzinger and Weinberg, *Fighting Poverty,* pp. 50–77.

80. Roberta M. Spalter-Roth, Heidi I. Hartmann, and Linda Andrews, *Combining Work and Welfare: An Alternative Anti-poverty Strategy* (Washington, DC: Institute for Women's Policy Research, 1992); Heidi Hartmann, Roberta Spalter-Roth, and Jacqueline Chu, "Poverty Alleviation and Single-Mother Families," *National Forum,* Vol. 76, No. 3, 1996, pp. 24–27.

81. Leonard Goodwin, "Can Workfare Work?" *Public Welfare,* Vol. 39, Fall 1981, pp. 19–25.

82. *Ibid.*

83. Judith M. Gueron, *Reforming Welfare with Work* (New York: Ford Foundation, 1987).

84. Gayle Hamilton and Daniel Friedlander, *Final Report on the Saturation Work Initiative Model in San Diego* (Washington, DC: Manpower Demonstration Research Corporation, November 1989), quotes are from pp. x and vii.

85. This paragraph relies on Daniel Friedlander and Gary Burtless, *Five Years After: The Long-Term Effects of Welfare-to-Work Programs* (New York: Russell Sage Foundation, 1995), quote from p. 35.

86. Jan L. Hagen and Irene Lurie, "How 10 States Implemented Jobs," *Public Welfare,* Vol. 50, Summer 1992, p. 13.

87. Some of this section relies on Committee on Ways and Means, *1993 Green Book,* Section 7, especially pp. 624–644.

88. Robert B. Hudson, personal communication.

89. Stephen Freedman and Daniel Friedlander, *The JOBS Evaluation: Early Findings on Program Impacts in Three Sites,* Executive Summary (New York: Manpower Demonstration Research Corporation, 1995), also cited in Committee on Ways and Means, *1996 Green Book* (Washington, DC: U.S. House of Representatives), p. 428.

90. U.S. General Accounting Office, *Welfare to Work: Most AFDC Training Programs Not Emphasizing Job Placements,* GAO/HEHS-95-113 (Washington, DC: Author, May 1995). Retrieved February 18, 2010, from http://www.gao.gov/archive/1995/he95113.pdf

91. James Riccio, Daniel Friedlander, and Stephen Freedman, *GAIN: Benefits, Costs, and Three-Year Impacts of a Welfare-to-Work Program* (New York: Manpower Research Development Corporation, 1994).

92. Peter Passell, "Like a New Drug, Social Programs Are Put to the Test," *New York Times,* March 9, 1993, pp. C1, 10. For more in-depth information on welfare-to-work programs see Dan Bloom, *After AFDC: Welfare to Work, Choices and Challenges for States* (New York: Manpower Demonstration Research Corporation, 1997).

93. Administration for Children and Families, "Temporary Assistance for Needy Families (TANF), 1936-1998" (Washington, DC: U.S. Department of Health and Human Services, May 1998).

94. Administration for Children and Families, "Aid to Families with Dependent Children (AFDC), Temporary Assistance for Needy Families (TANF),

1960–1998" (Washington, DC: U.S. Department of Health and Human Services, August 1998).

95. Social Security Administration, *Social Security Bulletin, Annual Statistical Supplement, 1991* (Washington, DC: U.S. Department of Health and Human Services, 1992), p. 305.

96. Committee on Ways and Means, "Aid to Families with Dependent Children and Related Programs (Title IV-A)," *1996 Green Book,* (Washington DC: House of Representatives), p. 459.

97. See U.S. Bureau of the Census, *Statistical Abstract of the United States: 1997* (Washington, DC: U.S. Government Printing Office, 1997), Table 477, p. 299.

98. Committee on Ways and Means, "Aid to Families with Dependent Children and Related Programs (Title IV-A)," *1996 Green Book,* p. 442.

99. *Ibid.,* pp. 435, 437.

100. This description of methods used to determine standards of need is based on Kathryn A. Larin and Kathryn H. Porter, *Enough to Live On* (Washington, DC: Center for Budget and Policy Priorities), cited in "Study Faults State AFDC 'Need Standards,'" *NASW News,* Vol. 38, July 1993, p. 11.

101. Committee on Ways and Means, "Aid to Families with Dependent Children and Related Programs (Title IV-A)," *1996 Green Book,* pp. 436–438, 451–453.

102. Center on Budget and Policy Priorities, "The Cato Institute Report On Welfare Benefits: Do Cato's California Numbers Add Up?" (Washington: March 7, 1996). Retrieved on September 26, 2009 from http://epn.org/cbpp/cbcato.html

103. Executive Office of the President, Office of Management and Budget, *A Program for Economic Recovery* (Washington, DC: U.S. Government Printing Office, 1981), p. 1-11.

104. John L. Palmer and Isabel V. Sawhill, Eds., *The Reagan Record* (Cambridge, MA: Ballinger, 1984), p. 364.

105. "AFDC Cuts Hurt," *ISR Newsletter,* University of Michigan, Spring-Summer 1984, p. 3.

106. Executive Office of the President, *Budget of the United States Government, Fiscal Year 1991* (Washington, DC: U.S. Government Printing Office, 1990), p. 176.

107. Much of this section relies on Jeffrey L. Katz, "Clinton's Welfare Reform Plan to Be Out in Fall, Aides Say," *Congressional Quarterly,* Vol. 51, July 10, 1993, p. 1813; National Association of Social Workers, "Policy Recommendations of the Clinton Administration's Working Group on Welfare Reform,

Family Support and Independence" (Washington, DC: May 6, 1994); also see Executive Office of the President, Office of Management and Budget, Budget of the United States Government, Fiscal Year 1995 (Washington, DC: U.S. Government Printing Office, 1994).

108. David T. Ellwood, "Welfare Reform As I Knew It: When Bad Things Happen to Good Policies," *The American Prospect,* No. 26, May-June 1996, pp. 21–29. Retrieved from http://epn.org/prospect/26/26ellw.html

109. Robert A. Rankin, "Clinton Steers to the Middle, and Traditional Welfare Falls," *Austin American-Statesman,* August 4, 1996, pp. D1, 6.

110. Committee on Ways and Means, "Temporary Assistance for Needy Families (TANF)," *2008 Green Book,* pp. 7-5–7-7.

111. For a description of the change to TANF, see Committee on Ways and Means, *1996 Green Book,* Appendix L; see also David A. Super, Sharon Parrott, Susan Steinmetz, and Cindy Mann, "The New Welfare Law" (Washington, DC: Center on Budget and Policy Priorities, August 13, 1996). Retrieved September 20, 2009, from http://www.cbpp.org/archiveSite/WECNF813.HTM

112. Committee on Ways and Means, "Temporary Assistance for Needy Families," 2008 Green Book, pp. 7-10–7-11.

113. *Ibid.,* pp. 7-6–7-7.

114. *Ibid.,* p. 7-89.

115. *Ibid.* p. 7-5.

116. *Ibid.,* pp. 7-7–7-8.

117. Committee on Ways and Means, "Temporary Assistance for Needy Families," *2004 Green Book,* (Washington, DC: U.S. House of Representatives, 2004) p. 7-22.

118. Committee on Ways and Means, "Temporary Assistance for Needy Families," *2008 Green Book,* pp. 7-95–7-96.

119. For more information on these topics, see Committee on Ways and Means, *2008 Green Book;* Margy Waller, "TANF Reauthorization: Options and Opportunities," Presentation to the U.S. Conference of Mayors Annual Meeting, June 15, 2002. Retrieved September 20, 2009, from http://www.brookings.edu/speeches/2002/0530metropolitanpolicy_waller.aspx

120. Committee on Ways and Means, U.S. House of Representatives, *2008 Green Book,* p. 7-60–7-61.

121. This and other state rules are found in Gretchen Rowe, Mary Murphy, and James Kaminski, *Welfare Rules Databook: State TANF Policies as of July 2007* (Washington, DC: The Urban Institute, December

2008). Retrieved September 20, 2009, from http://anfdata.urban.org/wrd/databook.cfm

122. Committee on Ways and Means, *2008 Green Book,* pp. 7-81–7-84.

123. *Ibid.,* pp. 7-64–7-65.

124. *Ibid.,* Table 7-27, pp. 7-61–7-62.

125. *Ibid.,* p. 7-75.

126. U.S. Department of Health and Human Services, *Final Synthesis Report of Findings from ASPE's "Leavers" Grants* (Washington, DC: Office of the Secretary, Office of the Assistant Secretary for Planning and Evaluation, November 27, 2001). Retrieved February 18, 2010, from http://aspe.hhs.gov/hsp/leavers99/synthesis02/

127. Committee on Ways and Means, "Temporary Assistance for Needy Families," *2008 Green Book,* pp. 7-56–7-58, 7-74.

128. *Ibid.,* 7-66–7-67.

129. *Ibid.,* p. 7-87.

130. Thomas M. Fraker, Dan M. Levy, Irma Perez-Johnson, Alan M. Hershey, Demetra S. Nightingale, Robert B. Olsen, and Rita A. Stapulonis, "The National Evaluation of the Welfare-to-Work Grants Program: Final Report" (Princeton, NJ: Mathematica Policy Research, Inc., September 2004). Retrieved September 21, 2009, from http://aspe.hhs.gov/hsp/wtw-grants-eval98/final04/index.htm

131. Committee on Ways and Means, "Temporary Assistance for Needy Families," *2008 Green Book,* pp. 7-95–7-96.

132. Committee on Ways and Means, "Appendix J: The Experimental Evidence of Welfare-Related Initiatives," *2008 Green Book,* p. J-26.

133. Elizabeth Bauchner, "Bush Marriage Initiative Robs Billions from Needy," *Women's eNews,* September 10, 2003. Retrieved September 21, 2009, from http://www.womensenews.org/article.cfm/dyn/aid/1519/context/archive

134. Committee on Ways and Means, *2008 Green Book,* "Temporary Assistance for Needy Families," Table 7-22.

135. *Ibid.,* pp. 7-56–7-58.

136. Administration for Children and Families, "Characteristics and Financial Circumstances of TANF Recipients," *TANF Eighth Annual Report to Congress* (Washington, DC: Department of Health and Human Services), p. x. Retrieved September 28, 2009, from http://www.acf.hhs.gov/programs/ofa/data-reports/annualreport8/TANF_8th_Report_111908.pdf

137. Linda Rosenberg, Michelle Derr, LaDonna Pavetti, Subuhi Asheer, Megan Hague Angus, Samina Sattar, and Jeffrey Max, "A Study of States' Diversion Programs: Final Report" (Princeton, NJ: Mathematica Policy Research, Inc., 2008). Retrieved July 8, 2009, from http://www.acf.hhs.gov/programs/opre/welfare_employ/identify_promise_tanf/reports/tanf_diversion/tanf_diversion.pdf

138. Committee on Ways and Means, "Temporary Assistance for Needy Families," *2008 Green Book,* pp. 7-13–7-14.

139. Administration for Children and Families, *TANF Financial Data* (Washington, DC: U.S. Department of Health and Human Services). Retrieved September 20, 2009, from http://www.acf.hhs.gov/programs/ofs/data/chart1_1997.html; Committee on Ways and Means, U.S. House of Representatives, "Temporary Assistance for Needy Families," *2008 Green Book,* p. 7-17.

140. Committee on Ways and Means, "Temporary Assistance for Needy Families," *2008 Green Book,* p. 7-87.

141. See, for example, "Work First 105—Federal 60 Month Time Limit" (Raleigh, NC: North Carolina Department of Health and Human Services, August 1, 2008). Retrieved September 21, 2009, from http://info.dhhs.state.nc.us/olm/manuals/dss/csm-95/man/WF105.htm

142. The National EITC Outreach Partnership, "The Earned Income Tax Credit—A Fact Sheet" (Washington, DC: Center on Budget and Policy Priorities). Retrieved February 18, 2010, from http://www.cbpp.org/eitc-partnership/eitcfactsheet.htm

143. These paragraphs draw from Sondra G. Beverly, "What Social Workers Need to Know About the Earned Income Tax Credit," *Social Work,* Vol. 47, No. 3, July, 2002, pp. 259-266; Elaine Maag, "Disparities in Knowledge of the EITC," *Tax Notes (*Washington, DC: Tax Policy Center, Urban Institute and Brookings Institution, March 14, 2005). Retrieved September 21, 2009, from: http://www.urban.org/publications/1000752.html; Katherine Ross Phillips, *"Who Knows About the Earned Income Tax Credit?",* Series B, No. B-27 (Washington, DC: Urban Institute, January 2001). Retrieved September 21, 2009, from http://www.urban.org/UploadedPDF/anf_b27.pdf; Paul Trampe, "The EITC Disincentive: The Effects on Hours Worked from the Phase-out of the Earned Income Tax Credit," *Econ Journal Watch,* Vol. 4, No. 3, September, 2007, pp. 308–320.

144. "Policy Basics: The Earned Income Tax Credit" (Washington, DC: Center for Budget and Policy Priorities, December 4, 2009). Retrieved February

18, 2010, from http://www.cbpp.org/cms/index.cfm?fa=view&id=2505

145. "TANF Childcare in 2007: New Data Released" (Washington, DC: Center for Law and Social Policy, 2009). Retrieved July 16, 2009 from: http://www.clasp.org/issues/in_focus?type=child_care_and_early_education&id=0024

146. Akemi Kinukawa, Lina Guzman, and Laura Lippman, "National Estimates of Childcare and Subsidy Receipt for Children Ages 0 to 6: What Can We Learn from the National Household Education Survey?" (Washington, DC: Child Trends, October 2004). Retrieved September 21, 2009, from http://www.childtrends.org/Files/NHES_Research_brief_10_19_04.pdf

147. On the topic of childcare, see Jennifer Mezey and Brooke Richie, *Welfare Dollars No Longer an Increasing Source of Childcare Funding: Use of Funds in FY 2002 Unchanged from FY 2001* (Washington, DC: Center for Law and Social Policy, August 6, 2003); "Welfare Reform: States Provide TANF-Funded Work Support Services to Many Low-Income Families Who Do Not Receive Cash Assistance," GAO-02-615 (Washington, DC: General Accounting Office, April 10, 2002), especially p. 8. Retrieved September 21, 2009, from http://www.gao.gov/new.items/d02615t.pdf; Committee on Ways and Means, "Temporary Assistance for Needy Families," *2008 Green Book,* pp. 7-15–7-16; 7-88–90.

148. Communication Workers of America, *109th Congress Reauthorizes Temporary Assistance Program: Contentious Legislative Process Concludes,* March 2, 2006. Retrieved October 29, 2008, from http://www.cwa-legislative.org/fact-sheets/page.jsp?itemID=27482970

149. *United States: Use of TANF and Maintenance of Effort (MOE) Funds in Fiscal Year 2006* (Washington, DC: Center for Law and Social Policy). Retrieved May 18, 2010, from http://www.clasp.org/admin/site/publications_states/files/0597.pdf

150. *Ibid.*

151. See, for example, Michael Sherraden, Mark Schreiner, and Sondra Beverly, "Income, Institutions, and Saving Performance in Individual Development Accounts," *Economic Development Quarterly,* Vol. 17, No. 1, February, 2003, pp. 95–112.

152. Committee on Ways and Means, "Temporary Assistance for Needy Families (TANF)," *2008 Green Book,* pp. 7-11, 7-13–7-14.

153. Calculations based on Administration for Children and Families Office of Family Assistance Caseload data. Retrieved September 21, 2009, from: http://www.acf.hhs.gov/programs/ofa/data-reports/caseload/caseload_recent.html

154. Center for Law and Social Policy, *United States: Use of TANF and Maintenance of Effort (MOE) Funds in Fiscal Year 2006.*

155. See, for example, Government Accounting Office, "Welfare Reform: Information on Changing Labor Market and State Fiscal Conditions," GAO-03-977 (Washington, DC: Author, July 2003). Retrieved September 21, 2009, from http://www.gao.gov/new.items/d03977.pdf

156. Administration for Children and Families, Combined TANF AND SSP-MOE: Total Number of Recipients Fiscal Year 2009 (Washington, DC: U.S. Department of Health and Human Services, January 28, 2010). Rretrieved February 6, 2010, from http://www.acf.hhs.gov/programs/ofa/data-reports/caseload/2009/2009_recipient_tanssp.htm

157. The remainder of this paragraph relies on Elizabeth Lower-Basch, "Looking Ahead to TANF Reauthorization" (Washington, DC: Center for Law and Social Policy, July, 2009). Retrieved September 21, 2009, from http://www.clasp.org/admin/site/publications/files/Looking-Ahead-to-TANF-Reauthorization.pdf

158. Committee on Ways and Means, "Temporary Assistance for Needy Families," *2008 Green Book,* pp. 7–4.

159. Administration for Children and Family Assistance, TANF: Total Number of Families (Washington, DC: U.S. Department of Health and Human Services, January 29, 2010). Retrieved February 20, 2010, from http://www.acf.hhs.gov/programs/ofa/data-reports/caseload/2009/2009_family_tan.htm

160. Joyce Foundation, *Welfare to Work: What Have We Learned* (Chicago: Author, March 2002). Retrieved September 21, 2009, from http://www.joycefdn.org/pdf/welrept/welfarereport.pdf

161. Committee on Ways and Means, "Temporary Assistance for Needy Families (TANF)," *2004 Green Book,* p. 7-31.

162. *Ibid.*

163. Gregory Acs and Pamela J. Loprest, *TANF Caseload Composition and Leavers Synthesis Report* (Washington, DC: Urban Institute, March 28, 2007). Retrieved September 21, 2009, from http://www.acf.hhs.gov/programs/opre/welfare_employ/tanf_caseload/reports/tanf_caseload_comp/tanf_caseload_final.pdf

164. Committee on Ways and Means, "Temporary Assistance for Needy Families," *2008 Green Book,* pp. 7-78–7-79; 7-82–7-83.
165. Margy Waller, "TANF Reauthorization: Options and Opportunities"; Committee on Ways and Means, "Temporary Assistance for Needy Families," *2008 Green Book,* p. 7-85.
166. General Accounting Office, "Welfare Reform: Information on Changing Labor Market and State Fiscal Conditions"; Acs and Loprest, *TANF Caseload Composition and Leavers Synthesis Report.*
167. Pamela J. Loprest, *Fewer Welfare Leavers Employed in Weak Economy* (Washington, DC: Urban Institute, August 21, 2003), No. 5 in Series, "Snapshots of America's Families III." Retrieved September 21, 2009, from http://www.urban.org/urlprint.cfm?ID=8550
168. General Accounting Office, "Welfare Reform: Information on Changing Labor Market and State Fiscal Conditions"; Acs and Loprest, *TANF Caseload Composition and Leavers Synthesis Report.*
169. General Accounting Office, "Welfare Reform: Information on Changing Labor Market and State Fiscal Conditions"; Alan Weil, *"Ten Things Everyone Should Know about Welfare Reform"* (Washington, DC: The Urban Institute, May, 2002). Retrieved September, 21, 2009, from http://www.urban.org/UploadedPDF/310484.pdf
170. Joyce Foundation, *Welfare to Work;* General Accounting Office, "Welfare Reform: Information on Changing Labor Market and State Fiscal Conditions."
171. Committee on Ways and Means, "Temporary Assistance for Needy Families (TANF)," *2008 Green Book,* pp. 7-85–7-86.
172. Committee on Ways and Means, "Appendix J," *2008 Green Book,* p. J2-3.
173. Pamela J. Loprest, *Fewer Welfare Leavers Employed in Weak Economy.*
174. Pamela J. Loprest, *Disconnected Welfare Leaver Face Serious Risks* (Washington, DC: The Urban Institute, August 21, 2003); Gregory Acs & Pamela J. Loprest, *TANF Caseload Composition and Leavers Synthesis Report.*
175. Waller, "TANF Reauthorization"; Michael Wiseman, "Food Stamps and Welfare Reform," Welfare Reform Policy Brief #19 (Washington, DC: Brookings Institution, March 2002).
176. Joyce Foundation, *Welfare to Work.*
177. Committee on Ways and Means, "Temporary Assistance for Needy Families," *2008 Green Book,* pp. 7-59, 7-61; Communication Workers of America, *109th Congress Reauthorizes Temporary Assistance Program: Contentious Legislative Process Concludes.*
178. National Women's Law Center, "$5 Billion in Additional Funding for Temporary Assistance to Needy Families Now Available to States to Meet Urgent Needs" (Washington, DC: Author, April 13, 2009). Retrieved July 21, 2009, from http://www.nwlc.org/details.cfm?id=3552&section=child%20and%20family%20support
179. Sharon Parrott, "Despite Critics' Over-Heated Rhetoric, the Economic Recovery Bill Does Not Undermine Welfare Reform" (Washington, DC: Center on Budget and Policy Priorities, February 17, 2009). Retrieved September 29, 2009, from http://www.cbpp.org/cms/index.cfm?fa=view&id=2648
180. Michael Grabell and Chris Flavelle (ProPublica), "States: We can't afford costs tied to $5B emergency fund," *USA Today,* September 8, 2009. Retrieved September 29, 2009, from http://www.usatoday.com/news/nation/2009-09-07-stimulus_N.htm
181. Olivia Golden and Sheila R. Zedlewski, "Reject Proposal to End Welfare" (Washington, DC: Urban Institute, June 14, 2009). Retrieved September 29, 2009, from http://www.urban.org/publications/901261.html
182. Liz Schott, "Policy Basics: An Introduction to TANF" (Washington, DC: Urban Institute, March 19, 2009). Retrieved September 29, 2009, from http://www.cbpp.org/cms/?fa=view&id=936
183. Ron Haskins, "Elite Opinion and Welfare Reform" (abstract), Thirty-first Annual Association for Public Policy Analysis and Management Research Conference, *Evidence Based Policy Making in the Post-Bush/Clinton Era.* Retrieved February 18, 2010, from https://www.appam.org/conferences/fall/search_results.asp

8 | FINANCING HEALTHCARE: CAN ALL AMERICANS BE INSURED?

David H. Johnson
Diana M. DiNitto

Health policy in the United States exemplifies many of the problems of rational policymaking. Political issues intervene at every stage of decision making—in defining the goals of health policy, in identifying alternative courses of action, in assessing their potential costs, and in selecting policy alternatives that maximize the quality and accessibility of healthcare while containing costs. Efforts at comprehensive federal healthcare policy have been part of the U.S. political landscape for nearly a century. From those first efforts at universal care in the Progressive Era to the raging healthcare reform debates of 2009, those efforts illustrate the U.S. political system at its best and at its worst.

HEALTHCARE: CROSSROADS OF POLITICS AND SOCIAL WELFARE POLICY

Healthcare is a basic human need. No one should suffer or die for lack of financial resources to obtain medical attention. But how much are Americans willing and able to pay for healthcare? If healthcare is a scarce resource, how do we decide who will get what care and how? These are largely political questions that do not lend themselves easily to rational planning.

Before the 1940s, few people had private health insurance.[1] When they needed medical care, they arranged payment with their local doctor or hospital. Early in the Great Depression, hospitals began offering prepaid hospital service benefit plans that became known as Blue Cross to provide ongoing revenue to hospitals during the economic crisis. A little more than a decade later, physician-owned plans (Blue Shield) developed to cover costs of physician services. In these plans, a monthly premium entitled the consumer to reimbursement for healthcare services. Along with greater sophistication of medical practice and technology, and the influence of both private medical insurance plans and government plans such as Medicare and Medicaid, also came rapidly increasingly healthcare costs. Healthcare is among the most pressing social welfare issues in the United States. The cost of healthcare for all citizens is so high that policymakers can no longer be concerned about how to provide healthcare for the poor and elderly alone. Politicians, healthcare providers, employers, and citizens are concerned about healthcare for the entire nation.

GOOD HEALTH OR MEDICAL ATTENTION?

The first obstacle to a rational approach to health policy is deciding on our goal. Is health policy a question of good health—that is, whether we live at all, how well we live, and how long we live? Or are we striving for good medical care—that is, frequent and inexpensive visits to doctors, well-equipped and accessible hospitals, and equal access to medical attention by all citizens?

Good medical care does not necessarily mean good health. Good health is related to many factors over which medical personnel and facilities have no control—heredity (the health of one's parents and grandparents), lifestyle (smoking, eating, drinking, exercise, stress), and the physical environment (sewage disposal, water quality, conditions of work, and so forth). Of course, doctors can set broken bones, stop infections with drugs, and remove swollen appendixes. Anyone suffering from health problems certainly wants the careful attention of skilled physicians and the best of medical facilities. But in the long run, infant mortality, sickness and disease, and life span are affected surprisingly little by the quality of medical care.[2] If you want to live a long, healthy life, choose parents who have lived long, healthy lives, and then do all the things your mother always told you to do: Don't smoke, don't drink too much, get lots of exercise and rest, don't overeat, relax, and don't worry.

The access to healthcare that many Americans enjoy is not the same as good health, but it does play a role in who is able to maintain good health. The differences in healthcare access and in healthcare outcomes are referred to as *health disparities.*

Health status and death rates differ considerably among segments of the population:

1. On average, the poor and older adults require more medical attention than the general population; indeed, "the prevalence of many chronic conditions is directly related to age and inversely related to financial status."[3]

2. Racial and ethnic minorities frequently have much poorer access to preventive, diagnostic, and treatment services than non-Hispanic whites. They are less likely to receive appropriate cancer diagnostic tests, treatment for cancer, diagnosis and treatment of asthma, or appropriate pain management. They are more likely to suffer the more dire consequences, such as lower-limb amputations and invasive surgeries, of unmanaged chronic illnesses.[4] Major differences in health among racial and ethnic groups persist even when income is controlled.

3. The healthcare delivery system (facilities and personnel) is particularly disorganized and inadequate in poor communities—both inner cities and rural areas.

Infant mortality rates are considered to be especially sensitive to the adequacy of healthcare and are frequently used as a general indicator of well-being. Figure 8.1 shows the wide discrepancies in infant mortality rates, ranging from 4.4 infant deaths per 1,000 live births for Cubans to 13.6 for blacks.[5] Even among Native Americans, who have very high poverty rates, the infant mortality rate of 8.1 is considerably lower than it is for blacks. Also of interest is that Hispanics and non-Hispanic whites have nearly identical infant mortality rates, even though Hispanics have much higher poverty rates and much lower rates of health insurance coverage. For example, the infant mortality rate for Mexican Americans is 5.5, while the rate for non-Hispanic whites is 5.8 per 1,000 live births. This phenomenon is called the Hispanic paradox.[6] Hispanics are also more likely than other groups to go without seeing a doctor. In 2007, 25 percent of Hispanics made no visits to healthcare professionals, compared with 22 percent of Native Americans and Asians, and 16 percent of blacks and whites.[7]

Blacks see doctors as often as whites, and they have been making greater gains in life expectancy than whites, but blacks' life expectancy is still about five years shorter than whites.[8] Blacks also have an infant mortality rate that is more than twice as high as whites or Hispanics. Blacks also experience an annual AIDS case rate that is three times that of Hispanics and nearly nine times that of whites.[9] In addition to relatively low infant mortality, Hispanics also have a lower age-adjusted cancer incidence than whites and blacks. Hispanics are slightly more likely than whites to be obese, while Asian Americans and Pacific Islanders have the lowest rate of overweight and obesity. Asian Americans are among the healthiest population groups in the United States. Gender is also an important factor in health outcomes. For example, men are 50 percent more likely than women to die of heart disease or cancer, but there is very little gender difference in deaths from strokes or other cerebrovascular disease.[10]

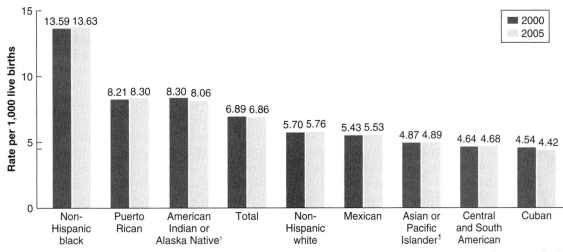

FIGURE 8.1   **Infant Mortality Rates by Race and Ethnicity: United States, 2000 and 2005**   *Source:* Marian F. McDorman and T. J. Mathews, "Recent Trends in Infant Mortality in the United States" (Atlanta: Centers for Disease Control and Prevention, October 2008). Retrieved December 24, 2009, from http://www.cdc.gov/nchs/data/databriefs/db09.htm

The overarching goals of the federal government's Healthy People 2010 initiative were to (1) "increase quality and years of healthy life" and (2) "eliminate health disparities among different segments of the population."[11] There were also many specific goals for various groups of Americans. As 2010 dawned, the federal government reported that the 2010 goals had perhaps been too ambitious. Most had not been met, although improvements were made in vaccination rates, reduced workplace injuries, and lower death rates from stroke, cancer, and heart disease. However, more Americans are obese, more suffer from high blood pressure, and more children have untreated tooth decay.[12] The overarching goals of the Healthy People 2020 initiative are to:

1. attain high quality, longer lives free of preventable disease, disability, injury, and premature death.
2. achieve health equity, eliminate disparities, and improve the health of all groups.
3. create social and physical environments that promote good health for all.
4. promote quality of life, healthy development and healthy behaviors across all life stages.[13]

HOW AMERICANS PAY FOR HEALTHCARE

Americans use four primary means of paying for healthcare. In 2008, government insurance covered 29 percent of the population.[14] Employment-based group health insurance covered 59 percent. Private, individually purchased health insurance covered about 9 percent. Some Americans have more than one source of health insurance, but 15 percent, or about 46 million Americans, had no health insurance coverage at all. They had to pay out-of-pocket or ignore health care bills.

A common feature of private plans, group plans, and most government plans is that they do not cover "first-dollar" expenses. In other words, most plans require that patients pay something out of pocket before their insurance plan begins to pay anything. These out-of-pocket expenses are called deductibles or co-payments. They are usually subject to a maximum per person and a maximum per family amount. Their purpose is to prevent people from "overutilizing" healthcare so that they don't go running off to the doctor for every minor complaint.

One problem with deductibles and co-payments is that they discourage many poorer people who have coverage from accessing preventive care services. They may also cause people to delay seeking medical attention until the condition becomes much more serious. In these cases, an earlier visit might have saved the person's life, or, at the least, saved the system considerable money. Delaying vital medical attention is one factor that drives medical costs higher. This is borne out by examining the nation's total annual healthcare expenditures. In 2006, Americans whose healthcare expenses exceeded $41,580 were the top one percent of the population by healthcare spending. This group was responsible for just over 21 percent of all healthcare expenditures, while the bottom 50 percent, those with less than $776 in expenses, accounted for just over 3 percent of healthcare expenditures.[15] Many of the leading causes of death, such as cancer, stroke, and heart disease, are preventable or controllable by activities such as diet, exercise, and lifestyle changes like smoking cessation. Shifting just 5 percent of spending to that bottom 50 percent in the form of preventive dollars might go a long way toward lowering the nation's total healthcare bill.

Medicare: Healthcare for Virtually All Older Americans

Social welfare policy has made considerable strides in meeting the income and healthcare needs of older Americans. Prior to Medicare (enacted in 1965 as Title XVIII of the Social Security Act), less than half of elderly people had any health insurance. Even with Medicare, out-of-pocket healthcare costs for older Americans are substantial. In 2006, this amount averaged nearly $3,000 per enrollee.[16] Estimates are that a couple that was aged 65 in 2009 and had Medicare will pay about $240,000 in out-of-pocket healthcare costs over the rest of their lives.[17] This represents a 50 percent increase in out-of-pocket costs since 2002.

Most Medicare beneficiaries are people aged 65 or older who receive Social Security retirement benefits (or are eligible even if they have not claimed their Social Security benefits yet). Some younger people also qualify for Medicare, mostly former workers who have been receiving Social Security Disability Insurance (SSDI) for at least two years. The program covers another group of people regardless of age—those with end-stage renal disease (kidney failure). As part of the Social Security system, Medicare compels employers and employees to pay into the program during working years in order for workers to enjoy the benefits of health insurance after retirement or long-term disability. Since Medicare is a social insurance program, participation is not contingent on income. Even older people who do not qualify for Social Security can buy into Medicare.

About 38 million older individuals and 7 million disabled younger people were enrolled in Medicare in 2008. Federal spending was about $468 billion.[18] This is a huge increase from Medicare's $157 billion cost in 1995. There is constant concern about the Medicare trust fund's ability to keep up with healthcare costs (see Chapter 5). This concern mounts as the baby boom generation begins claiming its Medicare benefits.

MEDICARE PART A: HOSPITAL INSURANCE   The Medicare program has two basic parts—hospital insurance (HI), called Part A, and supplemental medical insurance (SMI), called Part B. Part A pays for beneficiaries' hospital care, skilled nursing care following a hospital stay, some (usually short-term) home healthcare, and hospice care. Part A is financed by a portion of the Social Security payroll tax (also see Chapter 5). This compulsory 1.45 percent tax is now levied on all the wages of current workers and is matched by the employer, for a total tax of 2.9 percent of wages. Older people who do not qualify for Social Security and want to participate in Part A can pay premiums (in 2010 monthly premiums were as much as $461, depending on work history).

Under Part A, beneficiaries incurring a hospital stay must pay a deductible ($1,100 in 2010), after which Medicare pays for the remainder of the first 60 days in the hospital and a portion of additional days. For days 61 through 90 in 2010, the patient's coinsurance payment was $275 per day, with the federal government paying the remainder during each benefit period. For days 91 to 150, the coinsurance payment was $550 a day (these 60 days are reserves that can only be used once but can be spread out over a beneficiary's lifetime). If more hospital days are needed, the patient must assume all the costs. If a patient needs skilled nursing home care, there is no charge for the first 20 days in each benefit period. There is a coinsurance fee of $137.50 per day for days 21 through 100. Medicare does *not* cover nursing home care after 100 days in a benefit period. A benefit period starts when a Medicare patient enters a hospital or skilled nursing facility and ends after the patient has not received hospital or skilled nursing home care for 60 days in a row. There is no limit on the number of benefit periods a Medicare patient can have.

MEDICARE PART B: SUPPLEMENTAL MEDICAL INSURANCE Medicare Part B is a voluntary component that covers physician services, outpatient hospital services, certain home healthcare services, and durable medical equipment. Medicare Part A beneficiaries who wish to participate in Part B are assessed premiums. In 2010, Part B premiums were $96.40 per month per individual for individual beneficiaries with an adjusted gross income of less than $85,000 and $170,000 for a couple. The small number of beneficiaries with higher incomes pay a higher premium. This cost is so low compared to private insurance that almost all Part A participants are enrolled in Part B. Part B premiums can be deducted automatically from Social Security retirement or disability checks. Even those aged 65 and older who are not insured under Part A can participate in Part B. After Part B beneficiaries pay an annual deductible ($155 in 2010), Medicare pays 80 percent of most services and the patient pays the remaining 20 percent. The federal government's general revenue funds are also used to subsidize Part B.

From 2004 through 2006, Part B premiums for all Medicare beneficiaries were set at 25 percent of actual costs. Beginning in 2007, the percentage began to increase gradually for those in higher income brackets and will increase again in 2011. For example, in 2011, individuals with incomes from $80,000 to $100,000, indexed for inflation, will pay 35 percent of actual costs. Those with incomes greater than $200,000, indexed for inflation, will pay the most—80 percent of the actual costs of Part B premiums.[19]

COVERING "MEDIGAPS" A serious problem with the U.S. healthcare system is the inadequate coverage most types of health insurance—both public and private—provide. Private health insurance plans may limit payments to the first 30 or 60 days of hospital care; place caps on the dollar amounts paid to hospitals and physicians for a patient during her or his lifetime; exclude various diagnostic tests, outpatient care, or office visits; and so on. Moreover, private insurance has often excluded people initially found to be in poor health, who most need insurance. Perhaps the most serious concern about private insurance is that it frequently fails to cover "catastrophic" medical costs—costs that can easily run into the tens and even hundreds of thousands of dollars for serious, long-term illnesses. If such a catastrophe occurred, most people would lose everything they owned.

The gaps in Medicare coverage are referred to as "medigaps." Medicare does not pay for custodial nursing home care, most dental care (including dentures), private-duty nursing, eyeglasses and eye examinations, most routine physician examinations, hearing tests and hearing devices, and very long hospital stays. Until 2004, Medicare did not help with prescription drug costs.

To cover at least some of these gaps, some Medicare beneficiaries purchase supplemental policies. Some of these policies cover medigaps better than others. To prevent unscrupulous individuals from taking advantage of older Americans' fears of impoverishment from illness, Congress passed legislation to regulate the sale of Medicare supplemental or "medigap" policies. Medigap insurance carriers must offer 12 levels of policies from A to L. At any given level, the same types of benefits are supposed to be offered. Level A offers the fewest benefits and costs the least. Level J offers the most benefits at the highest cost. Levels K and L are lower-cost alternatives that cover a portion of many of the co-insurance or co-payment requirements of Medicare Parts A and B. This structure makes it easier to compare policies, but costs and coverage still vary widely depending on several factors, including the state in which the policy is purchased.

MEDICARE ADVANTAGE (PART C)   Every November, Medicare beneficiaries are mailed information on Medicare's current benefits and the types of plans from which they can choose. As part of the Balanced Budget Act (BBA) of 1997, Medicare beneficiaries were given managed care options in addition to health maintenance organizations that might cover some "medigaps" and were intended to contain healthcare costs. These options were called Medicare+Choice or Part C. Under the 2003 Medicare legislation, Part C, now called Medicare Advantage, also offers Medicare beneficiaries various private managed care arrangements in lieu of traditional fee-for-service Medicare. These plans vary substantially in terms of costs and benefits to participants, such as whether participants are limited to using "in-network" physicians if they want costs covered. In 2005, these managed care arrangements actually cost about 12 percent *more* than traditional Medicare,[20] and in 2008 these private fee-for-service (PFFS) plans under Medicare Advantage averaged nearly 17 percent *more* than costs in traditional Medicare.[21] Under the Medicare Improvements for Patients and Providers Act of 2008, Congress made changes in how these PFFS plans must operate. The Congressional Budget Office projects these changes will slow growth in PFFS plan enrollments.

ADDING D (PRESCRIPTION DRUGS) TO THE A, B, Cs OF MEDICARE   When Medicare was first enacted, drug costs were not the major expense they are today. Proposals to include prescription drugs in Medicare were rejected.[22] Momentum for a prescription drug benefit gained steam during the Clinton administration. In 2003, Congress narrowly passed the controversial Medicare Prescription Drug, Improvement, and Modernization Act. The House vote was 220 to 215; the Senate vote was 54 to 44.

As of January 2006, the Modernization Act allows Medicare participants to join a private drug plan by paying a monthly premium. Although participation is voluntary, not signing up during the first six months that one is eligible may result in higher fees. Monthly premiums vary according to the plan selected. Costs and coverage also differ for each plan, but all must provide a minimum level of coverage set by Medicare. In a typical plan, an individual might pay the first $310 of drug costs themselves. After that, the beneficiary may pay a co-payment and the plan would pay the rest of the cost until the plan and the beneficiary together had paid out $2,830. After that, the beneficiary is solely responsible for all costs until he or she has spent a total out-of-pocket of $4,550. This gap in coverage has been dubbed the "doughnut hole." After a beneficiary spends $4,550, the catastrophic benefit takes over—the beneficiary pays a small copayment, perhaps 5 percent, for each prescription and the Medicare drug plan covers the rest of the costs. Medicare beneficiaries with limited income and assets may be able to get more help.

Prescription drug coverage is a major change in Medicare policy, and it generated bitter battles. Part D has helped many older people with prescription drug costs, but many contend that the biggest beneficiaries are prescription drug companies and the insurance industry. The law prohibits the federal government from negotiating prices with pharmaceutical companies, an obvious concession to the drug industry. Needless to say, drug companies lobbied to ensure that any legislation Congress passed would benefit them. Under Part D, it is up to private insurance plans to negotiate prices with the drug industry. Drug companies contend that prices are regulated de facto, because insurance companies and HMOs use all their negotiation powers to keep drug prices down. But these insurers also benefit because they offer the plans. Others think that the government should just step in and regulate prescription drug costs and benefits like they do most other Medicare services.

As part of the package of national healthcare reform legislation passed in 2010, Senator Max Baucus (D-MT), chairman of the Senate Finance Committee, announced that he had reached an agreement with pharmaceutical companies to pay half the costs of seniors' prescriptions in the "doughnut hole," at an estimated cost of $80 billion over the next 10 years. Such "voluntary" agreements frequently arise when Congress begins talking about major changes in how healthcare will be paid for and regulated in the United States. As a result of the legislation, out-of-pocket expenses in the "doughnut hole" will gradually be reduced through a combination of discounts agreed to by pharmaceutical manufacturers and subsidies from the federal government. The changes begin in 2011 and ramp up over succeeding years.[23]

LONG-TERM CARE   Although older Americans now get help paying for prescription drugs, long-term care remains a major "medigap." People need these services when they cannot care for themselves due to difficulties with activities such as dressing, bathing, eating, shopping, and money management. Long-term care services include both healthcare and supportive services and may be provided in nursing homes, community-care residences, or at home.

Nursing home care is provided at three levels—skilled, intermediate, and custodial. Skilled is the highest level and the only type Medicare reimburses. It is generally needed for a short time, for example, following some surgeries. Supplemental Medicare policies cover only what Medicare covers, so they do not help with intermediate and custodial nursing home care, yet this type of care is often needed.

Home healthcare includes a variety of services provided in the individual's own home or in homelike community-based programs. Home health is a fast-growing Medicare service. Medicare covers some in-home care, but not care needed on a 24-hour basis. Rather than paid services, it is spouses, children, and other informal caregivers who provide the vast majority of in-home care (see Chapter 10).

Individuals who need nursing home care not covered by Medicare may pay out of their own pocket, but even a modest nursing home is beyond many people's financial reach. The average cost of a semiprivate room in a nursing home is approximately $183 per day or $66,795 per year, with daily rates for a private room averaging $206 ($75,190 per year).[24] Many people enter a nursing home with some funds, but with costs like this, savings can easily be depleted. The costs of 24-hour a day in-home care can be much more.

Medicaid (the government healthcare program for some poor Americans) is the primary source of government funding for long-term care. To qualify for nursing home care under

Medicaid, applicants must meet their state's definition of being poor. States' definitions vary considerably. Previously, when there was a spouse at home, both the nursing home patient and the spouse had to deplete their assets to qualify. Under Medicaid impoverishment provisions passed in 1988, the spouse of a Medicaid nursing home patient is allowed to keep considerably more assets and income. A non-institutionalized spouse may keep 50 percent of the couple's assets up to as much as $109,560 in 2009, plus a monthly income allowance. States may recoup Medicaid payments by taking proceeds from the sale of nursing home patients' homes or other parts of their estate after their death. Little has actually been recovered in this way because states are prohibited from recovering on a lien against the home if it is the residence of the person's spouse or certain other qualified family members. One concern is older people transferring assets ("Medicaid estate planning" as it has been called) in order to qualify for nursing home care at public expense. To address this, an individual's eligibility may be delayed if assets were transferred or sold for less than fair market value in the five years prior to application.[25]

As people become more worried about needing care in their old age, sales of long-term care insurance have grown.[26] These policies may cover nursing home and home healthcare. Between 1987 and 2002, 9 million policies were sold. As one ages, the policy price increases. According to America's Health Insurance Plans, in 2002, to obtain a policy that pays a $150 per day benefit with 5 percent inflation protection and four years of coverage, the average annual premium for a 50-year old purchaser was $1,134; for a 65-year old purchaser, $2,346; and for a 79-year old purchaser, $7,572.[27] Low-income individuals are least likely to be able to afford the premiums. In fact, those who would quickly qualify for Medicaid upon entering a nursing home may not think long-term care insurance is worth the cost. High-income individuals may assume the risk of paying out-of-pocket should they need long-term care. Long-term care policies might be most attractive to middle-income individuals who want to protect their assets for family members. Employer-sponsored policies may be offered not only to the worker, but also the worker's spouse, parents, and parents-in-law. Employer-sponsored policies encourage younger people to participate, and spread the risk over a larger group of people. The federal government is the largest employer to offer long-term care insurance.

To make purchasing long-term care policies more attractive, employer contributions are excluded from employees' taxable income, and benefits paid are also exempt from taxes. In addition, long-term care expenses can be included with other medical expenses and taken as itemized tax deductions if they exceed 7.5 percent of adjusted gross income. Long-term care insurance premiums can also be included as part of this deduction, based on an amount that increases with an individual's age. These policies are still relatively new, and people might be wary about what will and will not be provided should they need care.

In 2006, public and private expenditures for long-term care (nursing home and home healthcare services) were nearly $178 billion, or about 10 percent of all personal healthcare expenditures. This includes funds spent for intermediate care facilities for people with mental retardation (ICFs/MR). Medicaid paid for 41 percent ($72 billion) of long-term care, Medicare paid for 23 percent, consumers' paid for 22 percent of costs from their own pockets, private health insurance for 9 percent, and other sources paid for 3 percent.[28]

More could be done to help older people (and younger disabled people) remain in their own homes by shifting more public funding to in-home care. More could also be done with tax breaks and governmentally supported services like respite services to help families keep older and disabled members at home (see also Chapter 6). Studies suggest that home-based care may not result in cost savings, because elderly persons cared for at home may enter hospitals more frequently than those in institutions.[29] However, elderly people, their caregivers, service providers, and policymakers express satisfaction with home and community-based care. That may be reason enough to pursue these options.

Private options for meeting long-term care needs are growing rapidly. *Assisted living facilities*, for example, offer help (e.g., meals, housekeeping, transportation, and perhaps assistance with personal care, medications, socialization, and recreation) in accord with each resident's needs and desires, although they do not provide extensive medical or nursing care.[30] Another option, *continuing care retirement communities*, are really multiple facilities located on the same property. Residents may start out in their own apartment, which may be purchased or leased and may include an entrance fee in addition to monthly fees. As residents' needs change, the level or amount of care they receive increases. Ultimately, they may require care in the community's skilled or custodial nursing component. These alternative arrangements can be very expensive and require a clear understanding of costs and the legal commitment one is making. Some are more modestly priced because religiously affiliated groups or other organizations with a desire to serve members or older adults in general operate them.

Concerns about long-term care costs mount with each passing year as the population ages. From 2010 to 2030, those aged 65 and older will grow from about 13 percent of the U.S. population to about 20 percent.[31] This population will also double from 35 million in 2000 to 70 million in 2030; 33 million will be aged 75 and older; and almost 9 million will be aged 85 and older. By 2035, demand for institutional care like nursing homes and alternative living facilities is expected to increase by 70 percent and demand for home care by 85 percent.

Medicaid: Healthcare for Some of the Poor

Congress enacted the Medicaid program in 1965 as Title XIX of the Social Security Act. Every state operates a Medicaid program, although Arizona held out until 1982. Medicaid rapidly grew to be the federal government's most expensive public assistance program. The costs of Medicaid now easily exceed the costs of the other major "welfare" (public assistance) programs (SSI, TANF, and SNAP) combined.[32]

In 1970, total Medicaid costs were about $5 billion; by 1990 they had risen to about $72 billion. Estimated costs for 2008 were $339 billion. The federal government covers approximately 57 percent of Medicaid costs; the states provide the other 43 percent. In 2007, an average of 49 million persons were covered by Medicaid at any given time at a cost of just under $6,800 per person. The Centers for Medicare and Medicaid Services projected an annual average growth rate in Medicaid expenditures of 7.9 percent, reaching expenditures of $674 billion for the year 2017.[33]

The federal government pays its share of Medicaid costs from general tax revenues. The states also use their own revenues to fund Medicaid, and they are under constant pressure to raise more funds to pay their share and to draw down more federal matching funds. States may receive from 50 to 83 percent of total Medicaid service expenditures from the federal government, with poorer states (as determined by per capita income) receiving the most. This percentage is calculated annually. In 2009, eight states and the District of Columbia received at least 70 percent of their Medicaid benefit funds from the federal government; Mississippi received the highest rate at nearly 76 percent.[34] Sixteen states received 50 percent or slightly more. The U.S. territories receive 50 percent for their Medicaid programs. In the face of the country's economic downturn that began in late 2008, the federal share to states was increased temporarily. All jurisdictions are reimbursed for 50 percent of administrative costs for most services rendered.

The House Committee on Ways and Means acknowledges that many people regard Medicaid as an enigma. Not only is the program complex, it does not serve most poor people. Each state administers its own program and sets it own rules, and each state has many different Medicaid components that may offer different services depending on the category under which one qualifies. This chapter can only hope to scratch the surface at describing Medicaid.

Each state must designate a single state agency (generally the state's health or welfare agency) to carry out its Medicaid program. The state can process its own claims or contract for this service. Each state determines the reimbursement rates it will pay for Medicaid services. Since 1989, federal guidelines say that reimbursement rates must be sufficiently adequate so that services will be as available to Medicaid recipients as they are to the general population in the area. Recipients are also supposed to have some freedom in choosing service providers. This does not mean that providers are anxious to accept Medicaid payments. Most physicians do not participate because payments are so low, the paperwork is burdensome, and reimbursement often takes too long.

Who Gets Medicaid?

Like the Supplemental Security Income (SSI) program and the Supplemental Nutrition Assistance Program (food stamps), Medicaid is an entitlement program; all qualified applicants must be served. Federal statutes actually define more than 50 distinct groups that can qualify for Medicaid. Without intimate knowledge of a state's Medicaid program, it would be difficult to say exactly who qualifies and who does not. Even in states with the most generous Medicaid programs, many poor people do not fit any of the eligibility categories and therefore have no claim to Medicaid. This is especially true for poor, able-bodied adults with no dependent children. In 2006, nearly 13 percent of the U.S. population was enrolled in Medicaid, including 40 percent of all those in poverty. Of all who received Medicaid, 42 percent had incomes below poverty, while 58 percent had incomes above poverty. Nearly half (46 percent) of Medicaid recipients are dependent children, their parents are 22 percent, those aged 65 and older are 8 percent, disabled recipients are 14 percent, and the remaining 10 percent fall in other categories.[35]

PEOPLE WHO ARE AGED OR DISABLED   Although states determine many eligibility requirements, they must still cover certain categories of people, such as most SSI recipients. Should SSI recipients earn enough to make them ineligible for SSI, they can receive Medicaid for an extended period (also see Chapter 6). States may also cover individuals who are aged or disabled if their incomes do not exceed 100 percent of the poverty guideline and up to 250 percent of the poverty guideline for those with disabilities if they are working.

Through their Medicaid programs, states must pay Medicare premiums, coinsurance, and deductibles for "qualified Medicare beneficiaries"—those with incomes below 100 percent of the federal poverty level and limited assets ($4,000 for an individual and $6,000 for a couple). States must also provide more limited assistance by paying Part B Medicare premiums for other low-income Medicare recipients. States must also use Medicaid funds to pay Part A Medicare premiums (hospital insurance) for those who previously received Medicare and Social Security Disability Insurance but have returned to work, as long as they are still disabled, their income is not more than 200 percent of the poverty level, their resources do not exceed $4,000, and they are not otherwise entitled to Medicaid.

CHILDREN AND THEIR PARENTS   Prior to welfare reform in 1996 (see Chapter 6), states were required to cover all those receiving AFDC. AFDC was replaced with the Temporary Assistance for Needy Families (TANF) program. There is no automatic link between Medicaid and TANF, but in general, states must cover all those who meet AFDC financial eligibility criteria in place in their state on July 16, 1996, so that low-income families continue to have healthcare. States have some options for increasing or decreasing their previous AFDC income and resource standards if they wish. Most states have chosen to include more low-income families by loosening eligibility requirements.

States can terminate Medicaid benefits to adults who do not meet TANF work requirements, but their children must continue to be covered. Should TANF recipients earn enough or get sufficient income from child or spousal support to make them ineligible for TANF, they can continue to receive Medicaid for certain lengths of time so that their medical benefits are not abruptly terminated.

States must also cover pregnant women and children under age 6 with incomes up to 133 percent of official poverty guidelines. These women are entitled only to pregnancy-related services, but children receive all Medicaid benefits.

All children over age 5 and under age 19 in families with incomes less than 100 percent of poverty guidelines are also entitled to Medicaid. Medicaid must also cover a few other categories of poor children such as children under age 18 who are receiving adoption and foster care assistance. States can extend this assistance to children who have "aged out" of foster care until they reach age 20.

States may also provide Medicaid to other groups of children such as those living in certain types of institutions. They may also provide 12 months of continuous coverage to children once they become Medicaid participants even if their circumstances change and they would otherwise not be eligible.

CHILDREN UNDER SCHIP   An important development in healthcare coverage for low-income children is the State Children's Health Insurance Program, referred to as SCHIP or CHIP. SCHIP is related to Medicaid, but it is a block grant program established by the Balanced Budget Act of 1997 as Title XXI of the Social Security Act. Children qualify for SCHIP if they are not eligible for Medicaid, are not covered by other health insurance, and live in low-income families.

The states can provide SCHIP to children whose family income is up to 200 percent of poverty guidelines. States that already covered children with incomes greater than 200 percent of poverty can raise their previously established income level by as much as 50 percentage points. States can cover SCHIP-eligible children by expanding their Medicaid program, creating a new program, or using a combination of approaches.

There is some perversity in the relationship of SCHIP and Medicaid.[36] Most states get a substantially bigger federal return for covering the higher-income children eligible under SCHIP than they do for covering poorer Medicaid-eligible children. SCHIP's funding formula reimburses states, in part, based on the number of uninsured children. This penalizes states that had already made more progress in insuring low-income children. However, states with higher per-capita incomes get a higher percentage increase to insure children under SCHIP than states with lower per capita incomes.

Since its inception, a primary concern is that states should do more to enroll eligible children in SCHIP as well as Medicaid. In Texas, for example, the state with the highest rate of uninsured children, there were claims of unwarranted delays in implementing SCHIP. Additionally, the state's Republican (and female) comptroller joined many child advocates and Democrats in complaining that federal funds were being left on the table after 107,000 children were dropped from the program.[37] The Republican (and female) Chair of the House Select Committee on State Healthcare Expenditures' response was that given the state's record budget deficit at that time, the legislature did the right thing in tightening SCHIP's asset (not income) test. She suggested that families with expensive vehicles purchase less expensive transportation instead.[38] The Comptroller suggested a $1 increase on each pack of cigarettes to raise money that would provide a needed transfusion to the state's healthcare budget. A lawsuit also erupted over whether the state was providing sufficient access to preventive services for children under Medicaid. In addition, the state was accused of ignoring Medicaid outreach while focusing on SCHIP outreach, and making SCHIP enrollment much easier than Medicaid enrollment (which has since been simplified). All this controversy came amid claims that the state had overpaid hospitals for services under Medicaid and might have to pay back $300 million.

By 2007, 81 percent of all eligible children nationwide were participating in Medicaid or SCHIP, but 5 million eligible uninsured children (64 percent of all uninsured children) were still not enrolled.[39] Medicaid and SCHIP participation rates vary greatly by region of the country. Many children do not get recertified once their initial enrollment period ends.[40] Barriers to enrollment and re-enrollment procedures "may include face-to-face interviews, confusing application forms and onerous documentation requirements to verify income and assets."[41] The Deficit Reduction Act of 2005 added a new requirement that current Medicaid recipients and future applicants provide proof of identity and citizenship.

The Agricultural Risk Protection Act of 2000 encourages schools to use their federally subsidized school meal programs to identify children who might be eligible for Medicaid or SCHIP. Since the economic crisis that erupted in 2008, states may be hesitant to take on new Medicaid and SCHIP participants, but just two weeks into his new administration, President Obama signed the Children's Health Insurance Program Reauthorization Act of 2009. It reauthorized SCHIP and expanded it to include an additional four million children. The bill passed the House of Representatives by a vote of 290–135. The new law makes it easier to enroll children in the program because substantial numbers of parents do not know their children are eligible or face difficulties with application and reapplication processes.[42] For example, the new law contains "express lane" provisions that allow states to use information in their databases to enroll children since many eligible children reside in families that receive other public benefits or file income tax returns.

MEDICALLY NEEDY   Thirty-five states and the District of Columbia also provide Medicaid to people categorized as "medically needy." These individuals and families are similar to other groups covered by Medicaid except that their income and assets exceed eligibility requirements to some degree. The states have some discretion in defining the groups considered medically needy, but if a state provides a medically needy program, it must include all children under age 18 who would qualify under a mandatory Medicaid category as well as pregnant women who would qualify under a mandatory or optional category, if their income and resources were lower (generally not more than 133 1/3 percent of the state's AFDC payment as of July 16, 1996).

IMMIGRANTS   Many legally admitted immigrants are not eligible for Medicaid. Those admitted after August 22, 1996, cannot receive Medicaid for five years, although permanent residents who have earned 40 work credits under Social Security (see Chapter 5) can. States can opt to cover those residing in the United States before August 22, 1996, if they were receiving Medicaid as of that date or if they become disabled. States must provide Medicaid for up to seven years to those admitted as asylees or refugees. Immigrants with past or current U.S. military service and their dependents may also qualify. States must provide emergency Medicaid services to all noncitizens regardless of whether they are residing legally in the United States if they meet eligibility requirements.

OTHERS States may also choose to cover certain low-income women while they are being treated for breast or cervical cancer if they do not have other healthcare coverage; 42 states do so. Eight states have also exercised the option to cover low-income individuals receiving tuberculosis treatment.

What Services Can Medicaid Beneficiaries Receive?

The federal government requires that states make certain services available to most Medicaid enrollees: inpatient and outpatient hospital care; physicians' services; laboratory and x-ray services; nursing home services for those over age 21; home healthcare (for those entitled to nursing home care); dental surgery; family-planning services and supplies; nurse midwife services; early and periodic screening, diagnosis, and treatment (EPSDT) services for those under age 21, which includes dental services and a variety of other services; family and pediatric nurse practitioner services; and pregnancy and postpartum services. States can limit many services (e.g., the number of days of hospital care or the number of visits to physicians), but they cannot limit certain services to children.

States may offer other benefits to Medicaid beneficiaries such as prescription drugs, eyeglasses, psychiatric services to those under age 21 or over age 65, or special services to elderly people with disabilities or to others with developmental disabilities. States generally offer at least some optional services. In 2005, at least 40 states offered prescription drugs; dental services; optometrist services and eyeglasses; physical therapy; speech, hearing, and language therapies; occupational therapy; audiology services; intermediate care services for people with mental retardation; mental health services; podiatry; prostheses; skilled nursing facility care for those under age 21; case management; and transportation.[43]

In 2006, about 17 percent of Medicaid payments were for nursing facility services (21 percent if residential facilities for people with intellectual disability are included); this is the largest category of Medicaid expenditures. Almost 14 percent went to inpatient hospital services. Prescription drugs accounted for nearly 11 percent of Medicaid spending. In 2006, Medicaid services cost an average of approximately $13,300 for each aged recipient, $14,000 for each disabled recipient, $1,700 for each dependent child, and $2,600 for each parent of these children.[44] While children are the largest category of Medicaid recipients, they are the least costly to serve (see Figure 8.2).

How Are Medicaid Services Delivered?

Medicaid services are provided in-kind. Physicians and other healthcare providers serve patients, and the government directly reimburses these providers. A number of states do use some type of program cost sharing, such as requiring recipients to pay small deductibles or copayments for services, but they cannot impose cost-sharing requirements on services for children under age 18, or for emergency, pregnancy, and family-planning services. People in custodial nursing facilities and intermediate-care facilities are not charged copayments. Virtually all their income already goes toward their care.

Most states use both fee-for-service arrangements and managed care plans to cover Medicaid recipients. In order to (1) control costs and (2) improve service quality, more states have turned to managed care, but as the House Committee on Ways and Means notes, there is a good deal of uncertainty over whether either goal has been achieved.[45] Managed care plans tend to come and go because of insurance company consolidations and bankruptcies. Some of their difficulties may stem from low reimbursement rates or unsuccessful risk-sharing methods (covering many

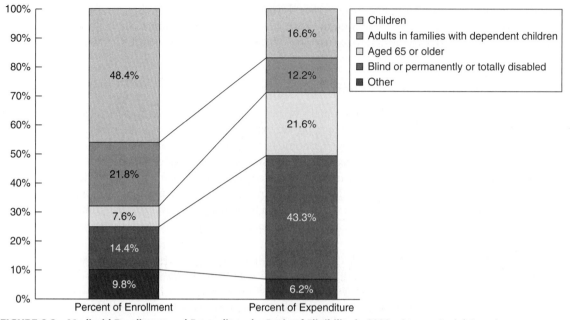

FIGURE 8.2 **Medicaid Enrollment and Expenditure by Basis of Eligibility in 2006** *Source:* Social Security Administration, Annual Statistical Supplement, 2008, released March, 2009: Table 8.E2. Retrieved January 2, 2010, from http://www.socialsecurity.gov/policy/docs/statcomps/supplement/2008/

beneficiaries with high medical care needs). In 1991, about 10 percent of Medicaid beneficiaries were covered under managed care. By 2008, this number had grown to 71 percent.[46]

Many states use more than one managed care arrangement. For example, to serve most children and families, who generally need only routine care, states may use a risk-based managed care organization (MCO). The MCO is paid a set fee to provide a defined set of benefits and is responsible for any additional costs incurred in serving the patient. States may also use a prepaid health plan for a particular type of service like mental health services. Some states use primary care case management (PCCM) to coordinate services for recipients, especially those who have greater healthcare needs. This method can also provide more continuity when there is a turnover in plans. Fee-for-service arrangements are mostly used for aged or disabled recipients, who need more care, and for those who live in rural areas with limited access to managed care options.

States are testing various methods to improve healthcare delivery under their Medicaid programs. Some of this activity occurs under waiver programs (many under what is called Section 1115) that allow states to deviate from certain Medicaid rules. For example, states can offer a comprehensive benefit package to Medicaid-eligible individuals and other low-income individuals as well.

Other Routes to Healthcare for the Poor

Block grants are also used to provide medical care, primarily to low-income people. The Maternal and Child Health Services Block Grant, administered by the U.S. Department of Health and Human Services's (DHHS's) Health Resources and Services Administration, assists additional low-income pregnant women and young children. The Preventive Health and Health Services (PHHS) Block Grant, administered by DHHS's Centers for Disease Control, provides funds for a variety of services. States have a great deal of say in how they use the funds. Funds are often used for educational services and risk reduction programs, such as smoking cessation programs and nutrition advice; to treat those with specific health problems, such as hypertension and tuberculosis; and to provide some emergency medical services and rodent-control programs.[47] A portion of PHHS funds must be used for rape prevention and treatment. The federal government also offers many other health and health-related programs. States and communities also search for creative ways to meet health needs and stretch their healthcare dollars.

Employer-Sponsored and Private Health Insurance

The Kaiser Family Foundation and Health Research and Educational Trust reports that the average annual health insurance premium for a family increased from $5,791 in 1999 to $13,375 in 2009, a 131 percent increase. Over the same time period, the average worker contribution for that coverage increased by 128 percent from $1,543 in 1999 to $3,515 in 2009. The employer share in 2009 averaged $9,860; for most full-time employees this amounts to an extra $4.93 per hour in non-taxable benefits. For individual coverage, the average annual premium rose 120 percent from $2,196 in 1999 to $4,824 in 2009. Employee contributions rose from $318 to $779 over the same period. The $4,045 average annual employer contribution for employee-only coverage amounts to just over $2.00 per hour in additional *non-taxable* compensation.[48] Since World War II, health benefits have received very favorable tax treatment for employers and employees—employers get a tax deduction for providing these benefits, and employees are not taxed on these benefits.

Types of Employer-Based Plans

Employer-based plans, often called "true group" plans, generally fall into one of four types: preferred provider organizations (PPOs), health maintenance organizations (HMOs), point-of-service plans (POS), and high deductible health plans with a savings option (HDHP/SOs). Eighty-six percent of firms that offer health insurance benefits offer only one type of plan. This is important because much of the 2009 debate about healthcare reform was about maintaining choice, while almost half of those receiving healthcare benefits from their employers have no choice of health plans.

PREFERRED PROVIDER ORGANIZATIONS (PPO)   Many employer-based group plans are built on a preferred provider organization (PPO) arrangement. In PPOs, the insurer contracts with doctors, hospitals, and other providers to offer services for the PPO plan participants. In many cases, the PPO contract price is expressed as a percentage of what Medicare would pay for the same service. Such contractual arrangements mean that changes to Medicare reimbursement rates have broader-ranging effects on private plans such as PPOs.

Typically, PPO plan participants can choose from a range of primary care physicians and specialists; sometimes they also have a choice of hospitals and other medical care providers. These providers are known as "in-network" providers, meaning that they have contracted with the insurance company to provide their services at a predetermined price. Plan participants who use an in-network provider usually cannot be charged in excess of this predetermined price.

Participants may also use "non-network" providers for their healthcare needs. However, such choices typically mean that the plan will pay only a portion, typically 80 percent, of charges. The plan participant is responsible for any difference between the charges and what the plan pays the provider. This means that participants generally have a major incentive to stick with in-network providers.

HEALTH MAINTENANCE ORGANIZATIONS (HMO)   Health maintenance organizations (HMOs) have been available in the United States since the early part of the twentieth century.[49] These organizations, an approach to healthcare cost management, initially utilized salaried doctors and plan-owned hospital facilities to offer healthcare to their plan participants. Today, most HMOs contract with primary care physicians who act as the gatekeeper for all other medical services. In many ways, HMOs have become almost identical to PPOs. Typically, HMO customers are not permitted to see a specialist unless their primary care physician refers them, and the choice of providers is limited. In return, participants pay very little out-of-pocket for doctor visits and many other services. HMOs got their first real boost with the Health Maintenance Organization Act of 1973, which, at that time, placed some requirements on employers that offered a traditional health insurance plan to offer an HMO option. The HMO act, proffered by the Nixon administration, was passed with the idea of controlling rising healthcare costs in the wake of the implementation of Medicare and Medicaid in 1966.

The politics surrounding the HMO Act of 1973 provide a glimpse into the way social welfare often gets addressed politically. Initially, President Nixon favored a national healthcare proposal. However, when Senator Edward Kennedy (D-MA) endorsed such a plan, Nixon dropped his support for it. Edgar Kaiser, of the large HMO Kaiser-Permanente, lobbied the Nixon White House extensively for the HMO Act.

In February 1971, White House Aide John Ehrlichman met with President Nixon about healthcare plans, and about the Kaiser proposal in particular. The president was disinterested in plans *until* Ehrlichman told him that the Kaiser plan was "a private enterprise one." The conversation was captured on the now infamous, and once legally embattled, Nixon White House tapes. In what may be one of the more revealing political conversations ever held about healthcare, Ehrlichman pointed out to Nixon that "[a]ll the incentives are toward less medical care because— the less care they give them, the more money they make . . . and the incentives run the right way." Nixon's response? "Not bad."[50]

POINT OF SERVICE (POS) PLANS   Point of Service plans are a hybrid of HMOs and PPOs. Participants in a POS plan select a primary care physician (PCP) from a list of participating physicians provided by the plan, just like an HMO. This doctor becomes the plan member's "point of service," meaning that he or she directs all medical services for the participant. If a specialist is needed, the PCP attempts to refer the participant to an in-network provider. Most networks have a broad base of providers.

In POS plans, participants can also see out-of-network providers as they can in a PPO plan. However, in most POS plans, participants must cover charges up front out-of-pocket, complete their own claims forms, submit them for reimbursement, and then wait for whatever amount the POS plan reimburses them. In many cases, the participant does not know in advance how much reimbursement will be paid. Like the PPO plans, the percentage that the insurance company pays for out-of-network charges is lower than what they pay for in-network providers. Most POS plans require that the PCP refer participants to in-network providers; participants who self-refer to an out-of-network provider may receive little or no reimbursement for that provider's services

HIGH-DEDUCTIBLE HEALTH PLANS WITH SAVINGS OPTIONS (HDHP/SO)   As health insurance premiums have more than doubled over the past ten years, some companies have begun offering plans that have very high deductibles and, consequently, much lower premiums, in an effort to contain employee benefit costs. These companies typically offer employees a portion of the premium savings, which the employee can deposit into a tax-favored Health Savings Account (HSA). Employees can then pay health expenses from their HSA until their high deductible is met.

The tax advantages of an HSA go beyond tax-deductibility. Any amount that remains unused at the end of the year can stay in the account and continue to grow on a tax-deferred basis. Once the owner reaches age 65, the account balances can essentially be used just like any other Individual Retirement Account (IRA).

Of course, the increased risk of an HDHP/SO plan is that the employee or covered family member may incur a major, unexpected medical expense before the HSA has sufficient funds to cover the high deductible. In that case, the employee must come up with the money to cover the plan deductible and co-payments out-of-pocket.

How Do People Choose a Plan?

Only about 53 percent of employees have a choice of employer-sponsored health insurance plans. Most of these employees work for large firms (200 or more employees). The employer makes the choice for the other 47 percent of employees. For those who have a choice, plan options can sometimes be quite confusing. Which plan is best is a matter of such factors as how often the employee or covered family members see a doctor, whether any have a chronic illness, and whether they anticipate any major expenses, such as surgeries, in the upcoming plan year. Employees who don't anticipate major expenses often choose the plan that leaves them with the most money in their net paycheck, resulting in assuming more risk on their own. This may or may not pay off for them in the long run since illnesses and accidents (by definition) are generally unpredictable.

Individual Private Insurance Plans

Approximately 9 percent of the U.S. public is covered by individually purchased private insurance plans. These plans operate much like the "true group" employer-sponsored plans in terms of how medical expenses are covered. There are, however, important differences between individual and group plans.

The first major difference is how they are underwritten. *Underwriting* is the process by which an insurance company decides whether, and at what price, to offer insurance coverage. Most group plans do not require individual participants to provide proof of good health. Especially among larger firms, insurers assume that the composition of people in the company is roughly equivalent to the composition of the population at large in terms of health risks. (This, of course, is not true if the company is engaged in work that results in increased risks to employees such as mining or tall-building construction.)

Individual plans, on the other hand, generally require that applicants at least complete a medical questionnaire. The company may also require a medical examination prior to offering the policy to the applicant. This additional, and more restrictive, underwriting is necessary given that people who know they are likely to incur major medical expenses will be more likely to try to purchase individual coverage if they do not have a group plan available to them. Insurers call this *adverse selection risk*. Premiums, deductibles, co-payments, and out-of-pocket maximums are usually higher in private plans than in group plans. This is because of the increased adverse selection risk associated with private plans.

Another major difference involves pre-existing conditions. Group plans may have a *general* provision that excludes *any* condition for which the participant has received treatment during a specific period of time in the past. Individual plans may name *specific* conditions that they will exclude if the insured has admitted to having them or which are discovered in the course of underwriting the policy. Excluding pre-existing conditions permits insurers to offer

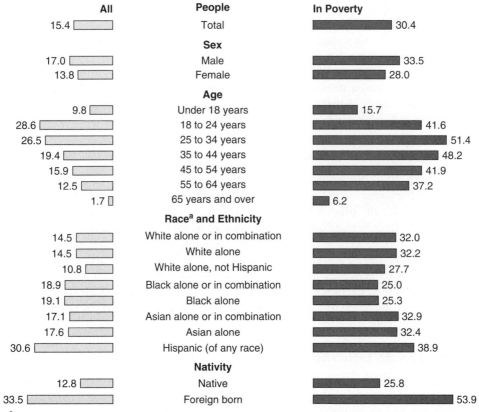

	All	People	In Poverty	
	15.4	**Total**	30.4	
		Sex		
	17.0	Male	33.5	
	13.8	Female	28.0	
		Age		
	9.8	Under 18 years	15.7	
	28.6	18 to 24 years	41.6	
	26.5	25 to 34 years	51.4	
	19.4	35 to 44 years	48.2	
	15.9	45 to 54 years	41.9	
	12.5	55 to 64 years	37.2	
	1.7	65 years and over	6.2	
		Race[a] and Ethnicity		
	14.5	White alone or in combination	32.0	
	14.5	White alone	32.2	
	10.8	White alone, not Hispanic	27.7	
	18.9	Black alone or in combination	25.0	
	19.1	Black alone	25.3	
	17.1	Asian alone or in combination	32.9	
	17.6	Asian alone	32.4	
	30.6	Hispanic (of any race)	38.9	
		Nativity		
	12.8	Native	25.8	
	33.5	Foreign born	53.9	

[a]In race categories, "alone" means respondents reported only one race, and "in combination" means they reported more than one race.

FIGURE 8.3   People without Health Insurance for the Entire Year by Selected Characteristics, 2008
Source: U.S. Census Bureau, Current Population Survey, 2008 Annual Social and Economic Supplement.

coverage for unforeseen risks while limiting their exposure to known risks of the insured. Although health care legislation passed by Congress in 2010 will no longer allow insurers to deny coverage because of pre-existing conditions, this change will not affect adults applying for health insurance until 2014.

The Uninsured: Pay As You Go

With all the forms of public and private insurance, you might think that all Americans would have health insurance from some source. During the three-year period from 2006 to 2008, an average of 46 million people, approximately 15 percent of the U.S. population, had no health insurance coverage at any point in time (see Figure 8.3).[51] Who are the people without health insurance, and how do they obtain their healthcare?

As you might imagine, poor and low-income people are much more likely to be uninsured than their wealthier counterparts. In 2008, about 27 percent of people living in households with less than $25,000 in annual income had no health insurance, while approximately 7 percent of those living in households with annual incomes of $75,000 or more were uninsured.

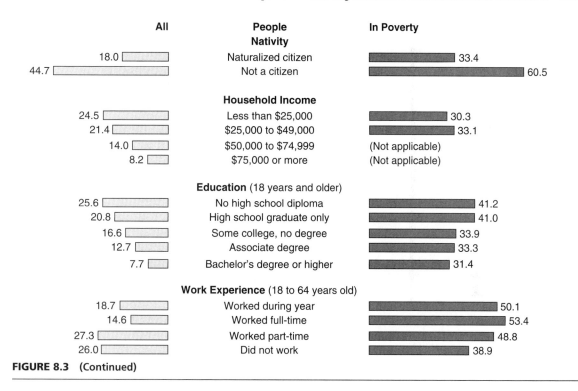

	All	People	In Poverty
		Nativity	
	18.0	Naturalized citizen	33.4
	44.7	Not a citizen	60.5
		Household Income	
	24.5	Less than $25,000	30.3
	21.4	$25,000 to $49,000	33.1
	14.0	$50,000 to $74,999	(Not applicable)
	8.2	$75,000 or more	(Not applicable)
		Education (18 years and older)	
	25.6	No high school diploma	41.2
	20.8	High school graduate only	41.0
	16.6	Some college, no degree	33.9
	12.7	Associate degree	33.3
	7.7	Bachelor's degree or higher	31.4
		Work Experience (18 to 64 years old)	
	18.7	Worked during year	50.1
	14.6	Worked full-time	53.4
	27.3	Worked part-time	48.8
	26.0	Did not work	38.9

FIGURE 8.3 (Continued)

Even worse, the uninsured rate for those in poverty was 30 percent compared to 15 percent for the population as a whole. As Figure 8.3 shows, those in poverty are much less likely to have insurance compared to the general population regardless of their age, race, education, or other characteristics.

More than half of uninsured adults are the "working poor," and those numbers are increasing. In 2007, nearly 27 million (18 percent) of those between ages 18 and 64 who worked at some time during the year were uninsured. By 2008, that number had climbed to nearly 19 percent or almost 28 million people. As Figure 8.3 shows, individuals who worked full-time but still had poverty-level incomes had an uninsured rate of 53 percent.

Race also plays a factor. Among non-Hispanic whites, almost 11 percent are uninsured. Blacks have an uninsured rate of about 19 percent, Native Hawaiians and Other Pacific Islanders are uninsured at a rate of about 17 percent, and 18 percent of Asians have no health insurance. Hispanics have the highest rate at 31 percent.

In 2008, about 10 percent of children under 18 years old were uninsured. This is the lowest uninsured rate among children since 1987. Even with Medicaid and SCHIP, 16 percent of children in poverty were uninsured compared to 10 percent for the general population. Race also plays a factor in uninsured status for children. Less than 7 percent of non-Hispanic white children are uninsured, while almost 11 percent of black children and Asian children are uninsured. More than 17 percent of Hispanic children were uninsured in 2008 (see Figure 8.4).

Uninsured people generally delay going to a doctor until the pain or the extent of illness makes further delay impossible, and they often use the hospital emergency room as their "general

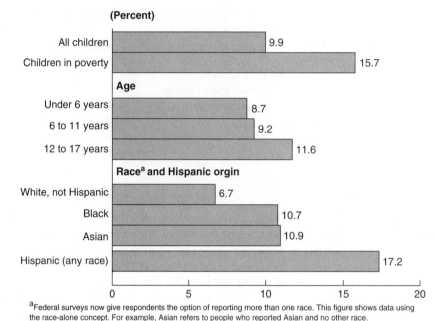

FIGURE 8.4 Uninsured Children by Poverty Status, Age, and Race and Hispanic Origin: 2008
Source: Carmen DeNavas-Walt, Bernadette D. Proctor, and Jessica C. Smith, *Income, Poverty, and Health Insurance Coverage in the United States: 2008*, U.S. Census Bureau, Current Population Reports, P60-236 (Washington, DC: U.S. Government Printing Office, 2009). Retrieved December 19, 2009, from http://www.census.gov/prod/2009pubs/p60-236.pdf

practitioner." This is the most expensive form of care available. Costs are driven even higher because these individuals could likely have received far less expensive treatment if they had a way to pay for it (note that after one's name, the next question most providers ask is about insurance coverage, and many providers have signs at the front desk that say payment is due at time of service). Unlike those with insurance, no one is negotiating prices with doctors, hospitals, and other medical providers on behalf of the uninsured. Therefore, they typically pay *higher* prices for medical services than those with insurance. One study showed that, in 2007, 62 percent of all bankruptcies in the United States were due to medical problems.[52] Medical bankruptcies increased by almost 50 percent since 2001. Most of those filing for bankruptcy *had* health insurance.

WHAT AILS HEALTHCARE?

There is no doubt that Americans' access to medical care has increased with Medicaid, Medicare, and more employer-based coverage. Unfortunately, this increase in access to healthcare has not been met with a concomitant improvement in health. Evidence from the early 1970s on this point was particularly bleak—there seemed to be no relationship between increased healthcare expenditures and improved health for vulnerable groups.[53] Improvements in general health statistics were just as great prior to Medicaid and Medicare as they were following these programs' enactment.

Rather than more medicine, Americans need a more rational means of distributing a scarce resource—medical care—in an efficient fashion to improve the nation's health. We cannot really hope to provide all of the healthcare that everyone might want, but we could channel more funds to help Americans adopt healthier lifestyles. This might be one of the best uses of healthcare dollars. The greatest benefits to health and reductions in healthcare costs would accrue if people would eat healthier diets, exercise more, and stop smoking, all things that are apparently easier said than done. Debate also ensues over where responsibility for adopting healthier lifestyles lies—with the government, with the manufacturers of food and tobacco products, or with the individual.

Healthcare in International Perspective

Most people would expect a highly developed society to invest a substantial amount in healthcare. The United States does just that, exceeding healthcare spending over all other developed nations. Table 8.1 provides information on overall healthcare spending in several countries. No other country comes close to the $7,290 per person the United States spent on healthcare in 2007. The closest is Norway at $4,763, followed by Switzerland at $4,417.[54] The United States also spends more on healthcare as a percent of gross domestic product (GDP) than other countries. At 16 percent in 2007, it exceeded France and Switzerland's 11 percent. Less than half (45 percent) of U.S. healthcare expenditures comes from public sources. Except for Switzerland, public funds account for more than two-thirds of healthcare expenditures in the other countries shown in Table 8.1. Nearly everyone in these other countries has publicly sponsored health insurance. The United States and South Africa are the only industrialized countries that do not have some form of national health insurance.

The cost of healthcare in the United States might not be so hard to swallow if Americans could boast that they were healthier than people in other countries, but this is hardly the case. Despite access to the most advanced healthcare technology, Americans have a lower life

TABLE 8.1 Healthcare Expenditures per Capita and as a Percentage of Gross Domestic Product (GDP) and Public Expenditures as a Percentage of Total Healthcare Expenditures for Selected Countries, 2007

Country	Per Capita Expenditure in U.S. Dollars	Expenditures as Percent of GDP	Public Expenditures as a Percentage of Total Healthcare Expenditures
Australia[a]	$3,137	8.7	67.7
Canada	3,895	10.1	70.0
Finland	2,840	8.2	74.6
France	3,601	11.0	79.0
Germany	3,588	10.4	76.9
Ireland	3,424	7.6	80.7
Italy	2,686	8.7	76.5
Japan[a]	2,581	8.1	81.3
Norway	4,763	8.9	84.1
Spain	2,671	8.5	71.8
Sweden	3,323	9.1	81.7
Switzerland	4,417	10.8	59.3
United Kingdom	2,992	8.4	81.7
United States	7,290	16.0	45.4

[a] Data in all categories for Australia and Japan are for 2006

Source: Organization for Economic Cooperation and Development, *OECD in Figures 2009*, p. 8, www.oecd.org/infigures

expectancy than those in many other industrialized countries (ranking 23rd for women and 22nd for men out of 30 countries) and higher infant mortality (ranking 25th).[55]

The Nation's Healthcare Bill

It would be much easier to offer healthcare benefits to all Americans if medical costs were not so high. National healthcare expenditures have risen rapidly in the United States. In 1965, prior to Medicare and Medicaid, the country's total (public and private) healthcare bill was $42 billion; in 1990 it was $698 billion, and in 2008, healthcare expenditures (not counting construction and research) were more than $2.3 trillion (see Table 8.2). In 2008, for every dollar spent on health-care, private insurance and other private spending combined accounted for 41 cents, government spending (federal, state, and local including expenditures for Medicare, Medicaid, and SCHIP) for 47 cents, and out-of-pocket expenditures for 12 cents (see Figure 8.5).

Employers are passing more health insurance costs on to employees, and some employees who have coverage cannot afford the additional premiums to insure their family members. Some people work only to maintain healthcare coverage because they are afraid to do without it.

Several factors have contributed to escalating medical costs:

1. Third-party financing, including the expansion of private insurance (especially through employers) and public insurance (Medicaid and Medicare), has contributed to these rapidly increasing health costs. All have increased the demand for healthcare.
2. The rapidly growing number of older people is another contributor, since those over age 65 use more healthcare services than the rest of the population.
3. Advances in medical technology also contribute. Amazing improvements have occurred in the diagnosis and treatment of many illnesses—including heart disease and cancer—which not long ago were invariably considered fatal. Equipment such as computerized axial tomography (CAT) scanners and magnetic resonance imaging (MRI), and techniques such as organ transplants and other extraordinary means of sustaining life also add to costs. The technology that continues to be developed has allowed for increased survival rates of the tiniest infants and people with the most serious ailments.
4. There has also been a vast expansion of medical facilities, including hospital beds that are expensive to maintain (although rural areas may not have a doctor, let alone a hospital). Medicaid funding has spawned many new nursing home facilities and resulted in many more people being placed in them.
5. Litigation is another contributor. The threat of malpractice suits results in doctors ordering more tests, even if their utility is questionable. Patients generally want all the best services available, and so do their physicians. Given the threat of lawsuits (and lawyers seeking to pursue cases), malpractice insurance costs increase. These costs are also passed on to consumers.
6. Healthcare cost inflation remains a concern. The double-digit healthcare cost inflation of the 1980s has abated due to managed care, more competition, and providers' efforts to avoid greater government intervention in the healthcare arena. Healthcare costs for 2009 were projected to increase at a rate of 7.4 percent, making 2009 the third straight year of declines in healthcare inflation.[56] However, the total cost against which this percentage of increase is calculated continues to grow, and healthcare inflation continues to exceed general price inflation. As healthcare costs continue to increase, the effect of compounding rates of growth combined with the aging of the baby boomer population predicts an uncertain future for healthcare in the United States if measures are not taken to "bend the cost curve."

TABLE 8.2 U.S. National Healthcare Expenditures, 2008 (in billions of dollars).

Spending Category	Amount
Health services and supplies	$2,181.3
Personal healthcare	1,952.3
Hospital care	718.4
Physician and clinical services	496.2
Dental services	101.2
Other professional services	65.7
Home healthcare	64.7
Nursing home care	138.4
Prescription drugs	234.1
Nondurable medical products	39.0
Durable medical equipment	26.6
Other personal healthcare	68.1
Government administration and net cost of private health insurance	159.6
Government public health activities	69.4
Research	43.6
Structures and equipment	113.9
Total	$2,338.8

Source: Centers for Medicare and Medicaid Services, Office of the Actuary. Retrieved May 22, 2010, from http://www.cms.hhs.gov/NationalHealthExpendData/02_NationalHealthAccountsHistorical.asp#TopOfPage

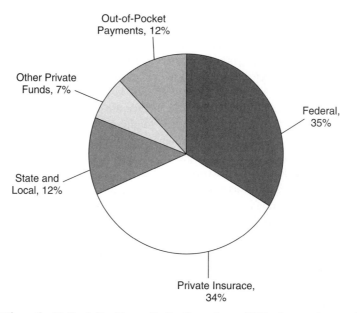

FIGURE 8.5   Where the Nation's Healthcare Dollar Came From: 2008   *Source:* Centers for Medicare and Medicaid Services, Office of the Actuary. Retrieved May 22, 2010, from http://www.cms.hhs.gov/NationalHealthExpendData/02_NationalHealthAccountsHistorical.asp#TopOfPage

Trying to Control Healthcare Costs

In the 1980s, the federal government took action to curb rapidly escalating public healthcare costs. Since Medicaid reimbursement rates were already so low, the initial target of these efforts was the Medicare program.

REINING IN MEDICARE   The major vehicles enacted to rein in rapidly growing Medicare costs were diagnosis-related groups (DRGs) and Medicare assignment. In 1983, Congress adopted its controversial DRG system. Prior to this, there were some restrictions on what Medicare would reimburse hospitals, but generally hospitals were reimbursed for the "reasonable" costs incurred in treating a patient. This was a *retrospective* (after-the-fact) method of paying for hospital care. Despite strong opposition, the DRGs introduced a *prospective* reimbursement method in which the federal government specifies in advance what it will pay hospitals for the treatment of 487 different illnesses, or diagnosis-related groups. A reimbursement formula was devised to include the average cost of treating a Medicare patient in the hospital, the average cost of treating the particular DRG, whether the hospital is in a large urban area or other area, and hospital wages in the area compared to the national average hospital wage. Greater reimbursement is provided for very costly cases, to hospitals that serve a large number of low-income patients or are the only providers in the area, and to regional referral centers and cancer treatment centers. Anyone who takes time to read the rules will be dazzled by the complexity of the DRG system. When a hospital spends more to treat a patient, it must absorb the additional costs, but when the hospital spends less than the DRG allows, it can keep the difference. Participating hospitals are not allowed to charge Medicare patients more than the DRG. Obviously, the purpose of DRGs is to make hospitals more cost efficient, and immediate drops in hospital stays along with cost savings were seen.

Containing physicians' charges was more difficult to achieve. Medicare traditionally paid physicians what was "usual, customary, and reasonable" in their community. Opposition from physicians and the AMA to controlling fees was a formidable obstacle to overcome.[57] Cost control provisions have included freezes on the amount that participating physicians can charge Medicare patients. Participating physicians and other providers agree to accept Medicare reimbursement as payment in full, while nonparticipating physicians may charge patients more than the amount covered by Medicare. Some physicians are not taking new Medicare patients, presumably because reimbursement is low and paperwork is high. Each year the U.S. Department of Health and Human Services determines the fees that will be paid to physicians under the Medicare program. Incentives used to increase the number of participating physicians include higher payments, prompter reimbursement, and distribution of participating physician directories.

In 1989, Congress reckoned further with the AMA by instituting major changes to control physicians' fees. One such change was to pay physicians according to a fee schedule for about 7,000 different services beginning in 1992.

In spite of Congress's attempts to hold down expenditures, the government's share of healthcare costs increased substantially during the 1990s relative to that paid by the private sector and by households.[58] Most troubling was that the Medicare trust fund was headed for exhaustion even though Congress had taken measures to control costs and to raise more funds by levying the Medicare tax on all workers' earned income. As Congress searched for ways to bring the federal budget into balance, healthcare became a prime target of the Balanced Budget Act of 1997.

THE BALANCED BUDGET ACT   The Balanced Budget Act of 1997, or BBA, made cost savings changes in Medicaid and Medicare. The vast majority of savings have come from smaller increases in payment updates to providers. Medicare savings were projected to be $115 billion in the first five years and about $15 billion in Medicaid. The act also repealed the Boren amendment, which required states to make "reasonable and adequate" payments to hospitals and nursing homes. This gives states more flexibility but was particularly controversial because Medicaid nursing home reimbursement rates were already very low in many places.[59]

The savings to be gained from disproportionate share hospital (DSH) payments has also been controversial. In the past, hospitals and physicians made up for the costs of providing services to those who could not pay their bills by shifting these costs to third-party payers (government programs and private health insurers) and to patients who could afford the bills. Today, this is increasingly difficult to do because of public and private cost-containment strategies. DSHs serve many Medicaid enrollees and many poor people who have no health insurance. Disproportionate share payments have been used to compensate hospitals for this service. The BBA and previous legislation passed during the 1990s limit DSH payments in order to save the government money through more efficient service delivery.

Under the BBA, Medicare beneficiaries assumed more out-of-pocket costs, like higher Part B premiums. The BBA also sought to achieve savings through greater use of managed care and other healthcare options for poor and older people. According to the House Committee on Ways and Means, the BBA "achieved significant savings to the Medicare program by slowing the rate of growth in payments to providers and by enacting structural changes to the program."[60] The BBA might have done too good a job. Claims were that payment reductions were greater than intended, causing some facility closures and limiting some beneficiaries' access to care. Subsequent measures were taken to increase payment rates. But there have also been additional efforts to limit spending. For example, in 2003, Congress decided to reduce the amount of services that Medicare beneficiaries could get in a year from physical, speech, and occupational therapists.

Why Americans Do Not Have Universal Healthcare

Ever since the presidency of Teddy Roosevelt, progressives have sought to introduce universal healthcare to the United States. Why, if U.S. healthcare spending tops all other countries, are 46 million Americans without health insurance?

There have been many responses to this particular question. Perhaps the best comes from an idea called path-dependence theory. This economic theory, founded in biology, holds that early decisions in a process become reinforced by later decisions. Initial conditions are very important to the ultimate outcomes.[61]

Most other countries have public policies that make healthcare a universal benefit, paid for, in one form or another, by general national tax revenues.[62] In Britain, Canada, and many other countries, decisions to adopt national healthcare were made relatively early on in the formulation of the welfare state, but these countries have adopted several variations of the idea. Great Britain has its National Health System in which the Crown owns the nation's hospitals, and doctors are government employees. This type of "national" system is often called "socialized medicine." The Canadian system is much different. Hospitals are privately owned, and doctors are not government employees. Canadians have a single-payer insurance system in which the provincial governments pay all claims and costs to these private providers. Care is considered quite good and the system reportedly functions efficiently by centralizing services and equipment.[63] Physicians maintain substantial incomes under the Canadian plan. Before the Canadian national government adopted universal hospital insurance in 1958 and universal physician insurance in 1968, some provinces were already insuring their residents.

The United States has had a more individualized system from its earliest days. President Franklin D. Roosevelt backed off from the idea of including national health insurance in the original Social Security Act after his advisors convinced him that any attempt to include national healthcare would jeopardize Social Security retirement insurance. Presidents Harry S. Truman and Bill Clinton failed in their attempts at universal health insurance. In each case opponents raised the specter of "socialized medicine" as something foreign to the American way of life.

During the Great Depression of the 1930s, private Blue Cross and Blue Shield plans provided a funding stream to hospitals and doctors when patients had a difficult time paying for services. As the United States found itself in World War II, runaway cost inflation was an imminent danger. The Wage Stabilization Act of 1942 prohibited employers from raising wages for most employees. In lieu of wage increases, unions (organized labor) encouraged employers to provide fringe benefits, largely in the form of health insurance, to their employees. The federal government permitted this to occur. Thus was born the connection between employment and health insurance in the United States.

President Johnson considered Medicare to be a first step toward recognizing healthcare as a basic right. In his 1971 memoirs, he expressed his hope that it would eventually lead to universal healthcare.[64] More than two decades passed before a serious attempt at insuring all Americans was made.

During his first race for the presidency, Bill Clinton's number one campaign promise was national health insurance. The president was so invested in the issue that he appointed his wife First Lady Hillary Rodham Clinton to chair the large task force that helped devise the plan. Advocates hoped that it would provide all Americans the opportunity to get preventive and early treatment while simultaneously keeping national health costs in check using expenditure controls.

Under the plan all citizens and legal immigrants would have received a "health security card" guaranteeing them comprehensive healthcare benefits, including preventive care, for life.[65] No one would have been denied coverage, and coverage would have been continuous regardless of employment. Eligibility and reimbursement rules would have been standardized across the country, replacing the myriad rules under the many healthcare policies and plans that exist today. Competition was a main theme of the plan, with participants buying into large purchasing pools (healthcare alliances) to get the best value for their healthcare dollar. Each alliance would have offered a choice of plans. Employers would have paid 80 percent of the premiums for the standard benefit package and workers would have paid the rest. Premium targets would have been set to protect against cost inflation. Poor individuals would have received premium discounts or would not have been charged. Medicaid would have covered premiums for the poorest individuals, who would also receive discounts on coinsurance payments, but they, too, would have been served by an alliance. Medicare would have remained, but individuals could have chosen Medicare or a regional alliance. Prescription drug benefits would have been added to Medicare. A federal-state long-term care benefit including home- and community-based services for people with disabilities, regardless of age and income, would have been established.

About three-quarters of funding for the Health Security Act was expected to come from current sources—employers and the insured—with additional funding from cost-savings measures in Medicare and Medicaid. As healthcare expert Uwe Reinhardt put it:

> The president's proposal . . . [was] not a clean, simple design tailored to a single dominant philosophy as are, for example, the Canadian and German health systems. True to American tradition, it . . . [was] a complex compromise that has been bent and twisted onto the Procrustean bed of a pluralistic set of ethical precepts and of an equally pluralistic set of narrow economic interests pursued by politically powerful groups.[66]

Dozens of competing proposals were offered. Many of a more liberal ilk advocated greater government regulation, including a single-payer system in which the federal government would collect all funds used to pay for healthcare and would pay all claims. Single-payer proponents wanted to eliminate the two-tier system of healthcare in which the rich receive the best treatment and the poor get second-class care. But the fear was that without competition, there would be no incentive for efficiency.

At the other end of the spectrum were those who felt that the Clinton plan was too much government regulation. They complained that many healthcare decisions would be made by bureaucrats rather than between doctor and patient. Conservatives wanted to leave far more to the competition that flows from natural market forces, and they wanted to take a much more incremental approach. The political stakes overwhelmed the public's support of the plan. With the First Lady leading the charge, a victory on the Health Security Act would have been too much for the Republicans to hand to the Democrats. Representative Newt Gingrich (R-GA) recognized this as an opportunity to hand the President and the Democrats a major defeat and allow Republicans to retake control of the House and Senate. Using healthcare reform to set up his Contract With America (limiting government and social welfare), Gingrich succeeded in both defeating national healthcare reform and seeing Republicans retake control of both houses of Congress. For his efforts, Gingrich's reward was being elected Speaker of the House.[67] In the end:

> One need look no further than America's previous failures to reform the health system to recognize that it is a complex undertaking. The challenge is daunting because it must attract broad political support in a nation that has never achieved consensus on an overriding social ethic (universal coverage) to which all other worthwhile goals in healthcare must take second place … The result of this ambivalence—open espousal of a lofty goal, but open hostility to the only means of achieving that goal—has led to the perennial stalemate that is the hallmark of congressional wrangling over universal health insurance.[68]

Any ray of hope for national health insurance quickly faded. It remained off the table until 2009.

INCREMENTALISM AND THE 2009–2010 EFFORT FOR UNIVERSAL HEALTHCARE

Nowhere is the United States' unique approach to social welfare policy more evident than it is in healthcare. Americans are accustomed to the healthcare status quo, and campaigns by vested healthcare interests, such as physicians, pharmaceutical companies, hospitals, and insurance companies, encourage Americans to fear greater government intervention in healthcare. In 2010, President Barack Obama and the Democratic-led 111th Congress overcame unified Republican opposition to pass the first major national healthcare reform bill since Medicare was passed in 1965.

The problems of the U.S. healthcare system are obvious. Costs are high. Government expenditures for Medicare and Medicaid threaten the stability of the economy. Employers are facing ever-increasing costs to provide both employee and, in the case of some larger companies, retiree benefits. General Motors, prior to its bankruptcy filing, faced a $15 billion healthcare liability. Ford Motor Company pays out more than $3 billion a year for healthcare costs.[69] The number of Americans without health insurance grows during times of economic recession. The expenses of providing healthcare to the uninsured are borne by the rest of society. In addition, the uninsured population is a moving target. While some individuals gain health insurance through employment, others may lose their job, and along with it their health insurance. Public health insurance for all but older Americans is no better. An individual insured by Medicaid today may not be covered tomorrow due to increased income or other changes in circumstances.

In the face of these daunting policy challenges, one might presume that the government would take swift and massive corrective action. However, even in the face of massive need, the U.S. system of government tends to discourage sweeping changes in favor of an incrementalist approach. This is often desirable since it prevents taking actions without thorough and thoughtful discourse; however, some problems call for major change, and many would include healthcare in that list. Such change is very hard to achieve, as evidenced by the failed attempts at national health insurance over the past 100 years.

Most Americans have a decent source of healthcare, and although they may complain about some facet of their health plan, the majority is satisfied with the current system. A poll conducted by three reputable groups found that "Americans favor building on the current system as a way of improving healthcare; they are not eager to make sweeping changes."[70] The Institute of Medicine (IOM) has tried to persuade Americans otherwise, saying that "incremental approaches to extend coverage are insufficient."[71] The AMA and the Health Insurance Association of America also joined the call for some type of universal health insurance. A number of years ago the AMA began endorsing mandatory employer-supported healthcare. But these organizations criticized aspects of President Clinton's national health insurance proposal, especially spending controls.[72]

Elements of the Healthcare Reform Debate

The U.S. system of paying for healthcare is complex. It involves many political and economic interests, not all of which are directly related to providing better or even more healthcare. These interests compete for the attention of Congress and the public in the hope of influencing the outcome of debates over healthcare. The 2009–2010 debate had three primary themes: (1) the extent to which Americans should have choice in healthcare; (2) whether health insurers should be prohibited from excluding people from coverage based on pre-existing conditions or post-claims underwriting; and (3) whether making access to adequate, affordable healthcare a right rather than a privilege would lead to rationing healthcare.

HEALTHCARE CHOICE   Americans have a cultural history that embraces a rugged individualist national concept. Americans like to believe that they have choices and that they exercise control over their own lives. In the debate over healthcare reform, this point is evident in the push for choice of coverage, choice of providers, and protecting the doctor-patient relationship. Opponents of healthcare reform framed the debate in terms that evoked the image of a government bureaucrat standing between patient and doctor. Americans' suspicion of government, especially "big government" is deep-rooted. Opponents knew that they could play on this suspicion in their efforts to defeat ideas like a government-run option to cover uninsured Americans, not to mention a single-payer system.

In actuality, very few Americans exercise full choice or control over their healthcare decisions. Those not covered by a government plan are mostly covered by employer-provided insurance plans. As noted earlier in this chapter, only about half of those covered by employer-sponsored plans are offered a choice of plans. Even for those who have a choice, the choices are often relatively limited and difficult to compare. Under most plans, patients can choose their own physician, hospital, and other providers, but they pay a hefty penalty to choose a provider who is not under contract to the insurance plan. As for control over healthcare decisions, this ultimately, or at least theoretically, rests with the patient. However, the patient's insurance plan may refuse to cover certain procedures. In this case, it is not government bureaucrats who make healthcare decisions for them. It is bureaucrats who work for profit-driven insurance companies that make many of the decisions about healthcare payments and procedures (see Illustration 8.1).

ILLUSTRATION 8.1
Too Little, Too Late

The 2009 debate over healthcare reform had many human faces, and one of the more compelling was that of Nataline Sarkisyan, a 17-year-old girl whose liver had failed as a result of complications of a bone marrow transplant to treat leukemia. In December 2007, CIGNA HealthCare initially refused to pay for a liver transplant for Sarkisyan in spite of a request from her doctors to do so. CIGNA claimed that the procedure was not covered since it was experimental in nature. As media pressure intensified, teenagers and nurses rallied outside CIGNA's Philadelphia headquarters to demand that the insurer reverse its decision. On December 21, 2007, the company relented and said that it would "make an exception in this rare and unusual case." Nataline Sarkisyan died just hours after the company announced its agreement to pay for her liver transplant.

Source: Based on various media stories; see, for example, "Family Sues Insurer Who Denied Teen Transplant," MSNBC, December 21, 2007. Retrieved January 2, 2010, from http://www.msnbc.msn.com/id/22357873

Since a single-payer system is an impossibility given the scope and influence of the private insurance system in the United States, many individuals pushed for what has been termed a "robust public option" or choice in the recent healthcare debate (see Illustration 8.2). A public option could take many forms. Medicaid or Medicare could be expanded to include the uninsured by allowing them to buy into these programs. Those deemed unable to afford the premiums in part or in full could be provided government subsidies to pay the premium. Although many have argued that a government-run option would be a fiasco, in truth, Medicare and Medicaid are highly successful programs. Without them, many more Americans would be uninsured.

In addition to a public option, the Obama administration favored insurance "exchanges," a type of marketplace where individuals, families, and small businesses could compare plans offered by private insurance companies as well as a public option and choose a plan that is best for them. Since private insurers have not stepped up to the plate in the past to make a serious dent in covering the millions of Americans without health insurance, one point of view is that a public option might provide the competition needed to help them cover more Americans. Another point of contention in the healthcare debate concerned what has been termed an "individual mandate," i.e., requiring that all Americans obtain health insurance. Many proposals made to Congress included such a mandate. Various arguments were made against it. One is that it would place too great a financial burden on many low-income individuals because they would likely have to shoulder some of the costs of their health insurance premiums. Another argument is that it is simply too much government interference—the government should not have the right to tell people that they have to be insured. In countries that have true national health insurance, the government does not mandate that people obtain health insurance; by virtue of being a citizen or resident, people automatically have coverage. They can choose to use the coverage or not.

PRE-EXISTING CONDITIONS   A second major point in the healthcare debate concerned health insurance practices such as limiting coverage for pre-existing conditions. Insurance is based on pooling risk, i.e., people pay premiums when they don't have a need for the coverage so that they

ILLUSTRATION 8.2
The Battle Over the Public Option

In the 2009–2010 healthcare reform debate, one of the major differences between legislation initially passed by the House and that passed by the Senate was the "robust public option." The House Bill, H.R. 3200, contained provisions for a public option. The original Senate Finance Committee bill had no such option. However, after the bills were reported out of various Senate committees, Majority Leader Harry Reid (D-NV) attempted to insert a public option in his "Leader's Mark" version of the bill.

In the course of negotiations with various Democratic and Independent senators to obtain the necessary votes for the cloture motion to end the filibuster over the proposed legislation, Leader Reid's efforts were stymied by Senator Joe Lieberman (I-CT), who insisted that he would not vote for cloture on any bill that contained a public option. Lieberman represents a state where many health insurance companies are either headquartered or have large corporate centers that employ many of his constituents. Majority Leader Reid initially proposed to back off of the public option in favor of reducing the eligibility age for Medicare to age 55 with a premium buy-in by those wishing to access Medicare between ages 55 and 64. However, Lieberman refused to go along with this proposal as well. In the end, Reid was forced to forgo the public option or any Medicare buy-in option for those under age 65 to secure Lieberman's vote for the bill.

Many progressives saw the loss of the public option in the Senate bill as a major disappointment. In mid-September 2009, Wendell Potter, former Vice President for Communications for CIGNA, one of the largest health insurers in the nation, testified before the House Democratic Steering and Policy Committee. In his opening statement, Potter, now the Senior Fellow on Health Care for the Center for Media and Democracy, told Congress that if it "fails to create a public insurance option to compete with private insurers, the bill it sends to the president might as well be called the Insurance Industry Profit Protection and Enhancement Act."

Although Potter joined many others in expressing disappointment in the Senate bill that was passed at 7:00 a.m. on Christmas Eve, 2009, he stopped short of advocating ultimate defeat of the bill. Instead, he called for reform supporters to "realize that for all its disappointing compromises and flaws, even the Senate-passed bill should be viewed as a foundation that can be built upon in years to come."

Sources: This illustration relies on news reports on CNN.com and MSNBC.com as well as The Huffington Post online edition. Both Wendell Potter quotes are from The Huffington Post. Retrieved January 2, 2010, from http://www.huffingtonpost.com/2009/09/15/wendell-potter-public-opt_n_287733.html and http://www.huffingtonpost.com/wendell-potter/why-im-not-joining-the-ca_b_403176.html, respectively.

can be covered when the need for healthcare arises. For insurance to work, the pool must be protected from those who would take advantage by not paying (or having coverage) until they have an "insurable event." Allowing people to buy health insurance without limitations at any time would be analogous to letting them purchase fire insurance on their home once they actually have a fire in progress. It just doesn't make economic sense.

One way to eliminate pre-existing conditions limitations is by making sure that everyone, including those who think they are too young and healthy to need coverage, participates in the risk pool. This, too, raises the idea of an individual mandate. An individual mandate would help to eliminate the problem of people buying insurance only when they know they are about to have claims. Everyone would share in the costs of the system. Under the current private health insurance system, it would be very difficult, if not impossible, to control premium costs if pre-existing condition limitations were eliminated *unless* an individual mandate is included.

Proponents of healthcare reform emphasized the very sad stories of people who need coverage but can't get it because of pre-existing conditions. They also used the equally sad stories of people who have their insurance cancelled once they have a claim, usually from something called "post-claims underwriting." In post-claims underwriting, an insurer takes money for the coverage; then, when the insured has a claim, the company checks back to see if the insured may have had a pre-existing condition that he or she failed to disclose when the policy was purchased. Used legitimately, post-claims underwriting helps to protect insurers from paying large claims to consumers who fraudulently claimed they did not have a pre-existing condition. Undoubtedly, some insurers may have also abused post-claims underwriting to simply avoid paying out large claims. The extent to which such abuse has occurred, however, has not been well documented beyond anecdotal evidence. Individual mandates would help to eliminate the need for post-claims underwriting.

PRIVILEGE, RIGHT, OR RATIONING?   The third major point of debate is whether access to quality, affordable healthcare ought to be a right or a privilege in the United States. In other developed nations, this matter has long been resolved. Under either socialized medicine or national health insurance, healthcare is a right because everyone is entitled to access. One argument against making healthcare a right or universal entitlement in the United States is that it would lead to rationing of care. This is true, but it is an incomplete picture. Since healthcare is a scarce commodity everywhere, every country, including the United States, rations healthcare in one way or another.

Under socialized healthcare in Britain and national health insurance in Canada, healthcare is rationed in part by time rather than money. Patients may have to wait hours to see a doctor and months to undergo nonemergency surgeries. It is those who are willing and able to wait rather than to pay who are served. There is some dissatisfaction with these systems, and in Great Britain, some private practice by physicians has been permitted for patients willing and able to pay. In the U.S. system, care is rationed by whether one is insured, underinsured, or uninsured; in other words, Americans ration care based on ability to pay. It is very doubtful that any country accustomed to universal healthcare coverage would opt for a system like that in the United States. It is equally doubtful that the United States will ever adopt a system like Britain's. The free enterprise system prevails—physicians, drug companies, other healthcare providers, and insurance companies are powerful enough to resist that much government control. On the other hand, most Americans would likely agree that the country should strive to see that more Americans have continuous, comprehensive health insurance, including vision and dental care (see Illustration 8.3).

The Politics of Healthcare Reform 2009–2010

In November 2008, Democrats regained control of the White House and both houses of Congress for the first time since 1994. Healthcare reform was a major plank in the party's election platform, and for most of 2009, Congress wrestled with a variety of plans and proposals.

Barack Obama was sworn in as the 44th President of the United States on January 20, 2009, in the midst of the worst recession since the Great Depression some 80 years earlier. The financial sector of the economy was on the verge of collapse. General Motors filed bankruptcy soon afterwards. Among the first bills to be passed under the new administration was a $797 billion stimulus package, on the heels of the $700 billion Troubled Asset Relief Program (TARP) that had been passed at the request of Treasury Secretary Henry Paulson in the waning days of the George W.

ILLUSTRATION 8.3
The Uninsured Pay the Price

If health insurance is difficult for some people to get, dental insurance is even more difficult. Even people with "good" private dental insurance are often charged substantial co-payments. And even though Medicaid is supposed to provide children with dental care, it may be difficult to find a dentist who accepts Medicaid due to factors such as low reimbursement rates. Patients may also lack transportation to appointments, especially when the nearest dentist that will see them is far away. In his short life, Deamonte Driver did not have regular dental care. While his mother was trying to get dental care for his brother who had several rotted teeth, Deamonte had an abscessed tooth that developed into a brain infection. The family's Medicaid coverage had expired, perhaps because paperwork had been sent to a homeless shelter where they were no longer staying. Deamonte's mother took him to a hospital. Soon after, he had brain surgery. Although Deamonte was making progress at first, he died a tragic death that may have been prevented with a simple tooth extraction.

Source: Based on various media stories, see especially, Mary Otto, "For Want of a Dentist," *The Washington Post,*" February 28, 2007. Retrieved January 31, 2010, from http://www.washingtonpost.com/wp-dyn/content/article/2007/02/27/AR2007022702116.html

---

Bush administration. In spite of the overwhelming economic problems he confronted, or perhaps because of them, President Obama made clear his desire to move forward on a plan for national healthcare reform.

Unlike President Clinton, President Obama had no intention of writing the healthcare reform legislation himself. Clinton has since revealed that he wanted Congress to write the legislation in 1993, but then-Chairman of the House Ways and Means Committee Dan Rostenkowski (D-IL) convinced Clinton that his administration should prepare the legislation and then let Congress negotiate it.[73] Obama apparently realized the futility of such an approach and encouraged Congress to bring him a bill to sign by the summer of 2009.

Neither the House nor the Senate met the President's summer deadline. As committees wrestled with multiple versions of the bill, the opposition was marshalling its forces. To say that emotions ran high during the healthcare reform debate would be an understatement. Conservative radio and television personalities joined forces with conservative lawmakers and others to promote a series of events, beginning in spring 2009, to protest stimulus spending and the healthcare reform package. These events, called "tea parties" by their organizers (after the American colonists' Boston tea party waged to protest "taxation without representation"), drew significant crowds in what was portrayed as a grassroots movement. Nobel prize–winning economist and syndicated columnist Paul Krugman called them:

> AstroTurf (fake grass roots) events, manufactured by the usual suspects. In particular, a key role [was] played by FreedomWorks, an organization run by Richard Armey, the former House majority leader, and supported by the usual group of right-wing billionaires . . . and being promoted heavily by Fox News.[74]

As the long summer of 2009 wore on without a bill, Senators and Congress members headed home for the summer recess, a time when the nation's legislators return home to raise campaign funds, tend the home fires, and, in most cases, hold town hall meetings to discuss issues with their constituents. For many of them, mostly Democrats, these town hall meetings turned into shouting matches and occasional physical scuffles as anger erupted over healthcare reform. At an event in Lebanon, Pennsylvania, hosted by Democratic Senator Arlen Specter (formerly a Republican who switched parties in 2009), shouting led to shoving. Senator Claire McCaskill (D-MO) was repeatedly shouted down at a forum she hosted in her home state of Missouri. Representative David Scott (D-GA), who is black, received letters that contained "N-word" references against him and that referred to President Obama as a Marxist. A sign outside Representative Scott's office was painted with a swastika as civil discourse became increasingly less civil.[75]

Congress had just returned from the summer recess when President Obama delivered a speech on healthcare to a joint session of the Congress on September 9, 2009, outlining broad concepts for what he hoped to achieve in healthcare reform. The President apparently touched a sensitive point when he stated that the legislation would not include free healthcare for illegal immigrants, at which point Representative Joe Wilson (R-SC) stunned everyone when he shouted, "You lie!" at the President. Wilson issued an apology for the outburst, though not for the sentiment of it.[76] Leaders from both parties denounced the Wilson outburst, but Wilson added more than $700,000 to his campaign war chest within 48 hours of the outburst.[77]

Both the House of Representatives and the Senate set about drafting their versions of legislation. The House version included a robust public option, defined as a government-run plan that would not be required to produce a profit and that would offer coverage primarily to those who were not otherwise covered. This much-discussed public option would have been paid for by cuts in Medicare spending combined with an income surtax on individuals making more than $500,000 per year or married couples making more than $1 million per year. The Senate version would have been financed with a combination of Medicare cuts and a 40 percent tax on so-called "Cadillac" health plans—plans that mostly cover union members who have negotiated better benefits in lieu of larger salary increases.

In the Senate, five different committees had jurisdiction over the bill that emerged. It was primarily the Senate Finance Committee, in consultation with Senate Majority Leader Harry Reid (D-NV), that made most of the decisions about what was presented on the Senate floor. The Finance Committee, chaired by Senator Max Baucus (D-MT), initiated its work by hearing from some 45 witnesses who gave expert testimony regarding their recommendations for the format the reform should take. Progressive and liberal members of the Democratic Party who supported a single-payer plan, one in which the federal government would act as the insurer for all Americans, were dismayed that not a single witness was called to support such an option. Baucus had made it clear that a single-payer plan was "off the table."

The U.S. Senate has often been referred to as "the most deliberative body in the world." Senate rules concerning filibusters have made it even more deliberative in recent times. Any senator can filibuster a bill, that is, "talk it to death." In order to invoke cloture—end the debate—a "supermajority" of three-fifths of the Senate (60 members) must vote in favor of the cloture motion.

On November 21, 2009, the Senate voted 60–39 to open full debate on the healthcare legislation.[78] Over the next month, Majority Leader Reid negotiated with numerous senators in an effort to reach the 60 votes needed to invoke cloture. In the 111th Congress, the 58 Democratic senators plus the two Independents, who caucus with the Democrats, were needed to provide the necessary 60 votes. Since the Republicans were able to maintain complete solidarity in the voting process, Reid had to ensure that every member of his caucus would vote for cloture or the bill would die in filibuster.

One point of contention during the healthcare debate was that Congress had to grapple with bills in excess of 1,000 pages written in technical, or even obtuse, language in very short timeframes. There were many complaints that Democrats were trying to ram legislation through without sufficient time for consideration of provisions that could radically change the face of healthcare and cost hundreds of billions of dollars.

The last senator to come on board for the cloture motion was Ben Nelson (D-NE), a so-called "Blue Dog" or fiscally conservative Democrat. Nelson, a strong supporter of the pro-life movement, insisted that the bill contain language that would restrict any use of federal funds to pay for an abortion, particularly under the "insurance exchanges" that would be established through private for-profit corporations but partially funded by federal subsidies for those who qualify on the basis of income. The end result of the negotiations between Majority Leader Reid and Senator Nelson is that women who are covered under the exchange and wish to have coverage for abortions will have to write two separate checks each month—one to cover their part of the regular premium and one for a separate rider to cover abortion. In addition to the abortion language in the bill, Nelson also secured an amendment (referred to derisively as the "Cornhusker Kickback") that would have exempted Nebraska from having to pay its share of the increased Medicaid costs called for under the bill, while other states would have to begin paying their share of those costs in 2016.[79] In the end, the Cornhusker Kickback was eliminated.

At 1:00 a.m. on December 21, 2009, the Senate voted 60 to 40, on a strictly partisan basis, to end debate, setting the stage for a Christmas Eve vote to pass the Senate version of the bill. On the afternoon of December 21, Majority Leader Reid and Finance Committee Chairman Baucus held a press conference. Also present was Dr. Cecil Wilson, an internist from Winter Park, Florida, and the President-elect of the American Medical Association (AMA). Expressing the AMA's support for the Senate bill, Dr. Wilson said:

> America has the best health care in the world, if you can get it. But, for far too many people, access to care is out of reach because they lack insurance, and this is just not acceptable to physicians who provide high quality care in an often-fragmented system that doesn't work for them or their patients.[80]

On December 24, 2009, the Senate approved its $871 billion bill—the Patient Protection and Affordable Care Act. The vote was again strictly partisan—58 Democrats and two Independents voted for approval; 39 Republicans voted against it.

Normally, a conference committee composed of both House and Senate members would try to reach consensus on a final bill and report it out in a Conference Report. House and Senate Democratic leaders, along with the White House, were concerned that Senate Republicans would filibuster the bill required to name the Senate's conferees to the committee. In view of that concern, they began meeting behind closed doors in December 2009, and early January 2010, to try to craft a compromise bill that could be brought to the floor of both houses and carry all the votes in the Senate Democratic caucus to defeat a Republican filibuster. Keeping the Democratic caucus together is no small task. Senators Nelson and Lieberman both said that they would vote to block the bill if provisions for which they fought were changed substantially. Progressive Democrats in the House of Representatives, meanwhile, struggled over the public option and the original abortion language to prohibit using federal funds to directly pay for abortions but allow insurance policies subsidized with government funds to offer abortion coverage.

While Democratic leaders were wrangling over this, a special election was taking place in Massachusetts to fill the seat left vacant following the death of Senator Edward Kennedy (D-MA) in August 2009. Kennedy, Congress's most ardent supporter of universal healthcare, was elected to Congress in 1962 and served more than 46 years. In a stunning blow for the Democrats, their stronghold was broken when State Representative Scott Brown, the Republican candidate, defeated Massachusetts Attorney General Martha Coakley, the Democratic candidate, for the seat. Brown, who campaigned against healthcare reform, became the forty-first vote that Republicans would need to sustain a filibuster of any bill in the Senate.[81]

Many, if not most, political analysts considered Brown's election to be the death knell for President Obama's attempt at healthcare reform. Immediately after Brown's election, there were calls for Democrats to rush a vote before Brown could be seated. President Obama advised against such an action. Others proposed that the House of Representatives simply pass the Senate's bill. While constitutionally possible, House Speaker Nancy Pelosi (D-CA) indicated she did not have the votes to pass the Senate's version without amendment.[82] Short of being able to persuade at least one Republican senator to vote to end the filibuster, the only remaining avenue seemed to be including the final negotiated bill in a "reconciliation" bill. Under Senate rules, reconciliation bills cannot be filibustered. Following a period of debate, they are guaranteed a vote. If this option were utilized, only 51 votes would be required to pass the bill. Ironically, Bill Clinton wanted to use the reconciliation process to pass healthcare reform in 1993. At that time, he was blocked from doing so by then-Majority Leader Robert Byrd (D-WV), who argued that healthcare was far too complex and far-reaching an issue to cut short debate in a reconciliation process. First Lady Hillary Rodham Clinton, who headed the Clinton task force, found herself agreeing with Senator Byrd later, although she was disappointed at the time.[83]

On March 21, 2010, following nearly 12 hours of floor debate, the House of Representatives passed the Senate's healthcare reform bill by a vote of 219–212. Every one of the 178 Republicans and 34 of the 253 Democratic Congress members voted against the bill. The House then voted on a separate reconciliation bill to amend the Senate bill. The reconciliation bill sought to reconcile differences between the Senate bill, now passed by the House, and the original House bill. This reconciliation bill then went back to the Senate, where it could be passed by a simple majority vote, since reconciliation bills are not subject to filibuster. Four days later, the Senate passed the reconciliation bill.

Neither the original Senate bill nor the reconciliation bill contains a public option for health insurance. In spite of this, the bills represent a major step towards insuring all Americans. Of the 46 million currently uninsured, the Congressional Budget Office (CBO) projects that 32 million will be insured under the new law by 2019. This means that 94 percent of nonelderly American citizens and other legal residents would have health insurance coverage compared to approximately 83 percent at present.[84] The bill also ended the denial of coverage on the basis of a preexisting condition for children six months after enactment and for anyone starting in 2014. Children are permitted to stay on their parent's insurance plans until age 26 under the new law.

Medicare beneficiaries will see the "doughnut hole" in the Medicare Part D Prescription Drug Plan closed by 2020. Seniors hitting the doughnut hole in 2010 will receive a $250 rebate, and beginning in 2011, those in the gap will receive a 50 percent discount on prescription drugs. However, the law also includes $500 billion in Medicare cuts between 2010 and 2020.

Medicaid is expanded under the new law to cover persons with incomes up to 133 percent of the federal poverty line. The new law also requires states to begin covering childless adults who are otherwise eligible for Medicaid by 2014. The federal government will pay 100 percent of costs for newly eligible insured persons through 2016.

The law establishes a mandate for most U.S. residents to carry health insurance by 2014. Those who are uninsured or self-employed would be permitted to purchase insurance through state-based exchanges. The premiums will be subsidized for individuals and families with income between 133 percent and 400 percent of the federal poverty line. Starting in 2014, separate exchanges will be created for small businesses to purchase coverage for their employees. The federal government will provide funding to the states for the establishment of the exchanges within one year of enactment and until January 1, 2015.[85]

The CBO estimates that the new law will *reduce* the federal deficit by $143 billion between 2010 and 2019, not increase it as critics had claimed. Projections beyond the 10-year window are much more difficult and the CBO rarely makes them. However, the CBO indicated that the effects of the law will be an additional reduction in the federal deficit of between one-quarter and one-half percent of gross domestic product over the second decade (2020–2029).[86]

The bills contain many insurance reforms—an individual mandate, subsidies for purchase of health insurance for the working poor, and establishment of insurance exchanges to allow the consolidation of purchasing power among small employers. In spite of these significant steps, many progressives remain disappointed that the bill does not provide universal healthcare for all Americans.

MEANWHILE, BACK AT THE STATES

Given that no national health insurance plan has yet emerged in the United States, the problem of how to insure those not covered by an employer, Medicaid, Medicare, or other plans has fallen mostly to state governments. States have tried various means such as insurance pools to help people gain access to lower-cost plans or employer mandates to cover employees. Today, Massachusetts is being hailed as the state most successful in covering its population. It has used a combination of Medicaid, private insurance plans, and an individual mandate to see that more of its residents are covered. In 2008, more than 94 percent of Massachusetts' residents were covered by health insurance, making Massachusetts the state with the lowest percentage of its population uninsured. Texas, by contrast, has the highest percentage of its residents uninsured at just over 25 percent one in every four.[87] Other states have also made efforts to increase the number of insured residents, most notably Tennessee, Oregon, and Maine.

In the wake of the recently signed healthcare reform bills, states are scrambling to meet their new obligations, while many of them are also applying pressure for repeal of some or all of the new provisions. Twenty-one states have filed or joined in a health care repeal lawsuit, and thirty have filed health care repeal legislation.[88]

Until the lawsuits and repeal measures are concluded, states will still have to devote resources to the creation of state exchanges where persons who are not covered by an employer can purchase insurance. These exchanges are to be established by 2014, and if a state declines to open an exchange, the federal government can open one in that state.[89] The new laws also provide $5 billion to the states for implementing or expanding high-risk pools for those who cannot obtain health insurance. As of mid-May 2010, 28 states and the District of Columbia had already done so. Nineteen states chose to have the federal government handle the high risk pool for them, and three states had not yet decided which course to take.[90]

HEALTHCARE: MORE ETHICAL DILEMMAS

In addition to seeing that all Americans have a source of health insurance, there are many other ethical issues to consider in the health arena from issues of health insurance portability and medical information privacy to stem cell research and cloning.

Portability and Privacy

Under the Consolidated Budget and Reconciliation Act (COBRA) of 1986, many employees who lose their jobs have been able to continue their group health insurance coverage if they can afford to pay the premiums. The Health Insurance Portability and Accountability Act (HIPAA) of 1996 also provides opportunities for enrolling in group plans when changing jobs or in the case of life events such as marriage, divorce, or the birth of child. HIPAA also limits new employers' ability to exclude coverage for pre-existing conditions. The law also prohibits discrimination against employees or their dependents based on health factors and guarantees that certain individuals have access to, and can renew, individual health insurance policies. Some states have laws that are more generous than HIPAA, but HIPAA provisions are the minimum requirements for the nation. The health insurance reform bills of 2010 eliminate pre-existing condition limitations, but they do not take effect for adults until 2014.

HIPAA addresses healthcare privacy as well as insurance portability. Most people would probably prefer that their medical history be treated confidentially. The U.S. Department of Health and Human Service website describes HIPAA as the first federal standards to provide a uniform floor of privacy protections for patients' medical records.[91] If you have received health-care services or had a prescription filled since April 14, 2003, you have undoubtedly been asked to sign a HIPAA notice. But the law has as much to do with letting patients know how their medical information will be released to other parties (primarily to "coordinate," "manage," or seek reimbursement for treatment) as it does in protecting privacy.[92]

As healthcare reform progresses, many are calling for standardization of medical records in electronic format. The benefits of such a change include reduction in administrative costs, ease of sharing information between providers, and potentially better outcomes as providers can be aware of a patient's entire medical history through the electronic medical record. In the era of the Internet, however, we also know that electronic data can be compromised by those wishing to utilize the data for purposes neither intended, nor approved of, by the owners of those records. Patient medical record privacy will be an important concern in developing any such electronic system. In the face of changing technology, HIPAA regulations must be continuously updated.

Healthcare Rationing

As seen in the country's 2009–2010 healthcare debate, bioethical dilemmas like healthcare rationing are also social welfare concerns. Since there are limits to the amount of healthcare that can be provided, what factors should be considered in rationing? For example, should we forgo life support for the very old in favor of more preventive healthcare for children? This is an extremely difficult question, and there is no consensus on how healthcare procedures should be ranked or rationed. In fact, some people insist that spending 16 percent or more of the country's GDP on healthcare should not be an issue at all; the country should avoid rationing services. But healthcare is rationed by a number of factors—whether an individual has third-party coverage or can otherwise afford care; whether those who are ill present themselves for treatment; and whether the medical community treats indigent patients rather than refusing to treat or "dumping" them. In other situations, desperate parents have tried to influence rationing decisions by using television to plead for a transplant donor for their terminally ill child when they felt that existing networks were not responding quickly enough. Without a substantial amount of money up front, transplants are out of reach for many patients. Some Medicaid programs no longer pay for transplants.

Costs are not the only basis on which rationing must be considered. Sheer availability of resources is likely to become even more of a challenge in the years ahead, particularly as more people acquire health insurance and as people continue to live longer. Limited numbers of general practitioners, barriers to establishing new hospitals or expanding existing hospitals, and limited availability of laboratory facilities, especially those requiring large financial investments (such as magnetic resonance imaging machines) all could add to the need to ration care as the country both grows and ages.

Futile Care

None of us wants to think that we might be in a situation in which we would be unable to make decisions about our own medical care. That is why Americans are urged to have advance directives to clarify their wishes. But even individuals with advance directives cannot be assured that their medical wishes will be carried out. Family members, medical professionals, or the courts might disagree about the intent of those wishes, or they may disagree on what, if anything, should be done. An issue in point is "futile care policies" or "futile care theory" where hospitals reserve the right to refuse treatment to individuals who are terminally ill or in persistent vegetative states, even over their objection or their family's. The topic of what constitutes futile care is widely discussed in the medical literature. Apparently, "physicians do not have a responsibility to provide futile care even if a patient or surrogate insists on it."[93] Critics contend that decisions to stop treatment, despite the objections of patients and their families, are motivated by the high costs of providing such care.[94] These decisions raise even more suspicions under managed care.[95] Most hospitals have an ethics committee that often includes community members such as clergy to help address the difficult decisions that patients, family members, and hospital staff face.[96] Medical personnel must also uphold their own codes of ethics and obey state and federal laws. The AMA's Council on Ethical and Judicial Affairs recommends a process for addressing futile care cases, but it also recognizes that "the patient or proxy and the physician [may] have discrepant values or goals of care" and that "universal consensus on futile care is unlikely to be achieved."[97]

Futile care was raised in the 2009 healthcare reform debate in the form of so-called "death panels." Former Alaska Governor Sarah Palin, John McCain's vice-presidential running mate on the failed 2008 Republican ticket, charged (on twitter.com) that the House bill contained a provision for "death panels" to decide whether grandma lives or dies. In reality, the bill's provision, which was inserted by Republicans, called for Medicare to pay for a consultation with a patient's physician regarding end-of-life medical directives. In the end, Democrats removed the language from the bill rather than face down the resulting anger.

Euthanasia and Assisted Suicide

Those who believe in the individual's right to determine when life should end point to the Netherlands, which allows physicians to help patients with voluntary, active euthanasia in which the physician administers or prescribes drugs to promote death.[98] Active euthanasia was technically illegal but was practiced in the Netherlands for some time and seldom resulted in serious legal repercussions if the physician followed guidelines developed as a result of judicial decisions made in the 1970s. For example, the patient must make the request, the physician must have known the patient previously, and the physician is not compelled to honor the request. The Dutch parliament was deeply divided on the morality of the issue, but in 1993 it supported the practice, and in 2001, the parliament legalized it, making it the world's most liberal euthanasia policy.[99] Those opposed to the law believe that condoning the practice promotes the idea of social Darwinism (survival of the fittest) and could be used inappropriately.

In the United States, the Oregon legislature passed a law in 1994 that allowed doctors to assist patients with lethal doses of medication. The law requires that an individual be mentally competent, have less than six months to live, make a written request that is witnessed, drink a cocktail of drugs rather than be administered an injection, and wait 15 days to be given the cocktail. Two physicians must concur, and a physician must discuss alternatives with the patient. In 1995, a federal judge ruled the law unconstitutional to prevent error, abuse, and discrimination.

In 1996, the Ninth Circuit Court of Appeals overturned a Washington state law making it a felony to assist in a person's death by ruling that a mentally competent person who is terminally ill has a constitutional right to commit suicide with a doctor's help. In 1996 a federal appeals court found New York's law against physician-assisted suicide unconstitutionally discriminatory. Unlike the Washington decision, it did not find a constitutional right to assisted suicide based on the Fourteenth Amendment's guarantees of liberty and privacy. Instead, it said that while those on life support can hasten death by turning off machines that sustain their life, others in terminal situations have no such recourse, thus violating the Constitution's equal protection clause.

The U.S. Supreme Court agreed to hear appeals of the Washington and New York cases, a surprising move in that the high court had usually tried to avoid the issue. In June 1997, it concluded that there is no constitutional right to physician-assisted suicide. The ruling allows states to ban physician-assisted suicides but does not stop states from allowing them in narrowly defined cases. The high court refused to hear an appeal of the Oregon law, but in November 1997, the issue was again put to Oregon voters. By a 20 percent margin, Oregonians affirmed approval of access to physician-assisted suicide.

In 2008, in a state ballot initiative, Washington voters approved the use of physician assisted suicide, similar to Oregon's Death with Dignity Act. On December 31, 2009, the Montana Supreme Court upheld physician-assisted suicide in that state, making it the third state to allow such practices.[100] This is likely not the end of the discussion in Montana. The decision may be challenged in the state legislature or a voter referendum.

Retired pathologist Dr. Jack Kevorkian devoted himself to assisting in suicides of ill individuals (or at least in helping them end their suffering). Kevorkian was prosecuted in a few of these cases and acquitted each time. A Michigan ban on assisted suicide and an attempt to invoke unwritten common law failed to stop him. Neither did the time he spent in jail. In late 1998, Kevorkian was charged and later convicted after a tape he provided to the TV show *60 Minutes* showed him administering a lethal injection of potassium chloride to a man with Lou Gehrig's disease. He served eight years of a 10-to-25 year prison sentence before being released on parole for good behavior on June 1, 2006. Kevorkian's parole was conditioned on his agreement to refrain from participating in any future suicides.[101]

Compassion and Choices (formerly the Hemlock Society), an organization interested in "the freedom to choose a dignified death and for individual control concerning death," states that it "support[s] the right of terminally ill, mentally competent adults to hasten death under careful safeguards."[102] On the other side of the issue, the National Right to Life Committee works to block efforts that support the right to choose death. Physician-assisted death has been likened to the issue of abortion, not only on constitutional grounds, but also because of the groups (like anti-abortion, "right to life" organizations) that have rallied around the issue and the fervor with which they have pursued their positions. Ethical, moral, and legal questions have been raised. Among them is the issue of discrimination. Many refer to it as a slippery slope bound to go further than most intend. For example, some fear that assisted suicide laws may turn into a duty to die, because in the United States a terminal illness, as well as a chronic, long-term illness, can bankrupt a family (unlike other countries where national health insurance protects families from financial disaster due to medical conditions). Another concern is that assisted suicide devalues the lives of people with severe disabilities. Still another concern is cases in which patients' requests to end their lives may be due to inadequate medical attention such as lack of sufficient pain medication and other palliative care that can ease suffering. In this case, the answer may lie in better education of medical professionals to treat such cases. Others contend that doctors fear repercussions for prescribing sufficient doses of potentially addictive pain-relieving narcotic medications.

The Assisted Suicide Funding Restriction Act of 1997 expressed the opinion of Congress and President Clinton by making it illegal to use federal funds to support physician-assisted suicide. The two largest physician organizations in the United States, the American Medical Association (AMA) and the American College of Physicians, also oppose physician-assisted suicide.

Stem Cell Research and Cloning

As medical science advances further, the list of bioethical concerns grows. Stem cell research holds promise for curing many illnesses like Alzheimer's disease, to which President Reagan and many others have succumbed, and offers hope to repair spinal cord injuries like the one that left actor Christopher Reeve paralyzed. Some people support stem cell research but draw the line at the use of embryonic stem cell research, which they believe denigrates the sanctity of human life. Another issue is cloning. Now that animals have been cloned, human cloning cannot be far behind, and that thought is especially disturbing.

Summary

Many of the leading causes of death for those in all income brackets are related to heredity and lifestyle rather than lack of medical care. The United States spends more for healthcare than other industrialized nations, yet fewer Americans have health insurance, and U.S. adult and infant mortality rates exceed those of most of these countries. Black, Hispanic, Native Americans, and poor Americans continue to experience disparities in health insurance coverage and in many health outcomes. By branding them as "socialized medicine," opponents delayed major federal healthcare proposals for 50 years before Medicaid and Medicare were adopted to provide healthcare to poor and older Americans, respectively.

Given the expansion of public and private health insurance, healthcare makes up an increasing amount of the country's gross domestic product. Rapidly growing medical technology also adds to health care costs. Health maintenance organizations and other managed care arrangements are attempts at keeping healthcare costs under control.

With millions of Americans still uninsured, President Clinton wanted to create a national healthcare program to ensure that all Americans have continuous healthcare coverage, but his plan was defeated. Healthcare reform recaptured the attention of the nation following President Barack Obama's 2008 election. It was a major plank in the 2008 Democratic Party platform. A summer of political turmoil and civil unrest failed to derail the 2009 reform effort, and Democrats were able to unilaterally pass healthcare reform in March 2010. Projections are that when fully in effect, 96 percent of Americans will have health insurance.

Healthcare ethics issues abound. Technology has raised issues about healthcare privacy. It has also challenged us to consider how to extend life, but this opens the door to debates about who should have the right to decide when life-saving practices should be terminated or when they should be extended.

Discussion Questions and Class Activities

1. What percent of your state's population is currently uninsured and how does this figure compare with the rest of the country? Identify factors that affect the rate of uninsured individuals in your state. Invite health experts from the public sector, such as an employee of the state's Medicaid program, and/or a representative of private health insurance companies to discuss issues in seeing that all persons in the state have health insurance. What methods has your state used to try to see that more people have health insurance? How does the state intend to implement the new federal healthcare legislation passed in 2010. Has your state challenged the new laws?

2. Have a class discussion about including a "robust public option" in national healthcare reform. What is your perspective about the reliance that should be placed on government and private health insurers to help the many Americans who do not have health insurance? You may also wish to debate whether the country should adopt a universal, single-payer healthcare system that would cover all Americans and be run by the federal government. Among the issues to consider is whether access to healthcare should be considered a right or a privilege.

3. Healthcare is a limited resource. How would you go about rationing this resource? How would you go about rationing this resource even if everyone has health insurance? How would your plan differ from what Americans currently do to ration care? In what ways is it better than the current system? Invite an economist to discuss the effects of various modes of rationing resources.

4. Invite an individual who serves on a hospital committee that considers futile care cases to discuss the types of cases they address, the dilemmas they pose, and how the committee goes about its work.

5. Divide the class into groups and have each group investigate an ethical dilemma in healthcare such as stem cell research, cloning, genetic testing, or assisted suicide. Have each group make a presentation on the issues that have been raised on all sides of these topics. Or have a medical ethicist come to class to discuss these issues.

Websites

Centers for Disease Control and Prevention, http://www.cdc.gov, provide individuals and communities the information and tools they need to protect their health "through health promotion, prevention of disease, injury and disability, and preparedness for new health threats."

Centers for Medicare and Medicaid Services, http://www.cms.hhs.gov, provide federal administration of the Medicare and Medicaid programs and extensive information about these major publicly supported health insurance programs in the United States.

National Institutes of Health (NIH), http://www.nih.gov, composed of 27 institutes and centers, is part of the U.S. Department of Health and Human Services. NIH is the main federal agency that conducts and supports medical research to prevent disease and identify the causes, treatments, and cures for common and rare diseases.

The Henry J. Kaiser Family Foundation, http://www.kff.org, provides reports, graphs, PowerPoint slides, and a host of other tools to help people better understand topics such as healthcare reform, Medicaid/SCHIP, Medicare, employer-based insurance, prescription drugs insurance, state policies on health, minority healthcare, and women's health policy.

Notes

1. For an extensive consideration of the history of healthcare, including health insurance, see Paul Starr, *The Social Transformation of American Medicine* (New York: Basic Books, 1982).

2. Although this point may seem arguable, the research literature is extensive. See, for example, Victor R. Fuchs, *Who Shall Live? Health, Economics, and Social Choice* (New York: Basic Books, 1974); Victor R. Fuchs, "The Clinton Plan: A Researcher Examines Reform," *Health Affairs,* Vol. 13, No. 1, Spring I, 1994, pp. 102–114; Nathan Glazer, "Paradoxes of Healthcare," *Public Interest,* No. 22, Winter 1971, pp. 62–77; Leon R. Kass, "Regarding the End of Medicine and the Pursuit of Health," *Public Interest,* No. 40, Summer 1975, pp. 11–42; John B. McKinlay and Sonja M. McKinlay, "Medical Measures and the Decline of Mortality," in Peter Conrad and Rochelle Kern, Eds., *The Sociology of Health and Illness: Critical Perspectives* (New York: St. Martin's Press, 1994), pp. 10–23.

3. Committee on Ways and Means, *2004 Green Book* (Washington, DC: U.S. House of Representatives, 2004), Appendix B, p. B-2. Retrieved May 23, 2010, from http://waysandmeans.house.gov/singlepages.aspx?NewsID=10489; see also Robert Sapolsky, "How the Other Half Heals," *Discover,* April 1998, pp. 46, 50–52.

4. "Eliminating Racial and Ethnic Health Disparities: A Business Case Update for Employers" (Washington DC: National Business Group on Health, Center for Prevention and Health Services Issue Brief, February 2009). Retrieved January 2, 2010, from http://www.businessgrouphealth.org/pdfs/Final%20Draft%20508.pdf

5. Most of this paragraph relies on T. J. Mathews and Marian F. McDorman, "Infant Mortality Statistics from the 2004 Period Linked Birth/Infant Death Data Set," *National Vital Statistics Reports,* Vol. 55, No. 14, June 13, 2007. Retrieved December 24, 2009, from http://www.cdc.gov/nchs/data/nvsr/nvsr55/nvsr55_14.pdf; Marian F. McDorman and T. J. Mathews, "Recent Trends in Infant Mortality in the United States" (Atlanta: Centers for Disease Control and Prevention, October 2008). Retrieved December 24, 2009, from http://www.cdc.gov/nchs/data/databriefs/db09.htm

6. Kyriakos S. Markides and Jeannine Coreil, "The Health of Hispanics in the Southwestern United States: An Epidemiologic Paradox," *Public Health Reports,* Vol. 101, No. 3, 1986, pp. 253–265.

7. U.S. Census Bureau, Statistical Abstract of the United States: 2010 (Washington, DC: U.S. Government Printing Office, 2009), Table 160. Retrieved December 19, 2009, from http://www.census.gov/compendia/statab/cats/health_nutrition/health_care_utilization.html

8. Jiaquan Xu, Kenneth Kochanek, and Betzaida Tejada-Vera. "Deaths: Preliminary Data for 2007" *National Vital Statistics Reports,* Vol 58, No. 1, 2009. Retrieved December 30, 2009, from http://www.cdc.gov/nchs/data/nvsr/nvsr58/nvsr58_01.pdf

9. "Key Health and Health Care Indicators by Race/Ethnicity and State," publication #7633-02 (Menlo Park, CA: The Henry J. Kaiser Family Foundation, 2009). Retrieved January 1, 2010, from http://www.kff.org/minorityhealth/upload/7633-02.pdf

10. "State Health Facts for 2006" (Menlo Park, CA: The Henry J. Kaiser Family Foundation). Retrieved January 1, 2010, from http://www.statehealthfacts.org

11. "Healthy People 2010, What Are Its Goals?" (Washington, DC: U.S. Department of Health and Human Services), Retrieved May 23, 2010, from http://www.healthypeople.gov/About/goals.htm

12. Mike Stobbe. "CDC: Nation failing to meet most 2010 health targets; getting worse on obesity, blood pressure," *Chicago Tribune,* December 31, 2009. Retrieved January 2, 2010, from http://www.chicagotribune.com/health/sns-ap-us-med-healthy-people,0,3405888.story

13. "Healthy People 2020 Public Meetings: 2009 Draft Objectives" (Washington, DC: U.S. Department of Health and Human Services), Retrieved January 1, 2010, from http://www.healthypeople.gov/hp2020/Objectives/files/Draft2009Objectives.pdf

14. Figures are from Carmen DeNavas-Walt, Bernadette D. Proctor, and Jessica C. Smith, *Income, Poverty, and Health Insurance Coverage in the United States: 2008,* U.S. Census Bureau, Current Population Reports, P60-236 (Washington, DC: U.S. Government Printing Office, 2009). Retrieved December 19, 2009, from http://www.census.gov/prod/2009pubs/p60-236.pdf. These percentages add up to more than 100 percent because about 10 percent of people have multiple sources of insurance coverage (e.g., covered by Veterans Affairs benefits in addition to employer-provided coverage).

15. "Concentration of Health Care Spending in the U.S. Population, 2006" (Menlo Park, CA: The Henry J.

Kaiser Family Foundation); calculations are based on data from U.S. Department of Health and Human Services, Agency for Healthcare Research and Quality, Medical Expenditure Panel Survey (MEPS), 2006. Retrieved December 19, 2009, from http://facts.kff.org/chart.aspx?ch=822

16. Richard Johnson and Corina Mommaerts, "Are Health Care Costs a Burden for Older Americans?", Brief Series, No. 26 (Washington, DC: Urban Institute, July 2009). Retrieved December 30, 2009, from http://www.urban.org/publications/411924 .html

17. Fidelity Investment, Fidelity Facts. Retrieved December 30, 2009, from http://personal.fidelity.com/myfidelity/ InsideFidelity/NewsCenter/quickFacts/quickFacts .shtml.cvsr

18. "2009 Annual Report of The Boards of Trustees of the Federal Hospital Insurance and Federal Supplementary Medical Insurance Trust Funds" (Washington, DC: Centers for Medicare and Medicaid Services, 2009). Retrieved May 11, 2009, from http://www.cms.hhs.gov

19. "CMS Announces Medicare Premiums, Deductibles for 2009," press release of September 19, 2008, Centers for Medicare and Medicaid Services, Office of Public Affairs. Retrieved December 19, 2009, from http://www.cms.hhs.gov

20. Brian Biles, Lauren Hersch Nicolas, Barbara S. Cooper, Emily Adrion, and Stuart Guterman, "The Cost of Privatization: Extra Payments to Medicare Advantage Plans–Updated and Revised," Issue Brief (New York: Commonwealth Fund, November 2006). Retrieved July 20, 2008, from http://www .commonwealthfund.org/usr_doc/Biles_costprivatiz ationextrapayMAplans_970_ib.pdf?section=4039

21. Brian Biles, Emily Adrion, and Stuart Guterman, "Issue Brief: Medicare Advantage's Private Fee-for Service Plans: Paying for Coordinated Care Without the Coordination" (New York: The Commonwealth Fund, October 2008). Retrieved December 19, 2009, from http://www.commonwealthfund.org/~/media/Files/ Publications/Issue%20Brief/2008/Oct/Medicare%20 Advantages%20Private%20Fee%20for%20Service%20 Plans%20%20Paying%20for%20Coordinated%20 Care%20Without%20the%20Coordinat/Biles_ MedicareAdvantageprivatefeeforserviceplans_ib%2 0pdf.pdf

22. David H. Johnson, *A Structure by No Means Complete: A Comparison of the Path and Processes Surrounding Successful Passage of Medicare and Medicaid under Lyndon Baines Johnson and the Failure to Pass National Health Care Reform under William Jefferson Clinton.* Dissertation. The University of Texas at Austin, 2009.

23. "Explaining Health Care Reform: Key Changes to the Medicare Part D Drug Benefit Coverage Gap" (Menlo Park, CA: The Henry J. Kaiser Family Foundation, March, 2010). Retrieved May 12, 2010, from http://www.kff.org/healthreform/upload/8059 .pdf/

24. A. Tumlinson and S. Woods, "Long-Term Care in America: An Introduction" (Washington, DC: Avalere Health LLC for the National Commission for Quality Long-Term Care, 2007). Retrieved November 30, 2009, from http://www.qualitylongtermcarecom- mission.org/pdf/ltc_america_introduction.pdf

25. "Guide to Choosing a Nursing Home" (Washington, DC: Centers for Medicare and Medicaid Services, November 2008). Retrieved May 13, 2009, from http://www.medicare.gov/Publications/Pubs/pdf/ 02174.pdf

26. Much of this information on long-term care insur- ance relies on Committee on Ways and Means, *2004 Green Book*, Appendix B, pp. B-40–B-44.

27. "America's Health Insurance Plans Guide to Long-Term Care Insurance" (Washington, DC: America's Health Insurance Plans, 2004). Retrieved December 30, 2009, from http://www.ahip.org/content/default.aspx? docid=21018

28. "Health, United States, 2008" (Atlanta, GA: Centers for Disease Control, 2009). Retrieved November 27, 2009, from http://www.cdc.gov/nchs/data/hus/ hus08.pdf

29. The remainder of this paragraph relies on William G. Weissert, Cynthia Matthews Cready, and James E. Pawelak, "The Past and Future of Home- and Community-Based Long-Term Care," *Milbank Quarterly*, Vol. 66, No. 2, 1988, pp. 309–386.

30. For information on alternative living and care arrangements, see the websites of the AARP (http:// www.arp.org) and ThirdAge (http://www.thirdage .com).

31. This paragraph relies on Committee on Ways and Means, *2004 Green Book*, Appendix B, pp. B- 27–B-29.

32. Most of the remainder of this section relies on Committee on Ways and Means, Section 15, "Medicaid," *2004 Green Book*.

33. Office of the Actuary, "2008 Actuarial Report on the Financial Outlook for Medicaid" (Washington, DC: Centers for Medicaid and Medicare Services, 2008). Retrieved November 20, 2009, from http:// www.cms.hhs.gov/ActuarialStudies/downloads/ MedicaidReport2008.pdf

34. Federal Matching Rate (FMAP) for Medicaid with American Recovery and Reinvestment Act (ARRA) Adjustments, FY2009 (Menlo Park, CA: The Henry J. Kaiser Family Foundation). Retrieved December 30, 2009, from http://www.statehealthfacts .org/comparemaptable.jsp?ind=695&cat=4

35. "Medicaid: Recipients," *Social Security Bulletin, Annual Statistical Supplement, 2008.* Retrieved December 24, 2009, from http://www.ssa.gov/policy/ docs/statecomps/supplement/2008/8e.pdf

36. Frank Ullman, Brian Bruen, and John Holahan, "The State Children's Health Insurance Program: A Look at the Numbers" (Washington, DC: Urban Institute, March 1, 1998). Retrieved May 23, 2010, from http://www.urban.org/publications/307470 .html

37. "Federal Funds Left on the Table," *Fiscal Notes* (newsletter of the Texas Comptroller's office), March 2004, p. 4. Retrieved May 23, 2010, from http://www .window.state.tx.us/comptrol/fnotes/fn0403/news .html

38. Dianne White Delisi, "Assets Test for CHIP Won't Hurt Texas' Neediest Children," *Austin American-Statesman*, April 2, 2004, p. A19.

39. Genevieve M. Kenney, Allison Cook, and Lisa Dubay, *Progress Enrolling Children in Medicaid/CHIP: Who Is Left and What Are the Prospects for Covering More Children?* (Washington, DC: Urban Institute, December 14, 2009). Retrieved December 30, 2009, from Urban Institute website: http://www.urban .org/publications/411981.html

40. Ian Hill and Amy Westpfahl Lutzky, "Is There a Hole in the Bucket?" Occasional Paper 67 (Washington, DC: Urban Institute, May 16, 2003). Retrieved December 19, 2009, from http://www.urban.org

41. Lauren Necochea, "The Challenge of Enrolling and Retaining Low-Income Children in SCHIP," Robert Wood Johnson Foundation Research Brief, Number 3, March 2007. Retrieved December 20, 2009, from http://www.rwjf.org/grants/product.jsp?id=18636

42. Kenney et al., *Progress Enrolling Children in Medicaid/CHIP: Who Is Left and What Are the Prospects for Covering More Children?*

43. "Medicaid At-a-Glance 2005" (Baltimore, MD: Centers for Medicare & Medicaid Services). Retrieved November 4, 2009, from http://www.cms .hhs.gov/MedicaidDataSourcesGenInfo/downloads/ maag2005.pdf

44. Fiscal Year 2004 National MSIS Tables. Source: Medicaid Statistical Information System State Summary FY2004. Created 06/22/2007 (Baltimore, MD: Centers for Medicare & Medicaid Services).

Retrieved November 17, 2009, from http://www.cms. hhs.gov/MedicaidDataSourcesGenInfo/downloads/ MSISTables2004.pdf

45. Committee on Ways and Means, "Medicaid," *2004 Green Book*, p. 15-39.

46. National Summary of Medicaid Managed Care Programs and Enrollment as of June 30, 2008 (Washington, DC: Centers for Medicaid and Medicare Services). Retrieved December 23, 2009, from http:// www.cms.hhs.gov/MedicaidDataSourcesGenInfo/ downloads/08Trends508.pdf

47. National Center for Chronic Disease Prevention and Health Promotion, "Preventive Health and Health Services Block Grant, A Critical Public Health Resource: At a Glance 2009" (Atlanta, GA: Centers for Disease Control and Prevention). Retrieved December 20, 2009, from http://www.cdc.gov/ chronicdisease/resources/publications/AAG/block-grant.htm

48. "Employer Health Benefits: 2009 Annual Survey" (Menlo Park, CA: The Henry J. Kaiser Family Foundation and Chicago, IL: Health Research & Educational Trust, 2009). Retrieved December 21, 2009, from http://ehbs.kff.org/pdf/2009/7936.pdf

49. Much of this section on employer-based and private insurance plans arises out of one of the authors' (DHJ) eleven years of experience in the life and health insurance industry. Other information comes from The Henry J. Kaiser Family Foundation website at http://www.kff.org, or the FamiliesUSA website at www.familiesusa.org

50. Rector and Visitors of the University of Virginia (2003). Transcript of tape number 450-23 of a White House meeting between Richard M. Nixon and John Ehrlichman, February 17, 1971. Miller Center of Public Affairs, University of Virginia, Presidential Recordings Program, as cited in David H. Johnson, *A Structure by No Means Complete: A Comparison of the Path and Processes Surrounding Successful Passage of Medicare and Medicaid under Lyndon Baines Johnson and the Failure to Pass National Health Care Reform under William Jefferson Clinton.* Dissertation. The University of Texas at Austin, 2009.

51. Except as otherwise noted, this section relies on DeNavas-Walt et al., *Income, Poverty, and Health Insurance Coverage in the United States: 2008,* Current Population Reports, P60-236.

52. The remainder of this paragraph relies on David U. Himmelstein, Deborah Thorne, Elizabeth Warren, and Steffie Woolhandler, "Medical Bankruptcy in the United States, 2007: Results of a National Study," *The American Journal of Medicine*, in press. Retrieved

January 1, 2010, from http://www.pnhp.org/
new_bankruptcy_study/Bankruptcy-2009.pdf

53. Paul Starr, "Healthcare for the Poor: The Past Twenty
Years," in Sheldon H. Danzinger and Daniel H.
Weinberg, Eds., *Fighting Poverty: What Works and
What Doesn't* (Cambridge, MA: Harvard University
Press, 1986), pp. 106–137.

54. "OECD Health Data 2009: How Does Canada
Compare" (Paris: Organization for Economic
Cooperation and Development, 2009). Retrieved
December 21, 2009, from http://www.oecd.org/
dataoecd/46/33/38979719.pdf

55. "OECD Health Data 2008—Frequently Requested
Data" (Paris: Organization for Economic Cooperation
and Development, December 10, 2008). Retrieved
May 15, 2009, from http://www.oecd.org/document/
16/0,3343,en_2649_34631_2085200_1_1_1_1,00
.html

56. "Health Care Cost Inflation Appears to Slow, but
Statistics Can Be Misleading" *Workforce Management*,
May 18, 2009. Retrieved December 21, 2009, from
http://www.workforce.com/section/00/article/26/43/
62.php

57. Paul Starr, "Healthcare for the Poor: The Past Twenty
Years," in Sheldon H. Danzinger and Daniel H.
Weinberg, Eds., *Fighting Poverty: What Works and
What Doesn't* (Cambridge, MA: Harvard University
Press, 1986), pp. 109–110.

58. Cathy A. Cowan and Bradley R. Braden, "Business,
Households, and Government: Healthcare Spend-
ing, 1995," *Healthcare Financing Review*, Vol. 18,
No. 3, 1997, pp. 195–206.

59. Joshua M. Wiener and David G. Stevenson, *Long-
Term Care for the Elderly and State Health Policy*
(Washington, DC: Urban Institute, November 1,
1997). Retrieved May 23, 2010, from http://www
.urban.org/publications/307048.html

60. The remainder of this paragraph relies on
Committee on Ways and Means, *2004 Green Book*,
Appendix D, "Medicare Payment Policies," p. D-2.

61. For a more thorough exploration of path-dependence theory, see W. Brian Arthur, *Increasing Returns
and Path Dependence in the Economy* (Ann Arbor,
MI: University of Michigan Press, 1994).

62. Most of the remainder of this section relies on the
work of Jacob Hacker. For a complete explanation of
the path-dependent nature of U.S. healthcare systems see Jacob S. Hacker, "The Historical Logic of
National Health Insurance: Structure and Sequence
in the Development of British, Canadian, and U.S.
Medical Policy," *Studies in American Political
Development*, Vol 12, 1998, pp. 57–130.

63. George Anders, "Canada Hospitals Provide Care as
Good as in U.S. at Lower Costs, Studies Show," *Wall
Street Journal*, March 18, 1993, p. B5.

64. Lyndon B. Johnson, *The Vantage Point: Perspectives
of the Presidency 1963–1969* (New York: Holt,
Rinehart and Winston, 1971).

65. This account of the Clinton proposal relies on
*Budget of the United States Government, Fiscal Year
1995* (Washington, DC: Executive Office of the
President, 1994), Chapter 4.

66. Uwe E. Reinhardt, "The Clinton Plan: A Salute to
American Pluralism," *Health Affairs*, Vol. 13, No. 1,
Spring I, 1994, p. 116.

67. Haynes Johnson and David Broder, *The System: The
American Way of Politics at the Breaking Point*
(Boston: Little, Brown and Company, 1997).

68. Uwe E. Reinhardt and John K. Iglehart, "From the
Editor, the Policy Makers' Dilemma," *Health Affairs*,
Vol. 13, No. 1, Spring I, 1994, pp. 5–6.

69. Laurence Kotlikoff, *The Healthcare Fix: Universal
Insurance for All Americans.* (Cambridge, MA: The
MIT Press, 2007).

70. "NPR/Kaiser/Kennedy School Poll on Healthcare,"
June 5, 2002. Retrieved December 19, 2009, from
http://www.npr.org/news/specials/healthcarepoll

71. "Incremental Approaches to Extend Coverage
Are Insufficient," *Uninsurance Facts & Figures*
(Washington, DC: Institute of Medicine of the
National Academies, n.d.). Retrieved February 6,
2010, from http://www.iom.edu/~/media/Files/
Report%20Files/2004/Insuring-Americas-Health-
Principles-and-Recommendations/Factsheet1uni-
versal.ashx

72. "Can Anything Resist Hillary Clinton? Time Will
Tell," *New York Times*, October 3, 1993, Section 3, p.
2; Robert Pear, "Insurers End Opposition to Health
Reform," *Austin American-Statesman*, December 3,
1992, pp. A1, 17.

73. Chip Hirzel (Writer), "Interview with Bill Clinton by
Sanjay Gupta," 2009. In H. Waters (Producer), Larry
King Live: CNN.

74. Paul Krugman, "Tea Parties Forever," *New York
Times*, April 12, 2009. Retrieved December 22, 2009,
from http://www.nytimes.com

75. Michael Saul, "Rage Boils Over at Town Hall
Meetings Over Health Care," *New York Daily News*,
August 11, 2009. Retrieved December 22, 2009, from
http://www.nydailynews.com

76. "Rep. Wilson shouts, 'You lie' to Obama during
speech." CNNPolitics.com, September 10, 2009.
Retrieved December 22, 2009, from http://www.cnn
.com/2009/POLITICS/09/09/joe.wilson/index.html

77. John McArdle, "Wilson's fundraising tops $700,000 after outburst," *Roll Call News*, September 11, 2009. Retrieved December 22, 2009, from http://www .rollcall.com/news/38422-1.html

78. David Herszenhorn and Robert Pear, "Senate Votes to Open Health Care Debate." *New York Times*, November 21, 2009. Retrieved December 21, 2009, from http://www.nytimes.com

79. Huma Khan, "President Obama Hails Senate Health Care Bill as Ben Nelson Jumps on Board" (Washington, DC: ABC News, 2009). Retrieved December 19, 2009, from http://abcnews.go.com

80. "Andrea Mitchell Reports," MSNBC, December 21, 2009.

81. Michael Cooper, "G.O.P. Senate Victory Stuns Democrats," *New York Times*, January 20, 2010. Retrieved January 31, 2010, from http://www .nytimes.com/2010/01/21/us/politics/21elect.html

82. Shailagh Murray and Paul Kane, "Pelosi: House Won't Pass Senate Bill to Save Health-care Reform," *The Washington Post*, January 22, 2010. Retrieved January 31, 2010, from http://www.washingtonpost.com/ wp-dyn/content/article/2010/01/21/AR2010012101604. html

83. Hillary Rodham Clinton, *Living History* (New York: Simon & Schuster, 2003).

84. Douglas W. Elmendorf, Director of Congressional Budget Office, March 20, 2010, Letter to Honorable Nancy Pelosi, Speaker of the House of Representatives. Retrieved May 14, 2010, from http:// www.cbo.gov/ftpdocs/113xx/doc11379/Manager%27 sAmendmenttoReconciliationProposal.pdf

85. This section relies heavily on information contained on the U.S. Department of Health and Human Services web site devoted to the changes under the healthcare reform laws of 2010. Retrieved May 14, 2010, from http://www.healthreform.gov

86. Douglas W. Elmendorf, Director of Congressional Budget Office, March 20, 2010, Letter to Honorable Nancy Pelosi, Speaker of the House of Representatives. Retrieved May 14, 2010, from http:// www.cbo.gov/ftpdocs/113xx/doc11379/Manager%27 sAmendmenttoReconciliationProposal.pdf

87. U.S. Census Bureau, *2009 Annual Social and Economic Supplement,* Table HI06. Retrieved January 3, 2010, from http://www.census.gov/hhes/www/ cpstables/032009/health/h06_000.htm

88. Linda Bergthold, "Repeal health care reform? 41 states think so," The Huffington Post, May 7, 2010. Retrieved May 22, 2010, from http://www.huffingtonpost.com/ linda-bergthold/repeal-health-care-reform_b_568472 .html

89. Peter Grier, "Health care reform bill 101: What's a health 'exchange'?" *The Christian Science Monitor*, March 20, 2010. Retrieved May 22, 2010, from http:// www.csmonitor.com/USA/Politics/2010/0320/Health- care-reform-bill-101-What-s-a-health-exchange

90. "Coverage of High Risk Individuals: State and Federal High Risk Pools" (National Conference of State Legislatures, May 17, 2010). Retrieved May 22, 2010, from http://www.ncsl.org/IssuesResearch/Health/ StateHighRiskPoolsforHealthCoverage/tabid/14329/ Default.aspx

91. "Fact Sheet: Protecting the Privacy of Patients' Health Information" (U.S. Department of Health and Human Services, April 14, 2003). Retrieved December 22, 2009, from http://www.hhs.gov/news/ facts/privacy.html; "FAQs About Portability of Health Coverage and HIPAA" (Washington, DC: U.S. Department of Labor). Retrieved December 26, 2009, from http://www.dol.gov/ebsa/faqs/faq_con- sumer_hipaa.html

92. "Fact Sheet 8a: HIPAA Basics: Medical Privacy in the Electronic Age" (San Diego, CA: Privacy Rights Clearinghouse, August 2009). Retrieved January 2, 2010, from http://www.privacyrights.org/fs/fs8a- hipaa.htm

93. John M. Luce, "Making Decisions about the Forgoing of Life-Sustaining Therapy," *American Journal of Respiratory and Critical Care Medicine*, Vol. 156, No. 6, 1997, pp. 1715–1718; quote from p. 1715.

94. "Hospitals Reserve the Right to Refuse Service," *Mouth: Voice of the Disability Nation*, September 2003. Retrieved December 22, 2009, from http:// www.mouthmag.com/news.htm

95. Luce, "Making Decisions about the Forgoing of Life- Sustaining Therapy."

96. Arlene Orhon Jech, "Hard Choices: Ethics Committees Grapple with Complex Issues," *Health Week*, Vol. 5, No. 18, 2003, pp. 20–21.

97. Council on Ethical and Judicial Affairs, American Medical Association, "Medical Futility in End-of- Life Care, Report of the Council on Ethical and Judicial Affairs," *Journal of the American Medical Association*, Vol. 281, 1999, pp. 937–941.

98. Alan L. Otten, "Fateful Decision: In the Netherlands, the Very Ill Have Option of Euthanasia," *Wall Street Journal*, August 21, 1987, pp. 1, 6; Carol J. Williams, "Netherlands Legalizes Euthanasia," *Austin American- Statesman*, April 11, 2001, p. A5.

99. Tamara Jones, "Dutch Set Euthanasia Guidelines," *Austin American-Statesman*, February 10, 1993, p. A12; on the case of the Netherlands and on assisted

suicide and euthanasia in general, see Michael M. Uhlmann, Ed., *Last Rights? Assisted Suicide and Euthanasia Debated* (Washington, DC: Ethics and Public Policy Center, 1998).

100. Matt Gouras, "Montana Becomes Third Sstate to Allow Physician-Assisted Suicide after State's High Court Rules" *Chicago Tribune,* December 31, 2009. Retrieved January 2, 2010, from http://www .chicagotribune.com/business/sns-ap-us-physician-assisted-suicide,0,673120.story

101. Monica Davey, "Kevorkian Freed After Years in Prison for Aiding Suicide," *New York Times*, June 2, 2007. Retrieved January 1, 2010, from http://www.nytimes.com/2007/06/02/us/02kevor kian.html?_r=1

102. Compassion & Choices. Retrieved December 22, 2009, from http://www.compassionandchoices .org; see also Derek Humphry, *Final Exit* (New York: Dell, 1991).

9 PREVENTING POVERTY: EDUCATION AND EMPLOYMENT POLICY

Peter A. Kindle
Diana M. DiNitto

Education and employment go hand-in-hand. Public education policy in the United States began as a local affair. In many respects, it still is, but over the decades, there has been increased state and federal intervention in the local educational arena. Today political battles ensue over a wide range of issues such as how K through 12 schools should be funded, the teaching of evolution and creationism, standardized testing and national educational standards for students, and how loans for higher education should be administered.

Employment policy seeks to ensure that the United States has a work force that is prepared to fill jobs in today's labor market. Employment policy must also respond to the vicissitudes of the labor market as employment and unemployment wax and wane and to many other concerns such as what constitutes a decent wage and other fair labor standards and the effects of immigration, offshoring, and outsourcing on employment. As this chapter indicates, there are many views on just what education and employment policies should be and who should be responsible for them.

EDUCATION FOR THE FEW OR THE MANY?

Public education in the United States has deep roots. As early as 1647, the Massachusetts colony was the first western government to pass a compulsory public education law requiring communities with 50 homes to employ a schoolmaster and communities with 100 homes to establish grammar schools.[1] With American independence and the development of a representative form of government, schools were considered the best setting in which "a national identity must be formed"[2] (a sentiment that continues to resonate today).

In 1779, Thomas Jefferson, a strong proponent of a meritocratic system of local education, proposed "A Bill for the More General Diffusion of Knowledge" in Virginia. He envisioned a three-tiered system of locally supported public schools that would provide equality of opportunity for young, white, and male children who could advance through competition to higher levels of education, thereby reproducing the elitist model of European education but providing male children increased access.

Jefferson's focus on local initiative led to an informal education system that contained tuition-supported schools for the children of well-off parents and, in the more compassionate localities, to charity schools for children living in poverty. In contrast with this informality, a movement to provide free, tax-supported schools for all children developed under the leadership of Horace Mann of Massachusetts. The "common schools" Mann advocated were based on the educational system Prussia instituted in the eighteenth century.[3] As Secretary of the new Massachusetts Board of Education in 1837, Mann promoted free non-sectarian schools, a trained educational profession, and state control over local schools.[4] Under the Prussian pattern, common schools provided basic literacy and introductory arithmetic skills through eighth grade. At the time, school attendance was rarely compulsory in the United States, and, in keeping with the Jeffersonian intent of advance through competitive merit, dropout rates were quite high in most areas of the country.[5] Where education was available, students received the same, "common" instruction regardless of their social class or gender because the goal was clear–to prepare citizens to participate in the new democracy.

By 1860 the successes of the common school movement were obvious. Over 70 percent of white children aged 5 through 15 were enrolled in 13 states (Connecticut, Illinois, Maine, Massachusetts, Michigan, New Hampshire, New York, Ohio, Pennsylvania, Rhode Island, Vermont, Washington, and Wisconsin). The failures were just as prominent in the 14 states with enrollments under 50 percent (Alabama, Arkansas, Florida, Georgia, Kansas, Louisiana, Maryland, Mississippi, Nebraska, North Carolina, South Carolina, South Dakota, Texas, and Virginia).[6] Disparities were greater for free black children. Over 67 percent attended school in the New England states, but these states contained less than 5 percent of the free black children in the country. The South Atlantic region (Virginia through Florida) contained almost half of the free black children in the country, but less than 4 percent attended school.[7]

Reconstruction (1865–1877) of the southern states following the Civil War led to massive expansion of public education in that region. Federal participation in public education began through the new Department of Education (1867) and the Bureau of Refugee, Freedmen, and Abandoned Lands known as the Freedmen's Bureau. The Freedmen's Bureau started schools for the children of freed slaves, because prior to the Civil War, the southern states had laws making it illegal to educate slaves. Black children were not the only southern children lacking an education. Charity schools for poor white children were rare as well. Racial rivalry resulted in the establishment of public schools throughout the south–primarily to ensure that white children were not disadvantaged in comparison to black children. The Freedman's Bureau's educational initiatives established a precedence that northern church-based organizations maintained after the end of Reconstruction. Northern religious denominations sponsored thousands of educational missionaries to teach in schools for African Americans, and founded what today are known as Historically Black Colleges and Universities.

The removal of federal troops from the south in 1877, however, opened the door to segregation and Jim Crow laws that isolated African Americans from white society, educational institutions, and businesses. Under Jim Crow laws, "separate but equal" significantly curtailed quality public education for African Americans. There was also little concern for equity or proportionality. For example, in Alabama, teachers at black and white schools were comparably paid in 1890, but by 1910, salaries for teachers in white schools were more than double salaries for teachers in black schools.[8] Public expenditures in 1910 for education in Alabama's Lowndes County were $33.40 per white child and only $1.00 per black child.[9] It was no longer illegal for black children to be educated in the southern states, but the quality of the free public education available to them was highly questionable.

PUBLIC EDUCATION: THE PROGRESSIVE ERA TO WORLD WAR II

Industrialization followed Reconstruction, and by 1890 the United States was the world's leading manufacturing country. Jobs in the new manufacturing centers were plentiful, and immigrants flooded the country. By 1910, 15 percent of the U.S. population was foreign born; 15 percent were children of immigrants; and another 7 percent had one immigrant parent.[10] By 1920, more than two-thirds of the inhabitants of New York, Chicago, Boston, and Detroit were immigrants or children of immigrants.[11] The demands placed on public schools to first assimilate, and then educate, these children were overwhelming. The task of "Americanizing" the millions of foreign-born immigrants and their children fell to the public schools. U.S. participation in World War I in 1914 seemed to underscore the importance of nationalization rather than scholarship.

Child labor was a significant deterrent to educating the nation's youth. During the turn of the twentieth century, the movement to halt child labor resulted in the organization of the National Child Labor Committee in New York in 1904 and its chartering by Congress in 1907.[12] Not until the New Deal of the 1930s did the federal government pass sustainable child labor legislation because of pro-business conservatism on the U.S. Supreme Court, but the states made significant progress in limiting child labor. By 1910, 41 states had enacted minimum age restrictions on manufacturing employment.[13] Children who were not working could more easily be enrolled in schools. Enrollments increased significantly. By 1918, all states had legislation requiring some form of compulsory school attendance as well.[14] In 1870, 53 percent of all children aged 5 to 15 were enrolled in school; by 1920, 80 percent were enrolled, including over 60 percent of black children.[15] In addition, the number of years of schooling was increasing.

Prior to the Civil War, high schools were tuition-supported preparatory academies for the elite few who were preparing for college. In 1876, the first move toward public, tax-supported high schools began in Kalamazoo, Michigan. From 1900 to 1920, national high school enrollment increased from 200,000 to over 2.5 million students.[16] The United States was the first country in the world to establish universal secondary education.

Public schools were poorly prepared for such massive and rapid growth. Classrooms, especially in the immigrant-dominated urban centers of the northern states, were overcrowded, and individual students' developmental needs were rarely the teacher's focus. The success of the scientific management approach associated with Frederick Taylor's time and motion studies[17] led to consolidating one-room schoolhouses into larger educational facilities so that teachers could specialize in educating children of specific age groups.

Regimentation in the classroom was the norm. Intelligence testing, first utilized on a large-scale basis with Army draftees at the onset of U.S. entry into World War I, provided a tool for student sorting and differentiated educational programs,[18] the precursors of "tracking" in public schools. Tracking became a controversial issue as the following quote indicates:

> The emerging industrial nation needed a new workforce, people who would fit into jobs in an increasingly elaborate division of labor and who would be socialized to work together in a new, efficient social order. . . . Teaching according to a child's nature [i.e., differentiated instruction] easily became teaching according to a child's position in the social order.[19]

Some form of differentiated education may have been appropriate had it been implemented fairly, but racial and ethnic animosity, in the south directed mostly against African Americans and in the north mostly against immigrants, resulted in disparities based on race, then gender and wealth.[20] According to one perspective, segmentation of public schools into those with a focus on academic preparation for the children of the affluent, and those with a focus on vocational preparation for racial minorities, immigrants, and children from low income households, "has plagued instruction ever since."[21] The first federal legislation to provide funding for public schools, the Smith-Hughes Act of 1917, effectively ended the *de facto* common curriculum of the nineteenth century by paying teachers whose job it was to teach vocational skills. With the financial prosperity of the 1920s, the cessation of large-scale immigration by 1924,[22] and the ensuing economic challenges of the Great Depression in the 1930s, education dropped from U.S. public discourse.

When the United States entered World War II in 1944, state regulations and uneven local school board implementation dominated public education. Accountability, to the extent it existed, was informal and directed to pleasing the idiosyncratic interests of civic and business leaders. Widespread unemployment in the 1930s led to increasing high school enrollment and graduation rates. From 1920 to 1954, the proportion of 17-year-olds with a high school education grew from 17 percent to 60 percent,[23] although the academic rigor in most high schools was significantly weaker than in the few preparatory academies that existed for the affluent half a century earlier. The U.S. political system had not yet addressed differences in educational access, quality, and achievement along class and racial lines.

THE POST WORLD WAR II ERA: INCREASED FEDERAL INVOLVEMENT IN EDUCATION

The U.S. Constitution is silent on the federal government's role in public education; thus, under the Tenth Amendment, education is presumed to be the purview of the individual states, and funding for public education has historically been a local and state responsibility. Until the late 1950s, no major federal legislation was directed at primary and secondary public education. The Cold War and the Space Race gave birth to the National Defense Education Act

(NDEA), and the War on Poverty spawned the Elementary and Secondary Education Act (ESEA). Both significantly increased federal involvement in public education.

National Defense Education Act (1958): The Cold War Influences Education

After World War II, local school districts struggled to provide the resources to meet the needs of the growing student population. The "baby boom" was on the way. Primary and secondary enrollments grew from 26 million students in 1946 to 36 million in 1954.[24] Funding for public education increased by more than 140 percent in the decade before 1950 and by another 170 percent in the decade before 1960.[25] Local education agencies responded to the need for school expansion by increasing property taxes by more than 440 percent from 1940 to 1960. This led to substantial public sentiment in favor of directing more state and federal funding to schools. Enrollments were increasing, and educational aspirations were, too. Parents began to demand more rigorous academic standards for all children. When *Why Johnny Can't Read*[26] was published in 1955, a receptive audience kept it on the bestseller's list for weeks.[27] Undoubtedly, "moving upward [economically] . . . had become more central in American life and education had become the main way to move upward."[28] Since that time, educational "tracking" of students has been continuously criticized by some sectors of the public and some sectors of the educational establishment.

Internationally, the United States and its allies were involved in Cold War hostilities with the Soviet Bloc countries. The U.S. public was already primed to question the academic quality of public schools. It greeted with dismay the Soviet Union's successful Sputnik satellite launch in 1957. President Eisenhower had extensive public support when he signed the National Defense Education Act (NDEA) into law in 1958 as a defensive reaction to the perception of Soviet superiority. NDEA set a precedent for allocating federal funds to states using a formula based on student population and state income levels. States then distributed the funds to local education agencies. State education agencies were required to get federal approval for their distribution priorities in advance, and state or local matching funds were required after the first year.

NDEA was the first federal attempt to improve academic rigor in public schools, an emphasis that has enjoyed broad public support for the last 50 years. By establishing mechanisms for federal funding of local schools, NDEA gave the federal government a voice in local educational decisions and established the precedent that federal involvement in local schools would occur through the "carrot" of funding rather than the "stick" of legal restrictions or penalties.

Elementary and Secondary Education Act (1965): Access and Diversity

Unlike NDEA, which was primarily concerned with academically talented students, President Lyndon Baines Johnson's War on Poverty in the 1960s shifted federal priorities to the disadvantaged in primary and secondary schools. As Walter Heller, the War on Poverty's chief architect, articulated, "equality of opportunity is the American dream, and universal education, [sic] is our noblest pledge to realize it.[29] The movement toward universal education planted in the common school movement of the early nineteenth century blossomed during the Americanization of immigrants in the early twentieth century, but the quality of public education was structurally and intentionally unequal by the 1950s. Few resources were devoted to educating African American students and other children living in poverty. The solution to the social problem was public school integration, that is, open access to the best public schools for all children regardless of race or socioeconomic class. Technically, integration of the public schools was under the direction of the federal district courts, but ESEA's passage in 1965 provided a powerful additional stimulus for integration–additional federal funding (also see Chapter 12 regarding school integration).

Title I of ESEA provided $1 billion in new federal funding to both private and public schools where low-income students comprised at least 40 percent of the enrollment. This funding was intended for programs specifically designed to compensate for the "culture of poverty" in which low-income students grew up. However, the legislation lacked restrictions on expenditures once schools qualified for the funding. In effect, Title I funding became general aid to schools that enrolled disadvantaged students.[30] Every congressional district had one or two schools that qualified, and therefore, there was broad-based legislative support. During the 1949–1950 school year, federal contributions to public education were less than 3 percent of the $5.4 billion spent on K–12 public school education. Approximately 57 percent of total public school revenues were provided through local property taxes. With NDEA in 1958 and ESEA in 1965, federal influence grew. The federal proportion of public school funding was 4.4 percent of nearly $15 billion in 1959–1960, peaking at nearly 10 percent of $97 billion in 1979–1980.[31] Although the federal share is still the smallest, it represents a significant influx of funds to schools. Figure 9.1 shows funding trends in public education.

Francis Keppel, Commissioner of the U.S. Office of Education, led the fight to pass ESEA against "Race, Republicans, Roman Catholics, and Reds."[32] Many southerners opposed ESEA because they correctly surmised that it would strengthen desegregation efforts. Republicans were opposed to every aspect of Johnson's War on Poverty, but held too few seats to prevent passage of ESEA. Roman Catholic leaders disapproved of additional tax outlays to public schools because separation of church and state was traditionally interpreted to exclude parochial schools from public funding. Others who believed that any centralized control over locally directed public

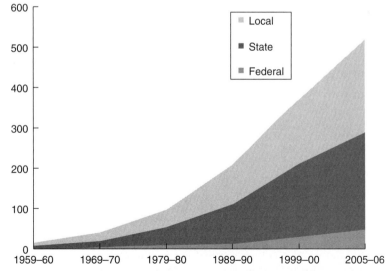

FIGURE 9.1 **Revenues by Government Source for Public Elementary and Secondary Schools (in billions of dollars)** *Source:* Compiled using data from U.S. Department of Education, National Center for Education Statistics, *Digest of Educational Statistics: 2008,* Table 32, Historical Summary of Public Elementary and Secondary School Statistics. Retrieved March 6, 2010, from http://nces.ed.gov/programs/digest/d08/tables/dt08_032.asp

schools would be a move toward socialism were mollified by explicit language in the original legislation prohibiting federal control over curriculum, program of instruction, administration, personnel, or instructional materials. Roman Catholic support for ESEA was won using the "child benefit" rationale or theory that the funds were to benefit the child and not the school, thus allowing parochial and other nonpublic schools to receive funding. The large Democratic majority in both houses of Congress enabled Johnson's proposed legislation to be approved with a single amendment, which established a national testing program termed the National Assessment of Educational Progress (NEAP).[33]

Title VI of the Civil Rights Act of 1964 empowered the federal government to withhold funds from school districts that did not desegregate, but this regulation had little impact before ESEA. Keppel's successor as Commissioner, Howard Howe II, implemented desegregation aggressively. The pull of federal funding and the push of federal district court decisions resulted in the proportion of black children attending schools with white children increasing from 11 percent in the 1964–1965 school year to 84 percent in 1970–1971 in the southern states.[34]

In a piecemeal fashion, other disadvantaged groups gained priority in additional federal legislation with corresponding impacts on public education. The Immigration and Nationality Act (1965) eliminated the immigration quota system in place since 1924. Once again immigration began to increase, resulting in growing student enrollments. The Bilingual Education Act, proposed in 1968 and eventually merged into ESEA's reauthorization, addressed the educational needs of children with low English proficiency (i.e., immigrant children) by providing funding for voluntary bilingual programming. The Education for All Handicapped Children Act (1975) promoted mainstreaming of children with mental and physical disabilities who had previously been relegated to special education programs (also see Chapter 6).[35] Not only did ESEA increase school desegregation and equal access to educational opportunity, it led to the embrace of diversity and an ethic of inclusion in primary and secondary educational systems.

ESEA Reauthorizations: From Access to Achievement

ESEA was originally authorized through 1970 and reauthorized approximately every five years since then. Each reauthorization provides the opportunity for a shift in federal funding mechanisms and priorities. Between 1965 and 1981, ESEA reauthorizations focused mainly on tracing funds to insure they were spent according to federal intent. Educational reformers in the Office of Education had never endorsed the unofficial conversion of ESEA funding from compensatory programming to general assistance. Gradually, reformers influenced ESEA implementation as well as ESEA legislation. In 1970 it was made clear that federal funds had to be used for *additional* programming for disadvantaged children *beyond* what would have been provided by state and local funding alone. This "supplement, not supplant" approach resulted in heavy bookkeeping requirements for local and state agencies.[36]

Perhaps more significantly for the classroom teacher and student, efforts to restrict use of ESEA funds to compensatory programs resulted in *pull-out* programs that provided intensive, personal, and out-of-classroom instruction for children identified as disadvantaged. By 1978, local schools and school districts that accepted ESEA funding had to create parental advisory councils and give them a formal role in educational decisions.[37] Teachers and local school district administrators did not take kindly to this new form of federal interference, however indirect and well intended it might have been.

The focus on achievement began under President Carter. Carter had pledged to elevate education to his cabinet in order to garner support from the teachers' unions during his 1976 election campaign, a pledge fulfilled by passage of the Department of Education (DOE) Organization Act in 1979. Carter appointed Joseph Califano, Jr., President Johnson's senior domestic policy aide, to be Secretary of the Department of Health, Education, and Welfare in 1977, but Califano was a strong advocate for the continuation of an *access first* educational agenda. He often publicly contradicted President Carter's policy preferences that were more balanced between access and achievement. Califano opposed even voluntary national standards and testing[38] as well as the elevation of the Office of Education to the presidential cabinet level Department of Education.[39] On the first issue, Califano prevailed; however, Carter perceived balance between access and achievement to be more difficult to maintain if health and welfare concerns remained conjoined with education. No one clearly anticipated the consequences. Eventually, "education programs operated in a vacuum, stressing achievement without so much as casting a glance at the environment in which the child lived."[40]

During the 1980 presidential race, incumbent Jimmy Carter and the Republican candidate, Ronald Reagan, disagreed sharply on educational reform. Reagan countered Carter's support among teachers by condemning the escalation of federal interference in public schools, especially court-imposed cessation of school prayers, and pledged to abolish the DOE if elected president. With Reagan's election, the 15-year history of presidential support for ESEA expansion was suspended.[41] The transition from a focus on access to educational achievement was gradual, but Reagan gave it new impetus with his critical orientation toward public education.

President Reagan's pledge to abolish the DOE, however, went unfulfilled because he lacked the votes in Congress. Federal debates over educational policy were largely contained within DOE during Reagan's administration,[42] but Reagan publicly championed a resurgence in conservative ideology that gave impetus to local and state controversies in the schools. Attempts to reinstitute school prayer, curricula modifications to include "creation science" or "intelligent design," and restrictions on sex education made national headlines. On the local level, Republican constituents, especially those represented by the Moral Majority and Christian Coalition, were quite successful in gaining a voice on local school boards. Ironically, political and religious conservatives who entered the education policy controversies in support of Reagan did not realize the fiscal retrenchment that occurred during his administrations. The federal proportion of revenues devoted to public education fell from 9.8 percent in 1979–1980 to 6.1 percent by 1989–1990.[43]

Educational policy on the state and local level quickly deteriorated into an argument over funding. Local property owners, the primary source of local school revenues, resisted property tax levy escalations. State governments were pressed to increase state support for local schools but often resisted increasing sales taxes and state income taxes to raise the required funds. The federal courts entered the fray when local districts with a weak property tax base challenged disproportionate funding in specific states. Texas, for example, continues to struggle with its controversial "Robin Hood" law, which redistributes property tax revenues between richer and poorer school districts in an attempt to achieve equitable funding for each school child in the state.[44]

Under Reagan, a symbolic turn toward achievement could be noted in the new title given ESEA in its 1981 reauthorization, the Education Consolidation and Improvement Act. This reauthorization also reduced federal funding and eliminated some of the heavy bookkeeping requirements by converting part of the funding to block grants. However, all other educational initiatives under Reagan pale when compared to the Commission on Excellence in Education's *A Nation at Risk: The Imperative for Educational Reform.*[45] The oft-quoted preamble of this landmark report on U.S. education seemed intended to shock: "If an unfriendly foreign power had attempted to impose on America the mediocre education performance that exists today, we might well have viewed it as an act of war."[46] Paradoxically, the report's recommendations were mild in comparison:

- Strengthen academic programs by requiring more years of secondary education in English, science, mathematics, social studies, and computer science.
- Elevate test scores for college admission.
- Require a longer school day and a longer school year.
- Raise teacher salaries.

What soon became clear was that concerns about equal opportunity and access no longer dominated federal involvement in the U.S. educational system. Academic excellence took precedence, especially in order for U.S. workers to maintain a competitive advantage in the global economy. The link between education and employment, suggested as early as 1917 in the Smith-Hughes Act, became entrenched in the public mindset. Enthusiasm for *A Nation at Risk* and a host of other studies critical of the country's educational outcomes[47] reversed the historical priorities for U.S. education by placing knowledge and academic achievement ahead of virtue, character, and citizenship "because many Americans feared that our economy was falling behind."[48] Fuel was added to the fire when *Why Johnny Can't Read* was reprinted in 1986.

ESEA's 1988 reauthorization, the Hawkins-Stafford Elementary and Secondary School Improvement Amendments, was a major step away from access first to a new focus on student achievement. It required states to (1) set educational goals for disadvantaged students in schools receiving Title I funds and (2) identify schools that failed to show progress. It also mandated that underperforming schools take remedial steps, including the development of improvement plans and, ultimately, state intervention and control if improvement was not achieved. Although the federal government was not directly involved in establishing educational outcome targets for disadvantaged students, ESEA's 1988 reauthorization established, for the first time, school-level accountability for disadvantaged students' educational outcomes. Educator opposition to this shift in federal policy was mitigated by adding new flexibility in the use of Title I funds in schools where 75 percent of students were disadvantaged and in schools that exceeded state-imposed educational outcome targets.[49]

Bipartisan Congressional support to raise the academic achievement of U.S. students echoed the broad public support for improvement. President George H. W. Bush's Charlottesville Education Summit in 1989, attended by then Arkansas governor Bill Clinton, produced six goals that were later expanded into eight in the Goals 2000 Act, passed in 1994 during the Clinton administration.[50] The eight goals can be summarized as:

- All children will start school ready to learn.
- High school graduation rates will increase to 90 percent.
- Fourth, eighth, and twelfth grade students will demonstrate competency in challenging subject matter to be prepared for citizenship, further learning, and productive employment.
- U.S. students will be first in the world in science and mathematics achievement.
- Every adult will be literate, globally competitive, and a responsible citizen.
- Every school will be free of drugs and violence.
- Every school will be free of firearms and alcohol with a disciplined environment conducive to learning.
- Every school will increase parental involvement and participation in the social, emotional, and academic growth of children.

At least five of these eight goals specifically focused on academic outcomes. The Goals 2000 Act required that states develop their own academic standards and initiate testing to see if students had achieved the established targets. The 1994 ESEA reauthorization, Improving America's Schools Act, disallowed separate educational targets for disadvantaged students and authorized funding for charter schools. Once again, opposition from educators was dampened by providing more flexibility in the use of Title I funds. Now restrictions were lifted if only 50 percent of students in a school were disadvantaged. For the first time, DOE was given the authority to waive federal requirements in certain circumstances. This enhanced state and local district control over spending priorities, especially in large urban districts.[51]

From Achievement to Accountability: Leave No Child Behind

From DOE's perspective, ESEA's reauthorization in 2001 in the No Child Left Behind (NCLB) Act was "based on stronger accountability for results, more freedom for states and communities, proven education methods, and more choices for parents."[52] From the perspective of state and local education agencies, NCLB was a disaster. Higher accountability for results, on the local school level, was mandated in the form of "annual yearly progress" assessed by mandatory student test-taking. The "proven" methods of education were curricula decisions made on the federal level. Implementation of the federally approved curricula on the local level was almost guaranteed by limiting use of federal funds, for example, to providing the Reading First program. Parents of children attending schools that did not maintain annual yearly progress were empowered to transfer their children to other schools. Teachers complained that educational priorities were being shifted away from academic excellence to "teaching to the test." Local administrators, accustomed since the 1980s to have broad discretion in the use of Title I funds, were not receptive to new guidance requiring extensive compensatory programs in underperforming schools. The cry of "unfunded mandates" was heard nationwide despite the original intent behind Title I funding—compensatory programming for disadvantaged students. The discretion states and communities had in the use of non-Title I federal funds was insufficient to quell this opposition.[53]

STANDARDS AND TESTING   Beginning as early as the Carter administration, there was growing national interest in elevating student outcomes by raising standards, and many states developed testing standards independently. Clinton's reauthorization of ESEA as the Improving America's School Act (IASA) of 1994 required states to submit a plan designed to comply with Goals 2000. Such a plan had to include "challenging content standards";[54] however, there was no requirement to submit these standards for review. States were required to assess student academic performance against state-defined standards as proficient, advanced, or partially proficient. Each year, states were also required to assess individual schools' progress toward meeting Goals 2000.

In effect, the structures necessary for implementing this "high risk" (also called "high stakes") testing required by NCLB were put into place in 1994. Because the flexibility afforded to states in ESEA did not lead to higher average scores on NAEP, and because gaps between white and minority students did not close (see Figure 9.2), NCLB imposed stricter standards for accountability on both the state and school level to see that all students achieve academic proficiency. NCLB's goal is to eliminate average academic proficiency gaps between student groups based on socioeconomic classes, race/ethnicities, disabilities, or limited English proficiency so that all student groups are academically proficient.[55] Initially focusing on reading and math proficiency, the academic standards outlined in NCLB continue to rise with every new regulation or

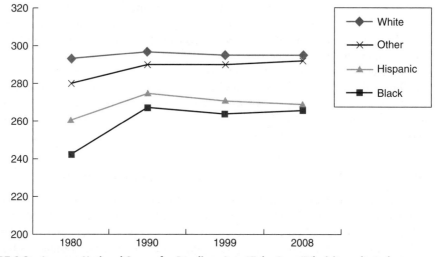

FIGURE 9.2 **Average National Scores for Reading, Age 17, by Race/Ethnicity, selected years**
Source: U.S. Department of Education, Institute of Education Sciences, National Center for Education Statistics, National Assessment of Educational Progress (NAEP), 1980, 1990, 1999, and 2008 Long-Term Trend Reading Assessments. Retrieved March 6, 2010, from http://nces.ed.gov/nationsreportcard/pdf/main2008/2009479.pdf

piece of legislation. Currently, the academic content has expanded to reading, math, and science, and the expectation is that all students and all schools will be assessed at grade level by 2014.[56] State educational standards and mandatory testing procedures must now be submitted to the U.S. Secretary of Education for review and approval. State sanctions against schools that are not making sufficient progress are required, and parents can transfer their children from underperforming schools to schools making adequate progress.

TEACHER IMPROVEMENT NCLB requires "highly qualified teachers" defined as those that have a baccalaureate degree, state certification or licensure, and can prove they know each subject they teach.[57] The National Council for Accreditation of Teacher Education (NCATE) responded to NCLB by publishing *Standards for Professional Development Schools* in 2001[58] and has since upgraded these standards.[59] All fifty states have either adopted NCATE professional content standards for teacher education or have aligned existing content standards to comply with NCATE. Escalation of standards for teachers has met with some resistance. Teachers consider assessment against new standards to be a potential threat to their tenure, and educational administrators often find it difficult to locate a sufficient number of qualified teachers for positions in the less desirable schools. Higher standards have also resulted in local and state fiscal problems as new teachers, educated in accordance with these new standards, command higher starting salaries.

CHARTER SCHOOLS AND SCHOOL VOUCHERS NCLB has a strong focus on educational innovation and encourages a variety of publicly funded efforts to evaluate and expand on private efforts. Charter schools, private educational institutions that receive public funding, are one approach to educational reform. Conceptually, charter schools operate with greater autonomy and higher accountability for student achievement than public schools, both legally and financially.

For some, this means charter schools have greater innovative potential and promise superior educational outcomes. In practice, this is not always the case with considerable difference, nationwide, in the quality and oversight provided to charter schools. By 2009, 40 states had passed legislation authorizing some form of charter schools.[60]

During the late 1980s and 1990s, private foundations like Annenberg, MacArthur, Carnegie, Pew, Ford, Rockefeller, Kellogg, Mellon, Mott, Hewlett, and most recently, the Bill and Melinda Gates Foundation, poured hundreds of millions of dollars into local and nationwide school reform efforts within the existing public school infrastructure. More conservative donors like The Lynde and Harry Bradley, Scaife, John M. Olin, Smith Richardson, and Walton Family foundations have supported voucher experiments. [61] Voucher experiments are an attempt to pressure schools to improve outcomes by placing school funding decision in the hands of the children's parents. Parents present the voucher to the school they select for their child, and the school obtains funds by redeeming the voucher. To date, program evaluations have not supported the conclusion that vouchers or many other innovations are warranted on a nationwide basis.[62]

As might be expected from a minority organization seeking a competitive advantage, Albert Shanker, leader of the teacher's union called the American Federation of Teachers, embraced the idea of "schools of choice" as early as 1988. The Center for Education Reform reported 1,156,874 students enrolled in 3,940 charter schools in 40 states and the District of Columbia in April 2007.[63] The larger teachers' union, the National Education Association, defends its dominance of public education by disapproving of charter schools and reports that assessments have not supported the presumption of superior educational outcomes through privatization.[64] NAEP scores tend to support this conclusion;[65] however, many studies are ongoing. For example, The Center for Research on Education Outcomes at Stanford University used a matched pairs design to compare 84 percent of charter school students in 16 states with regular public school students. Only 17 percent of charter school students outperformed the public school students in math with 37 percent underperforming. Closer examination of the findings suggests that charter schools may be most effective for elementary and middle schools and for children living in poverty.[66]

Teacher opposition to NCLB is understandable. State educational agencies accustomed to treating federal subsidies as general revenues face higher scrutiny over the use of federal funds. Local educational agencies face budget crises and taxpayer opposition while attempting to compensate for the decline in federal resources. Classroom teachers face larger class sizes, curricula mandates, and student proficiency expectations. The extent to which teachers should be held accountable for student educational outcomes when the classroom is only one of many variables impacting a child's readiness and capacity to learn raises a legitimate question. The National Education Association believes penalties that may include loss of employment for some teachers and school closures are draconian.[67] Yet NCLB has strong bipartisan support on the federal level. Implementation may need to be adjusted, but in the eyes of many, NCLB is both the logical conclusion of a 50-year trend toward higher accountability in public education as well as a competitive necessity for the United States in the global economy.

A more telling criticism of NCLB addresses the philosophical inconsistencies underlying the premise that no child can be left behind.[68] Shifting the locus of equality from access to educational outcomes, as measured by standardized testing, disregards differences in students' abilities and experiences and requires every child to be at least average (i.e., "on grade level"), an arithmetic impossibility. The NCLB goal of universal educational outcomes has resulted in a focus in many classrooms on assisting underperforming students. Although laudable, such an emphasis may detract from the quality of education available to top students, sacrificing excellence for mediocrity.

Early Childhood Education

Except for kindergarten, which was incorporated into the public school system in the second half of the twentieth century,[69] access to early childhood education (i.e., birth to 5 years) has not been a national priority. Bruce Fuller, Professor of Education and Public Policy at the University of California, Berkeley, traced this reluctance to parental discomfort with state or federal influence over a child's earliest years, a liberal-humanist tradition rooted in the early nineteenth century. According to this view, the early years are a period of character development and socialization (i.e., the inculcation of familial and cultural values) that is best accomplished through play and parent–child interaction rather than through classroom instruction, and the closely related issue of the mother's economic role in the family.[70] The first schools for children from birth through 5 years were organized in Boston, New York, and Philadelphia in the early nineteenth century. Initially designed to serve children from poor as well as affluent families, these so called "infant schools" took on a decidedly affluent-only flavor as their incorporation into the new public school systems had failed by the mid-nineteenth century.[71]

Early twentieth century efforts to aid low-income families led to local programs to provide care for children under school age while their mothers worked. These programs generally lacked a strong educational focus. By the 1930s, $10 million in federal funding was directed for nursery schools to provide poverty relief under the Works Progress Administration. This program expanded under the Lanham Act (1946), providing childcare services for 400,000 preschool children whose mothers worked in war-related industries during World War II. It became part of President Johnson's War on Poverty in the 1960s under the new name Operation Head Start.

Head Start was the most popular of the Office of Economic Opportunity's programs. The idea was to give children from families with low income a "head start" on formal schooling. In addition to education, Head Start emphasized social skills, nutrition, health and mental health services, and parental participation. Nearly all the nation's community action agencies operated a Head Start program. By the late 1960s, over one-half million children were enrolled throughout the country,[72] but Head Start never evolved into an entitlement program. As discussed in Chapter 2 of this book, evaluations of Head Start and other early childhood education programs are political issues in and of themselves. Among the latest, the National Head Start Impact Study, released in 2010, compared a large group of Head Start students to other children, some of whom received other early education services. The researchers found that "benefits of access to Head Start at age four are largely absent by 1st grade for the program population as a whole."[73] This and the more nuanced findings by subgroups of Head Start enrollees will provide more fuel for discussion about the best approaches for early childhood education, especially for children in low-income families.

The Child Care and Development Block Grant, established in 1990, extended federal support for the cost of childcare services for low-income working families by authorizing $2.5 billion in its first three years,[74] increasing to $5 billion in 2008,[75] not including Head Start. Much of the federal support is distributed by providing vouchers to parents so they can pay for childcare and serves as a form of income redistribution. Funds can be used to secure formal or informal care of the parent's choice. Care provided by grandparents (23 percent), non-relative home care (14 percent), and licensed family childcare homes (6 percent) exceeds the 20 percent of children enrolled in day care or preschool centers.

Estimates are that the federal government pays for one-fourth to one-third of the total cost of preschool childcare each year.[76] Childcare use produces a U-shaped distribution. Use is greatest among those in the highest and lowest income quintiles. Middle-class families with incomes just over the national median pay the highest proportion of their income for childcare because they do not qualify for federal support. They are less likely to use formal care, and when they do, have fewer choices of facilities because they are more cost conscious in selecting childcare. The quality of affordable childcare can also be an issue for middle-class parents because in more affordable centers, class size tends to be higher and teachers' education levels lower.[77] Despite these challenges, with so many mothers and fathers working, preschool enrollment for 3- and 4-year-olds has increased dramatically. Today, almost 70 percent of 4-year-olds attend a preschool center at some point prior to kindergarten.[78]

The movement toward academic outcomes and accountability that came to dominate public education has had a significant impact on childcare and early childhood education in the United States. Under the leadership of individuals like Rob Reiner and Warren Buffet, and the influence of The Pew Charitable Trusts and Pre-K Now, advocacy for the institutionalization of universal pre-K is ongoing. This movement, reminiscent of the common school movement in the early nineteenth century, seeks to make publicly funded preschool available for all 3- and 4-year-olds whose parents desire it. The movement embraces an academic emphasis on the use of numbers and preliteracy skills thought to be essential for future academic success.[79]

Not everyone is convinced that the evidence supports universal pre-K.[80] Researchers are just beginning to comprehensively assess whether pre-K classroom experiences are in the best interest of the child and lead to lasting educational advantages, and whether the pre-K emphasis should be on cognitive development rather than socialization and character development.

Higher Education

In contrast with primary and secondary public education, higher education in the United States has a long history of federal support. The Northwest Ordinance of 1787 was the first to provide land for the establishment of educational institutions, but it was the Morrill Act of 1862 that established the land-grant universities that many students attend today. [81] Events associated with World War II revolutionized U.S. higher education. Jewish émigrés and other academics from Nazi-controlled Europe brought the higher research standards of Europe to America in the pre-war years; federal funding for war-related research like the Manhattan Project created the modern American research universities; and the Serviceman's Readjustment Act of 1944, commonly known as the GI Bill, increased college and university enrollments.[82] The GI Bill gave returning military unprecedented opportunities to obtain a college education. College enrollments doubled from 1.5 million students in 1940 to 3 million in 1950.[83] Eventually, eight million veterans received educational assistance through this legislation.[84] In 1947, the GI Bill funded 49 percent of those enrolled in college.[85] Registrars were completely unprepared to deal with the mass of applicants, and the Educational Testing Service (ETS) responded by designing the Scholastic Aptitude Test (SAT) to assess the large influx of nontraditional students. There were over half a million test-takers by 1957.[86] Mass enrollment in post-secondary education and the testing apparatus to facilitate this enrollment began to change two things about the United States—educational aspirations and academic expectations.

Increased access to undergraduate and graduate education was inherent in the NDEA of 1958. Title II created the National Defense Student Loan Program, which provided almost $443 million to approximately 600,000 needy students in its first six years. Annual and cumulative limits were established for student borrowing with repayment deferred until one year after leaving college. Interest rates were fixed at 3 percent, and partial loan forgiveness was possible based on years of service for those taking jobs as elementary or secondary school teachers. This new student loan program aimed to support academically gifted students and financially needy students. This dual focus diluted the impact of this loan for the financially needy with most of the loans benefitting gifted students. Results were mixed with little evidence that college enrollment increased among lower-income applicants; however, students were highly receptive to paying for college with loans.[87]

President Johnson's War on Poverty also focused on increased access to higher education. The Economic Opportunity Act (1964) established what is now called the Federal Work Study Program for students who needed financial aid. In 1965, the Higher Education Act (HEA), a complement to ESEA, also expanded access. Title IV was clearly the most significant part of this legislation. Title IV created the Educational Opportunity Grant Program that provided the first public funds for student grants and the Guaranteed Student Loan Program that provided federal insurance for private loans to students.[88]

Like ESEA, HEA has been reauthorized regularly with modifications. In 1972, the reauthorized Title IV converted the NDEA loan program into the National Direct Student Loan Program (renamed the Perkins Loan in 1986) and created the Basic Educational Opportunity Grant Program (renamed Pell grants in 1980). The Guaranteed Student Loan Program was renamed the Federal Stafford Loan Program and grouped with smaller loan programs as the Federal Family Education Loan (FFEL) program in 1992. Funding for all Title IV programs was constrained, especially during the retrenchment of the Reagan years in the 1980s, with restrictions on the size of Pell grants and lower subsidies to reduce interest rates on student loans as eligibility standards began favoring lower-income households. Pell grants did not expand again until the 1998 reauthorization of HEA under the Clinton administration.[89]

Controversy always accompanies HEA reauthorization, especially surrounding Title IV programs. Pell grants are clearly the dominant source of student aid. In the late 1970s, a Pell grant paid almost 100 percent of the tuition, fees, and room and board of a public two-year institution and over 70 percent of the same costs for a public four-year institution, but the purchasing power of these grants has eroded significantly.[90] Congress has not appropriated full funding of Pell grant authorized limits since the 1970s.[91] Controversy has also plagued the loan programs, most currently with accusations of lender kickbacks to college personnel and inadequate DOE supervision of the repayment process and collections.[92] On March 30, 2010, President Obama signed the Health Care and Education Reconciliation Act of 2010. Among the things it did was eliminate federal subsidies to banks for providing student loans, transferred all student loan administration directly to the DOE, and increased the Pell grant award.[93] Illustration 9.1 discusses the controversies over the student loan changes.

Higher education grew tremendously in the latter half of the twentieth century. In 1949–1950 there were 1,851 degree-granting institutions with revenues of $2.4 million and 2.7 million students. In 2005–2006 there were 4,276 institutions with nearly $400 billion in revenues and 17.5 million students[94] (Figure 9.3 shows the sources of higher education funding). The proportion of recent high school graduates enrolling in college increased from 45 percent in 1960 to 66 percent in 2006, with women's enrollment increasing the most.[95] Looking at this growth internationally, "Today more than one-third of American adults have attended post-secondary institutions compared to about one-fifth of the Japanese and about one-tenth of those in Western Europe."[96] Although there have been debates as to the quality of higher education provided when access is so high, the *International Adult Literacy Survey* measured prose literacy, document literacy, and quantitative literacy in 22 nations from 1994 to 1998. Only two nations outperformed adults in the United States on the prose scale and only three on the document and quantitative scales.[97]

ILLUSTRATION 9.1
Who Should Make Loans to Students for Higher Education?

THE DEBATE ON FFEL VS. DIRECT LENDING PROGRAMS

We know you're tired after a long school year and you don't feel like pondering higher education politics when the summer hot spots are calling your name. However, the latest legislation is almost certain to affect college parents and students who use federal financial aid. Part of President Obama's higher education budget proposes that, starting in academic year 2010–2011, all new student loans be originated through the Direct Student Loan program, thereby marching all Federal Family Education Loan program (FFELP) student loan lenders to their demise. You can explore the proposed changes at http://edlabor.house.gov/newsroom/education/higher-education/, but we've outlined some of the arguments on both sides below:

MOVING FEDERAL LOANS ENTIRELY THROUGH THE DIRECT LENDING PROGRAM WILL ELIMINATE COMPETITION AND CHOICE

In the past, banks and other student loan lenders have competed for your federal loan business. Student loan borrowers have benefited from this competitive environment through better customer service, efficient processes and additional borrower incentives, like interest rate reduction rewards for making on-time payments. Although interest rates on federal student loans are the same everywhere, it is the varying array of lender incentives that have often been the deciding factor for families selecting a loan product.

The most spirited capitalists would discourage the government from taking over any industry and eliminating choice for the customer. If the legislation becomes law, students' and parents' only option if they need federal student loans will be to apply for a loan with the Department of Education through the William D. Ford Direct Loan Program. Have you ever been forced to use a company because it had a monopoly on the market? The reality is

that if you are unhappy with the service it provides you, there are no alternatives. Until the government finds a way to provide great service that is on par with the private sector, this will probably remain a negative point.

On the flip side, according to the Congressional Budget Office, the Department becoming the sole provider of federal student loans saves taxpayers' money—money the Department of Education plans to use to increase Pell Grant scholarship and provide for other forms of student aid and still save $1 billion in taxpayers' money. If the CBO's budget calculations are correct (and this is being debated), over the next ten years shifting loans from the private sector to the Department would save taxpayers almost $100 billion dollars. Rep. George Miller, chairman of the House Education and Labor Committee, says that these billions of dollars in savings can "be used to further boost college aid and reduce our deficit," while also "making our nation more competitive" in the long run.

IS THE GOVERNMENT BETTER AT COLLECTING ON STUDENT LOAN DEBTS THAN PRIVATE BANKS AND LENDERS?

According to recent data from the Department of Education, they are. Only 5.3 percent of borrowers in the direct loan program default compared to 7.3 percent in the bank-based program. The accuracy of this data has been disputed by lenders who noted that the data came out one day before the proposed legislation and similar program comparison numbers have not been published for several years. School type (such as for profits, versus not-for profits), can skew this as well, and most for-profit schools have trended higher in default rates and are often not Direct Loan Program participants. Sallie Mae has recently pointed out that its borrowers, who participate in default prevention programs through state loan guarantee agencies, are 30 percent less likely to default than Direct Loan borrowers.

(Continued)

HOW WOULD THE LEGISLATION IMPACT SCHOOLS AND ULTIMATELY STUDENTS?

All schools currently in the FFEL program would be required to change their operational systems to support the Direct Lending model. For schools currently in the FFEL program, this would mean investing staff time and money to change systems and processes at a time where budgets have been cut to the core. It's realistic to imagine that those costs may have to be absorbed through increased tuition and student fees.

CAN THE GOVERNMENT FINANCE EVERY FEDERAL STUDENT LOAN DOLLAR LENT?

The recent crisis in the credit markets made it very difficult for private banks and lenders to raise money to lend to students. A loan access crisis was averted by the creation of a stopgap government financing and loan purchase program, allowing the FFEL program to continue to function during the credit crunch. But, the argument goes, if banks are using government money to lend to students today, it makes sense that the government could just step in and lend the money directly to students itself through the Direct Loan program.

On the other hand, just how much more money would the government need to lend if it discontinues the FFEL program and transitioned all new loan volume into Direct lending? Well, the number is growing every year, but it is now about $60 billion annually. That's a big jump for the Direct Lending program to make in one year. If you're a student and the legislation passes, expect the first few years to have some bumps along the way as the government ramps up. Just make sure you stay on top of your student loan paperwork and disbursements.

Source: College Loan Corporation, "The Debate on FFEL vs. Direct Lending Programs." Retrieved March 6, 2010, from http://www.collegeloan.com/college-loan-corp-news/student-loan-articles/the-debate-on-ffel-vs-direct-lending-programs/ This excerpt is copyrighted material of College Loan Corporation (www.collegeloan.com) and is used by permission.

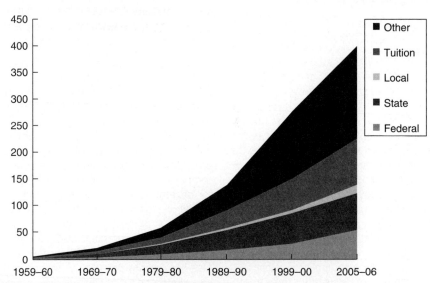

FIGURE 9.3   Revenues by Source for Higher Education (in billions of dollars)

Other includes endowments, gifts, and revenues from auxiliary enterprises including hospitals.
Source: Compiled using data from U.S. Department of Education, National Center for Education Statistics, *Digest of Educational Statistics: 2008,* Tables 348-350. Retrieved March 6, 2010, from http://nces.ed.gov/programs/digest/2008menu_tables.asp

WAS THIRTY YEARS OF EDUCATIONAL REFORM NECESSARY?

Since World War II there has been an undercurrent of public and political dissatisfaction with the quality of the U.S. educational system. Is this perception accurate? A report by the Strategic Studies Center, Sandia National Laboratories, in 1991 contained surprising findings.[98] On-time, high school graduation rates had been stable for 20 years and were among the highest in the world. NAEP standardized test scores had been steady or improved over the same time period with the largest improvements occurring in basic skills. The decline in SAT scores from the 1950s to the 1970s was clearly attributed to an increase in the number of test-takers from the lower quartiles of high school achievement, a laudable indicator of improved access. International comparisons indicated that the United States had the highest rates of college enrollment and graduation in the world. Significant progress had also been made in the diversity of college enrollment with all "minority" groups, including women, demonstrating an accelerated rate of post-secondary participation. The researchers' analysis of job-related compensatory programs did not support anecdotal claims that U.S. high school graduates were unprepared for employment. Employers in both Japan and Germany, countries reputedly with better educational systems, outspent U.S. employers in workplace training.[99]

Sandia's findings did not support President George H. W. Bush's education reform policies, which were predicated on the public perception that the U.S. educational system was in crisis. This led to significant obstacles in distributing the report with publication delayed for two years. The academic response to the report was replete with methodological criticism, but the findings were largely upheld. According to education professor Lawrence C. Stedman:

> In spite of several problems in their analyses and argument, the Sandia analysts deserve great credit for restoring a balance in the discussion of U.S. education. In broad outlines, their perspective is right—performance generally has been stable over the last two decades, there have been improvements in some areas, the United States is a world leader in high school and college graduation, and ethnic and racial groups need to be targeted for assistance because they continue to lag behind. Their data-driven analyses are a welcome counterpoint to the critics' insistent trumpeting of a decline in excellence.[100]

Politically, Sandia's findings were unpalatable to the U.S. public. Harold Bloom's *The Closing of the American Mind,* a surprise on the *New York Times* bestseller list for four months, may best exemplify popular criticism of U.S. higher education.[101] Even Stedman, who spoke laudably of the Sandia report, joined the chorus critical of U.S. public education in a overly scathing review of *The Manufactured Crisis: Myths, Fraud, and the Attack on American Public Schools.*[102]

Recent analyses underscore the strength of U.S. education. Since 1980, the secondary or high school dropout rate for 16- to 24-year-olds has declined from 14.1 percent to 8.7 percent.[103] The Organization for Economic Cooperation and Development (OECD), an international collaboration of the 30 most economically developed countries, reported that the United States has the highest college graduation rate (34.5 percent) in the world for adults 25 to 64 years of age.[104] Furthermore, as Harvard University president Derek Bok summarized:

> Whether one looks at the number of Nobel Prize winners, the share of articles in scientific journals, or the frequency with which scientific results are cited, the United States has plainly had great success in promoting the discovery of new knowledge.[105]

EDUCATION AND THE OBAMA ADMINISTRATION

Organizing for America, a national organization supportive of President Barack Obama, and the direct successor of his election campaign, ascribes this stance to the forty-fourth U.S. president:

> [P]reparing our children to compete in the global economy is one of the most urgent challenges we face. We need to stop paying lip service to public education, and start holding communities, administrators, teachers, parents and students accountable. We will prepare the next generation for success in college and the workforce, ensuring that American children lead the world once again in creativity and achievement.[106]

To the dismay of the many educators opposed to NCLB who supported his candidacy, Obama is clearly aligning himself with the general trends of the last thirty years—access, achievement, and accountability.

In general, educators have supported Obama's focus on *access* and college affordability. The "American Opportunity" Tax Credit, part of the American Recovery and Reinvestment Tax Act of 2009, raised the maximum education tax credit to $2,500 and made a portion of it refundable based on taxpayer income. The Tax Policy Center estimates that this will direct $13.9 billion to support higher education over the next ten years.[107] The recently signed Health Care and Education Reconciliation Act of 2010 eliminated $68 billion in student loan subsidies for private lenders. Half of it was used to increase Pell grants to $5,550 per student in 2010 and will link future Pell authorizations to inflation through 2017.[108]

With regard to *achievement,* educators have been less enthusiastic. The Obama administration's "blueprint" for reauthorizing the Elementary and Secondary Education Act calls for softening the school-based annual yearly progress assessments in favor of a broader goal, that every student "graduate from high school ready for college and a career." [109] Advocates of eliminating achievement gaps between socioeconomic and racial/ethnic groups have expressed concern that this signals a retreat from a focus on achievement; however, a better conclusion is that the blueprint represents a shift in focus from school-based to student-based accountability.

Student-based *accountability* is a significant escalation of the standards under NCLB. The administration's blueprint calls for "a new generation of assessments" that measure individual student progress and enable teacher and principal evaluation based on that student progress. It proposes converting the state-established education standards permissible under NCLB to a single national standard of proficiency. Republicans, educators, and state governments have opposed such a move as far back as the 1965 passage of ESEA. The blueprint also intends to encourage state and local innovation by converting most federal funding for public education from per pupil formulas to competitive grants, another controversial move. The 2009 stimulus package already included the largest discretionary funding for education in history—$4.35 billion in competitive state funding known as "Race to the Top." States will not be eligible to apply for this funding without first eliminating any state legislation that prohibits basing teacher compensation on student academic performance or that restricts charter schools. States must also establish remediation programs for low performing schools that include closure, conversion to charter schools, and/or complete replacement of administration and faculty.

A top priority in Race to the Top is the creation of systems to track student progress, as measured by national standardized tests, and to link this progress to specific teachers and principals. Both teachers' unions have been strongly critical, calling the Race to the Top proposal "Bush III."[110] There is some truth to this claim. The primary differences between

George W. Bush's educational policy and Barack Obama's appears to the latter's preference for revenue enhancements rather than sanctions and the movement of accountability downward from school to individual classroom teacher. Legislation to reauthorize ESEA and the extent to which this reauthorization may implement the blueprint has yet to be determined. Considerable opposition from the educational establishment is expected, and many voices have already entered the fray.[111]

FEDERAL RELUCTANCE IN EMPLOYMENT POLICY

Historically, the federal government was as reluctant to get involved in labor markets as it was to intervene in public education. Since colonial times the prevailing sentiment was that America was a land of opportunity for anyone willing to work. As recently as 1889 when the first parts of the Oklahoma territory were opened, the primary American solution to unemployment was land. The Homestead Act of 1862 signed into law by Abraham Lincoln offered a quarter section (160 acres) to anyone who had not borne arms against the United States and who was willing to apply, improve, and reside on the land. After six months, deed passed for a mere $1.25 per acre. By 1900, 80 million acres had been purchased.[112]

Prior to establishment of the U.S. Department of Labor (DOL) in 1913, public response to unemployment was relegated to local and state governments. In the seventeenth century, some American colonies established almshouses and workhouses after the English tradition[113] that were essentially punishment for the indolent. "Pauperism," a nineteenth-century term for the growing unemployment in northern urban centers in the mid-1800s, was addressed with the same reluctant and judgmental spirit. In part, the birth of the U.S. labor movement can be traced to the untenable position of common laborers in these northern urban centers who had no recourse against unreasonable and unregulated work rules in dangerous factory employment except stigmatized residence in a workhouse.

Workers organized into local unions as early as the 1820s, but a national and sustainable labor movement did not survive the periodic nineteenth-century economic downturns until Samuel Gompers and the American Federation of Labor (AFL) came on the scene in 1886. The AFL advocated for an eight-hour work day, higher wages to keep the skilled laborer from "sinking to the level of pauper wages,"[114] and ultimately for a seat for labor in the President's cabinet. In 1913, the Organic Act of the Department of Labor (DOL) began providing labor a voice. The DOL's purpose was "to foster, promote and develop the welfare of working people, to improve their working conditions, and to advance their opportunities for profitable employment."[115] The first Secretary of Labor, William B. Wilson, was a strong advocate for labor and interpreted this charge to mean that the department was created in the interest of the wage earner. By 1915 he had converted 80 immigration offices across the country into employment offices, and by 1917, over 287,000 people had found employment with DOL assistance.[116] Wilson was a controversial figure. In 1920, he was threatened with impeachment for refusing to deport the majority of the 4,000 labor activists arrested under the Anarchist Exclusion Act of 1918. Legislative support for his pro-labor agenda was minimal.

Early social workers were intimately involved in advocacy for improved working conditions and labor organizing. In 1899, social workers Jane Addams and Josephine Shaw Lowell tapped their colleague Florence Kelley to be the first executive secretary of the National Consumers League (NCL).[117] In this capacity until 1932, Kelley's primary responsibility was organizing local NCL chapters. She was instrumental in promoting state regulations that were the precursors to the 1938 Fair Labor and Standards Act, which is best known for its minimum wage, overtime pay, and child labor provisions.[118] Federal reluctance to regulate work and intervene in labor markets ended with the devastating unemployment caused by the Great Depression and the 1932 election of Franklin Delano Roosevelt who intended to put people back to work.

RELUCTANCE OVERCOME: THE NEW DEAL

When Roosevelt took office, 25 percent of Americans were unemployed. The Gross Domestic Product, a measure of the size of the U.S. economy, had fallen by nearly 48 percent.[119] Social worker Francis Perkins, the first woman to serve in a president's cabinet, was Secretary of DOL from 1933 until 1945. The first legislation passed during her tenure was the Emergency Conservation Work Act of 1933 that created the Civilian Conservation Corps. This popular program ultimately relocated three million 18- to 25-year-old urban men to rural camps where they were paid one dollar a day to work on a variety of conservation efforts on public lands.[120] In addition to the Fair Labor Standards Act, other major employment legislation that passed with Perkins's leadership included the Wagner-Peyser Act of 1933 that established the U.S. Employment Service and the National Labor Relations Act (or Wagner Act) of 1935 that legalized collective bargaining.[121]

Harry Hopkins, another social worker Roosevelt appointed, became head of the Federal Emergency Relief Administration (FERA) in 1933 and moved to the subsequent Work Progress Administration (WPA) in 1935. FERA was primarily a public assistance program, but the WPA made it a low-wage public works program. The WPA employed eight million people prior to World War II. The National Youth Administration, part of WPA, provided work study jobs for those enrolled in high school and college, and a variety of temporary job programs were available to those not enrolled in school.

Despite the proliferation of New Deal programs, the unemployment and economic crisis of the 1930s was not resolved until the United States entered World War II.[122] From 1940 to 1944, 10 million men entered the U.S. military, and 5 million women took their places in the workforce.[123] When World War II ended, the GI Bill helped to smooth men's reintroduction to the labor force, but no corresponding provisions were made for women who were expected to return to their traditional role of homemaker. As the challenge of rebuilding Europe through the Marshall Plan stimulated U.S. economic growth, the federal government's focus on employment waned. The Taft-Hartley Act (1947), for example, placed significant restrictions on labor unions.

THE WAR ON POVERTY: THE SEARCH FOR A CURE

By the middle of the twentieth century, the United States had attempted several strategies to address poverty and hardship during the course of its history. It had adopted the *alleviative* strategy of public assistance through programs such as Aid to Families with Dependent Children, which attempted only to ease the hardships of poverty. It had adopted the social insurance strategy through programs such as Social Security and unemployment insurance to compel people to save money in order to *prevent* economic problems that are likely to result from old age, death, disability, sickness, and unemployment. And it had directly employed people who could not find work in the private sector through programs such as the Civilian Conservation Corps and the Works Progress Administration.

During the War on Poverty of the 1960s, the federal government adopted another approach, this time a *curative* strategy to help the poor become self-supporting by bringing about changes in these individuals and in their environment. The War on Poverty's curative strategy was supposed to break the cycle of poverty and allow economically disadvantaged Americans to move into the country's working classes and eventually its middle classes. The strategy was "rehabilitation and not relief." The Economic Opportunity Act of 1964, the centerpiece of the War on Poverty, was to "strike at the causes, not just the consequences, of poverty."

In his influential 1958 book *The Affluent Society,* John Kenneth Galbraith, who became President John F. Kennedy's economic advisor, called attention to poverty in the midst of a generally affluent society.[124] Galbraith distinguished between *case poverty* and *area poverty.* Case poverty was largely a product of some personal characteristic of the poor—old age, illiteracy, inadequate education, lack of job skills, poor health, race—which prevented them from participating in the nation's prosperity. Area poverty was a product of economic deficiency relating to a particular sector of the nation, such as West Virginia and much of the rest of Appalachia. "Pockets of poverty" or "depressed areas" developed because of technological change or a lack of industrialization—for instance, decline in the coal industry, the exhaustion of iron ore mines, and the squeezing out of small farmers from the agricultural market. Area poverty has also resulted from declines in the automobile, steel, and petroleum industries in regions that came to be called the country's "rust belt," and in deteriorated inner city neighborhoods as economic enterprise moved to the suburbs.

Area Poverty: Addressing Economic Deficiencies of Place

The Economic Opportunity Act included several mechanisms to address area poverty.

ECONOMIC DEVELOPMENT ADMINISTRATION (EDA)   The initial forays in the War on Poverty begun in the Kennedy administration included the fight against area poverty. The Area Redevelopment Act of 1961, for example, authorized federal grants and loans to governments and businesses in designated "depressed areas" to promote economic activity. This program was later revised in the Public Works and Economic Development Act of 1965. This legislation has been criticized as a "trickle-down" approach to alleviating poverty, contending that most benefits went to business and not to the poor. Republicans have also called it a pork barrel program to aid Democrats in getting reelected. The Economic Development Administration (EDA), part of the U.S. Department of Commerce, has long defended its work, saying that its efforts pay for themselves by generating jobs and related tax revenues in distressed communities. EDA's two major goals are "attracting private capital investment and creating higher-skill, higher-wage jobs."[125] Today, the EDA states that its work with state and local governments, regional economic development districts, public and private nonprofit organizations, and Indian tribes "is guided by the basic principle that distressed communities must be empowered to develop and implement their own economic development and revitalization strategies."[126]

President Reagan tried to abolish the EDA. The agency's annual appropriations continued to dwindle under the George W. Bush administration. But the unfolding economic crisis that became apparent in 2008 resulted in a significant expansion of the EDA's appropriations, which grew from $280 million in 2007[127] to more than $779 million in 2008 to create a sustaining fund for economic development in domestic regions suffering natural disasters.[128] The Obama administration's American Recovery and Reinvestment Act (ARRA) of 2009 provided another $150 million for job creation and economic development in regions hardest hit by the economic crisis.[129]

COMMUNITY DEVELOPMENT BLOCK GRANT (CDBG)   Since 1974, the federal government has also provided funds to local Community Development Corporations to aid depressed areas through economic development efforts and a variety of other neighborhood revitalization activities.[130] The CDBG, administered by the Department of Housing and Urban Development, has come under the same criticisms as the EDA for poor targeting. For example, the George W. Bush administration said that while the CDBG was "designed to boost low-income communities, its effectiveness is diluted by the inclusion of some of the richest cites in the country."[131] Apart from disaster relief funding, CDBG appropriations were on a slight downward trajectory until President Obama's election. With an additional $1 billion in ARRA funding, CDBG appropriations increased by more than 26 percent in 2009.

ENTERPRISE ZONES   In response to The Heritage Foundation's advocacy of "supply-side economics" in the 1970s, Republican and conservative opposition to federal efforts to address area poverty began to abate. From Heritage's perspective, enterprise zones were an opportunity to demonstrate the economic efficiency and effectiveness of tax reductions and business deregulation.[132] Enterprise zones were expected to encourage businesses to locate in economically distressed areas in order to boost employment and the local economy and increase community services. Despite strong support by then-President Reagan in the 1980s, Congress was slow to give these zones financial support because the tax breaks would cause a loss in federal revenue. In the wake of the 1992 Los Angeles riots following the acquittal of white police officers in the beating of African American Rodney King, Congress reconsidered.

In 1993 Congress funded nine empowerment zones or EZs (six in urban and three in rural areas) and 95 enterprise communities or ECs (65 in urban and 30 in rural areas), opening competition for $3.5 billion in federal funding. Each empowerment zone selected got tax incentives, including as much as $20 million in tax-exempt bonds. For each area resident a business in the zone hired, it was able to deduct up to $3,000 (20 percent of the first $15,000 of the employee's income) and some training expenses from its taxes. Each urban empowerment zone also got a $100 million social service block grant (for services such as child development, drug treatment, and job training), and each rural zone got $40 million; the enterprise communities received about $3 million each for these purposes. Zone applicants were required to submit a plan for supplementing the federal funding with state and local resources.

Congress eventually appropriated funds for a second round of EZs and ECs in 1999 and a third round in 2001, bringing the total to 30 urban EZs, 10 rural EZs, 65 urban ECs, and 50 rural ECs. The 2001 legislation also designated 40 renewal communities (RCs) in place of ECs. In the last round, communities got federal tax incentives to hire residents and improve business operations, but no grant funding. A 2008 Yale University report gave the urban EZs high marks for improving local labor participation rates and improving rental housing occupancy in comparison to rejected EZ applicants.[133] Less pro-business analysts believe the evidence is mixed:[134] Employment growth and income growth is rare, with employment shifting to the EZ rather than expanding regionally. Those economic benefits that do occur tend to be short-lived. Federal funding of this initiative was due to end in 2009; however, President Obama recommended extension of the EZ and RC designations through December 2010.[135]

Case Poverty: Addressing Economic Deficiencies of Persons

In addition to area poverty, the War on Poverty also addressed case poverty.

LBJ AND THE ECONOMIC OPPORTUNITY ACT   When Lyndon B. Johnson assumed the presidency in 1963 after the assassination of President Kennedy, he saw an opportunity to distinguish his administration and to carry forward the traditions of Franklin D. Roosevelt. Johnson, a former public school teacher, believed that government work and training efforts, particularly those directed at youth, could break the cycle of poverty by giving people the basic skills to improve their employability and make them self-sufficient adults. To accomplish this, he championed the Economic Opportunity Act.

The Office of Economic Opportunity (OEO) was originally intended to support antipoverty programs devised by the local community action agency. Projects could include literacy training, health services, legal aid, neighborhood service centers, vocational training, childhood development activities, or other innovative ideas.

YOUTH TRAINING AND EMPLOYMENT The Economic Opportunity Act of 1964 established three primary youth programs: the Job Corps, the Neighborhood Youth Corps, and the Work-Study program. Each program was designed to mimic Depression-era programs like the Civilian Conservation Corps and National Youth Administration that ended with World War II. The Job Corps provided education, vocational training, and work experience in rural conservation camps for unemployable youth aged 16 to 24 years. Job Corps trainees were to be "hard core" unemployables who could benefit from training away from their home environment—breaking habits and associations that were obstacles to employment while learning reading, arithmetic, and self-healthcare, as well as auto mechanics, clerical work, and other skills. The Job Corps was transferred to the Department of Labor in 1969. It continues to operate 122 Job Corps centers across the country. The Neighborhood Youth Corps was designed to provide work, counseling, and on-the-job training for young people in or out of school who were living at home. The Neighborhood Youth Corps was to serve young people who were more employable than those expected in the Job Corps. The Work-Study program helped students from low-income families remain in high school or college by providing them with federally paid, part-time employment in conjunction with cooperating public or private agencies.

Job Corps: Expensive and Ineffective. Today, the Job Corps serves nearly 60,000 youth aged 16 to 24 per year at 122 centers located throughout the country.[136] The Job Corps is the government's most expensive job training program for youth with spending at more than $1.6 billion in 2009.[137] Services are usually provided in residential programs and include rather intensive basic education, vocational training, and work experience as well as interpersonal skill development, healthcare, recreational, and other support services. The Job Corps is intended to be attractive to youth. Computer-managed instruction is used to teach reading, math, writing, and thinking skills. Services and length of participation are geared to each youth's needs.

The DOL has commissioned two large evaluations of the Job Corps at different times in the program's history. The final report of the most recent study was published in 2006.[138] The study is based on a random sample of 11,313 Job Corps applicants (not just those who actually received services) from late 1994 through 1995 and followed them for four years. The control group could not enroll in the Job Corps, but they were free to access other services. Study results are based upon all applicants who completed a fourth-year interview (this included about 80 percent of both experimental and control group members).

The researchers estimated that the government spends about $25,000 per Job Corps enrollee.[139] If the gains in year four earnings were sustained, Job Corps participation would produce benefits of about $31,000 over the enrollee's lifetime, a negligible net gain to society. However, gains did not persist after the first four years, according to annual earnings records from 1998 to 2004. Thus, costs associated with the Job Corps programs cannot be justified on the basis of participants' future earnings alone. Whether reductions in public assistance and lower levels of involvement in the criminal justice system warrant maintenance of the Job Corps program are questions yet to be carefully addressed. The Job Corps seems to serve participants with serious obstacles to employment, but participants' future earnings do not significantly rise and "the program's costs exceed its benefits."[140] Perhaps it is time to try some new approach as Illustration 9.2 suggests.

ILLUSTRATION 9.2
A Better Way to Get Educated, Employed
Robert Lerman

With a 10 percent national unemployment rate looming, the race is on to create jobs quickly and to skill-train the workforce so the next recession hurts less. President Obama's policy is to help millions more young people and laid-off workers attend community colleges. But community colleges already are swamped by job-seekers' stepped-up demand for training, and government funds for higher education already are stretched perilously thin.

As cash-strapped states struggle to sustain support or minimize cuts to community colleges, federal stimulus money and Pell grants can help more students and displaced workers enroll. But the end result could well be crowded classrooms presided over by less qualified teachers. Worse, many eager applicants will be turned away.

Is there a grade A solution? Luckily, yes. Demonstrably more effective at increasing earnings than a community college education is the nation's apprenticeship system. One model getting off the ground in South Carolina expands apprenticeship and blends it with technical college.

If you think apprenticeship sounds like a relic from centuries past—good enough for Ben Franklin but a no-go in a twenty-first-century economy—think again. Nearly all advanced economies still incubate skills in the workplace. In Germany, the world's leading exporter of advanced goods, 60 percent to 70 percent of young people enter formal apprenticeships, signing up for years of rigorous on-the-job learning combined with academic coursework.

Apprenticeship is expanding significantly in the United Kingdom, Australia and other countries too. And the European Commission is calling for the public and private sectors to create 5 million apprenticeships by the end of 2010.

Largely unnoticed, the U.S. apprenticeship system currently trains over 500,000 workers. Apprentices learn while they earn, working as a regular employee, contributing to companies' output and mastering skills under the wing of trainers, who themselves learned mainly by doing. Apprentices take formal courses too, sometimes at community colleges or their work site with community college instructors. After two to four years of work, job-based training, and classes, apprentices get a well-recognized occupational credential that documents their new expertise.

Research suggests that apprenticing raises a worker's earnings far more than just taking community college courses does. In Washington State, apprentices' annual earnings rose by nearly $12,000, more than double the gains for former community college students.

Apprenticeship's appeal is especially great in today's cash-poor environment. Government costs—for marketing and oversight—are low, since employers pay most training costs. The skills learned are what the market demands, bolstering the worker's career prospects. Unlike full-time students, apprentices get wages that increase with skills. And many apprentices earn credit toward a college degree, which still matters in many jobs that workers-in-training hope to land.

Given their low costs and high long-term payoffs, what's the best way to beef up apprenticeship programs? First, increase the pittance—$21 million nationwide—allocated to the Labor Department's Office of Apprenticeship so its staff can help employers set up new programs. Doubling the budget means thousands of new apprenticeship positions. Besides earnings gains, an upward bump of that size would fuel increases in payroll and income tax revenue that far exceed the added program costs.

South Carolina's success in expanding registered apprenticeship drives the story home. Thanks go to the state's business community, modest state funding (about $1 million a year) and annual S.C. employer tax credits of $1,000 per apprentice starting in 2007. The Apprenticeship Carolina Division of the S.C. Technical College System has registered an average of one new employer-sponsored apprenticeship program per week and more than doubled the number of apprentices. Career opportunities have been created in advanced manufacturing, healthcare, information technology, and other hot sectors.

As another stimulus to apprenticeship, the federal government could reimburse employers for the classroom training. After all, federal subsidies to students taking community college classes that may or may not lead to jobs top $4.5 billion.

In an economy shedding jobs, it's penny- and pound-wise to subsidize apprenticeships to create jobs and help more workers build high-quality careers. A cost-effective subsidy might be, say, $3,000–$5,000 for each apprentice hired beyond 80 percent of last year's level.

Higher learning deserves its high place in the nation's workforce-development strategy. But for the growing numbers who would be best served by learning and earning at the same time, policymakers and business leaders must form partnerships that deliver on apprenticeship's promise—job creation and more rewarding careers for more American workers.

Dr. Lerman is an institute fellow at the Urban Institute in Washington and an economics professor at American University.

Source: thestate.com (Columbia, S.C.), August 3, 2009. "A Better Way to Get Educated, Employed" by Robert Lerman is reprinted by permission. This article was retrieved March 6, 2010, from the Urban Institute website, http://www.urban.org/publications/901274.html

AmeriCorps: Boosting Education and Employment Through Service. Established under the Clinton Administration, AmeriCorps provides various options for Americans 18 years and older to earn money for college or vocational education in exchange for service within the United States. AmeriCorps subsumed the former VISTA program in a program now called AmeriCorps*VISTA, which is committed to bringing low-income individuals and communities out of poverty. Other AmeriCorps programs include AmeriCorps*State and National (funding goes to nonprofit organizations that sponsor volunteers) and AmeriCorps*National Civilian Community Corps (NCCC) (participants, aged 18 to 24, live together in one of several designated communities to provide service, and they receive leadership training and team building similar to the military). VISTA and NCCC members are prohibited from maintaining outside employment during a full-time commitment, but the State and National program is more flexible.[141]

AmeriCorps participants can choose an educational award of $4,725 or $1,200 in cash for a year of community service (they may serve for two years). They also get a modest living allowance that varies by state if they work 1,700 hours in a nine- to 12-month period). Part-time work is also permissible for half the stipend. Volunteers serve in educational, public safety, environmental, health, and social welfare positions. They get healthcare benefits, student loan deferment, and, if needed, childcare benefits. There is no maximum age limit, and people of any income may participate in the VISTA and State and National programs.

In addition to AmeriCorps, the Corporation for National and Community Service[142] is responsible for the Senior Corps and Learn and Serve America programs. Senior Corps includes the Foster Grandparent Program, the Retired Senior Volunteer Program (RSVP), and the Senior Companion Program, all designed to encourage Americans aged 55 and older to serve their communities. Learn and Serve America encourages community service by elementary, secondary, and college students. In 2008, the Corporation reported that there were 500,000 Senior Corps volunteers.[143] Since 1993, Senior Corps members have provided over 1 billion volunteer service hours, over 400,000 individuals have served through AmeriCorps, and more than 1 million high school students have participated through Learn and Serve. President Obama is a strong proponent of the federal volunteer programs with $210 million being directed at program expansion through the ARRA.

FEDERAL JOB PROGRAMS The fight against case poverty began with the Manpower Development and Training Act (MDTA) of 1962—the first large-scale, federally funded job training program. Eventually, MDTA was absorbed into the Comprehensive Employment and Training Act of 1973 and later into the Reagan administration's Job Training Partnership Act of 1982. Today, these program fall under the Workforce Investment Act of 1998.

Comprehensive Employment and Training Act (CETA). Initially, CETA was directed at the structurally unemployed—the long-term, "hard-core" unemployed who have few job skills, little experience, and perhaps other barriers to employment. But later, particularly in response to the economic recession of 1974–1975, Congress included people affected by "cyclical" unemployment—temporary unemployment caused by depressed economic conditions. The U.S. Department of Labor was given overall responsibility for consolidating these job-training programs and distributing funds to city, county, and state governments to administer them. CETA provided job training for over 3.5 million people per year. Programs included classroom training, on-the-job experience, and public-service employment. "Prime sponsor" local governments contracted with private community-based organizations (CBOs) to help recruit poor and minority trainees, provide initial classroom training, and place individuals in public-service jobs.

As it turned out, cities used a major share of CETA funds to pay individuals to work in regular municipal jobs. In some cases, cities facing financial stress used CETA funds to cut back on their own spending without laying off large numbers of their employees. Estimates were that local governments had originally funded about half of CETA jobs. As a result, CETA was criticized for failing to target those who needed the assistance most—the economically disadvantaged and long-term, hard-core unemployed. One estimate was that only one-third of all CETA workers came from families receiving public assistance. Prime sponsors tended to skim off the most skilled of the unemployed. Nonetheless, according to federal figures, about 45 percent of participants had less than a high school education, 39 percent were age 21 or younger, about 40 percent were minorities, and 73 percent were classified as "low income."[144]

The Humphrey-Hawkins Act of 1978 "guaranteed" jobs to every "able and willing" adult American. The ambitious language of the act reflects the leadership of its sponsor, the late Senator Hubert H. Humphrey (D-MN). The act viewed the federal government as "the employer of last resort" and pledged to create public-service jobs and put the unemployed to work on public projects. Lowering the unemployment rate to 3 percent was to be a national goal. The Humphrey-Hawkins Act seems more symbolic of liberal concerns than a real national commitment. Even in the strongest of economic times, it is unlikely that the national unemployment rate will ever be reduced to 3 percent. Rather than public service jobs, Congress is more concerned with the creation of what has been called "real," permanent, private-sector jobs.

Job Training Partnership Act (JTPA). To address criticisms, the Reagan administration allowed CETA legislation to expire and replaced it with the Job Training Partnership Act (JTPA) of 1982. The unlikely team of Senators Edward "Ted" Kennedy (D-MA) and Dan Quayle (R-IN), who was later Vice President during the George H. W. Bush administration, coauthored the bill. Funds were provided in the form of state block grants. JTPA's goals were familiar: to increase employment and earnings and thereby reduce poverty and welfare dependency among unemployed and underemployed people by providing them with skill training, job search assistance, counseling, and related services. About 600 Private Industry Councils (PICs) composed of volunteers from the business sector with knowledge of job skills needed in their communities were established. The PICs advised job training centers established by state and local governments with federal funds.

Did JTPA work? The National JTPA Study of 20,000 randomly assigned participants at 16 different sites found that the program was cost effective for adult participants but not for youth and young adults (under age 22).[145] The researchers concluded "that JTPA works reasonably well for adults," with $1.50 returned in earnings for every $1.00 invested in the program.[146] JTPA participation, however, had little effect on the AFDC benefits received by female members of the experimental group, and food stamp benefits were not affected for men or women. On-the-job training and job search assistance seemed particularly helpful for the AFDC mothers. The findings for youth were disappointing. The males in the experimental group had *lower* earnings than controls, and the females had only small earnings gains that were not statistically significant compared to controls. For both groups of youths, JTPA produced net social *costs*. The researchers also considered subgroups of youths and could not find any group that had earnings gains from JTPA participation.

Workforce Investment Act (WIA).   During his terms in office, President Clinton pledged to "make the welfare office look more like an employment office" and to "make work pay." To do this, Clinton, like President George H. W. Bush before him, endorsed the idea of "one-stop shopping"—multiservice centers that would consolidate the "crazy quilt" of "150 federal job programs run by twenty-four agencies."[147] Getting 24 agencies to consolidate or coordinate unemployment insurance claims, job training, job search, and other employment-related services is no easy feat. The task is made more difficult by the different work requirements of the Temporary Assistance for Needy Families (TANF) program (see Chapter 7) and the Supplemental Nutritional Assistance Program, as well as efforts to help people with disabilities receiving Supplemental Security Income secure employment (see Chapter 5).

The current version of the federal government's job training and employment programs is the Workforce Investment Act (WIA) of 1998, which replaced JTPA and amended the Wagner-Peyser Act. WIA includes adult programs and youth programs, including the Job Corps. WIA is intended to "increase employment, retention, and earnings of participants, and in doing so, improve the quality of the workforce to sustain economic growth, enhance productivity and competitiveness, and reduce welfare dependency."[148]

Under WIA, adults aged 18 or older can receive core services such as skills and need assessments, job search, and placement assistance.[149] More intensive services like training may be available to those who need them to obtain or maintain employment. In 2006, nearly 76 percent of low-income adults who received intensive or training services were employed within three months after exiting services, and their average earnings in that quarter were $4,687. In 2008, nearly $849 million was spent to serve about 276,800 adults. WIA appropriations to serve adults have fallen more than 10 percent since the peak in fiscal year 2002, with the number of adults served falling by almost 42 percent from 2002 to 2008.

Among the youth services under WIA are tutoring, study skills training, alternative high school services, and summer activities. In 2008, about $924 million was spent to provide these services to about 323,300 youth, a decline of more than 18 percent in appropriations and youth served since the peak year of 2002.

The most recent assessment of WIA implementation in eight selected states[150] indicated that WIA funding was not sufficient to provide higher cost training services to all applicants, leading to "creaming"—enrolling those applicants considered the easiest to serve and most likely to quickly obtain employment. The provision of seamless services in One-Stop Centers has been impaired by conflicting goals and cultures in the TANF, Vocational Rehabilitation, and Veteran's Employment and Training Service programs. The evaluators noted a distinct inability to match state-level policy decisions with local Workforce Investment Board (WIB) implementation. Specifically, WIBs often adopt a *work-first* or *human capital development* priority without regard to whether a state prefers to develop a more technically proficient or highly educated workforce.

MINIMUM WAGES AND LIVING WAGES

The federal Fair Labor Standards Act of 1938 was intended to guarantee a wage that would sustain a decent standard of living for all workers. The minimum wage began at 25 cents per hour and has increased gradually over time. The labor act also established a 40-hour work week; employees can work longer, but for hourly-wage workers, overtime usually requires additional pay. The law covers 90 percent of nonsupervisory personnel with certain exceptions (e.g., some farm workers, youth during a 90-day initial training period, and workers who receive tips). In 2008, 2.2 million workers (3 percent) of the labor force aged 16 and older who were paid hourly wages earned at or below the federal minimum wage.[151] About half were over 25 years of age. Minimum-wage jobs generally lack benefits like health insurance that can help with a worker's cost of living.

Certainly, a high minimum wage helps the person who has a job, particularly an unskilled or semiskilled worker who is most likely to be affected by minimum-wage levels. Liberals have consistently argued for a higher minimum wage. Until the last two decades, conservatives and many economists vigorously denounced this position. Their classic argument was that higher minimum wages lead to higher unemployment. A growing body of research based on the natural experiment of state minimum wage changes and the federal escalations in the 1990s hase resulted in less unanimity among economists. While the debate continues, it is clear that the evidence does not unequivocally connect the minimum wage with unemployment.[152] Recent increases in the minimum wage have not resulted in any substantial job loss. Other benefits of a higher minimum wage include higher productivity in the low-wage labor market, decreased absenteeism, increased morale, and increased consumer spending.[153]

Those who might be excluded from jobs by a higher minimum wage are teenagers, whom some feel have not yet acquired the skills to make their labor commensurate with the minimum wage. A higher minimum wage might induce employers such as fast-food chains, movie theaters, and retail stores to reduce their teenage help to cut costs. Accordingly, the Fair Labor Standards Act of 1996 established a lower, 90-day training rate of $4.25 that remains in force.[154] At a lower minimum wage, more teens might be expected to find work. The teenage unemployment rate is about three times the adult rate.

Because federal minimum wage legislation does not include cost-of-living adjustments, any increase requires congressional action—action that pits conservative, business interests opposed to minimum wage increases against liberal advocates for income redistribution. For example, upon taking office, President Clinton wanted to increase the minimum wage, but with healthcare and welfare reform legislation on the table at that time, Congress did not mount a serious effort to give the minimum wage another hike until 1996. By this time the minimum wage was reported to be at a near 20-year low in purchasing power (see Figure 9.4). Proponents of a higher wage argued that it was needed to "make work pay," especially to encourage more people to leave welfare for work. They also argued that the pay of CEOs and other high-end workers had

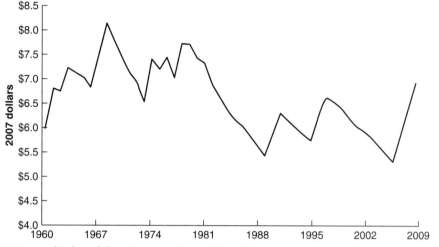

FIGURE 9.4   Real Value of the Minimum Wage, 1960–2009   *Source:* Reprinted from Lawrence Mishel, Jared Bernstein, Heidi Shierholz, The State of Working America, 2008/2009. Copyright © 2009 by Cornell University. Used by permission of the publisher, Cornell University Press.

risen much more rapidly than for workers at the low end of the pay scale and that Congress has been far more generous in voting itself pay raises. One argument against the increase was that higher-wage workers would also demand a raise. All these raises would increase employers' costs and result in lost jobs, higher prices to consumers, or both.

There was much political maneuvering over the issue. Democrats tried unsuccessfully to tack the minimum wage measure on to a Republican-favored bill to increase the government's borrowing authority and on an immigration bill. Then Senate Majority Leader Bob Dole, who had voted for raising the minimum wage in the past, wanted to package the new minimum wage bill with other Republican-supported economic measures. President Clinton said he would veto the bill if it included an amendment to exempt new hires and businesses that make less than $500,000 a year. In the end, Congress raised the minimum wage to $4.75 initially and then to $5.15 in July 1997. The additional costs to businesses were cushioned because the bill also included various tax breaks for them. A subsequent Congressional effort to raise the minimum wage failed in 2000 largely because it was tied to tax cuts that Democrats opposed.

The battle began anew after the 2006-midterm elections that provided a Democratic majority in the House. To get the Fair Minimum Wage Act of 2007 passed, it was attached to a bill supplementing funding for the Iraqi War and over $4 billion in tax breaks over 10 years to small businesses to overcome the objections of the lobbyists for the National Restaurant Association and the National Federation of Independent Business.[155]

Many believe that the minimum wage is the most direct and comprehensive way to increase the earnings of the working poor. But given today's minimum wage, if only one person in a household is employed, minimum-wage earnings generally fall well below the official poverty level. For example, in 2008, the poverty threshold for a family of four (two adults and two children) was about $21,200[156] while a full-time (40 hour per week) worker earning the federal minimum wage ($5.85 through July 23, 2008; $6.55 thereafter) earned a gross salary of $12,784. With two adults working full-time, the family would still have been living close to the poverty level.

On July 24, 2009, the third and last increase to the federal minimum wage under the Fair Minimum Wage Act of 2007 took effect. Thirteen states and the District of Columbia already have minimum wage laws that exceed the new federal level of $7.25 an hour.[157] In other areas, "prevailing" wages may also exceed the federal minimum. The Economic Policy Institute estimates that 76 percent of the beneficiaries of the higher minimum wage are adults over 25 years of age and that 4.5 million workers, those currently earning the minimum and those earning slightly more than the minimum, will benefit from the 2009 increase in the federal minimum wage by adding $1.6 billion to earned wages.[158] Among the groups that will benefit most are single parents, particularly women, and people of color.

Many advocates for higher minimum wages want legislation that would provide automatic cost-of-living raises to the minimum wage rather than the continual political haggling that is required at the present. Arizona, Colorado, Florida, Missouri, Montana, Oregon, Vermont, and Washington have adopted some form of annual cost-of-living adjustments to their state minimum wage.[159]

Another idea for increasing the earnings of low-wage workers is to set the minimum wage at half of the national average wage, which in July, 2009, was $18.46 per hour for production workers in private industry.[160] This would boost the current minimum wage, but it is not clear why half the national average wage is an appropriate figure. It might make more sense to pay a living wage. An organization called Universal Living Wage (ULW) and many others believe that an individual working full time should be able to afford basic housing.[161] ULW calculates living wages based on fair market rental rates and the Department of Housing and Urban Development's guideline that housing should not consume more than 30 percent of low-income individuals' budget (also see Chapter 4). Since housing costs vary from community to community, ULW's living wage calculations also vary. For example, ULW's 2010 estimate is that the wage needed for a 40-hour a week worker to secure a one-bedroom apartment in Little Rock, Arkansas, was $8.67 per hour, and in Boulder, Colorado, $14.75 per hour.

ECONOMIC CRISIS AND THE OBAMA STIMULUS PLAN

As a result of the economic crisis of 2008, the unadjusted nonfarm unemployment rate grew from 4.7 percent in December 2007 to 10.0 percent in November 2009.[162] During that period of time, the United States lost more than 7.9 million jobs.[163]

> The six months between October 2008 and March 2009 saw the U.S. economy contract more rapidly than during any other half-year since 1958. In April [2009] the unemployment rate reached a 25-year peak and it is forecast to rise through at least the end of this year. In short, the U.S. economy today is mired in a deep recession.[164]

Two presidents have attempted to address the 2008 economic crisis, the Republican George W. Bush and the Democrat Barack Obama. Bush's response to the crisis was the Troubled Asset Relief Program (TARP), a $700 billion bailout of financial institutions authorized by the Economic Emergency Stabilization Act of 2008. This legislation provided some taxpayer protections in the form of limitations on executive compensation and partial federal ownership of some financial institutions benefitting from the receipt of bailout funds. TARP is essentially a trickle-down mechanism for dealing with the recession. By stabilizing financial institutions, TARP assumed that credit flows would normalize and produce general economic growth to increase jobs.[165] While TARP may be credited with avoiding a more catastrophic failure of the banking system, credit remains tight, especially for small businesses and home-buyers.

Barack Obama's approach to dealing with the crisis was the $787 billion American Recovery and Reinvestment Act (ARRA) signed into law on February 17, 2009.[166] ARRA was a potpourri of programs aimed at economic recovery within two years, including individual tax cuts of $237 billion and business tax cuts of $51 billion. However, individuals would not see many of the benefits until after they filed their 2009 tax returns in 2010. Particularly effective has been the $144 billion in assistance to local and state governments, which has mitigated the negative impact of the recession on public employment. Although only 32 percent of ARRA funds had been dispersed through October 2009, this stimulus plan is already being credited with having a modest positive influence on the economy claiming over 640,000 jobs saved or created by October 2009.[167]

The working poor gained substantially in the Obama administration's stimulus plan. The ARRA increased the Earned Income Tax Credit (EITC) to a maximum of $5,657. EITC is a refundable federal tax credit for low-wage workers that has proved to be one of the strongest federal antipoverty programs (also see Chapter 7). Eligibility requires married taxpayers to file jointly, which may result in higher household earned income and lower EITC refunds. ARRA modified the refund tables to soften this "marriage penalty." ARRA also created a new Making Work Pay (MWP) refundable tax credit that refunds up to $400 per individual ($800 per couple) to reduce the regressive effects of payroll taxes and reduced the income threshold for the $1,000 refundable Child Tax Credit (CTC) from $12,550 to $3,000 so that many more low-wage and even part-time workers will quality to receive the CTC.

These ARRA measures rely on the tax system rather than on employers to provide more money to the working poor who can potentially receive up to $7,457 in refundable tax credits under new legislation.[168] They demonstrate the continuing and distinct preference for poverty relief to (1) reward work and (2) to be distributed through the federal tax system rather than in the form of public assistance (also see Chapters 1 and 7). These refundable tax credits are among the most significant labor policies benefitting people with low incomes. Unfortunately for many workers, these new tax provisions were a response to the country's economic recession and available for only two years, expiring with the 2010 tax year.

Summary

Federal involvement in U.S. educational systems and labor markets increased dramatically during the twentieth century. This involvement has its supporters and its detractors. Federal involvement in public school education has evolved from a focus on access to education to one concerned with quality, increased standards, and student achievement as is evident in the No Child Left Behind Act. This has caused many tensions with state and local governments where the major responsibility for elementary and secondary education still lies. The federal government has engaged in a series of job programs with various successes in helping Americans secure jobs. The current major federal job program legislation is the Workforce Investment Act (WIA).

The 2010 federal budget provided the Department of Education and the Department of Labor with discretion over government funding of approximately $47 billion and $13 billion, respectively. As this overview of educational and labor policy has shown, federal expenditure decisions are guided by political considerations more often than by reason. Some education and job programs initiated during the War on Poverty in the 1960s have been politically resilient for almost 50 years, but rigorous evaluations raise serious questions about whether programs such as Head Start and the Job Corps are worthy federal investment choices. In a national atmosphere supportive of higher levels of accountability on the personal and institutional levels, there is a certain degree of irony in the reluctance of federal decision makers to apply the same standards to their own deliberations.

Discussion Questions and Class Activities

1. Contact the superintendent of a local public school district or the principal of a low-performing public school in your area. Visit the school district's administrative offices or the public school or ask the superintendent or principal to visit class to discuss implementation of the No Child Left Behind (NCLB) Act and testing standards in his or her district or school. Ask the superintendent or principal to discuss NCLB's impact, especially with regard to children's socioeconomic backgrounds. What aspects of testing standards do she or he consider useful? In what ways can they be improved? After hearing the speaker, hold a class discussion or debate on what the most important purpose or purposes of public education should be—acculturation, academic skills, or employability? Why?

2. Invite the principal from a highly regarded charter school in your area to speak to your class. Ask the principal to discuss what he or she considers the critical differences between the charter school and the public schools. You may wish to include parents of charter school students or students themselves in the discussion. Before hearing the speaker(s), read articles about charter schools from the academic literature, including evaluation studies so you can be prepared to ask questions.

3. Contact a nonprofit community development corporation (CDC) in your area. Ask if your class can visit the CDC or if a speaker from the CDC can come to your class. Ask that individual to discuss the mission of the organization, its history, funding sources, programs, successes, and challenges, especially with regard to employment of residents of low-income areas.

4. Invite a speaker from your state's workforce commission or agency that is responsible for implementing the major federal and state job training and employment programs in your area. Ask the speaker to describe the programs, whom they serve, and how successful the programs have been. Be prepared to ask questions by learning about these programs before the speaker's visit. Examine the agency's website and search for any recent evaluations that have been conducted of the programs.

5. Invite the head of a nonprofit organization dedicated to helping refugees, ex-offenders, or other disadvantaged groups gain employment to speak about the organization's successes and challenges. Ask his or her opinion of the effectiveness of the state agency responsible for implementing job training and employment programs in serving the organization's clientele.

6. If possible, visit a Head Start program or other early education program for children from low-income families. Ask the director to describe the population of children served, the services provided, and the impact she or he believes the program has on the children who attend and their parents. Prior to your visit, read evaluations of Head Start (see, for example, Head Start Impact Study and Follow-up, 2000-2010 at http://www.acf.hhs.gov/programs/opre/hs/impact_study/index.html) or other preschool programs and prepare questions based on your reading to ask the director. You may also wish to invite a faculty member at your university with expertise in early childhood or preschool education to speak to the class.

7. Invite a speaker from a living wage organization in your community to speak to the class about the organization's advocacy efforts, such as the strategies the organization is using to increase wages in the community. Prior to the speaker's visit, investigate whether your state has a legislatively established minimum wage that exceeds the federal minimum wage. If so, how does that wage compare with what it takes to live in your area? For example, if there is a Universal Living Wage calculation or Self-sufficiency Standard for your area (see Chapter 4 for information on the Self-Sufficiency Standard), compare your state's minimum wage to that standard.

8. Look at the research that has been done that supports minimum wage legislation and research that suggests that a minimum wage has a negative impact on employment. Have a class discussion on the strengths, weaknesses, and ramifications of this research. What approaches do class members believe are viable for seeing that workers are paid fair wages?

9. Invite your university or college's director of financial aid to discuss trends in student financial aid and what the Health Care and Education Reconciliation Act of 2010, which transferred administration of all student loans to the Department of Education, means for students at your institution and other universities and colleges.

Websites

American Federation of Teachers, http://www.aft.org/, a trade union and affiliate of the AFL-CIO, represents the interests of pre-K through 12th-grade teachers and other school personnel; higher education faculty and professional staff; federal, state, and local government employees; and nurses and other healthcare professionals.

Economic Policy Institute, http://www.epi.org/, is a nonprofit Washington DC think tank that conducts research on economic policy with a special interest in policies that affect low- and middle-income workers.

National Center for Education Statistics, http://nces.ed.gov/, is the primary federal entity for collecting and analyzing data related to education.

National Education Association, https://www.nea.org/, represents education professionals (public school teachers, faculty members, education support professionals, retired educators, and students preparing to become teachers) and is concerned that public education prepares students to succeed.

U.S. Department of Education (DOE), http://www.ed.gov/index.jhtml, is a federal agency whose mission "is to promote student achievement and preparation for global competitiveness by fostering educational excellence and ensuring equal access." DOE establishes federal education funding policies, distributes funds, and monitors their use; collects data and oversees research on U.S. schools; addresses major issues in education; and enforces federal laws that prohibit discrimination in programs that receive federal funds.

U.S. Department of Labor (DOL), http://www.dol.gov/, seeks to improve conditions for U.S. workers in the areas of finding employment, retirement and healthcare benefits, and free collective bargaining. DOL tracks changes in employment, prices, and other economic measures and administers federal labor laws concerning safe and healthful working conditions, minimum hourly wage and overtime pay, freedom from employment discrimination, unemployment insurance, and other income supports.

Notes

1. See discussion of The Olde Satan Deluder Act in Carl L. Bankston and Stephen J. Caldas, *Public Education — America's Civil Religion: A Social History* (New York: Teachers College Press, 2009), p. 21.
2. Patricia Albjerg Graham, *Schooling America: How the Public Schools Meet the Nation's Changing Needs* (New York: Oxford University Press, 2005) p. 18.
3. Jonathan Messerli, *Horace Mann: A Biography* (New York: Knopf, 1972).
4. Bankston and Caldas, *Public Education–America's Civil Religion: A Social History*, pp. 31–34.
5. Graham, *Schooling America: How the Public Schools Meet the Nation's Changing Needs*, pp. 12–13.
6. Bankston & Caldas, *Public Education—America's Civil Religion: A Social History*, Table 2.1, Percentages of White Youth Aged 5 through 15 in School, by State or Territory, 1860, p. 31.
7. *Ibid.*, pp. 36–37.

8. Graham, *Schooling America: How the Public Schools Meet the Nation's Changing Needs,* p. 22.

9. *Ibid.,* p. 22.

10. Bankston and Caldas, *Public Education–America's Civil Religion: A Social History,* p. 43.

11. Graham, *Schooling America: How the Public Schools Meet the Nation's Changing Needs,* p. 14.

12. See the National Child Labor Committee website at http://www.nationalchildlabor.org/index.html.

13. Robert Whaples, "Child Labor in the United States," *EH Net Encyclopedia.* Retrieved August 10, 2009, from http://eh.net/encyclopedia/article/whaples.childlabor

14. "Compulsory Education," *Encyclopedia of Everyday Law* (Seattle, WA: eNotes). Retrieved August 12, 2009, from http://www.enotes.com/everyday-law-encyclopedia/compulsory-education

15. Bankston and Caldas, *Public Education–America's Civil Religion: A Social History,* p. 54.

16. Graham, *Schooling America: How the Public Schools Meet the Nation's Changing Needs,* p. 37.

17. Sudhir Kakar, *Frederick Taylor: A Study in Personality and Innovation* (Cambridge, MA: MIT Press, 1970).

18. Graham, *Schooling America: How the Public Schools Meet the Nation's Changing Needs,* p. 27.

19. Bankston and Caldas, *Public Education–America's Civil Religion: A Social History,* p. 54.

20. Graham, *Schooling America: How the Public Schools Meet the Nation's Changing Needs,* p. 27.

21. *Ibid.,* p. 44.

22. Bankston and Caldas, *Public Education–America's Civil Religion: A Social History,* p. 63.

23. *Ibid.,* p. 75.

24. Graham, *Schooling America: How the Public Schools Meet the Nation's Changing Needs,* p. 104.

25. *Digest of Educational Statistics: 2008, Table 32: Historical summary of public elementary and secondary school statistics: Selected years, 1869–70 through 2005–06* (Washington, DC: National Center for Education Statistics, March 2009). Retrieved November 1, 2009, from http://nces.ed.gov/programs/digest/d08/tables/dt08_032.asp?referrer=list

26. Rudolph F. Flesch, *Why Johnny Can't Read: And What You Can Do About It* (San Francisco: Harper & Brothers, 1955).

27. Bankston and Caldas, *Public Education–America's Civil Religion: A Social History,* p. 84.

28. *Ibid.,* p. 98.

29. Bankston andCaldas, *Public Education—America's Civil Religion: A Social History,* p. 115.

30. John F. Jennings, "Title I: Its Legislative History and Its Promise" in Geoffery D. Borman, Sam Stringfield, and Robert E. Slavin (Eds.), *Title I: Compensatory Education at the Crossroads* (Mahwah, NJ: Erlbaum, 2001), p. 9.

31. *Digest of Educational Statistics: 2008, Table 32: Historical summary of public elementary and secondary school statistics: Selected years, 1869–70 through 2005–06* (Washington, DC: National Center for Education Statistics, March 2009). Retrieved November 1, 2009, from http://nces.ed.gov/programs/digest/d08/tables/dt08_032.asp?referrer=list

32. Graham, *Schooling America: How the Public Schools Meet the Nation's Changing Needs,* p. 134.

33. *Ibid.,* pp. 134–136, 144.

34. Graham, *Schooling America: How the Public Schools Meet the Nation's Changing Needs,* p. 139.

35. *Ibid.,* pp. 144–145.

36. Jennings, "Title I: Its Legislative History and Its Promise," p. 10.

37. *Ibid.,* p. 11.

38. Deanna L. Michael, *Jimmy Carter as Educational Policymaker* (Albany: State University of New York Press, 2008), pp. 93–95.

39. *Ibid.,* p. 95.

40. *Ibid.,* p. 133.

41. Jennings, "Title I: Its Legislative History and Its Promise," pp. 12–16.

42. *Ibid.,* pp. 14–17.

43. *Digest of Educational Statistics: 2008, Table 32: Historical summary of public elementary and secondary school statistics: Selected years, 1869–70 through 2005–06* (Washington, DC: National Center for Education Statistics, March 2009). Retrieved November 1, 2009, from http://nces.ed.gov/programs/digest/d08/tables/dt08_032.asp?referrer=list.

44. Terrence Stutz, "Robin Hood law touches record number of schools," *Dallas Morning News,* August 21, 2008. Retrieved March 4, 2010, from http://www.dallasnews.com/sharedcontent/dws/dn/education/stories/082108dntexrobinhood.41bd1a5.html.

45. The National Commission on Excellence in Education, *A Nation at Risk* (Washington, DC: U.S. Department of Education, April 1983). Retrieved October 31, 2009, from http://www.ed.gov/pubs/NatAtRisk/index.html.

46. *Ibid.,* second paragraph.

47. See, for example, Diane Ravitch, *The Troubled Crusade: American Education, 1945–1980* (New York: Basic Books, 1983) and Theodore R. Sizer, *Horace's Compromise: The Dilemma of the American High School* (Boston: Houghton Mifflin, 1984).

48. Graham, *Schooling America: How the Public Schools Meet the Nation's Changing Needs,* p. 161.
49. Jennings, "Title I: Its Legislative History and Its Promise," pp. 14–15.
50. Bankston and Caldas, *Public Education–America's Civil Religion: A Social History,* p. 143.
51. Jennings, "Title I: Its Legislative History and Its Promise," pp. 16–17.
52. See "Four Pillars of NCLB" (Washington, DC: U.S. Department of Education). Retrieved March 4, 2010, from http://www.ed.gov/nclb/overview/intro/4pillars.html
53. See the ESEA Committee 2009 RA Report (Washington, DC: National Education Association, July 1, 2009). Retrieved March 4, 2010, from http://www.nea.org/home/NoChildLeftBehindAct.html. This 60-page memorandum documents NEA opposition to NCLB and current efforts to influence educational policies on the national level.
54. Title I—Improving America's Schools Act, Part A—Improving Basic Programs Operated by Local Educational Agencies, Section 1111(b)(1)(A). Retrieved October 31, 2009, from http://www.ed.gov/legislation/ESEA/sec1111.html
55. "Four Pillars of NCLB."
56. "Standards and Assessment Group and Accountability Group" (Washington, DC: U.S. Department of Education, January 16, 2009). Retrieved August 17, 2009 from http://www.ed.gov/admins/lead/account/saa.html#plans
57. "No Child Left Behind Flexibility: Highly Qualified Teachers" (Washington, DC: U. S. Department of Education, November 29, 2005). Retrieved August 17, 2009, from http://www.ed.gov/nclb/methods/teachers/hqtflexibility.html
58. National Council for Accreditation of Teacher Education, *Standards for Professional Development Schools* (Washington, DC: Author, Spring 2001). Retrieved August 17, 2009 from http://www.ncate.org/documents/pdsStandards.pdf
59. National Council for Accreditation of Teacher Education, *Professional Standards for the Accreditation of Teacher Preparation Institutions* (Washington, DC: Author, February 2008). Retrieved August 17, 2009 from http://www.ncate.org/documents/standards/NCATE%20Standards%202008.pdf
60. "State by State Overview" (Chicago: National Association of Charter School Authorizers). Retrieved March 2, 2010, from http://www.qualitycharters.org/i4a/pages/index.cfm?pageid=3305
61. Graham, *Schooling America: How the Public Schools Meet the Nation's Changing Needs,* pp. 180–181.
62. *Ibid.,* p. 182.
63. "Charter School Enrollment and Closures, by State" (Washington, DC: The Center for Education Reform, April 20007). Retrieved August 16, 2009, from http://web.archive.org/web/20070819170450/www.edreform.com/_upload/CER_charter_numbers.pdf
64. National Education Association, "For-Profit Management of Public Schools" (Washington, DC: Author, July 8, 1998). Retrieved August 16, 2009, from http://www.corpwatch.org/article.php?id=886
65. National Center for Education Statistics, *A Closer Look at Charter Schools Using Hierarchical Linear Modeling* (U.S. Department of Education, NCES No. 2006-460, August 2006). Retrieved August 16, 2009, from http://nces.ed.gov/nationsreportcard//pdf/studies/2006460.pdf
66. Center for Research on Educational Outcomes, *Multiple Choice: Charter School Performance in 16 States* (Stanford, CA: Author, June 2009).
67. See "No Child Left Behind Act (NCLB)/ESEA: Background" (Washington, DC: National Education Association). Retrieved October 31, 2009, from http://www.nea.org/home/NoChildLeftBehindAct.html
68. See Bankston and Caldas, *Public Education–America's Civil Religion: A Social History,* chapter 8 for an extensive critique.
69. See Barbara Beatty, *Preschool Education in America: The Culture of Young Children from the Colonial Era to the Present* (New Haven, CT: Yale University Press, 1996) for details.
70. Bruce Fuller, *Standardized Childhood: The Political and Cultural Struggle over Early Education* (Stanford, CA: Stanford University Press, 2007), chapter 2.
71. *Ibid.,* pp. 1–4.
72. Laura Lein, "Child Care Services," *Encyclopedia of Social Work* (New York: NASW Press, 2008), pp. 240–243.
73. Administration for Children and Families, *Head Start Impact Study. Final Report* (Washington, DC: U.S. Department of Health and Human Services, January 2010). Retrieved May 25, 20110, quote from p. xxvi, from http://www.acf.hhs.gov/programs/opre/hs/impact_study/reports/impact_study/executive_summary_final.pdf. Findings through the third grade will be published in the future. See "Head Start Impact Study and Follow-up, 2000–2010" (Washington, DC: Administration for Children and Families) at http://www.acf.hhs.gov/programs/opre/hs/impact_study/index.html

74. "Factsheet Number 19: The Child Care and Development Block Grant Program" (Chapel Hill, NC: National Resource Center for Respite and Crisis Care Services, February 1993). Retrieved October 31, 2009, from http://www.archrespite.org/archfs19.htm

75. Administration for Children and Families, "About the Child Care and Development Fund" (Washington, DC: U.S. Department of Health and Human Services, December 23, 2009). Retrieved March 5, 2010, from http://www.acf.hhs.gov/programs/ccb/ccdf/index.htm

76. Fuller, *Standardized Childhood: The Political and Cultural Struggle over Early Education,* p. 12.

77. *Ibid.,* pp. 12–14.

78. "Child Care Arrangements of 3- to 5-year-old Children Who Are Not Yet in Kindergarten, by Age and Ethnicity" (Washington, DC: National Center for Education Statistics). Retrieved March 5, 2010, from http://nces.ed.gov/fastfacts/display.asp?id=4

79. Fuller, *Standardized Childhood: The Political and Cultural Struggle over Early Education,* pp. 9–11.

80. See *ibid.,* chapter 6, for a critical look at the evidence.

81. Scott L. Thomas, "Finance, Higher Education—Overview," *The Encyclopedia of Higher Education* (New York: Macmillan Reference USA, 2003), p. 870.

82. Graham, *Schooling America: How the Public Schools Meet the Nation's Changing Needs,* pp. 221–224.

83. Bankston and Caldas, *Public Education—America's Civil Religion: A Social History,* p. 85.

84. "The Federal Role in Education," U. S. Department of Education (May 6, 2009). Retrieved August 12, 2009, from http://www.ed.gov/about/overview/fed/role.html

85. Bankston and Caldas, *Public Education—America's Civil Religion: A Social History,* p. 84.

86. *Ibid.,* p. 86.

87. Pamela Ebert Flattau et al., *The National Defense Education Act of 1958: Selected Outcomes,* section 2 (Washington, DC: Institute for Defense Analyses, Science & Technology Policy Institute, March 2006). Retrieved May 25, 2010, from https://www.ida.org/stpi/pages/D3306-FINAL.pdf

88. See "History of Financial Aid" (Fort Collins, CO: Center for Higher Education Support Services, July 17, 2003). Retrieved November 1, 2009, from http://www.chessconsulting.org/financialaid/history.htm

89. *Ibid.*

90. Charmaine Mercer, "Federal Pell Grant Program of the Higher Education Act: Background and Reauthorization" (Washington, DC: Congressional Research Service, January 30, 2008), p. 19. Retrieved May 25, 2010, from http://leahy.senate.gov/imo/media/doc/CRSFederalPellGrant.pdf

91. *Ibid.,* p. 10.

92. Kelly Field, "Education Department Proposes New Rules for Student-Loan Programs," *Chronicle of Higher Education,* June 15, 2007, Vol. 53, No. 41, p. A19.

93. Peter Baker and David M. Herszenhorn. "Obama Signs Overhaul of Student Loan Program," *New York Times,* March 30, 2010. Retrieved May 17, 2010 from http://www.nytimes.com/2010/03/31/us/politics/31obama.html?scp=5&sq=health%20care%20and%20education%20reconciliation%20act%20of%202010&st=cse

94. *Digest of Educational Statistics: 2008,* "Table 187. Historical Summary of Faculty, Students, Degrees, and Finances in Degree-granting Institutions: Selected Years, 1869-1870 through 2006–2007" (Washington, DC: National Center for Education Statistics, March 2009). Retrieved November 1, 2009, from http://nces.ed.gov/programs/digest/d08/tables/dt08_187.asp?referrer=list

95. *Digest of Educational Statistics: 2008,* "Table 191. College Enrollment and Enrollment Rates of Recent High School Completers, by Sex: 1960 through 2006" (Washington, DC: National Center for Education Statistics, March 2009). Retrieved November 1, 2009, from http://nces.ed.gov/programs/digest/d07/tables/dt07_191.asp

96. Graham, *Schooling America: How the Public Schools Meet the Nation's Changing Needs,* p, 226.

97. "Adult Literacy and Lifeskills Survey" (Washington, DC: National Center for Educational Statistics). Retrieved March 5, 2010, from http://nces.ed.gov/surveys/all/index.asp

98. Charles C. Carson, Robert M. Huelskamp, & Thomas D. Woodall, "Perspectives on Education in America," *The Journal of Educational Research,* Vol. 86, 1993, pp. 259–310.

99. Robert M. Huelskamp, "Perspectives on Education in America," *The Phi Delta Kappan,* Vol. 74, Issue 9, 1993, pp. 718–721.

100. Lawrence C. Stedman, "The Sandia Report and U. S. Achievement: An Assessment," *The Journal of Educational Research,* Vol. 87, Issue 3, 1994, p. 144.

101. Harold Bloom, *The Closing of the American Mind: How Higher Education has Failed Democracy and Impoverished the Souls of Today's Students* (New York: Simon & Schuster, 1987).

102. David C. Berliner, *The Manufactured Crisis: Myths, Fraud, and the Attack on American Public Schools*

(Reading, MA: Addison-Wesley, 1995). Stedman's review was published in *Education Policy Analysis Archives,* Vol. 4, Issue 1, with a response by Berliner in Vol. 4, Issue 3.

103. National Center for Education Statistics, *The Condition of Education 2009* (Washington, DC: U. S. Department of Education, 2009). Retrieved November 1, 2009, from http://nces.ed.gov/fastfacts/display.asp?id=16

104. Education, Attainment, OECD Index of Statistical Variables (Paris: Organization for Economic Cooperation and Development, February 2009). Retrieved November 1, 2009, from http://www.oecd.org/dataoecd/26/40/38785295.htm#E

105. Quoted in Graham, *Schooling America: How the Public Schools Meet the Nation's Changing Needs,* p. 234.

106. Issues: Education, Organizing for America. Retrieved November 1, 2009, from http://www.barackobama.com/issues/education/index.php

107. Urban-Brookings Tax Policy Center, "Tax Stimulus Report Card: Conference Bill" (Washington, DC: Urban Institute). Retrieved November 1, 2009, from http://www.urban.org/UploadedPDF/411839_conference_reportcard.pdf

108. Peter Baker and David M. Herszenhorn. "Obama Signs Overhaul of Student Loan Program," *New York Times,* March 30, 2010. Retrieved May 17, 2010, from http://www.nytimes.com/2010/03/31/us/politics/31obama.html?scp=5&sq=health%20care%20and%20education%20reconciliation%20act%20of%202010&st=cse

109. *A Blueprint for Reform: The Reauthorization of the Elementary and Secondary Education Act* (Washington, DC: U.S. Department of Education, March 2010), quotes from pp. 3 and 4. Retrieved May 25, 2010, from http://www2.ed.gov/policy/elsec/leg/blueprint/index.html

110. Nick Anderson, "Unions Criticize Obama's School Proposals as Bush III," *Washington Post,* September 25, 2009. Retrieved November 1, 2009, from http://www.washingtonpost.com/wp-dyn/content/article/2009/09/24/AR2009092403197.html

111. For the opinions of various organizations, see NCLB Reauthorization Database on Education Commission of the States website at http://ecs.org/ecsmain.asp?page=/html/IssueCollapse.asp

112. "Homestead Act," Web Guides, Library of Congress. Retrieved August 19, 2009 from http://www.loc.gov/rr/program/bib/ourdocs/Homestead.html

113. Phyllis J. Day, "History (Colonial Times to 1900)," in Terry Mizrahi and Larry E. Davis, Eds., *Encyclopedia of Social Work,* 20th ed. , Vol. 4, pp. 66–68 (New York: NASW Press and Oxford University Press, 2008).

114. "A Brief History of American Labor," adapted from the *AFL-CIO American Federationist,* March 1981. Retrieved August 19, 2009, from http://www.albany.edu/history/history316/LaborMovementHistory1.html

115. "Chapter 1: Start-up of the Department and World War I, 1913-1921," *History at the Department of Labor* (Washington, DC: U.S. Department of Labor). Retrieved August 19, 2009, from http://www.dol.gov/oasam/programs/history/dolchp01.htm

116. *Ibid.*

117. Dorothy Rose Blumberg, *Florence Kelley: The Making of a Social Pioneer* (New York: August M. Kelley, Publishers, 1966).

118. "An Overview of the Fair Labor Standards Act" (Washington, DC: U. S. Office of Personnel Management). Retrieved August 19, 2009, from http://www.opm.gov/flsa/overview.asp

119. Iris Carlton-LaNey, "Social Policy History (1900-1950)," in Mizrahi and Davis, *Encyclopedia of Social Work,* 20th ed., Vol. 4, p. 73.

120. "Chapter 3: The Department in the New Deal and World War II, 1933–1945," *History at the Department of Labor.* Retrieved August 19, 2009, from http://www.dol.gov/oasam/programs/history/dolchp01.htm

121. *Ibid.*

122. Paul Krugman, *The Return of Depression Economics and the Crisis of 2008* (New York: W. W. Norton, 2008).

123. Susan E. Shank, "Women and the Labor Market: The Link Grows Stronger," *Monthly Labor Review,* March 1988, p. 3. Retrieved January 3, 2010, from http://www.bls.gov/opub/mlr/1988/03/art1full.pdf

124. John Kenneth Galbraith, *The Affluent Society* (Boston: Houghton Mifflin, 1958).

125. Economic Development Administration, *Fiscal Year 2008 Annual Report* (Washington, DC: U.S. Department of Commerce). Retrieved September 18, 2009, from http://www.eda.gov/PDF/FY08%20EDA%20Annual%20Report.pdf

126. "Mission" (Washington, DC: Economic Development Administration). Retrieved September 18, 2009, from http://www.eda.gov/AboutEDA/Mission.xml

127. Economic Development Administration, *Fiscal Year 2007 Annual Report* (Washington, DC: U.S. Department of Commerce), p. 7. Retrieved August 24, 2009, from http://www.eda.gov/PDF/2007AnnualReport.pdf

128. Economic Development Administration, *Fiscal Year 2008 Annual Report,* p. 7.

129. Economic Development Administration, *$150 Million in U.S. Economic Development Administration Funds Now Available Via the American Recovery and Reinvestment Act to Create Jobs and Boost Development in Areas Hard Hit by Recession* (Washington, DC: U. S. Department of Commerce, March 11, 2009). Retrieved August 24, 2009, from http://www.eda.gov/xp/EDAPublic/NewsEvents/PressReleases/PRWashington031109.xml

130. Information on the Community Development Block Grant is available at http://www.hud.gov

131. Office of Management and Budget, *Budget of the United States Government, Fiscal Year 2003* (Washington, DC: Executive Office of the President, 2002), p. 173.

132. Andrew Blasko, "Reagan and Heritage: A Unique Partnership" (Washington, DC: The Heritage Foundation, June 27, 2004). Retrieved January 3, 2010, from http://www.heritage.org/Press/Commentary/ed060704e.cfm

133. Matias Busso and Patrick Kline, "Do Local Economic Development Programs Work? Evidence from the Federal Empowerment Zone Program," Working Paper No. 36 (New Haven, CT: Yale University, Economics Department, February 2008). Retrieved January 3, 2010, from http://papers.ssrn.com/sol3/papers.cfm?abstract_id=1090838

134. Don Hirasuna and Joel Michael, "Enterprise Zones: A Review of Economic Theory and Empirical Evidence" (Policy Brief, Minnesota House of Representatives, Research Department), p. 13. Retrieved August 27, 2009, from http://www.house.leg.state.mn.us/hrd/pubs/entzones.pdf

135. "Welcome to the Community Renewal Initiative" (Washington, DC: U.S. Department of Housing and Urban Development, July 15, 2009). Retrieved August 27, 2009, from http://www.hud.gov/offices/cpd/economicdevelopment/programs/rc/index.cfm

136. For additional information, see the Job Corps website at http://www.jobcorps.gov/Home.aspx

137. "Detailed Assessment on the Job Corps Assessment" (Washington, DC: Office of Management and Budget, Fall 2007). Retrieved January 3, 2010, from http://www.whitehouse.gov/omb/expectmore/detail/10002372.2007.html

138. This description of the Jobs Corps and the study's findings are based on Peter X. Schochet, John Burghardt, and Sheena McConnell, *National Job Corps Study and Longer-term Follow-up Study: Impact and Benefit-Cost Findings Using Survey and Summary Earnings Records Data* (Washington, DC: U.S. Department of Labor, 2006). Retrieved July 21, 2009, from http://www.mathematica-mpr.com/publications/PDFs/jobcorpimpactbenefit.pdf

139. "Detailed Assessment on the Job Corps Assessment."

140. "Program Assessment: Job Corps" (Washington, DC: Office of Management and Budget). Retrieved January 3, 2010, from http://www.whitehouse.gov/omb/expectmore/summary/10002372.2007.html

141. Information on these programs is from the AmeriCorps website. Retrieved August 27, 2009, from http://www.americorps.gov

142. Information in this paragraph is based on the National & Community Service website. Retrieved August 27, 2009, from http://www.nationalservice.gov/Default.asp

143. Corporation for National and Community Service, *Fiscal Year 2008 Annual Performance Report* (Washington, DC, 2008). Retrieved August 27, 2009, from http://www.nationalservice.gov/pdf/2008_budget_justification.pdf

144. Executive Office of the President, *Budget of the United States Government, Fiscal Year 1982* (Washington, DC: U.S. Government Printing Office, 1981), p. 220.

145. Larry L. Orr, Stephen H. Bell, and Jacob A. Klerman, "American Lessons on Designing Reliable Impact Evaluations, from Studies of WIA and Its Predecessor Programs," paper presented at What Can the European Social Fund Learn from the WIA Experience, Washington, DC, October 30, 2009, p. 3. Retrieved January 3, 2010, from http://www.umdcipe.org/conferences/WIAWashington/Papers/Orr%20-%20American%20Lessons%20on%20Designing%20Reliable%20Impact%20Evaluations.pdf

146. Larry L. Orr, Howard S. Bloom, Stephen H. Bell, Fred Doolittle, Winston Lin, and George Cave, *Does Training for the Disadvantaged Work? Evidence from the National JTPA Study* (Washington, DC: Urban Institute Press, 1996).

147. Clinton Proposes Changes in Unemployment, Training," *Austin American-Statesman,* March 10, 1994, p. A2.

148. Workforce Investment Act (Washington, DC: U.S. Department of Labor). Retrieved September 18, 2009, from http://www.doleta.gov/regs/statutes/finalrule.htm.

149. This paragraph relies on Committee on Ways and Means, Section 15: Other Programs, "Workforce Investment Act," *2008 Green Book* (Washington, DC: U.S. House of Representatives, 2008). Retrieved

May 25, 2010, from http://waysandmeans.house
.gov/singlepages.aspx?NewsID=10490

150. See Burt S. Barnow and Christopher T. King, *The Workforce Investment Act in Eight States* (New York: The Nelson A. Rockefeller Institute of Government, February 2005). Retrieved July 21, 2009, from http://www.rockinst.org/pdf/workforce_welfare_and_social_services/2005-02-the_workforce_investment_act_in_eight_states.pdf

151. Bureau of Labor Statistics, "Characteristics of Minimum Wage Workers, 2008," Table 1 (Washington, DC: U.S. Department of Labor). Retrieved August 25, 2009 from http://www.bls.gov/cps/minwage2008tbls.htm

152. Liana Fox, "Minimum Wage Trends: Understanding Past and Contemporary Research" (Washington, DC: Economic Policy Institute, October 24, 2006). Retrieved January 3, 2010, from http://www.epi.org/publications/entry/bp178

153. Kai Filion, "Minimum Wage Issue Guide" (Washington, DC: Economic Policy Institute, July 21, 2009), p. 4. Retrieved August 25, 2009, from http://epi.3cdn.net/9f5a60cec02393cbe4_a4m6b5t1v.pdf

154. "Fact Sheet #32: Youth Minimum Wage-Fair Labor Standards Act" (Washington, DC: U.S. Department of Labor, July 2008). Retrieved January 3, 2010, from http://www.dol.gov/whd/regs/compliance/whdfs32.pdf

155. Paul K. Sonn, "The Fight for the Minimum Wage," *American Prospect,* June 4, 2007. Retrieved August 27, 2009, from http://www.prospect.org/cs/articles?article=the_fight_for_the_minimum_wage

156. "Annual Update of the HHS Poverty Guidelines," *Federal Register,* January 23, 2008, Vol. 73, No. 15, pp. 3971–3972. Retrieved September 18, 2009, from http://aspe.hhs.gov/POVERTY/08fedreg.htm

157. Filion, "Minimum Wage Issue Guide."

158. *Ibid.*

159. Employment Standards Administration, "Minimum Wage Laws in the States" (Washington, DC: U.S. Department of Labor, July 24, 2009). Retrieved August 27, 2009, from http://www.dol.gov/esa/minwage/america.htm#Consolidated

160. Bureau of Labor Statistics, Table B-2. Average hours and earnings of production and nonsupervisory workers on private nonfarm payrolls by major industry sector, 1964 to date (Washington, DC: U.S. Department of Labor). Retrieved August 27, 2009, from ftp://ftp.bls.gov/pub/suppl/empsit.ceseeb2.txt

161. See the Universal Living Wage website at www.UniversalLivingWage.org

162. Bureau of Labor Statistics, "Labor Force Statistics from the Current Population Survey" (U.S. Department of Labor, August, 27, 2009). Retrieved August 27, 2009, from http://data.bls.gov/PDQ/servlet/SurveyOutputServlet

163. Bureau of Labor Statistics, "Employment Situation Summary" (U. S. Department of Labor, December 4, 2009). Retrieved January 4, 2010, from http://www.bls.gov/news.release/empsit.nr0.htm

164. "Economic Performance" (Economic Policy Institute, no date). Retrieved August 27, 2009, from http://www.epi.org/issues/category/economic_performance/

165. See Troubled Asset Relief Program website at http://troubled-asset-relief-program.net

166. This paragraph relies on John Irons and Ethan Pollock, "The Recovery Package in Action," Briefing Paper #239 (Washington, DC: Economic Policy Institute, August 13, 2009). Retrieved August 28, 2009, from http://www.epi.org/publications/entry/recovery_package_in_action

167. "Track the Money" (Washington, DC: Recovery.gov, January 4, 2010). Retrieved January 4, 2010, from http://www.recovery.gov/Pages/home.aspx

168. "Tax Stimulus Report Card" (Washington, DC: Urban-Brookings Tax Policy Center, February 13, 2009). Retrieved August 27, 2009, from http://www.taxpolicycenter.org/UploadedPDF/411839_conference_reportcard.pdf

10

PROVIDING SOCIAL SERVICES: HELP FOR CHILDREN, OLDER AMERICANS, AND INDIVIDUALS WITH MENTAL AND SUBSTANCE USE DISORDERS

Jessica A. Ritter
Mary Margaret Just
Diana M. DiNitto

Social welfare programs are often equated with programs for the poor, but people may benefit from social services regardless of their income and social status. This chapter briefly reviews governments' roles in social services as well as the involvement of religious, nonprofit, and profit-making organizations in providing social services. Three major areas of social service provision are highlighted: child welfare, assistance for older adults, and the treatment of people with mental illness and alcohol and drug problems.

SOCIAL SERVICES IN THE UNITED STATES

Information, referral, advocacy, and consumer services are among the social services that can be helpful to people of all socioeconomic groups. A list of all the social services available in the United States would include services for individuals, families, groups, and communities.[1] Among the services for individuals are those that target children, including community youth centers, child protective services, foster home care, adoption assistance, and voluntary guidance programs such as Big Brothers and Big Sisters of America. Other services are for individuals who are disabled or elderly, such as transportation, homemaker and chore services, opportunities for socialization at senior citizen centers or other community programs, adult protective services, community residences, and long-term care. Services aimed at family units include family planning, marital and family counseling, daycare and after-school care for children, assessments for courts and schools, family preservation and reunification services when abuse or neglect has occurred, and respite care to provide relief to caretakers of older or disabled family members.

Other services involve assisting or mobilizing groups such as community residents concerned about drugs and crime, mothers receiving welfare, migrant workers, newly arrived immigrants, tenants, individuals with disabilities and their families, and even gang members, to achieve beneficial goals for themselves and their communities. Some services, such as education, consultation, and neighborhood rehabilitation are offered to meet needs at the community level. Organizations such as churches, schools, general hospitals, workplaces, youth centers, and community mental health centers often address community needs as well as individuals' and families' needs.

Social Service Providers

There are five types of organizations that provide social services: (1) public agencies, (2) private not-for-profit corporations, (3) private for-profit corporations, (4) mutual-help groups, and (5) religious organizations. Services such as daycare may be provided by all these types of organizations. Other services, such as child and adult protection, are provided by public agencies because these agencies have the legal right to intervene in cases of neglect or abuse. But even public child welfare agencies contract with private entities to provide some services once thought to be solely in the public domain.

Public agencies are established by law and are operated by federal, state, or local governments. The U.S. Department of Health and Human Services (DHHS) is the major federal agency responsible for social welfare services, although many other federal agencies also offer social services. Some states also have large umbrella agencies for the many departments that deliver the states' social services. In other states, several separate agencies administer the various social welfare programs. Many counties and cities also operate social welfare agencies.

Private not-for-profit corporations, also called voluntary agencies or nonprofit agencies, are governed by boards of directors or trustees. These agencies may receive funds from endowments and donations; client fees; other community organizations such as the United Way; or local, state, and federal governments in the form of grants, contracts, or fees for service. Private not-for-profit agencies provide a multitude of services such as daycare for children, mental health services, and nursing home care. Many of these agencies charge clients fees on a sliding scale, based on their ability to pay for the service. Other not-for-profit agencies, such as rape crisis centers, generally do not charge their clients. Some not-for-profit corporations act as advocates for their clientele by informing policymakers and the public of their clients' needs. The Arc (formerly the Association for Retarded Citizens of the United States) and its local affiliates, the Child Welfare League of America, and the National Council on Alcoholism and Drug Dependence are examples of private not-for-profit organizations.

Private profit-making organizations, also called proprietary agencies, provide services like childcare, nursing home care, and mental health care. They usually charge customers for services at the current market rate. Government agencies sometimes purchase services from private agencies, because the government may not directly provide services a client needs and cannot obtain it from a not-for-profit agency. For example, Medicaid covers two out of three residents in larger intermediate care nursing homes,[2] many of which are proprietary.

Mutual-help groups also provide social services but generally do not accept government funding at all. Their structure is less formal than other social service agencies. Alcoholics Anonymous (AA), the best known mutual-help group, was founded in 1935 and assists people with drinking problems. The only requirement for membership is the desire to stop drinking. The group relies solely on its members for financial support.

The mutual-help category also includes cooperatives where people band together to share childcare, to purchase groceries more economically, or achieve other mutual goals. Other mutual-help organizations have emerged to assist people with mental illness and their families, including the National Alliance for the Mentally Ill and Recovery, Inc. These groups may be organized as not-for-profit corporations, but their focus is on mutual aid provided by those who share a common problem, rather than reliance on professional service providers.

Finally, religious organizations have a long history of providing social services. Although their services are generally (but not always) provided by the clergy or lay members of a particular religious sect, they may be available to people regardless of their personal religious beliefs. Among the services religious groups offer are childcare, crisis pregnancy counseling, adoption, mental health counseling, food and shelter for people who are homeless or poor, and outreach to those who are incarcerated.

When different types of agencies provide services, consumers have greater choice in selecting services. Many alternative service organizations have emerged because the public sector was not providing needed services such as rape crisis or substance abuse services or it was not sensitive to the concerns of particular clientele such as African Americans, women, or lesbian, gay, bisexual, or transgendered individuals.

Privately operated and faith-based social service organizations often accept public funds in order to fill service gaps and sustain their missions. In some cases, agencies have modified their original goals and procedures to meet standards for receiving funds from government sources.[3] Other agencies reject public funding because they fear accepting it will impinge on the way they provide services and even change the character of their organization.

Social Service Development

Before the 1900s, social services were provided by family members, neighbors, church groups, private charitable organizations, and local governments in the form of indoor and outdoor relief (see Chapter 3). In fact, the Charity Organization Societies of the late 1800s, which helped poor people, preferred to provide social services rather than financial aid. During the first half of the twentieth century, most of the federal and state government assistance provided to destitute people was cash and in-kind assistance (e.g., food). Although child welfare services were part of the original Social Security Act of 1935, most social services remained outside federal purview until 1956 when Congress amended the Social Security Act to provide social services to families on relief.[4]

More social service amendments were added to the Social Security Act in 1962 and 1967 (also see Chapter 7). The rationale was to rehabilitate poor people, help them overcome their personal problems, and thereby reduce their dependence on welfare. The federal government began giving the states three dollars for every dollar the states spent on these services, with virtually no limit on spending. The federal government's enthusiasm for subsidizing social services was a boon to the states that were willing to increase the services available to clients. But the costs of social services increased so fast—from $282 million in 1967 to $1.7 billion in 1973—that Congress decided to curb spending.[5]

In 1975, Title XX was added to the Social Security Act to place a ceiling on expenditures and ensure that the majority of federally funded social services went to the poor. In 1981, the Reagan administration convinced Congress to replace the original Title XX with the Social Services Block Grant. The goals of the block grant are to increase economic self-support and self-sufficiency, reduce abuse and neglect of children and adults, reduce inappropriate institutional care, and secure institutional care when needed. The grant is based on the premises that economic and social needs are interrelated and that states know best what services their residents need. State matching requirements were eliminated, and block grant funds are now allocated to states on the basis of population. But under the block grant, federal contributions to social services have decreased considerably.

Unlike the open-ended funding that social services received when it had "entitlement" status, the Title XX Social Services Block Grant (SSBG) is capped. Congress not only sets the spending cap for social services, it also has the power to appropriate more or less than the cap if it deems necessary, and in several years it has appropriated less. When expressed in 2007 constant dollars, the amount appropriated has declined from an equivalent of $4.9 billion in 1983 to $1.7 billion in 2008.[6] Most funds do go to assist low-income clients, and states are most likely to use their block grant funds for child welfare and related family services as well as adult protective services.[7]

Since the Reagan era, block grants have become the federal government's primary tool for supporting social services. In addition to the Title XX SSBG, the Preventive Health and Health Services Block Grant, the Maternal and Child Health Services Block Grant, the Substance Abuse Prevention and Treatment Block Grant, the Community Mental Health Services Block Grant, the Low-Income Home Energy Assistance Block Grant, the Developmental Disabilities Basic Support and Advocacy Grants, the Older Americans Act, and many other pieces of federal, state, and local legislation have provided social service funding.

A significant development in social welfare is the recognition that those who are not poor can also benefit from social services. The growth of private social service agencies that cater to middle- and upper-class groups is an indication that many Americans need social services. People with problems of child abuse and neglect, the frailties that may accompany old age, mental illness, and alcohol and other drug dependence, are among those who have received increased attention from social service providers since the 1960s.

CHILD WELFARE POLICY AND SERVICES

Americans place a high value on privacy, and governmental interference in the private matters of the home is generally considered an unwelcome intrusion. As a result, the United States has no official national family policy. Instead, a number of federal, state, and local laws govern various aspects of family relations. A critical area of family policy concerns child welfare, also known as child protection.

State child welfare systems are often in a difficult position since many Americans believe that they do not do enough to adequately protect the nation's children from abuse and neglect, while others believe they tear families apart unnecessarily. Funding for child welfare services is complicated and involves a variety of federal funding streams along with state and local government funds. This section focuses on one of the most controversial areas of child welfare—the policies and services that address child abuse and neglect.

Discovering Child Abuse

Following the tradition of English common law, children in colonial America were considered chattels—the possessions of their parents.[8] Parents who severely punished their children, even beat them, were not defying community standards or breaking the law; they were merely making sure their children obeyed. Eventually case law allowed for criminal prosecution of parents in very severe cases, but in reality, little was done to protect children. Children in need of care were subject to the same demeaning forms of social welfare as adults—often almshouses or poorhouses, and they were also subject to indenture. This tradition prevailed in America until the Industrial Revolution brought an abundance of new social problems. Among them were the conditions of urban cities, which were often overcrowded and unsanitary and where hunger and disease were not uncommon.

During this period a prevailing philosophy was that children from poor homes might be better raised in institutions. Institutions such as the New York House of Refuge were established for neglected, abandoned, and delinquent youth. But the emphasis was not on protecting children from parents who harmed or neglected them. Institutional placement was intended to reverse the trend of poverty by teaching children proper social values and good work habits. Some organizations, like the Children's Aid Society founded by Charles Loring Brace in 1853 and the Children's Home Society founded by Martin Van Buren Van Arsdale in 1883, decided that children would best be served in rural areas, and they sent thousands of them to live and work with families, generally Christian families, away from the cities and their own families.

In 1874 the famous case of Mary Ellen Wilson brought public attention to the plight of severely mistreated children. The folklore surrounding the little girl's plight is that the laws protecting animals were stronger than those protecting children, so Henry Bergh of the New York Society for the Prevention of Cruelty to Animals (NYSPCA) decided to plead her case on the basis that the child was a member of the animal kingdom. Historical records do reflect Mr. Bergh's intervention, but apparently as a private citizen who presented the girl as a child in need of protection, not as a member of the animal kingdom.[9] The story, however, raised public consciousness about child abuse and has become woven into the history of child welfare (see Illustration 10.1).

Despite efforts of the settlement houses and eventually the Charity Organization Societies to focus on services to the family unit, the prevailing philosophy in the early twentieth century remained removing children from their homes rather than rehabilitating parents. The establishment of juvenile courts during this period did little to change this, but as the century progressed, more concern was expressed for the children themselves. Orphanages and foster homes became the preferred alternatives for child placement. New state mothers' aid programs provided some financial means to children in their natural homes, and slowly, child welfare philosophy in the twentieth century came to reflect "the great discovery . . . that the best

ILLUSTRATION 10.1
Little Mary Ellen

Before 1875, U.S. authorities had no legal means to interfere in cases of battered children. The laws were changed with the help of the Society for the Prevention of Cruelty to Animals (SPCA).

A 9-year-old named Mary Ellen became the exemplar of the battered children's plight. Indentured to Francis and Mary Connolly (and rumored to be the daughter of Mary's ex-husband), the girl was whipped daily, stabbed with scissors and tied to a bed. Neighbors reported the situation to Etta Wheeler, a church worker, in 1874. When Wheeler found that there was no lawful way to rescue the child from her brutal guardians, she went to Henry Bergh of the SPCA for help.

Under the premise that the child was a member of the animal kingdom, the SPCA obtained a writ of habeas corpus to remove Mary Ellen from her home. On April 9, 1874, she was carried into the New York Supreme Court, where her case was tried. She was pitifully thin, with a scissor wound on her cheek. Mrs. Connolly was sentenced to a year in prison. Mary Ellen was given a new home. The following April, the New York Society for the Prevention of Cruelty to Children (NYSPCC) was incorporated.

Before-and-after photos of Mary Ellen (as a pathetic waif upon her rescue and as a healthy child a year later) still hang at the New York SPCA, framed with Mrs. Connolly's scissors.

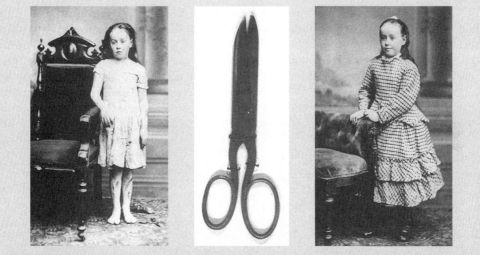

ASPCA's before and after photos of Mary Ellen, with scissors used to punish her.   *Source:* First published in *Parade* magazine, Nov. 29, 1981 issue. Copyright © 1989 Amy Wallace, Irving Wallace and David Wallechinsky. All rights reserved. Reprinted by permission. Photos courtesy of ASPCA Archives.

place for normal children was in their own homes."[10] Still, abusive parents were not themselves the targets of social policies or social programs, and the public largely condoned parents' use of physical force on their children.

According to Stephen Pfohl, it was not the social reformers, nor the juvenile court authorities, nor the public at large who finally "discovered" child abuse.[11] It was pediatric radiologists who identified the problem or "syndrome," gave it legitimacy, and aroused public concern. Beginning in 1946, the work of pediatric radiologist John Caffey led to the identification of parents as the cause of many of the bone fractures seen in children. Although emergency room and family physicians (not radiologists) were the first to come into contact with abused children, at least four factors prevented them from recognizing the problem: (1) Child abuse was not a traditional diagnosis; (2) doctors may have found it difficult to believe that parents would perpetrate such acts; (3) if the family, rather than just the child, was the doctor's patient, reporting abuse may have constituted a violation of patient confidentiality; and (4) physicians may have been unwilling to report criminal behavior because of the time-consuming nature of criminal cases and their dislike for serving as witnesses in legal proceedings. Pediatric radiologists exposed child abuse because they did not deal directly with the child and the family. Issues regarding confidentiality and court proceedings were not their primary concerns. This "discovery" also elevated the position of radiologists, who held lower status since they did not provide direct patient care.

To keep child abuse under the purview of the medical profession, it had to be viewed as a medical rather than a social or legal problem. In 1962, Dr. Henry Kempe and his associates labeled child abuse with the medical terminology "the battered-child syndrome," which legitimized its recognition by physicians.[12] Magazines, newspapers, and television programs, such as *Ben Casey* and *Dr. Kildare*, publicized the problem. Today, child abuse legislation is aimed more at rehabilitating parents than punishing them, and local child welfare agencies, rather than law enforcement, handle most cases.

Child Maltreatment

Child maltreatment consists of both abuse and neglect. Abuse occurs when severe harm is inflicted on a child such as bruises, broken bones, or burns. Abuse can also be emotional or sexual. Neglect occurs when a parent or caretaker fails to provide a child with the essentials needed to live adequately, including neglecting the child's medical needs, or it may result from psychological deprivation, such as isolating the child from others. Other types of maltreatment can include abandonment (see Illustration 10.2), not providing adequate parental supervision, threats of harm to the child, exploitation, and congenital drug addiction.

ILLUSTRATION 10.2
"Baby Moses" or Safe Haven Laws

In 1999, Texas was the first state to pass a law to address the problem of mothers in crisis abandoning their babies. These babies were sometimes found in dumpsters where they had perished. The law is nicknamed "Baby Moses" from the ancient story of baby Moses who was placed in a wicker basket by his mother to be saved from death. Today, all 50 states have enacted safe haven laws, which allow mothers to relinquish their baby at designated places such as hospitals and fire stations so that the baby can receive appropriate care until a permanent home is found. These laws allow the parent to remain anonymous and to be shielded from prosecution in exchange for surrendering the baby to a safe haven.

Laws sometimes have unintended consequences. In 2008, various media outlets reported that a new safe haven law in Nebraska was being misused. Even though the law was intended to meet the needs of abandoned infants, a number of parents began dropping off older children whom they were having difficulty parenting. One Omaha man left his nine children (ages 1 to 17) at a medical center after his wife died. Nebraska was the only state that lacked an age limit on leaving children under its law.

State laws mandate that professionals serving children (such as teachers, nurses, doctors, law enforcement personnel, daycare providers, and social workers) report even the suspicion of abuse or neglect to the local child protective services (CPS) agency. In 2008, professionals were responsible for 58 percent of the reports that were investigated.[13] Family and community members reported most other cases.

CPS workers are supposed to respond to suspected cases within established time frames, although this is not always possible when caseloads are high and agencies are not fully staffed. High-priority cases require a response within 24 hours. Lower priority cases require a response within a few days to a few weeks, depending on the state. In 2008, the average response time to a report of abuse or neglect nationally was 80 hours.

In 2008, child protective services (CPS) agencies across the country received 3.3 million reports of suspected child abuse and neglect, involving nearly 6 million children. Sometimes reports are not investigated at all because the situation does not fall under the state's rules for investigation, or the case is not given a high priority and the state lacks the resources to follow up on every report. After screening, approximately 63 percent of these cases were investigated, and of those, approximately 24 percent were substantiated (evidence of maltreatment was found) or indicated (there was reason to suspect maltreatment). The other 76 percent of cases were not substantiated because CPS investigations found either no evidence, or insufficient evidence, to indicate that the children were maltreated. Substantiation rates vary considerably by state. In total, across the United States, approximately 772,000 children were identified as victims of child abuse or neglect in 2008.

Data on the types of maltreatment in substantiated cases have been relatively consistent over time. In 2008, the National Child Abuse and Neglect Data System (NCANDS) reported that 73 percent of cases were neglect, including medical neglect; 16 percent were physical abuse; and 9 percent fell into the category of "other," which includes abandonment, threats of harm, and congenital drug addiction (see Table 10.1). Nine percent of cases were sexual abuse and 7 percent were psychological abuse. Younger children are more likely to be maltreated (see Figure 10.1). Nearly half (45 percent) of reported child victims are white, while 22 percent are African American, and 21 percent are Hispanic. African American and Native American or Alaskan Native children were overrepresented among reported abuse and neglect cases, with rates of 17 per 1,000 and 14 per 1,000, respectively (see Figure 10.2). The lowest rate is for Asian children. Approximately 15 percent of victims had a disability. In most cases (81 percent), children were abused or neglected by one or both parents. An estimated 1,740 children died as a result of abuse or neglect in 2008. Most (80 percent) of these children were under 4 years of age. Forty percent of the fatalities were due to multiple types of maltreatment, one-third to neglect, and one-fourth to physical abuse.

TABLE 10.1 Child Maltreatment by type, 2008[a]

Neglect	73%
Physical Abuse	16%
Sexual Abuse	9%
Other	9%
Psychological Maltreatment	7%

[a]Total does not equal 100% since some children are counted in more than one category.

Source: Administration for Children and Families, Administration on Children, Youth, and Families, Children's Bureau, *Child Maltreatment 2008* (Washington, DC: U.S. Department of Health and Human Services, 2010). Retrieved May 31, 2010, from http://www.acf.hhs.gov/programs/cb/pubs/cm08/index.htm

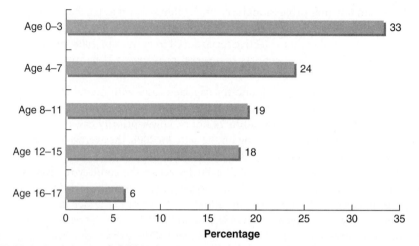

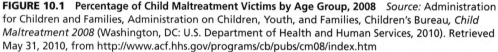

FIGURE 10.1   Percentage of Child Maltreatment Victims by Age Group, 2008   *Source:* Administration for Children and Families, Administration on Children, Youth, and Families, Children's Bureau, *Child Maltreatment 2008* (Washington, DC: U.S. Department of Health and Human Services, 2010). Retrieved May 31, 2010, from http://www.acf.hhs.gov/programs/cb/pubs/cm08/index.htm

The figures on child abuse and neglect reported above are based on all states and the District of Columbia. Because states differ in their definitions of problems and the procedures they use to screen calls and investigate cases, there are inconsistencies or gaps in the picture these data present. Many cases of abuse and neglect never come to the attention of authorities. The cases of child molestation by clergy members also remind us that even the most trusted members of society can be responsible for harming children.

A Brief History of Child Protection Legislation

The federal government's initial concern about children's welfare began with the first White House Conference on Children in 1909 called by President Theodore Roosevelt and the establishment of the Children's Bureau in 1912 under President William Howard Taft. The bureau was charged with addressing a broad range of child welfare issues, from health and child labor to delinquency and orphaned children. The Social Security Act of 1935 authorized the first federal grants for child welfare services and allowed states to develop local agencies and programs. Services were expanded, primarily during the 1960s. The AFDC-Foster Care program was established in 1961 to provide out-of-home care to poor children after the state of Louisiana dumped 23,000 black children from the AFDC program. The state considered their own homes "unsuitable" because the mothers had borne a child out of wedlock. This move led to the growth of the foster care system.[14] Child welfare services originally included under Title V of the Social Security Act were expanded and became Title IV-B, Child Welfare Services, in 1967.

Between 1963 and 1967 every state passed child abuse reporting legislation. Then, in 1974, Congress passed the Child Abuse Prevention and Treatment Act (CAPTA), landmark legislation that provided federal funding to the states to aid them in the prevention, assessment, identification, and treatment of child abuse and neglect. It also provided a minimum definition of child abuse and neglect and clarified the federal government's role in supporting efforts related to research and evaluation, data collection, and technical assistance. CAPTA was passed exactly 100 years after the famous child abuse case of Mary Ellen Wilson. CAPTA has been amended a number of times over the years, most recently by the Keeping Children and Families Safe Act of 2003.

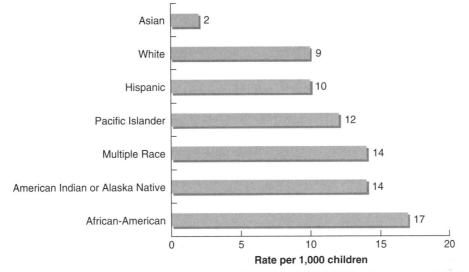

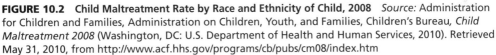

FIGURE 10.2   Child Maltreatment Rate by Race and Ethnicity of Child, 2008   *Source:* Administration for Children and Families, Administration on Children, Youth, and Families, Children's Bureau, *Child Maltreatment 2008* (Washington, DC: U.S. Department of Health and Human Services, 2010). Retrieved May 31, 2010, from http://www.acf.hhs.gov/programs/cb/pubs/cm08/index.htm

In 1975, when Title XX was added to the Social Security Act, the intent was to reduce fragmentation and to provide a more comprehensive approach to funding services for children and families. States had flexibility in how they used funds to achieve Title XX goals. Today, critics argue that expenditures are capped at a level that limits states' ability to positively impact the lives of children and families.

In 1978, the Indian Child Welfare Act (ICWA) created new requirements for child welfare agencies in serving Native American children and gave tribal governments authority in child custody proceedings. The goal of this law is to help preserve Native American culture and to give tribes a voice in legal proceedings involving the care and custody of Native children. Prior to ICWA, more Native children were removed, not only from their family, but also their community and culture.

In 1993, Title IV-B, child welfare services, was amended to create a new Family Preservation and Family Support Program. The goal was to dedicate funding to child welfare prevention programs such as family preservation, community-based family support services, time-limited reunification services, and adoption promotion and support. In 1997, it was renamed Promoting Safe and Stable Families (PSSF). Nine years later, Congress passed The Child and Family Services Improvement Act of 2006, reauthorizing the PSSF program for five years from 2007 through 2011. This legislation provides $345 million in mandatory funds each year (without going through the annual appropriation process) and $200 million in discretionary grants (Congress must approve this amount each year). It also includes a state grant program of $5 million to $20 million for child welfare workforce initiatives designed to help states reach the goal of providing monthly visits to children in foster care, funding for two $10 million court improvement grants, and a competitive grant program to address parental methamphetamine abuse. While some PSSF funding is competitive, other funds are allocated to the 50 states, the District of Columbia, and the U.S. territories on a formula basis, and a percentage is set aside for Native American and Native Alaskan tribes.[15]

CAPTA was reauthorized through 2008 under the Keeping Children and Families Safe Act of 2003. As the end date neared, the Child Welfare League of America (CWLA), a prominent child welfare advocacy organization, again called for reauthorizing CAPTA, including its three main programs: state grants, discretionary grants, and the Community-Based Child Abuse Prevention Grants. CWLA recommended the following:

- Strengthen funding for innovative approaches to address child abuse and neglect.
- Use CAPTA reauthorization to focus attention on the lack of adequate front-end child abuse and neglect prevention services and their role in the overrepresentation of children of color in the system.
- Fully fund CAPTA and the Community-Based Child Abuse Prevention grants at authorized levels so that child abuse and neglect protection programs and services can be implemented.
- Strengthen funding for research and program evaluation efforts to help advance the field of prevention of child abuse and neglect toward more evidence informed and evidence-based programs and practices.[16]

In 2008, a new law, The Fostering Connections to Success and Increasing Adoptions Act, was passed that has been lauded as the most important piece of child welfare legislation in more than a decade. It is intended to make important improvements to the child welfare system and includes the following components:

- Kinship Care: States are allowed to use Title IV-E funds to aid kinship guardianship families, and they must notify close relatives when children are placed in foster care. The act also funds "family connection" grants to help children establish or maintain ties with biological family members.
- Foster Youth: States can extend Title IV-E foster care to children until age 21. Child welfare agencies are required to help youth develop a transition plan during the 90-day period immediately before the youth exits care.
- Tribal: For the first time, tribal governments and consortia may apply to run their own Title IV-E foster care, adoption assistance, and kinship programs.
- Adoption: The law provides states with a larger incentive grant if they increase the number of adoptions of "older" children (aged 9 and older) and children with special needs. States are also required to inform prospective adoptive parents that they are entitled to an adoption tax credit.
- Healthcare: States must work with their Medicaid programs to ensure more extensive planning and coordination to meet the health needs of children in care. This includes how and when healthcare screenings will be conducted.
- Siblings: States must make reasonable efforts to place siblings together unless doing so would jeopardize the safety of any of the siblings. If siblings are not placed together, the state must make reasonable efforts to provide frequent visitation between the siblings.
- Education: New case plan requirements direct states to develop an agreement or arrangement with local school agencies so that children can remain in the same school even when they move out of the district as long as it is in the child's best interest. When a child does have to move, arrangements must be made for immediate school enrollment. States are now allowed to include in their foster care rates (payments) the cost of transportation to school.

Although the federal government has substantially increased its role in remedying abuse and neglect, there is still no single definition of these problems, and no single piece of legislation that uniformly addresses them throughout the nation. Child abuse and neglect statutes remain the states' prerogative. Available model legislation often serves as the basis for state statutes, but it is still difficult to achieve consensus on definitions. Even if there were agreement on definitions, the best strategies for intervention are often unclear, and funding to provide all needed services is clearly inadequate to meet the needs of vulnerable children. This is true despite the federal government's 2004 allocation of $7.6 billion specifically for child welfare services. Federal and state funding under the Title XX Social Services Block Grant and the TANF and Medicaid programs also support child welfare services. Not-for-profit agencies and foundations devoted to improving the lives of children, such as the Annie E. Casey Foundation and Court Appointed Special Advocates (CASA), also provide a good many child welfare services.

Foster Care and Adoption

Each year, approximately 500,000 children remain in foster (substitute) care in the United States.[17] The number of children in the care and custody of the state has received increased attention in recent years by policymakers in Washington. Perhaps the most significant recent development is the Adoption Assistance and Child Welfare Act of 1980, also known as the "permanency planning law." Amendments to the law were made by the Adoption and Safe Families Act (ASFA) of 1997. The basic idea behind the 1980 and 1997 laws is that children have the right to a permanent home as soon as possible, and that it is not healthy for them to linger for years in foster care while their parents make efforts at rehabilitation.

The 1980 law was a reaction to scathing indictments of the child welfare system, and was intended to prevent the drift of so many children into foster care for long periods. Critics alleged that federal policy had unwittingly encouraged the removal of children from their homes by providing much more funding for foster care and much less for prevention and in-home services. Thus, the goal of the Adoption Assistance and Child Welfare Act was to reduce the numbers of children entering care by focusing more on prevention and reunification, to reduce the time that children spend in care, and, when necessary, to find permanent placements for children as soon as possible. The federal government may impose financial penalties on states that do not comply with the act. The act also created a new entitlement program, Title IV-E Foster Care and Adoption Assistance, to help fund these new policies and programs.

Child welfare agencies have been required to follow new policies including making "reasonable efforts" to prevent removal of a child from the home and to return those who have been removed as soon as possible. The child must be placed in the "least restrictive setting" and close to the parent's home if the child will benefit. States were also required to have written plans for every child and to review each case at least every six months. Within 18 months (later reduced to 12 months) of placement, each case was required to have a permanency planning hearing to determine whether the child will be returned home, placed for adoption, or referred for another permanent living arrangement. Finally, states must provide adoption assistance payments to parents who adopt a child with special needs or is considered difficult to place (e.g., older children, those with physical and mental disabilities, and sibling groups).

Like the Adoption Assistance and Child Welfare Act of 1980, the Adoption and Safe Families Act (ASFA) of 1997, signed into law by President Clinton, was passed due to concerns about the performance of state child welfare systems and criticisms that they were often not operating in children's best interests. Some child rights advocates alleged that CPS systems were focusing too much on family reunification at the expense of children's safety. ASFA made a number of important changes to child welfare practice. The law (1) clarified that safety and permanence are paramount when making placement decisions for children, (2) addressed the growing number of children waiting for adoption by offering bonuses to states that increase the number of adoptions in their states and remedy barriers to the adoption process, (3) shortened the timeline for filing termination of parental rights (with some exceptions, states must begin procedures to terminate parental rights if a child has been in foster care 15 of the past 22 months); (4) shortened the timeframe for the permanency hearing from 18 to 12 months; and (5) clarified a number of circumstances where CPS would not be required to make "reasonable efforts" to reunify children with their parents (e.g., the parent has caused seriously bodily injury or murdered a child).

A longstanding problem of the child welfare system is finding enough foster homes. The system is always in need of more good homes in which to place vulnerable children. Foster parents are often portrayed negatively since the majority of stories in the media involve cases where a child is abused in a foster home. Being a foster parent can be challenging and stressful since children in care often have a range of emotional and behavioral problems due to the abuse or neglect they have suffered. It is important that foster parents be screened carefully and receive sufficient training and support from child welfare agencies. Many children benefit tremendously from the care they receive while in foster care. Foster parents are crucial in providing temporary care to children. They are also crucial in providing permanent care since foster parents adopt approximately 60 percent of children placed in their care.[18]

Another inaccuracy is that foster parents are well paid and that many foster parents "do it for the money." States pay foster parents to help cover the cost of caring for children until they are returned to their families or are adopted, although many children remain in foster care until adulthood. Payment rates vary widely across states and are generally higher for children who have special needs. According to a 2007 study, a foster parent caring for a 9-year-old child received as little as $275 a month in Ohio or as much as $869 in the District of Columbia. The average reimbursement was $509 a month.[19]

In 2007, more than 51,000 children were legally adopted from the public foster care system, and nearly 134,000 were waiting to be adopted.[20] In 2007, subsidies to adoptive families varied from $250 a month in Ohio to as much as $848 in Utah.[21] According to the Administration for Children and Families, in FY 2008, the federal government spent just over $2 billion for adoption assistance payments, services, and associated costs, and an average of 381,000 children were served each month. Title IV-E also includes continued Medicaid eligibility for these adopted children.

In addition to Title IV-E adoption assistance, Congress has made other efforts to promote adoption, including tax credits to defray adoption costs. In 2001, this tax credit became a permanent part of the federal tax code, doubled the amount that parents could claim from $5,000 to $10,000, doubled the amount adoptive parents can earn and still claim the full credit from $75,000 to $150,000, and provided a cost-of-living adjustment (COLA) for this credit. In recent years, the federal adoption tax credit has increased. The per-child tax credit was $11,650 for adoptions finalized in 2008, and $12,150 for those finalized in 2009, and families have six years to use the entire credit. Since 2003, families that have finalized adoptions for special-needs children can claim the tax credit even if their adoption expenses were less than this amount. In 2006, Congress also passed the Safe and Timely Interstate Placement of Foster Children Act, which speeds the placement of adoptive children across state lines.

For many youth in the foster care system, placement in a permanent home is not possible due to legal and other barriers. In 2007, approximately 29,000 youth reached adulthood ("aged out") while in foster care.[22] Studies have demonstrated poor outcomes for these emancipated youth and have found them to be at high risk for unemployment, poor educational outcomes, health and mental health problems, early parenting, poverty, incarceration, and homelessness.[23] Title IV-E provides services to help foster children make a better transition to independent living once they reach adulthood.

To improve independent living services, the John H. Chafee Foster Care Independence Program (CFCIP) was established under the Foster Care Independence Act of 1999. Youth aged 18 to 21 can receive financial and housing assistance, counseling, and other supportive services to assist them in moving from foster care to independent living.[24] The legislation doubled federal funding for independent living programs from $70 million to $140 million a year. In 2001, this law was amended to provide funding for a new educational and vocational training program for foster youth.

Controversial Issues in Child Welfare

Child welfare services are fraught with controversies. The federal government and the states have chosen to address them in various ways.

CONTROVERSY 1: ARE TRANSRACIAL ADOPTIONS APPROPRIATE? One of the most heated debates in child welfare practice is transracial adoption. Since finding adoptive homes for children who are permanently removed from their families can be difficult, child welfare agencies have resorted to practices such as placing pictures and stories of these children in the newspaper, on television, and on websites to attract interest. Many people are interested in adopting, but the preference is often for healthy, white infants. Children in foster care generally do not fit this description. Many are older, of ethnic minority backgrounds, and enter care with behavioral, developmental, medical, or other problems, and many of them live in a number of foster homes before they reach adulthood. There has been controversy over placing African American, Hispanic, and Native American children with white parents.[25] In 1972 the National Association of Black Social Workers (NABSW) famously called the adoption of black children by white families "cultural genocide." NABSW's position is that children are best served when they are placed with families that match and can preserve their cultural background. The organization faulted the states' child welfare systems for not doing a better job of recruiting families of color. Today, NABSW focuses more on advocating for kinship care, or placing children with relatives, which they view as a "continuation of the African tradition of caring, supporting, and providing cultural continuity for families." [26]

The other side of this argument is that due to the disproportionate numbers of children of color, primarily African American children, in foster care, transracial and transcultural adoptions can ensure that more children have a permanent home. Some believe that matching children and parents should be a "colorblind" process and that a loving home is a good home, despite any racial differences that might exist within the family. In response to this growing national controversy, Congress passed the Multi-Ethnic Placement Act (MEPA) in 1994, which prohibited states from delaying or denying adoption and foster placements on the basis of race or ethnicity, but allowed states to consider race as one of many factors in making placement decisions. In 1996, the Inter-Ethnic Placement Provisions Act made it illegal for states to include race as a factor at all.[27]

The controversy continues as a 2008 report released by the Evan B. Donaldson Institute recommends overhauling MEPA and the inter-ethnic adoption provisions act and permitting race to be one factor (although not the sole factor) when making placement decisions for a child who is eligible for adoption.[28] The Institute bases this recommendation on a study that concludes very little progress has been made in reaching equality for African American children awaiting adoption and makes the case that current law contradicts accepted best practices in adoption. The Institute also states that sufficient resources should be provided to agencies to aid in recruiting adoptive families that match the ethnic backgrounds of children in foster care. Other prominent child welfare organizations such as the Child Welfare League of America, the North American Council on Adoptable Children, and the Dave Thomas Foundation for Adoption have endorsed the report.

CONTROVERSY 2: SHOULD CHILD WELFARE SYSTEMS FOCUS MORE ON PREVENTION? A major criticism of child welfare policy and practice is that child welfare agencies devote insufficient resources to prevent child abuse and neglect. Children who come to child welfare agencies' attention may benefit from a variety of services. Some states invest most of their funds in post-investigation services and fewer in preventive services. This may occur because states have large caseloads of children in need of foster care or family preservation services.

In 2008, nearly 3.3 million children "at risk" for neglect or abuse or their parents received preventive services. [29] Services to prevent child abuse and neglect may include respite care, parenting education, housing assistance, substance abuse treatment (see Illustration 10.3), daycare, home visits, individual and family counseling, homemakers' services, and transportation. Many services are offered on a voluntary basis, and the family has the right to refuse them. In contrast to preventive services, post-investigation services are meant to ensure against future episodes of abuse and neglect. In 2008, more than one million, or slightly more than half of children whose cases were investigated or their parents received post-investigation services. These services may include individual and family counseling, family-based or in-home services (such as family preservation), family reunification services, court services, foster care, and adoption services.

Home visiting programs have received increased attention in recent years. Many see them as an important tool in child abuse prevention. Nurses, social workers, or other trained professionals make frequent home visits to families with young children from birth to age 5, since these early years are the most critical in terms of healthy child development. Goals include reducing parental stress and depression and promoting positive parenting skills, health and child development, and school readiness. There are a number of home visiting programs around the country including Parents as Teachers, Nurse-Family Partnership, Early Head Start, Home Instruction for Parents of Preschool Youngsters (HIPPY), and Healthy Families America. In the 108th, 109th, and 110th Congress, Senator Kit Bond (R-MO) introduced the Education Begins at Home Act to make grants to the states so they can implement home visiting programs, but it has yet to pass. Representative Jim McDermott (D-WA) introduced the Early Support for Families Act in the 111th Congress with the same goal.

Prevention and early intervention services are laudable. Questions arise, however, about too much interference in family matters and whether the mandates violate confidentiality and civil liberties, such as the right to privacy.

CONTROVERSY 3: SHOULD CHILD WELFARE SYSTEMS OPERATE FROM A SOCIAL WORK OR CRIMINAL JUSTICE FRAMEWORK? Some child advocates contend that children are poorly treated because the United States lacks a comprehensive profamily policy that sees that every family has the basic resources it needs to help children become healthy, functioning adults. Others see these problems as rooted in the wanton acts of a group of parents who are too immature or too impaired by mental or substance use disorders to care for their children. Thus, the question becomes whether we should have a "child welfare system" focused on the basic needs of

ILLUSTRATION 10.3
Substance Abuse: Risk Factor for Child Abuse and Neglect

Most children enter placement due to abuse or neglect. For more than 15 years, substance abuse has been a major contributor to removing children from their homes. Estimates indicate that substance abuse is a factor in two-thirds of foster care cases.[a] The introduction of crack cocaine in the 1980s and the recent methamphetamine epidemic have been blamed for the huge increases in the number of child maltreatment cases and out-of-home placements. However, there is a great deal of controversy surrounding prenatal drug exposure and how the child welfare system should respond to parental substance abuse.

The perspective of child welfare professionals and many others is that parental substance abuse leads to impaired judgment and places children at increased risk of maltreatment and impaired attachment. It often contributes to child neglect when parents spend money needed for housing and food on drugs or lose their jobs because of alcohol or illicit drug use. Also cited are the devastating consequences of prenatal drug exposure such as fetal alcohol syndrome and a range of cognitive and behavioral deficits.

Rather than attempt to prosecute women who use drugs during pregnancy, advocates for these women believe that rehabilitation or treatment is a much better alternative. They are concerned that the shortened timeframes set by the Adoption and Safe Families Act do not give parents enough time to successfully complete drug and alcohol treatment.

An additional perspective is that the effects of in utero drug exposure have been exaggerated as part of the country's ill-conceived drug war and that children can be removed from their parent's care and custody with insufficient proof of abuse or neglect. They cite recent research that shows that there is great variability in harm to exposed infants, ranging from no detectable negative effects to the rare outcome of severe harm.[b]

Over 8 million children live with substance-abusing or dependent parents.[c] The U.S. Department of Health and Human Services (DHHS) recognizes the many barriers to providing child welfare services to substance-abusing parents. There is a shortage of substance abuse treatment facilities, and state and federal laws often make it difficult to coordinate substance abuse treatment and child welfare services. Child welfare may expect a "cure," while chemical dependency professionals recognize that relapses are a part of the recovery process. DHHS has identified key program features important to comprehensively attending to the substance treatment and child welfare needs of families. Among these needs are better training for caseworkers, more preventive services, and better access to substance abuse treatment and support during recovery. The Child Welfare League of America recommends increased funding for the Substance Abuse Prevention and Treatment Act and the passage of the Family-Based Meth Treatment Access Act (H.R. 405/S. 884).

[a]Child Welfare League of America, 2008 Children's Legislative Agenda (Washington, DC). Retrieved July 30, 2008, from http://www.cwla.org/advocacy/2008legagenda.pdf
[b]Steven J. Ondersma, Sharon M. Simpson, Elizabeth V. Brestan, and Martin Ward, "Prenatal Drug Exposure and Social Policy: The Search for an Appropriate Response," *Child Maltreatment*, Vol. 5, No. 3, 2000, pp. 93–108.
[c]Substance Abuse and Mental Health Services Administration, Office of Applied Studies, National Household Survey on Drug Abuse. *Children Living with Substance-Dependent or Substance-Abusing Parents: 2002–2007, The NSDUH Report* (Washington, DC: Author, April 16, 2009). Retrieved May 30, 2010, from http://oas.samhsa.gov/2k9/SAparents/SAparents.htm

children and their families, or a "child protection system" focused on those who cause serious harm to children.[30] In other words, should the system be in the hands of social welfare authorities who seek to make the family better, or in the hands of law enforcement officials who seek to punish and obtain retribution from adults who harm children in their care?

Of course, both approaches are needed—basic services for families when parents need help in performing their role, and legal intervention when they flagrantly violate society's standards. Of utmost importance is addressing the "best interests" of the child. To prevent child abuse and neglect, the child welfare system uses two types of programs to strengthen families at–risk or families in crisis: family preservation services and family support services.

Family preservation programs, such as the Homebuilders Model, provide short-term, intensive services designed to prevent the removal of a child from the home. Services such as counseling, parenting skills, child development, and behavior management are provided in the home. Family preservation caseworkers have small caseloads (two to six families) and spend up to 20 hours a week with a family for four to 12 weeks. Family support programs are different since they focus on making services available to all families in a community, not just those in crisis. These community-based services are designed to increase the number of children living in safe and stable family environments, increase parents' confidence in their parenting abilities, and enhance child development. Examples of services are daycare, respite services, parenting classes, child development programs, individual and family counseling, housing assistance, recreation, and job training programs. Another focus is preserving families through the use of kinship care (see Illustration 10.4).

ILLUSTRATION 10.4
Preserving Families with Kinship Care

Removing children from their homes even temporarily can be traumatizing for the child, and finding an appropriate placement can be difficult. Kinship care is one approach that may reduce trauma to children when they are separated from their parent or parents. Staying with "grandma" or "auntie" may not be unusual for a child, but being sent to stay with total strangers can be confusing to children at best, and traumatic at worst. Kinship care was once eschewed because it left the child unavailable for adoption or was believed to increase the risk of recurring maltreatment due to ease of access by abusive parents. But kinship care has grown in use because it keeps children connected to their family, preserves children's cultural heritage, and helps address the dire shortage of foster and adoptive families. Some rules prohibiting relatives from obtaining foster care payments have been removed, thus making this arrangement more financially viable for many family members who want to care for the child. Children cared for by relatives are apparently less likely to incur repeated maltreatment than children placed with nonrelatives.[a] Having undergone a major reversal of policy, almost all states now give preference to relative caregivers over nonrelatives.

According to the 2000 U.S. Census, some 6 million children lived with relatives, 4.5 million of whom lived with a grandparent. African American grandparents were more likely to be a primary caregiver than whites or Hispanics.[b] Although most children living with relatives are not involved with the child welfare system,

[a]See Reid M. Jonson, "Foster Care and Future Risk of Maltreatment," *Children and Youth Services Review,* Vol. 25, No. 4, April 2003, pp. 271–294.
[b]U.S. Census Bureau, *Grandparents Living with Grandchildren: 2000* (Washington, DC, October 2003). Retrieved May 30, 2010, from http://www.census.gov/prod/2003pubs/c2kbr-31.pdf

in 2007, 25 percent of children placed in out-of-home care by the state were living with a relative, and in some states the figure is as high as 50 percent.[c]

It is fortunate that so many grandparents have assumed the primary caregiving role, but this presents a new family model and raises new concerns. Income usually diminishes as people retire, and these grandparent-headed families often live on fixed incomes and have economic hardships. Health and energy levels are often not what they were at a younger age. Grandparents may need support services such as respite care, transportation, in-home assistance, and in-kind or cash assistance to raise their grandchildren. In a study of grandparent caregivers in New York, grandparents suffered "extreme" levels of stress that they attributed to fears of not being able to raise their grandchildren into adulthood, or they feared that their grandchildren would be taken from them.[d]

In the past, the federal government did not provide any steady funding to assist

relatives with children in their care and custody, and many relatives went without any financial support. This has changed with the passage of the Fostering Connections to Success and Increasing Adoptions Act of 2008, which allows states to use Title IV-E funds to support kin families. It also extends the funds available to provide education to kinship parents to help them in their role. States will have to create a system of notification to relatives when a child enters care. The new kinship section also provides at least $5 million a year for competitive grants to create a navigator system for all kin families in the state whether they receive Title IV-E funding or not. Kinship navigator programs assist grandparents and other relative caregivers in learning about, finding, and using programs and services to meet the needs of the children they are raising, as well as their own needs. Finally, the bill clarifies that states may waive certain licensing standards, as determined by the state, on a case-by-case basis in order to eliminate barriers to placing children with relatives.

[c]Child Welfare League of America, *National Fact Sheet 2010*, Special tabulation of the Adoption and Foster Care Analysis Reporting System (AFCARS) by National Data Archive for Child Abuse and Neglect (NDACAN) and CWLA (Arlington, VA: Author, 2007). Retrieved May 30, 2010, from http://www.cwla.org/advocacy/statefactsheets/2010/nationalfactsheet10.pdf; Child Welfare League of America, Special tabulation of the Adoption and Foster Care Analysis Reporting System (Washington, DC: Author, 2006).
[d]Gerard Wallace, "Grandparent Caregivers: Emerging Issues in Elder Law and Social Work Practice," *Journal of Gerontological Social Work*, Vol. 34, No. 3, 2001, pp. 127–136.

Interest in family preservation has resulted in a number of studies to determine its efficacy; however, findings have been mixed. According to a recent meta-analysis of research on intensive family preservation services (IFPS):

Although some of the studies . . . report promising results, the field still needs additional evidence that IFPS programs prevent unnecessary child placement and more data about which types of family-based services programs are most effective with different client sub-populations, including racial and ethnic minorities and those involved in physical abuse, neglect, and other parenting problems. We also need a better understanding of the effectiveness of IFPS with different age groups of children, of program components that contribute to success with different families (e.g., in-home services, client goal-setting, concrete services), and of nonprogram components that may be important for certain families (e.g., other community supports, specialized treatment services).[31]

CONTROVERSY 4: DOES THE CHILD WELFARE SYSTEM CAUSE MORE HARM THAN GOOD? Child welfare agencies have had their share of problems, and many individuals and organizations question whether they sometimes do more harm than good. Every child should have a safe and happy home, but this goal is not easily achieved. With high demands for services, state child protective service agencies cannot respond to the numbers of children and parents in need, so they resort to prioritizing cases. The more serious cases get the attention while others may not get addressed unless, or until, they become as serious.

The public is particularly outraged when a child is not removed from the home and is later severely injured or dies as a result of abuse or neglect. This is a rare occurrence, but when it does happen, it captures media attention, and overshadows the successful cases that rarely make the news.

At the other end of the spectrum are stories of families destroyed by child welfare workers who remove children without just cause (Illustration 10.5 describes a controversial example of this issue). Courts may mandate that parents accused of abusing their children get

---

ILLUSTRATION 10.5
State of Texas v. the Fundamentalist Church of Jesus Christ of Latter Day Saints (FLDS), Yearning for Zion Ranch

In April 2008, the nation was riveted by the story of child welfare officials in Texas who removed more than 450 children from a Mormon polygamist compound.[a] An anonymous report was made, allegedly by a 16-year-old girl who told authorities that she was pregnant for the second time and was being physically and sexually abused by her husband. After interviewing a few of the minors who were or had been pregnant, CPS removed all of the children, arguing that the beliefs of the FLDS resulted in the males being groomed to be perpetrators and the females to be victims of sexual abuse. When CPS workers interviewed the girls, they were told that it was their belief that no age was too young to be married or "spiritually united" with a man of any age.

Americans had various opinions on whether the state did the right thing by removing these children from their families. Many were horrified when they heard the allegations and felt that CPS had acted correctly in protecting children from this harmful family environment. Others were critical of CPS and its handling of the case. They argued that it was traumatic to the children to be removed from their families and separated from their siblings, many of whom had never been outside the walls of their 1,700-acre ranch. Some

children had to be placed in cities far from home, making it difficult for their parents to visit them. Many also argued against the logic that all of the children were in "imminent danger" based on the allegations of a few children. The ACLU said it was concerned that the basic rights of the children and women were violated. Finally, the identity of the original reporter was never ascertained. Some believe it was a 33-year-old woman in Colorado, with a history of making false reports to authorities. The FLDS parents denied all allegations that their children were victims of physical and sexual abuse and believed they were being persecuted for their religious beliefs.

Thirty-eight mothers sued the state, and an appeals court ruled in their favor stating, "Evidence that children raised in this particular environment may someday have their physical health and safety threatened is not evidence that the danger is imminent enough to warrant invoking the extreme measure of immediate removal prior to full litigation of the issue." This is just one example of the ambivalence and conflicting feelings that arise for many Americans about when it is appropriate to remove children from the care and custody of their parents in order to protect their health, safety, and well-being.

[a]For *New York Times* coverage of this situation, see http://topics.nytimes.com/topics/reference/timestopics/subjects/f/fundamentalist_church_of_jesus_christ_of_latterday_saints/index.html

professional help, but parents are often frustrated when they cannot afford private treatment and there are long waits for services at community mental health and substance abuse treatment centers.

CONTROVERSY 5: WHY ISN'T THE CHILD WELFARE WORKFORCE BETTER PREPARED?   "Social workers" often take the blame for problems in the child welfare system, but in reality, many child welfare workers are not professionally qualified and may lack the education and experience necessary to do the job.[32] According to the Child Welfare League of America (CWLA), less than one-third of staff in state child welfare agencies have a formal social work education.[33] Some child welfare experts argue that a major impediment to improving the child welfare system is the difficulty in recruiting and retaining child welfare caseworkers. Child welfare work is very stressful. CPS agencies have a high caseworker turnover rate, and many state agencies find it difficult to maintain a stable and competent workforce.

CWLA sets standards for child welfare practice and recommends that child protection investigative workers carry a maximum caseload of 12 active cases per month. Advocates argue that more federal funds are needed to increase salaries, hire more caseworkers to keep caseloads manageable, and provide high-level training and loan forgiveness to students in social work (or a related field) who become child welfare workers. Another strategy to recruit and retain competent caseworkers includes developing more training partnerships between university social work programs and state child welfare agencies.

CONTROVERSY 6: ARE LAWSUITS THE BEST WAY TO CHANGE THE CHILD WELFARE SYSTEM?   When mistakes are made, the threat of lawsuits hangs over the head of child welfare workers and administrators. Rhode Island is one of several states that have come under intense scrutiny for the failings of its child welfare system. In 2007, the Child Advocate of Rhode Island (a state agency that protects the legal rights of children in state care) and an advocacy organization called Children's Rights sued the state. They allege that children are frequently abused and neglected while in state care, that foster parents are not adequately screened, and that caseloads are dangerously high, which prevents caseworkers from making home visits and ensuring that children are safe and receiving appropriate care. It is debatable how effective this strategy of lawsuits is in improving child welfare systems; however, some argue that they can lead to needed systems reforms.

In 1989 the U.S. Supreme Court ruled six to three that public employees could not be held liable for failure to protect citizens from harm by other private citizens. The case involved the Winnebago County, Wisconsin, department of social services and Joshua DeShaney, who suffered severe, permanent brain damage as a result of abuse by his father after the department failed to remove him from his home.[34] Many child advocates were shocked by this decision, although it was surely a relief to child welfare workers who make tough decisions every day about the lives of the children in their care. Greater threats of legal repercussions would likely cause an exodus of child welfare professionals. It is already difficult to find people who are willing to take these jobs or keep them for long. Child welfare workers can, however, be sued for clear civil rights violations.

In 1994 the U.S. Supreme Court again granted protections to social workers by saying that they are immune from being sued even if their accusations against parents are wrong. The high court's ruling stemmed from a Kentucky case in which the 6th U.S. Court of Appeals stated that social workers should "not [be] deterred from vigorously performing their jobs as they might if they feared personal liability."[35]

CONTROVERSY 7: WHY ISN'T THE CHILD WELFARE SYSTEM BETTER FUNDED? A major complaint of child welfare advocates is that child welfare systems are grossly underfunded. Most federal child welfare funding categories are entitlements (although some are capped) and require state matching funds. Between 1995 and 2004, total federal child welfare spending increased nearly 200 percent. In 2004, funding for child welfare services was more than $23 billion; 50 percent of these funds were federal dollars, 39 percent were state funds, and 11 percent were local funds.[36]

Although it may sound like a lot of money goes to child welfare services, it pales in comparison to the money spent on other social service programs such as Social Security or funds dedicated to national security. Child welfare experts argue that more funding is needed to ensure that all abused children receive the services they need, caseloads are kept low, more prevention programs are offered, and children are moved through the system to adoption or other permanent option in a timelier manner. Child welfare services may lack funding because children lack a direct voice in the political system.

CONTROVERSY 8: WHAT MUST BE DONE TO IMPROVE FOSTER CARE SERVICES? Perhaps the most criticized part of the child welfare system is the foster care system. Over the years, state foster care programs have been accused of causing instability in the lives of children in foster care who are bounced from home to home. Among the accusations are failing to meet foster youth's educational needs, failing to monitor foster youth's care closely enough, and concerns that a disproportionate number of African American children are in foster care due to bias and the higher poverty rate among African Americans.

More than 20,000 youth age out of the foster care system each year and must make the transition to independent living. Given the chaotic life of many foster care children, they face an uphill battle when at age 18 or 21 they are simply left to make it on their own. Substantial numbers of foster youth reside in homeless shelters after leaving foster care. Some ethnographic researchers suggest that the "drift" of youth in and out of homelessness after leaving foster care is a continuation of the drift they experienced in foster care.[37] Children who have the greatest difficulty transitioning to independent living have had multiple foster care placements and have less education. In recent years, there has been increased attention to better serving children in foster care by reducing the number of foster home moves and speeding up legal proceedings so children reach "permanency" as quickly as possible.

Most young people learn the skills needed to function as adults during the natural course of growing up in a family. Due to frequent moves from foster home to foster home or living in alternative settings such as children's group homes, many foster care youth did not acquire these skills. Today, the most common service older foster youth receive is independent living (IL) programs. While still in care, many foster youth attend classes focused on building the competencies needed for successful family and community life and participation in the workforce (e.g., budgeting, cooking, how to secure housing and healthcare, job application and interview skills, making lasting connections with caring adults). Many states will pay for a foster child's or former foster child's college education at a public university; unfortunately, the majority of foster youth are not college ready.

Ten years after IL programs began, DHHS found that large numbers of youth "aging out" of foster care had never received IL services.[38] Even many who received them had trouble maintaining employment and were living on the streets or involved in the criminal justice system. Many children reported that IL programs provided little concrete assistance, and they had difficulty recalling what the content of the IL program was. With funding provided by the Foster Care

Independence Act of 1999, a number of states have developed innovative programs that provide support for transitioning foster youth in the areas of housing, education, employment, and career development.

Despite the increase in funding and programs, youth leaving foster care continue to experience many challenges. A 2005 report on older youth in the states of Illinois, Iowa, and Wisconsin found that former foster youth were twice as likely as youth in the general population to report not having enough money to pay their rent or pay utility bills. In addition, youth who aged out of foster care reported sometimes or often not having enough food to eat.[39] A study by Casey Family Programs found that one in four foster youth were still coping with symptoms of posttraumatic stress disorder (PTSD) after leaving foster care.[40] This is double the PTSD rate of veterans returning from recent wars, and over six times the rate among the general U.S population. Many child welfare advocates call for a greater investment of time and resources to help this highly vulnerable population.

CONTROVERSY 9: WHY AREN'T CHILDREN'S RIGHTS BETTER PROTECTED? Another controversy in child welfare concerns the rights that should be afforded children and the rights that should be afforded parents. The United Nations (UN) Convention on the Rights of the Child (CRC) is an international human rights treaty that outlines the basic rights and protections all children should have, regardless of their country of residence. The CRC promotes a child's right to healthcare, protection from all forms of violence, an adequate standard of living, the right to develop to his or her fullest potential, and much more.

Advocates argue that the CRC is a useful framework that leaders of all countries can use to create comprehensive and cost effective policies and programs that address the specific needs of children and their families. By adhering to the reporting requirements contained in the CRC, the United States and other countries would be compelled to assess the state of children's well-being and undertake crucial efforts to improve their lives. The UN General Assembly adopted the CRC in 1989, and it was instituted in international law in 1990. As of 2009, 193 countries had ratified the CRC; the United States and Somalia are the only two countries that are a party to the UN who have not.[41]

In the early 1990s, resolutions were introduced in the U.S. Senate calling for CRC ratification. In 1995, Secretary of State Madeline Albright signed the CRC signaling the United States' intention to ratify. However, since this time it has not been forwarded to the Senate Foreign Relations Committee for consideration due to procedural and political barriers. The U.S. review process for ratifying international treaties is quite lengthy, and some fear that ratifying such treaties threatens national sovereignty. Additionally, a small number of conservative and religious groups and individuals allege that CRC ratification would undermine parental rights. They argue that that CRC would dictate to parents how they should raise their children and would enable children to do as they please (e.g., take legal action against their parents; choose their own religion; and have abortions without parental consent). Currently, a national campaign, The Campaign for U.S. Ratification of the Convention on the Rights of the Child, headquartered in Washington, DC, is working to pressure the United States to ratify the CRC.[42]

The Future of Child Welfare Policy

President Barack Obama's election brought a new sense of optimism in the child welfare arena as advocates press for legislation that would benefit children and their families. The Child Welfare League of America (CWLA) has called on the president to convene a White House Conference on Children and Youth as soon as possible. Legislation to this effect has been introduced in the House and the Senate. Advocates have also asked the federal government and state governments to protect human services and provide needed supports for vulnerable families during the country's economic crisis. The Children's Defense Fund has asked the president and Congress to find a way to expand healthcare to all children in the United States.

Social workers and other professionals are continually searching for more effective ways to help children and their families. Federal and state governments are concerned not only on humanitarian grounds but also because they foot most of the bill for remedying social problems. Federal grants and waivers that allow states to bend established rules are approved by Congress and provided through many government offices in order to test experimental approaches to address social problems. Since 1994, Congress has approved a number of waivers to test innovative approaches for delivering child welfare services. As of May 2007, 23 states have implemented one or more demonstrations under these initiatives. They include new funding mechanisms for state agencies, services to parents with substance abuse problems, post-adoption services, intensive care systems, tribal administration, managed care payment systems, assisted guardianship/kinship permanence, and training for child welfare staff. Most projects are still being evaluated. While some completed projects showed promising results, others have not.

One innovative child welfare practice is called *family group decision making* (FGDM) or *family group conferencing*. It offers a fresh approach to working with families. FGDM recognizes that families are the experts on their own situation and are often the best judge of what is needed to solve their problems. FGDM gives parents more power in the process of developing their family service plan. A trained child welfare professional convenes a "family conference," which includes family friends, extended family members, and community members who can serve as resources to assist the parents in reaching the goals identified on the family service plan.

Given the growing recognition that not all cases require formal investigation, another rapidly expanding child welfare practice is *alternative or differential response*. Although this practice varies slightly in how it is carried out, the basic idea is to permit states more flexibility in how they respond to reports of abuse and neglect. Where differential response is used, high-risk cases are formally investigated, whereas in low- and moderate-risk cases, families are offered needed assistance and services in lieu of a formal investigation.

Despite the many challenges child welfare systems face, they have an important mission and a vital role to play in protecting children from abuse and neglect. Child welfare policy and practice are constantly evolving as new interventions are tested with the goal of better outcomes for the children and families served by child protection systems across the country.

SOCIAL SERVICES FOR OLDER AMERICANS

Family members and friends are the major source of aid for older adults who need help with activities of daily living. In 2007, an estimated 52 million individuals assisted an older American at some time during the year.[43] When family and friends cannot meet all these needs, federal, state, and local agencies try to respond.

Over the last century, older Americans' quality of life has improved considerably. Public policies have contributed to these gains. The Social Security program (see Chapter 5) is an important source of income for most older Americans. Supplemental Security Income (see Chapter 7) is another source of income support. Medicare and Medicaid (see Chapter 8) are crucial in maintaining health. However, a significant number of older Americans still spend the last portion of their lives in need. As life spans increase, even those in higher income brackets are likely to need publicly supported healthcare services, assistance in independent living, protection, and long-term care services.[44]

The Older Americans Act

Social services are a vital component in meeting the needs of older people. Perhaps the most important legislation in this regard is the Older Americans Act (OAA) of 1965, reauthorized in 2006 until 2011.[45] The OAA and the "aging network" are adjuncts to the major cash assistance and health programs for older Americans. These social service programs provide links to the community and help to keep older Americans involved in the mainstream of U.S. life and out of institutions. Advocacy groups for older Americans are concerned that services be well publicized to ensure they are utilized.

The objectives listed in the Older Americans Act are suitable for virtually any group in the world.[46] The objectives are the following:

- An adequate income in retirement in accordance with the U.S. standard of living
- The best possible physical and mental health that science can make available without regard to economic status
- Suitable housing that is independently selected, designed, and located, with reference to special needs and available at costs older citizens can afford
- Full restorative services for those who require institutional care
- Opportunity for employment with no discriminatory personnel practices because of age
- Retirement in health, honor, and dignity—after years of contribution to the economy
- Pursuit of meaningful activity within the widest range of civic, cultural, and recreational opportunities
- Efficient community services, including access to low-cost transportation, that provide a choice in supported living arrangements and social assistance in a coordinated manner and that are readily available when needed
- Immediate benefit from proven research knowledge that can sustain and improve health and happiness
- Freedom, independence, and the free exercise of individual initiative in planning and managing one's own life.

The OAA provides a framework and funding for an array of services to older citizens. Services for the most vulnerable older adults and their family caregivers are a special concern of the OAA. The 2000 amendments to the act established the National Family Caregiver Support Program. The 2006 amendments added an initiative, "Choices for Independence," which promotes better healthcare choices and more services directed toward helping older adults remain in their own homes.

Progress toward achieving OAA objectives is documented in an annual performance report. Recent reports (2004–2007) indicate that over 80 percent of annual program targets were met.[47] For example, one indicator was to "increase the number of clients served per million dollars of AoA funding." The target for FY 2007 was to serve 7,110 clients per million dollars. This target was exceeded with 8,346 clients served per million dollars of funding.

The OAA created an "aging network" to meet the needs of older Americans (see Figure 10.3). The network operates at the federal, regional, state, and local levels. At the federal level is the Administration on Aging (AoA), which is part of the U.S. Department of Health and Human Services.[48] The AoA's primary function is to provide technical assistance to state and local governments in developing and implementing services for older people. It also conducts some program evaluations and research on aging and acts as a national clearinghouse on information about older people. To assist in its efforts, the AoA has ten regional offices across the United States.

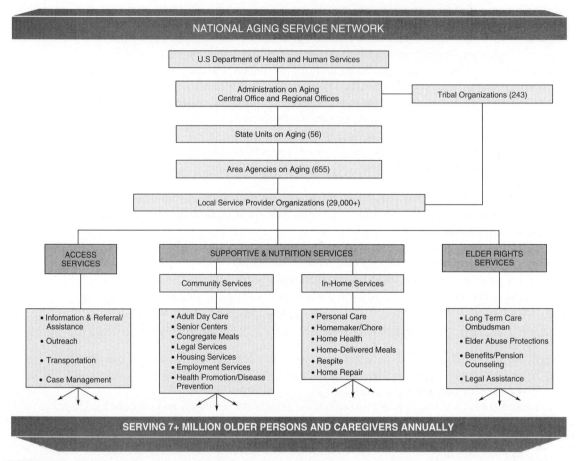

FIGURE 10.3 **National Aging Services Network** *Source: Administration on Aging: Emergency Assistance Guide* (Washington, DC: U.S. Department of Health and Human Services). Retrieved February 9, 2010, from http://www.aoa. gov/AoARoot/Preparedness/Resources_Network/pdf/Attachment_1357.pdf

At the state level, the entity concerned with services for older individuals may be part of the state's human services or welfare department or a free-standing cabinet-level agency or department. These state offices assist in implementing federal policies and act as advocates for older citizens. They make older adults needs known to the AoA, and also to their own state legislatures, which determine how state programs to address these concerns will be funded and administered.

The programs available to older Americans and their caregivers vary from region to region and county to county throughout the United States. At the local level there are about 655 Area Agencies on Aging (AAAs). Each AAA is guided by an advisory council primarily composed of older people. The Area Agencies assess the needs of older people in their communities and distribute funds to community agencies. The OAA prohibits state agencies and Area Agencies from providing direct services other than information and referral. Instead, they must contract with local agencies to deliver services.[49]

Among the services local agencies provide are nutrition programs such as home-delivered meals ("meals on wheels") and meals provided at sites such as senior centers, socialization and other activities at senior centers, transportation, homemaker and chore services, legal counseling, escort services, home repair and renovation, home health aide services, shopping assistance, visitation, and telephone assurance (phone calls to the elderly for reassurance and to check on their needs). In FY 2009, nearly 40 percent of Older Americans Act funds went to nutrition services and 31 percent went to community service employment to help older Americans maintain adequate income (see Figure 10.4).

In addition to services for older citizens, family caretakers of the elderly may also need services if they are to continue to be a mainstay of support. For example, respite care provides relief to spouses, adult children, and other caretakers, so they can go shopping, have a few hours of free time, or take a vacation. Many families cannot afford or prefer not to purchase respite care and do without it or rely on other family members and friends when relief is needed. In 2009, the Administration on Aging allocated more than $154 million to the National Family Caregiver Support Program for services to those caring for ill or disabled family members.[50]

The Family and Medical Leave Act signed by President Clinton in 1993 (also see Chapter 11) allows employees of larger employers to take up to 12 weeks of job and health benefit-protected unpaid leave to care for a parent, child, or spouse. Some states expand the definition of family to include domestic partners and in-laws.[51]

Public policies that might encourage greater family involvement in elder care include allowing Medicaid and Medicare to cover more home healthcare costs and income tax deductions or credits for providing care to older family members. Paying family members to provide this care is another option. Such changes would be especially helpful to lower-income families

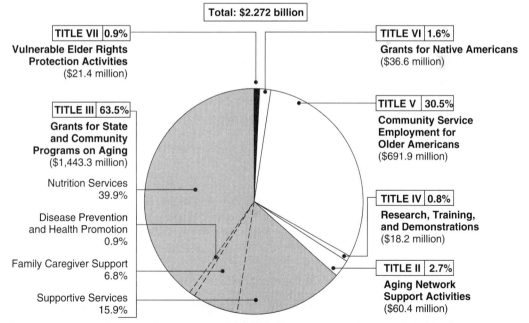

FIGURE 10.4   Older Americans Act, Fiscal Year 2009 Appropriations   *Source:* From Carol O'Shaughnessy, "The Basics: Older Americans Act of 1965" (Washington, DC: National Health Policy Forum, October 8, 2009). Retrieved February 10. 2010, from http://www.nhpf.org/library/the-basics/Basics_OlderAmericansAct_10-08-09.pdf, based on appropriations data in Angela Napili, "Older Americans Act (OAA): Funding," Congressional Research Service, Report RL33880.

who wish to care for an older or disabled family member but who could not otherwise afford to do so. These options may provide cost savings for federal and state governments over institutional care.

White House Conferences on Aging

There have been five White House Conferences on Aging, with older Americans from across the United States participating as delegates. The last one was held in 2005.[52] The next is scheduled for 2015. The conferences have reiterated many of the goals of the Older Americans Act.

The 2005 conference delegates adopted 50 resolutions. In addition to support for the Older Americans Act, Social Security, Medicare, Medicaid, long-term care services, improved mobility and transportation options, and research on aging, the 2005 conference focused on the graying of the Baby Boomer generation. A summary of the 2005 conference states:

> In areas such as Social Security, health care planning, and the workforce, we are already behind the curve. While experience is always important, it is unlikely that we will find all the answers to future problems in the past because tomorrow's older population can be expected to differ in distinct ways from prior generations:

> They will be healthier and wealthier.

> They will be better educated and desire to make contributions beyond traditional retirement.

> They will be more racially and ethnically diverse.

> The average age of the older population will increase as the number of centenarians continues to grow, and there will be longer life expectancy.

> People are likely to stay in the workforce longer than in the last seven decades.[53]

The U.S. House of Representatives had a Select Committee on Aging from 1974 to 1992. The Senate has had a Special Committee on Aging since 1961.[54] These special committees have no legislative authority, but they can bring attention to issues of concern. State legislatures generally have committees whose functions also include consideration of the needs of older individuals. Over the years about half the states have periodically convened "Silver-Haired Legislatures" composed of older residents who discuss the needs of their age cohort and report to the governors and state legislatures.

In addition to these advisory groups, older people throughout the country have organized in an effort to make their needs known. Perhaps the best known organization of older Americans is the nonpartisan AARP (formerly called the American Association of Retired Persons). With more than 40 million members, it can be called the country's largest advocacy group.[55] A smaller but also vocal association is the Gray Panthers, which has a particular interest in intergenerational issues. The number of groups in states and communities addressing the concerns of older people is likely to grow as the baby boomers become the older population.

Protective Services for Older Americans

When older people can no long care for themselves or when caretakers are unable to encourage them to eat or perform other self-care activities, their situation is termed "self-abuse." Another serious situation is maltreatment by others. Most states have statutes that prohibit physical and psychological abuse of elders and exploitation of their resources (unauthorized use of their income or assets). These types of abuse may occur in the older person's home, the home of a caretaker, or in an institution such as a nursing home. Penalties for citizens who do not report elder abuse vary, and in many cases, there is no real penalty.[56]

It is difficult to say how many older Americans are abused, neglected, or exploited each year. Since 1986, the National Center on Elder Abuse (NCEA), a part of the Administration on Aging, has collected data from all 50 states and the District of Columbia. Although the rate of reporting has risen, sources vary in the quality of information provided. The 32 states that were able to differentiate elder abuse reports from abuse of younger vulnerable adults reported more than 253,000 incidents in fiscal year 2003. There were 8.3 reports of elder abuse for every 1,000 older persons.[57]

The identification of elder abuse is complicated by several issues. For example, even those older people capable of reporting the abuse may not do so for fear that loss of their caretaker will result in their being placed in an institution. When the abuser is a loved one, the older person may not want to risk intervention by social service workers or law enforcement. Elder abuse laws are not as well developed as child abuse laws, but in most areas, adult protective service workers or law enforcement officers can be asked to intervene.

Guardianship

An important civil rights issue for the elderly is guardianship or conservatorship. Guardianship may empower an individual to make personal and/or financial decisions for another individual, while conservatorship provides only for financial decisions.[58]

The courts may appoint a guardian when it appears that an older person is no longer competent to manage his or her daily affairs. In most states these are probate courts that also deal with child custody and adults in need of treatment for mental illness. Once a guardian is appointed, the older person may be stripped of rights and decision-making power over where to live, how to spend money, whether to receive treatment, and so forth. Guardianship is defined under state law, and these laws have come under increased scrutiny as more older people are subjected to guardianship. Concerns are that many guardianship decisions are made without sufficient information. Decisions may be based on the viewpoint of the individual who believes guardianship is needed rather than on any convincing evidence. The older person may not even be given an opportunity for legal representation. In many cases, supervision of guardians is also lax. The elderly can be robbed of assets and treated poorly by guardians who may be relatives or perhaps someone previously unknown to them.

Fee-for-service guardianship is a particular concern with regard to exploitation. In 2006, eight states tightened regulation of guardianship. Family members, financial institutions that serve older persons, AARP, and the American Bar Association have instituted efforts to reduce or eliminate instances of misuse of guardianship. The primary need is for systematic, ethical oversight of guardianships.[59]

In a striking example, economist Mollie Orshansky, the original developer of federal poverty thresholds (see Chapter 4), was the object of guardianship proceedings in the District of Columbia. The dramatic story of a niece's successful rescue of Ms. Orshansky includes forced hospitalization that resulted in new risks to Ms. Orshansky's health, clandestine escape across state lines, unresolved lawsuits, and Ms. Orshansky's eventually living out the rest of her life in her New York apartment close to her family.[60]

A Government Accounting Office report on guardianships, generated in part by Ms. Orshansky's plight, looked at what state courts do in respect to guardianships, identified exemplary guardianship programs, and made recommendations as what state courts and federal agencies can do to better protect vulnerable individuals. The report called for more collaboration between courts and social welfare agencies. The U.S. Department of Health and Human Services is working to implement suggested changes, while the Social Security Administration said it was unable to do so, citing concerns about interagency data sharing and privacy laws.[61]

Nursing Home Care

Older persons, their families, community service providers, and activists for the protection of elders all say that nursing home care should be a last resort, to be delayed as long as possible and avoided if at all possible. However, in the real world, most persons who need full-time supervision and care are served in residential facilities. Medicare covers only a limited period of skilled care after a hospitalization. Intermediate care facilities, usually called nursing homes, do provide full-time care, although rates in even modest facilities are easily a $100 a day or more. Once people who need long-term care have exhausted their personal resources, they generally must turn to Medicaid, the federal-state health insurance program for very low-income individuals. Given the high costs of care, many residents become Medicaid eligible during their nursing home stay.

The Nursing Home Reform Act was part of the 1987 Omnibus Budget and Reconciliation Act. The act mandated regular evaluation of resident care plans, substantially less use of physical restraints, and greater protections of nursing home patients' rights.[62] Even 20 years after reform, nursing home surveyors find more than occasional instances of patient abuse and violations of care procedures. Care providers argue that low reimbursement rates from Medicaid and other sources limit their ability to hire well-qualified employees and provide quality care. Whether older adults reside in the community or in residential facilities, social workers and other human service professionals seek to meet their basic needs; prevent, reduce, or eliminate mistreatment; and promote protection of their civil rights and human dignity.

SOCIAL SERVICES FOR INDIVIDUALS WITH MENTAL AND SUBSTANCE USE DISORDERS

Everyone experiences emotional stress at some time in his or her life. With the passage of time and the support of family and friends, most make it through these difficult times. Significant numbers of Americans, however, develop mental health and substance abuse problems that require professional care. Changing cultural norms and celebrity endorsements of treatment for mental and substance use disorders have reduced some of the stigma attached to receiving professional assistance for these problems. The development of psychotropic medications has also strongly influenced the ability of persons with mental health problems to function in society, and some medications, like methadone, are available to aid those with drug addiction.

Today's mental health professionals would prefer to focus on preventing mental health problems and providing early intervention. Budget constraints often preclude intervention until problems become severe, and use of some public funds is restricted to providing services to those who have serious mental illness like severe anxiety, depression, schizophrenia, or significant difficulty in adapting to society's expectations for their behavior. Professionals in the private sector often have more flexibility in deciding whom they will serve. They often assist people adapting to divorce, the death of a loved one, or other life changes. They may also treat individuals with severe mental illnesses, but often these individuals have no way to pay for private care and must rely on publicly supported services.

Despite the efforts of those who advocate for increased utilization of mental health services, the costs of care, lack of public education about mental illness, and social stigma are factors in service underutilization.[63] Other obstacles to providing mental health and substance abuse services are a lack of consensus about how to define these problems, how to ensure that those in need have access to services, and what the preferred treatment and prevention approaches are.

A Brief History of the Response to Mental Illness

People with mental illness were once thought to be possessed by the devil and were hidden away from public view, but by the nineteenth century treatment began to take different forms.[64] Phillipe Pinel, a French physician, introduced "moral treatment," which consisted of caring for patients with kindness and consideration, providing the opportunity for discussion of personal problems, and encouraging an active orientation to life. This was a far more humane approach to treating mental illness, but it was not the treatment offered to most patients. Institutionalization or incarceration was the typical method for dealing with mental illness. Dorothea Dix, a social reformer during the mid-1800s, sought to improve the plight of severely mistreated mental patients. Dix succeeded in improving conditions within mental institutions, but with increasing numbers of people being labeled mentally ill, institutions grew larger and less capable of helping patients.

The Industrial Revolution increased many social problems, including mental illness. People came to the cities seeking jobs and wealth; instead, many found overcrowding, joblessness, and misery. Coping with urban problems was difficult, and new arrivals were often without the support of family and friends. Immigrants from other countries also flocked to the cities. Those who did not acculturate or assimilate quickly into U.S. society were often labeled deviant or mentally ill. City dwellers, overwhelmed with problems, had little tolerance for behavior they considered abnormal. This increased the number of people sent to mental institutions.[65]

Apart from state institutions, there was little in the way of social policies and public programs for people with mental illness. Following Dix's efforts, Clifford Beers introduced the "mental hygiene movement" in the early twentieth century. In 1909 he founded the National Mental Health Association. Beers knew well the dehumanizing conditions of mental institutions; he himself had been a patient. His efforts to expose the inhumane conditions of the institutions, like Dix's, resulted in better care, but the custodial and institutional philosophies of mental health treatment continued.

During World War II, a large number of young men were needed for military service. Part of the screening procedure for new recruits was a psychiatric examination. The number of young men rejected as unfit for military service or later discharged for psychiatric reasons was alarming. Although these psychiatric screening procedures have been criticized, the identification of so many young men with mental problems brought renewed concern for mental health. This concern was reflected in the Mental Health Act of 1946. The act established the National Institute of Mental Health (NIMH), with its focus on training, education, and research.[66]

In the 1950s, the development of improved psychotherapeutic drugs reduced many of the troubling symptoms (such as hallucinations) that patients experienced. This allowed hospital staffs to reduce restrictions placed on patients and made patients more acceptable to the community. Psychotropic medications can have serious side effects, and the appropriate use of drug therapy has been debated, but it is evident that they have reduced the need for hospitalization for many patients. New and better drugs are being developed all the time, but they are often costly, thus prohibiting more people from obtaining them.[67]

The use of psychotherapeutic drugs helped to lay the groundwork for the Mental Retardation Facilities and Community Mental Health Centers Construction Act of 1963. The act was a key element of an emerging community mental health movement. It emphasized more federal support for community-based care, better coordination between hospitals and community services, improved services to people with serious mental illness, a reduction in state hospital treatment, and an increase in community treatment consistent with deinstitutionalization and normalization (also see Chapter 6) as well as education and prevention services.[68]

Prevalence and Treatment of Mental and Substance Use Disorders

Mental health professionals have long debated the best way to define mental illnesses, but laypeople may conceptualize mental health and mental illness as two ends of a continuum. At one extreme are people who behave in an acceptable manner. At the other extreme are people who are unable to cope with reality and cannot function within the community. Despite conventional divisions between problems of mind and body, most sources acknowledge that mental and substance use disorders are strongly affected by biological and social factors.[69]

The National Institute of Mental Health lists mood disorders, schizophrenia, anxiety disorders, eating disorders, attention deficit hyperactivity disorder, autism, and Alzheimer's disease as major categories of mental disorders.[70] In each category, NIMH identifies a range of severity. The definitions of mental illness that mental health professionals commonly use are found in the American Psychiatric Association's *Diagnostic and Statistical Manual of Mental Disorders (DSM)*.[71] The diagnostic codes in the DSM match the codes in the *International Classification of Diseases 9th Edition Clinical Modification* (ICD-9-CM) published by the World Health Organization. Medicare, Medicaid, and many insurers require that professionals use these codes to be reimbursed for providing treatment. The *DSM* determines the way mental health professionals diagnose patients and also how they are paid for their services. Those who favor the current system argue that consistent nomenclature is helpful for research and reimbursement purposes.[72] Critics argue that these practices promote categorizing and labeling people even when they may not specifically fit DSM categories, or when labeling may be counterproductive.[73]

Since 1980, the National Institute of Mental Health has funded three major studies of the incidence and prevalence of mental health problems among the U.S. population. Through face—to-face interviews, professional interviewers gathered data about the prevalence, severity, and burden of disorders and the use of mental health services.[74] According to the latest NIMH-sponsored study called the National Comorbidity Survey Replication (NCS-R), about one-quarter of the U.S. population aged 18 and older experienced a mental illness during the course of the past year. The NCS-R found that "45% of those with one mental disorder met the criteria for two or more disorders." Comorbidity is having more than one mental disorder. Although the NCS-R researchers found that "mental disorders are widespread, serious cases are concentrated among a relatively small proportion of cases with high comorbidity."[75] NCS-R researchers also reported that among respondents with a mental disorder, the 40 percent classified as mild were unable to carry out normal activities about two days in the previous year. The 37 percent classified as moderate were unable to carry out normal activities about five days in the previous year. The 22 percent classified as serious lost an average of 88 days in the previous year.

The Substance Abuse and Mental Health Services Administration (SAMHSA), part of the U.S. Department of Health and Human Services, estimated that nearly 10 million adult Americans had a serious mental illness in 2008.[76] Approximately 60 percent received some type of mental health care, most often prescription medication followed by outpatient care. Among those who said they went without needed services, the largest group reported it was because they could not afford them.

The Methodology for Epidemiology of Mental Disorders in Children and Adolescents (MECA) Study estimated that almost 21 percent of U.S. children ages 9 to 17 have a diagnosable mental or addictive disorder associated with at least minimum impairment.[77] In 2008, SAMHSA reported that of the 2 million youth with major depressive episode, nearly 40 percent received treatment.[78]

SAMHSA has conducted the National Survey on Drug Use and Health (NSDUH) since 1971. Most people who try an illicit drug do not become problem users, but based on *DSM-IV* diagnoses, the 2008 NSDUH found that approximately 23 million indivduals (9 percent of the population) aged 12 or older met the criteria for alcohol or drug dependence or abuse during the past year.[79] Only 2.3 million (about 10 percent) of them received substance abuse treatment. Another one million thought they needed treatment but did not get it, most often because they said they were not ready to stop drinking or using or because they did not have health coverage or income to pay for treatment. However, most people who meet the criteria for alcohol or drug disorders do not get care because they do not perceive that they have a problem or need treatment. One of the biggest public health challenges is encouraging people with substance use disorders to recognize the problem.

Some people have both mental and substance use disorders. The systems for treating mental illness and substance abuse are usually separate, not to mention fragmented and limited. While some communities have model programs to help people that have both a mental disorder and a substance use disorder, people with these "co-occurring" illnesses often experience significant difficulty in finding effective, coordinated services to meet their needs. The NSDUH indicates that in 2008, 2.5 million adults had co-occurring serious mental illness and substance use disorders. Nearly half (45 percent) received mental health treatment only; about 11 percent received treatment for both problems, and about 4 percent received only substance abuse treatment. The remainder went without treatment.

Paying for and Providing Care

Federal, state, and local agencies regulate the operation of residential, community-based, inpatient, outpatient, medical, criminal justice system, and other services for people with mental illness and substance use disorders. Governments also pay for most of this care. Social workers, counselors, nurses, psychologists, psychiatrists, and other health and mental health professionals provide the services. Most often nurses and social workers provide this care.[80] Social workers are sometimes the only mental health service providers in rural areas.[81]

Treatment for mental and substance use disorders make up 7.5 percent of the nation's healthcare spending.[82] Public funds pay for 61 percent of this treatment compared to 45 percent of all healthcare spending (see Figure 10.5). These figures do not include much of the cost of mental and substance use disorders, which are indirect, including "reduced labor supply, public income support payments, reduced educational attainment, and costs associated with other consequences such as incarceration or homelessness[,] . . . emergency room care, . . . and early mortality."[83]

Given that so many do not get care, treatment advocates want to increase access to services and promote more adequate and earlier treatment. The differences between the public and private tiers of the healthcare system are often more pronounced in the mental health and substance abuse treatment delivery systems. Although both sectors can provide quality service, those who have insurance or can afford to pay for services often have immediate access to services. There may be a wait for public mental health and substance abuse services, especially voluntary inpatient treatment. However, the public sector often offers clients a broader range of services than the private sector. For example, public mental health services may offer housing, childcare, and

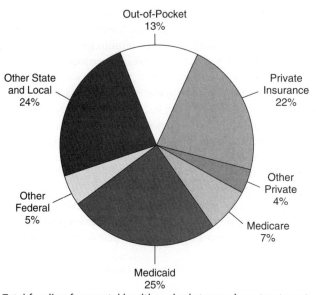

Total funding for mental health and substance abuse treatment services was $121 billion in 2003.

FIGURE 10.5 **Sources of Funding for Mental Health and Substance Abuse Treatment Services, 2003**
Source: Tami L. Mark, Katherine R. Levit, Rosanna M. Coffey, David R. McKusick, Henrick J. Harwood, Edward C. King, Ellen Bouchery, James S. Genuardi, Rita Vandivort-Warren, Jeffrey A. Buck, and Katheryn Ryan, *National Expenditures for Mental Health Services and Substance Abuse Treatment, 1993–2003,* SAMHSA Publication No. SMA 07-4227 (Rockville, MD: Substance Abuse and Mental Health Services Administration, 2007). Retrieved October 8, 2009, from http://www.samhsa.gov/spendingestimates/SAMHSAFINAL9303.pdf

other supportive services for clients and their families at low or no cost. The private sector may not provide these services, even if clients can afford to pay for them.[84]

INSURANCE COVERAGE FOR MENTAL AND SUBSTANCE USE DISORDERS. Many believe that more could be done to treat Americans with mental and substance use disorders if more of them had health insurance, and if health insurance plans included the same coverage for mental and substance use disorders as for physical health problems. In 1996, Congress passed the Mental Health Parity Act, which mandated increased insurance coverage for mental health services, bringing it closer to the coverage offered for other health problems. One viewpoint is that anything less than parity for mental illness (and substance use disorders) is discriminatory since these problems have biological bases like other health problems.[85]

In 1998, the RAND Corporation estimated that overall, premium costs for unlimited mental health care under managed care would increase premiums by about $1 per employee per year.[86] A SAMHSA-sponsored study of state programs also found that the costs of mental health parity were indeed minimal.[87] Additional costs were so small because increased mental health benefits had not resulted in increased use of mental health services. This is unfortunate because a more recent RAND Corporation publication indicates that health maintenance organizations (HMOs) whose members had a higher volume of mental health services use had significantly better outcomes (e.g., greater use of post-psychiatric hospitalization follow-up) than HMOs with a lower volume of use of mental health services.[88]

State and watchdog groups post public policies that govern mental health coverage on their Internet sites.[89] Since state and federal policies regarding insurance coverage tend to change along with political and economic cycles, those concerned with current service availability find that they must review these sites regularly.

In 1999, President Clinton issued an Executive Order requiring parity for mental health coverage in federal employees' health insurance coverage. Many other working Americans have not had this type of coverage for mental health care.

Medicaid and Medicare have in effect expanded the public mental health system beyond community mental health centers (CMHCs) to other mental health providers, many in private practice, who are willing to accept these public payments. Today, the public mental health system is a mix of private providers who accept government payment for services, CMHCs, veterans hospital psychiatric services, and state mental health facilities such as psychiatric hospitals and residential treatment centers. Although the cost of treatment for mental illness may be offset by the savings accrued from a healthier and more productive workforce, those with major mental health problems are less likely to be employed than the general population. Therefore, those with the greatest treatment needs are not usually those who are covered by employer insurance plans.[90]

INSURANCE PARITY.   Congress passed a new mental health and substance abuse parity law in 2008 that became effective on January 1, 2010. A major improvement is that this time it includes substance abuse treatment; however, it does not specifically define mental health and substance abuse treatment benefits. The 1996 parity act prohibited more restrictive annual or lifetime limits for mental health care compared to medical and surgical benefits, but plans often had different caps on the number of mental health sessions or days of hospitalization covered regardless of medical necessity and imposed higher out-of-pocket costs. The new law moves Americans further along the road to parity but requires parity only in plans that include mental health and substance abuse coverage.[91] Plans can exclude substance abuse and mental health treatment entirely, and parity is not mandatory for businesses with fewer than 50 employees, if those businesses even offer health insurance.

In the first year of the Obama administration, the major issues in mental healthcare provision were part of the struggle over national healthcare reform.[92] The legislation that emerged, the Patient Protection and Affordable Health Act of 2010, is intended to provide coverage for mental illness and substance use disorders to more Americans. Nevertheless, without further reform, it is likely that many people with mental disorders and alcohol and drug problems will remain underserved. To ensure that all Americans have access to the care they need, a universal health insurance program that includes parity for mental health and substance abuse services may be the most efficacious approach. Without it, the United States will need a more extensive array of publicly supported programs equitably distributed throughout the country to see that people with mental and substance use disorders get the treatment they deserve.

CHOICE IN SERVICES.   The National Association of Social Workers states "social workers should act to expand choice and opportunity for all people, with special regard for vulnerable, disadvantaged, oppressed, and exploited people and groups."[93] In keeping with this principle, health insurance, public or private, should cover a wide range of treatment options across the continuum of care for people seeking treatment for mental and substance use disorders and give people a choice in the treatment options they wish to pursue.

Substance abuse treatment professionals, for example, generally take the position that the selection of services should be based on consultation between the client and treatment providers and with regard to criteria like the American Society of Addiction Medicine's Patient Placement criteria.[94] The continuum of care for substance use disorders includes inpatient and outpatient detoxification, inpatient and outpatient treatment, residential programs (e.g., halfway houses), and other services. Whether people receive treatment for mental or substance use disorders through the public or private sector, their choice of treatment options is often limited, either by what is available in the public system or what insurance will pay for under various managed care arrangements.

Of course, the most basic services are those that meet survival needs (food, shelter, and healthcare). While the deinstitutionalization of people with severe mental illness and substance use disorders that began in 1960s was considered a humane policy, it has also been blamed for increases in homelessness because services to meet people's needs in the community have never been anywhere near adequate. People with severe mental and substance use disorders may not have the ability to cope with the complications and frustrations involved in applying for Social Security Disability Insurance, qualifying and requalifying at intervals for public assistance benefits like Supplemental Security Income and SNAP (food benefits), obtaining a place in a group home or other residential facility, or engaging in the social interactions necessary to reside in these environments. "Housing first" options, which provide living quarters to those who are not engaged in treatment, are intended to reduce the public cost of caring for those who strain healthcare, criminal justice, and other service systems. Opponents believe that providing such services does nothing to encourage people to pursue recovery and become abstinent.

Treatment and Civil Rights

Some persons seek treatment voluntarily, but many cannot locate services or are unable to recognize a need for treatment. State and local policies stipulate the conditions under which an individual may be compelled to accept mental health services. Involuntary admission to a psychiatric hospital is generally reserved for those who are deemed dangerous to themselves or others and decline treatment.

Involuntary commitment laws are controversial.[95] Some argue that involuntary hospitalization infringes on civil rights. Others argue that a lack of mandatory treatment condemns too many people to a life of homelessness, and less often to incidents such as the shooting deaths at Virginia Tech in which a formerly hospitalized student killed 32 people, wounded 17, then committed suicide.

People with severe mental and substance use disorders who are unable to recognize their need for treatment may be ordered to participate in outpatient treatment, or they may be hospitalized involuntarily. Involuntary hospitalization restricts an individual from moving about the community and participating in normal, daily activities. These restrictions on one's liberties mean that great care should be taken to prevent unnecessary confinement. Although the U.S. Constitution is necessarily concerned with protecting individual liberties, the states have primary responsibility for providing mental health services, and it is often courts at the state level that have intervened to offer civil rights protections.

Until the mid-1880s, involuntary commitment was mostly done through informal procedures rather than state statute; then, in 1845, "the Massachusetts Supreme Court established the precedent that individuals could be restrained only if dangerous to themselves or others and only if restraint would be conducive to their restoration."[96] In practice, patients had few means to contest their confinement. Some remained hospitalized for decades, even if their placement was no longer necessary or they had been placed inappropriately (such as those confined because they were mentally retarded, not mentally ill). In 1960, California's Lanterman-Petric-Short Act, and in 1972, Wisconsin's *Lessard v. Schmidt* decision, restricted the grounds for involuntary commitment and established stringent due process procedures. Soon after, in 1975, the U.S. Supreme Court ruled in Florida's *Donaldson* case, reinforcing the view that it is unjust to confine patients who are not dangerous in psychiatric institutions when they are not provided treatment and they can survive on their own. In 1980, Congress passed the Civil Rights of Institutionalized Persons Act to better protect people held in state and local institutions.

Thomas Szasz, in his well-known book *The Myth of Mental Illness,* called psychiatric illnesses "stigmatizing" labels, phrased to resemble medical diagnoses and applied to persons whose behavior annoys or offends others. Szasz took the position of the true libertarian in denouncing all involuntary treatment as "crimes against humanity." [97] Most people do not share this position; every community contains individuals whom other members of society feel are in need of protection. But it is sometimes difficult to know when involuntary treatment should be applied.

Mechanic's assessment is that except for previous dangerous behavior, the conditions that qualify as dangerous to self or others have not been clearly identified.[98] Psychiatry is hardly an exact science, and the "system" often fails even those who get treatment such as Andrea Yates, the Houston, Texas, mother who drowned her five children, and too many others illustrate.

Many people with mental illness and substance use disorders have been mistreated or harmed, and occasionally people with these illnesses mistreat or harm others due to delusions or other symptoms of their illness. The issue is to protect all those involved to the extent possible. The rights guaranteed to those receiving mental health services and the mechanisms for ensuring their rights are protected vary from state to state. Sometimes the problems victims and perpetrators with mental health problems face are due to difficulties communicating with law enforcement officers and court staff, and finding or continuing mental health treatment with competent providers.

The Public Mental Health System

The Mental Retardation Facilities and Community Mental Health Centers Construction Act of 1963, often called the Community Mental Health Act, was a watershed event in establishing community services. Community mental health centers (CMHCs) were required to provide five essential services: inpatient care, outpatient care, emergency services, partial hospitalization (daycare), and consultation and education. CMHCs were to be a "mental health safety net" and make mental health services available to community members, regardless of ability to pay.[99] CMHC funding was originally provided for construction only, and CMHCs were supposed to become self-sufficient.

Beginning in 1975 CMHCs were required to provide more essential services, including special programs for children and the elderly, aftercare and halfway house services for patients discharged from mental hospitals, and screening services to courts and related agencies to identify those in need of treatment. In 1977, NIMH began the Community Support Program, which established federal-state partnerships to encourage long-term care for those with serious mental illness.[100]

In the 1970s, a number of studies evaluated the success of community mental health centers.[101] The General Accounting Office and the Senate Committee on Labor and Public Welfare discussed the positive effects of CMHC programs, including an increase in the availability of community care. Other reports were less complimentary. A 1974 report by Ralph

Nader stated that CMHCs had not reduced the number of people admitted to state mental hospitals and accused psychiatrists of benefiting unfairly from the programs and of neglecting services to the poor.

To improve services, the Mental Health Systems Act of 1980 was intended to continue many provisions of the Community Mental Health Act. The act also included recommendations of the President's Commission on Mental Health, appointed by Jimmy Carter in 1977 and headed by First Lady Rosalyn Carter. There were provisions for people with serious mental illness, severely disturbed children and adolescents, and others who were unserved or underserved. The act was rescinded in 1981 shortly after President Ronald Reagan took office and attention was directed back to the states.[102]

Today, CMHCs are no longer required to provide the essential services formerly identified, and federal funds are channeled through block grants to state-run facilities and non-profit agencies. Each state must now develop a State Comprehensive Mental Health Services Plan. These three-year plans cover services to individuals with serious mental illness, individuals who are homeless and mentally ill, and children with severe disturbances. NIMH recommends one or more of the following services for them: residential services (e.g., short-term crisis stabilization units and longer-term supported housing options); client and family support (e.g., counseling, medication services, and emergency screening); psychosocial habilitation or rehabilitation (for developing vocational, social, and independent living skills); case management (coordination of multiple services needed by clients and outreach). Special initiatives such as the PATH and ACCESS programs are efforts to prevent or remedy homelessness among individuals with mental illness.[103]

Although the funding structure of CMHCs has evolved over the years, their main goals remain the same—provide mental health services to low-income and uninsured people, especially community-based services to people with serious mental illness. Achieving these goals has been increasingly challenging.[104] In the 1980s, when federal funding changed from categorical grants made directly to CMHCs to block grants to states, federal funding shrank. To keep their doors open and continue to serve the poor, CMHCs have had to balance serving clients unable to pay with serving "paying" clients. This has made it more difficult for those without Medicaid, Medicare, or private insurance to obtain care.

Increasing pressure to make clients with serious mental illness a service priority has also made it difficult for CMHCs to provide mental services to community members with less severe disorders. CMHCs remain committed to serving low-income community members, but they often have waiting lists and may turn people away. Events such as the September 11, 2001, terrorist attacks, the ensuing war on terrorism, and a series of natural disasters including Hurricane Katrina, placed increased demands on the mental health system. The public mental health system was asked to develop crisis response plans in the event of future terrorist attacks and natural disasters, but CMHCs are already overwhelmed with serving clients who are poor and those who have severe mental illnesses.[105]

In response to increasing mental health needs, President George W. Bush issued an executive order establishing the New Freedom Commission on Mental Health in April 2002 and charged it with conducting a "comprehensive study of the United States mental health service delivery system, including public and private sectors providers, and to advise the President on methods of improving the system." After a year of study and input from nearly 2,500 people, including consumers, mental health professionals, and national experts, the commission issued its final report in July 2003.[106] The commission concluded that the system is not oriented toward recovery and recommended a transformation of the public mental health system. The National Alliance for Mental Illness questioned whether there would be a "wholesale transformation" or whether the recommendations would "prove just to be another Washington report gathering dust on shelves."[107]

After five decades of publicly supported community mental health services, some people are served well enough by existing public, nonprofit, and private service providers, but the difference between the number who need services and those who get the services they need remains quite large. Advocates for increasing and improving mental health and substance abuse services will be looking to see how the nation's health care reform legislation affects this gap.

The War on Drug Addicts

The war on drugs began at the beginning of the twentieth century. The 1914 Harrison Narcotics Act essentially criminalized opiate and cocaine addiction, prescribing these drugs for addicts, and distributing these drugs except for limited medical and scientific purposes. Alcohol prohibition followed in 1919 under the Volstead Act and the Eighteenth Amendment to the U.S. Constitution, which was ratified in 1920 and repealed in 1933. With these laws, the United States established a new underclass composed of people with alcohol and drug problems. The Controlled Substances Act of 1970, passed during the Nixon administration, provides penalties for illicit drug possession, manufacture, and distribution, and ushered in the contemporary drug war.[108]

The National Institutes of Health (NIH), part of the Department of Health and Human Services, include the National Institute on Alcohol Abuse and Alcoholism (NIAAA), founded in 1970, and the National Institute on Drug Abuse, founded in 1973. These institutes, which support research and training, were the beginning of federal efforts to address problems related to alcohol and drug abuse through scientific study. Countervailing forces were also brewing.

In the 1980s during the Reagan administration, funding for alcohol, drug abuse, and mental health services was combined under a single block grant to states. President Reagan supported a "war on drugs" or law enforcement approach to curtailing drug use and First Lady Nancy Reagan introduced her "Just Say No to Drugs" campaign. Public awareness of AIDS added to concern about drug abuse. President Reagan's Commission on the Human Immunodeficiency Virus Epidemic called for "treatment on demand" for drug abusers to help prevent the spread of HIV.

In 1986 and 1988 Congress passed omnibus drug abuse legislation to wage the drug war. The 1988 Anti-Drug Abuse Act established the Office of National Drug Control Policy (ONDCP), headed by a cabinet-level "drug czar" in the Executive Office of the President. ONDCP's emphasis was on interdiction (stopping the flow of drugs into the United States) and on stiffer legal penalties for drug-related crimes (including the possibility of the death penalty when a murder is involved).

These provisions are said to strike at the *supply side* of the drug problem. Prevention, education, and treatment efforts were also included in the act in an attempt to influence the *demand side* of the drug problem. There are numerous other provisions in the 1988 act, including those for drug-free workplaces and eviction of public housing residents who engage in or permit drug use on or near the premises. After the Reagan years, the "war on drugs" theme continued, but even the most casual observer will probably agree that the law enforcement approach has not substantially stemmed drug trafficking. No matter how many tons of drugs are seized, the enticement provided by the lucrative drug trade causes more to be produced. Many people in the United States and elsewhere are lured into this underground economy.

The United States leads the world in incarceration rates. In 2008, 7.3 million people in the United States were in jail, in prison, on probation or parole. Thirty percent (about 2.2 million) were incarcerated in prisons or jails. Those imprisoned are disproportionately black and Hispanic. In 2007, over half (53 percent) of federal inmates were serving sentences for drug-related offenses.[109] Due to the difference between federal sentencing guidelines for convictions related to powder cocaine and those related to crack cocaine (which is cheaper), a disproportionate number of those serving long sentences for crack cocaine use are black, causing many individuals to call the policy racist. Advocacy efforts have resulted in reducing, but have not yet eliminated, the substantial differences in sentencing guidelines for the two forms of the same drug.

The FY 2010 federal budget included over $80 million for the Bureau of Prisons drug treatment programs, since approximately 40 percent of current inmates have a diagnosis of a drug use disorder.[110] State jails and prisons are also overwhelmed with an influx of people incarcerated for relatively low-level drug crimes. Prisons are responding with more drug treatment. Some prisons are devoted entirely to rehabilitating drug offenders. Privately operated corrections companies have benefitted from the boom in incarceration. Nevertheless, many individuals with drug problems do not receive services while incarcerated.[111]

During the Reagan administration, 82 percent of the federal budget for drug control went to law enforcement efforts and 18 percent to treatment, education, and prevention. George H. W. Bush's administration budgeted 30 percent for treatment, education, and prevention. Today about two-thirds of the national drug control budget is directed to law enforcement and interdiction, and one-third to prevention, treatment, and education.[112] In May 2009, the Obama administration's new head of the White House Office of National Drug Control Policy Gil Kerlikowske said that the administration was discarding the "war on drugs" terminology for an emphasis on treatment.[113]

To help more nonviolent drug offenders get treatment, the Violent Crime Control and Law Enforcement Act of 1994 supports the use of diversion programs, including drug courts, and Title I of the Omnibus Crime Control and Safe Streets Act of 1994 provided funds to states, tribes, and local courts to create drug court programs. These 1994 acts recognized that incarceration has little impact on substance abuse.[114] By July 2009, nearly 2,038 drug courts were operating across the 50 states, with another 226 projected to open in the near future.[115]

Among the key components of the drug court model are the following:

- Creating a non-adversarial relationship between the defendant and the court.
- Identifying defendants in need of treatment and referring them to treatment.
- Providing access to a continuum of treatment and rehabilitation services.
- Monitoring abstinence through frequent, mandatory drug testing.
- Maintaining judicial interaction with each drug court participant.
- Continuing interdisciplinary education to promote effective drug court operations.
- Enhancing local support and drug court effectiveness through partnerships among drug courts, public agencies, and community-based organizations.[116]

According to Steven Belenko of the National Center on Addiction and Substance Abuse, "drug courts have been quite successful in bridging the gap between the court and the treatment/public health systems and spurring greater cooperation among the various agencies and personnel within the criminal justice system, as well as between the criminal justice system and the community."[117] In 2000, California voters approved Proposition 36, which diverts all first- and second-time nonviolent drug possession offenders to treatment rather than incarceration.[118]

Success of the drug court model has prompted the creation of similar courts for individuals arrested for driving under the influence (DUI) and domestic violence and individuals with mental illness arrested for relatively minor infractions. These courts are also creating new pathways between treatment centers and the criminal justice system.[119] While these models are useful, the criminal justice system has become the *de facto* mental health and substance abuse treatment system for too many individuals.

While some progress was being made in offering social services through models like drug courts, those with alcohol or drug problems were being denied other social welfare services. As part of welfare reform legislation in 1996, those with alcohol or drug disabilities are no longer entitled to any benefits from the Social Security Disability Insurance (see Chapter 5) or Supplemental Security Income (see Chapter 6) programs unless they have a disabling condition in addition to alcoholism or drug addiction. Those who lost these benefits were also cut from the Medicare and Medicaid programs, making it more difficult to get treatment for alcohol or drug problems. Those forced off SSI were less likely to receive mental health and medical care, had higher rates of substance abuse, and were more likely to commit drug-related crimes compared to those who retained their SSI benefits because they had a disability in addition to alcohol or drug abuse.[120] Participation in substance abuse treatment also declined substantially among former SSI recipients with alcohol and drug disabilities.[121]

Those with felony drug convictions can be banned forever from participating in the Temporary Assistance for Needy Families program and Supplemental Nutrition Assistance Program (food stamps). Public housing residents can be evicted if someone they know uses drugs on or near the premises, even if the resident did not know that person was using or could not control his or her use.

The Higher Education Act (HEA) also singles out students who have committed drug crimes. Students with adult drug convictions were denied federal financial aid for varying lengths of times, including forever, depending on the type and number of convictions. Students can still be denied aid, but the law was changed in 2006 to apply only to convictions (any possession or sale charges) during periods when federal financial aid was being received. Completing an approved rehabilitation program may reduce the length of ineligibility.[122]

The U.S. public is ambivalent about the drug war. A May 2009 Rasmussen poll found that 54 percent of U.S. voters think illegal drug use is more of a criminal justice than a public health issue, while 37 percent saw it as "mostly a public health issue."[123] The public is more evenly divided on the issue of marijuana legalization: "41% . . . think the United States should legalize and tax marijuana to help solve the nation's fiscal problems," while 49 percent oppose this approach.[124] Individuals on many fronts have proposed or supported drug legalization in some form or another for some time, including legal philosophers,[125] law enforcement officers,[126] economists,[127] conservatives,[128] and libertarians.[129] One approach would be to employ a model similar to that used for regulating alcohol sales. Except for some movement to permit the use of marijuana for medical purposes, legalization of what are now illicit drugs is not in the offing in the United States.

Even many forms of harm reduction remain controversial or have been rejected.[130] Methadone maintenance therapy has helped many opiate addicts lead productive lives, but it is controversial because rather than a "drug-free" approach, it leaves users dependent on the drug methadone. Needle exchange programs have largely been rejected in the United States. In 1998, the British medical journal *The Lancet,* along with other groups, implored the Clinton administration to lift the ban on the use of federal funds to pay for needle exchange programs for intravenous drug users.[131] In July 2009, the U.S. House of Representatives finally voted to remove the ban, but it remains in place despite evidence that needle exchange programs stop the spread of HIV and do not encourage illicit drug use. Needle exchange programs do operate in some

U.S. cities, often underground without official sanction. America's ambivalence about how to address drug problems is reflected in the lack of a political groundswell for even clearly effective harm reduction practices. Hope for a more humane response to people with drug problems may more realistically be placed in an expanded social services approach. Illustration 10.6 provides a bill of rights intended to improve the public policy response to people who have alcohol and drug disorders.

ILLUSTRATION 10.6
Recovery Bill of Rights

Faces & Voices of Recovery is an organization founded to give people most affected by alcohol and drug problems a voice in public policy. The organization has developed the following Recovery Bill of Rights.

We will improve the lives of millions of Americans, their families and communities if we treat addiction to alcohol and other drugs as a public health crisis. To overcome this crisis, we must accord dignity to people with addiction and recognize that there is no one path to recovery. Individuals who are striving to be responsible citizens can recover on their own or with the help of others. Effective aid can be rendered by mutual support groups or healthcare professionals. Recovery can begin in a doctor's office, treatment center, church, prison, peer support meeting, or in one's own home. The journey can be guided by religious faith, spiritual experience, or secular teachings. Recovery happens every day across our country and there are effective solutions for people still struggling. Whatever the pathway, the journey will be far easier to travel if people seeking recovery are afforded respect for their basic rights:

1. **We have the right to be viewed as capable of changing, growing** and becoming positively connected to our community, no matter what we did in the past because of our addiction.

2. **We have the right—as do our families and friends—to know about the many pathways to recovery, the nature of addiction** and the barriers to long-term recovery, all conveyed in ways that we can understand.

3. **We have the right, whether seeking recovery in the community, a physician's office, treatment center, or while incarcerated, to set our own recovery goals,** working with a personalized recovery plan that we have designed based on accurate and understandable information about our health status, including a comprehensive, holistic assessment.

4. **We have the right to select services that build on our strengths,** armed with full information about the experience and credentials of the people providing services and the effectiveness of the services and programs from which we are seeking help.

5. **We have the right to be served by organizations or healthcare and social service providers that view recovery positively,** meet the highest public health and safety standards, provide rapid access to services, treat us respectfully, understand that our motivation is related to successfully accessing our strengths, and will work with us and our families to find a pathway to recovery.

6. **We have the right to be considered as more than a statistic,** stereotype, risk score, diagnosis, label, or pathology unit —free from the social stigma that characterizes us as weak or morally flawed. If we relapse and begin treatment again, we should be treated with dignity and respect that welcomes our continued efforts to achieve long-term recovery.

7. **We have the right to a healthcare and social services system that recognizes**

the strengths and needs of people with addiction and coordinates its efforts to provide recovery-based care that honors and respects our cultural beliefs.

8. **We have the right to be represented by informed policymakers** who remove barriers to educational, housing, and employment opportunities once we are no longer misusing alcohol or other drugs and are on the road to recovery.

9. **We have the right to respectful, nondiscriminatory care from doctors** and other healthcare providers and to receive services on the same basis as people do for any other chronic illness, with the same provisions, copayments, lifetime benefits and catastrophic coverage

in insurance, self-funded/self-insured health plans, Medicare, and HMO plans. The criteria of "proper" care should be exclusively between our healthcare providers and ourselves; it should reflect the severity, complexity, and duration of our illness and provide a reasonable opportunity for recovery maintenance.

10. **We have the right to treatment and recovery support in the criminal justice system** and to regain our place and rights in society once we have served our sentence.

11. **We have the right to speak out publicly about our recovery** to let others know that long-term recovery from addiction is a reality.

Source: Faces & Voices of Recovery, "The Recovery Bill of Rights," retrieved February 9, 2010, from http://www.facesandvoicesofrecovery.org/pdf/Advocacy_Toolkit/RBOR_legal.pdf

Summary

Social services include many types of programs, including child welfare programs, services to older Americans, mental healthcare, and treatment for alcohol and drug abuse. People from all walks of life may benefit from social services. Public agencies, private not-for-profit and profit-making organizations, religious organizations, and mutual-help groups all provide social services. The Title XX Social Services Block Grant is a major vehicle for funding social services.

The United States has no comprehensive social policy for families and children, largely because of the belief that families should be relatively free from governmental intervention. However, state laws govern various aspects of family relations, such as intervention in cases of child abuse and neglect. The 1980 Adoption Assistance and Child Welfare Act, along with amendments to the act in 1997, are currently considered the most important child welfare legislation. This legislation focuses on keeping families together whenever possible and finding other permanent homes when children cannot be returned to

their original families, but many children, especially African American children, languish in foster care until they reach adulthood.

The most important legislation that recognizes the social service needs of the elderly is the Older Americans Act of 1965. The act emphasizes nutrition programs and services that increase the ability of the elderly to remain in the community. The Administration on Aging is the federal agency that administers this act by determining the needs of older Americans and by encouraging states and communities to provide services that address these needs.

The Community Mental Health Act of 1963 was the landmark legislation that encouraged the development of community mental health centers across the country. States are a major funding source of community mental health and substance abuse treatment services. The federal government also contributes, largely through the Community Mental Health Services Block Grant and the Substance Abuse Prevention and Treatment Block Grant. Many people with mental and substance use disorders do not get treatment. Among the many issues in mental health treatment are homelessness and the appropriate use of involuntary treatment in cases of severe mental illness. The "war on drugs," which has led to the incarceration of many people with drug problems, is another highly controversial issues in addressing substance use disorders.

Discussion Questions and Class Activities

1. Investigate federal block grant funding to your state, such as the Title XX Social Services Block Grant, for various social welfare programs. What percentage of the block grant funding is allocated to your state and community for social services? What services are most often provided with the funding? How does your state contribute to these programs?

2. Investigate funding from the Child and Family Services Improvement Act of 2006 to your state. How much funding is allocated for caseworker visits? How much is allocated for addressing parental drug abuse problems, and what measures to address these particular problems are funded? What are your reactions about the adequacy of the level of funding and services available?

3. Invite child protective services workers and foster care and adoption workers to class to talk about services and the challenges they face in their work. Ask them about the methods used to investigate cases, the priority given to cases, the time from report to investigation, rates of substantiation, and the disposition of cases. You may also wish to invite staff and volunteers of organizations such as Court Appointed Special Advocates to discuss their work, experiences, and perspectives on the child welfare system, or invite a family court judge to discuss her or his role in child welfare cases and perspectives on the child welfare system.

4. On page 380 of this chapter, proposed legislation entitled "Education Begins at Home Act" and "Early Support for Families Act" is mentioned. Learn more about the content of these bills, determine what has happened to them, and search for similar bills introduced to Congress or your state legislature and determined how they have fared. Have a class discussion on whether you think such pieces of legislation should be passed and whether they have a chance of passage, and why. You may also wish to follow up to see what the current status of the U.N. Convention on the Rights of the Child is. You may wish to write a letter or send an e-mail to your elected representatives expressing your opinion on any of these proposed policies.

5. Investigate the local Area Agency on Aging's service delivery contracts. How does the agency deliver information and referral services? How are nutrition programs such as meals on wheels and congregate meal sites, senior centers, transportation, homemaker and chore services, legal counseling, escort services, home repair and renovation, home health aides, shopping assistance, visitation, and telephone assurance provided? Invite a staff member from a component of the "aging services network" (see Figure 10.3) to discuss the range of services to older adults and the policy and service delivery challenges faced in adequately serving the older adult population.

6. Investigate costs and payment sources in for profit, not-for-profit, luxury, and basic nursing homes in your community. What factors contribute to higher costs per month? What factors contribute to the amount of private pay, insurance-covered, and Medicaid-reimbursed care in these homes? If you have not had many opportunities to visit nursing homes, select a nursing home in a low-income community and arrange to spend some visiting with residents, or your class may wish to sponsor an activity such as a holiday party at a local nursing home. What are your observations about nursing home care, especially those that may be addressed by public policy?

7. Investigate services available in your community to persons with mental and substance use disorders. Are the service agencies and providers predominately tax supported and state or locally administered, such as a state mental hospital, not-for-profit organizations that accept payment from as many sources as possible, or private providers who serve those who are insured or able to pay costs? Determine if there is a waiting list for the various services available and how long the wait is likely to be. What do reports in the media or other local information sources indicate about public acceptance of treatment providers and treatment recipients? Invite state and local officials to class to discuss policy and service challenges in assisting people with mental and substance use disorders.

8. Invite a panel of people recovering from mental and substance use disorders and/or family members of individuals who have mental and substance use disorders to

discuss their experiences with policies and services. From the consumers' and family members' points-of-view, what are their recommendations for improving policies and services in order to help more people get treatment and recover? How closely do their suggestions match the recovery bill of rights in Illustration 10.6 of this chapter?

8. If there is a local mental health or drug court in your area, call the administrator to see if you or your class may visit the court to observe how it is conducted. Prior to attending, read more about these courts and

their rates of success in helping people get treatment, pursue recovery, and avoid further legal involvement. How did the operation of the court compare with your expectations?

9. Discuss the similarities and differences you find in the lists of rights and desirable services suggested for children, older persons, and individuals with mental or substance use disorders. What do these similarities and differences suggest for the way policies and services should be developed, administered, and evaluated?

Websites

The Administration on Aging, http://www.aoa.gov, part of the U.S. Department of Health and Human Services, works to develop comprehensive, coordinated, and cost-effective systems of home and community-based services to help older adults maintain their health and independence in their homes and communities.

The Children's Bureau, http://www.acf.hhs.gov/programs/cb/index.htm, part of the U.S. Department of Health and Human Services, Administration on Children and Youth, works with state and local agencies to develop programs that focus on preventing the abuse of children in troubled families, protecting children from abuse, and finding permanent

placements for those who cannot safely return to their homes.

The Child Welfare League of America, http://www.cwla.org, is a long-standing coalition of private and public agencies working to improve the lives of vulnerable children and families through policies, programs, and practices.

The Substance Abuse and Mental Health Services Administration, http://www.samhsa.gov/index.aspx, part of the U.S. Department of Health and Human Services, works to reduce the impact of mental illness and substance abuse through the delivery and financing of prevention, treatment, and recovery support services.

Notes

1. This overview of services relies on a classic policy text, Alfred J. Kahn, *Social Policy and Social Services* (New York: Random House, 1979), pp. 12–13.

2. James R. Farris, "The 20th Anniversary of OBRA '87: Nursing Home Quality, Staffing and Enforcement Issues." Testimony before the Senate Special Committee on Aging, May 2, 2007. Retrieved December 17, 2009, from http://www.cms.hhs.gov/apps/media/press/testimony.asp?Counter=2177&intNumPerPage=10&checkDate=&checkKey=&srchType=1&numDays=3500&srchOpt=0&srchData=&ke

ywordType=All&chkNewsType=7&intPage=&showAll=365&pYear=&year=0&desc=false&cboOrder=date

3. For information on funding opportunities for faith-based and community organizations, see U.S. Department of Health and Human Services, "Faith-Based and Neighborhood Partnerships" at http://www.hhs.gov/fbci/funding/ for information on federal funding policy.

4. See Robert Morris, *Social Policy of the American Welfare State: An Introduction to Policy Analysis* (New York: Harper & Row, 1979), p. 120.

5. U.S. Department of Health, Education and Welfare, *First Annual Report to Congress on Title XX of the Social Security Act* (Washington, DC: Department of Health, Education, and Welfare, 1977), p. 1; Martha Derthick, *Uncontrollable Spending for Social Services Grants* (Washington, DC: The Brookings Institution, 1975).

6. Committee on Ways and Means, "Section 10–Title XX Social Services Block Grant Program," *2008 Green Book* (Washington, DC: U.S. House of Representatives), p. 10–2. Retrieved May 30, 2010, from http://waysandmeans.house.gov/singlepages .aspx?NewsID=10490

7. *Ibid.,* p. 10–8.

8. This historical account relies on Stephen J. Pfohl, "The Discovery of Child Abuse," *Social Problems,* Vol. 24, No. 3, 1977, pp. 310–323; Diana M. DiNitto and C. Aaron McNeece, *Social Work: Issues and Opportunities in a Challenging Profession* (Englewood Cliffs, NJ: Prentice Hall, 1990), Chapter 9; Sallie A. Watkins, "The Mary Ellen Myth: Correcting Child Welfare History," *Social Work,* Vol. 35, No. 6, 1990, pp. 500–503.

9. Watkins, "The Mary Ellen Myth: Correcting Child Welfare History."

10. Robert H. Bremner, Ed., *Children and Youth in America: A Documentary,* Vol. 2 (Cambridge, MA: Harvard University Press, 1974), pp. 247–248.

11. The remainder of this section relies on Pfohl, "The Discovery of Child Abuse."

12. Dr. Henry Kempe et al., "The Battered-Child Syndrome," *Journal of the American Medical Association,* Vol. 181, July 7, 1962, pp. 105–112.

13. Unless otherwise noted, figures in this section are from Administration for Children and Families, Administration on Children, Youth and Families, Children's Bureau, *Child Maltreatment 2008* (Washington, DC: U.S. Department of Health and Human Services, 2010). Retrieved May 30, 2010, from http://www.acf.hhs.gov/programs/cb/pubs/ cm08/

14. Kasia O'Neill Murray and Sara Gesiriech, *A Brief Legislative History of the Child Welfare System* (Washington, DC: Pew Commission on Children in Foster Care, June 25, 2008). Retrieved June 11, 2009, from http://www.pewfostercare.org/research/docs/ Legislative.pdf

15. P.L. 109–288 Child and Family Services Improvement Act of 2006. Retrieved February 2, 2010, from http:// www.acf.hhs.gov/programs/fysb/content/docs/06_ improvementact.pdf; Administration for Children and Families, "Promoting Safe and Stable Families,"

Justification of Estimates for Appropriations Committees (Washington, DC: U.S. Department of Health and Human Services). Retrieved May 30, 2010, from http://www.acf.hhs.gov/programs/olab/budget/ 2008/cj2008/sec3i_pssf_2008cj.pdf

16. See Child Welfare League of America, *2008 Children's Legislative Agenda* (Washington, DC: Author). Retrieved July 30, 2008, from http://www.cwla.org/ advocacy/2008legagenda.pdf

17. Committee on Ways and Means, Section 11: "Child Welfare," *2008 Green Book* (Washington, DC: U.S. House of Representatives), Table 11-44. Retrieved May 30, 2010, from http://waysandmeans.house.gov/ singlepages.aspx?NewsID=10490

18. Child Welfare League of America, *2008 Children's Legislative Agenda* (Washington, DC: Author). Retrieved July 30, 2008, from http://www.cwla.org/ advocacy/2008legagenda.pdf

19. Diane DePanfilis, Clara Daining, Kevin D. Frick, Julie Farber, and Lisa Levinthal, *HITTING THE M.A.R.C.: Establishing Foster Care Minimum Adequate Rates for Children, Technical Report* (Tacoma, WA: Children's Rights, National Foster Parent Association, and University of Maryland School of Social Work, October 2007). Retrieved February 2, 2010, from http://www.nfpainc.org/ uploads/MARCTechReport.pdf

20. Child Welfare League of America, *National Fact Sheet 2010,* Special tabulation of the Adoption and Foster Care Analysis Reporting System (AFCARS) by National Data Archive for Child Abuse and Neglect (NDACAN) and CWLA (Arlington, VA: Author, 2007). Retrieved May 30, 2010, from http:// www.cwla.org/advocacy/statefactsheets/2010/ nationalfactsheet10.pdf

21. *Special Tabulation from the National Data Analysis System housed at the Child Welfare League of America.* Retrieved June 11, 2009, from http://ndas.cwla.org

22. Child Welfare League of America, *National Fact Sheet 2010,* Special tabulation of the Adoption and Foster Care Analysis Reporting System (AFCARS) by National Data Archive for Child Abuse and Neglect (NDACAN) and CWLA.

23. See Child Welfare League of America, *Youth After Foster Care* (Washington, DC: Author). Retrieved February 2, 2010, from http://www.cwla.org/pro- grams/fostercare/factsheetafter.htm

24. Kasia O'Neill Murray and Sara Gesiriech, *A Brief Legislative History of the Child Welfare System.*

25. See Arnold Silverman, "Outcomes of Transracial Adoption," in The Center for the Future of Children, Ed., *The Future of Children* (Los Altos, CA: David

and Lucille Packard Foundation, 1993), pp. 104–118; Ruth G. McRoy, "An Organizational Dilemma: The Case of Transracial Adoptions," *Journal of Applied Behavioral Science,* Vol. 25, No. 2, 1989, pp. 145–160.

26. National Association of Black Social Workers, "Kinship Care Position Paper," adopted by the NABSW National Steering Committee, January 10, 2003. Retrieved January 30, 2010, from http://www.nabsw.org/mserver/KimshipCare.aspx

27. Kasia O'Neill Murray and Sara Gesiriech, *A Brief Legislative History of the Child Welfare System.*

28. Susan L. Smith, Ruth McRoy, Madelyn Freundlich, and Joe Kroll, "Finding Families for African American Children: The Role of Race & Law in Adoption from Foster Care" (New York: Evan B. Donaldson Adoption Institute, May 2008). Retrieved August 15, 2008, from http://www.adoptioninstitute.org/publications/MEPApaper20080527.pdf

29. Unless otherwise noted, figures in this section are from Children's Bureau, *Child Maltreatment 2008* (Washington, DC: U.S. Department of Health and Human Services, 2008).

30. See Bruce Bellingham and Joseph Byers, "Foster Care and Child Protection Services," in Allen W. Imershein, Mary K. Pugh Mathis, C. Aaron McNeece, and Associates, *Who Cares for the Children: A Case Study of Policies and Practices* (Dix Hills, NY: General Hall, 1995), pp. 101–121.

31. See Kristine Nelson, Betty J. Blythe, Barbara Walters, Peter J. Pecora, and Don Schweitzer, *A Ten Year Review of Family Preservation Research: Building the Evidence Base* (Seattle, WA: Casey Family Programs, January 4, 2009), quote from p. 2. Retrieved June 11, 2009, from http://www.casey.org/NR/rdonlyres/18F7CBE5-CD62-41D1-A27A-3CEA123FF5B7/809/FamilyPreservationpaperFINAL2009.pdf

32. John V. O'Neill, "GAO Affirms Need for High-Quality Staff," *NASW News,* June 2003, p. 7.

33. Child Welfare League of America, *Research to Practice Initiative, Child Welfare Workforce,* Research Roundup (Washington, DC: Author, September 2002). Retrieved August 20, 2008, from http://www.cwla.org/programs/r2p/rrnews0209.pdf

34. See Rudolph Alexander, Jr., "The Legal Liability of Social Workers after DeShaney," *Social Work,* Vol. 38, No. 1, 1993, pp. 64–68.

35. David S. Savage (*Los Angeles Times* Service), "Court Gives Social Workers Immunity from Lawsuits," *Austin American-Statesman,* April 26, 1994, p. C20.

36. Cynthia Andrews Scarcella, Roseana Bess, Erica H. Zielewski, and Rob Geen, *The Cost of Protecting Vulnerable Children: Understanding State Variation in Child Welfare Financing* (Washington, DC: Urban Institute, May 24, 2006). Retrieved May 30, 2010, from http://www.urban.org/publications/311314.html

37. Rose Marie Penzerro, "Drift as Adaptation: Foster Care and Homeless Careers," *Youth and Family Care Forum,* Vol. 32, No. 4, August 2003, pp. 229–244.

38. See, for example, Committee on Ways and Means, Section 11: "Child Protection, Foster Care, and Adoption Assistance," *2004 Green Book* (Washington, DC: U.S. House of Representatives, 2004). Retrieved May 30, 2010, from http://www.gpoaccess.gov/wmprints/green/2004.html

39. Mark E. Courtney, Amy Dworsky, Gretchen Ruth, Tom Keller, Judy Havlicek, and Noel Bost, *Midwest Evaluation of the Adult Functioning of Former Foster Youth: Outcomes at Age 19* (Chicago, IL: Chapin Hall Center for Children at the University of Chicago, May 2005). Retrieved May 30, 2010, from http://www.chapinhall.org/sites/default/files/ChapinHallDocument_4.pdf

40. Peter J. Pecora, Ronald C. Kessler, Jason Williams, Kirk O'Brien, A. Chris Downs, Diana English, et al., *Improving Family Foster Care: Findings from the Northwest Foster Care Alumni Study* (Seattle, WA: Casey Family Programs, 2005).

41. See UNICEF Convention on the Rights of the Child at http://www.unicef.org/crc/

42. The website of the U.S. Campaign for Ratification of the U.N. Convention on the Rights of the Child (CRC) is http://childrightscampaign.org/crcindex.php

43. AARP Public Policy Institute, *Valuing the Invaluable: The Economic Value of Family Caregiving* (Washington, D.C.: Author, 2008). Retrieved December 16, 2009, from http://www.aarp.org/research/ppi/ltc/care/

44. See Kentucky Governor Paul Patton's March 21, 2002 testimony before the Senate Special Committee on Aging on Broken and Unsustainable: The Cost Crisis of Long-term Care for Baby Boomers; and Medicaid: The Nation's Unintended Financier of Long-Term Care. Retrieved December 21, 2009, from http://www.nga.org/portal/site/nga/menuitem.0f8c660ba7cf98d18a278110501010a0/?vgnextoid=36de9e2f1b091010VgnVCM1000001a01010aRCRD

45. For information on the Older Americans Act, see the website of the Administration on Aging, http://www.aoa.gov/AoARoot/AoA_Programs/OAA/Reauthorization/Index.aspx; *The Basics: Older Americans Act of 1965* (Washington, DC: National Health Policy Forum, October 8, 2009). Retrieved November 22, 2009, from http://www.adrc-tae.org/tiki-download_file.php?fileId=27290

46. For the Administration on Aging's unofficial compilation of the Older Americans Act of 1965 as amended in 2006 (Public Law 109-365) see http://www.aoa.gov/AoARoot/AoA_Programs/OAA/oaa_full.asp

47. Administration on Aging, *2008 Annual Performance Report* (Washington, DC: U.S. Department of Health and Human Services). Retrieved December 16, 2009, from http://www.aoa.gov/AoARoot/Program_Results/docs/2008/2008_AoA_Annual_PerformanceReport.pdf

48. See Administration on Aging, "Aging Network." Retrieved November 23, 2009, from http://www.aoa.gov/AoARoot/AoA_Programs/OAA/Aging_Network/Index.aspx

49. Administration on Aging, *2008 Annual Performance Report.*

50. "National Family Caregiver Support Program" (Washington, DC: Administration on Aging, November 18, 2009). Retrieved February 7, 2010, from http://www.aoa.gov/AoARoot/AoA_Programs/HCLTC/Caregiver/index.aspx

51. U.S. Department of Labor Wage and Hour Division, *Fact Sheet #28: The Family and Medical Leave Act of 1993* (Washington, DC: Author, revised January 2009). Retrieved December 16, 2009, from http://www.dol.gov/whd/regs/compliance/whdfs28.pdf

52. *Report of the 2005 White House Conference on Aging, The Booming Dynamics of Aging: From Awareness to Action*, Executive Summary (Washington, DC: U.S. Department of Health and Human Services, Administration on Aging). Retrieved February 7, 2010, from http://www.whcoa.gov

53. *Ibid.*, pp. 1–2.

54. See United States Senate Special Committee on Aging website at http://aging.senate.gov/about/index.cfm

55. AARP's website is http://www.aarp.org; the Gray Panthers' website is http://www.graypanthers.org

56. The Administration on Aging's National Center on Elder Abuse website (http://www.ncea.aoa.gov/ncea-root/Main_Site/index.aspx) provides a wealth of information on elder abuse.

57. *Abuse of Adults Aged 60+, 2004 Survey of Adult Protective Services* (Washington, DC: National Center on Elder Abuse, February 2006). Retrieved December 17, 2009, from http://www.ncea.aoa.gov/NCEAroot/Main_Site/pdf/2-14-06%2060FACT%20SHEET.pdf

58. George H. Zimny and George T. Grossberg, *Guardianship of the Elderly: Psychiatric and Judicial Aspects* (New York: Springer, 1998).

59. Judy McKee and Sean M. Douglass, "Protecting the Protected: Overseeing Adult Guardianship" (Washington, DC: National Association of Attorneys General), *NAA Gazette*, Vol. 3, No. 4, May 29, 2009. Retrieved December 17, 2009, from http://www.naag.org/protecting-the-protected-overseeing-adult-guardianship.php

60. Jane M. Pollack, written statement before the United States Senate Special Committee on Aging, February 11, 2003. Retrieved December 17, 2009, from http://aging.senate.gov/events/hr93jp.pdf

61. Government Accountability Office, *Guardianships: Collaboration Needed to Protect Incapacitated Elderly People* (GAO-04-655) (Washington, DC: Author, July 13, 2004). Retrieved December 17, 2009, from http://www.gao.gov/products/GAO-04-655.

62. For a timeline of the first 20 years of Nursing Home Reform see http://aging.senate.gov/events/hr172tl.pdf

63. *APA Poll: Most Americans Have Sought Mental Health Treatment but Cost, Insurance Still Barriers* (Washington, DC: American Psychological Association, May 13, 2004). Retrieved February 7, 2010, from http://www.apa.org/news/press/releases/2004/05/apa-poll.aspx

64. Much of this section relies on David Mechanic, *Mental Health and Social Policy* (Boston: Allyn and Bacon, 2007); also see Theodore Millon, *Masters of the Mind: Exploring the Story of Mental Illness from Ancient Times to the New Millennium* (Hoboken, NJ: Wiley, 2004).

65. Gerald N. Grob, *The State and the Mentally Ill: A History of Worcester State Hospital in Massachusetts, 1830–1920* (Chapel Hill: University of North Carolina Press, 1966), cited in Mechanic, p. 53; see also Gerald N. Grob, *The Mad Among Us: A History of the Care of Americas Mentally Ill* (Cambridge, MA: Harvard University Press, 1995).

66. See the *NIH Almanac*, "Important Events in NIMH History" (Bethesda, MD: National Institute of Mental Health, March 16, 2009). Retrieved December 26, 2009, from http://www.nih.gov/about/almanac/organization/NIMH.htm

67. See *Mental Health Medications* (Bethesda, MD: National Institute of Mental Health, September 17, 2009). Retrieved December 26, 2009, from http://www.nimh.nih.gov/health/publications/mental-health-medications/complete-index.shtml

68. Steven S. Sharfstein, "Whatever Happened to Community Mental Health?," *Psychiatric Services,*

Vol. 51, 2000, pp. 616–620. Retrieved February 7, 2010, from http://psychservices.psychiatryonline.org/cgi/content/full/51/5/616

69. See Catherine G. Greeno and Phyllis Solomon, "Mental Health," in Terry Mizrahi and Larry E. Davis, Eds., *Encyclopedia of Social Work*, 20th ed. (e-reference edition) (Oxford, UK: Oxford University Press; National Association of Social Workers, October 31, 2009). Retrieved December 26, 2009, from http://www.oxford-naswsocialwork.com/entry?entry=t203.e243

70. National Institute of Mental Health, *The Numbers Count: Mental Disorders in America* (Bethesda, MD: Author, May 28, 2010). Retrieved May 30, 2010, from http://www.nimh.nih.gov/health/publications/the-numbers-count-mental-disorders-in-america/index.shtml

71. See Juan E. Mezzich, "International Surveys on the Use of ICD-10 and Related Diagnostic Systems," *Psychopathology*, Vol 35, Nos. 2-3, 2002, pp. 72–75.

72. Ronald C. Kessler, Wai Tat Chiu, Olga Demler, and Ellen E. Walters, "Prevalence, Severity, and Comorbidity of Twelve-Month DSM-IV Disorders in the National Comorbidity Survey Replication (NCS-R)," *Archives of General Psychiatry*, Vol. 62, No. 6, 2005, pp. 617–627. Retrieved May 30, 2010, from http://archpsyc.ama-assn.org/cgi/content/full/62/6/617

73. For a critique of the *Diagostic and Statistical Manual of Mental Disorders,* see Stuart A. Kirk and Herb Kutchins, *The Selling of the DSM: The Rhetoric of Science in Psychiatry* (Hawthorne, NY: Aldine de Gruyter, 1992); Herb Kutchins and Stuart A. Kirk, *Driving Us Crazy: DSM, the Psychiatric Bible and the Creation of Mental Disorders* (New York: Free Press, 2003).

74. See National Institute of Mental Health, *Questions and Answers About the National Comorbidity Survey Replication* (NCSR) Study (Bethesda, MD: Author, March 31, 2009). Retrieved May 30, 2010, from http://www.nimh.nih.gov/health/topics/statistics/ncsr-study/questions-and-answers-about-the-national-comorbidity-survey-replication-ncsr-study.shtml#q7

75. Kessler et al., "Prevalence, Severity, and Comorbidity of Twelve-month DSM-IV Disorders in the National Comorbidity Survey Replication (NCS-R)."

76. Office of Applied Studies, *Results from the 2008 National Survey on Drug Use and Health: National Findings* (Washington, DC: Substance Abuse and Mental Health Services Administration, 2009). Retrieved October 1, 2009, from http://oas.samhsa.gov/nsduh/2k8nsduh/2k8Results.pdf

77. *Mental Health: A Report of the Surgeon General* (Washington, DC: Department of Health and Human Services 1999), Chapter 3, "Children and Mental Health." Retrieved February 7, 2010, from http://www.surgeongeneral.gov/library/mental-health/chapter3/sec1.html

78. Office of Applied Studies, *Results from the 2008 National Survey on Drug Use and Health: National Findings* (Washington, DC: Substance Abuse and Mental Health Services Administration, 2009). Retrieved October 1, 2009, from http://oas.samhsa.gov/nsduh/2k8nsduh/2k8Results.pdf.

79. *Ibid.*

80. Daniel J. Foley, Ronald W. Manderscheid, Joanne E. Atay, James Maedke, Jeffrey Sussman, and Sean Cribbs, "Table 19.7, Number and Percent Distribution of Full-Time Equivalent Staff in All Mental Health Organizations by Staff Discipline: United States, Selected Years, 1972–2000," in Ronald W. Manderscheid and Joyce T. Berry, Eds., *Mental Health, United States, 2004*, DHHS Pub No. (SMA) 06-4195 (Rockville, MD: Substance Abuse and Mental Health Services Administration, 2006). Retrieved May 30, 2010, from http://mentalhealth.samhsa.gov/publications/allpubs/SMA06-4195/chp19table7.asp

81. Catherine N. Dulmus, Albert R. Roberts, Marlys Staudt, and Lonnie R. Snowden, "Mental Illness," in Terry Mizrahi and Larry E. Davis, Eds., *Encyclopedia of Social Work*, 20th ed. (e-reference edition) (Oxford, UK: Oxford University Press, National Association of Social Workers). Retrieved October 31, 2009 from http://www.oxford-naswsocialwork.com/entry?entry=t203.e244

82. Tami L. Mark, Katherine R. Levit, Rosanna M. Coffey, David R. McKusick, Henrick J. Harwood, Edward C. King, Ellen Bouchery, James S. Genuardi, Rita Vandivort-Warren, Jeffrey A. Buck, and Katheryn Ryan, *National Expenditures for Mental Health Services and Substance Abuse Treatment, 1993–2003,* SAMHSA Publication No. SMA 07-4227 (Rockville, MD: Substance Abuse and Mental Health Services Administration, 2007). Rretrieved October 8, 2009, from http://www.samhsa.gov/spendingestimates/SAMHSAFINAL9303.pdf.

83. Thomas R. Insel, "Assessing the Economic Costs of Serious Mental Illness," *American Journal of Psychiatry*, Vol. 165, June 2008, pp. 663–665. Retrieved February 7, 2010, from http://ajp.psychiatryonline.org/cgi/content/full/165/6/663

84. Peter J. Delany, Joseph J. Shields, and Dana L. Roberts, "Program and Client Characteristics as Predictors of the Availability of Social Support Services in Community-based Substance Abuse Treatment Programs," *Journal of Behavioral Health Services & Research,* Vol. 36, No. 4, 2009, pp. 450–464; Mesfin S. Mulatu, "Ancillary and Transitional Assistance Services at Substance Abuse Treatment Facilities: Effects of Facility Characteristics and Implications to Policy," presented at the 135th American Public Health Association Annual Meeting & Exposition, Washington, DC, November 6, 2007. Retrieved June 24 2010, from http://apha.confex.com/apha/135am/techprogram/paper_163757.htm

85. See, for example, A. Thomas McLellan, David C. Lewis, Charles P. O'Brien, and Herbert D. Kleber, "Drug Dependence, A Chronic Medical Illness: Implications for Treatment, Insurance, and Outcomes Evaluation," *JAMA,* Vol. 284, 2000, pp. 1689–1695.

86. RAND Corporation, "How Does Managed Care Affect the Cost of Mental Health Services?", Research Highlights from RAND Health, Report RB-4515 (Santa Monica, CA: Author, 1998). Retrieved June 25, 2009, from http://www.rand.org/publications/RB/RB4515

87. Merrile Sing, Steven Hill, Suzanne Smolkin, and Nancy Heiser, *The Costs and Effects of Parity for Mental and Substance Abuse Insurance Benefits* (DHHS Publication No. MC99-80) (Rockville, MD: U.S. Department of Health and Human Services, March 1998). Retrieved February 7, 2010, from http://mentalhealth.samhsa.gov/publications/allpubs/Mc99-80/prtyfnix.asp

88. RAND Corporation, "The Relationship Between Volume and Quality in Mental Health Care," Research Highlights from RAND Health (Report RB- 9105) (Santa Monica, CA: Author, 2005). Retrieved June 25, 2009, from http://www.rand.org/pubs/research_briefs/RB9105/index1.html

89. For example, see MassLegalHelp. Retrieved December 26, 2009, from http://masslegalhelp.org/mental-health/mental-health-parity

90. Sing et al., *The Costs and Effects of Parity for Mental and Substance Abuse Insurance Benefits.*

91. *The New Mental Health Parity Act: What It Does and Doesn't Do* (Nashville: Bass, Perry, & Sims, January 7, 2009). Retrieved February 7, 2010, from http://www.bassberry.com/sitesearch.aspx?qu=mental%20health%20parity

92. For current information on legislative action on mental health issues, see the Legislative Action Center at the website of the National Alliance on Mental Illness at http://capwiz.com/nami/home/

93. National Association of Social Workers, *Code of Ethics of the National Association of Social Workers* (Washington, DC: Author, 2008). Retrieved October 16, 2009, from http://www.socialworkers.org/pubs/code/code.asp

94. David Mee-Lee, Gerald D. Shulman, Marc Fishman, David R. Gastfriend, and Julia Harris Griffith, *ASAM Patient Placement Criteria for the Treatment of Substance-related Disorders,* 2nd ed., rev. (Chevy Chase, MD: American Society of Addiction Medicine, 2001).

95. See the Treatment Advocacy Center's website at http://www.treatmentadvocacycenter.org for pro-commitment material. See the website of PsychRights at http://psychrights.org/index.htm for anti-commitment material. For an example of a grievance process for mental health service consumers, see the website of the state of Maine's office of Adult Mental Health Services at http://www.state.me.us/dhhs/mh/GrievanceMH/basic-rights.html. For information about mental health care and people involved in the criminal justice system see *Criminal Justice Primer for State Mental Health Agencies* (National Technical Assistance Center for State Mental Health Planning, September 2002). Retrieved February 7, 2010, from http://www.nasmhpd.org/general_files/publications/ntac_pubs/reports/Primer.pdf

96. This paragraph relies on Mechanic, *Mental Health and Social Policy,* pp. 215–217; quote is from p. 215.

97. Thomas S. Szasz, *The Myth of Mental Illness: Foundations of Theory of Personal Conduct,* rev. ed. (New York: Harper & Row, 1974), pp. 267–268.

98. Mechanic, *Mental Health and Social Policy,* pp. 228–230.

99. Walter E. Barton, "Trends in Community Mental Health Programs," *Journal of the American Psychiatric Association,* Vol. 17, No. 9, 1966, pp. 253–258.

100. David Hartley, Donna C. Bird, David Lambert, and John Coffin, *The Role of Community Mental Health Centers as Rural Safety Net Providers,* Working Paper #30 (Portland, ME: Maine Rural Health Research Center, Edmund S. Muskie School of Public Service, November 2002). Retrieved February 7, 2010, from http://muskie.usm.maine.edu/publications/rural/wp30.pdf

101. See Lucy D. Ozarin, "Community Mental Health: Does It Work? Review of the Evaluation Literature," in

Walter E. Barton and Charlotte J. Sanborn, Eds., *An Assessment of the Community Mental Health Movement* (Lexington, MA: Health, 1977), pp. 122–123.

102. Gerald N. Grob, "Mental Health Policy in 20th-Century America," in Ronald W. Manderscheid and Marilyn J. Henderson, Eds., *Mental Health, United States, 2000*, Chapter 2 (DHHS Publication No. SMA 3938) (Rockville, MD: Center for Mental Health Services, Substance Abuse and Mental Health Services Administration, 2002). Retrieved February 7, 2010, http://mentalhealth.samhsa.gov/publications/allpubs/SMA01-3537/chapter20.asp

103. "How State Mental Health Agencies Use the Community Mental Health Services Block Grant to Improve Care and Transform Systems: 2007" (Rockville, MD: Substance Abuse and Mental Health Services Administration, December 3, 2007). Retrieved January 1, 2010, from http://download.ncadi.samhsa.gov/ken/pdf/MHBGReportSection508-5-6-08.pdf

104. For information on financing for mental health care, see the website of the Office of Survey, Analysis and Financing, National Mental Health Information Center, Substance Abuse and Mental Health Services Administration at http://mentalhealth.samhsa.gov/cmhs/ManagedCare/about.asp

105. For information on mental health and terrorism and natural disasters see "Disasters & Terrorism" (Washington, DC: American Psychological Association, 2010). Retrieved February 8, 2010, from http://www.apa.org/helpcenter/disaster/index.aspx

106. New Freedom Commission on Mental Health, *Achieving the Promise: Transforming Mental Health Care in America. Final Report* (DHHS Pub. No. SMA-03-3832) (Rockville, MD: U.S. Department of Health and Human Services, July 2003). Retrieved February 8, 2010, from http://www.mentalhealthcommission.gov/reports/FinalReport/downloads/downloads.html

107. "President's New Freedom Commission on Mental Health" (Arlington, VA: National Alliance on Mental Illness). Retrieved February 8, 2010, from http://www.nami.org/Content/NavigationMenu/Inform_Yourself/About_Public_Policy/New_Freedom_Commission/Default1169.htm

108. Diana M. DiNitto, "Ending America's Ambivalence in the War on Drugs," Robert J. O'Leary Memorial Lecture, School of Social Work, The Ohio State University, October 26, 2009. Retrieved June 25, 2010, from http://csw.osu.edu/research/oleary/

109. William J. Sabol and Heather West, *Prisoners in 2007* (Washington, DC: U.S. Department of Justice, December 11, 2008) (NCJ224280), Appendix Table 12, p. 22. Retrieved June 25, 2010, from http://bjs.ojp.usdoj.gov/content/pub/pdf/p07.pdf

110. Drug Enforcement Administration, *National Drug Control Strategy FY 2010 Budget Summary* (Washington, DC: U.S. Department of Justice). Retrieved December 20, 2009, from http://www.whitehousedrugpolicy.gov/publications/policy/10budget/justice.pdf

111. Lori Whitten, "Research Addresses Needs of Criminal Justice Staff and Offenders," *NIDA Notes, 22*(3), 2009, pp. 4–5. Retrieved May 30, 2010, from http://www.nida.nih.gov/NIDA_notes/NNvol22N3/nidaatwork.html

112. Drug Enforcement Administration, *National Drug Control Strategy FY 2010 Budget Summary.*

113. Gary Fields, "White House Czar Calls for End to 'War on Drugs,'" *Wall Street Journal*, May 14, 2009. Retrieved December 18, 2009, from http://online.wsj.com/article/SB124225891527617397.html

114. National Institute of Justice, *Drug Courts: The Second Decade*, NCJ 211081 (Washington, DC: US Department of Justice, June 2006). Retrieved December 20, 2009, from http://www.ncjrs.gov/pdffiles1/nij/211081.pdf

115. "Drug Courts–Facts and Figures" (Washington, DC: U.S. Department of Justice, December 4, 2009). Retrieved December 20, 2009, from http://www.ncjrs.gov/spotlight/drug_courts/facts.html

116. The National Association of Drug Court Professionals, *Defining Drug Courts: The Key Components* (Washington, DC: Office of Justice Programs, January 1997). Retrieved December 27, 2009, from http://www.ndci.org/sites/default/files/ndci/KeyComponents.pdf; National Criminal Justice Reference Service, "Drug Courts-Summary" (Washington, DC: U.S. Department of Justice, September 10, 2009). Retrieved December 27, 2009, from http://www.ncjrs.gov/spotlight/drug_courts/summary.html

117. Steven Belenko, "Research on Drug Courts: A Critical Review," *National Drug Court Institute Review*, Vol. 1, No. 1, Summer 1998, p. 47.

118. "California Proposition 36" (Sacramento, CA: Drug Policy Alliance). Retrieved December 20, 2009, from http://www.prop36.org

119. "Drug Courts—Facts and Figures."

120. James A. Swartz, Zoran Martinovich, and Paul Goldstein, "An analysis of the Criminogenic Effects of Terminating the Supplemental Security Income Impairment Category for Drug Addiction and Alcoholism," *Contemporary Drug Problems, 30*(1/2), 2003, pp. 391–424.

121. James A. Swartz, Kevin M. Campbell, Jim Baumohl, and Peggy Tonkin, "Drug Treatment Participation and Retention Rates Among Former Recipients of Supplemental Security Income for Drug Addiction and Alcoholism," *Contemporary Drug Problems, 30*(1/2), 2003, pp. 335–364.
122. "FAQs: Eligibility" (Washington, DC: Department of Education, September 22, 2009). Retrieved October 1, 2009, from http://www.fafsa.ed.gov/faq003.htm#faq003_5
123. "54% Say Illegal Drug Use Is Primarily a Criminal Problem, Not Health Issue" (Vienna, VA: Rasmussen Reports, May 18, 2009). Retrieved October 4, 2009, from http://www.rasmussenreports.com/public_content/politics/general_politics/may_2009/54_say_illegal_drug_use_is_primarily_a_criminal_problem_not_health_issue
124. "41% Favor Legalizing and Taxing Marijuana" (Vienna, VA: Rasmussen Reports, May 19, 2009). Retrieved October 4, 2009, from http://www.rasmussenreports.com/public_content/business/taxes/may_2009/41_favor_legalizing_and_taxing_marijuana
125. Douglas Husack, *Legalize This! The Case for Decriminalizing Drugs* (London: Verso, 2002).
126. Jack A. Cole, "This Is Not a War on Drugs—It's a War on People" (Medford, MA: Law Enforcement Against Prohibition, February 2009). Retrieved October 21, 2009, from http://leap.cc/Publications/End_Prohibition_Now.pdf
127. Milton Friedman, "Prohibition and Drugs," *Newsweek*, May 1 1972. Retrieved October 18, 2009, from http://druglibrary.org/special/friedman/prohibition_and_drugs.htm
128. Willian F. Buckley, Jr., *National Review,* February 12, 1996. Retrieved October 18, 2009, from http://www.nationalreview.com/12feb96/drug.html
129. James Ostrowski, "Thinking About Drug Legalization" (Washington, DC: Cato Institute, May 25, 1989). Retrieved October 18, 2009, from http://www.cato.org/pub_display.php?pub_id=981&full=1
130. C. Aaron McNeece and Diana M. DiNitto, *Chemical Dependency: A Systems Approach,* 3rd ed. (Boston: Allyn and Bacon, 2005).
131. "Needle-Exchange Programmes: Time to Act Now," *The Lancet, 351,* January 10, 1998, p. 75.

11 THE CHALLENGES OF A DIVERSE SOCIETY: GENDER AND SEXUAL ORIENTATION

Ninety years after women in the United States won the right to vote, sexism remains a contentious issue in social welfare policy, and gay rights have emerged on the social policy agenda. Rip Van Winkle might be surprised at the progress that women have made in advancing their rights, and he might be surprised that gay rights have made it to the political agenda, but frustrations over inequality remain. This chapter examines political issues in the quest for women's rights and gay rights.

THE FEMINIZATION OF POVERTY

During the 1980s, "the feminization of poverty"[1] became a catch phrase, but this situation was hardly new. Most poor adults and public assistance recipients have always been women. Social welfare in the United States developed along two separate tracks: the less generous public assistance programs (e.g., mothers' aid, Aid to Families with Dependent Children) were instituted largely to help women and children, while the more generous social insurance programs (Social Security, unemployment compensation) targeted male workers.[2] Traditionally, women "went on welfare" because they were expected to remain at home to care for their young children when their husbands were unable or unwilling to support the family. Women who did go to work to support themselves and their children were generally forced into low-paying jobs.

As the number of female-headed households increased, especially during the 1970s and 1980s, their poverty rates and public assistance receipt became a topic of intense policy debate. Chapter 4 clearly shows that female-headed households are most vulnerable to poverty, and that women who are members of certain racial and ethnic groups are extremely vulnerable. Women continue to be the vast majority of adult recipients in the Temporary Assistance to Needy Families program (see Chapter 7). They are also the majority of Supplemental Security Income (SSI) recipients, especially among aged recipients, because their Social Security benefits are generally less than men's, they are less likely to have other sources of income such as pensions, and they live longer than men (see Chapter 6). The original Social Security program also conceived of women as dependents of their spouses, and as discussed in Chapter 5, gender inequities persist in the program. Many of the economic and social inequities women face are a direct result of decisions and non-decisions in social welfare policy.

The Wage Gap and Comparable Worth

The terms *feminism* or *feminist* may conjure up images of angry white women burning their bras at protest rallies in the 1960s. This image has been invoked to trivialize the subject of women's rights. The core feminist belief is that women should have the same social, economic, and political rights as men. Although the point might be debatable, both women and men can be feminists. Feminism, however, is not a unified school of thought, and feminists are not a unified group of people. There are many branches of feminism, and adherents of each branch see the route to equality differently. Briefly, liberal feminists might be considered the most conservative among them because they espouse working within the confines of mainstream society to achieve equality for women. Radical feminism, the type associated with the women's rights movement of the 1960s and 1970s, may be seen as more militant. Radical feminists generally believe women's oppression underlies all forms of societal oppression. Marxist feminists see the economic system as the root cause of equality and believe women will not have equal rights until the capitalist system is overthrown.[3]

While some believe the feminist movement is dead, largely because women have gained many rights according to law, this does not mean that women have gained equality with men. This section looks more closely at the inequality in earnings between the genders.

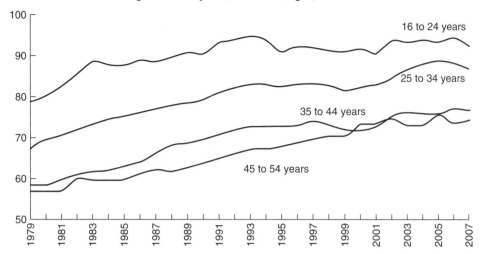

Women's weekly earnings as a percent of men's by age, workers aged 16 to 54 years, annual averages, 1979–2007

FIGURE 11.1   The Wage Gap by Gender and Age, 1979–2007   *Source:* U.S. Bureau of Labor Statistics, "Women's Earnings as a Percentage of Men's, 1979–2007" (Washington, DC: Department of Labor, October 2008). Retrieved February 7, 2010 from http://www.bls.gov/opub/ted/2008/oct/wk4/art03.htm

In 1955 the Bureau of Labor Statistics calculated that women earned 64 cents for every dollar earned by men. By 1961 the figure had dropped to 59 cents.[4] As it hovered there, "59 cents" became a well-known refrain of the equal rights movement. It was not until the 1980s that women's earnings again consistently exceeded the 60 percent mark. Figure 11.1 shows that the wage gap has narrowed slowly over the years and that the gap is greater for older than younger women. Progress in closing the gap continues to be slow. In 2008, among full-time workers, women's earnings were 80 percent of men's.[5] In the 25 to 34 age bracket, women earned 89 percent of what men earned. Figure 11.2 also shows that there are differences between women and men's earnings for each of the major ethnic groups in the United States, with women consistently earning less.

The wage gap may be greater than estimated because it is based only on wages and does not take into account health insurance, retirement, and other benefits that workers, especially men, receive. Estimates are that over the life of a full-time female worker, the earnings gap will result in a loss of $700,000 for a high school graduate, $1.2 million for a college graduate, and $2 million for a professional school graduate.[6]

Over the years, many reasons have been offered to explain the difference in women's earning power:

1. Traditionally, women were not the family's major wage earners, nor did they earn salaries comparable to men's if they did work.
2. Women's wages were considered secondary or as a supplement to their spouses' wages.
3. Women were considered temporary employees who would leave their jobs to marry and have children; they were not seen as serious about careers.
4. Women's work outside the home was considered an extracurricular activity to fill free time.
5. Women had fewer opportunities to obtain education that would lead to better-paying jobs.
6. Women were forced into certain occupations on the low end of the wage scale.

7. Women had limited job choices because they were forced to accept employment that did not conflict with their husband and children's routines.
8. "Women's work"—cleaning and child rearing in their own homes—does not pay a wage.
9. Some argued that women "preferred" lower-level employment because these jobs were more compatible with characteristics they associated with women, such as nurturing qualities and lack of aggressiveness.

Although many of these explanations are readily dismissed, and some are even laughable today, others contain elements of truth. Women may terminate their employment on a temporary or long-term basis to raise families. The unfortunate term "mommy track" has been used to describe women who interrupt their careers or try to juggle both career and children. The term implies that women who want or need careers pay the price, because their multiple responsibilities diminish their chances of career advancement. For example, in an often-cited case, in 1994, a trial court found that Vassar College (historically a women's college) discriminated against a married woman with children when she was denied tenure in the biology department.[7] In the past 30 years, no married woman in the "hard sciences" had been tenured there, but an appellate court overturned the decision and the Supreme Court refused to hear the faculty member's appeal.

Women are now 47 percent of the civilian labor force.[8] Women's paid employment is often essential to their families' support. Women are the sole heads of 18 percent of U.S. families,[9] and many two-earner families would be in serious financial difficulty without the wife's economic contribution. Most two-parent families today are dual-earner families. Only a minority of U.S. families fit the traditional or "Ozzie and Harriet" perception of a mother at home caring for children and the father as sole wage earner.[10]

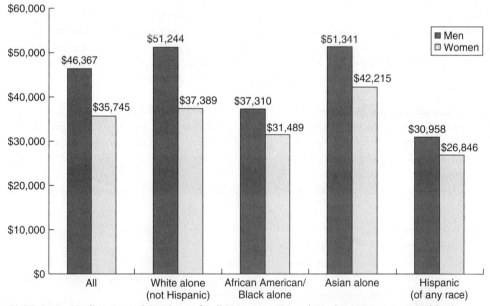

FIGURE 11.2 Median Annual Earnings of Full-Time, Year-Round Workers 15 Years and Older by Gender and Race, 2008 *Source:* U.S. Census Bureau, Historical Income Tables—People, Table P-38. Retrieved June 30, 2010, from http://www.census.gov/hhes/www/income/histinc/incpertoc.html

Today, slightly more men than women hold a bachelor's degree or a graduate or professional degree, but younger women are more likely to be college educated than men.[11] Although education has helped women obtain better jobs, it has not closed the earnings gap between men and women (see Table 11.1). Of full-time workers with a high school education, women earn about $10,600 less than men or about 73 percent of men's wages. At higher educational levels, women also earned less, ranging from 71 to 74 percent of men's wages.

Earnings differences also persist among men and women in the same occupations who worked full-time, year-round, although inequality is greater in some professions than others (see Table 11.2). Even in traditional women's jobs such as nursing, women earned only 87 percent of men's wages, and in postsecondary education they earned only 85 percent. In professions such as financial management and real estate sales, the picture was worse. Equality was greater in social work, but this is another "women's profession" where salaries are generally modest. In a very few occupations like special education, women earn a little more than men.

Not everyone believes there is a wage gap. Some contend that when years of work experience and factors like lifestyle choices (e.g., decisions to leave the workforce to raise children) are considered, the wage gap nearly disappears.[12] Determining just how much various factors contribute to pay differences between men and women is a difficult task for economists and other social scientists. Past scholarly analyses find that even after including "human capital variables" such as education and job experience, 30 to 50 percent of the variance or difference in pay between men and women remains unexplained.[13] Including occupation and type of industry explains some, but not all, of the remaining gap. The amount of unexplained variance may be due to gender discrimination or other factors.

As more women delay marriage and childbearing or never marry, they are obtaining more education and spending more time in the workforce.[14] Pay differentials become increasingly difficult to justify, when, for example, a male accountant is paid more than a female accountant for jobs that entail the same responsibilities. To close the wage gap, women have resorted to political action. According to the Equal Pay Act of 1963, men and women who do the *same* work are supposed to be paid equally. To further ensure that laws like this are upheld, the federal government established the Equal Employment Opportunity Commission (EEOC) to help employees address gender and other forms of discrimination in the workplace.

TABLE 11.1 Median Annual Earnings of Full-Time, Year-Round Workers Age 25 and Older by Gender and Educational Attainment, 2008

	Men	Women	Women's Earning as a Percent of Men's
Doctorate degree	$100,000	$74,025	74
Professional degree	100,000	71,297	71
Master's degree	80,962	57,512	71
Bachelor's degree	65,800	47,026	71
Associate's degree	50,147	36,760	73
Some college	45,821	32,626	71
High school diploma	39,009	28,382	73
Some high school	29,678	20,405	69
Less than ninth grade	24,255	18,634	77

Source: U.S. Census Bureau, Historical Income Tables—People, Table P-24. Retrieved June 3, 2010, from http://www.census.gov/hhes/www/income/histinc/incpertoc.html

TABLE 11.2 Median Weekly Earnings of Full-time Workers by Selected Occupations and Gender, 2008 Annual Averages

Occupation	Men	Women	Women's Earnings as a Percentage of Men's
Financial managers	$1,457	$945	65
Real estate brokers and sales agents	$952	$682	72
Computer and information systems managers	$1,641	$1,260	77
Police and sheriff's patrol	$929	$731	79
Butchers & meat/fish processors	$512	$430	84
Postsecondary teachers	$1,245	$1,056	85
Registered nurses	$1,168	$1,011	87
Food preparation workers	$368	$338	92
Social workers	$812	$779	96
Special education teachers	$914	$949	104

Source: Bureau of Labor Statistics, "Highlights of Women's Earnings in 2008" (Washington, DC: U.S. Department of Labor, July 2009). Retrieved June 3, 2010, from http://www.bls.gov/cps/cpswom2008.pdf

Another approach to reducing the gap in earnings between women and men (as well as between members of different racial and ethnic groups), is "comparable worth" or "pay equity." According to this concept, workers should be paid equally when they do *different* types of work that require the same level of responsibility, effort, knowledge, and skill.[15] Many jobs done by men provide greater monetary compensation because the "dual" or "gender-segregated" labor market creates a situation in which "women's professions" are regarded less highly than professions dominated by men. In discussing comparable worth, we are really asking whether the jobs in question are of equal value to society. Given the gender-segregated job market, it is commonly believed that the pay gap won't close until more women move into professions dominated by men, both "blue collar" and "white collar."[16]

Comparable worth or pay equity has been called everything from radical to rational.[17] In the views of some, pay equity for women is long overdue, while others believe it would create havoc with the supply and demand forces that regulate the free market, reduce demand for female workers, increase unemployment among women, and cause a great deal of litigation.[18]

By 1985, twenty states had passed laws or resolutions making comparable worth a requirement or a goal of state (not private) employment. Minnesota and Washington state are the prime examples. Deciding the value or worth of jobs is an arduous task. In Minnesota, state jobs are assigned points based on work requirements, skill levels, and other factors in order to assess the comparable value of job categories. For example, in 1982, the state of Minnesota's job evaluation ratings for a delivery van driver (most were men) and a clerk typist (most were women) were the same—117 points; however, the monthly state salary for the van driver was $1,900 while the clerk typist salary was $1,400.[19] The Minnesota legislature approved pay equity wage adjustments for state jobs found to be undervalued and underpaid, amounting to an average annual increase of $2,200 for these positions.[20] The National Committee on Pay Equity reports that most of these salary increases went to women, while 10 percent went to men in undervalued jobs. It also reported that an independent evaluation found that the wage gap between male and female state employees closed by 9 percentage points, and there was no significant negative affect on women's employment. Other economists see it differently saying that in Minnesota the result was less employment growth in jobs held mostly by women compared to jobs held mostly by men.[21] They also report that following Washington state's implementation of comparable worth, the number of jobs in areas that got adjustments dropped, especially those that received the largest adjustments. The Independent Women's Forum says that most states abandoned comparable worth efforts because of implementation problems—those responsible for the task could not agree on job classification systems.[22]

The U.S. Commission on Civil Rights has not supported comparable worth, agreeing that it would wreak havoc on the marketplace, and the courts have generally not favored comparable worth, finding that paying prevailing market rate salaries is not illegal. For example, in a case against Brown University, a male faculty member accused the university of paying an equally qualified female faculty member a higher salary. The First Circuit Court ruled in favor of the university, which argued that the female professor was paid more because she had planned to take a position at another school that had offered her a higher salary. Brown wanted to retain her. The university contended that she had greater market value than the male professor, and the court agreed. In another case, nursing faculty at the University of Washington filed suit stating that they were paid less than male faculty in other departments. The Ninth Circuit Court ruled that under Title VII of the Civil Rights Act, suits cannot be brought before the court if salary inequities are due to labor market conditions.

The executive, judicial, and legislative branches of government are all involved in pay equity. For example, in 2000, the U.S Department of Labor instituted new affirmative action regulations to promote equal pay, requiring all federal contractors to report hiring, termination, promotions, and compensation by gender and minority status.[23] Court cases also continue to test the principle of pay equity. In a case that received national attention, Lilly Ledbetter won a pay discrimination suit against Goodyear Tire and Rubber. Goodyear appealed the verdict. Eventually the U.S. Supreme Court heard the case, ruling that Ledbetter was not entitled to compensation because she had not filed her suit in a timely manner. To correct this technicality, Congress passed the Lily Ledbetter Fair Act of 2009 to ensure the intent of civil rights legislation with respect to pay equity. Ledbetter got no monetary compensation, just the satisfaction of knowing that an act that bears her name states that time limits for filing a pay discrimination suit accrue after the *last* discriminatory paycheck or compensation practice, not after the *first* discriminatory paycheck or compensation practice. The Ledbetter Act was among the very first bills President Barack Obama signed after taking office.

Public policy rarely ends controversy over an issue. Workplace discrimination suits continue to be filed, the courts continue to hear appeals, and sometimes Congress finds that it must pass a law to clarify the intent of previous legislation.

The Institute for Women's Policy Research (IWPR) estimates that at the current rate, the pay gap nationwide won't be closed for another 50 years.[24] The IWPR also reports that among the best economies for women are the District of Columbia, Maryland, and New Jersey; among the worst are Arkansas, West Virginia, and Louisiana.[25]

WOMEN IN POLITICAL OFFICE

Women began organizing, demonstrating, and risking arrest to gain equality through political participation long before the suffragette movement, although it was not until 1920 that the Nineteenth Amendment to the U.S. Constitution finally gave women the right to vote. Even with this right, women remain grossly underrepresented in elected and appointed offices compared to their numbers in the population. Illustration 11.1 describes some notable firsts for women in politics, and

ILLUSTRATION 11.1
Some Notable Firsts of Women in Politics

Women have been making political history in major elected and appointed positions since at least the mid-1800s. For example, in 1866, Elizabeth Cady Stanton was the first woman to run for the U.S. House of Representatives. In 1884, three women were elected to the Colorado House of Representatives, becoming the first women ever to serve in a state legislature. In 1916, four years before the Nineteenth Amendment to the U.S. Constitution gave women the right to vote, Jeanette Rankin, a Republican from Montana, was elected to the U.S. House of Representatives. In 1933, President Franklin Delano Roosevelt appointed Frances Perkins Secretary of Labor, making her the first woman to hold a cabinet post. Margaret Chase Smith was the first woman ever elected to both houses of Congress, and in 1964, she became the first Republican woman to be nominated for President of the United States. Also in 1964, Patsy Takemoto Mink, Democrat from Hawaii, became the first woman of Asian origin and the first woman of color elected to the U.S. House of Representatives. In 1968, Shirley Chisholm was elected to the House, making her the first African American woman to serve in Congress. In 1972, she became the first woman to be nominated for President of the United States at the Democratic National Convention and the first African American major-party candidate for President. In 1977, Patricia Roberts Harris became the first African American woman to hold a cabinet-level post when she was appointed to head the Department of Housing and Urban Development.

Since the 1980s, women have realized many more notable firsts in elected and appointed offices. For example, in 1981, President Reagan appointed Sandra Day O'Connor as the first woman to serve on the U.S. Supreme Court. In 1984, Democratic Congresswoman Geraldine Ferraro was the first woman to be nominated as the vice presidential candidate on a major party ticket. In 1989, Ileana Ros-Lehtinen (R-FL) was the first

Hispanic woman and first Cuban American elected to Congress. In 1992, Carol Moseley-Braun (D-IL) become the first African American woman and the first woman of color elected to the U.S. Senate, and California became the first state to have elected two women senators simultaneously—Barbara Boxer and Dianne Feinstein (both Democrats). In 1993, President Clinton appointed Janet Reno the first woman U.S. Attorney General, and in 1997, Aida Alvarez became the first Hispanic woman to hold a cabinet-level post when she was appointed to head the Small Business Administration. In 1997, President Clinton also appointed Madeleine Albright Secretary of State, making her the highest ranking woman ever appointed to serve in the federal government.

In 2001, President George W. Bush appointed Condoleezza Rice the first woman to serve as National Security Advisor, and in 2007, she became the first African American woman and the first Republican woman to serve as Secretary of State. In 2001, Elaine Chao became the first Asian American woman to serve as a presidential cabinet member when President Bush appointed her Secretary of Labor; and President Bush appointed Gale Norton the first female Secretary of the Interior and Ann Veneman the first woman to serve as Secretary of Agriculture. Representative Nancy Pelosi (D-CA) has held several firsts—in 2001, she became the highest ranking woman ever to serve in the U.S. Congress when she was elected House Democratic Whip; in 2002 she became the first woman to head a Congressional party when she was elected House Democratic Leader; and in 2007, she became the first woman to serve as Speaker of the U.S. House of Representatives. In 2008, Senator Hillary Rodham Clinton (D-NY) became the first woman to be a presidential candidate in every state's primary election and caucus, and Alaska Governor Sarah Palin became the first woman to run as the Republican party's vice presidential nominee. Perhaps these firsts and the presence of more women running for office, being elected to office, and being appointed to high-level offices will inspire many more women to seek careers in politics.

Source: Center for American Women and Politics, Eagleton Institute of Politics, "Firsts for Women in U.S. Politics" (New Brunswick, NJ: Rutgers, The State University of New Jersey). Retrieved May 31, 2009, from http://www.cawp.rutgers.edu/fast_facts/resources/Firsts.php.

Table 11.3 shows that despite their underrepresentation, the proportion of women in the U.S. Congress has grown steadily, from 3 percent in 1979 to 17 percent in 2009.[26] In 2009, 17 women served in the U.S. Senate, 13 Democrats and four Republicans. Of the 73 women from 31 states in the U.S. House of Representatives, 56 are Democrats and 17 are Republicans; in addition, there are three women delegates representing the District of Columbia, Guam, and the Virgin Islands.

In statewide elective offices such as governor and lieutenant governor, the proportion of women has grown from 11 percent in 1979 to 23 percent (74 of the 314 positions) in 2009, but this is less than the 28 percent in 1999 (see Table 11.3). Of the 74 women, 50 are Democrats, 22 are Republicans, and two were elected in nonpartisan races. The number of women elected to state legislatures increased from 10 percent in 1979 to 24 percent in 2009. In 2009, women were mayors of 11 of the country's 100 most populous cities, and mayors of 17 percent of the country's 1,142 cities with populations of over 30,000.

RESUSCITATING THE EQUAL RIGHTS AMENDMENT

The women's rights movement of the 1960s and 1970s helped to spur several pieces of federal legislation that address the inequities women face in employment, education, and the marketplace. Some of the most notable achievements are the following:

1. The Equal Pay Act of 1963 requires employers to compensate male and female workers equally for performing the same jobs under similar conditions. The law does not cover all employment, but amendments have added to the types of jobs and employers that must comply.
2. Title VII of the Civil Rights Act of 1964 prohibits gender discrimination in employment practices and provides the right to court redress. The Equal Employment Opportunity Commission is charged with interpreting and enforcing Title VII.

TABLE 11.3 Percentages of Women in Elective Office, Selected Years, 1979–2009

Year	U.S. Congress	Statewide Elective Office	State Legislatures
1979	3%	11%	10%
1989	5	14	17
1999	12	28	22
2009	17	23	24

Source: "Women in Elective Office 2010," Center for American Women and Politics, December 2009. Retrieved February 2, 2010, from http://www.cawp.rutgers.edu/fast_facts/levels_of_office/documents/elective.pdf. Reprinted by permission.

3. Executive Order 11246, as amended by Executive Order 11375 in 1967, prohibits employers who practice gender discrimination from receiving federal contracts. Employers are also required to develop "affirmative action" plans to remedy inequities. The order established the Office of Federal Contract Compliance under the Department of Labor as an enforcement agency.

4. Title IX of the 1972 Education Amendments to the Civil Rights Act prohibits gender discrimination by elementary, secondary, vocational, and professional schools, colleges, and universities that receive federal funds.

5. The Equal Credit Act of 1975 prohibits discrimination by lending institutions based on gender or marital status.

6. The Pregnancy Discrimination Act of 1978, another amendment to the Civil Rights Act, protects women from employment discrimination as a result of childbearing.

It may seem that with all these pieces of legislation there should be no question that women are protected under the law. But battles over these laws are fought again and again. Title IX is a prime example. Much of the debate concerns whether school's athletic programs continue to discriminate against female students or whether Title IX hampers men's athletics by requiring that women be given equitable opportunities to participate in sports, receive scholarships proportional to their participation, and be treated equally with regard to recruitment, facilities, coaching, housing, tutoring, and other benefits and resources.[27]

Perhaps most discouraging to women's rights activists is that an equal rights amendment to the U.S. Constitution has never been ratified. In 1923 at the Seneca Falls Women's Rights Convention, Alice Paul first introduced language for an equal rights amendment (ERA) to the U.S. Constitution. Virtually every year thereafter the ERA was introduced into Congress, but it did not pass both houses of Congress until 1972. This 51-word amendment simply stated:

> **Section 1.** Equality of rights under the law shall not be denied or abridged by the United States or by any state on account of sex.
>
> **Section 2.** Congress shall have the power to enforce by appropriate legislation the provisions of this Article.
>
> **Section 3.** This amendment shall take effect two years after the date of ratification.

By 1978, the amendment still had not been ratified by the required 38 states. Congress extended the deadline to June 30, 1982. Despite the endorsement of 450 organizations with 50 million members—unions, churches, civil rights groups, legal associations, educational groups, and medical organizations—ERA ratification fell short by three states.[28]

ERA proponents argued that this guarantee of equality under law should be part of the Constitution—"the supreme law of the land"— and that until this happens, there is tacit consent to discriminate on the basis of gender. While a number of federal and state laws already prohibit gender discrimination, ERA proponents contend that like many other social policy issues, gender discrimination is best addressed by an overarching national policy rather than by a multitude of federal, state, and local laws, each subject to modification or repeal.

Others beg to differ. Conservative Phyllis Schlafly founded the "Stop ERA Movement" shortly after Congress approved the ERA in 1972. The movement was based on fears about what might happen if the traditional roles of women in society were disrupted. There was speculation that the ERA would lead to a military draft and combat duty for women, that women's rights to financial support and child custody would be weakened, and even that restrooms would become unisex. None of these concerns were specifically mentioned in the ERA. Schlafly and the Eagle Forum remain opposed to the ERA, which is reintroduced in almost every session of Congress.

The United States remains one of the few democratic nations without constitutional protection of women's rights, and many women still believe the ERA should still become law. Some ERA advocates hope that Congress will extend the ERA ratification deadline.[29] They point to an amendment on Congressional pay raises that was ratified in 1992—203 years after Congress passed it. No ratification deadline was imposed on this pay raise amendment. Congress did impose an initial ratification deadline on the ERA. Since it extended this deadline once, some believe that Congress could extend it again.

In the eyes of these ERA advocates, Congress could also apply the U.S. Supreme Court's "reasonable" and "sufficiently contemporaneous" tests indicating the amendment is still vital, timely, and relevant, and allow the ERA to become a constitutional amendment with the ratification of three more states.[30] Many Americans may not realize there is an active movement to revive the ERA, and some question whether it is still vital, timely, or relevant. For example, in 2003, when Representative Carolyn Maloney (D-NY) and Senator Edward Kennedy (D-MA) reintroduced the ERA to the 108th Congress, Anita Blair, the executive vice president and general counsel of the Independent Women's Forum (a conservative Republican organization) declared, "Normal women don't want it and don't need it."[31]

FAMILY CARE

More assistance with childcare and other family responsibilities would certainly promote greater equality for women. This topic is so important that it has been discussed more than once in this book. Proposals to increase tax credits for childcare run into opposition from those that claim that this approach is unfair to families that choose to use nonpaid care while working, including those in which one parent stays at home with the children. They support a larger child tax credit for dependents that would help families regardless of their employment and childcare choices. The 1997 Balanced Budget Act included a modest child tax credit. The 2001 tax cut under the George W. Bush administration gradually increased this credit to $1000 by 2010 (see Chapter 2), and the American Recovery and Reinvestment Act (ARRA) passed in the early days of the Obama administration makes the credit available to more low-income families, even those that owe no income tax.

Chapter 7 addressed increased funding for childcare under the Child Care and Development Fund (CCDF), established as part of the 1996 Personal Responsibility and Work Opportunity Reconciliation Act. The act instituted large-scale welfare reform and requires most families receiving assistance to work or participate in work-related activities. ARRA funds are also being directed at the CCDF. The ARRA also increased funding for Head Start programs, which provide childcare and educational programs for children before they reach school age (see Chapters 2 and 9).

Childcare affordability, quality, and monitoring, as well as the low pay afforded childcare workers that results in difficulties recruiting and retaining staff, are issues of concern to everyone who uses care or provides it. Many low-income parents must use whatever childcare they can find, either because they must work to make ends meet or because TANF requires them to work. The "catch-22" is that many families cannot afford or find decent childcare while they work.

Obtaining care for disabled adult and elderly family members also presents challenges, primarily to women who generally assume the major caretaker responsibilities. Community adult daycare centers help alleviate some of this burden, and many families obtain some form of home care through the private sector using Medicare, Medicaid, or their own funds.

During President George H. W. Bush 's administration, Congress twice passed family leave bills that would have required some employers to provide 12 weeks of unpaid leave to family members when a new baby arrives or when a spouse, parent, or child had a serious illness. The same leave would have been provided to employees with an illness. Despite strong public support, President Bush vetoed both bills, saying that while he favored family leave, the bills might force businesses to hire replacement help, which they might not be able to afford. Rather than preserve jobs, he feared that the bills might result in a net job loss.

President Clinton felt very differently about family leave legislation. On taking office, he moved swiftly to sign the Family and Medical Leave Act of 1993. However, the law exempts businesses with fewer than 50 workers (thereby excluding half the workforce and the vast majority of businesses), and covered businesses are not required to provide leave to upper-echelon employees.

In 1994, California became the first state to enact a law entitling many private and public sector workers to six weeks of paid leave at 55 percent of their salary (in 2008, no more than $917 per week), to care for a new child or a family member.[32] To finance the program, the amount employees pay to the state's insurance program for disabled workers was increased. As of 2009, Washington and New Jersey also had paid family leave programs.[33] Employers continue to argue that family leave disrupts business and is too costly.

According to a McGill University study of 173 countries, the United States lags behind other high-income countries and many middle- and low-income countries when it comes to supports for working families.[34] In total, 168 of the countries offer paid maternity leave, and 98 of them provide at least 14 weeks of paid leave. Only the United States, Lesotho, Liberia, Swaziland, and Papua New Guinea do not guarantee mothers paid leave. Sixty-five of the countries also offer fathers paid paternity leave.

President George W. Bush voided a Clinton-era regulation that allowed states to use unemployment insurance to help parents take job leave when they have a baby or adopt a child.[35] Some states do provide unemployment insurance benefits when workers must take leave for family reasons. The Obama administration has tried to entice more states to expand their unemployment insurance programs to include benefits for those who need to care for a family member.

NO MIDDLE GROUND ON ABORTION RIGHTS

Abortion is a key issue in the nation's culture wars. Before the 1960s, abortions were rarely permitted in any states, except in cases where the mother's life was in danger. Then about a quarter of the states made some modifications in their abortion laws, extending them to cases of rape, incest, or when the mother's physical or mental health was in jeopardy. Obtaining an abortion was still difficult because each case had to be reviewed individually by physicians and by the hospital where the abortion was to be performed.

The Supreme Court and *Roe v. Wade*

In 1970, four states (New York, Alaska, Hawaii, and Washington) further liberalized their abortion laws, permitting women to obtain an abortion on the woman's request with her physician's agreement. In 1973 the U.S. Supreme Court made decisions that fundamentally changed abortion policy. In the cases of *Roe v. Wade* and *Doe v. Bolton,* the Court ruled that the Fifth and Fourteenth Amendments to the Constitution, which guarantee all people "life, liberty and property," did not include the life of the unborn fetus. In addition, the First and Fourteenth

Amendments guaranteeing personal liberties were said to extend to childbearing decisions. The Court did stipulate some conditions under which the states could and could not restrict abortions: (1) During the first three months of pregnancy, the states cannot restrict the mother's decision for an abortion; (2) from the fourth through sixth months of pregnancy, the states cannot restrict abortions, but they can protect the mother's health by setting standards for how and when abortions can be performed; (3) during the last three months of pregnancy, the states can prohibit all abortions except those to protect the mother's life and health.

Prochoice and Antiabortion Forces

Abortion rights proponents, who often call themselves the "prochoice" movement, believe that a woman should have the right to make decisions about her own body, including abortion. Without recourse to legal abortions, they fear that women may turn to illegal abortions that can result in health risks or even death for the woman. Proponents believe that misery and suffering may be avoided when a woman can choose to end an unwanted pregnancy. Prochoice groups, including the National Abortion Rights Action League and Planned Parenthood, hold "speakouts" across the country to counteract the antiabortion movement.

Abortion opponents, often referred to as "right-to-life" groups, oppose the freedom to obtain an abortion and generally base their arguments on religious, moral, and biological grounds, contending that abortion is tantamount to taking a human life. "Prolifers" demonstrate annually in Washington on the anniversary of the *Roe v. Wade* decision. Norma McCorvey, the plaintiff in the *Roe v. Wade* case, who later became a born-again Christian, now speaks out against abortion. McCorvey never had the opportunity to have an abortion because it took the courts so long to rule in her case.

Emily's List (Early Money Is Like Yeast; it helps the dough rise) is the PAC dedicated to electing prochoice Democratic women to office at all levels of government. The Wish (Women In the Senate and House) List is the PAC dedicated to electing prochoice Republican women.

Medicaid and Abortion

Following the *Roe* and *Doe* decisions, poor pregnant women were able to obtain federally funded abortions under the Medicaid program. But in 1976, antiabortion groups, with the unflagging support of conservative Representative Henry J. Hyde (R-Illinois), successfully pushed through what is known as the Hyde Amendment. The amendment prohibited the federal government from paying for abortions except in cases where the mother's life was endangered. It did not prevent states from financing abortions with their own funds. The Hyde amendment also did not restrict women from obtaining privately funded abortions, but necessarily limited their ability to do so if they were unable to cover the costs. The U.S. Supreme Court upheld the Hyde Amendment, declaring that a poor woman does not have the right to a federally financed abortion except when her life is in danger. In 1977, the federal funding ban was lifted in promptly reported cases of rape and incest and in cases where "severe and long-lasting" harm would be caused to the woman, but in 1981 the language was again restricted to permit federally funded abortions only to save the mother's life. In 1989, Congress again approved legislation to add cases of rape and incest, but President George H. W. Bush vetoed it, and Congress could not muster the two-thirds vote needed in both chambers to override the veto.

The Clinton administration viewed abortions in cases of rape or incest as "medically necessary," and in October 1993, President Clinton signed a law reinstating access to Medicaid-financed abortions in cases of rape or incest. Six states already permitted state-funded abortions for poor women with certain restrictions, and 13 others provided state-funded abortions for poor women on request. A protest quickly arose over whether the intent of the law was to *allow* or to *require* states to pay for these abortions. Antiabortion activists called the directive an attempt to challenge laws in states with more restrictive abortion policies. Today, under federal Medicaid regulations, abortions continue to be available in cases of rape, incest, or when the mother's life is in danger. The Clinton administration's failed national health insurance plan included coverage for abortions. Access to abortion was a sticking point in the nation's 2010 healthcare reform legislation. The legislation will allow many Americans to obtain healthcare coverage under government supported health care exchanges that help people locate coverage. A Chapter 8 noted, women covered under the exchange who wish to have abortion coverage included must write two separate checks each month—one to cover their part of the regular premium and one for a separate rider to cover abortion. Since women generally do not expect to have an abortion and may not wish to deal with a separate rider due to cost or other reasons, the effectiveness of this provision in providing access to abortion will likely be limited.

Changing Tenor of the Supreme Court

Interpreting abortion rights has kept the U.S. Supreme Court busy. In 1983, it reaffirmed the landmark 1973 decisions concerning the right to abortion and also extended some provisions. Abortions early in the second trimester do not have to be performed in hospitals, because medical advances now make it possible to conduct these procedures safely on an outpatient basis. The Court also struck down regulations adopted in Akron, Ohio, that made it more difficult to obtain an abortion, such as requiring minors to get parental consent and imposing a 24-hour waiting period between the time a woman signed an informed consent form and the time the abortion was performed. In 1986, the Court acted again. This time it struck down a Pennsylvania law aimed at discouraging women from obtaining abortions.

Then the tenor of the Court began to change. In its 1989 decision in *Webster v. Reproductive Health Services,* the Court upheld a Missouri law that (1) prohibits public hospitals and public employees from performing abortions and from counseling a woman to obtain an abortion unless her life is in danger; (2) requires physicians to determine whether a woman who is at least 20 weeks pregnant is carrying a fetus that is viable (able to survive outside the womb); and (3) declares that life begins at conception. The ruling opened the door for states to pass more restrictive abortion laws. Pennsylvania quickly adopted new regulations, including notification of husbands, 24-hour waiting periods, and prohibition of third-trimester abortions. A wave of additional attempts at more restrictive state laws ensued. In contrast, Maryland passed a law shoring up abortion rights. Although it met with some stiff opposition, abortion rights advocates hoped it might protect the right to abortion in Maryland should the Supreme Court fail to protect access to abortions in the future.

Prochoice groups grew increasingly concerned about abortion rights during the Republican presidential administrations of the 1980s. The 1973 U.S. Supreme Court decision upholding abortion rights was supported 7-2, the 1983 decision 6-3, and the 1986 decision 5-4. In 1989, the restrictions in the Missouri law were also upheld 5-4. President Reagan made three appointments to the Court during his terms in office—Sandra Day O'Connor, Anthony Kennedy, and Antonin Scalia. All voted to uphold the Missouri law in 1989. It was the older members of the Court who defended abortion rights. Prochoice advocates also feared that President George H. W. Bush's appointees to the high court, David Souter and Clarence Thomas, would further imperil their cause.

In 1992, the U.S. Supreme Court heard another case, this time concerning Pennsylvania's new abortion law. In another 5-4 decision, the Court again protected the right to an abortion, but in a 7-2 decision upheld the provisions requiring parental consent for women under age 18, 24-hour waiting periods for almost everyone seeking an abortion, and requirements that physicians inform women of their options; it did, however, strike down provisions that required notification of husbands.

In 1993, President Clinton appointed Ruth Bader Ginsburg, a well-known women's rights advocate, to the Supreme Court, renewing prochoice proponents' hope for stronger support of abortion rights. Clinton made one additional Supreme Court appointment and President George W. Bush made two. It is unclear what effect President Obama's Supreme Court appointee, Sonia Sotomayor might have on any abortion decisions since she has not previously decided abortion cases. The media have frequently referred to Elena Kagan, President Obama's most recent U.S. Supreme Court appointee, as pro abortion rights. Antiabortion advocates are naturally wary of how Obama administration appointees will affect abortion policy, just as prochoice advocates are wary of Republican presidential appointments.

Protests and Violence

In their efforts to prevent abortions, antiabortion activists have used a number of tactics such as Internet "wanted posters" with pictures of doctors who perform abortions. This activity was apparently protected by constitutional guarantees of free speech,[36] but Internet service providers shut down various websites because they were so threatening.[37] Prolifers also use images of developing fetuses on TV, the Internet, and billboards in efforts to demonstrate that a fetus is a human life. They have also tried to entrap abortion clinic staff into agreeing to violate the law by keeping confidential that an adult boyfriend had impregnated a minor.

Other tactics prolife advocates use include blockades of abortion clinics that have resulted in the arrests of hundreds of members of antiabortion groups. In an effort to stop harassment at abortion clinics, the National Organization for Women (NOW) tried several strategies. It was unsuccessful in invoking an 1871 civil rights law that had been used in cases involving the Ku Klux Klan. But NOW filed another lawsuit to invoke federal racketeering and antitrust laws directed at organized crime (called the Racketeer Influenced, Corrupt Organization [RICO] Act of 1970) to prohibit Operation Rescue and similar organizations from protesting at abortion clinics. The suit was initially dismissed because the protests involved a political activity, not a commercial activity for profit. Operation Rescue hailed it as a victory for free speech, but when the issue reached the Supreme Court, the justices unanimously agreed that RICO could be invoked if illegal activities are involved. In 1998, under RICO, a Chicago jury found three antiabortion activists guilty of using threats and violence in an attempt to prevent abortions at clinics. Believing that other Supreme Court decisions did not go far enough in protecting entrances to clinics, Congress passed a "buffer zone" law in 1994 that makes it a federal offense to block the entrances to abortion clinics and also to use or threaten force against those seeking or performing abortions.

In 1994 Operation Rescue and another antiabortion group were ordered to pay $1 million in damages to a Planned Parenthood clinic in Texas, the largest such award to date. The U.S. Supreme Court's job is to interpret the U.S. Constitution. Sometimes these interpretations change. In 2003 and 2006, the U.S. Supreme Court reversed its RICO decision saying that federal racketeering statutes cannot be used as a basis for action against abortion protestors.[38] Antiabortion forces had prevailed.

Some individuals have gone beyond protests and demonstrations by bombing or setting fire to abortion clinics. Even if the vast majority of antiabortion activists decry such violence, the murders of several physicians and abortion clinic staff members have raised serious concerns about how far fanatics will go in name of the movement. In May 2009, Dr. George Tiller, one of a handful of U.S. doctors who performed late-term abortions, was shot to death while serving as an usher at his church. Tiller had previously been shot in both arms, his clinic has been bombed, and he had been continually harassed and intimidated. Some called him a hero, and some called him a murderer, but Tiller had continued to serve women.

Congress, the Presidents, and Abortion

In the tug of war over abortion, presidents have also resorted to rulemaking. Rulemaking requires a 30-day comment period, but it can circumvent the legislative process when a president wishes to act quickly or believes Congress won't approve the content of the rule. While in office, President Reagan issued a rule banning federal funding to domestic family-planning clinics that so much as discussed abortion with patients through what came to be called the "gag rule" or "domestic gag rule." Planned Parenthood said it would give up its federal funding rather than obey the rule. The U.S. Supreme Court upheld the gag rule. Congress disagreed, but it was unable to override President George H. W. Bush's veto of its legislation. The Bush administration did soften the rule by allowing physicians to discuss abortion if there was a medical need for it, but other personnel could make referrals only if women asked for information about abortion. Upon taking office, President Clinton lifted the domestic gag rule. Today, federally funded clinics can provide information on all options available to women, including abortion, but they cannot promote or provide abortions.[39]

Just before leaving office, President George W. Bush issued a rule that expanded existing protections to health workers who do not want to take part in healthcare services they find objectionable on religious or moral grounds. President Obama has signaled his intention to reverse the rule.

U.S. efforts to curtail women's reproductive rights also extend internationally under a provision called the "global gag rule" or the "Mexico City Policy" because it was discussed at an international conference there. President Reagan initiated this rule, which prevents international groups that receive U.S. aid from providing information on abortion or performing abortions. Republican administrations have enforced the ban, and Democratic administrations have lifted it (President Obama did so upon taking office in 2009). Antiabortion forces support the ban, saying that the taxes of those who oppose abortion should not be used to promote it. If this argument sounds logical at first blush, just think of the tax dollars that support activities that some Americans oppose, such as the war in Iraq. Prochoice forces continue to argue that access to abortion in the United States reduces back-alley and self-performed abortions and preserves women's health. They also argue that women in poor countries where healthcare is sparse also need access to a range of family planning options and other reproductive healthcare services.

In recent years, the U.S. Congress has taken direct action on abortion policy. In November 2003, Congress passed, and President George W. Bush signed into law, the first ban on a specific abortion procedure called "intact dilation and evacuation (or extraction)." To the chagrin of prochoice advocates, this late-term abortion procedure is also referred to as "partial-birth abortion." Few abortions of this nature are conducted, but debate about whether the procedure should be allowed and the appropriate term for the procedure has been heated.[40] The ban makes it a criminal offense for doctors to knowingly perform such abortions, except to save the woman's life. The American Medical Association and the American College of Obstetricians and Gynecologists opposed the legislation. *Boston Globe* columnist Ellen Goodman called the law a "public relations coup" for antiabortion forces, made worse by the picture of the bill's signing.[41] It showed the president and a group of smiling legislators—all male. In 2007, the Supreme Court upheld the ban 5–4.

A more indirect Congressional attempt to affect abortion rights is the Unborn Victims of Violence Act, which President George W. Bush signed in 2004. This act made it a crime to harm an "unborn child" during an assault of a pregnant woman. Laws such as these may appear justified in order to punish criminals. Prochoice groups see them as subterfuge or thinly veiled attempts to undermine the *Roe* and *Doe* decisions that constitutional rights do not extend to the unborn fetus.

Contraceptive Drugs

The availability of contraceptive drugs and devices is also a public policy issue. Some women have had to sue their health plans to cover birth control, even though these plans cover men's sexual performance drugs like Viagra. It took a 2000 Equal Employment Opportunity Commission ruling to get some employer-sponsored health plans to cover birth control.

Although not a public policy issue per se, in 2009, the British medical journal *The Lancet* took issue with Pope Benedict XVI, calling "outrageous and wildly inaccurate" his statement that Africa's fight against HIV/AIDS "cannot be overcome by the distribution of condoms: on the contrary, they increase it."[42] Making condoms available in U.S. high schools is a public policy issue, and it can raise parents' ire. A study published in the *Journal of Public Health* found that "adolescents in schools where condoms were available were . . . less likely to report lifetime or recent sexual intercourse. Sexually active adolescents in those schools were twice as likely to use condoms, but less likely to use other contraceptive methods, during their most recent sexual encounter."[43] These are interesting research findings, but they hardly settle the question of whether schools should distribute condoms.

In 1988 France granted women access to RU-486 (called mifepristone in the United States), a drug that induces an abortion in the early weeks of pregnancy. To avoid boycotts of companies that made mifepristone available, the French drug company gave the nonprofit Population Council marketing rights for the drug in the United States. The United States did not approve mifepristone's use until 2000, four years after it said the drug was safe. Mifepristone allows women to avoid abortion clinics and to obtain a physician's help to terminate a pregnancy more privately. Medicaid does not provide the drug unless a woman would otherwise qualify for an abortion under Medicaid, and those cases are limited.

Other emergency contraception issues erupted in 2005 over a drug called levonorgestrel or Plan B® or, more commonly, the "morning after" pill. (Mifepristone is used to terminate pregnancies, while Plan B helps to prevent pregnancy after intercourse.) Instructions indicate that plan B may be taken up to 72 hours after intercourse, but the sooner it is taken, the more effective it is.[44] One reason Plan B became controversial is that some pharmacists refused to fill prescriptions for the drug based on religious objections. The battle over whether pharmacists must fill prescriptions has been fought at the state level, with some states passing laws that require pharmacists to fill all legitimate prescriptions presented to them.

Plan B also became controversial because the Food and Drug Administration (FDA) refused to make it available over the counter (i.e., without a prescription) despite scientific evidence of its safety and recommendations by the FDA's joint advisory committee and FDA review staff to do so. A Government Accountability Office report found the FDA did not use usual practices in making its decision on Plan B.[45] This is the only case from 1994 to 2000 in which a request to switch a drug from prescription to over-the-counter sales was rejected after the advisory committee recommended it. The FDA commissioner explained a subsequent delay in making the drug available over the counter by citing concerns that women under age 18 might not use Plan B properly. Reproductive rights advocates called it politics before science, and Susan Wood, then head of the

FDA's Office of Women's Health, resigned in protest of the delay. Following a 2005 lawsuit filed by the Center for Reproductive Rights and other groups, the FDA made Plan B available over the counter to adults (aged 18 and over) in 2006. In 2009, a federal judge ordered that the age be lowered to 17 (girls younger than age 17 must still have a prescription to obtain Plan B).[46] The judge also told the FDA to consider removing all restrictions on the drug's over-the-counter availability. Conservatives called lowering the age a political decision that disregards parental rights.[47]

Will Abortion Rights Survive?

Following the *Roe v. Wade* decision, the number of legal induced abortions performed annually nearly doubled from an estimated 763,000 in 1974 to about 1.4 million in 1980.[48] The number has since declined. In 2005, about 820,000 legal abortions were performed, and the abortion rate has dropped from 25 per 1,000 women aged 15 to 44 in 1980 to 15 per 1,000 in 2005. Many reasons might explain this drop, including increased contraception use, a decrease in unintended pregnancies, and more limited access to abortion services due to factors such as parental consent or notification laws and mandatory waiting periods.[49] More women are apparently carrying their pregnancies to term, and in many areas, especially rural areas, there are no abortion providers (the state of Mississippi reportedly has only one abortion provider).[50] Whether crisis pregnancy centers, which reach out and offer pregnant women help, have any affect on the number of women seeking abortions is questionable. Many of these centers are controversial because prochoice advocates see them primarily as an effort to dissuade women from considering abortion.

Thirty-three states now require that women be counseled before receiving an abortion, and 24 states require a waiting period before an abortion can be performed.[51] Prolife activists would like to push the envelope further by, for example, requiring that women have an ultrasound of the fetus before an abortion can be performed. Nebraska has taken abortion restrictions a step further with 2010 laws that ban most abortions after 20 weeks, contending that fetuses feel pain, and require health professionals to determine whether a woman might develop mental or physical problems following an abortion or was pressured to seek an abortion.[52] As more states whittle away at abortion rights, the prochoice movement has become increasingly concerned about the future of abortion policy.

The vast majority of states require parental consent or notification before a minor can obtain an abortion.[53] Parental consent is an especially sensitive issue because minors generally cannot receive medical care without a parent's permission. Some believe that abortion should be treated differently because young women may fear parental reprisal for becoming pregnant, became pregnant through incest, or believe their parents won't permit them to have an abortion.

Rather than continue to challenge restrictive state abortion laws in the courts, prochoice advocates would like to see abortion rights protected through federal law. Since 1989, the Freedom of Choice Act has been introduced to every Congress in an effort to codify the *Roe* decision into law and provide greater protection of women's right to choice. Senator Barbara Boxer (D-CA) introduced a sweeping new version of the Freedom of Choice Act in 2004.[54] Under the act, women would have statutory reproductive rights as articulated by the Supreme Court in *Roe v. Wade*. Among other provisions, Medicaid would cover abortions; public hospitals could not prohibit abortions; women would not be subjected to waiting periods or other efforts to dissuade them from having an abortion; military women serving outside the United States would have access to abortions; and women denied access to an abortion or who are discriminated against while seeking an abortion would have legal redress.

President Barack Obama has called for "a fresh conversation on family planning, working to find areas of common ground to best meet the needs of women and families at home and around the world."[55] He has directed his "staff to reach out to those on all sides of this issue to achieve the goal of reducing unintended pregnancies." Such common ground has proven elusive. Despite studies showing that abstinence-only programs do not reduce teens' sexual activity or rates of unprotected sex,[56] Americans cannot agree on how to educate young people in their own country about sexual activity, and they certainly have not agreed on abortion policy. These topics remain key issues in the culture wars.

CONFRONTING VIOLENCE AGAINST WOMEN

Violence against women can take several forms. Broadly conceived, it includes rape and other forms of sexual assault and emotional as well physical abuse by intimate partners. It can also include sexual harassment.

Sexual Assault

Law enforcement reports provide an incomplete picture of rape and sexual assault because many victims do not report these crimes due to embarrassment and stigma. Based on a confidential survey that is probably the most widely cited study of the incidence of rape and sexual assault ever conducted in the United States, each year more than 300,000 women and nearly 93,000 men are raped.[57] The researchers also found that nearly 18 percent of women (one in six) and 3 percent of men (one in 33) had experienced a rape (defined as "forced vaginal, oral, and anal sex") or attempted rape in their lifetime.

In the 1970s a rape crisis movement developed that has substantially affected the way women and men are treated after being raped or sexually assaulted. Today, law enforcement agencies take reports of rape much more seriously and treat victims with greater respect and dignity. The judiciary is also more likely to prosecute such crimes. Every state now has a "rape shield" law or court policy that is used in criminal cases. Rape shield laws or policies prevent information about a victim's past sexual conduct or other behavior from being introduced in court. The extent of the protection varies. Some states allow more flexibility based on the information's relevance to the case in order to protect the rights of the accused.[58] In most states, rape shield laws do not apply in civil cases where victims may attempt to get monetary compensation from perpetrators. To protect victims' identities, many newspapers do not print their names.

Many communities have social service systems that help victims from the time the rape is reported until the case makes its way through court proceedings. Support services may also be provided at no cost as long as the victim wishes. Hospital emergency departments usually give rape cases top priority and may have private waiting areas for victims. "Rape kit" protocols have been established to ensure better evidence collection for use in prosecution. These protocols are really best described as evidence collection procedures, which can be intrusive, and are separate from medical care the victim may need. In some jurisdictions, sexual assault nurse examiners (SANEs), who are specifically trained to collect the evidence and be supportive of victims, are called.

Law enforcement agencies and district attorney's offices may have personnel or units dedicated to working on sex crime cases in order to build expertise in investigations and prosecutions. They may also have units that provide support services to victims. Sexual assault response teams (SARTs), composed of representatives of social service, law enforcement, prosecutorial, and other agency staff, are designed to see that victims are served appropriately and in a coordinated manner by all involved at each step in the process.[59]

Intimate Partner Violence

Domestic violence includes violence perpetrated against an intimate partner (heterosexual or same-sex) or any other family member. In the broadest sense, this violence can be physical, sexual, emotional, and include other forms of abuse such as denying a family member financial resources. It also includes stalking and threats of harm. Witnessing such violence can also be very harmful to children. This section focuses on what is often called spouse abuse or intimate partner violence to distinguish it from other forms of domestic or family violence.

A widely cited national study calls intimate partner violence "pervasive."[60] Of survey respondents, 25 percent of women and nearly 8 percent of men reported being raped or physically assaulted by an intimate partner (including a date) during their lifetime, with 1.5 percent of women and nearly one percent of men reporting an occurrence in the past year. Based on these data, each year in the United States, 1.5 million women and more than 800,000 men are raped or physically assaulted by an intimate partner. Many are victimized more than once in a year. In addition, approximately 500,000 women and nearly 200,000 men are stalked by an intimate partner or former intimate partner each year. The Bureau of Justice reports that in 2005, 1,181 women and 329 men were killed by an intimate partner.[61]

In the late 1970s, some states began to officially recognize that battered women were not receiving adequate legal protection, and they adopted the position that this amounted to gender discrimination.[62] All states now have some type of legislation to protect abused spouses. Battered spouses have two types of legal recourse: civil and criminal. Civil laws are used to "settle disputes between individuals and to compensate for injuries," while criminal laws are used to "punish acts which are disruptive of social order and to deter other similar acts."[63]

In the early 1980s, Duluth, Minnesota, introduced a policy of mandatory arrest in domestic violence cases, which many jurisdictions adopted. This approach requires arrest in cases where police officers have probable cause to believe that an individual has assaulted a current or previous intimate partner or family member. The police officer retains discretion to determine if there is probable cause to arrest, but if visible injuries are present, the officer must arrest the alleged perpetrator.

In 1984, the Minneapolis Domestic Violence Experiment tested whether mandatory arrest reduced subsequent domestic violence incidents compared to requiring the alleged perpetrator to leave for at least 8 hours, or advising the alleged perpetrator or the couple on how to resolve the situation.[64] A classic experimental design was used and the study was limited to misdemeanor minor assault cases, which constitute most domestic violence calls to police (serious injury cases were excluded). Arrest was the most effective approach, resulting in repeat incidents in 10 percent of cases in which police were called. Least effective was police requiring the alleged perpetrator to leave; 24 percent of these cases had repeat incidents. Victims also reported fewer repeat incidents following arrest.

Findings of the Minneapolis experiment were hailed "as among the most influential results ever generated by social science," but subsequent studies of mandatory arrest policies did not provide consistent results.[65] In some studies, the men arrested were more likely to engage in repeat violence. Since research methods used in these studies were not consistent, a study using a consistent methodology was designed to test mandatory arrest in five jurisdictions in various parts of the United States. Arrest was compared to other methods (mediation, being ordered to leave the scene, a warning, or a restraining order). Arrest was associated with less repeat offending, but the difference was statistically significant only for measures based on victims' reports, not for police reports. During the follow-up period, more than half of the men did not harm the woman again, and a minority reoffended, no matter which intervention they got. Personal characteristics such as the perpetrator's age and criminal record explained more of the variance in reoffending than did being arrested. The researchers did conclude, however, that there is "good evidence of a consistent and direct, though modest, deterrent effect of arrest on aggression."

Today, some states have a mandatory arrest policy; others use preferred arrest (arrest is preferred but not mandatory) or discretionary arrest (officers have more leeway in deciding to arrest).[66] A more recent and controversial policy is "dual arrest" in which both parties in domestic violence cases are arrested because the officer cannot determine who is at fault or believes both are at fault. (Many people think such policies are unfair because one party, often the woman in a heterosexual couple, may have been trying to defend herself.) Primary aggressor policies provide guidelines for identifying the true or main offender. A large study found that jurisdictions with primary aggressor policies or laws had 75 percent fewer dual arrests than those without such policies or laws. Only 2 percent of intimate violence cases in areas with primary aggressor policies resulted in dual arrests, but same-sex partners were much more likely to experience dual arrest than heterosexual couples. The same study found that mandatory arrest policies do increase the number of arrests, but they reduce the number of convictions, perhaps because prosecutors are overwhelmed with the number of cases referred to them. Thus a policy that produces what some consider a positive effect (more arrests) may result in an unintended negative consequence (fewer prosecutions). Identifying more effective approaches once officers are called is important, but even better is preventing the violence in the first place.

Victims may employ protective or restraining orders in an effort to prevent future violence against them. There has been controversy over whether these tools further enrage male partners and promote repeat assault. A Seattle study found that women with "permanent" orders (lasting about one year) were significantly less likely to report a subsequent assault to police than those with no order, while short-term orders were associated with greater likelihood of reporting psychological abuse (including stalking) to police.[67] Research on protective orders is difficult to conduct because victims cannot be randomly assigned to take out protective orders. According to a report for the National Institute of Justice, given "numerous studies indicating consistent victim satisfaction with orders, complimented by studies that have consistently found that orders do not appear to significantly increase the risk of reabuse and may deter some abusers," "victims should be encouraged to take out protective orders and retain them but should also be advised that the orders do not deter all abusers and may be more effective when accompanied by criminal prosecution of the abuser."[68]

Another issue concerns the effectiveness of treatment programs for batterers. A systematic review of court-ordered batterer intervention programs (BIPs), either cognitive-behavioral or psychoeducational programs, was conducted. Overall, experimental studies showed a modest reduction in official reports of domestic violence but no effect based on victims' reports. The results from quasiexperimental studies were mixed. Overall, the authors concluded that "the findings . . . raise doubts about the effectiveness of court-mandated batterer intervention programs in reducing re-assault among men convicted of misdemeanor domestic violence."[69]

Violence Against Women Act

The Violence Against Women Act (VAWA) is part of the Violent Crime Control and Law Enforcement Act of 1994. Prior to this law, the federal response to violence directed at women was considerably weaker. The National Office on Violence Against Women, part of the Department of

Justice, was created in 1995 and is responsible for oversight and implementation of the federal mandates included in VAWA. VAWA strengthens protective orders through interstate enforcement, prohibits those with restraining orders from possessing a firearm, and bolsters restitution orders and rape shield laws.

VAWA established the National Domestic Violence Hotline (1-800-799-SAFE). It also provided funds to strengthen and streamline the criminal justice system's approach to helping victims, including education for law enforcement officers, prosecutors, and judges, and to encourage pro-arrest policies and community policing techniques. Guidelines have also been developed to require sex offenders to register with local authorities.

VAWA encourages cooperation between the criminal justice system and agencies such as shelters for battered women, rape crisis programs, and victim-witness programs that have provided the front-line services to victims. The community response is crucial because women rely on local law enforcement agencies and courts for protection and to see that justice is served through setting appropriate bail, serving warrants, arresting suspects, and meting out appropriate punishment.

Many social service agencies that assist women, such as rape crisis centers, have small budgets and little consistent support. They can help only a fraction of those in need. Services for sexual assault and domestic violence victims are often crisis-oriented with insufficient long-term help in the form of transportation, housing, and other services such as psychotherapy for women, their children, and the perpetrators. Model programs for helping women who have experienced violence, particularly domestic violence, focus on providing comprehensive legal, medical, employment, housing, counseling, and child-related services to help women re-establish their lives. Domestic violence courts are another response to the problem (see Illustration 11.2).

ILLUSTRATION 11.2
Domestic Violence Courts in New York

WHAT ARE THEY?

Domestic violence victims face many barriers to safety and independence. Incomprehensible and complex court processes should not be among these barriers. Traditionally, victims had to face several judges in up to four different courtrooms to have their criminal, family, and matrimonial matters heard. These "one family/one judge" courts are designed to respond to the unique nature of domestic violence with one judge handling all criminal domestic violence cases and related family issues, such as custody, visitation, civil protection orders, and matrimonial actions. Integrating criminal and civil response systems is the critical next step in improving victim safety and offender accountability. IDV [integrated domestic violence] Courts hold offenders to a higher level of accountability by concentrating responsibility for defendant oversight in the hands of a single judge who can monitor compliance with court orders and program mandates. In addition, victims gain a greater voice in their cases and are better able to address critical family issues—such as safe visitation and timely support—that often impede safety and independence. Additionally, services to the victim are often on-site and coordinated. Currently, there are more than 40 integrated domestic violence courts operating in New York counties that include Rensselaer, Westchester, the Bronx, Rochester, Syracuse, Richmond, Queens, Tompkins, Erie, Franklin, and Suffolk. Additionally, the Center has provided national and international technical assistance in planning and implementing integrated domestic violence court responses.

HOW THEY WORK

Integrated domestic violence courts improve the handling of domestic violence cases through:

One Family/One Judge: A single presiding judge has been cross-trained to handle all matters—both criminal and civil—relating to a family. In the past, a Family Court judge might never hear about an order of protection issued in Criminal Court, or a Criminal Court judge might never learn about relevant issues that arise in Family Court. By concentrating responsibility with a single judge, the court speeds decision making, improves defendant accountability, enhances victim safety, and eliminates the potential for conflicting judicial orders.

Defendant Monitoring: By bringing all aspects of a domestic violence case before a single judge, the court increases coordination among criminal justice and community-based social service agencies. In addition, through scheduling regular compliance dates, the court keeps close tabs on defendants and responds quickly to allegations of noncompliance.

Informed Decision Making: By working with a wide spectrum of stakeholders—from civil attorneys, law enforcement, probation, and parole—judges gain greater access to necessary information.

Greater Efficiency: By handling both criminal and civil matters in a single hearing, the integrated domestic violence courts aims to reduce the number of court appearances for litigants. This speeds dispositions and streamlines the process for all participants.

Services for Victims: The court works closely with community based victim advocates to coordinate services for victims such as crisis counseling, housing, and job training.

Source: "Integrated Domestic Violence Courts in New York: What Are They?" (New York: Center for Court Innovation). Retrieved June 7, 2009, from http://www.courtinnovation.org/index.cfm?fuseaction=Page.ViewPage&PageID=604&currentTopTier2=true

Originally, VAWA allowed victims to sue perpetrators for monetary damages in federal court based on the premise that gender-based violence affects women's ability to engage in interstate commerce. In 2000, the U.S. Supreme Court overturned that provision saying that Congress had no business regulating "non-economic, violent criminal conduct based solely on [its] effect on interstate commerce."

VAWA was reauthorized in 2000 under the Victims of Trafficking and Violence Protection Act of 2000 (also called the Violence Against Women Act of 2000). Dating violence was added to the law, along with funds to educate and train law enforcement personnel about making arrests in dating violence cases. "Cyberstalking" was added to the definition of interstate stalking. A new grant program was added to develop transitional housing assistance for domestic violence victims. Elders who are abused, neglected, or exploited are now included as a protected group, along with funds for training law enforcement officers about elder abuse. New protections and services for battered immigrants were added, as well as a mandate for cracking down on human trafficking, especially with regard to "sex trade, slavery and slavery like conditions." VAWA was reauthorized again in 2005. In addition to continuing previous programs under the act, it expanded the definition of cyberstalking, added new housing provisions, provided the first federal funding stream for sexual assault programs, and broadened service provisions for children and teenagers.

Many women's organizations hail VAWA and its reauthorizations as a success story for women and children. Some men's organizations and conservative groups are critical of at least some aspects of the act. Respecting Accuracy in Domestic Abuse Reporting (RADAR) says VAWA "blatantly discriminates against men" because it fails to recognize that men are often the victims of domestic violence, judges may issue restraining orders on the word of a woman without sufficient evidence that violence has occurred, and it unjustly promotes the separation of men from their children.[70] The counterarguments are that women are overwhelming the victims of domestic violence and that men who are domestic violence victims can also seek assistance under VAWA.

Sexual Harassment

The Equal Pay Act, the Equal Credit Act, the Family and Medical Leave Act, and similar policies are important to women, but other areas of public policy require attention if women are to enjoy true economic and social equality. One of these issues is sexual harassment. The definition found in the Code of Federal Regulations and employed by the Equal Employment Opportunity Commission is:

> Unwelcome sexual advances, requests for sexual favors, and other verbal or physical conduct of a sexual nature constitute sexual harassment when
>
> 1. Submission to such conduct is made either explicitly or implicitly a term or condition of an individual's employment or admission to an academic program,
> 2. Submission to or rejection of such conduct is used as the basis for decisions affecting an individual's employment status or academic standing, or
> 3. Such conduct has the purpose or effect of substantially interfering with an individual's performance on the job or in the classroom, or creating an intimidating, hostile, or offensive work or study environment.[71]

Title VII of the Civil Rights Act of 1964 and Title IX of the 1972 Educational Amendments to the Act prohibit sexual harassment, but for many years, such behavior was considered harmless and was taken for granted. Public policy now recognizes the damaging effects of such behavior on women, men, and the workplace. Under the Civil Rights Act of 1991, those who suffer sexual harassment may collect from $50,000 to $300,000 in damages, depending on the size of the company involved. But making accusations of sexual harassment may involve risks, as evidenced by law professor Anita Hill when she accused then Supreme Court nominee and now Supreme Court Justice Clarence Thomas of such behavior. The poor treatment Hill received during Thomas' Senate confirmation hearings outraged many people. Since then, the number of harassment suits has increased, extending even to a U.S. president.

Among the publicized cases of sexual harassment was that of Dr. Frances Conley. She resigned her position at Stanford University Medical School after becoming fed up with the sexual harassment she and female medical students had endured over the years (she later returned to her job). The Navy's Tailhook scandal involved sexual behavior unbecoming servicemen or any men. Such behavior can cross the line into sexual assault.[72] In Tailhook's aftermath, the country learned of situations in other branches of the service in which women who did not go along with such behavior were denied career advancement or left the service altogether. It is probably no coincidence that once publicized, these scandals were followed by significant promotions of female military personnel, and roles and duties once off limits to women were expanded.

The U.S. Supreme Court's first major sexual harassment decision came in 1986 in *Meritor Savings Bank v. Vinson,* which stated that Title VII of the Civil Rights Act of 1964 does include sexual harassment. Some lower courts interpreted this decision rather narrowly, applying it only in situations where women were psychologically harmed or no longer able to work in that environment. The second major case came in 1993 when the Court broadened this interpretation. Teresa Harris first brought her sexual harassment case against Forklift Systems in the mid-1980s. Lower courts rejected her case because it did not meet the restrictive definition of sexual harassment they had adopted. Supreme Court Justice Ruth Bader Ginsburg countered, arguing that those of one gender should not be subjected to conditions in which they are treated differently from the other gender in the workplace. Justice Sandra Day O'Connor also noted that there should be recourse before the behavior becomes psychologically damaging and that sufficient proof should be that "the environment would be perceived, and is perceived, as hostile or abusive."

Sexual harassment cases are generally divided into two types. The "quid pro quo" type occurs when sexual favors are demanded or required as a basis for employment decisions. The "hostile environment type" occurs when sexual conduct unreasonably interferes with work performance. On the hostile environment type, controversial author, humanities professor, and self-described feminist Camille Paglia writes, "the fanatic overprotection of women is fast making us an infantile nation."[73]

In 1998, the Supreme Court ruled in the sexual harassment cases of *Burlington Industries v. Ellreth* and *Farragher v. City of Boca Raton.* In each case, the vote was 7 to 2 (Justices Thomas and Scalia dissented) that employers are liable for sexual harassment in both types of cases even if they did not know of the harassment and even if the threats or abuses were not acted on, as long as the harassment is pervasive or severe. The rulings also indicate that employers may limit their liability by showing that they took care to prevent or correct harassment and that the worker was unreasonable in not trying to correct the situation. In another case, the justices ruled that schools receiving federal funds can be sued for damages if a student sexually harasses another student and if the school is "deliberately indifferent" to the situation. Title IX of the Civil Rights Act allows schools the opportunity to correct problems. Title VII does not grant this stipulation to employers.

In 2008, the EEOC and state and local Fair Employment Practices Agencies that work in conjunction with the Commission received nearly 14,000 sexual harassment complaints (down from the nearly 16,000 received in 1998); men filed 16 percent of these complaints.[74] Nearly 12,000 cases were resolved, and $47 million in monetary benefits recovered, not including monetary benefits obtained through litigation. Although the definition of sexual harassment may be vague, court rulings have encouraged more employers to educate employees about the types of behaviors that may lead to lawsuits and have made them less tolerant of employees who engage in these behaviors.

A NEW ERA FOR GAY RIGHTS

Forty years ago, there was no "gay rights" agenda in this country, only the taboos placed on gay and lesbian relationships. Then, in 1969, a police raid on a gay bar called Stonewall, in Greenwich Village in New York City, set off riots that culminated in the birth of the gay rights movement. For some people, gay rights is more a moral or religious issue than a legal or political issue. This adds to the difficulties in reaching public policy solutions. But no matter how one defines it, the gay rights agenda now has the attention of the media, and federal, state, and local governments, including the judiciary.

An End to Sodomy Laws

For almost 20 years, the U.S. Supreme Court refused to hear gay rights cases, leaving sodomy laws (which make certain types of sexual acts illegal) and other laws affecting gay men and lesbians to the states. In 1985, the Court broke its silence and heard the case of *Oklahoma City Board of Education v. National Gay Task Force.* The case involved an Oklahoma law that permitted school boards to bar from employment teachers who publicly advocated homosexuality. The Gay Rights Task Force criticized the law as a First Amendment violation of free speech, while the Board of Education contended that the law was only concerned with those who publicly endorsed certain sexual acts between homosexuals. In its evenly divided 4-4 decision (Justice Powell was ill), the Supreme Court upheld a lower court's ruling that public school teachers cannot be forbidden from advocating homosexuality but that homosexuals can be prohibited from engaging in homosexual acts in public. Shortly after, in 1986, the U.S. Supreme Court dealt a serious setback to the rights of gay men and lesbians in its decision in *Bowers v. Hardwick* by refusing to strike down Georgia's sodomy law.[75]

In 1992, the Kentucky Supreme Court became the first since the *Hardwick* decision to overturn its state's anti-sodomy law when it ruled that the law violated its state's constitutional rights to privacy and equal protection. A decade later, the U.S. Supreme Court decided to hear the case of *Lawrence v. Texas.* Lawrence was arrested when police responded to a call, made by a third party at a private residence. Upon arrival, the police discovered Lawrence in a sexual relationship with another man. Both were arrested for violating Texas's sodomy law. Two lower courts upheld the men's prosecution. Then in March 2003, the U.S. Supreme Court delivered its historic ruling, overturning *Bowers v. Hardwick* by invoking the constitutional rights to privacy, equal protection, and due process. In doing so, the U.S. Supreme Court cited two previous decisions, *Romer* (1996) and *Casey* (1992). Drawing upon *Casey,* Justice Kennedy expressed the court's conclusion that "Our obligation is to define the liberty of all, not to mandate our own moral code," and that "It is a promise of the Constitution that there is a realm of personal liberty which the government may not enter." In *Romer,* the Court concluded that the case was "born of animosity toward the class of persons affected." The *Lawrence* decision asserted that "*Bowers* was not correct when it was decided, and it is not correct today.... Their [homosexuals'] right to liberty under the Due Process Clause gives them the full right to engage in their conduct without intervention of the government."

The decision was a major victory for the gay community. Civil rights groups hailed it as a huge step forward. At the time of the *Lawrence* decision, 13 states still had anti-sodomy laws. The *Lawrence* decision invalidated these laws, giving consenting adults of the same gender the same rights of intimate sexual expression as those of the opposite gender.

Expanding the Gay Rights Agenda

The gay rights agenda has moved well beyond freedom of sexual expression. Various municipalities have addressed gay and lesbian rights in employment, housing, and other matters, with cities such as San Francisco and St. Louis leading the way in passing antidiscrimination measures. In 1992 there was a flurry of state activity over gay rights, much of it spurred by fundamentalist Christians and other conservative groups. A Colorado law attempted to prohibit the state from enacting gay rights protections and would have caused the repeal of existing local laws supporting gay rights, but the state's supreme court declared it unconstitutional. The U.S. Supreme Court concurred that the law violated the U.S. Constitution's equal protection clause. This marked a first for the high court in treating gay rights as a civil rights issue. When Oregonians failed to approve a tough anti-gay state law that would have condemned homosexuality and forbidden protections to gay men and lesbians, some Oregon towns adopted their own anti-gay measures. In 1997, Maine joined ten other states and the District of Columbia with laws supporting gay rights. Sexual orientation was added to the state's laws banning discrimination in employment, housing, credit, and public accommodations. In 1998 anti-gay forces were successful in overturning the Maine law at the polls.

As of February 2010, 21 states and the District of Columbia ban employment discrimination based on sexual orientation and 12 of these states and the District of Columbia also ban employment discrimination based on gender identity (designed to protect those who are transgendered).[76] These laws pertain to both public and private employers, although there may be some exceptions.

Bill Clinton was the first president to address gay rights. He issued a directive banning discrimination against federal employees who are gay. Most federal agencies already had similar nondiscrimination policies. The executive order was intended to make the policies uniform. A 1998 challenge to the order failed in the House of Representatives.

There is still no federal law that protects all employees, regardless of where they work, from discrimination based on sexual orientation and gender identity. The Employment Non-Discrimination Act (ENDA) was first introduced to Congress in 1994. It has gained support but has yet to pass.[77] The current version includes both sexual orientation and gender identity.

As of June 2009, 31 states and the District of Columbia have hate crime statutes that include sexual orientation; 12 states and the District of Columbia also include gender identity as a protected class.[78] Hate crime statutes generally add enhancements (extra penalties) to existing laws if the victim is targeted because he or she is a member of a racial, religious, or other group.

Many advocates feel that the lack of laws protecting the rights of gay men, lesbians, bisexuals, and transgendered individuals and laws that deny them protections not only make them targets for discrimination but also for physical attacks or other hate crimes. The brutal murder of Matthew Shepard, a gay man, in Laramie, Wyoming, is a dramatic example of a hate crime. In 2008, the FBI reported a total of nearly 7,800 hate crimes; of them, about 17 percent were attributed to the victim's sexual orientation.[79] Opponents of hate crime laws believe that bills that include special classes of people are unfair because they do not treat all classes of people equally. Proponents believe that such legislation is needed to root out the discrimination that certain classes of people continue to suffer. In 2009, Congress passed an expanded hate crimes law that includes actual or perceived gender, sexual orientation, and gender identity. It also includes crimes that target people based on disability. A *Washington Post* staff writer called efforts to pass the bill "a decade-long proxy war between liberal groups that want to expand gay rights and conservative groups that do not."[80] President Obama signed the bill, saying that "No one in America should ever be afraid to walk down the street holding the hands of the person they love."

Domestic Partnerships and Same-Sex Marriage

Perhaps the hottest issue on the gay rights agenda is same-sex marriage. Opponents believe that marriage is a sacred union between a man and a woman and that same-sex marriage would harm the institution of marriage. Supporters believe that a same-sex marriage prohibition violates the U.S. Constitution's equal protection provisions and prevents some individuals from enjoying the benefits of marriage. They point to the lack of credible evidence that the institution of marriage would be harmed by allowing people of the same sex to marry.

In the late 1980s, a handful of cities decided to extend bereavement leave to domestic partners not in traditional marriages, including gay and lesbian partners. Since then, the number of municipal governments and private companies (IBM, American Express, and Walt Disney Co. are among them) extending healthcare or other benefits to the live-in partners of employees, both gay and straight, has grown. In 2008, the Human Rights Campaign reported that nearly 9,400 companies offered some type of domestic partner benefits, with the largest employers more likely to offer them.[81]

In 1996, a judge ordered the state of Oregon to provide insurance benefits to the domestic part-ners of its gay workers, saying that doing otherwise was discriminatory and violated the state's consti-tution. In June 2002 President George W. Bush signed the Mychal Judge Police and Fire Chaplains Public Safety Officers' Benefit Act of 2002, providing federal payments to beneficiaries of public safety officers killed in the line of duty on September 11, 2001. The bill was named after the New York Fire Department chaplain killed in the September 11th terrorist attacks. It allowed benefits to be paid to same-sex partners if there was no surviving spouse or children. The inclusion of same-sex partners in this federal law was modeled after a similar state law passed in New York in May 2002. Eighteen states and the District of Columbia offer some type of same-sex partner benefits to state employees.[82]

In June 2009, President Obama extended a few same-sex partner benefits to federal employees, but the federal Defense of Marriage Act prevents offering health insurance and retire-ment or survivor's benefits to them. While recognition of domestic- or same-sex partnerships in these ways is a start, these provisions, and even legally recognized civil unions, are not the same as marriage. Many same-sex partners are still not recognized as next-of-kin in making healthcare and other important decisions for each other should the need arise, and they are restricted in many other family matters such as custody and adoption. Americans disagree, however, about whether it is time to permit same-sex marriages.

In 1991, two lesbian couples and a gay male couple sued the state of Hawaii because it refused to issue them a marriage license. A number of U.S. Congress members became alarmed that Hawaii might legalize such unions and that the U.S. Constitution's "full faith and credit clause" might require other states to recognize same-sex marriages performed in Hawaii or other states. In response, Congress eventually passed the Defense of Marriage Act (DOMA) in 1996. DOMA does not prohibit states from recognizing or legalizing same-sex marriages. It does say that states cannot be forced to recognize such unions performed in other states. Although Hawaii's courts upheld same-sex marriages, in 1998, voters in Hawaii, and also in Alaska, failed to approve them.

In 2000, the Vermont Supreme Court ruled that denying homosexual couples the same benefits of married couples violated the Common Benefits Clause of the Vermont Constitution. Vermont's high court ordered the legislature to craft appropriate legislation to meet the constitu-tional mandate, warning that failure to do so would open the way for the plaintiffs to again peti-tion the court for the right to marry. The legislature responded with a law, effective January 1, 2005, that recognized civil unions (but not marriage) for gay and lesbian couples and provided them with all the "benefits and burdens" of married couples. In April 2009, the Vermont legisla-ture became the first state legislature to approve same-sex marriage. The bill garnered enough support from legislators to override the Republican governor's veto.

In November 2003, the New Jersey Supreme Court upheld that state's gay marriage ban. In essence, the court found that marriage is a fundamental right, but not when the parties are of the same sex, suggesting that there can be two standards of civil rights, one for opposite-sex couples and one for same-sex couples.[83] In April 2004, 13 same-sex couples sued the state of New York, claiming that denying them access to marriage denied their basic civil rights.[84]

In 2003, seven same-sex couples also petitioned the Massachusetts Supreme Court for the right to marry. Unlike Vermont, the Massachusetts Constitution does not have a Common Benefits Clause; therefore, the court had to consider the case on the basis of marriage as an institution, and not marital benefits. The Massachusetts court denounced the exclusion of same-sex partners from the right to marry and concluded that assigning a different status to same-sex unions by using a civil unions provision in effect relegates same-sex partners to a "second-class status." The Massachusetts Supreme Court stated that denial of the right to marry "works a deep and scarring hardship on a very real segment of the community for no rational reason." It gave the state legislature 180 days to respond with appropriate legislation. The state legislature tried to sidestep the marriage mandate by passing a bill that provided the right to civil union with "all the benefits, protections, rights and responsibilities" of marriage, but the court said "no," declaring same-sex couples would not only be denied the "full protection of the laws," they would also be "excluded from the full range of human experience." On May 1, 2004, Massachusetts became the first state to issue marriage licenses to same-sex couples.

Civil unions and gay marriage have been issues in California for many years. In 2000, voters approved Proposition 22; it affirmed that "only marriage between a man and a woman is valid in California." But the state began offering domestic partnerships in that year. In 2005, these unions became nearly equivalent to marriage.

In February 2004, San Francisco Mayor Gavin Newsom directed the county clerk to begin issuing marriage license to same-sex couples, claiming that to do otherwise violates due process and equal protection clauses of the state of California's Constitution. In the days following the directive, 3,000 same-sex couples were married. The problem was that the state of California defined marriage as a civil contract between a man and a woman.

In May 2008, the California Supreme Court overturned the state's gay marriage ban, and that June same-sex couples began marrying. But anti-gay forces were able to get the issue before voters. Gay marriage supporters raised $38 million and opponents $32 million in the hotly contested issue over what was called Proposition 8.[85] In November 2008, Californians rejected gay marriage with a 52 percent majority. The 18,000 marriages of same-sex couples already performed were allowed to stand. The California battle continued in a federal trial over the ban's constitutionality. (The U.S. Supreme Court ruled 5 to 4 that the trial would not be broadcast because those testifying against gay marriage might suffer "irreparable harm."[86]) In August 2010, the federal judge ruled the ban unconstitutional saying it violated equal protection and due process clauses. The case will likely reach the U.S. Supreme Court.

In 2006, Arizona voters defeated a gay marriage ban, but in 2008, Arizona voters and New Jersey voters enacted constitutional amendments against same-sex marriages. In Maine in 2009, voters rejected a law passed earlier that year legalizing same-sex marriage.

With pressure from the far right, President George W. Bush called for an amendment to the U.S. Constitution banning same-sex marriage. The Federal Marriage Act, introduced to the Senate on March 22, 2004, was intended to do that. Civil rights groups said that if such an amendment were ratified, it would be the first time a discriminatory measure had been written into the U.S. Constitution. President Bush called "the union of a man and a woman...the most enduring human institution, honored and encouraged in all cultures and by every religious faith." He claimed that "marriage cannot be severed from its cultural, religious and natural roots without weakening the good influence of society."[87] The Log Cabin Republicans (a group of gay Republicans) took exception. The president was accused of using the issue to fuel his reelection campaign, but he did endorse the right of same-sex couples to form civil unions, causing some backlash from conservatives.

As of late June 2010, prompted by either a state supreme court decision or through legislative action, four northeastern states, Connecticut, Massachusetts, New Hampshire, and Vermont, and one heartland state, Iowa, as well as the District of Columbia, permit same-sex couples to marry.[88] Most other states have statutes, constitutional language, or both banning same-sex marriage, but five of them allow same-sex unions that are very similar to marriage. The country can expect much more political activity on same-sex marriage.

Child Custody and Adoption

Many gays, lesbians, bisexuals, and transgendered people have biological children. They are generally entitled to the same child custody rights as other parents, although "courts and agencies in [some] states retain discretion to consider a parent's sexual orientation in adoption and custody disputes."[89] There is no credible evidence that sexual orientation affects one's ability to be a good parent. In a democracy it seems that any court decision about suitability for parenting would be made on an individual basis; however, deciding who is entitled to adopt children or become a foster parent is a state matter, and states' laws and policies in these areas differ.[90]

Most states allow single people to adopt regardless of their sexual orientation as long as they meet criteria for being an adoptive parent. States' policies are less consistent and often less clear on joint adoption and second-parent adoptions. Joint adoption occurs when an unmarried couple (domestic partners) adopts a child together. A second-parent adoption occurs when a parent has custody of a child (biological or adopted) and his or her partner adopts the child, giving both parental rights. A second-parent adoption helps ensure that the partner will have custody should the first parent die or be unable to care for the child. (A second-parent adoption cannot take place if the child already has two parents with legal rights to him or her.)

A few states (e.g., Illinois, New Jersey, New York) clearly permit both joint and second-parent adoptions. In 2000, the New Jersey Supreme Court ruled that same-sex partners who raise a child have the same custody rights as other parents. A few states clearly disagree. For example, in 1977, the Florida legislature passed a law prohibiting gays and lesbians (singles or couples) from adopting, and in November 2008, Arkansas voters passed Act 1 prohibiting unmarried couples, gay or straight, from adopting or being foster parents. In January 2004, the 11th U.S. Circuit Court of Appeals upheld Florida's ban on gay adoption, ruling that it did not violate the Constitution's due process and equal protection clauses. The U.S. Supreme Court refused to hear the case, but in November 2008, a Miami-Dade circuit court judge ruled that the law is not in children's best interest and violated the equal protections that should be afforded children and prospective adoptive parents.[91] As of late June 2010, the state was awaiting a ruling on its appeal of the decision.

States' laws or policies about who can be a foster parent have also been debated. Given the dire need for foster and adoptive parents (see Chapter 10), gay and lesbian individuals and couples have been called an underutilized resource who can give children the homes they need and deserve while saving governments money.[92]

Gays in the Military: Don't Ask, Don't Tell

Another hotly debated gay rights issue is service in the military and in national security positions. In 1949, the U.S. Department of Defense implemented a rule intended to prevent gay men and lesbians from serving in the military. For several decades there was no major policy change. In 1988 the U.S. Supreme Court did tell the Central Intelligence Agency that it could not dismiss a gay man without justifying the reason for its action, but the Court avoided the issue of whether gay men and lesbians have employment rights under the Fourteenth Amendment (equal protection clause) of the U.S. Constitution, including the right to serve in the military.

Beginning in the early 1990s, some things began to change. In 1991 the case of Sergeant Perry Watkins, a gay soldier, was settled after years in court when he was awarded back pay, an honorable discharge, and full retirement benefits. In 1992 a federal judge ordered the Navy to reinstate Petty Officer Keith Meinhold, who stated he is gay, but the ruling was based on a technicality and hardly settled the question of gays in the military.

As the various branches of the military faced increasing pressure to stop discriminating against gay men and lesbians, President Clinton's desire to drop the ban caused a heated national debate that included some serious Democratic opposition to lifting the ban. The President of the United States is also commander-in-chief of the armed forces, and Clinton could have overturned the ban. So much furor arose that rather than lift the ban himself, President Clinton attempted to use the well-known political strategies of negotiation and compromise. In 1993, Congress passed U.S. Code Title 10, Subtitle G, Section 654 "Policy Concerning Homosexuality in the Armed Forces," with bipartisan support. It states, "The prohibition against homosexual conduct is a longstanding element of military law that continues to be necessary in the unique circumstances of military service." The law was also dubbed "don't ask, don't tell, don't pursue" because as part of the compromise, recruits are not to be asked to reveal their sexual orientation, and investigations to determine service members' sexual orientation without cause that sexual conduct codes have been violated are prohibited.[93] The guidelines also prohibit harassment of gay and lesbian military personnel, but homosexual conduct can be grounds for discharge. According to Pentagon guidelines, the definition of homosexual conduct includes acknowledgment of being gay, lesbian, or bisexual. In many circumstances, physical contact, such as holding hands and kissing, can also be construed as homosexual conduct. However, going to gay bars, marching in gay rights demonstrations in civilian attire, or having gay publications would generally not be considered homosexual conduct.

Although President Clinton intended for a new spirit to be reflected in the policy, one view is that the regulations broadened the definition of homosexual conduct and resulted in more discharges.[94] The number discharged peaked at 1,227 in 2001, falling to about half that number in years 2006 to 2008 (since 1993 about 13,000 service members have been discharged for being gay).[95] Some claim that the numbers have dropped because of the need for troops to fight the Iraq and Afghanistan wars.[96]

The courts have not ruled consistently on gays in the military. Some judges take the view that the military has a vested interest in keeping gays and lesbians from serving. Others believe Congress and the president should decide. The U.S. Supreme Court has not resolved the issue. In June 2009, it refused to hear a challenge to the current policy.

Everyone knows that gay men and lesbians are serving honorably in the military. In 1999, a ruling by a European Court of Human Rights forced Britain to allow those who are openly gay or lesbian to serve in the military. A number of European countries allow those who are openly gay to serve in the military. Gay rights advocates in the United States are vehement that sexual orientation is not related to service and using it to exclude qualified individuals is discriminatory.

Opposition to gays serving in the military has not abated. In 2009, more than 1,000 retired officers signed a letter to President Obama asking him to let the ban against gays serving in the military stand. The *Washington Post* published a letter from four of these retired officers reiterating arguments about sexual attraction in close living quarters, diminished team cohesion, and negative effects on recruitment and reenlistment.[97]

President Obama promised to see that the ban was lifted. Gay rights advocates were critical when he did not act on his promise soon after taking office. The new president called for a study to determine the effects on the military and to increase Congressional support for lifting the ban.[98] In his 2010 state of the union message, President Obama stepped up his language to make good on ending the ban. Now it looks as though Congress will soon allow Pentagon officials to end the ban and permit gays to serve openly in the military. Illustration 11.3 provides an

ILLUSTRATION 11.3
Writing Congress About "Don't Ask, Don't Tell"

This is an example of The Human Rights Campaign's efforts to encourage Congress to allow gay men and lesbians to serve openly in the military.

Tell Congress it's time to put an end to "Don't Ask, Don't Tell."

In his State of the Union address, President Obama pledged to work with the Congress and military this year to repeal "Don't Ask, Don't Tell" (DADT).

To make this a reality, we need to capitalize on this momentum immediately. Ask your representative to sponsor legislation to repeal "Don't Ask, Don't Tell" and to move the bill swiftly!

MESSAGE

Please help end "Don't Ask, Don't Tell"

Dear [Decision Maker],

[Please personalize your message]

As your constituent, I urge you to move quickly to repeal the discriminatory "Don't Ask, Don't Tell" law.

The House legislation to repeal the ban, the Military Readiness Enhancement Act (H.R. 1283), will hopefully be echoed by a similar bill in the Senate soon. I ask that I can count on your support to repeal the "Don't Ask, Don't Tell" law.

Although the main purpose of this legislation is to repeal the U.S. military's "Don't Ask, Don't Tell" law so that lesbian and gay troops would be allowed to serve openly, the bill is much more than a civil rights law. It is a bill that would protect national security and strengthen our military, while saving taxpayers and our armed forces millions of dollars and countless resources that could be put to better use.

Military readiness is enhanced when every qualified American who wants to serve in the military is allowed to do so. It is estimated that at least 66,000 lesbian and gay Americans are currently serving in the U.S. military. More than 13,000 have already been discharged under "Don't Ask, Don't Tell." Given the current needs of the armed forces, which are already stretched thin and are facing serious problems in recruiting and retaining troops, we must repeal the law that keeps able-bodied Americans from serving.

"Don't Ask, Don't Tell" weakens our national security. According to a report released by the General Accounting Office, nearly 800 specialists with critical skills have been fired, including more than 300 linguists, more than 60 of whom specialized in Arabic. It has been estimated that enforcement of this law has cost between $290 million and half a billion, although that number does not include costs associated with discharging officers or other highly skilled specialists. Not included in the GAO report are the estimated 4,000 service members who choose not to reenlist each year because of the law, or the effects that ripping a service member away from the unit so unnecessarily can have on cohesion, morale, or combat readiness. The GAO report is further evidence that "Don't Ask, Don't Tell" must be repealed.

Please support our Armed Forces by supporting this critical legislation. I look forward to receiving your response.

Sincerely,

[Your Name]

[Your Address]

[City, State ZIP]

Source: Human Rights Campaign, "A National Campaign to Repeal 'Don't Ask, Don't Tell.'" Retrieved February 9, 2010, from https://secure3.convio.net/hrc/site/Advocacy?cmd=display&page=UserAction&id=673 Reprinted by permission of Here Media, Inc.

example of how one organization has encouraged advocates to contact Congress members to repeal the ban.

Gay, Lesbian, Bisexual, and Transgendered Youth

Many states lack laws that specifically protect gay, lesbian, bisexual, and transgendered (GLBT) youth,[99] although many school districts are demonstrating increased sensitivity to the needs of GLBT youth and youth unsure of their sexual identity. Most important is seeing that every child is safe at school. In many areas, the history of tolerance and acceptance has been rocky at best.

In 1996, the Salt Lake City School Board terminated all student groups on campus rather than allow a gay organization because the federal Equal Access Act of 1984, which arose to support Bible groups, also seemed to support the gay student organization.[100] The Utah legislature came to the school board's aid with a law supporting the board's efforts to outlaw gay student groups. In 1997, a federal appeals court invalidated an Alabama law barring lesbian, gay, and bisexual student groups from university campuses on the grounds that it was unenforceable because it violated the students' First Amendment rights.[101] In Kentucky, in 2004, a district court found in favor of students wanting to form a gay-straight alliance club, declaring that the school district must treat all student clubs equally and conduct anti-harassment training for all middle and high school staff and students.

GLBT students also face discrimination in other areas. The ACLU reports that it often gets calls from students saying they are not allowed to have same sex prom dates or that girls cannot wear tuxedos to the prom or school dances despite court decisions to the contrary.[102] For example, in the 1980 case of *Fricke vs. Lynch,* a district court ruled that prohibiting a student from bringing a same-sex date to the prom was a free speech violation.

Decisions in other lawsuits also support GLBT students' rights to be free from harassment. For example, in 1998, Alana Flores, a bisexual high school student, complained after receiving graphic death threats on her school locker.[103] The assistant principal told her to return to class, saying, "Don't bring me this trash anymore, this is disgusting." After years of harassment, threats, and physical violence, Alana and several of her classmates sued the school for ignoring and promoting homophobia that led to harassment and violence. The students' suit sought damages and training for district personnel and students. Six years later, the 9th District Court of Appeals found in favor of the students.

Gay students continue to file lawsuits over discrimination. Lawyers often invoke federal protection rights to win their suits (generally Title IX of the Education Amendments Act of 1972, the Equal Protection Clause of the U.S. Constitution, and the Equal Access Act of 1984). In 2009, the American Civil Liberties Union sued two Tennessee school districts claiming it unconstitutionally blocked access to online information about GLBT issues.[104] Apparently, they permitted access to anti-GLBT speech but not pro-GLBT speech, such as the websites of Parents, Families, And Friends of Lesbians and Gays (PFLAG), the Gay Lesbian Straight Education Network (GLSEN), and the Human Rights Campaign (HRC).

The Boy Scouts of America's credo requires that members be "morally straight." In 2000, the U.S. Supreme Court ruled 5–4 that the Boy Scouts, a private organization, could exclude gay members and leaders. The Lambda Legal Defense and Education Fund, the Human Rights Campaign, the American Civil Liberties Union, and other organizations are working to end discrimination based on sexual orientation.

Summary

Women won the right to vote in 1920, but an Equal Rights Amendment to the U.S. Constitution has eluded them. In recent decades, the executive, legislative, and judicial branches of government have come to recognize the serious consequences of abuses such as domestic violence and sexual harassment. Other recent efforts to secure equality for women include passage of the Family and Medical Leave Act of 1993. A particularly contentious issue is abortion. The U.S. Supreme Court has upheld the right of women to abortions since its 1973 decision in *Roe v. Wade,* but in recent years, abortion rights have been threatened by some court decisions and state and federal legislation that limits access to abortions.

The rights of gay men, lesbians, bisexuals, and transgendered people have made their way to the public policy agenda. Gay men and lesbians have made some progress on the state and local level in gaining equal treatment, and the U.S. Supreme Court finally overturned state sodomy laws. The much watered-down version of a policy allowing gay men and lesbians to serve in the military, and efforts to ban antidiscrimination laws for gay men and lesbians, attest to the deep-seated controversies that remain over the gay rights agenda in this country. Marriage of same-sex couples has not only made its way to the public policy agenda, a handful of states now allow same-sex couples to marry.

Discussion Questions and Class Activities

1. Compare and contrast the views of groups with different perspectives on women and family issues such as the National Organization for Women and the Eagle Forum. Think about your own views on issues such as an equal rights amendment and reproductive rights. How did you arrive at those views? Have your views changed over time? If so, what influenced those changes? You may wish to invite a panel of women from different age cohorts to class to discuss their views of sexism and feminism, discrimination against women, and the progress women have made in gaining equality.

2. Look at where your state or community ranks with respect to issues such as pay equity and legal protections for women. Information on this topic can be found at websites of organizations such as the Institute for Women's Policy Research. Have a class discussion on what efforts might increase equity and legal protections at this juncture in the nation's and your state's history, including whether an Equal Rights Amendment to the U.S. Constitution is needed.

3. Invite local law enforcement officers to class to discuss their agency's arrest policy in cases of domestic violence and a prosecutor to discuss his or her work in domestic violence cases. Do their agencies have special units or staff that handle domestic violence cases? Does the community have a domestic violence court? You may wish to sit in on some domestic violence court proceedings or invite a judge who hears these cases to class. You may also wish to invite representatives of the local battered women's shelter or other domestic violence agencies to discuss their work and the community's response to domestic violence victims, and invite domestic violence survivors to discuss their experiences with the legal and social service systems.

4. Invite community professionals to discuss the way rape and sexual assault cases are addressed in your community. Do law enforcement agencies and the prosecutor's office have a special sex crimes unit or personnel that specialize in these cases? What types of rape crisis or sexual assault services are available? Is there a rape crisis agency, a sexual assault response team (SART), sexual assault nurse examiners (SANEs), or other specialized services? What is the "rape shield law" in your state or the court's policy on this issue? You may also wish to invite rape survivors to discuss their experiences with the legal and social service systems.

5. Have a class discussion on gay rights. Debate various policy issues such as whether same-sex couples should have the right to marry, or whether openly gay individuals should be allowed to serve in the military. If your state legislature is considering same-sex marriage, attend committee meetings or hearings on the issue. Invite a representative of one or more advocacy groups working on these issues to discuss the strategies they are using to promote or defeat gay rights legislation. You may also wish to invite lesbian, gay, bisexual, or transgendered individuals to discuss their experiences with discrimination and the ways they have addressed

these experiences on an individual level and through groups, organizations, and the political process.

6. Ask local school district personnel if they believe bullying or other harassment of gay, lesbian, bisexual, or transgender students is a problem. Determine what policies or programs are in place to see that students are treated fairly and protected from bullying or other unfair treatment based on what their sexual orientation or gender identity is or is perceived to be. How effective do they believe these policies and programs are in promoting fair treatment

7. Does your state or community have a hate crimes law? If so, what groups are covered? Discuss whether hate crimes laws are needed, that is, whether any group should be singled out for special protection and whether criminal penalties should be enhanced when a crime is targeted at an individual or individuals due to gender or sexual orientation or at a group or organization based on its views of gender or sexual orientation.

Websites

GLSEN, the Gay, Lesbian and Straight Education Network, http://www.glsen.org/cgi-bin/iowa/all/home/index.html, is a national education organization dedicated to ensuring that schools are safe for all students regardless of their sexual orientation or gender identity/expression and are places where difference and diversity are valued for the positive contributions they make to society.

Human Rights Campaign, http://www.hrc.org/, is a national civil rights organization that works to promote equal rights for gay, lesbian, bisexual, and transgendered individuals and their families, supports candidates who share its values, and educates the public about GLBT issues.

Institute for Women's Policy Research, http://www.iwpr.org/index.cfm, is an independent, nonprofit organization that conducts research to address the needs of women, families, and society. It focuses on issues of poverty and welfare, employment and

earnings, work and family issues, health and safety, and women's civic and political participation.

Lambda Legal, http://www.lambdalegal.org/, is a national civil rights organization that works to promote equal rights for lesbian, gay, bisexual, and transgendered individuals and those with HIV and their families through education, public policy, and litigation.

League of Women Voters, http://www.lwv.org//AM/Template.cfm?Section=Home, is a nonpartisan, grassroots, political organization working at national, state, and local levels to improve government and public policies through citizen education and advocacy.

National Organization for Women (NOW), http://www.now.org/, is a feminist organization that works for women's equality through efforts to end discrimination, harassment, and violence in all sectors of society, secure reproductive rights, and eradicate racism, sexism, and homophobia.

Notes

1. Diana Pearce, "The Feminization of Poverty: Women, Work, and Welfare," *The Urban and Social Change Review* (Special Issue on Women and Work), Vol. 11, 1978, pp. 28–36, 1978. Republished in Vol. 4, Women's Studies Yearbook, *Working Women and Families* (Thousand Oaks, CA: Sage, 1979).

2. See, for example, Barbara J. Nelson, "The Origins of the Two-Channel Welfare State: Workmen's Compensation and Mothers' Aid," in Linda Gordon, Ed.,

Women, the State, and Welfare (Madison: University of Wisconsin Press, 1990), pp. 123–150.

3. For discussions of feminist theories, see books such as Linda Nicholson, *The Second Wave: A Reader in Feminist Theory* (New York: Routledge, 1997); Christine Flynn Saulnier, *Feminist Theories and Social Work: Approaches and Applications* (Binghamton, NY: Haworth Press, 1996).

4. For information on the wage gap, see National Committee on Pay Equity, "The Wage Gap Over

Time: In Real Dollars, Women See a Continuing Gap" (Washington, DC: Author, August, 2008). Retrieved May 30, 2009, from http://www.pay-equity .org/info-time.html

5. U.S. Bureau of Labor Statistics, "Highlights of Women's Earnings in 2008" (Washington, DC: U.S. Department of Labor, July 2009). Retrieved June 1, 2010, from http://www.bls.gov/cps/cpswom2008.pdf

6. Evelyn Murphy, *Getting Even: Why Women Don't Get Paid Like Men and What to Do About It* (New York: Touchstone, 2005).

7. Catherine Hill and Sarah Warbelow, "Tenure Denied: Cases of Sex Discrimination in Academia," *American Academic,* Vol. 4, March, 2008, pp. 65–104.

8. U.S. Census Bureau, *The 2010 Statistical Abstract,* Table 603. Employed Civilians by Occupation, Sex, Race, and Hispanic Origin: 2008. Retrieved June 1, 2010, from http://www.census.gov/compendia/ statab/2010/tables/10s0603.pdf

9. U.S. Census Bureau, *The 2010 Statistical Abstract,* Table 59. Households, Families, Subfamilies, and Married Couples: 1980 to 2008. Retrieved June 1, 2010, from http://www.census.gov/compendia/ statab/2010/tables/10s0059.pdf

10. See Rebecca A. Clay, "Making Working Families Work," *APA Monitor on Psychology,* Vol. 36, No. 11, December 2005, p. 54.

11. U.S. Census Bureau, "Educational Attainment, 2005-2007." Retrieved May 30, 2009, from http:// factfinder.census.gov/servlet/STTable?_bm=y&-geo_ id–01000US&-qr_name=ACS_2007_3YR_G00_ S1501&-ds_name=ACS_2007_3YR_G00_

12. Denise Venable, "The Wage Gap Myth" (Dallas, TX: National Center for Policy Analysis, April 12, 2002). Retrieved May 31, 2009, from http://www.ncpa.org/ pub/ba392

13. The remainder of this paragraph relies on Rosemary Hays-Thomas, "Pay Equity," *Encyclopedia* (Chestnut Hill, MA: Boston College, The Sloan Work and Family Research Network, September 7, 2006). Retrieved May 31, 2009, from http://wfnetwork .bc.edu/new/encyclopedia_entry.php?id=3829&area =All

14. Marisa DiNatale and Stephanie Boraas, "The Labor Force Experience of Women from 'Generation X,'" *Monthly Labor Review,* March 2002, pp. 3-15. Retrieved February 5, 2010, from http://www.bls. gov/opub/mlr/2002/03/art1full.pdf

15. M. Anne Hill and Mark R. Killingsworth, Eds., *Comparable Worth: Analyses and Evidence* (Ithaca, NY: ILR Press, New York State School of Industrial and Labor Relations, Cornell University, 1989); Elaine Sorensen, *Comparable Worth: Is It a Worthy Policy?* (Princeton, NJ: Princeton University Press, 1994).

16. Linda Chavez, "Comparable Worth," *The Wall Street Journal,* August 27, 2005. Retrieved May 31, 2009, from http://www.opinionjournal.com/editorial/ feature.html?id=110007168

17. Hays-Thomas, "Pay Equity."

18. See, for example, David Theroux, "'Comparable Worth' Harms Women and Minorities," *The Beacon,* February 2, 2009. Retrieved May 31, 2009, from http://www.independent.org/blog/?p=1137

19. "Pay Equity and Comparable Worth" (Saint Paul: Minnesota Management and Budget, 2005–2009). Retrieved June 1 2009, from http://www.mmb.state .mn.us/comp-pay-equity

20. National Committee on Pay Equity, "Two Progressive Models on Pay Equity: Minnesota and Ontario" (Washington, DC: Author, no date). Retrieved June 2, 2010, from http://www.pay-equity .org/PDFs/ProgressiveModels.pdf

21. June Ellenoff O'Neill, "Comparable Worth," *The Concise Encyclopedia of Economics* (Indianapolis: Liberty Fund, 2002). Retrieved June 1, 2010, from http://www.econlib .org/library/Enc1/ComparableWorth.html

22. "IWF Busts the Wage Gap" (Washington DC: Independent Women's Forum, June 1, 2001). Retrieved June 1, 2009, from http://www.iwf.org/ iwfmedia/show/18729.html

23. "The History of Affirmative Action Policies," *In Motion Magazine* (Washington, DC: Americans for a Fair Chance, October 12, 2003). Retrieved June 1, 2009, from http://www.inmotionmagazine.com/aahist.html

24. "Still a Man's Labor Market: The Long-term Earnings Gap" (Washington, DC: Institute for Women's Policy Research, February 2008). Retrieved June 7, 2009, from http://www.iwpr.org/pdf/C366_RIB.pdf

25. Heidi Hartmann, Olga Sorokina, and Erica Williams "The Best and Worst State Economies for Women" (Washington, DC: Institute for Women's Policy Research, December 2006). Retrieved June 7, 2009, from http://www.iwpr.org/pdf/R334_BWState Economies2006.pdf

26. Information in this paragraph relies on Center for American Women and Politics, Eagleton Institute of Politics, "Women in Elective Office 2009" (New Brunswick, NJ: Rutgers, The State University of New Jersey, 2009). Retrieved May 31, 2009, from http:// www.cawp.rutgers.edu/fast_facts/levels_of_office/ documents/elective.pdf

27. "Title IX Frequently Asked Questions" (Indianapolis, IN: National Collegiate Athletic Association, 2010). Retrieved February 5, 2010, from http://www.ncaa.org/wps/wcm/connect/ncaa/ncaa/about+the+ncaa/diversity+and+inclusion/gender+equity+and+title+ix/faq.html

28. National Organization for Women, "ERA Ratification Status Summary," in ERA *Countdown Campaign* (Washington, DC: NOW, 1981), p. A.

29. For a history of efforts to pass the ERA, see Roberta W. Francis, "The History Behind the Equal Rights Amendment" (Washington, DC: National Council of Women's Organizations, no date). Retrieved May 31, 2009, from http://www.equalrightsamendment.org/era.htm

30. See Allison L. Held, Sheryl L. Herndon, and Danielle M. Stager, "The Equal Rights Amendment: Why the ERA Remains Legally Viable and Properly Before the States," *William & Mary Journal of Women and the Law,* Vol. 3, 1997, pp. 113–136. Retrieved May 31, 2009, from http://www.equalrightsamendment.org/W&M%20law%20article.pdf

31. Quoted in Chris Lombardi, "Equal Rights Amendment Introduced in Congress" (Washington, DC: National Organization for Women, April 10, 2001), *Women's eNews.* Retrieved May 31, 2009, from http://www.womensenews.org/article.cfm/dyn/aid/506/context/archive

32. "California's Paid Family Leave Law," Workplace Flexibility 2010 (Washington, DC: Georgetown University Law Center, 2004). Retrieved May 31, 2009, from http://www.law.georgetown.edu/workplaceflexibility2010/law/ca.cfm

33. Eve Tahmincioglu, "Paid Family Leave Becomes Hot Workplace Issue," MSNBC.com, June 2, 2008. Retrieved May 31, 2009, from http://www.msnbc.msn.com/id/24893369

34. Jody Heymann, Alison Earle, and Jeffrey Hayes, *The Work, Family, and Equity Index: How Does the United States Measure Up?* (Boston, MA and Montreal, QC: Project on Global Working Families, 2007). Retrieved June 1, 2009, from http://www.mcgill.ca/files/ihsp/WFEIFinal2007.pdf

35. "Women's Rights Advocates Decry Bush's Family Leave Decision" (Washington, DC: National Organization for Women, December 9, 2002). Retrieved May 31, 2009, from http://www.now.org/issues/family/120902ui.html

36. Gene Sanchez *(Washington Post),* "Court: Antiabortion Web Site Protected by First Amendment," *Austin American-Statesman,* March

29, 2001, p. A7; also see "Abortion Site Causes Free Speech Firestorm," *Cnet News,* March 12, 1999. Retrieved June 7, 2009, from http://news.cnet.com/Abortion-site-causes-free-speech-firestorm/2100-1023_3-222930.html

37. Frederick Clarkson, "New Version of Nuremberg Files Yanked off Web," *Women's eNews,* December 15, 2003. Retrieved February, 5, 2010, from http://www.womensenews.org/story/the-nation/031205/new-version-nuremberg-files-yanked-web

38. "Supreme Court Rules Against Abortion Clinics," *WorldNetDaily,* February 28, 2006. Retrieved June 3, 2009, from http://www.wnd.com/news/article.asp?ARTICLE_ID=49041

39. Marilyn Keefe, "Domestic Gag Rule? Déjà Vu All Over Again," *RH Reality Check,* May 13, 2008. Retrieved June 3, 2009, from http://www.rhrealitycheck.org/blog/2008/05/13/domestic-gag-rule-deja-vu-all-over-again

40. Douglas Johnson, "The Partial-birth Abortion Ban Act—Misconceptions and Realities" (Washington, DC: National Right to Life Committee, November 5, 2003). Retrieved June 3, 2009, from http://www.nrlc.org/abortion/pba/pbaall110403.html

41. Ellen Goodman, "Out of the Picture on the Abortion Ban," *Boston Globe,* November 13, 2003. Retrieved February 5, 2010, from http://www.boston.com/news/globe/editorial_opinion/oped/articles/2003/11/13/out_of_the_picture_on_the_abortion_ban/

42. "Redemption for the Pope?" *Lancet,* Vol. 373, March 28, 2009, p. 1054.

43. Susan M. Blake, Rebecca Ledsky, Carol Goodenow, Richard Sawyer, David Lohrmann, and Richard Windsor, "Condom Availability Programs in Massachusetts High Schools: Relationships With Condom Use and Sexual Behavior," *American Journal of Public Health,* Vol. 93, No. 6, 2003, pp. 955–962.

44. "Plan B® One-Step" (Woodcliff Lake, NJ: Teva Women's Health, Inc., 2010). Retrieved June 26, 2010, from http://www.planbonestep.com/

45. Food and Drug Administration, "Decision Process to Deny Initial Application for Over-the-Counter Marketing of the Emergency Contraceptive Drug Plan B Was Unusual," GAO-06-109 (Washington, DC: November 14, 2005). Retrieved June 2, 2009, from http://www.gao.gov/new.items/d06109.pdf

46. "FDA Violated Law by Restricting Over-the-Counter Sales of Plan B, District Court Rules" (Cambridge, MA: Union of Concerned Scientists, March 23, 2009). Retrieved June 2, 2009, from http://www.ucsusa.org/news/press_release/fda-violated-law-by-0208.html

47. "FDA to OK Over-the-counter Plan B for 17-year-olds," *USA Today,* April 22, 2009. Retrieved June 2, 2009, from http://www.usatoday.com/news/health/2009-04-22-morning-after-pill_N.htm

48. Figures in this paragraph are from Sonia B. Gamble et al., "Abortion Surveillance—2005" (Atlanta: Centers for Disease Control, November 28, 2008). Retrieved May 2, 2009, from http://www.cdc.gov/mmwr/preview/mmwrhtml/ss5713a1.htm?s_cid=ss5713a1_e#tab3

49. Lilo T. Strauss et al., "Abortion Surveillance—United States, 2003 (Atlanta: Centers for Disease Control, November 24, 2006). Retrieved June 27, 2010, from http://www.cdc.gov/mmwr/preview/mmwrhtml/ss5511a1.htm; "U.S. Abortions Decline to Lowest Level Since 1974," MSNBC.com, January 17, 2008. Retrieved June 3, 2009, from http://www.msnbc.msn.com/id/22709609/

50. Nancy Gibbs, "Why Have Abortion Rates Fallen?", *Time Magazine,* January 21, 2008. Retrieved June 3, 2009, from http://www.time.com/time/nation/article/0,8599,1705604,00.html; also see "Decreasing Number of Abortion Providers" (Washington, DC: NARAL Prochoice Washington, May 1, 2008). Retrieved June 3, 2009, from http://www.prochoicewashington.org/issues/factsheets/200307084.shtml

51. "Counseling and Waiting Periods for Abortion" (New York: Guttmacher Institute, June 1, 2009). Retrieved June 3, 2009, from http://www.guttmacher.org/statecenter/spibs/spib_MWPA.pdf

52. Nate Jenkins, "Nebraska Abortion Law: Mental, Physical Screening Required For Women and No Abortion After 20 Weeks," *The Huffington Post,* April 12, 2010. Retrieved June 2, 2010, from http://www.huffingtonpost.com/2010/04/12/nebraska-abortion-law-men_n_534740.html

53. "An Overview of Minors Consent Law" (New York: Guttmacher Institute, June 1, 2009). Retrieved June 3, 2009, from http://www.guttmacher.org/statecenter/spibs/spib_OMCL.pdf

54. "Boxer Introduces Legislation to Codify *Roe v. Wade* on the 31st Anniversary of the Decision," Thursday, January 22, 2004. Retrieved June 3, 2009, from http://boxer.senate.gov/news/releases/record.cfm?id=217321

55. "Statement released after the President rescinds 'Mexico City Policy,'" January 24, 2009. Retrieved June 3, 2009, from http://www.whitehouse.gov/statement-released-after-the-president-rescinds

56. Christopher Trenholm, Barbara Devaney, Kenneth Fortson, Melissa Clark, Lisa Quay, and Justin Wheeler, "Impacts of Abstinence Education on Teen Sexual Activity, Risk of Pregnancy, and Risk of Sexually Transmitted Diseases," *Journal of Policy Analysis and Management,* Vol. 27, No. 2, 2008, pp. 255–276.

57. Patricia Tjaden and Nancy Thoennes, *Full Report of the Prevalence, Incidence, and Consequences of Violence Against Women* (Washington, DC: U.S. Department of Justice, November 2000). Retrieved June 26, 2020, from http://www.ncjrs.gov/pdffiles/nij/183781.pdf

58. "FAQ: Rape Shield Laws" (Washington, DC: National Center for Victims of Crime, 2007). Retrieved June 7, 2009, from http://www.ncvc.org/ncvc/main.aspx?dbID=DB_FAQ:RapeShieldLaws927

59. "Sexual Assault Response Teams" (Minneapolis: Minnesota Advocates for Human Rights, February 2009). Retrieved June 7, 2009, from http://www.stopvaw.org/Sexual_Assault_Response_Teams.html

60. Patricia Tjaden and Nancy Theonnes, *Extent, Nature and Consequences of Intimate Partner Violence* (Washington, DC: U.S. Department of Justice, July 2000). Retrieved June 5, 2009, from http://www.ncjrs.gov/pdffiles1/nij/181867.pdf

61. "Intimate Homicide Victims by Gender" (Washington, DC: U.S. Department of Justice, no date). Retrieved June 5, 2009, from http://www.ojp.usdoj.gov/bjs/homicide/tables/intimatestab.htm

62. U.S. Commission on Civil Rights, *The Federal Response in Domestic Violence* (Washington, DC: U.S. Government Printing Office, January 1982), pp. iv–v; see also Anne Sparks, "Feminists Negotiate the Executive Branch: The Policing of Male Violence," in Cynthia R. Daniels, Ed., *Feminists Negotiate the State: The Politics of Domestic Violence* (Lanham, MD: University Press of America, 1997), pp. 35–52.

63. Lisa G. Lerman, "Legal Help for Battered Women," in Joseph J. Costa, Ed., *Abuse of Women: Legislation, Reporting, and Prevention* (Lexington, MA: Lexington Books, 1983), p. 29.

64. Lawrence W. Sherman and Richard A. Berk, "The Minneapolis Domestic Violence Experiment" (Washington, DC: Policy Foundation, 1984). Retrieved June 5, 2009, from http://www.policefoundation.org/pdf/minneapolisdve.pdf

65. This paragraph relies on Christopher D. Maxwell, Joel H. Garner, and Jeffrey A. Fagan, "The Effects of Arrest on Intimate Partner Violence: New Evidence from the Spouse Assault Replication Program" (Washington, DC: U.S. Department of Justice, July 2001). Retrieved June 5, 2009, from http://www.ncjrs.gov/pdffiles1/nij/188199.pdf

66. Much of this paragraph relies on David Hirschel, "Domestic Violence Cases: What Research Shows About Arrest and Dual Arrest Rates (Washington, DC: National Institute of Justice, July 25, 2008). Retrieved June 6, 2009, from http://www.ojp.usdoj. gov/nij/publications/dv-dual-arrest-222679/dv-dual-arrest.pdf

67. Victoria Holt, Mary A. Kernic, Thomas Lumley, Marsha E. Wolf, and Frederick R. Rivara, "Civil Protection Orders and Risk of Subsequent Police-Reported Violence," *Journal of the American Medical Association,* Vol. 228, 2002, pp. 589–594.

68. Andrew R. Klein, *Practical Implications of Current Domestic Violence Research: For Law Enforcement, Prosecutors and Judges,* Chapter 7, "Judicial Responses, Section 11, "Protective Orders" (Washington, DC: National Institute of Justice, June 2009). Retrieved June 3, 2010, from http://www.ojp.usdoj. gov/nij/topics/crime/intimate-partner-violence/ practical-implications-research/ch7/protective-order-effectiveness.htm

69. Lynette Feder, David B. Wilson, and Sabrina Austin, "Court-Mandated Interventions for Individuals Convicted of Domestic Violence" (Oslo, Norway: Campbell Collaboration, August 29, 2008). Retrieved June 7, 2009, from http://db.c2admin.org/ doc-pdf/Feder_DomesticViolence_review.pdf

70. "Analysis of the Violence Against Women Act" (Rockville, MD: Respecting Accuracy in Domestic Abuse Reporting, July 5, 2005). Retrieved June 7, 2009, from http://www.mediaradar.org/RADAR_ Analysis_of_VAWA.pdf

71. *Code of Federal Regulations,* Vol. 29, Sec. 1604.11.

72. On sexual assault and the military, see Terri Spahr Nelson, *For Love of Country: Confronting Rape and Sexual Assault in the U.S. Military* (Binghamton, NY: Haworth Maltreatment and Trauma Press, 2002).

73. Camille Paglia, "A Call for Lustiness: Just Say No to the Sex Police," *Time,* March 23, 1998, p. 54.

74. U.S. Equal Employment Opportunity Commission, "Sexual Harassment," March 11, 2009. Retrieved June 1, 2009, from http://www.eeoc.gov/types/ sexual_harassment.html

75. Many books describe the history of sodomy laws. See, for example, David A. J. Richards, *The Case for Gay Rights from Bowers to Lawrence* (Lawrence, KS: University Press of Kansas, 2005). Supreme Court decisions can be found at the FindLaw website: http://www .findlaw.com/casecode/supreme.html

76. "Employment Policies & Laws" (Washington, DC: Human Rights Campaign, February 17, 2010).

Retrieved June 2, 2010, from http://www.hrc. org/documents/Employment_Laws_and_Policies.pdf

77. "Employment Non-Discrimination Act" (Washington, DC: Human Rights Campaign, February 26, 2010). Retrieved June 2, 2010, from http://www.hrc.org/ issues/workplace/enda.asp

78. "State Hate Crimes Laws" (Washington, DC: Human Rights Campaign, June 1, 2009). Retrieved June 2, 2010, from http://www.hrc.org/documents/hate_ crime_laws.pdf.

79. "Hate Crime Statistics, 2008" (Washington, DC: U.S. Department of Justice, November 2009). Retrieved June 2, 2010, from http://www.fbi.gov/ucr/hc2008/ index.html

80. Perry Bacon, Jr., "After 10-year Dispute, Expansion of Hate Crimes Law to Gays Signed," *Washington Post,* October 29, 2009. Retrieved February 5, 2010, from http://www.washingtonpost.com/wp-dyn/ content/article/2009/10/28/AR2009102804909.html

81. "Domestic Partner Benefits: Prevalence Among Private Employers" (Washington, DC: Human Rights Campaign, February 12, 2009). Retrieved June 8, 2009, from http://www.hrc.org/issues/work-place/benefits/11612.htm

82. "States Offering Benefits for Same-Sex Partners of State Employees" (Washington, DC: National Conference of State Legislatures, 2010). Retrieved February 4, 2010, from http://www.ncsl.org/Default.aspx?TabId=16315

83. Joanna Grossman, "Are Bans on Same-Sex Marriage Constitutional? New Jersey Says Yes, but Massachusetts, in a Landmark Decision, Says No," *FindLaw's Legal Commentary,* November 20, 2003. Retrieved June 7, 2009, from http://writ.news.find-law.com/grossman/20031120.html

84. Anthony J. Sebok, "What Gay Couples Lack—Besides Marriage: The Crucial Rights under Tort Law that Only Spouses Can Assert," *FindLaw's Legal Commentary,* April 9, 2004. Retrieved June 7, 2009, from http://writ .news.findlaw.com/sebok/20040409.html

85. Tamara Audi, Justin Scheck, and Christopher Lawton, "California Votes for Prop 8," *Wall Street Journal,* November 5, 2008. Retrieved February 4, 2010, from http://online.wsj.com/article/SB122586056759900673 .html

86. David G. Savage, "Supreme Court Cites 'Irreparable Harm' in Blocking Prop. 8 Trial," *Los Angeles Times,* January 14, 2010. Retrieved February 5, 2010, from http://articles.latimes.com/2010/jan/14/nation/la-na-court-cameras14-2010jan14

87. "Bush Calls for Ban on Same-Sex Marriages" (Washington, DC: CNN.com, February 25, 2004).

Retrieved February 5, 2010, from http://www.cnn.com/2004/ALLPOLITICS/02/24/elec04.prez.bush.marriage

88. This paragraph relies on "Marriage Equality & Other Relationship Recognition Laws" (Washington DC: Human Rights Campaign, April 2, 2010). Retrieved June 72, 2010, from http://www.hrc.org/documents/Relationship_Recognition_Laws_Map.pdf; "Same-sex Marriage, Civil Unions and Domestic Partnerships" (Washington, DC: National Conference of State Legislatures, April 2010). Retrieved June 2, 2010, from http://www.ncsl.org/IssuesResearch/HumanServices/SameSexMarriage/tabid/16430/Default.aspx

89. "Adoption Issues for Gay and Lesbians and Same-Sex Couples," Adoption & Child Welfare Lawsite (Columbus, OH: The National Center for Adoption Law and Policy, 2009). Retrieved June 8, 2009, from http://www.adoptionchildwelfarelaw.org/faq_detail.php?id=95

90. See "Adoption Laws: State by State" (Washington, DC: Human Rights Campaign, 2009). Retrieved June 8, 2009, from http://www.hrc.org/issues/2375.htm; Ramon Johnson, "Where is Gay Adoption Legal?", About.com. Retrieved June 8, 2009, from http://gaylife.about.com/od/gayparentingadoption/a/gaycoupleadopt.htm; "State-by-State Gay Adoption Laws" (Boston: Family Equality Council). Retrieved June 8, 2009, http://www.familyequality.org/resources/publications/aoption_withcitations.pdf

91. Yolanne Almanzar, "Florida Gay Adoption Ban Is Ruled Unconstitutional," *New York Times,* November 25, 2008. Retrieved June 8, 2009, from http://www.nytimes.com/2008/11/26/us/26florida.html?_r=1

92. Gary Gates, Lee M. V. Badgett, Jennifer Ehrle Macomber, and Kate Chambers, "Adoption and Foster Care by Lesbian and Gay Parents in the United States" (Washington, DC: The Urban Institute, March 23, 2007). Retrieved June 8, 2009, from http://www.urban.org/publications/411437.html

93. Also see David F. Burrelli and Jody Feder, *Homosexuals and the U.S. Military: Current Issues* (Washington, DC: Congressional Research Service, July 22, 2009). Retrieved June 2, 2010, from http://www.fas.org/sgp/crs/natsec/RL30113.pdf

94. Michelle M. Benecke, cited in "Challenges to Old Gay Ban Spark Questions on Military's New Policy," *Miami Herald,* December 19, 1993, p. 7A; this paragraph also relies on "Clinton: Let Military Bar Gay Conduct," *Miami Herald,* July 17, 1993, p. 11A; "Pentagon Outlines Revised Conduct Code for Gays in Military," *Miami Herald,* December 23, 1993,

p. 4A; Steven Lee Myers *(New York Times),* "More Gays Forced Out of Service Than before 'Don't Ask,'" *Austin American-Statesman,* January 23, 1999, p. A21.

95. Bryan Bender, "Continued Discharges Anger 'Don't Ask, Don't Tell' Critics," *Boston Globe,* May 20, 2009. Retrieved June 8, 2009, from http://www.boston.com/news/nation/washington/articles/2009/05/20/continued_discharges_anger_dont_ask_dont_tell_critics

96. Ann Scott Tyson, "Sharp Drop in Gays Discharged from Military Tied to War Need," *Washington Post,* March 14, 2007, p. A3. Retrieved June 8, 2009, from http://www.washingtonpost.com/wp-dyn/content/article/2007/03/13/AR2007031301174.html

97. James J. Lindsay, Jerome Johnson, E. G. "Buck" Schuler, Jr., and Joseph J. Went, "Gays in the Military: A Bad Fit," *Washington Post,* April 15, 2009. Retrieved June 9, 2009, from http://www.washingtonpost.com/wp-dyn/content/article/2009/04/14/AR2009041402704.html

98. Bryan Bender, "Obama Seeks Assessment on Gays in Military," *Boston Globe,* February 1, 2009. Retrieved June 9, 2009, from http://www.boston.com/news/nation/washington/articles/2009/02/01/obama_seeks_assessment_on_gays_in_military

99. "Youth and Campus Activism: Laws" (Washington, DC: Human Rights Campaign, 2009). Retrieved June 9, 2009, from http://www.hrc.org/issues/youth_and_campus_activism/youth_and_campus_activism_laws.asp

100. See, for example, Associated Press, "Salt Lake City School Board Bans Clubs After Request for Gay Group," *Daily News,* 1996. Retrieved June 9, 2009, from http://www.thefreelibrary.com/SALT+LAKE+CITY+SCHOOL+BOARD+BANS+CLUBS+AFTER+REQUEST+FOR+GAY+GROUP-a083919706

101. "Federal Appeals Court Strikes Down Alabama Law Barring Gay Student Groups from Campus," *American Civil Liberties Freedom Network,* April 30, 1997.

102. "Prom Resources for LGBT Students" (New York: American Civil Liberties Union, April 24, 2009). Retrieved June 3, 2010, from http://www.aclu.org/lgbt-rights_hiv-aids/prom-resources-lgbt-students

103. "Case Background: *Flores v. Morgan Hill Unified School District*" (New York: American Civil Liberties Union, January 6, 2004). Retrieved June 9, 2009, from http://www.aclu.org/lgbt/youth/11947res20040106.html

104. "ACLU Sues to Stop Tennessee Schools from Censoring Gay Educational Web Sites" (New York: American Civil Liberties Union, May 19, 2009). Retrieved June 9, 2009, from http://www.aclu.org/lgbt/youth/39616prs20090519.html

12 | THE CHALLENGES OF A DIVERSE SOCIETY: RACE, ETHNICITY, AND IMMIGRATION

By 2050 the United States will look quite different from the way it does today—non Hispanic whites may be less than 50 percent of the U.S. population, rather than the 65 percent they are now. Hispanics are projected to make up 30 percent and blacks 15 percent of the population by 2050.[1] Such major changes will certainly be reflected in the country's politics, but where does the country stand with regard to equality among racial and ethnic groups?

RACIAL EQUALITY: HOW FAR HAVE WE COME?

Some people would have us think that race relations have improved tremendously in the United States. They point to the progress that people of color have made in virtually all realms of U.S. life, and they see the election of the nation's first African American president as further affirmation that racism is no longer an obstacle to success. Others sway us to believe that the country remains deeply divided along racial lines, pointing to racial profiling and police brutality, disproportionate arrest and conviction rates, economic inequities, and infringements on voting rights.[2] They see the actions taken against innocent people of particular ethnic and religious groups, such as those following the September 11, 2001, terrorist attacks, as further evidence of the racism embedded in U.S. society.

Perhaps the fairest thing that can be said about the living conditions of people of color in the United States, especially blacks and Hispanics, is that they have improved substantially, but not on a par with whites. On the average, blacks are in poorer health than whites, and they do not live as long; they earn less and are more likely to be in poverty, and they are overrepresented in public assistance programs. Poverty and lower earnings also contribute to a less adequate lifestyle for many Americans of Hispanic origin and for Native Americans.

As described in Chapter 4, poverty rates are still nearly three times higher for black and Hispanic Americans than for whites. Chapter 4 also showed that while educational attainment is closely related to income for all ethnic groups, even after controlling for education, blacks and Hispanics are more likely to be poor and less likely to earn as much as whites. Blacks are approximately 13 percent of the total U.S. population, but they head 39 percent of families receiving TANF[3] and are 29 percent of noninstitutionalized SSI recipients.[4] Although the General Accounting Office found that blacks were more likely to be rejected for disability benefits than whites (see Chapter 5), the proportion of blacks in public assistance programs reinforces stereotypes that they prefer welfare to work. According to one report, "surveys show that racial attitudes are the most important reason behind white opposition to welfare programs. Political issues, such as crime and welfare, are viewed as 'coded issues' as they stimulate white Americans' anti-black feelings without explicitly raising racial discrimination."[5] Racial discrimination is so firmly entrenched in U.S. society that the term *institutional racism* has been used to refer to these practices.

THE CIVIL RIGHTS ACTS

The first federal legislation passed with "civil rights" in the title was the Civil Rights Act of 1866, and Congress had to override President Andrew Johnson's veto to do so. The act gave citizenship to all persons born in the United States, except "Indians not taxed," regardless of race, color, or having been a slave, and accorded them the same rights as white citizens. Penalties for failure to obey the act were a fine of not more than $1,000, up to a year of imprisonment, or both. The law was highly ineffective. Congress passed another civil rights act in 1875, but the U.S. Supreme Court declared it unconstitutional. Nearly 200 years after the United States of America was founded, Congress passed the Civil Rights Act of 1964, and gave it some teeth, but Congress exempted itself from complying with the Civil Rights Act until 1988. According to this act:

1. It is unlawful to apply unequal standards in voter registration procedures, or to deny registration for irrelevant errors or omissions on records or applications.
2. It is unlawful to discriminate or segregate persons on the grounds of race, color, religion, or national origin in any public accommodation, including hotels, motels, restaurants, movies, theaters, sports arenas, entertainment houses, and other places that offer to serve the public. This prohibition extends to all establishments whose operations affect interstate commerce or whose discriminatory practices are supported by state action.
3. The attorney general shall undertake civil action on behalf of any person denied equal access to a public accommodation to obtain a federal district court order to secure compliance with the act. If the owner or manager of a public accommodation should continue to discriminate, he (or she) would be in contempt of court and subject to peremptory fines and imprisonment without trial by jury.
4. The attorney general shall undertake civil actions on behalf of persons attempting orderly desegregation of public schools.
5. The Commission on Civil Rights, established in the Civil Rights Act of 1957, shall be empowered to investigate deprivations of the right to vote, study, and collect information regarding discrimination in America, and make reports to the president and Congress.
6. Each federal department and agency shall take action to end discrimination in all programs or activities receiving federal financial assistance in any form. This action shall include termination of financial assistance.
7. After 1965, it shall be unlawful for any employer or labor union with twenty-five or more people to discriminate against any individual in any fashion in employment because of his race, color, religion, sex, or national origin, and an Equal Employment Opportunity Commission shall be established to enforce this provision by investigation, conference, conciliation, persuasion, and if need be, civil action in federal court.

In 1968 the Fair Housing Act, which prohibits discrimination in housing sales and rentals, was passed an amendment to the Civil Rights Act. Support for the bill solidified following the assassination of Dr. Martin Luther King, Jr. In this chapter we take a closer look at civil rights policies, past and present, and their effects.

SCHOOL DESEGREGATION

In 1868, The Fourteenth Amendment to the U.S. Constitution, which guarantees all citizens equal protection under the law, was adopted. This amendment served as legal grounds for the *separate but equal doctrine* set forth in the U.S. Supreme Court decision in *Plessy v. Ferguson* in 1896. Segregation of blacks and whites in public schools, on public buses, and in other public (and private) places was official policy. This doctrine, ingrained in the minds of many Americans, perpetuated racial discrimination for more than another half century. Although public facilities for blacks were supposed to be equal to facilities for whites, this was generally not the case.

A growing dissatisfaction with the separate but equal doctrine resulted in the 1954 U.S. Supreme Court ruling that marked the official recognition of racial inequality in the United States and ignited the civil rights movement. Schools in Topeka, Kansas, were segregated but essentially equal in terms of physical conditions and quality of education. However, in the case of *Brown v. Board of Education of Topeka, Kansas,* the Supreme Court ruled that separate was *not* equal. In its decision, the Court took the position that "the policy of separating the races is usually interpreted as denoting the inferiority of the Negro Group." The Court also stated that "segregation with the sanction of law, therefore, has a tendency to retard the education and mental development of Negro children."

The *Brown* decision remains a landmark case in the history of equal rights, but additional actions were needed to remedy both *de jure* and *de facto* segregation. *De jure* segregation results from laws specifying separate facilities for people by race. In southern states, public schools were often segregated by law. *De facto* segregation results form other factors. For example, since neighborhoods are generally divided along racial (and socioeconomic) lines, neighborhood schools attended only by children residing in the neighborhood are segregated *de facto*. *De facto* segregation was often the case in northern states. In discussing the long, complicated, and often bitter battles over *de jure* and *de facto* school desegregation, attorney Alfred Lindseth labels the 1950s "massive resistance," the 1960s "accommodation," the 1970s "forced busing," the 1980s "voluntary desegregation," and the 1990s (and beyond) a period focused on educational quality.[6]

From Resistance to Accommodation

The *Brown* case actually resulted in two decisions that addressed *de jure* segregation. In 1954, in *Brown I,* the U.S. Supreme Court ruled that segregated schools violated the U.S. Constitution's Fourteenth Amendment or "equal protection" clause. In 1955, *Brown II* declared that desegregation was to be implemented with "all deliberate speed." Some school districts attempted to pass laws to circumvent integration or used other techniques to stall.[7] One of the most famous events in desegregation history occurred when Arkansas Governor Orval Faubus called out the National Guard to prevent African American students from integrating Central High School in Little Rock. In 1959, in Prince Edward County, Virginia, public schools closed rather than desegregate and did not open again until 1964.

In response to *Brown,* many school districts simply adopted "freedom of choice" plans that allowed parents to select the school their children would attend. Small numbers of black students enrolled in schools populated mostly by whites; virtually no white students enrolled in schools populated mostly by blacks.[8] Segregated schools were a way of life in the United States, and it was going to take more legal action to change that.

In 1968, the case of *Green v. School Board of Kent County* was intended to move school districts from passive nondiscrimination to affirmative action.[9] School districts were required to eliminate "all vestiges" of segregation on six dimensions that became known as the "Green factors": (1) assignment of students, (2) faculty, and (3) staff, (4) transportation, (5) extracurricular activities, and (6) facilities. Release from court supervision requires schools to meet all six factors, also called achieving "unitary status"—one school system for all children, not a *dual system* with separate schools for black children and white children.

Some schools continue to remain under court desegregation supervision. Some do not seek release even after attaining unitary status because it might mean a return to *de facto* segregation or a loss of state and federal revenue that schools receive while under court desegregation orders.[10] One viewpoint is that schools should be released from court order once they achieve unitary status because schools are intended to be under local control.[11] According to this view, remaining under court order also limits schools' flexibility in addressing changing demographics and other school district needs and ultimately harms students.

Busing and Mandatory Desegregation

In addition to the *Green* decision, forced busing has played an important role in school desegregation. In 1971, in the case of *Swann v. Charlotte-Mecklenburg Board of Education,* the U.S. Supreme Court approved "mandatory student reassignment" or court-ordered busing of children to achieve integration in school districts that had a history of discrimination. Among the most vivid examples of opposition to school busing is protestors in parts of Boston who attacked buses carrying African American children, throwing rocks and injuring some.

Most policies have spillover effects. The irony of forced school integration was "white flight"—white families moving to avoid busing, and increased private-school enrollments, which also thwarts efforts to integrate public schools. Parents—generally white parents—who purposely purchased homes in the school districts they preferred were often angered when their child was bused to a school they deemed inferior. Evidence supported the assertion that white flight was a real phenomenon, but mandatory reassignment did increase integration.[12] Even today, where forced busing does exist, parents often strenuously object to sending their child to a school that is miles from their home when another school is nearby.

It was not long before the high court began to soften its stance on busing. In 1974, in *Milliken v. Bradley,* the Court ruled that mandatory busing across city-suburban boundaries to achieve integration is not required unless segregation has resulted from an official action. The court's 1991 decision in *Board of Education of Oklahoma City v. Dowell* also eased rules on forced busing once unitary status was achieved and affirmed that school desegregation orders were not intended to last forever. In this same vein, in 1992, in *Freeman v. Pitts,* the high court declared that *de facto* neighborhood segregation is not a reason for denying schools unitary status.

Voluntary Desegregation and Educational Adequacy

Telling parents which school their child would attend was clearly an unpopular policy. To further the goal of integration, schools and the courts have tried to use more carrots (voluntary plans and incentives) than sticks (forced busing) to achieve desegregation.[13] Among these voluntary plans are magnet schools that specialize in a subject area (e.g., technology, science, performing arts) designed to entice students and parents to choose them. The plans are also often called "controlled choice" because they specify the percentages of racial groups to be enrolled in order to achieve integration. Educational enhancements (smaller class sizes, higher teacher pay, before- and after-school programs, etc.) are also used to attract students of all racial and ethnic groups. Evidence indicates that voluntary approaches do promote diversity by attracting middle-class students, and the courts have been favorable to them.[14]

Since voluntary programs can be costly to operate, those pressing for educational improvements for children in poor school districts often seek legal remedies from the state.[15] Some state constitutions include educational adequacy provisions. When some groups of students do not perform as well as others, this might be an indication of an inadequate education. School dropout rates continue to differ by race and ethnicity (see Figure 12.1). Today, it is more difficult to argue that differences in education attainment stem from the vestiges of discrimination rather than factors such as poverty, family dysfunction, or in the case of immigrant children, entering school without being able to speak English. Thus, state court action and achievement measures are replacing traditional desegregation suits and the Green factors in order to close gaps in educational outcomes.

In 2007, in a 5-4 opinion, the U.S. Supreme Court struck down the use of race as a criterion, or at least the sole criterion, for determining student assignment under voluntary (not mandatory) school desegregation plans in Seattle, Washington, and in Louisville, Kentucky (called the Parents

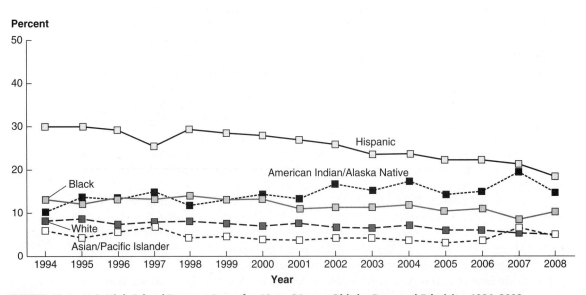

FIGURE 12.1 U.S. High School Dropout Rates for 16- to 24-year Olds by Race and Ethnicity, 1994–2008
Note: The dropout rate is the percentage of 16- to 24-year-olds who are not enrolled in high school and who have not earned a high school diploma or General Educational Development (GED) certificate. Race categories exclude persons of Hispanic ethnicity. *Source:* Data are from the U.S. Department of Commerce, Census Bureau, Current Population Survey, October supplement, 1994-2008, as compiled in Susan Aud, Willian Hussar, Michael Planty, Thomas Snyder, Kevin Bianco, Mary Ann Fox, M., Lauren Frohlich, Jana Kemp, and Lauren Drake, *The Condition of Education 2010* (NCES 2010-028) (Washington, DC: National Center for Education Statistics, Institute of Education Sciences, U.S. Department of Education, 2010), p. 69. Retrieved June 6, 2010, from http://nces.ed.gov/pubs2010/2010028.pdf

Involved in Community Schools or PICS cases). In issuing the majority opinion, Chief Justice Roberts took the color-blind stance, writing that "The way to stop discrimination on the basis of race is to stop discriminating on the basis of race." However, the opinions of the justices, including those in the majority, differ as to whether or how race may be used. School desegregation scholar Gary Orfeld described the decision as another blow to civil rights and school desegregation.[16] While schools were once forced to desegregate, today, assigning students on the basis of race may be construed as violating the Constitution's equal protection clause.

School "Resegregation"

Orfeld compliments U.S. public schools for their role in helping the children of European and Asian immigrants succeed, while he says that blacks, Latinos, and Native Americans often attend "'dropout factory' high schools."[17] He claims that schools are resegregating, especially in inner cities, and that in 2006, on average, black and Latino students attended schools where less than one-third of students were white, and approximately 40 percent attended intensely segregated schools. Although integration in some suburban school districts, particularly those with affordable housing, has increased,[18] Orfeld notes that other suburban areas are becoming increasingly segregated.

Educational Quality—a Matter of Equity or Adequacy?

A major source of elementary and secondary school funding is the local property tax. As a result, schools in middle- and upper-class areas are generally better funded than schools in poorer areas. To see that each child receives an equitable education, states usually provide more funding to poorer school districts than richer ones. The state of Texas is home to one of the country's most diverse student populations. The state government provides one of the lowest per student expenditures in the nation. To increase equity for school children, Texas's "Robin Hood" law takes money from richer school districts to help poorer ones. This controversial approach has met with continued legal challenges.

Students, parents, and civil rights groups continue to take states, including wealthy states, to court for failing to provide all students with equal educational opportunities. In 2000, in California, civil rights groups and attorneys, naming 46 school districts representing one million low-income students, filed a class-action suit against the state for failure to provide a basic education. The complaint alleged:

> Those schools lack[ed] the bare essentials required of a free and common school education that the majority of students throughout the State enjoy: trained teachers, necessary educational supplies, classrooms, even seats in classrooms, and facilities that meet basic health and safety standards. . . . Students who are forced to attend schools with these conditions are deprived of essential educational opportunities to learn.[19]

The State of California claimed that more money for poor schools would not fix educational differences because the problems are more deep-seated—in homes and neighborhoods.[20] The case was settled in 2004 and the plaintiffs prevailed. Following the settlement, the ACLU Foundation of Southern California and Public Advocates, Inc., reported substantial improvements in meeting students' needs for essential educational resources.[21]

Arguments about school funding are also moving from equity—that every child should be entitled to the *same* educational resources—to *adequacy*—that children who need more resources to achieve basic educational goals should receive them. Since the plaintiffs in many adequacy lawsuits have been successful, Lindseth predicts such lawsuits will increase "as plaintiffs' groups, disillusioned with the normal legislative process, turn to the courts as salvation for the problems plaguing inner-city schools serving large numbers of poor and minority children."[22] Experts lack a consensus about whether spending alone can increase achievement. Well-qualified and committed teachers, appropriate teaching materials, and other resources must be part of the equation.

School Desegregation Policy for the Future

In the twenty-first century, Americans are attempting to balance issues of diversity and integration, individual choice, and quality education. Public Policy Professor David Armor and his colleagues recognize there is no magic answer to these challenges, but they believe:

> School-choice programs such as interdistrict transfers (open enrollment), charter schools, or voucher programs, including vouchers for private and parochial schools, are ideally suited to solving this problem. Most of these programs enjoy broad popular support among white and minority families, unlike mandatory busing, controlled choice, or other policies that are based primarily on racial quotas.[23]

To make these choices viable for lower-income families, they suggest providing government assistance if needed and using income rather than race as a criterion to avoid issues raised by racial quotas or preferences. For example, transportation subsidies can help low-income inner-city families avail themselves of open enrollment programs so their children can attend suburban schools. They note the popularity of charter schools and voucher programs that allow children with limited financial resources to attend private and parochial schools and believe that when parents, regardless of race or ethnicity, select an educational option for their children, they will be more committed to seeing that it succeeds.

Orfeld, on the other hand, is more concerned about what he sees as the waning commitment to integration and fears there will be more failure for families and society at large if integration is not given higher priority.[24] He believes that the No Child Left Behind legislation (see Chapter 9), which focuses on educational achievement, lacks civil rights protections and has left many poor children and children of color worse off. He points to federal aid going to charter schools, which he calls "the most segregated sector of public schools," noting that they lack the mechanisms for promoting integration that magnet schools have. Orfeld favors magnet schools, which allow students in the majority to transfer to schools with high concentrations of minority students, and "controlled choice" plans that offer choice and simultaneously prohibit segregation.

HOUSING AND RACIAL DISCRIMINATION

When it comes to purchasing real estate, you've probably heard the phrase "location, location, location." In other words, a home's location is its most important feature. The Kirwan Institute, which studies race and ethnicity, explains why.

> Housing, in particular its location, is the primary mechanism for accessing opportunity in our society. Where you live is more important than what you live in. Housing location determines the quality of local public services, such as

schools, the degree of access to employment and transportation, and the degree of public safety. . . . [W]here you live also determines how much wealth you can build through homeownership.[25]

Because low-income communities, often populated largely by people of color, do not provide many of the benefits of more integrated communities, sociologists find that "racial residential segregation is the principal structural feature of American society responsible for the perpetuation of urban poverty and represents a primary cause of racial inequality in the United States."[26] This is a major reason why housing policy in the United States—public and private, formal and informal—is so important.

Housing Segregation

If housing were equally available to Americans regardless of race as the law intends, we might be able to tout it as a public policy success story. Evidence indicates this is not the case. Segregation and discrimination are still evident in the private housing market and in government housing programs. Racially segregated housing perpetuates itself despite recognition of the educational, employment, health, and other benefits that integrated neighborhoods provide.[27]

Between 1934 and 1968, whites received 98 percent of federally approved home mortgage loans.[28] The Fair Housing Act of 1968 was intended to end racial discrimination in housing. Section 235 of that act became the nation's "largest single subsidized housing program" designed to increase home ownership, but it also became "the most controversial."[29] According to the U.S. Civil Rights Commission, the Federal Housing Administration (FHA) contributed to the sale of inferior homes to blacks and others under section 235 by delegating too much authority to private industry, which had failed to comply with the spirit of the Housing Act and other civil rights legislation. The 1968 Fair Housing Act was a step in the right direction, but prior to passage, the act was stripped of strong enforcement mechanisms.

Public housing has also been a culprit in racial segregation. Public housing projects were originally built in racially segregated communities. Even today, much of the available subsidized housing is located in segregated communities because affordable housing is in limited supply in others areas, and mixed-income communities are rare. The city of Yonkers, New York, gained national notoriety in 1988 when it refused to implement a subsidized housing desegregation order. Vidor, Texas, earned a similar reputation in 1993 when it failed to integrate a public housing complex. In 2000, HUD took control of public housing in Beaumont, Texas, after years of attempts to encourage integration there.

To be fair, residential racial segregation has decreased. Figure 12.2 shows that from 2000 to 2006, black-white segregation decreased in 14 of 15 of the largest U.S. metropolises. Researchers also found that compared to Hispanics and Asians, blacks remain more segregated from whites.[30] Based on a measure of segregation called the "dissimilarity index,"[31] black/white residential segregation was highest in the Detroit metropolitan area at an index of 70, while it was 44 for Hispanics/non-Hispanic whites and 34 for Asians/whites. Segregation between blacks and whites in Detroit did decline between 2000 and 2006. Other metropolitan areas are less segregated than Detroit, but many still have a long way to go in achieving true integration for blacks and whites. The Riverside-San Bernadino area had the lowest level of black/white segregation, but segregation there increased between 2000 and 2006.

Redlining and Steering Past and Present

Redlining also contributes to inferior living arrangements for people of color. It occurs when a bank, mortgage company, home insurance company, or other enterprise refuses to finance or insure property in certain areas. Redlined areas are generally those occupied by people who are

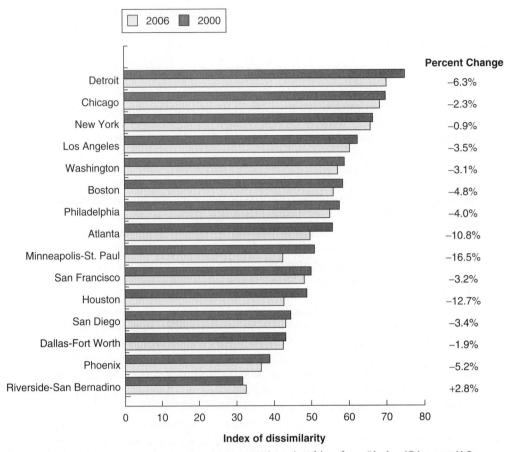

FIGURE 12.2 **Residential Segregation of Native-Born Non-Hispanic Whites from Blacks, 15 Largest U.S. Metropolises, 2000 and 2006** *Source:* Reynolds Farley, *The Kerner Commission Report Plus Four Decades: What Has Changed? What Has Not?* (Ann Arbor: Institute for Social Research, University of Michigan, September 2008). Retrieved February 18, 2010, from http://www.psc.isr.umich.edu/pubs/pdf/rr08-656.pdf. Used by permission.

poor and people of color. Another discriminatory practice is *steering,* which occurs when real estate agents direct members of particular racial and ethnic groups to housing in segregated areas, another Fair Housing Act violation. Fair housing and lending laws, opportunities to purchase housing with low down payments, and more recently, online mortgage applications have helped to eliminate some of these discriminatory housing practices.

Today, much of the redlining and steering of the past has been replaced by subprime mortgages. As discussed in Chapter 3, subprime mortgages have higher interest rates and other less favorable terms than traditional mortgages. Even after considering the effects of income, differences in mortgage rates seem to reflect racial bias. In 2004, Harvard University researchers reported that "relatively low shares of prime conventional [home] loans [are] going to African-American and Hispanic borrowers and neighborhoods, [and] race continues to be an important factor in determining the allocation of prime mortgage credit."[32] The Center for Responsible Lending also found that after controlling for "legitimate risk factors," people of color were 30 percent more likely to receive a higher-rate loan than whites.[33] The National

Urban League calls these practices "reverse redlining," pointing to the evidence that people of color are being steered to loans with higher interest rates (primarily subprime loans) when they could have qualified for lower interest home loan products.[34]

Enforcing Fair Housing Practices

Groups such as the National Fair Housing Coalition, the National Urban League, the American Civil Liberties Union, and the Lawyers' Committee for Better Housing believe that housing discrimination problems persist because laws designed to prevent it either continue to lack enforcement provisions or are not well enforced. In 1970, the U.S. Third Circuit Court and the Court of Appeals ruled that in keeping with the Fair Housing Act and the Civil Rights Acts of 1964 and 1968, HUD is responsible for assessing the racial impact of its decisions in order to prevent housing discrimination. Housing advocates complain that HUD has not met this responsibility, especially in the current era where more public housing is being demolished than is being made available to low-income households.[35] They believe that fair housing regulations lack "teeth" and that local housing authorities or landlords who fail to meet requirements face few, if any, consequences.[36]

In 1988, Congress toughened HUD's Fair Housing Act enforcement provisions and added protections against discrimination for people with disabilities and for families with children. In 1998, HUD proposed new regulations to strengthen fair housing requirements, but HUD retracted them in the face of strong opposition from the League of Cities.[37] The National Fair Housing Alliance (NFHA) contends that HUD's "partnerships with lenders, builders, real estate companies and apartment management companies" work against enforcement.[38]

The NFHA is comprised of nonprofit fair housing organizations (FHOs), state and local civil rights organizations, and individual members working to create "diverse, barrier free communities across the nation."[39] HUD contracts with FHOs and other nonprofit organizations to help individuals and families with housing discrimination complaints. Their work may involve "testers"—people of different racial and ethnic groups but the same financial qualifications—who determine whether housing providers treat equally qualified people of different racial or ethnic groups the same or differently.[40] A NFHA report suggests that FHOs do much of the work in addressing housing discrimination complaints. In 2008, nearly 31,000 housing complaints were filed based on race, disability, family status, and other factors; FHOs handled 66 percent of cases, state and local agencies 27 percent, HUD 7 percent, and the Justice Department handled less than one percent of cases.[41]

In 2008, four major civil rights groups formed the National Commission on Fair Housing and Equal Opportunity to make recommendations to address the "ongoing national catastrophes of housing discrimination and residential segregation . . . affect[ing] not only African-Americans, but also Latinos, Arab-Americans, Asian-Americans, families with children, and people with disabilities."[42] Two former HUD Secretaries, Republican Jack Kemp and Democrat Henry Cisneros, chaired the commission, which recommended that the federal government create an independent fair housing enforcement agency.[43]

Encouraging Neighborhood Integration

Many factors influence housing segregation,[44] such as racial discrimination, stereotyping, and distrust and housing affordability.[45] Some people seek to live in multiracial or multiethnic neighborhoods because their families are multiracial or multiethnic or because they feel that such neighborhoods enhance their lives. Proximity to work, quality of schools, access to shopping and recreation, and the type and density of housing may also be factors in housing choices.[46]

To increase choice, strong enforcement of fair housing policies is needed, but policymakers, community planners, members of the real estate industry, and community members should also consider how to encourage neighborhood integration on a voluntary basis.[47] These approaches may include education about housing choices and the advantages of integrated neighborhoods. Other approaches are to link school and neighborhood desegregation through affordable and mixed-income housing and job opportunities, including tax incentives and attractive home financing. Neighborhood amenities and neighborhood pride may also attract people of different races, ethnic groups, incomes, ages, and family compositions.

AFFIRMATIVE ACTION

Another aspect of equal rights is *affirmative action* policies designed to achieve equality in school admissions and employment for women and members of certain racial or ethnic groups. Affirmative action is based on the notion that women and minorities should be admitted, hired, and promoted in proportion to their representation in the population. To what extent should affirmative action policies be pursued? Is it enough to use policies that do not discriminate against people because of gender and racial and ethnic background, or should policies go much further in order to reduce imbalances in admissions and employment? Nondiscrimination simply means that preferential treatment will not be given to selected groups. Originally, the federal government chose a policy of nondiscrimination. Examples are President Truman's decision to desegregate the military in 1946 and Titles VI (federally assisted programs) and VII (employment) of the 1964 Civil Rights Act.

The slow progress in achieving equality spurred a debate as to whether quotas rather than goals should be used in affirmative action. In employment, for example, *quotas* are defined as "imposing a fixed, mandatory number or percentage of persons to be hired or promoted, regardless of the number of potential applicants who meet the qualifications," while a *goal* is a

> numerical objective, fixed realistically in terms of number of vacancies expected, and the number of qualified applicants available . . . . If . . . the employer . . . has demonstrated every good faith effort to include persons from the group which was the object of discrimination . . . but has been unable to do so in sufficient numbers to meet his goal, he is not subject to sanction.[48]

In addition, an employer is not obligated to hire an unqualified or less qualified person in preference to a prospective employee with better qualifications.

The Philadelphia Plan of 1967 issued by the U.S. Office of Federal Contract Compliance was one of the first examples of an affirmative action plan. It required that those bidding on federal contracts submit plans to employ specific percentages of minority workers. In 1971, the Federal Aviation Administration adopted another quota-type plan. It essentially placed a freeze on hiring any additional employees if a member of a minority group did not fill every fifth vacant position.

Reverse Discrimination

Opponents of quota setting generally believe that giving preferential treatment to members of particular groups violates the U.S. Constitution's Fourteenth Amendment (equal protection clause). In 1974 a federal court upheld this belief. It decided that the University of Washington Law School should admit Marco DeFunis, Jr., who had protested the university's decision to reject his application while admitting blacks with lower grades and test scores. In 1978, the U.S. Supreme Court issued a similar ruling in determining that Alan Bakke had been unfairly denied admission to the University of California Davis Medical School because his qualifications were stronger than those of some people of color admitted to the school. Proponents of the decision hoped the *Bakke* case would help change what they perceived to be a trend of "reverse discrimination" against whites. Opponents feared that the Bakke decision threatened the future of affirmation action.

Other reverse discrimination charges in California arose when the University of California at Berkeley was accused of discriminating against whites by favoring black, Hispanic, and Filipino applicants. Complaints were also leveled against the University of California system for using more stringent admissions requirements for Asian Americans. Asian Americans generally have higher test scores than other groups and have been admitted at rates higher than their representation in the population.

The Reagan Years

During the years of the Reagan presidency, civil rights advocates accused the administration of reversing a pattern of improvement in civil rights that began in the 1960s and that both Democratic and Republican administrations had supported. Reagan's recommendations for appointments to the U.S. Civil Rights Commission and his attempts to get rid of other members raised the ire of civil rights groups. Controversy also brewed in the U.S. Department of Justice. During the Carter presidency, the department was a strong proponent of civil rights. It had, for example, helped to implement a court decree requiring that the police and fire departments of Indianapolis establish quotas for hiring and promoting women and blacks. But in 1984, the U.S. Supreme Court ruled in the case of *Firefighters Local Union No. 1784 v. Stotts* that the jobs of blacks with less seniority cannot be protected at the expense of jobs of whites with more seniority. The Justice Department used this decision to get Indianapolis and 49 other jurisdictions to abandon the use of quotas. The National Association for the Advancement of Colored People (NAACP) and others called the Justice Department's action illegal.

The Reagan administration also challenged the use of *class action suits* to benefit groups of people. During Reagan's terms, the Equal Employment Opportunity Commission expressed its desire to address cases of discrimination against particular individuals rather than assisting classes of people who have been treated unfairly. William Bradford Reynolds, then head of the Department of Justice, declared that what was needed was a color- and sex-blind society rather than a color- and sex-conscious one. He contended that quotas are a form of discrimination.

The U.S. Supreme Court did deal a victory for affirmative action during the Reagan years with two 1986 decisions (one involved Cleveland firefighters, the other a New York sheet metal workers' union). According to these decisions, "federal judges may set goals and timetables requiring employers guilty of past discrimination to hire or promote specific numbers of minorities, even if the jobs go to people who are not themselves the proven victims of bias."[49]

But U.S. Supreme Court rulings in 1989 again put affirmative action on shaky ground. In *City of Richmond v. J. A. Croson Co.,* the high court struck down many state and local "set-aside" programs that gave preference to minority-owned firms in awarding contracts, saying that such programs should be used only to remedy discrimination. The decision reportedly resulted in a severe drop in the contracts awarded to minority-owned businesses. The court said *federal* set-aside programs were exempt because of the wide latitude that Congress has in determining what is needed to achieve equality nationally.

The 1989 U.S. Supreme Court decision in *Wards Cove Packing Co., Inc. v. Atonio* (a case primarily involving Asian American and Alaska Native employees of a salmon cannery in Alaska) placed the onus of proving that an employer intended to discriminate (rather than unintentionally discriminated) on the employee. This reversed the court's long-standing 1971 decision in *Griggs v. Duke Power,* in which the employer had the burden of showing that hiring criteria are directly related to the job. Other 1989 decisions also made it easier to challenge affirmative action programs and more difficult for employees to bring discrimination suits. Many called these decisions ironic given that higher unemployment rates and lower earnings among women, blacks, and Hispanics do not support the contention of reverse discrimination.

The George H. W. Bush Years

After years of what they considered unconscionable declines in civil rights protections and reductions in the number of discrimination cases pursued by the federal government in education, employment, and housing,[50] groups such as the NAACP and the National Organization for Women hoped that President George H. W. Bush's administration would reverse this trend. When the Bush administration failed to take the lead on these issues, Congress decided to pass new civil rights legislation to undo the 1989 Supreme Court rulings. Although the president expressed strong concern for civil rights, he used one of his trademark vetoes to overturn Congress's 1990 civil rights restoration effort, saying it would lead employers to use quotas to avoid lawsuits. The American Civil Liberties Union accused President Bush of using a "smokescreen of 'quotas' to prevent restoration of critically important civil rights laws that give minorities equal access to education, housing, employment and the ballot box."[51]

In 1991, the House of Representatives hammered out a bill to restore the original decision in the *Griggs* case while also strengthening antiquota language. President George H. W. Bush again rejected the bill, but eventually a compromise emerged. The bill eliminated a practice called "race norming" in which job-related test scores are adjusted for differences across racial or ethnic groups. It allowed punitive and compensatory damages to be collected for the first time in sexual discrimination (including sexual harassment) cases, as well as in cases of discrimination against people with disabilities and members of religious groups. The bill extended provisions to Senate and White House staff for the first time, with the stipulation that senators who violate the law are *personally* liable for damages.

Another civil rights issue that arose during the Bush administration was questioning whether college scholarships awarded solely on the basis of race violated Title VI of the Civil Rights Act. Since only a tiny fraction of the nation's scholarships were awarded on race alone (most include other criteria such as financial need and merit), there was concern that animosity among ethnic groups was being aroused over a nonissue. In 1993, President Clinton's Secretary of Education announced that such scholarships are a legal remedy to correct past inequities.

University Admissions

In the late 1990s, a number of ballot initiatives and court rulings challenged gender and racial preferences in public college and university admissions. In California (Proposition 209) and Washington state (Initiative 200), voters decided to ban gender and racial preferences in public education, employment, and contracting, effectively abolishing the states' affirmative action programs.

With regard to court rulings, in 1996, Cheryl Hopwood and three other white students who were denied admission to the University of Texas at Austin Law School sued the State of Texas for discrimination because students of color with lower qualifying scores were admitted. The U.S. Court of Appeals, Fifth Circuit's decision in *Hopwood v. Texas* declared the use of racial preferences in university admissions unconstitutional (see also *Johnson v. Board of Regents of University of Georgia*). Immediately following this decision, admissions of Hispanic and black students to the University of Texas at Austin and Texas A&M University dropped significantly. The concern was that this ruling sent a message that students of color were not welcomed on campuses.

In 1998, the Texas legislature adopted a plan to give Texas high school students placing in the top 10 percent of their high school graduating class automatic admission to the Texas public university of their choice. This corrected some of the loss of minority students following the *Hopwood* decision. After Proposition 209 passed, California began guaranteeing the top 12.5 percent of the state's high school graduates admission to a state university (but not necessarily to the school of their choice).

In 2002, The U.S. Commission on Civil Rights reported on Texas, California, and Florida's "percent plans." Overall, the commission found fewer admissions of students of color at these universities even on campuses that had increased outreach efforts. The commission concluded that "percentage plans alone do not improve diversity by reaching underrepresented minority groups and will only have their desired effect if affirmative action and other supplemental recruitment, admissions, and academic support programs remain in place."[52]

The Supreme Court's June 2003 decisions in *Grutter v. Bollinger* and *Gratz v. Bollinger*[53] added more food for thought to the affirmative action debate. Both were discrimination cases against the University of Michigan. Gratz was denied admission to the College of Literature, Science, and Arts and sued the university, claiming that minority students with lesser qualifications had been admitted. Grutter filed a similar case against the University of Michigan Law School. The Supreme Court heard the cases together but reached different conclusions in each. They agreed that Gratz suffered discrimination because the admission procedure automatically awarded 20 points to minority students. In the Grutter case, the court found in favor of the university, stating that its law school's admission procedures used race in a narrowly tailored way that furthered the school's compelling interest in obtaining the benefits accruing from a diverse student body. Thus, the court ruled against a point system, believing that it made race a deciding factor in admissions. In the Grutter case, among other admission requirements, students wrote an essay describing the diverse contributions they could make to the law school. The law school defined diversity broadly and had set educational goals dependent on a diverse student body. Race was one of many factors used in making admissions decisions, not the deciding factor.

Today, many universities go to great lengths to create procedures for ensuring diverse student populations based on multiple criteria for admission. The University of Michigan and other institutions have invested substantially in evaluating applications and other procedures and programs emphasized by the U.S. Commission on Civil Rights.

Affirmative Action in the Twenty-First Century

In 2009, the U.S. Supreme Court issued an important affirmative action ruling in the case of *Ricci v. DeStefano*, in which white firefighters in New Haven, Connecticut, claimed they were unfairly denied promotion. After a test to determine promotion was administered, one Hispanic and no blacks passed. The city decided that no promotions would be granted because it feared lawsuits from minority groups claiming that the test had an unfair or *disparate* impact on people of color. Others pointed to evidence that the test was not racially biased, claiming that the city unfairly denied the white firefighters a promotion they deserved. The Supreme Court agreed with the white firefighters.

One view is that the high court's decision presents a "catch-22" for New Haven and other employers because it did not address the inherent conflict between the U.S. Constitution's guarantee of equal protection for all and Title VII of the Civil Rights Act's disparate-impact provisions.

In addition to its importance, the *Ricci* decision piqued interest because President Obama's Supreme Court nominee Judge Sonia Sotomayor had joined with two other federal appeals court judges in a prior ruling that upheld the city's action. Some conservatives claimed her opinion was evidence that she was a "judicial activist," legislating from the bench, while some liberals said she had exercised judicial restraint because her decision was in keeping with other New York federal appeals court decisions and with the spirit of the Civil Rights Act.[54] A University of Texas legal scholar wrote:

> Ever since the Reagan Revolution, Republicans have been . . . committed to the (white) Southern position that the Constitution is colorblind . . . . Under a colorblind Constitution, laws assisting minorities—such as affirmative action—are suspect. Democrats, by contrast, believe that racial equality is such an important goal that outcomes should be scrutinized for racial fairness. Any Democrat nominated for the Supreme Court would have joined the Ricci dissenters, just as it is certain that if Sen. John McCain had won the presidency, he would have nominated a person who agreed with the Ricci majority.[55]

The NAACP is a strong supporter of affirmative action, but some African Americans take a very different position. For example, businessman Ward Connerly, who helped spearhead passage of California's Proposition 209, heads the American Civil Rights Institute (ACRI). ACRI "seeks to affect cultural change by challenging the 'race matters' mentality embraced by many of today's 'civil rights leaders'" and "believe[s] that government policies should not advocate group rights over individual rights."[56]

Some conservative blacks, including some black scholars, take the position that affirmative action helped blacks in the past, especially middle-class blacks, but that the future rests on blacks helping themselves.[57] When comedian Bill Cosby, who has an earned doctorate in education, said that blacks in undesirable circumstances need to take responsibility for themselves, he found his share of both critics and defenders.[58] Liberals who support affirmative action policies have been implored to "let race go" and to not make "race the organizing principle of our polity and civic culture."[59] Others believe that until gaps in areas such as education, wages, health coverage, and housing close, abandoning affirmative action would be foolish.[60]

VOTING RIGHTS

One way groups can achieve equity is to exercise their right to vote. Between 1970 and 2002, the number blacks or African Americans elected to local, state, and national offices increased from 1,469 to 9,430.[61] From 2002 to 2007, the number of blacks or African Americans elected in statewide elections for positions such as governor, lieutenant governor, state treasurer, judge, and university board members barely increased (from 40 to 43).[62] In 1989, Virginia voters elected Douglas Wilder the nation's first black governor. He was followed by Deval Patrick, elected Massachusetts governor in 2006. Among members of the 111th Congress in 2009, there were 42 black or African American U.S. representatives.[63] The only African American senator serving in the 111th Congress was Roland Burris (D-IL), who was appointed to fill the seat vacated when Barack Obama (D-IL) was elected President. In recent decades two other African Americans have served in the U.S. Senate—Edward Brookes (R-MA) and Carol Moseley Braun (D-IL). Some of the larger U.S. cities—Los Angeles, Detroit, Cleveland, New York, Atlanta, and Chicago—have elected blacks as mayors. African Americans overwhelmingly vote for Democratic candidates. Groups promoting the political agendas of blacks or African Americans include the National Association for the Advancement of Colored People and the National Urban League.

In 1994, 5,459 Hispanics held elective local, state, and national offices;[64] in 2008, that number had dropped to 5,240.[65] In the 111th Congress in 2009, there were 27 Hispanic representatives and three senators.[66] Florida, New Mexico, and Arizona have elected Hispanics as governor, and some large cities—Miami, San Antonio, and Denver—have had Hispanic mayors. Hispanics as a group may favor the Democratic party, but their political leanings also suggest that many favor conservative positions with respect to abortion and gay rights.[67] Groups promoting the political agenda of Hispanic Americans include the National Council of La Raza, the Mexican American Legal Defense and Education Fund (MALDEF), and the League of United Latin American Citizens (LULAC).

In the 111th Congress in 2009, six Asian Americans or Pacific Islanders served as U.S. representatives and two as U.S. senators (both from Hawaii). The *National Asian Pacific American Political Almanac* lists over 2,000 people of these ethnic groups holding elected or major appointed offices.[68] An analysis of Asian Pacific American political candidates indicates that they have "cross-over appeal" because those that run for office on the U.S. mainland are from political districts in which Asians are not the major ethnic group.[69] The same analysis notes that Asian and Pacific Americans often get little attention in "minority politics."

In recent decades, the only Native American to serve in the U.S. Senate was Ben Nighthorse Campbell (R-CO), a Cheyenne. He was a senator from 1993 until he retired in 2005 (he was formerly a U.S. representative and a Democrat). Since the 1950s, five Native Americans have served in the U.S. House of Representatives.[70] Native Americans and Alaska Natives comprise about 1.5 percent of the U.S. population. Congress members from states with the largest Native American populations often find challenges in representing their Native American constituents because their needs may conflict with those of larger and more powerful constituent groups,[71] a difficulty not uncommon in representing disenfranchised groups. In the November 2008 elections, one source counted 23 Native Americans from 11 states representing 16 tribes who were elected to state and local offices.[72]

Voter Discrimination Past and Present

In the course of U.S. history, the abolition of poll taxes and literacy tests (including ridiculous questions like "how many bubbles in a bar of soap") were important steps in assuring that Americans could exercise their voting rights.[73] Since the mid-1900s many more efforts have been made to ensure that all groups have the same voting opportunities. Especially important is the 1965 Voting Rights Act, designed to further protect and encourage the right to a voice in the electoral process. Congress periodically reviews and reauthorizes the act. Improvements have continually been made such as making it easier to register and cast one's vote.

Some Americans alive today remember the blatant racial voting discrimination of the past. Others took for granted that when they cast their vote, their vote was counted. That naiveté was lost during the 2000 presidential election, partly because of the numbers turned away from the polls because their names were improperly removed from the roles or whose votes went uncounted because of problems such as identifying individual voter's intent on punch card ballots. The U.S. Civil Rights Commission conducted an extensive investigation in

Florida, the most troublesome state during the 2000 election, and found that the votes of more than 14 percent of blacks were rejected, compared to less than two percent of other voters. The Commission concluded that although it found no conspiracy among the state's highest officials to disenfranchise voters, the responsible officials failed to "ensur[e] efficiency, uniformity, and fairness in the election."[74]

Whether they are isolated incidents, unintentional mistakes, or something more odious, accusations of various forms of discrimination in the voting process continue to be leveled.[75] Although we can cite just a few examples here, some of them have been called intimidation. For example, in 2002, Republican poll watchers in Arkansas were accused of photographing blacks as they voted,[76] and in 2006, reports were that 14,000 letters were mailed to Hispanic voters "falsely informing them that immigrants could be sent to jail for voting."[77] In 2001, a particularly egregious example allegedly occurred in Kilmichael, Mississippi (population 830), when "the all-white town council decided to cancel the municipal elections when it became clear that, for the first time in the town's history, a black candidate would win the mayoral election."[78]

Other accusations involve access and resources. For example, in 2003, Bexar County (Texas) officials were accused of failing to provide polling places in communities composed largely of Latinos during a special election when a Constitutional amendment was being considered.[79] In other examples, the federal government has filed complaints against jurisdictions for failing to provide voting education and voting materials in Spanish or to comply with other language assistance provisions of voting rights protections.[80] The language assistance provisions of the Voting Rights Act were intended to benefit foreign-born Americans as well as Native Americans and Alaska Natives who may use tribal languages.[81]

Voter identification measures have been called another means of disenfranchisement. Others say they are a way to prevent voter fraud. Identification procedures vary, but depending on the demands they impose, they have been likened to a poll tax because individuals may have to incur substantial costs in order to obtain the proper identification before they can vote.

Redistricting and Gerrymandering

The U.S. census is conducted every 10 years. Following the census, Congressional districts are redrawn to adjust for the allocation of the 435 seats in the U.S. House of Representatives based on changes in the U.S. population. This is called *redistricting* or *reapportionment*. It is done to ensure equal representation of Americans across the country based on the principle of "one person, one vote." Both Republicans and Democrats seek to redraw districts in their favor so they will have the votes necessary for members of their party to be elected to office. This partisan practice is widely recognized and widely accepted when it is done every 10 years following the census.[82] It is nonetheless a highly contentious process.

The U.S. Supreme Court struck down *gerrymandering* by using race as a principal or predominant factor to create voting districts. However, Section 5 of the Voting Rights Act and "a line of Supreme Court decisions have [also] worked to restrict the use of gerrymandering to dilute minority voting strength."[83] (Gerrymandering got its name from Massachusetts governor Elbridge Gerry, who in 1812 "approved a district that had been tortured for political purposes into the shape of a salamander."[84])

The state of Texas serves as an example of what The Brennan Center for Justice at New York University Law School called a case of "notorious 're-redistricting'" because it occurred in the middle of the decade, which no state had attempted to do since the Supreme Court mandated decennial redistricting. (Colorado also attempted "re-redistricting" in between decennial censuses, but the state's supreme court stopped it.) After the 2000 census, when the Texas legislature failed to agree on a redistricting plan, a federal court drew up a plan, which slightly favored Republicans. After the 2002 elections, Republicans gained control of the state legislature. In 2003, Republicans attempted to redistrict again. To avoid a vote on this redistricting, Democratic legislators literally fled the state. The Brennan Center filed an amicus (friend of the court) brief, which alleged that not only was there no need for the mid-decade redistricting, the effort was so partisan that "the new map would violate the state and federal constitutions, even if it had been adopted at the beginning of the decade."[85]

The Texas case made its way to the U.S. Supreme Court as *LULAC vs. Perry.* LULAC, the League of United Latin American Citizens, contended that the re-redistricting diluted the Hispanic vote. When the Supreme Court ruled in the case, LULAC called the decision a "vindication,"[86] even though the court found that in just one district had the redrawn boundaries resulted in "impermissible vote dilution under the Voting Rights Act."[87] The decision, however, left hanging the question of what constitutes permissible or impermissible redistricting in a country where attempts at gerrymandering occur with regularity.[88]

In the United States, *single-member districts* have allowed communities to elect candidates of the same racial or ethnic group as the majority of the population in that district. This was important because it was unlikely that a person of color would be elected in a white majority district. On the other hand, single-member districts may perpetuate racial divisions if voting districts are segregated by race.[89] Another approach used to promote minority representation is cumulative voting in which one person gets to cast several votes (usually the same number of votes as seats to be filled in a race). Voters can give all their votes to one candidate or spread them out over candidates. There is evidence that cumulative voting can result in increased minority representation.[90]

Today, one view is that any sort of racial gerrymandering is unnecessary and even counterproductive to people of all racial and ethnic groups. Individuals such as Abigail Thernstrom, Vice Chair of the U.S. Civil Rights Commission and scholar at the conservative American Enterprise Institute, point to the election of the nation's first African American president as evidence that the color barrier in electoral politics has been broken (although they acknowledge that this doesn't mean that racism has suddenly disappeared).[91] Perhaps this is so, but there is also a relationship between race or ethnicity and political party preference, so that partisan gerrymandering may also produce racially divided voting districts or districts in which a minority group's voice is diluted. With today's computer technologies, districts can be created to target groups by many characteristics that can favor the party in power. Political races have become increasingly less competitive because of partisan redistricting.[92]

The state of Iowa is perhaps the best example of nonpartisan redistricting, which promotes competitive elections. In Iowa, legislative staff draw up the redistricting plan without using prior voting data. The state legislature must approve the plan. Iowa's law has been described as one that "requires use of the old-fashioned redistricting principles of compactness, contiguity, and respect for local government boundaries, and more importantly, prohibits partisan considerations."[93]

Preclearance

A primary point of contention with regard to the Voting Rights Act in the twenty-first century is whether there is a need to continue to require jurisdictions that discriminated in the past to "preclear" with the U.S. Department of Justice any changes to their voting practices. Preclearance (Section 5 of the Voting Rights Act) began in 1965 and was originally intended to last for five years, unlike other provisions of the act that are permanent and apply to all states.

Jurisdictions can "bail out" of preclearance requirements after meeting specified criteria. Today, eight states, mostly in the South, and parts of eight other states, remain under preclearance requirements.

Congress last extended preclearance in 2006—this time for 25 more years. Today, some conservatives call parts of the Voting Rights Act "a period piece"[94] and preclearance "nonsensical," especially given the black voter turnout and election results in 2008.[95] They see no need to extend preclearance for another quarter of a century. Civil rights groups see it differently. Given how difficult voting rights protections were to come by, they insist that it would be a gamble to let any of them go.

TROUBLES IN INDIAN COUNTRY

No group in the United States has suffered a longer history of racially motivated violence and discrimination than Native Americans. As a direct result, Native Americans have endured tremendous social, economic, and health problems. Today it seems astonishing that Native Americans were not accorded citizenship until 1924, that some remained slaves until 1935, and that Utah, the last state to grant Native Americans voting rights, did not do so until 1956.[96]

Public policy decisions are at the heart of much suffering that Native Americans have endured. They have been robbed of land and minerals rights, thus depriving them of a livelihood. Many were displaced from their reservations and forced to adapt to urban life and to assimilate into the majority culture, even though their family structures, religions, and communication patterns differ substantially from those of whites.[97] Many Native American children were taken from their homes and placed in boarding schools where they were forbidden to speak their native language or to practice tribal customs.

To improve the lives of Native Americans, the Indian Self-Determination and Education Assistance Act of 1975 emphasized tribal self-government and the establishment of independent health, education, and welfare services, but the lives of many Native Americans have not improved substantially. Poverty rates among Native Americans remain much higher than for the U.S. population as whole; many Native Americans receive public assistance; about half of members of federally recognized tribes are unemployed; and nearly a third of those who are employed earn less than federal poverty guidelines.[98] Native Americans rates of diabetes, alcoholism, tuberculosis, suicide, and infant mortality are also much higher than that of the general population.[99]

Particularly degrading has been the removal of Native American children from their families to be raised by others, a practice rationalized by welfare professionals who viewed Native American child rearing practices as overly harsh.[100] The Indian Child Welfare Act of 1978 was designed to change the way Native American children are placed by restoring greater control over these decisions to the tribes. When a child must be placed, priority is now given to members of the child's own tribe rather than to non-Indian families.

In 1946, as part of a legislative reorganization act, the U.S. House of Representatives and Senate committees on Indian affairs were disbanded. Their responsibilities were transferred to other committees. In 1977, the Senate re-established a temporary committee. It became the permanent Committee on Indian Affairs in 1984 with responsibilities for all legislation pertaining to the "unique problems" of Native American, Native Hawaiian, and Alaska Native people, including education, economic development, land management and trusts, healthcare, and claims against the United States.[101] In the House, the Committee on Natural Resources has an Office of Indian Affairs that is responsible for many issues related to Native Americans. Representative Denny Rehberg (R-MT) has called for re-establishing a permanent House committee on Indian affairs.

Today, there are 564 federally recognized tribal governments.[102] Many Native American groups do not have this recognition, which is necessary for receiving the benefits and services that the federal government is required to provide to tribes and their members. The relationship of each of the 564 tribes to the U.S. government and the individual states is one of sovereigns (governments). Each tribe has the right to establish its own government and to make criminal and civil laws, determine tribal citizenship (membership), and undertake other functions.

The Bureau of Indian Affairs and the Indian Health Service

In 1775, the Continental Congress established three departments of Indian affairs to cover the northern, central, and southern parts of the country.[103] Today, the U.S. Assistant Secretary for Indian Affairs is responsible for the Bureau of Indian Affairs (BIA) and the Bureau of Indian Education (BIE). Both are part of the U.S. Department of the Interior. The BIA manages 66 million acres of land held in trust for Native Americans, Indian tribes, and Alaska Natives, and the BIE (formerly part of the BIA) is responsible for the education of about 48,000 Native American children.

The BIA's current mission "is to enhance the quality of life, to promote economic opportunity, and to . . . protect the trust assets of American Indians, Indian tribes, and Alaska Natives."[104] Almost all BIA employees are Native Americans. Under a policy established as part of 1934 Indian Reorganization Act, preference for these positions goes to Native Americans. The U.S. Supreme Court has approved this hiring preference, not as an affirmative action measure to redress past discrimination, but to promote self-governance and the unique trust relationship between Native Americans and the federal government.[105] This might sound like an ideal arrangement for promoting policies beneficial to Native Americans, but the BIA has long been criticized for its paternalistic and authoritarian attitude toward its clientele. Critics have said, "The BIA takes care of Indians' money, land, children, water, roads, etc. with authority [as] complete as that of a prison."[106]

Despite long-standing criticisms of the BIA, it was not until October 1987 that official action to investigate the BIA began. Senator Daniel Inouye (D-HI), then chairperson of the Senate Select Committee on Indian Affairs, called for full investigative hearings after an astonishing series of articles appeared in the *Arizona Republic* claiming "widespread fraud, mismanagement and waste in the almost $3 billion-a-year federal Indian programs."[107] Other accusations were that the government had assisted oil companies in bilking Native Americans of billions of dollars from oil and gas reserves.[108]

The Indian Health Service (IHS) is the federal government's main health program for Native Americans and Alaska Natives, and is part of the U.S. Department of Health and Human Services. The IHS was also criticized for inadequate and incompetent treatment of patients.[109] Allegations of abuse of students in boarding schools and educational facilities for Native American children were also widespread, and Native people continue to heal from these abuses.[110]

Cobell v. Salazar

The history of the BIA's relationship with Native Americans and a lengthy lawsuit, last known as *Cobell v. Salazar,* raised serious questions about the federal government's treatment of Native Americans. In 1887, the Dawes Act or General Allotment Act divided Native American lands into 80- to 160-acre portions and allocated them to individual Native Americans as part of the government's attempt to destroy reservations and force Native Americans to assimilate. The process also created Indian Individual Money (IIM) accounts that the Department of the Interior holds "in trust" (manages). These lands generate revenues from activities such as oil and gas leases.

In the United States, anyone with any type of trust account has a legal right to a full accounting, but IIM account management may best be described as a gigantic mess because the government could not provide a decent accounting of what is owed to Native Americans or even how many accounts there are (estimates are 300,000 to 500,000). The American Indian Trust Fund Management Reform Act of 1994 directed the Interior Secretary to provide an accounting, but this did not happen. In 1996 Elouise Cobell, a Blackfoot from Montana and a banker, and other Indians, filed a class-action suit *Cobell v. Babbit* (at that time Bruce Babbitt was Interior Secretary) to obtain an accounting and force the government to fulfill its fiduciary duty and pay Indians what is rightfully theirs. Other defendants in the case were the Treasury Secretary and the Assistant Secretary of Indian Affairs. As the lawsuit wore on, Cobell warned Indians not to make small individual settlements that would rob them of their just deserts and not to believe that a settlement would result in an end to spending on programs for Native Americans. The government spent millions defending itself; money that some argued could have gone to Native Americans instead.

In 2001, the lawsuit shut down the BIA website in order to ensure the security of individual trust account data. It was not until the summer of 2008 that the BIA was again fully connected to the Internet. In 2008, a district judge said an accurate trust fund accounting would be "impossible" given that the necessary records are unavailable and awarded nearly $456 million in the case. The judge also said:

> Whatever problems have existed in the history of this trust, and however serious the misfeasances and malfeasances of the trustees over 120 years, there has never been any evidence of such prodigious pilfering of assets from within the trust system itself. . . . The plaintiffs' model stands or falls with their legal theory, and it falls. The government's model, on the other hand, fits comfortably within the equitable principles that should be applied with respect to the IIM trust, because it offers a useful way of pricing the considerable uncertainty in the data. Plaintiffs presented no statistical testimony challenging the government's model, which I found to be sound.[111]

The plaintiffs appealed the decision contending that the $456 million was far from adequate. In December 2009, a settlement was finally reached in the case. The federal government will create a $1.4 billion Accounting/Trust Administration Fund, a $2 billion Trust Land Consolidation Fund, and a higher education Indian Education Scholarship fund of up to $60 million. This may sound like a lot of money, but the suit represents about 500,000 people. Most who are entitled to claims will receive no less than $1,500.[112]

In 1980, Edward Carpenter assessed Native Americans' status by stating "that a part of the problem is related to the Indian's cultural diversification and a history of limited tribal cooperation is probably true. However, the impact of the Indian's legal status, the failure of the Congress, and the concomitant administrative morass created by the BIA appear to be the critical variables."[113] Carpenter called for a hands-off policy by non-Indians and a return of authority to Native Americans. Ten years later, a special Senate committee recommended abolishing the BIA and replacing it with a program of direct financial grants to Native American tribes. This call was reportedly met by skepticism by Indians and non-Indians alike.[114] In November 2009, leaders of the nation's federally recognized Native American tribes were invited to meet with the president and his cabinet. They are looking to the Obama administration to ensure fair treatment of Native Americans in public policy arenas, such as the Indian health program overhaul Congress is considering. The Indian Health Care Improvement Act was reauthorized and the IHS permanently reauthorized as part of the nation's 2010 health care reform legislation package along with provisions to modernize the IHS.

RACIAL AND ETHNIC TARGETING

Racial and ethnic targeting can take different forms. Here we discuss racial profiling, hate crimes, and public policy responses to them.

Racial Profiling

Racial profiling may be defined as the practice of stopping, interrogating, searching, and/or arresting people based on their race or ethnicity or their presumed race or ethnicity. This practice is centered in stereotypical beliefs that people of certain racial or ethnic groups are more likely than others to commit crimes.[115] Racial profiling is not only upsetting to its victims, it can have significant, negative consequences in their lives and can affect law enforcement's relations with communities by undermining confidence in these agencies.[116] African American parents, for example, are often vigilant about instructing their sons about what to do if stopped by the police.

Racial profiling often occurs when people of color are pursuing ordinary everyday activities such as driving, walking, using airports, shopping, and even while they are at home (e.g., when residences are wrongly targeted for raids).[117] Racial profiling has likely occurred since people of different ethnic groups first encountered each other. It has long been recognized in the United States, but it was not until the late 1990s that the problem reached the public policy agenda. The issue emerged in the development of "drug courier" profiles.

Most people recognize the job that local, state, and federal law enforcement officers do requires them to make difficult decisions in virtually every case they encounter. In individual cases, it is often difficult to prove whether a law enforcement officer engaged in racial profiling or had a legitimate reason for taking action. For example, in 2009, when Harvard University Professor of African and African American Studies Henry Louis Gates, Jr., was arrested at his home for disorderly conduct (the charges were later dropped), the news media were full of commentaries about whether he had been a victim of racial profiling. Over beers at the Whitehouse with President Obama and Vice President Biden, Gates and the arresting officer respectfully agreed to disagree over what had transpired.[118]

Concerns about racial profiling are often based on multiple incidents. For example, in 2004, the ACLU accused the Charlottesville, Virginia, police force of detaining African American men "practically at random" in order to do DNA testing in their attempts to apprehend a serial rapist believed to be African American.[119] The ACLU said that while technically the men's constitutional rights against unreasonable search and seizure may not have been violated because they consented to provide saliva samples, "the racial aspect of the DNA search policy cannot be ignored." The ACLU encouraged the police department to better target its search and announced its intent to educate African American men about the extent of their rights to refuse searches.

Rather than attempt to determine individual law enforcement officers' motives, large numbers of traffic or pedestrian stops or other law enforcement activities are often studied to determine whether in the aggregate people of particular racial and gender groups are being stopped or detained disproportionate to their representation in the population and their involvement in illegal activities. These studies have often found evidence that supports the contention of racial profiling.[120] For example, a Government Accountability Office study of the U.S. Customs Service found that black female U.S. citizens were nine times more likely than white female U.S. citizens to be X-rayed following a frisk or pat down, but less than half as likely to be found with contraband.[121]

Systematic data collection can also be used to determine if any pattern of racial profiling seems to be confined to a particular officer or officers or if patterns are more pervasive throughout a law enforcement agency.[122] Even if data analysis does not definitively answer the question of whether racial profiling or another phenomenon is occurring, it can help identify issues and problems, and remedies can be undertaken such as education, supervision, and training.[123] Other suggestions to help curb racial profiling are combining internal monitoring with external efforts such as citizen complaint boards that address racial profiling and other complaints against law enforcement officers, enforcement of anti-profiling laws, and media attention.

The ACLU is often involved in racial profiling lawsuits and consent decrees (agreements reached between the plaintiffs and defendants). For example, in 2008, plaintiffs and the Maryland State Police (MSP) entered into a consent decree that included financial damages paid to the plaintiffs, the MSP's agreement to hire a consultant to assess progress in eliminating racial profiling, and a joint statement condemning racial profiling and stressing the need to act to prevent racial profiling in the future.[124]

A number of states have enacted laws to curb racial profiling. The human rights organization Amnesty International believes every state and the federal government should have a strong law prohibiting racial profiling (see Illustration 12.1). Since 2001, attempts at passing such a federal law have failed in Congress, and concerns about profiling have increased in light of Arizona's tough 2010 legislation targeting illegal immigrants.

ILLUSTRATION 12.1
Amnesty International's Recommendations for Legislation Prohibiting Racial Profiling

WHAT A GOOD LAW WOULD LOOK LIKE

After reviewing all existing and proposed state legislation addressing racial profiling (as of June 1, 2004), AIUSA determined that in order to effectively combat the most common forms of racial profiling, a statute should:

- Include a comprehensive effective ban on racial profiling. Such a ban would prohibit the profiling of individuals and groups by law enforcement agencies even partially on the basis of race, ethnicity, national origin, or religion, except when there is trustworthy information, relevant to the locality and timeframe, that links persons belonging to one of the aforementioned groups to an identified criminal incident or scheme.
- Ban pretextual stops (those instances in which police use minor/common traffic violations to inquire about drugs, guns, or other breaches of the law) of pedestrians and motorists.

- Criminalize violations of the racial profiling ban and specify penalties for officers who repeatedly engage in racial profiling.
- Require mandatory data collection for all stops and all searches (traffic and pedestrian) in all circumstances (citations and warnings given). Such data would include perceived race, perceived gender, perceived age, and whether immigration status was inquired about during the stop.
- Require data analysis and publication of the data collected.
- Create an independent commission to review and respond to complaints of racial profiling and regularly publish results of racial profiling investigations.
- Allow for individuals to seek court orders to stop individual departments from continuing to engage in racial profiling.
- Provide funds for periodically retraining officers and installing in-car video cameras for monitoring traffic stops.

Reprinted by permission of Amnesty International.

The War on Terror

Over the course of the nation's history, the federal government has also been accused of racial profiling. For example, during World War I, U.S. Attorney General A. Mitchell Palmer ordered the detention and deportation of large numbers of immigrants from Eastern Europe after extremists bombed his house. Federal agents were ordered to conduct "Palmer raids" by rounding up thousands of immigrants who were detained and some who were deported because of their ethnicity.[125]

The treatment of Japanese Americans after Japan attacked Pearl Harbor in 1941 and World War II erupted is another disturbing example of discrimination against Americans of foreign backgrounds. Following the attack, Japanese Americans were interned in ten relocation camps by President Franklin D. Roosevelt for fear that they might threaten U.S. security and to protect them from potential harm by Americans who were angered by Japan's attack. Japanese Americans believe that this action was neither necessary nor benevolent. They were forced to give up their jobs and their possessions. To prove they were indeed Americans, many volunteered for the armed services. Internment ended in 1943 with the recognition that citizenship and loyalty to one's country, not racial characteristics, make one an American. Not until 1983 did the U.S. government actually acknowledge wrongdoing. The statement came as a result of the work of the Commission on Wartime Relocation and Internment of Civilians. Reparation payments were later approved for the approximately 78,000 remaining survivors of internment.[126]

In February 2001, President George W. Bush called for an end to racial profiling,[127] but in the wake of the September 11, 2001, terrorist attacks, several thousand Arab, South Asian, and Muslim men residing in the United States were interviewed or sought for questioning because of national origin or religion. At least 1,200 were detained. Many lacked access to an attorney and other resources to fight arrest. Family, friends, and employers of many detainees did not know where these individuals were. Deportation hearings for Arabs were closed to the public and held in secret.[128] The ACLU filed suit in October 2001 under the Freedom of Information Act to force the government to release information about the prisoners. A federal judge ordered the government to provide information about detainees, noting that "secret arrests are a concept odious to a democratic society."[129] The federal government refused, and a higher court overturned the judge's ruling. The Inspector General's office in the Department of Justice found that arrests were indiscriminate and that detainees were denied access to counsel, detained in degrading conditions, and in some instances, verbally and physically abused.[130] Many were detained for months without charges, some in solitary confinement. For those with legal counsel, Attorney General John Ashcroft used "emergency authority" to order monitoring of attorney-client conversations, which many declared a violation of the Sixth Amendment (rights of the accused). Most detainees were eventually released, and large numbers were deported, but several hundred were held at the U.S. naval base in Guantanamo Bay, Cuba.[131] President George W. Bush declared these prisoners "enemy combatants." In June 2004, the Supreme Court told the President that the remaining Guantanamo detainees could challenge their detention. Military tribunals designated to hear the cases give the detainees only limited legal representation. Discussion continues over whether some of the remaining detainees will be tried in civilian courts or military tribunals (which afford them fewer rights) and whether some detainees can be held without trial indefinitely.

The ACLU remains highly critical of the federal government's efforts to prevent racial profiling, including the Justice Department's *2003 Guidance Regarding the Use of Race by Federal Law Enforcement Agencies*.[132] Amnesty International is also critical of the guidance, which is advisory rather than legally binding, because it "does not cover profiling based on religion, religious appearance, or national origin; does not apply to state or local law enforcement agencies; does not include any enforcement mechanisms; does not specify punishment for violating officers/agencies; and contains a blanket exception for 'national security' and 'border integrity' cases."[133]

Hate Crimes

Of the nearly 8,000 hate crimes against persons or their property included in official FBI reports in 2008, nearly two-thirds were motivated by bias due to race, ethnicity, or national origin and nearly one-fifth by religious bias.[134] Approximately 70 percent of racial bias incidents were motivated by bias toward blacks and 18 percent by bias toward whites. Of ethnically motivated incidents, nearly two-thirds were against Hispanics, and of religious motivated incidents, two-thirds were against Jews.

The Southern Poverty Law Center's (SPLC) Intelligence Project tracks hate groups in the United States. The project reports that between 2000 and 2008, the number of hate groups in the United States grew from 602 to 926 and calls Ku Klux Klan groups, neo-Nazis, and racist skinheads the "most active and dangerous white supremacist hate group sectors."[135] In recent years, the SPLC has attributed the growth of hate groups to "fears of Latino immigration" and more recently to the faltering economy and the successful presidential campaign of Barack Obama. With regard to the economy, the SPLC notes that misinformation that illegal immigrants are to blame for many mortgage defaults and that the Community Reinvestment Act provided loans to many people of color who defaulted on their mortgages added fuel to the fire.[136] The editor of the Intelligence Report adds that "Barack Obama's election has inflamed racist extremists who see it as another sign that their country is under siege by non-whites."[137]

Hate crime laws vary from state to state. As Chapter 11 noted, under these laws, bias-motivated crimes are generally not considered separate offenses. Instead, they include enhanced penalties for crimes against persons or property that are motivated by hate based on an individual's race, ethnicity, or other characteristic. Forty-five states and the District of Columbia have hate crime penalty enhancement laws.[138]

To further address hate groups and reduce hate crimes, the Leadership Conference on Civil Rights calls for three main actions.[139] First is constructive discussion on comprehensive immigration reform to counter efforts to demonize immigrants. Second is efforts by law enforcement to address hate-related violence, including passage of the Local Law Enforcement Hate Crimes Prevention Act to help local authorities combat hate-related violence and allow federal authorities to do so if local authorities do not. Third, the act calls for federally funded education and training programs to prevent and reduce prejudice. A well-known effort to reduce hate is the Southern Poverty Law Center's Teach Tolerance project for children in grades K through 12, designed to promote respect and appreciation for diversity.

IMMIGRATION AND SOCIAL WELFARE

When white men and women arrived to colonize what is now the United States, they became the first immigrants to set foot on this land. Today, well over 100 years after the Statue of Liberty—an enduring symbol of freedom for immigrants—was erected, people from virtually every country and every cultural, ethnic, racial, and religious group inhabit the United States of America. Most Americans are now the descendants of those who came to this country in search of a better life, but immigration has hardly faded from the public policy agenda.

In 1910, foreign-born residents were nearly 15 percent of the U.S. population.[140] In 2007, they were less than 13 percent.[141] This figure is expected to increase to 19 percent by 2050 with foreign-born residents and their descendants comprising the vast majority of population growth.[142] Figure 12.3 shows the world regions of origin of the foreign-born population.

Public policy concerns about immigration can be framed in terms of three main questions: how much immigration to allow, who should be allowed to immigrate, and how to enforce immigration policy. Before addressing these questions, we present a brief overview of some events in the history of U.S. immigration policy.

A Brief History of U.S. Immigration Policy

U.S. laws regulating immigration have existed since the 1800s. The Chinese Exclusion Act of 1882 and the Oriental Exclusion Act of 1924 severely restricted the entrance of Asian groups, as did the Quota System Law of 1921 and the Immigration Act of 1924. Chinese immigrants were brought to this country in 1864 to do the backbreaking work of building the nation's railroads, but as larger numbers of Asians entered the United States and began to prosper, their successes made Americans uneasy. Immigration policies were more favorable to others, such as northern Europeans, perhaps because of the greater similarity of their physical characteristics to those of many Americans. Nevertheless, immigrants from these and other countries faced bigotry, and epithets have been used to insult Irish, Germans, Italians, Japanese, Mexicans, and many other immigrant groups.

There have been four major waves of immigration to the United States.[143] In the country's early days, immigrants were primarily English or western Europeans seeking economic opportunity or political or religious freedom. The second wave, during the mid-1800s, was comprised largely of people from Britain, Germany, and Ireland who came for economic and political reasons. They helped settle the frontier. The third wave, from the late 1800s to 1914 (when World War I erupted), included southern and eastern Europeans and people from Asia. In 1965, during

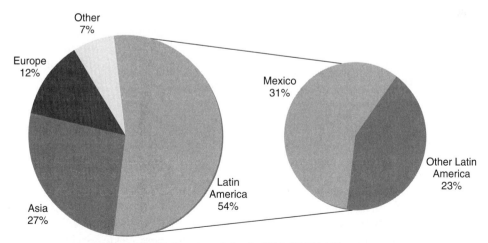

Total foreign-born population in 2008: 37,264,000

FIGURE 12.3 **World Region of Birth of the Foreign-born Population in the United States, 2008**
Source: U.S. Census Bureau, "Foreign-Born Population of the United States," *Current Population Survey—March 2008* Detailed Tables, Table 3.1. Retrieved February 16, 2010, from http://www.census.gov/population/www/socdemo/foreign/cps2008.html#birth

a period of sweeping civil rights reforms, Congress abolished stringent quotas limiting the number of entrants from various countries. This ushered in the fourth wave of immigration with preferences often going to family members of those already in the United States.

The Vietnam War displaced and impoverished many Vietnamese who later sought refuge in the United States. Of special concern were "Amerasian" children, children born to American servicemen and Vietnamese women. Several thousand of these children lived in poverty in Vietnam because it was difficult to establish their fathers' identities, a requirement for them to come to the United States. In other cases, fathers were unable to locate their children, or they faced bureaucratic problems in trying to get their children out of Vietnam. Under the Orderly Departure Program and the Amerasian Homecoming Act of 1987, the United States attempted to bring all these Amerasians (many of whom had reached adulthood) and their families to the United States.

Another immigration issue emerging in the 1960s was Cubans seeking refuge or asylum from the communistic Castro regime. As a result of the Cold War, U.S. immigration policy was more generous to those fleeing for fear of political persecution from communist governments. Freedom flights brought thousands of Cubans to the United States through the early 1970s. Then in 1980 Castro opened the port of Mariel and allowed thousands more Cubans to leave. To accommodate the new influx, President Jimmy Carter opened several refugee-processing centers in the United States. Many refugees came to join their families in the United States, but the convicted criminals and undesirables also sent caused criticism that Castro had used the United States as a dumping ground.

Cubans continue to risk their lives to come to the United States. In one dramatic escape, a Cuban flew a small plane from the United States and landed on a highway in Cuba to pick up his wife and sons and bring them to the United States. Others continue to brave shark-infested waters in small boats and makeshift rafts. In 1999, 5-year-old Elián Gonzalez captured the hearts of Americans when he survived a harrowing trip at sea to escape Cuba. His mother and others with them perished. A battle arose over whether the child should remain in the United States with relatives. Eventually, Elián was returned to his father in Cuba.

Cuban refugees are entitled to privileges not afforded other immigrants, such as temporary public assistance on arrival. After one year, most can become permanent residents. But 35 years after the first Cuban exodus, a new wave of immigrants and political pressures caused President Clinton to announce that Cuban refugees would be treated more like refugees from other countries. In 1994 many of those trying to flee were intercepted and detained at the U.S. naval base in Guantanamo Bay, Cuba. The Clinton administration reversed its position in 1996 and allowed them to enter the United States but said that those caught at sea in the future would be returned to Cuba. Immigration from other communist countries also made headlines, but for the opposite reason—the fall of many of these governments freed many individuals to leave.

Overwhelming poverty and the repressive Duvalier government spurred immigration from the tiny island of Haiti. The Duvaliers were eventually overthrown. A democratic election was held, but the elected leader, Jean-Bertrand Aristide, was ousted twice, first in 1991, less than a year after being elected, and then again in February 2004. Efforts to establish an acceptable governing structure during the 1991 uprising resulted in continued turmoil and violence.

Under the Immigration and Nationality Act of 1980, those seeking asylum or refugee status are admitted to the United States if they have "a well-founded fear of persecution on account of race, religion, nationality, membership in a particular social group or political opinion" (it excludes those who have had a role in persecuting others). In 1996, this definition was expanded to include those subjected to or persecuted for resisting coercive population control programs such as forced abortion or sterilization. The definition of refugee or asylee does not include those fleeing for "economic" reasons. The George H. W. Bush administration viewed those coming from Haiti as doing so for economic rather than political reasons, despite the country's brutal political situation. Many of those fleeing Haiti were sent to Guantanamo Bay (where many Cuban refugees were then being held). As Haitians fled in larger numbers and the camps there filled to capacity, George H. W. Bush ordered that Haitians intercepted at sea be immediately sent back to Haiti, without offering them legal counsel. There were court challenges to this policy and rulings pro and con amid concern about the plight of the Haitian people.

The Clinton administration continued the Bush policy, also encouraging the Haitians not to risk their lives at sea. In 1993 the U.S. Supreme Court upheld the practice of turning the Haitians back, stating that protections offered by the 1952 Immigration and Nationality Act pertain only to those who reach U.S. soil. During the 2004 uprising, President George W. Bush declared the United States' intent to continue these practices. Others believe this policy effectively ignores the legal and ethical obligations to refugees set forth in international law.[144]

The debate over political or economic refugee status also applied to those coming from Central America. Many blamed the United States for contributing to the political strife in Central America through foreign policies that increased the desire of Central Americans to immigrate to the United States. In 1990, Salvadorans already in the United States were temporarily granted stays of deportation, and their work permits were extended. This occurred after pleas from the Salvadoran president that his country's economy could not incorporate so many returning citizens.

In the 1980s, the "sanctuary" movement became another aspect of immigration concerns. Americans involved in the movement, many who were motivated by their religious convictions, provided food, clothing, shelter, and jobs to immigrants from El Salvador and Guatemala fleeing right-wing political movements. Sanctuary workers felt their actions were justified even if they were helping people who entered the country illegally. They believed that these individuals should have been treated as political refugees because they faced grave political oppression and persecution in their homeland. Immigration officials saw it differently, saying that transporting illegal immigrants and related acts violate the law.

Today, some U.S. cities are called sanctuary cities because they are more welcoming to undocumented individuals or because law enforcement does not pursue those who may be undocumented unless they commit a crime. A new sanctuary movement has developed to address what supporters consider unjust deportation and family breakup due to immigration issues.[145]

Between 1998 and 2002, following the breakup of the former Yugoslavia, nearly 100,000 Bosnians immigrated to the United States. Similarly, following U.S. involvement in the uprising in Somalia, the U.S. became a sanctuary for those fleeing oppression, as well as poverty, in Somalia. The litany of those seeking refuge or asylum in the United States continues, but events of September 11, 2001, marked another turning point in U.S. immigration policy.

Immigration Post-September 11th

Since the September 11, 2001, terrorist attacks in New York City and Washington, DC, immigration regulations have changed and enforcement has become more stringent. The United States has poured many more dollars into increased southern and northern border and port security to prevent terrorism and drug violence and to stop other illegal immigration by those motivated to enter the United States in search a better life. These efforts include increased numbers of border enforcement agents, erecting fences at the U.S. Mexico border, and using high-tech security devices and measures.

Most foreign nationals (citizens of countries other than the United States) who enter each year do so legally. These lawful entrants fall into two categories. *Immigrants* are allowed to enter for the purpose of becoming legal permanent residents (LPRs). About 1.1 million foreign nationals become LPRs each year. *Nonimmigrants* are allowed to enter on a temporary basis. They are the vast majority of lawful entrants. There were 163 million nonimmigrant admissions to the United States in 2009, mostly pleasure or business travelers; smaller numbers were temporary workers and their families (about 1.7 million), and students (about 1 million).[146] As in the past, substantial numbers of nonimmigrants continue to overstay their visas, but today they face much a greater threat of being caught and deported. Most of those who overstay work, support themselves and their families, live peacefully, and pose no U.S. security threat.

After September 11th, Americans realized that immigration authorities did not have good information on the whereabouts of many foreign nationals—those legally residing in the United States and those whose visas had expired. This raised concerns because it became apparent that even a relatively small number of well-organized terrorists could wreak havoc on the country. In response, the U.S. Attorney General implemented a new program in June 2002 called the National Security Entry Exit Registration System (NSEERS), requiring all males aged 15 and older from 25 countries to register with the U.S. government and be fingerprinted, photographed, and questioned. After one year, the Immigration and Naturalization Service (INS) had registered over 83,000 foreign nationals with nearly 14,000 being placed in deportation proceedings; none were publicly charged with terrorism.[147] Except for North Korea, all targeted countries were Arab or Muslim majority, making the program look more like another form of racial profiling rather than a program targeted to national security concerns. The program was poorly advertised. Many do not know about NSEERS or understand all its provisions, even though failure to comply can result in detention and deportation.[148]

A registration system called US-VISIT was also added to track the entry and exit of visitors to the United States holding nonimmigrant visas, regardless of country of origin.[149] This program, which uses digital, inkless, biometric finger scans and digital photographs, was greatly expanded in 2009 and is now required of nearly all those entering the United States whether to visit or reside permanently.[150]

After discovering that some of the September 11th terrorists had been admitted as foreign students, more policies were instituted. Students cannot enter the United States until they confirm that they have been accepted to the school they plan to attend. Foreign nationals already in the United States who wish to attend school in the United States must return to their home country before applying for a student visa. Today, immigration officials use the Student and Exchange Visitor Information System (SEVIS) to track students from other countries and ensure they do not overstay their visas. From January 2004 to January 2005, NSEERS, US-VISIT, and SEVIS produced over 300,000 "violator leads."[151]

As part of the federal government's approach to stronger enforcement of immigration laws as well as improved national security, in 2003, the U.S. Department of Homeland Security (DHS) was established. Within DHS, the U.S. Customs and Border Patrol (CBP) is responsible for enforcing immigration law at U.S. borders and ports of entry, and the U.S. Immigration and Customs Enforcement (ICE) is responsible for enforcing these laws inside U.S. borders. Also part of DHS is the U.S. Citizenship and Immigration Services (USCIS), formerly the U.S. Immigration and Naturalization Service (INS) of the Department of Justice. USCIS assists those wishing to immigrate and helps those who have immigrated, including helping them "naturalize" (become citizens).

Legal Immigration and Its Effects

Since World War II, the number of immigrants who become legal permanent residents (LPRs) of the United States each year has generally increased, from about 250,000 per year during the 1950s to slightly over one million per year from 2000 to 2009, reflecting expansions in immigration laws.[152] This has occurred despite the September 11, 2001, backlash over the entrance of "foreigners."

LPRs hold "green cards" that entitle them not only to permanently reside in the United States, but also to work, attend public educational institutions, own property, and join certain branches of the U.S. military. After lawfully residing in the United States for five years and completing English language, civics, and history tests, LPRs who are at least 18 years of age can apply for citizenship ("become naturalized"). Children under age 18 who are legal immigrants are automatically granted citizenship if their parents become citizens.

The Immigration Act of 1990 increased the number of people entering the country by making it easier for relatives of new immigrants to join them and easier for employers to bring in people with skills such as in science and engineering. It reduced favoritism toward immigrants from certain countries and made it more difficult to ban individuals from entering because of their political beliefs, sexual orientation, or health status. The law was called "the most sweeping revision of legal-immigration laws in a quarter century."[153]

Figure 12.4 shows that the majority (65 percent) of immigrants granted LPR status are based on family sponsorship.[154] Those with employment preferences and refugees and asylees also make up substantial numbers of LPRs. Refugees apply from outside the United States.

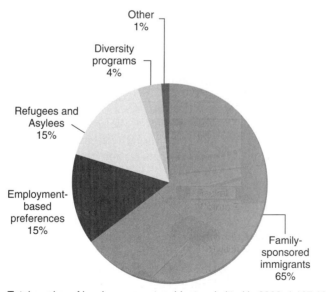

Total number of legal permanent residents admitted in 2008: 1,107,126

FIGURE 12.4   Basis of Legal Permanent Resident Admissions, 2008

Source: U.S. Department of Homeland Security, Computer Linked Application Information Management System (CLAIMS), "Legal Immigrant Data," reported in Randall Monger and Nancy Rytina, *U.S. Legal Permanent Residents: 2008* (Washington, DC: Office of Immigration Statistics, U.S. Department of Homeland Security, March 2009). Retrieved February 18, 2010, from http://www.dhs.gov/xlibrary/assets/statistics/publications/lpr_fr_2008.pdf

Asylees apply while within the United States or at a U.S. port of entry. In recent years, the largest numbers of refugees came from Iraq, Burma, and Bhutan, while the largest numbers of asylees came from China.[155] A smaller percentage of immigrants are admitted under diversity programs, which allow people from countries with low levels of immigration to the United States to apply for LPR status. While the number of immigrants granted LPR status each year may seem quite generous, the many rules, regulations, red tape, and often long waits to enter the United States are often discouraging to the many who want to enter the country and, in many cases, to the family members who await them. In 2009, the largest group of LPRs (17 percent) came from Mexico, followed by China, the Philippines, and India.[156] Most reside in California (20 percent), followed by New York, Florida, and Texas.

In a close look at the effects of *legal* immigration on the United States, the National Research Council found that immigration provided an overall economic benefit for the country but with some negative effect on the income of high school dropouts.[157] In the short run and on the average, immigrants used more public services than they paid for in taxes, although the situation varied depending on the immigrant's country of origin. From a macro perspective and in the long run, there were gains from immigration at the federal level, but losses for states and localities with large immigrant populations. In addition to country of origin, immigrants who entered during their working years and had higher levels of education made the greatest economic contributions. Another economist put it this way, "for the U.S. economy, immigration appears to be more or less a wash."[158]

A researcher who synthesized results of major studies of the impacts of immigration on the United States and other advanced economies drew similar conclusions:

- Immigrants with high skill levels make considerable fiscal contributions.
- Immigrants with low skill levels impose costs unless their stay is limited and they use few public services.
- Immigrants who do not become employed or who immigrate late in life are likely to impose fiscal costs.
- The net economic impact of immigration is small (approximately plus or minus one percent of the receiving country's gross domestic product).[159]

Despite the impassioned rhetoric over immigration, the conclusion was that given consistency across studies, there is no strong positive or negative argument to be made for immigration from an economic perspective and that immigration policy might better be made on other grounds.

The United States does give preference to many people who wish to enter on humanitarian grounds, such as uniting families and helping people escape persecution. Immigration policy also helps to meet employers' needs for workers. Some believe that families are paramount and that preference should be given to keep families together. Under current law, even nuclear families can be separated because children born in the United States are U.S. citizens even if their parents are not legally entitled to reside here. In addition, a foreign national married to a U.S. citizen or LPR may have difficulty immigrating to the United States.

Others believe that skilled workers should get immigration preference due to the economic contributions they make. A counterargument is that if the country lacks qualified workers to fill jobs, Americans should be trained for them. The League of United Latin American Citizens advocates "a family reunification component and a pathway to legalization for 11 million persons seeking documentation" and "ensur[ing that] strong worker protections are in place before any 'guest worker' type provisions are considered."[160]

Illegal Immigration and Its Effects

Since the September 11, 2001, terrorist attacks, the number of those removed from the United States has continued to rise to a high of 359,000 in 2008.[161] In 2008, ICE detained approximately 379,000 individuals.[162] Customs and Border Patrol (CBP) reported 724,000 apprehensions of individuals trying to enter the United States illegally compared to 1.7 million apprehensions in 2000.[163] Border apprehensions were at their lowest since 1976, perhaps due to the declining U.S. economy and increased border enforcement. Ninety-seven percent of CBP apprehensions were at the U.S.-Mexico border, and 91 percent of those apprehended were Mexican nationals.

The Department of Homeland Security estimates that 10.8 million "illegal," "undocumented," or unauthorized immigrants (about 3.5 percent of the U.S. population) were residing in the United States in January 2009, a decline from 11.6 million in 2008.[164] Most are from Mexico. The decline is likely due to the country's economic downturn, which made work less available. Whatever we call this type of immigration, let's step back for a moment and look at some of the evidence on whether it helps or harms Americans.

Undocumented workers are useful to farmers or others who hire them at crucial times, often at relatively low wages. But some believe that undocumented workers drive down wages and take jobs from legally admitted immigrants and American citizens. They object to providing services such as healthcare to undocumented immigrants and to a 1982 U.S. Supreme Court ruling that guarantees their children a public school education. Others counter that these costs are offset by the income taxes and Social Security taxes paid on undocumented workers' wages because these workers are not entitled to Social Security, public assistance, or many other benefits.

A Harvard University economist estimated that "by increasing the supply of labor between 1980 and 2000, immigration reduced the average annual earnings of native-born men by an estimated $1,700 or roughly 4 percent."[165] Although the effects are stronger on some groups, such as Americans with less education, he contends that such effects occur whether immigration is legal or illegal, temporary or permanent. A University of California economist notes that while there are concerns about illegal immigration, there are also benefits—illegal immigration is highly responsive to U.S. labor markets since it "provides U.S. businesses with the types of workers they want, when they want them, and where they want them."[166] He notes that those admitted legally on work visas lack the flexibility to respond to market conditions that illegal workers have, and attempts to legalize these workers, even through temporary worker programs, could reduce responsiveness.

"Internal" approaches to illegal immigration control occur within the United States, such as punishing employers who hire undocumented workers and enforcing provisions such as deportation of those who entered illegally.[167] "External" solutions focus on border enforcement to prevent illegal entry. It has been argued that external controls (keeping people out in the first place) are more effective in controlling immigration than internal controls that effectively turn those in the United States illegally into second-class citizens. Employers may be deterred from hiring them, and they are often taken advantage of because they are undocumented.

Anti-Immigration Rhetoric and the Culture Wars

Another issue is whether anti-immigration rhetoric is used to incite racial and ethnic discord rather than improve immigration policy. One example is the argument that immigration is especially harmful to African Americans and Hispanics who have higher poverty rates and unemployment rates than whites because it robs them of jobs and a higher standard of living. Other anti-immigration rhetoric is that efforts to provide legal status to those now residing in the United

States illegally would largely benefit Latinos at the expense of African Americans. The NAACP says that the "African American community and the immigrant community should not . . . be divided based on partisan politics," and the NAACP has stood with LULAC leaders to speak out against "anti-Hispanic attitudes . . . fueling racial and ethnic tensions."[168]

Even if people who think immigration should be greatly reduced were convinced that the net economic costs of immigration are small, something else is gnawing at them. They believe the fabric of American society is being lost. In addition to some members of the conservative media, former U.S. Representative Tom Tancredo (R-CO) has been among the most vocal in this regard. He contends that too much multiculturalism prevents children from learning American values in the classroom,[169] that minimal immigration should be allowed for work purposes only, and that most immigration visas should be granted to refugees and those seeking asylum (but no more than 25,000 a year).[170] The conservative Center for Immigration Studies recommends "fewer immigrants but a warmer welcome for those admitted."[171] Illustration 12.2 touches on fears about immigration.

ILLUSTRATION 12.2
Just Admit You're Scared, Ruben Navarrette Jr., *The San Diego Union-Tribune*, Wednesday, August 19, 2009

When talking about immigration, Americans need to get their stories straight.

The debate is about to start up again. Sen. Chuck Schumer (D-NY) has said that he intends to introduce, after Labor Day, legislation calling for comprehensive immigration reform. Schumer has an ally in Sen. Lindsey Graham (R-SC) who is working to rustle up support from his side of the aisle.

Recently, I was guest hosting a radio show and fielding calls on immigration. I remember two calls in particular that showed the disingenuousness of the debate. The first caller claimed: "No one is opposed to immigration . . . this is a country of immigrants . . . it's just illegal immigration that people are upset about." The second insisted: "The United States needs a moratorium on future immigration so we can sort out the people who are already here."

I'm glad we cleared that up: No one is opposed to immigration. . . . We just want to stop it.

It sounds noble to think that we care so much about the rule of law that we hold a grudge against anyone who enters the United States illegally—or, as with almost half the illegal population in the United States, overstays a visa. Imagine how much more unseemly it would be if we wanted a wholesale ban on all immigrants—even those who seek to come into the country legally.

But if you buy into the idea behind the second call—that it's time to stop all immigration—then you're obviously concerned with more than just illegal immigration. You can tell yourself that an immigration freeze is just a practical way to try to get a grip on the system or allow newcomers to assimilate. One restrictionist group, the Center for Immigration Studies, even argues that the United States needs an almost total ban on new immigrants so that those who are lucky enough to squeak through might get a warmer welcome.

So keeping out immigrants is for their own good? What nonsense. The only thing that legal, high-skilled immigrants from China or Pakistan or Russia have in common with illegal, low-skilled immigrants from Mexico, Brazil, or El Salvador is that they're all foreigners. So if you like the idea of keeping them all out of the United States, then it's hard to see how you're not simply anti-foreigner. And yet, even if you are, cheer up. You have company.

A recent Gallup poll found Americans to be less supportive of legal immigration than they were a year ago. Half of respondents

(50 percent) say immigration should be decreased, up from 39 percent last year. Close to another third (32 percent) say immigration levels should be kept the same, down from 39 percent. Only 14 percent say they should be increased, down from 18 percent. On the question of whether immigration is good or bad for the country, only a slim majority (58 percent) answered in the affirmative.

Pollsters haven't seen this kind of unwelcome attitude toward immigrants since shortly after the September 11, 2001, attacks. Back then, the concern was national security. This time, with unemployment high and the economy struggling, pundits insist that the backlash against immigrants is all about economic security.

They're wrong. First, it's a myth that Americans are aching to do the jobs that immigrants take. Besides, the same Gallup poll found the anxiety level about immigration was highest in regions where there are relatively few immigrants; 54 percent of people in the South want immigration decreased, while only 44 percent of people in the West feel that way. According to the theory advanced by the pundits—that the souring on immigrants is all economic—you'd have to infer that the employment picture is much bleaker in the South than in the West. But the jobless rates in those regions are comparable.

So what's the real reason so many Americans are increasingly anxious about immigration and want to cut back on it? It's all about changing demographics. Folks in the South have experienced in the last 10 years what those of us in the West experienced a generation or two ago. They see immigrants changing their surroundings and impacting the culture, and it scares the daylights out of them. That many of those immigrants came to this country legally doesn't do much to calm those fears.

Why not be honest and just admit what frightens us?

Source: "Immigration's Fear Factor" by Ruben Navarrette, from *The San Diego Union-Tribune,* Aug. 19, 2009, is reprinted by permission of the publisher.

When it comes to describing the U.S. population, no analogy is more common than the "American melting pot."[172] Concerns that more recent immigrants aren't assimilating like previous generations of immigrants have fueled calls for measures such as making English the official language of the United States. Others note that English is the language of the United States and that Americans appreciate signs and information in their native language when they visit other countries.

In 2005, foreign-born U.S. residents were about equally divided between naturalized citizens (35 percent), legally admitted non-citizens (33 percent), and unauthorized migrants (31 percent).[173] A major marker of assimilation among the foreign-born population is U.S. citizenship. In 1970, 64 percent of all legally admitted immigrants had become U.S. citizens (were naturalized); by 1990, the rate had dropped to 38 percent. Naturalization rates have been on the upswing. By 2005, the rate was 52 percent, and immigrants were naturalizing more quickly.

Naturalizations among immigrants increase along with lengths of stay, perhaps because it takes time to learn English, pass citizenship tests, and traverse other aspects of the naturalization process. Naturalizations are highest among Middle Easterners, and their naturalizations increased after 2001.[174] Mexicans have a lower naturalization rate than other groups, but from 1995 to 2005, the number of Mexicans who naturalized increased 144 percent, and from 20 to 35 percent of those eligible. The increase was higher than for any other major country of origin.

A number of ideas have been suggested to explain differences in naturalization rates.[175] Naturalization is less likely for those from countries close to the United States and if economic conditions in their country of origin are favorable. Naturalization is more likely if people enter as refugees, they were living under totalitarian rule, their home country allows dual citizenship, or if they can reclaim citizenship in their home country easily. The Mexican government has made claiming dual citizenship easier, a policy change that may have encouraged more Mexicans to obtain U.S. citizenship.

Amnesty

In 1986, after years of debate, Congress passed the Immigration Reform and Control Act. It incorporated both internal and external approaches to address illegal immigration. The law's main features were amnesty for some people who had entered the United States illegally, increased border enforcement, employer sanctions for hiring undocumented workers, and a temporary worker program.

Amnesty was the most controversial provision. Under this provision, those who had illegally resided in the United States before 1982, and could prove this, were allowed to remain and obtain citizenship. The irony was that undocumented entrants previously had to hide the fact that they were living in the United States and may have disposed of rent receipts or other records to verify their residence. To qualify for amnesty, applicants could not have received public assistance previously and were prohibited from doing so for five years after legalization. The number of people who initially applied for amnesty fell considerably short of official estimates, perhaps due to fear that family and friends who did not qualify for amnesty might be discovered and deported. There was also a substantial fee to apply for amnesty, which might have served as a deterrent, but nearly 3 million people gained citizenship through this provision.[176] Few people think that the 1986 law did much to deter illegal immigration.

In 2000, President Clinton signed the Legal Immigration and Family Equity Act. It allowed 640,000 undocumented individuals to apply for legal permanent resident status if an employer or close relative with U.S. citizenship or LPR status sponsored them. Proposals to provide amnesty to more immigrants remain on the table. Those who argue against amnesty contend that it flies in the face of established laws, unfairly penalizes those who had been waiting to enter the United States through legal channels, and might encourage even more individuals to enter illegally. Others point to reasons for providing amnesty—it offers a legal channel for those who have been residing and working in the United States to gain legal status and naturalize, keeps families together, and relieves people of second-class status. The Obama administration has been accused of supporting strict enforcement of immigration laws such as employer audits and sanctions in the hope of winning support for a new amnesty provision.[177] Immigration reform legislation would likely have received much more attention from the administration and Congress had it not been for the country's financial crisis, but it is likely to receive that attention soon.

Employer Sanctions

The 1986 immigration law requires employers to verify that employees are eligible to work in the United States. Violations can result in fines and prison terms if the employer has a pattern of hiring undocumented workers. For many years employers seemed to get off lightly, but enforcement has gotten tougher. As a concession to some employers, primarily farmers, the 1986 immigration law permits hiring foreign workers when domestic workers are not available. It also contains more liberal rules for agricultural workers who want to remain in the country. Employers complain that immigration law unfairly places the burden of proof on them and may cause them to do without needed workers. The government's current system of verification of employees' legal status, called E-Verify, has come under criticism for being inaccurate, but DHS has said that it has taken steps to improve its accuracy.

For many years, the National Council of La Raza (NCLR) said there was no shortage of agricultural workers in the United States and argued that guest workers desperate for jobs may be vulnerable to abuses by employers.[178] But in 2007, NCLR said it supported guest worker programs if they contained provisions such as pay at prevailing wages, the freedom to change jobs, and a route to citizenship as well as border enforcement to prevent illegal immigration.[179]

The debate over guest workers also includes the "high-tech" industries. Employers who claim that the number of work visas should be upped because they cannot find enough qualified Americans face opposition from those who counter that these employers want to bring in foreign workers because they can pay them less than Americans.

Immigrants and the Decennial Census

Every 10 years since 1790 the federal government has attempted to count every person residing in the United States regardless of whether they are in the country legally or illegally. No questions are asked about one's immigration status, and the U.S. Census Bureau, which collects and analyzes the information, is obligated to hold identifying information in strictest confidence.

One reason the census is serious business is because census figures are used to apportion the 435 seats in the U.S. House of Representatives. We have already discussed the contentious process of congressional and state redistricting. Congressional redistricting is the only constitutionally mandated purpose of the census, but the federal government also uses census figures to determine the amount of federal funds state, local, and tribal governments receive for various purposes (currently about $300 billion annually for services such as schools, social welfare programs, roads and other infrastructure, etc.).[180] States with large uncounted immigrant populations contend that undercounts unfairly burden state and local budgets with providing services. About two-thirds of the U.S. population participated in the 2000 census. Compared to whites, Asians were missed nearly twice as often, African Americans nearly three times as often, Hispanics four times as often, Native Hawaiians and other Pacific Islanders over six times as often, and Native Americans seven times as often.[181]

During the 2000 census, appeals were made to immigrants, especially the large numbers of Hispanics residing in the United States, urging their participation in the census. In addition to improving the direct count of hard-to-reach populations, including immigrants, Democrats wanted to use scientific sampling techniques, which they believed would also improve census counts. The National Academy of Sciences endorsed the approach recommended. Republicans claimed that the method would produce grossly erroneous results and that the Constitution requires a full enumeration, not sampling. In 1999 the U.S. Supreme Court ruled that an enumeration is necessary for apportioning seats in the U.S. House of Representatives. The ruling did not preclude using statistical adjustments for other purposes, but the Census Bureau refused to use the adjustment. In addition, the Commerce Secretary stripped the census director and demographers of the power to adjust census estimates. Democrats stress that undercounts rob communities of much needed funds, while "Republicans argue that Democrats seek to boost numbers in order to create extra congressional districts in urban areas and to bring in more federal money for their constituencies."[182] The 2010 census is the first in three decades to be conducted under a Democratic president. Debate again arose over any sampling methods to be used to adjust for undercounts.

The 2010 census has been portrayed as the toughest count in U.S. history. Americans are increasingly worried about their safety and privacy (e.g., identity theft), and immigrant groups may be more skeptical about participating than ever.[183] Immigrants, including older immigrants who are legally entitled to be in the country, may have long-standing and well-founded distrust of government officials. Younger immigrants may feel the same. Arabs may continue to fear reprisal following September 11, 2001. Crackdowns on illegal immigration, including raids at places of employment, neighborhood sweeps, use of state and local law enforcement to enforce immigration laws, and other local efforts, including attempts to pass ordinances that forbid renting to illegal immigrants, resulted in some calls for boycotts of the 2010 census.[184] The major Hispanic civil rights organizations encouraged Hispanics to participate in the census, in part because communities with large numbers of immigrants stand to lose significant sums of money if immigrants, legal or illegal, are not counted. Complete counts also allow each immigrant group to point to its presence in the United States and stress its political and consumer clout. Others are concerned that any emphasis on the growing immigrant presence may reinforce anti-immigrant sentiment, serve to reinforce crackdowns on illegal immigration, or change the balance with regard to the numbers of immigrants from various countries allowed to legally immigrate to the United States.

The federal government uses means such as public service announcements to encourage all residents to participate in the census. Churches, schools, and community organizations are also called on to get the word out that people should participate in the census, that doing so is safe, and that communities will benefit from accurate census counts. For the first time, census forms in English and Spanish were mailed to people in certain areas. This was done to increase participation, but it upset those who believe that such practices cater to illegal immigrants and to legal immigrants who fail to assimilate. Another strategy used to boost participation was to encourage people to mail in the short seven-question form in order to avoid a census taker visiting their home.

Summary

Black or African Americans and other people of color have faced numerous struggles in their fight for civil rights. Civil rights laws, especially the Civil Rights Act of 1964, which includes requirements for equal treatment in employment and access to public facilities, have contributed to gains in all areas of American life. Inequality, however, remains apparent, as demonstrated by issues such as poverty, graduation, and unemployment rates, racial profiling, and hate crimes. The place of policies and practices in areas such as school and neighborhood desegregation and affirmative action continue to be debated. The growing presence of groups such as Hispanics and people of Asian heritage also make them important considerations in U.S. politics. Perhaps no group is as disadvantaged as many members of the country's Native American population. They continue to suffer severe economic and social problems. The Indian Self-Determination and Education Assistance Act of 1975 was an attempt to restore to Native Americans planning power over social welfare issues. The *Cobell v. Norton* lawsuit was another attempt to return to Native Americans resources that are rightfully theirs.

New challenges to civil rights have emerged since the September 11, 2001, terrorist attacks on the World Trade Center and the Pentagon. Civil rights groups continue to file lawsuits and lobby Congress in an effort to reclaim lost civil rights, especially among citizens and noncitizens targeted because of national origin or religion. Immigration is a major U.S. policy concern. The large numbers of people entering both legally and illegally has resulted in debate over what immigration policy should be. Legislation in 1986 granted amnesty to many undocumented immigrants residing in the United States. In 1990 Congress again began permitting an increased number of people to enter the United States. Many immigrants fare quite well, finding jobs and becoming self-sufficient. Those concerned about immigration, however, believe that too many are entering the country to the disadvantage of those already here. A new round of immigration reform is likely in the offing.

Discussion Questions and Class Activities

1. What type of high school did you attend (e.g., public, private, faith-based, magnet, etc.)? What was the racial and ethnic composition of the student body, faculty, and staff compared to the population in your community? Discuss any tensions concerning race and ethnicity in your school. Do you know the history of school desegregation in the community where you attended school? If not, you may wish to learn about it. Discuss what, if any, school desegregation policies and procedures should be used today and what efforts should be taken to see that every child has the opportunity to receive a quality education.

2. Discuss whether or to what extent affirmative action policies should be used in admissions and employment. Consider questions such as: Do vestiges of discrimination remain in education and employment or have nondiscrimination, affirmative action, and other civil rights policies eliminated them to the extent that public policy can? If vestiges of discrimination remain, should racial preferences be used? If so, under what circumstances and to what extent?

3. Read further about the circumstances in the case *Ricci v. DeStefano*. What is your opinion about the appellate court decision and the U.S. Supreme Court's decision? Do you think the final decision was correct? What if the City of New Haven had promoted the white firefighters? Do you think the black and Hispanic firefighters would have filed suit, and do you think they would have won or lost the case? If you had been a New Haven city official, what position would you have taken upon learning of the test results?

4. Learn about the latest round of redistricting in your state. Discuss what principles and procedures should be used to determine voting districts.

5. Are you registered to vote and have you exercised your voting rights recently? Invite a local or state election official to speak to the class about the Voting Rights Act and how elections in the jurisdiction are conducted to ensure that the act's provisions are upheld. Ask the speaker to discuss any major problems that have arisen in conducting recent elections in that jurisdiction or to discuss problems that have occurred in national elections. You may wish to volunteer during a voter registration drive or at a polling place during an election to witness voting processes more closely.

6. Discuss how many immigrants you think should be granted legal permanent resident status each year in the United States and on what basis immigrants should be admitted, such as family preferences, employer preferences, refugee or asylee status, etc. What efforts do you think should be made to control illegal immigration? Follow media reports on efforts to change immigration policy since this book was published and discuss them in class.

7. Learn about the procedures necessary to become a naturalized U.S. citizen. Invite newly naturalized citizens from different countries who entered under different statuses (family member, refugee, etc.) to discuss their experience of immigrating to the United States, adapting to life in the United States, and becoming a citizen. Did they receive services or assistance from public and/or private sources? Ask them what they think should be done to assist immigrants in assimilating and what changes they would recommend in U.S. immigration policy. Attend a naturalization (citizenship) swearing in ceremony in your community. You may also wish to invite staff of public and private agencies or organizations that serve immigrants to learn about their work and the challenges immigrants face.

Websites

The League of United Latin American Citizens (LULAC), http://www.lulac.org/, is dedicated to promoting civil rights and equality for Hispanics in all areas of American life.

The National Association for the Advancement of Colored People (NAACP), http://www.naacp.org/home/index.htm, champions the civil rights of African Americans, is dedicated to ensuring equality for all people in all areas of society, and works to eliminate racial hatred and discrimination.

The National Congress of American Indians (NCAI), http://www.ncai.org/, represents tribal governments by monitoring and informing federal policy in the interests of American Indians and Alaska Natives and promotes understanding of the Indian people.

The U.S. Citizenship and Immigration Services (USCIS), http://www.uscis.gov/portal/site/uscis, part of the U.S. Department of Homeland Security, oversees lawful immigration to the United States and promotes understanding about immigration and citizenship by providing information and granting immigration and citizenship benefits.

Notes

1. Projections of the Population by Sex, Race, and Hispanic Origin for the United States: 2010 to 2050, Table 4 (Washington, DC: U.S. Census Bureau, August 14, 2008). Retrieved February 11, 2010, from http://www.census.gov/population/www/projections/summarytables.html

2. For a consideration of social policies and people of color, see King E. Davis and Tricia B. Bent-Goodley, Eds., *The Color of Social Policy* (Alexandria, VA: Council on Social Work Education, 2004).

3. Committee on Ways and Means, Section 7: "Temporary Assistance for Needy Families," *2008 Green Book* (Washington, DC: U.S. House of Representatives), Table 7-15. Retrieved June 4, 2010, from http://waysandmeans.house.gov/singlepages.aspx?NewsID=10490

4. Office of Policy, Characteristics of Noninstitutionalized DI and SSI Program Participants, Research and Statistics Note No. 2008-02 (Washington, DC: Social Security Administration, January 2008), Table 6. Retrieved February 11, 2010, from http://www.socialsecurity.gov/policy/docs/rsnotes/rsn2008-02.pdf

5. Martin Giles, "'Race Coding' and White Opposition to Welfare," *American Political Science Review*, Vol. 90, No. 3, 1996, pp. 593–604.

6. Alfred A. Lindseth, "Legal Issues Related to School Funding/Desegregation," in Christine H. Rossell, Davis J. Armor, and Herbert J. Wahlberg, Eds., *School Desegregation in the 21st Century* (Westport, CN: Praeger), pp. 41–65.

7. Much of this paragraph relies on Richard C. Hunter, "The Administration of Court-ordered School Desegregation in Urban School Districts: The Law and Experience," *The Journal of Negro Education*, 73(3), 2004, pp. 218–229.

8. Lindseth, "Legal Issues Related to School Funding/Desegregation."

9. Christine H. Rossell, "The Effectiveness of Desegregation Plans," in Rossell et al., *School Desegregation in the 21st Century*, pp. 67–105.

10. Lindseth, "Legal Issues Related to School Funding/Desegregation."

11. The remainder of this paragraph relies on Monika L. Moore, "Unclear Standards Create an Unclear Future: Developing a Better Definition of Unitary Status," *The Yale Law Journal*, Vol. 112, No. 2, November 2002, pp. 311–351.

12. Rossell, "The Effectiveness of Desegregation Plans."

13. Much of this paragraph relies on Lindseth, "Legal Issues Related to School Funding/Desegregation."

14. Rossell, "The Effectiveness of Desegregation Plans."

15. This paragraph relies on Lindseth, "Legal Issues Related to School Funding/Desegregation."

16. Gary Orfeld, *Reviving the Goal of an Integrated Society: A 21st Century Challenge* (Los Angeles: The Civil Rights Project/Proyecto Derechos Civiles at UCLA, 2009). Retrieved July 2, 2009, from http://www.civilrightsproject.ucla.edu/research/deseg/reviving_the_goal_mlk_2009.pdf

17. Most of this paragraph relies on *ibid*; see p. 10.

18. William A. V. Clark, "School Desegregation and Demographic Change," in Rossell et al., *School Desegregation in the 21st Century*, pp. 119–145; David J. Armor, Christine H. Rossell, and Herbert J. Walberg, "The Outlook for School Desegregation," in Rossell et al., *School Desegregation in the 21st Century*, see p. 328.

19. American Civil Liberties Union, *Williams v. State of California, Court Brief* (Sacramento, CA: May 17, 2000). Retrieved April 22, 2004, from http://www.aclunc.org/students/williams-brief.htm

20. Nanette Asimov, "Bitter Battle over Class Standards: State Spends Millions to Defeat Student Suit," *San Francisco Chronicle*, May 5, 2003. Retrieved June 29, 2009, from http://www.sfgate.com/cgi-bin/article.cgi?f=/c/a/2003/05/05/MN102341.DTL

21. ACLU Foundation of Southern California and Public Advocates, Inc., *Williams v. California: The Statewide Impact of Two Years of Implementation* (Los Angeles and San Francisco: August 2007). Retrieved June 29, 2009, from http://www.publicadvocates.org/docs/WilliamsReport2007_final_spread.pdf

22. Much of this paragraph relies on Lindseth, "Legal Issues Related to School Funding/Desegregation," p. 59.

23. Armor et al., "The Outlook for School Desegregation," p. 331.

24. Orfeld, *Reviving the Goal of an Integrated Society: A 21st Century Challenge.*

25. Kirwan Institute, "Fair Housing" (Columbus, OH: Ohio State University, 2009). Retrieved July 8, 2009, from http://kirwaninstitute.org/research/opportunity-communitieshousing/fair-housing.php

26. Douglas S. Massey and Nancy A. Denton, *American Apartheid: Segregation and the Making of the Underclass* (Cambridge, MA: Harvard University Press, 1993), p. viii.

27. *Ibid*; Ingrid Gould Ellen, "Supporting Integrative Choice," *Poverty and Race,* Vol. 17, No. 5, 2008, pp. 3–4, 10. Retrieved July 9, 2009, from http://www.prrac.org/pdf/SeptOct2008PRRAC.pdf; testimony of John Powell, cited in *The Future of Fair Housing: Report of the Commission on Fair Housing and Equal Opportunity.* (National Fair Housing Alliance, Leadership Conference on Civil Rights Education Fund, Lawyers' Committee for Civil Rights under Law, NAACP Legal Defense and Educational Fund, December 2008), pp. 5–6. Retrieved July 9, 2009, from http://www.prrac.org/projects/fair_housing_commission/The_Future_of_Fair_Housing.pdf

28. Testimony of George Lipsitz, cited in *The Future of Fair Housing: Report of the Commission on Fair Housing and Equal Opportunity,* p. 8.

29. Chester W. Hartman, *Housing and Social Policy* (Englewood Cliffs, NJ: Prentice Hall, 1975), pp. 136, 139.

30. Reynolds Farley, "The Kerner Commission Report Plus Four Decades: What Has Changed? What Has Not?" (Ann Arbor, MI: Institute for Social Research, University of Michigan, September 2008). Retrieved July 7, 2009, from http://www.psc.isr.umich.edu/pubs/pdf/rr08-656.pdf

31. Population Studies Center, "Residential Segregation: What It Is and How We Measure It (Ann Arbor: University of Michigan Population Studies Center, no date). Retrieved July 7, 2009, from http://enceladus.isr.umich.edu/race/seg.html; John Iceland and Daniel H. Weinberg with Erika Steinmetz, "Racial and Ethnic Residential Segregation in the United States: 1980-2000" (Washington, DC: U.S. Census Bureau, August 2002). Retrieved July 7, 2009, from http://www.census.gov/hhes/www/housing/resseg/pdf/censr-3.pdf

32. William C. Apgar and Allegra Calder, "The Dual Mortgage Market: The Persistence of Discrimination in Mortgage Lending" (Cambridge, MA: Joint Center for Housing Studies December 2005). Retrieved July 7, 2009, from http://www.jchs.harvard.edu/publications/finance/w05-11.pdf

33. Debbie Gruenstein Bocian, Keith S. Ernst, and Wei Li, "Unfair Lending: The Effect of Race and Ethnicity on the Price of Subprime Mortgages" (Washington, DC: Center for Responsible Lending, May 31, 2006). Retrieved July 7, 2009, from http://www.responsible-lending.org/mortgage-lending/research-analysis/rr011-Unfair_Lending-0506.pdf

34. "2008 Fair Housing Fact Sheet" (Washington, DC: National Urban League Policy Institute, April 11, 2008). Retrieved July 7, 2009, from http://www.nul.org/publications/policyinstitute/factsheet/2008-Fair-Housing-Fact-Sheet.pdf

35. "HUD's Fair Housing Duties and the Loss of Public and Assisted Housing" *Housing Law Bulletin* (Washington, DC: National Housing Law Project, 1999). Retrieved July 8, 2009, from http://www.nhlp.org/html/hlb/199/199fairhsg.htm

36. Testimony of Philip Tegeler, Legal Director, Connecticut Civil Liberties Union, on *Fighting Discrimination against the Disabled and Minorities through Fair Housing Enforcement* before the Oversight and Investigations Subcommittee and Housing and Community Opportunity Subcommittee of the House of Representatives Committee on Financial Services (Washington, DC, June 25, 2002). Retrieved July 8, 2009, from http://www.aclu.org/rightsofthepoor/housing/13423leg20020625.html

37. *Ibid.*

38. "Fair Housing Enforcement: Time for a Change" (Washington, DC: National Fair Housing Alliance, May 1, 2009). Retrieved July 7, 2009, from http://www.nationalfairhousing.org/Portals/33/2009%20Trends/2009%20Fair%20Housing%20Trends%20Report.pdf

39. "About NFHA" (Washington, DC: National Fair Housing Alliance, 2008). Retrieved July 8, 2009, from http://www.nationalfairhousing.org/AboutNFHA/tabid/2549/Default.aspx

40. "Fair Housing Initiatives Program" (Washington, DC: U.S. Department of Housing and Urban Development, Novemeber 8, 2007). Retrieved July 8, 2009, from http://www.hud.gov/offices/fheo/partners/FHIP/fhip.cfm

41. "Fair Housing Enforcement: Time for a Change."

42. "National Commission on Fair Housing and Equal Opportunity" (Washington, DC: Poverty and Race Research Action Council, no date). Retrieved July 8, 2009, from http://www.prrac.org/projects/fair_housing_commission/overview.php

43. *The Future of Fair Housing: Report of the Commission on Fair Housing and Equal Opportunity* (National Fair Housing Alliance, Leadership Conference on Civil Rights Education Fund, Lawyers' Committee for Civil Rights under Law, NAACP Legal Defense and Educational Fund, December 2008). Retrieved July 9, 2009, from http://www.prrac.org/projects/fair_housing_commission/The_Future_of_Fair_Housing.pdf

44. Maria Krysan, "Confronting Racial Blind Spots," *Poverty & Race*, Vol. 17, No. 5, September/October 2008, pp. 8–9. Retrieved July 10, 2009, from http://www.prrac.org/pdf/SeptOct2008PRRAC.pdf

45. *Ibid.*; Camille Zubrinsky Charles, "Who Will Live Near Whom?", *Poverty & Race*, Vol. 17, No. 5, September/October 2008, pp. 1–2, 5–7. Retrieved July 10, 2009, from http://www.prrac.org/pdf/SeptOct2008PRRAC.pdf

46. Charles, "Who Will Live Near Whom?"

47. Ellen, "Supporting Integrative Choice"; Krysan, "Confronting Racial Blind Spots"; Philip Tegeler, Susan Eaton, and Westra Miller, *Bringing Children Together: Magnet Schools and Public Housing Redevelopment* (Cambridge, MA: Harvard Law School, Charles Hamilton Houston Institute for Race & Justice and Washington, DC: Poverty & Race Research Action Council, January 2009). Retrieved July 10, 2009, from http://www.prrac.org/pdf/bringing_children_together.pdf

48. *Federal Policies on Remedies Concerning Equal Employment Opportunity in State and Local Government Personnel Systems,* March 23, 1973, cited in Felix A. Nigro and Lloyd G. Nigro, *The New Public Personnel Administration* (Itasca, IL: Peacock, 1976), p. 21.

49. See Frank Trippet, "A Solid Yes to Affirmative Action," *Time,* July 14, 1986, p. 22.

50. For a summary of reductions in litigation, see D. Lee Bawden and John L. Palmer, "Social Policy, Challenging the Welfare State," in John L. Palmer and Isabel V. Sawhill, Eds., *The Reagan Record* (Cambridge, MA: Ballinger, 1984), pp. 204–206.

51. From an undated letter to ACLU members from Ira Glasser, executive director of the American Civil Liberties Union, 132 West 43rd St., New York, NY 10036-6599.

52. Office for Civil Rights Evaluation, *Beyond Percentage Plans: The Challenge of Equal Opportunity in Higher Education* (Washington, DC: U.S. Commission on Civil Rights, November 2002). Retrieved July 12, 2009, from http://www.vpcomm.umich.edu/admissions/research/beyondpercentplns.pdf

53. Information on the Gratz case can be found at the U.S. Supreme Court website at http://www.supremecourt.gov/oral_arguments/argument_transcripts/02-516.pdf and on the Grutter case at http://www.supremecourt.gov/oral_arguments/argument_transcripts/02-241.pdf. Retrieved June 4, 2010.

54. Mark Sherman, "Supreme Court: White Firefighters Bias Victims," Associated Press, June 29, 2009. Retrieved July 12, 2009, from http://www.google.com/hostednews/ap/article/ALeqM5hdV4k6q8whNn7fJ_JhZb5tdIy4ZwD994IR900

55. Lucas Powe, "Sotomayor Will Be Confirmed," *Austin American-Statesman,* July 12, 2009, p. F3.

56. "About the American Civil Rights Institute" (Sacramento, CA: American Civil Rights Institute, 2007). Retrieved July 13, 2009, from http://www.acri.org/about.html

57. Glenn C. Loury, "The Moral Quandary of the Black Community," *Public Interest,* No. 79, Spring 1985, pp. 9–22; Loury has since modified his position; see Jenny Attiyeh, "Black Scholar Renounces Conservative 'Crown,'" *Christian Science Monitor,* September 5, 2002. Retrieved July 12, 2009, from http://www.csmonitor.com/2002/0905/p18s01-ussc.html

58. Thomas Sowell, "Friends of Blacks," Townhall.com, July 13, 2004. Retrieved July 12, 2009, from http://townhall.com/columnists/ThomasSowell/2004/07/13/friends_of_blacks. Other commentaries by economist Thomas Sowell of the Hoover Institute are posted at http://townhall.com/columnists/ThomasSowell/

59. Jim Sleeper, *Liberal Racism* (New York: Viking, 1997), p. 182.

60. Peter Dreier, "There's No Racial Justice without Economic Justice," in Chester Hartman, Ed., *Challenges to Equality: Poverty and Race in America* (New York: M. E. Sharpe, 2001), pp. 270–273.

61. U.S. Census Bureau, *Statistical Abstract of the United States: 2010,* 129th ed., Table 404 (Washington, DC: U.S. Department of Commerce, 2009). Retrieved June 4, 2010, from http://www.census.gov/compendia/statab/2010/tables/10s0404.pdf

62. "African Americans In Statewide Elective Office" (Washington, DC: Joint Center for Political and

Economic Studies, 2009). Retrieved June 4, 2010, from http://www.jointcenter.org/index.php/current_research_and_policy_activities/political_participation/black_elected_officials_roster_introduction_and_overview/african_americans_in_statewide_elective_office

63. "Minorities in the 111th Congress," *Infoplease.* Retrieved July 16, 2009, from http://www.infoplease.com/us/government/111-congress-minorities.html

64. U.S. Census Bureau, Table 399, *Statistical Abstract of the United States: 2009,* 128th ed. (Washington, DC: U.S. Department of Commerce, 2008). Retrieved July 15, 2009, from http://www.census.gov/compendia/statab/tables/09s0399.pdf

65. U.S. Census Bureau, Table 405, *Statistical Abstract of the United States: 2010,* 129th ed. (Washington, DC: U.S. Department of Commerce, 2009). Retrieved June 4, 2010, from http://www.census.gov/compendia/statab/2010/tables/10s0405.pdf

66. "Minorities in the 111th Congress."

67. Adam Nagourney and Janet Elder (*New York Times*), "Hispanic Praise Democrats and Bush," *Austin American-Statesman,* August 3, 2006, p. A6; "Results of 2005 National Hispanic Survey" (The Latino Coalition, January 5, 2006). Retrieved February 13, 2010, from http://www.ime.gob.mx/investigaciones/2005/articulos/politica/2005_national_latino_survey_results.pdf

68. "UCLA's New National APA Political Almanac Lists Over 2,000 Asian Pacific American Elected and Appointed Officials Nationwide" (Los Angeles: University of California at Los Angeles Asian American Studies Center, 2007). Retrieved July 16, 2009, from http://www.aasc.ucla.edu/archives/pa_07_08.htm

69. James S. Lai, Wendy K. Tam Cho, Thomas P. Kim, and Okiyoshi Takeda, "Asian Pacific-American Campaigns, Elections, and Elected Officials," *Political Science and Politics,* Vol. 34, 2001, pp. 611–617.

70. See Paula D. McClain and Joseph Stewart, Jr., *Can We All Get Along: Racial and Ethnic Minorities in American Politics,* 4th ed. (Boulder, CO; Westview, 2006), p. 147.

71. See Michael P. Shea, "Indians Skeptical of Report Urging Program Overhaul," *Congressional Quarterly,* Vol. 48, No. 2, 1990, pp. 98–100.

72. Courtney Ruark, "22 Natives From 11 States, 16 Tribes Win Elections," *Reznet,* November 5, 2008. Retrieved July 16, 2009, from http://www.reznetnews.org/blogs/tribalog/22-natives-11-states-16-tribes-win-elections-24190

73. Center for Oral History and Cultural Heritage, "August 6, 1965: Voting Rights Act," (Hattiesberg,

MS: University of Southern Mississippi, no date). Retrieved July 13, 2009, from http://www.usm.edu/crdp/html/cd/vra65.htm

74. U.S. Commission on Civil Rights, *Voting Irregularities in Florida during the 2000 Presidential Election* (Washington, DC: Author, June 2001). Retrieved February 18, 2010, from http://www.usccr.gov/pubs/vote2000/report/main.htm

75. Wade Henderson, "Voting Rights Act Reauthorization: What You Need to Know," *The National Voter,* June 2006. Retrieved July 16, 2009, from http://www.lwv.org/AM/Template.cfm?Section=Voting_Rights_Act&TEMPLATE=/CM/ContentDisplay.cfm&CONTENTID=5255; Caroline Fredrickson and Deborah J. Vagins, *Promises to Keep: The Impact of the Voting Rights Act in 2006* (Washington, DC: American Civil Liberties Union, March 2006). Retrieved July 16, 2009, from http://www.aclu.org/images/asset_upload_file516_24396.pdf

76. "Bad New Days for Voting Rights," *New York Times,* April 18, 2004. Retrieved February 18, 2010, from http://www.nytimes.com/2004/04/18/opinion/18SUN1.html?pagewanted=1

77. "How to Make Your Vote Count" (*New York Times* editorial), *Austin American-Statesman,* November 7, 2009, p. A7.

78. Henderson, "Voting Rights Act Reauthorization: What You Need to Know"; also see Melanie Eversley, "For a Mississippi Town, Voting Rights Act Made a Change," *USA Today,* August 5, 2005. Retrieved July 16, 2009, from http://www.usatoday.com/news/nation/2005-08-05-miss-town-voting_x.htm; letter from U.S. Department of Justice, Civil Rights Division to J. Lane Greenlee, Esq., Winona, Mississippi, December 11, 2001. Retrieved July 19, 2009, from http://www.usdoj.gov/crt/voting/sec_5/ltr/l_121101.php

79. "Why You Should Care About the Voting Rights Act," Civilrights.org (Washington, DC: Leadership Conference on Civil Rights and the Leadership Conference on Civil Rights Education Fund Civilrights.org, no date). Retrieved July 16, 2009, from http://www.civilrights.org/voting-rights/vra/why-you-should-care.html

80. Civil Rights Division, "Cases Raising Claims Under the Help America Vote Act" (Washington, DC: U.S. Department of Justice, July 25, 2008). Retrieved July 16, 2009, from http://www.usdoj.gov/crt/voting/litigation/recent_hava.php/\#bolivar

81. Henderson, "Voting Rights Act Reauthorization: What You Need to Know."

82. Kenneth Hwang, Micaela McMurrough, and Laura Chang, "*League of United Latin American Citizens*

v. Perry (05-204), consolidated with *Travis County, Texas v. Perry* (05-254), *Jackson v.*" (Ithaca New York: Cornell University Law School, March 1, 2006). Retrieved July 3, 2009, from http://topics.law.cornell.edu/supct/cert/05-204; "Political Process: Needs Repair," *Today's America: How Free* (Washington, DC: Freedom House, May 2, 2008). Retrieved July 16, 2009, from http://www.freedomhouse.org/template.cfm?page=384&key=142&parent=5&report=61

83. Hwang et al., "*League of United Latin American Citizens v. Perry* (05-204), consolidated with *Travis County, Texas v. Perry* (05-254), *Jackson v.*"

84. "Political Process: Needs Repair."

85. This paragraph relies largely on Brennan Center for Justice, "*LULAC v. Perry* (Sup. Ct. consolidated cases), *Session v. Perry* (E.D. Tex.)" (New York: New York University School of Law School, June 28, 2006). Retrieved July 13, 2009, from http://www.brennancenter.org/content/resource/lulac_v_perry_sup_ct_consolidated_cases_session_v_perry_ed_tex/; also see Hwang et al., "*League of United Latin American Citizens v. Perry* (05-204), consolidated with *Travis County, Texas v. Perry* (05-254), *Jackson v.*"

86. "Hispanic Voters Vindicated in *LULAC v. Perry* Texas Redistricting Case" (Washington, DC: League of United Latin American Citizens, June 28, 2006). Retrieved July 13, 2006, from http://www.lulac.org/advocacy/press/2006/perry1.html

87. Brennan Center for Justice, "*LULAC v. Perry* (Sup. Ct. consolidated cases), *Session v. Perry* (E.D. Tex.)."

88. Hwang et al., "*League of United Latin American Citizens v. Perry* (05-204), consolidated with *Travis County, Texas v. Perry* (05-254), *Jackson v.*"

89. For a discussion, see Stuart Taylor, "The Voting Rights Act and Its Wrongs," *National Journal Magazine,* May 2, 2009. Retrieved July 16, 2009, from http://www.nationaljournal.com/njmagazine/or_20090502_2469.php

90. Robert Richie, "Full Representation: Uniting Backers of Gerrymandering Reform and Minority Voting Rights," *National Civic Review,* 2004. Retrieved July 16, 2009, from http://www.ncl.org/publications/ncr/93-2/01_NCR93_2Richie.pdf

91. Abigail Thernstrom and Stephan Thernstrom, "Racial Gerrymandering Is Unnecessary" (Washington, DC: American Enterprise Institute for Public Policy Research, December 2008). Retrieved July 16, 2009, from http://www.aei.org/docLib/20081211_6723740OTIThernstrom_g.pdf

92. Richie, "Full Representation: Uniting Backers of Gerrymandering Reform and Minority Voting Rights."

93. Nonpartisan Redistricting (Washington, DC: The Democratic Leadership Council, May 8, 2004). Retrieved July 16, 2009, from http://www.ndol.org/ndol_ci.cfm?contentid=252625&kaid=139&subid=900083

94. Thernstrom and Thernstrom, "Racial Gerrymandering Is Unnecessary."

95. George Will, "Voting Rights Anachronism," *Washington Post,* January, 2009. Retrieved July 15, 2009, from http://www.washingtonpost.com/wp-dyn/content/article/2009/01/16/AR2009011603716.html

96. Daniel McCool, "Indian Voting," in Vine Deloria, Ed., *American Indian Policy in the Twentieth Century* (Norman, OK: University of Oklahoma Press, 1992), pp. 105–134; Gerald Thomas Wilkinson, "On Assisting Indian People," *Social Casework,* Vol. 61, No. 8, 1980, pp. 451–454.

97. See Vine DeLoria, Jr., "The Reservation Conditions," *National Forum:* The Phi Kappa Phi Journal, Vol. 71, No. 2, 1991, pp. 10–12.

98. Bureau of Indian Affairs, *2005 American Indian Population and Labor Force Report* (Washington, DC: U.S. Department of the Interior, no date). Retrieved July 4, 2009, from http://www.doi.gov/bia/docs/laborforce/2005%20American%20Indian%20Population%20and%20Labor%20Force%20Report.pdf

99. "Broken Promises: Evaluating the Native American Health Care System" (Washington, DC: U.S. Commission on Civil Rights, September 2004). Retrieved July 6, 2009, from http://www.usccr.gov/pubs/nahealth/nabroken.pdf

100. Joseph J. Westermeyer, "Indian Powerlessness in Minnesota," *Society,* Vol. 10, No. 3, 1973, pp. 45–47; also see Thomas H. Walz and Gary Askerooth, *The Upside Down Welfare State* (Minneapolis: Elwood, 1973), p. 31.

101. "History of the Committee on Indian Affairs" (Washington, DC: U.S. Senate, no date). Retrieved July 5, 2009, from http://indian.senate.gov/cominfo.htm

102. Indian Affairs, "Who We Are" (Washington, DC: U.S. Department of the Interior, January 7, 2010). Retrieved June 5, 2010, from http://www.bia.gov/WhoWeAre/index.htm

103. C. L. Henson, "From War to Self-Determination: A History of the Bureau of Indian Affairs" (Liverpool, UK: American Studies Resources Centre, Aldham Robarts Centre, Liverpool John Moores University, Mount Pleasant, 1996). Retrieved July 4, 2009, from http://www.americansc.org.uk/online/indians.htm

104. Indian Affairs, "Who We Are."

105. J. Kehaulani Kauanui, "A Time for Change? President Obama on Indian Country and Native Nations," *Diverse: Issues in Higher Education,* March 27, 2009. Retrieved July 6, 2009, from http:// diverseeducation.wordpress.com/2009/03/27/a-time-for-change-president-obama-on-indian-country-and-native-nations/

106. Thomas H. Walz and Askerooth, *The Upside Down Welfare State,* p. 25.

107. Chuck Cook, "BIA Ordered to Prepare for Inquiry," *Arizona Republic,* October 16, 1987, pp. A1, 5.

108. Chuck Cook, Mike Masterson, and M. N. Trahant, "Indians Are Sold Out by the U.S.," *Arizona Republic,* October 4, 1987, pp. A1, 18, 20.

109. Chuck Cook, Mike Masterson, and M. N. Trahant, "Child's Suffering Is Cry for Reform," *Arizona Republic,* October 7, 1987, p. A18.

110. DeLoria, "The Reservation Conditions"; Christina Good Voice, "Indians March to Mend Boarding School Hurt," *Reznet,* June 9, 2009. Retrieved July 5, 2009, from http://www.reznetnews.org/article/ indians-march-mend-boarding-school-hurt-35190; Andrea Smith, "Soul Wound: The Legacy of Native American Schools, *Amnesty International Magazine,* Summer 2003. Retrieved July 5, 2009, from http:// www.amnestyusa.org/amnestynow/soulwound.html

111. *ELOUISE PEPION COBELL, et al., Plaintiffs, v. DIRK KEMPTHORNE, Secretary of the Interior, et al.,* Defendants. Civil Action No. 96-1285 (JR) MEMO-RANDUM, August 7, 2008. Retrieved June 22, 2009, from http://www.usdoj.gov/civil/cases/cobell/docs/ pdf/08072008_courtmemo.pdf

112. "Frequently Asked Questions about the Settlement of *Cobell v. Salazar*" (Cobell v. Salazar, www. CobellSettlement.com, no date). Retrieved February 14, 2010, from http://www.cobellsettlement.com/ press/faq.php#settlement_2

113. Edward M. Carpenter, "Social Services, Policies, and Issues," *Social Casework,* Vol. 61, No. 8, 1980, pp. 455–461.

114. Shea, "Indians Skeptical of Report Urging Program Overhaul."

115. Leadership Conference on Civil Rights Education Fund, *Wrong Then, Wrong Now: Racial Profiling Before and After September 11, 2001* (Washington, DC: February 26, 2003). Retrieved July 12, 2009, from http://www.civilrights.org/publications/wrong-then/

116. See, for example, American Civil Liberties Union and the Rights Working Group, *The Persistence of Racial and Ethnic Profiling in the United States: A Follow-Up Report to the U.N. Committee on the Elimination of Racial Discrimination* (Washington,

DC: American Civil Liberties Union, June 30, 2009). Retrieved August 5, 2009, from http://www.aclu.org/ pdfs/humanrights/cerd_finalreport.pdf

117. See, for example, U.S. Domestic Human Rights Program, *Threat and Humiliation: Racial Profiling, Domestic Security, and Human Rights in the United States* (New York: Amnesty International, September 2004). Retrieved February 18, 2010, from http://www .amnestyusa.org/racial_profiling/report/rp_report.pdf

118. Jake Tapper, Karen Travers, and Huma Kahn, "Obama, Biden Sit Down for Beers with Gates, Crowley," *ABC News,* July 30, 2009. Retrieved August 4, 2009, from http://abcnews.go.com/Politics/ Story?id=8208602&page=1

119. This paragraph relies on "ACLU of Virginia Asks Charlottesville Police to Halt DNA Collection from African-American Males" (New York: American Civil Liberties Union, April 12, 2004). Retrieved August 4, 2009, from http://www.aclu.org/privacy/ genetic/15254prs20040412.html

120. See, for example, a summary of several traffic stop studies in Geoffrey P. Alper, Roger G. Dunham, and Michael R. Smith, "Investigating Racial Profiling by the Miami-Dade Policy Department: A Multimethod Approach," *Criminology and Public Policy,* Vol. 6, No. 1, 2007, pp. 25–56; also see Patricia Y. Warren and Donald Tomaskovic-Devey, "Racial Profiling and Searches: Did the Politics of Racial Profiling Change Police Behavior," *Criminology and Public Policy,* Vol. 8, No. 2, 2009, pp. 343–369.

121. General Accounting Office, *U.S. Customs Service: Observations on Selected Operations and Program Issues,* GAO/T-GGD/AIMD-00-150 (Washington, DC: April 20, 2000). Retrieved August 4, 2009, from http://www.gao.gov/archive/2000/g100150t.pdf

122. For more information on data collection, see the website of the Racial Profiling Data Collection Resource Center at Northeastern University's Institute on Race and Justice: http://www.racialprofilinganalysis.neu .edu/index.php

123. The remainder of this paragraph relies on Warren and Tomaskovic-Devey, "Racial Profiling and Searches: Did the Politics of Racial Profiling Change Police Behavior?"

124. "Landmark Settlement Reached with Maryland State Police in 'Driving While Black' Case" (New York: American Civil Liberties Union, April 2, 2008). Retrieved February 16, 2010, from http://www. aclu.org/racial-justice/landmark-settlement-reached-maryland-state-police-driving-while-black-case

125. Bruce Watson, "Crackdown: When Bombs Terrorized America, the Attorney General Launched

the 'Palmer Raids,' " *Smithsonian Magazine,* February 2002. Retrieved August 4, 2009, from http://www.smithsonianmag.com/people-places/redsquare.html; *Sanctioned Bias: Racial Profiling since 9/11* (New York: American Civil Liberties Union, February 2004). Retrieved August 4, 2009, from http://www.aclu.org/FilesPDFs/racial%20profiling%20report.pdf

126. Neil Skene, Ed., *Congressional Quarterly Almanac, 1992,* Vol. XLVIII (Washington, DC: Congressional Quarterly, 1993), pp. 335–336.

127. Leadership Conference on Civil Rights Education Fund, *Wrong Then, Wrong Now: Racial Profiling Before and After September 11, 2001.*

128. Testimony of Nadine Strossen, president of the American Civil Liberties Union, before the Senate Judiciary Committee, Department of Justice Oversight: *The Massive, Secretive Detention and Dragnet Questioning of People Based on National Origin in the Wake of September 11* (Washington, DC: American Civil Liberties Union, December 4, 2001). Retrieved February 18, 2010, from http://www.aclu.org/national-security/testimony-aclu-president-nadine-strossen-department-justice-oversight-senate-judic

129. *America's Disappeared: Seeking International Justice for Immigrants Detained After September 11* (New York: American Civil Liberties Union, January 2004). Retrieved February 14, 2010, from http://www.aclu.org/files/FilesPDFs/un%20report.pdf

130. "Statement, United States Senate Committee on the Judiciary Oversight Hearing: Lessons Learned–The Inspector General's Report on the 9/11 Detainees, June 25, 2003, The Honorable Patrick Leahy United States Senator, Vermont." Retrieved February 16, 2010, from http://www.fas.org/irp/congress/2003_hr/062503leahy.html; also see "Constitution at the Crossroads: Landmark 9/11 Cases Before Supreme Court Will Test America's Values of Fairness for All," Statement of ACLU Legal Director Steven R. Shapiro (New York: American Civil Liberties Union, April 12, 2004). Retrieved February 16, 2010, from http://www.aclu.org/content/constitution-crossroads-landmark-post-911-cases-supreme-court-will-test-americas-values-fair; Testimony of Nadine Strossen, president of the American Civil Liberties Union, before the Senate Judiciary Committee, Department of Justice Oversight: *The Massive, Secretive Detention and Dragnet Questioning of People Based on National Origin in the Wake of September 11.*

131. See, for example, "Constitution at the Crossroads: Landmark 9/11 Cases Before Supreme Court Will Test America's Values of Fairness for All," Statement of ACLU Legal Director Steven R. Shapiro.

132. American Civil Liberties Union and the Rights Working Group, *The Persistence of Racial and Ethnic Profiling in the United States: A Follow-Up Report to the U.N. Committee on the Elimination of Racial Discrimination.*

133. U.S. Domestic Human Rights Program, *Threat and Humiliation: Racial Profiling, Domestic Security, and Human Rights in the United States,* p. vii.

134. This paragraph relies on "Hate Crime Statistics, Incidents and Offenses, 2008" (Washington, DC: Federal Bureau of Investigation, November 2009). Retrieved August 5, 2009, from http://www.fbi.gov/ucr/hc2008/index.html

135. David Holthouse, "The Year in Hate: Number of Hate Groups Tops 900," *Intelligence Report,* Spring 2009. Retrieved August 5, 2009, from http://www.splcenter.org/intel/intelreport/article.jsp?aid=1027

136. Larry Keller, "Minority Meltdown: Immigrants Blamed for Mortgage Crisis," *Intelligence Report,* Spring 2009. Retrieved August 5, 2009, from http://www.splcenter.org/intel/intelreport/article.jsp?aid=1011

137. Quoted in "Confronting the New Faces of Hate: Hate Crimes in America 2009" (Washington, DC: Leadership Conference on Civil Rights Education Fund, June 2009). Retrieved August 5, 2009, from http://www.civilrights.org/publications/hatecrimes/

138. "Combating Hate" (Washington, DC: Anti-Defamation League, 2010). Retrieved February 14, 2010, from http://www.adl.org/combating_hate/

139. "Confronting the New Faces of Hate: Hate Crimes in America 2009."

140. "Nativity of the Population and Place of Birth of the Native Population: 1850-1990" (Washington, DC: U.S. Census Bureau, March 9, 1999). Retrieved August 2, 2009, from http://www.census.gov/population/www/documentation/twps0029/tab01.html

141. U.S. Census Bureau, "Table 40. Native and Foreign-Born Population by State: 2007," *Statistical Abstract of the United States: 2010* (Washington, DC: U.S. Department of Commerce, 2009). Retrieved June 4, 2010, from http://www.census.gov/compendia/statab/tables/09s0041.pdf

142. Jeffrey Passel and D'Vera Cohn, "Immigration to Play Lead Role in Future U.S. Growth" (Washington, DC: Pew Hispanic Center, February 11, 2008).

Retrieved August 2, 2009, from http://pewresearch
.org/pubs/729/united-states-population-projections

143. Most of this paragraph relies on Jeffrey S. Passel, "Growing Share of Immigrants Choosing Naturalizations" (Washington, DC: Pew Hispanic Center, March 28, 2007). Retrieved August 3, 2009, from http://www.pewtrusts.org/uploadedFiles/wwwpewtrustsorg/Reports/Hispanics_in_America/PHC_growing_share032807.pdf

144. "President Bush Finally Speaks the Truth about America's Unlawful Treatment of Haitian Refugees" (Washington, DC: U.S. Committee for Refugees and Immigrants, February 26, 2004). Retrieved June 5, 2010, from http://www.refugees.org/newsroomsub.aspx?id=1040

145. See the website of the New Sanctuary Movement at http://www.newsanctuarymovement.org/.

146. This paragraph relies on Randall Monger and Macreadie Barr, *Nonimmigrant Admissions to the United States: 2009* (Washington, DC; Office of Immigration Statistics, U.S. Department of Homeland Security, April 2009). Retrieved June 4, 2010, from http://www.dhs.gov/xlibrary/assets/statistics/publications/ni_fr_2009.pdf

147. *Sanctioned Bias: Racial Profiling since 9/11.*

148. For a critique of NSEERS, see Kareem Shora and Shoba Sivaprasad Wadha, *NSEERS: The Consequences of America's Efforts to Secure Its Borders* (Washington, DC: American-Arab Anti-Discrimination Committee, March 31, 2009). Retrieved June 5, 2010, from http://www.adc.org/PDF/nseerspaper.pdf

149. "US-VISIT Traveler Information" (Washington, DC: U.S. Department of Homeland Security, July 23, 2009). Retrieved July 28, 2009, from http://www.dhs.gov/files/programs/content_multi_image_0006.shtm

150. "Fact Sheet: Expansion of US-VISIT Procedures to Additional Travelers" (Washington, DC: U.S. Department of Homeland Security, January 14, 2009). Retrieved July 28, 2009, from http://www.dhs.gov/files/programs/gc_1231972592442.shtm

151. Office of Inspector General, "Review of the Immigration and Customs Enforcement's Compliance Enforcement Unit" (Washington, DC: Department of Homeland Security, September 2005). Retrieved February 21, 2010, from http://www.dhs.gov/xoig/assets/mgmtrpts/OIG_05-50_Sep05.pdf

152. Randall Monger, *U.S. Legal Permanent Residents: 2009* (Washington, DC: Office of Immigration Statistics, U.S. Department of Homeland Security, April 2010). Retrieved June 5, 2010, from http://www.

153. Neil Skene, Ed., "Sizable Boost in Immigration OK'd," *Congressional Quarterly Almanac,* 1990, Vol. XLVI (Washington, DC: Congressional Quarterly, 1991), pp. 474–485.

154. Monger and Rytina, *U.S. Legal Permanent Residents: 2008.*

155. Daniel C. Martin and Michael Hoefer, *Refugees and Asylees: 2008* (Washington, DC: Office of Immigration Statistics, U.S. Department of Homeland Security, June 2009). Retrieved July 24, 2009, from http://www.dhs.gov/xlibrary/assets/statistics/publications/ois_rfa_fr_2008.pdf; Daniel C. Martin, *Refugees and Asylees: 2009* (Washington, DC: Office of Immigration Statistics, U.S. Department of Homeland Security, April 2010). Retrieved June 5, 2010, from http://www.dhs.gov/xlibrary/assets/statistics/publications/ois_rfa_fr_2009.pdf

156. Monger, *U.S. Legal Permanent Residents: 2009.*

157. James P. Smith and Barry Edmonston, Eds., *The New Americans: Economic, Demographic, and Fiscal Effects of Immigration* (Washington, DC: National Academy Press, 1997), p. 51.

158. Gordon H. Hanson, *The Economic Logic of Illegal Immigration* (New York: Council on Foreign Relations, March 2007), p. 24.

159. Robert Rowthorn, "The Fiscal Impact of Immigration on the Advanced Economies," *Oxford Review of Economic Policy,* Vol. 24, No. 3, 2008, pp. 560–580.

160. "Immigration" (Washington, DC: League of United Latin American Citizens, no date). Retrieved July 28, 2009, from http://www.lulac.org/immigration.html

161. *Immigration Enforcement Actions: 2008* (Washington, DC: Office of Immigration Statistics, U.S. Department of Homeland Security, July 2009). Retrieved July 24, 2009, from http://www.dhs.gov/xlibrary/assets/statistics/publications/enforcement_ar_08.pdf

162. *Ibid.*

163. Nancy Rytina and John Simanski, *Apprehensions by the U.S. Border Patrol: 2005-2008* (Washington, DC: Office of Immigration Statistics, U.S. Department of Homeland Security, June 2009). Retrieved July 24, 2009, from http://www.dhs.gov/xlibrary/assets/statistics/publications/ois_apprehensions_fs_2005-2008.pdf

164. Michael Hoefer, Nancy Rytina, and Bryan C. Baker, *Estimates of the Unauthorized Immigrant Population Residing in the United States: January 2009*

(Washington, DC: Office of Immigration Statistics, U.S. Department of Homeland Security, January 2010). Retrieved June 6, 2010, from http://www.dhs.gov/xlibrary/assets/statistics/publications/ois_ill_pe_2009.pdf

165. George J. Borjas, "Increasing the Supply of Labor through Immigration" Washington, DC: Center for Immigration Studies, May 2004). Retrieved May 9, 2004, from http://www.cis.org/articles/2004/back504.html

166. Hanson, *The Economic Logic of Illegal Immigration;* quote from p. 5.

167. This paragraph relies on Jagdish N. Bhagwati, "Control Immigration at the Border," *Wall Street Journal,* February 1, 1985, p. 22.

168. "Building Bridges: African Americans and Immigration," *NAACP Advocate,* Vol. 1, No. 2, August 2006, p. 3. Retrieved July 30, 2009, from http://www.naacp.org/pdfs/advocate/NAACP_advocate_newsletter_2006-08.pdf

169. Tom Tancredo, "Immigration Policy," Speech to the House of Representatives (Washington, DC, February 24, 2004). Retrieved April 29, 2004, from http://www.limitstogrowth.org/WEB-text/tancredo-22404.html

170. "Rep. Tancredo Introduces an Immigration Moratorium Bill" (Washington, DC: Federation for American Immigration Reform, April 2003). Retrieved July 30, 2009, from http://www.fairus.org/site/PageServer?pagename=research_researchb210

171. "About the Center for Immigration Studies" (Washington, DC: Center for Immigration Studies, no date). Retrieved July 30, 2009, from http://www.cis.org/About

172. Nancy Foner, "The American Melting Pot Is a Rich Stew," *Phi Kappa Phi Forum,* Vol. 89, No. 2, 2009, pp. 7–10.

173. This paragraph relies on Passel, "Growing Share of Immigrants Choosing Naturalizations."

174. Much of this paragraph relies on *ibid.*

175. *Ibid.*

176. Smith and Edmonston, *The New Americans: Economic, Demographic, and Fiscal Effects of Immigration,* p. 29.

177. See, for example, James Walsh, "Immigration Reform: What Will the New Year Bring?," *Newsmax.com,* November 23, 2009. Retrieved June 6, 2010, from http://www.newsmax.com/JamesWalsh/immigration-reform/2009/11/23/id/336384

178. See, for example, "NCLR President Rallies Northwest Latino Community to Oppose Guestworker Legislation" (Washington, DC: National Council of La Raza, May 11, 2000). Retrieved June 4, 2010, from http://www.nclr.org/content/news/detail/2185/

179. Janet Murguía, "A Change of Heart on Guest Workers," *Washington Post,* February 11, 2007. Retrieved July 30, 2009, from http://www.nclr.org/content/viewpoints/detail/44671/

180. "What Is the Census?" (Washington, DC: U.S. Census Bureau, July 30, 2009). Retrieved August 2, 2009, from http://2010.census.gov/2010census/

181. U.S. Census Monitoring Board, Presidential Members, *Final Report to Congress* (Suitland, MD: Author, September 1, 2001). Retrieved August 2, 2009, from http://govinfo.library.unt.edu/cmb/cmbp/reports/final_report/FinalReport.pdf; see especially pp. 6 and 7.

182. Amy Sullivan, "Why the 2010 Census Stirs Up Partisan Politics," *Time,* February 15, 2009. Retrieved August 2, 2009, from http://www.time.com/time/nation/article/0,8599,1879667,00.html; also see U.S. Census Monitoring Board, Presidential Members, *Final Report to Congress.*

183. Haya El Nasser, "For 2010 Census, Counting Gets Tougher," *USA Today,* October 8, 2009. Retrieved August 2, 2009, from http://www.usatoday.com/news/nation/census/2008-10-08-Census_N.htm

184. See, for example, Haya El Nasser, "Hispanic Groups Call for Census Boycott," *USA Today,* April 15, 2009. Retrieved August 2, 2009, from http://www.usatoday.com/news/nation/census/2009-04-15-census_N.htm

CONCLUSION: POLITICS, RATIONALISM, AND THE FUTURE OF SOCIAL WELFARE POLICY

This book has described many of the policies and programs that form the U.S. social welfare system. We use the term "system" loosely since it is clear that there is no unifying system of social welfare policies and programs in the United States. The many titles and programs of the Social Security Act (Old Age Survivors and Disability Insurance, Supplemental Security Income, Temporary Assistance for Needy Families, Medicare, Medicaid, child welfare services, social services, and so forth),[1] and many other policies and programs try to address a wide range of social welfare needs.

As you have also seen throughout this text, social welfare policies and programs occasionally compliment each other. Oftentimes they are contradictory. For example, in Chapter 2, we discussed policies that encourage making it easier for Americans to apply for public assistance benefits. Other policies, however, discourage states from doing this because they fear it will cause their caseload error rates to rise and that the federal government will sanction them if this occurs. In Chapters 5 and 6, we discussed policies like Social Security Disability Insurance (SSDI) and Supplemental Security Income (SSI) that provide cash benefits to people who are disabled and deemed unable to engage in substantial gainful employment. We also discussed policies and programs that are supposed to complement SSDI and SSI by encouraging these individuals to work. Instead of complementing each other, these policies are often at odds because those who engage in work may risk losing all their cash and health benefits after a period of time. As you think about the chapters you have read in this book, other such contradictions in social welfare policy and programs likely come to mind.

This book has also emphasized that during the course of U.S. history, the prevailing ideas underlying social welfare programs have varied substantially. The terms *liberal* and *conservative* are often used to describe these varying approaches although social welfare policies fall along a wide continuum between these points of view. Centrists and libertarians also have their views about what a fair social welfare policy should be. In the area of public assistance for families, more conservative ideas have prevailed in recent decades, especially when these approaches are contrasted with the expansion of social welfare that occurred during the War on Poverty and Great Society programs of the 1960s.

There is also no consistent idea about whether many of the social welfare programs considered in this book should be funded and/or administered by the federal government, state or local governments, or whether nonprofit, for-profit, or religious organizations are better suited to delivering at least some social welfare services. Even more fundamental is the question of whether government should be involved at all in some areas of social welfare provision. The healthcare reform debate that has gone on in this country for decades, and culminated at this juncture with the Patient Protection and Affordable Care Act of 2010, is certainly testimony to the strong feelings about private versus public provision of services in the healthcare arena.

This book also notes that the U.S. welfare state differs substantially from the social welfare systems of other developed countries. In many other countries, healthcare, childcare, and parental leave when a baby arrives are universal policies. Americans generally regard their country as the greatest in the world for many reasons. One reason is that the capitalist or free enterprise system tends to reward hard work, ingenuity, and risk taking. It is doubtful, however, that individuals who live in countries where social services are available to all as a matter of right regardless of employment or wealth would trade those benefits for a social welfare system where obtaining these services is often as much a matter of luck as it is hard work and smart life choices.

Many people seek to immigrate to the United States for the opportunities that American capitalism provides. America is a land of opportunity, but it is also a land where misfortune like a serious illness can put an individual or family at risk of destitution. The Patient Protection and Affordable Care Act of 2010 is an incremental step in seeing that more Americans have health insurance, but it falls far short of a true national health insurance program that will cover all Americans equally and seamlessly throughout their lives.

In many areas, the United States favors a residual approach to social welfare in the form of means-tested public assistance programs. After all, the United States was founded on values such as rugged individualism. You may agree or disagree with the very definitions of the social problems that the major social welfare programs are supposed to address. You may feel the population the program is supposed to help is too narrowly or too broadly targeted. You may think that eligibility processes are demeaning to those they are supposed to help or that they are justified in insuring that only the truly needy receive assistance when billions of dollars in social welfare expenditures are at stake. Even among your classmates, family, and friends, it is likely that there are considerable differences of opinion on just what a desirable social welfare system should be. In fact, everyone seems to have an opinion on the topic of social welfare programs, whether they have studied these programs carefully or not, or whether they or people they know well have ever used a particular program. Much the same can be said about the civil rights policies that have aided women, people of color, people with disabilities, and gay men, lesbians, bisexuals, and transgendered individuals, also discussed in this book.

In the last few decades, there has perhaps been no time as exciting as the present to write about social welfare policy and to learn about it—at least that is what some of us social welfare policy wonks think. In 2008, the nation elected Barack Obama its first African American president, a significant event by itself. President Obama has led Congress to take major steps in social welfare policy. Congress adopted the American Recovery and Reinvestment Act, a major economic stimulus bill in 2009, and the Patient Protection and Affordable Care Act, significant healthcare reform legislation, in 2010.

Both the economic stimulus and healthcare bills are intended to assist millions of U.S. households. Both are also highly controversial. The stimulus bill focuses on economic relief following stock market and home mortgage lending failures. The lack of public oversight that contributed to these private market failures and the bailouts Congress passed, such as the Troubled Assets Relief Program, to help these industries and prevent further damage to many American individuals and families are sources of consternation to many Americans. Many are also concerned about how much the stimulus bill, bailouts, and other legislation add to the national debt that had already accumulated under Republican administrations. The non-partisan Congressional Budget Office projects that the 2010 healthcare bill will reduce budget deficits by $143 billion in the first ten years and nearly $1.3 trillion in the second ten years.[2] Many Republicans and others disagree. They believe the healthcare bill will increase rather than decrease the national debt and gives government too much control over a significant portion of the economy.

President Barack Obama's election, the country's present economic situation, and the battle over healthcare reform have all invigorated Americans' interest and participation in the political process. The political process and the policies and programs that flow from it affect every individual and family in the United States. Many times these effects are profound— from the millions of older adults who are spared from living in poverty because of Social Security to the many who have received lifesaving healthcare through Medicare, Medicaid, or the State Children's Health Insurance Program, from the children who were placed in a loving home through child welfare services to those who are in recovery from mental illness or substance use disorders because of publicly funded treatment services.

If you haven't followed social welfare issues closely before, perhaps this book or your social welfare policy course has motivated you to think about social welfare problems, policies, and programs more critically and to take action to register your opinion about them. Unfortunately, policymaking has been likened to watching sausage being made—less than a pretty picture. This book has focused on many of the political aspects of policymaking. In this regard, it seems that bipartisanship is at an all time low, and its absence is having a major effect on the shape of social welfare policy.[3] For example, no Republican representatives and only three Republican senators voted for the American Recovery and Reinvestment Act of 2009. The vote on the Patient Protection and Affordable Care Act was also drawn along party lines. This is far different from the nearly unanimous bipartisan support that the Social Security Act of 1935 received.[4] Medicare legislation did not enjoy the same level of support, but 51 percent of Republicans in the House and 43 percent of Republicans in the Senate joined Democrats in supporting it.

In a democracy, vigorous debate on issues is generally viewed as not only good, but as necessary. However, deep and even insurmountable partisan divides have become part of the political landscape. Sometimes these divides are marked by incivility, not only on the part of political pundits who shout at and talk over each other on television programs, but also on the part of some elected officials. It is perhaps these deep partisan divides that are also spurring more Americans to participate in the policy process. This may be occurring not only because people feel strongly about issues such as how health insurance should work, but because elected officials are having a much more difficult time reaching consensus on issues of major importance to Americans. Americans are frustrated with the inertia of the political process and with the continuing role of big business, money, and power in influencing policy decisions.

Policy is not made once; it is made and remade. In the upcoming months and years, we will be able to look at the results of legislation such as the stimulus bill and healthcare reform. Americans have done this with other major social welfare legislation from the New Deal of the 1930s to the War on Poverty of the 1960s and the Personal Responsibility and Work Opportunity Reconciliation Act of the 1990s. Whether we consider the results of formal analyses and policy evaluations or more informal assessments, people are likely to continue to disagree about whether these pieces of legislation and others were the right course of action for Americans. You may feel strongly about the course the country has charted. You may have creative ideas about how to change these policies and programs. It is never too trite to say that the best characteristic of democracy is the freedom to share and promote ideas in our quest for a more perfect union.

Discussion Questions and Class Activities

Hold a final discussion on what class members think should be done to improve the U.S. social welfare system. Ask class members if their views of social welfare programs have changed over the course of the semester or term. If so, how have they changed and why? If not, why not? If class members could make three changes to social welfare programs, what would they be? How similar or dissimilar are class members' points of view? What might account for these differences or similarities? Have class members taken any action about social welfare policies or programs on their own since the semester began? If so, ask them to discuss their experience, whether they accomplished their goal, and whether they would be likely to undertake such action again.

Notes

1. Also see Andrew W. Dobelstein, *Understanding the Social Security Act: The Foundation of Social Welfare for America in the Twenty-first Century* (New York: Oxford University Press, 2009).
2. For one commentary on this subject, see Christopher Beam, "Get Well Soon," *Slate Magazine,* March 23, 2010. Retrieved June 6, 2010, from www.slate.com/id/2248672/
3. For one view of bipartisanship today, see Nancy L. Cohen, "Death by Bipartisanship," *The Huffington Post,* June, 22 2009. Retrieved March 23, 2010, from http://www.huffingtonpost.com/nancy-cohen-phd/death-by-bipartisanship_b_219153.html
4. The remainder of this paragraph relies on Andrew Biggs, "What the Votes on the Social Security Act and Medicare Tell Us About Obamacare" (Washington, DC: American Enterprise Institute, March 18, 2010). Retrieved March 22, 2010, from http://blog.american.com/?p=11528

NAME INDEX

SUBJECT INDEX

new bill of rights for
individuals with
disabilities, 213, 215–19
Rehabilitation Act, 215
Civil rights for individuals with
mental and substance use
disorders, 398–99
Civil rights for poor, 20
Civil Rights of Institutionalized
Persons Act of 1980, 399
Class action suits, 21
Classic experimental design,
58, 58f
Climate change, Obama and,
100
Cloning, 316
Common Cause, 20
Community Choice Act
proposal, 213, 214
Community Development Block
Grant (CDBG), 345–46
Community Mental Health
Act of 1963, 393, 399, 400
Community mental health
centers (CMHCs), 399–401
Community Mental Health
Centers Construction
Act of 1963, 81
Community Reinvestment
Act of 1977, 135, 480
Comparable worth, 416–21
Compassionate
conservatism, 95
Comprehensive Employment
and Training Act (CETA)
of 1973, 350
Compulsory savings, 154–55
Congressional Budget Office
(CBO), 29–30, 36, 38
Conservative, defined, 15
Consolidated Budget and
Reconciliation Act
(COBRA) of 1986, 313
Consumer Price Index (CPI),
109
Contamination in social
science research, 58
Contraceptive drugs, 431–32
Control group, 58
Controlled Substances Act of
1970, 401

Convention on the Rights of
Persons with Disabilities,
218–19
Co-payments, 280
Corporate welfare, 28–29
Cost neutral policies, 38
Cost-of-living adjustments
(COLAs), 80
Court Appointed Special
Advocates (CASA), 375
Cranston-Gonzalez National
Affordable Housing Act
of 1990, 135
Culture of poverty, 123–24
Customs and Border Patrol
(CBP), 487
Cyberstalking, 437
Cyclical unemployment, 180

D

Dawes Act of 1887, 475
Deadbeat Parents Punishment
Act of 1998, 240
Death with Dignity Act
(Oregon), 315
Deductibles, 280
Defense Department, 21
Defense of Marriage Act
(DOMA) of 1996,
52, 442, 443
Defense spending
Balanced Budget and
Emergency Deficit
Reduction Act and, 87
capping, Budget
Enforcement Act and,
88
funding for, 26, 26f
National Defense Education
Act and, 327–28
U.S. spending priorities
and, 76–78, 77f
Deficit Reduction Act (DRA)
of 2006, 252, 265, 288
Dental insurance, 308
Department of Education
(DOE) Organization Act
of 1979, 330
Dependent care tax credit, 28
Dependency ratio, 165

Developmental Disabilities and
Facilities Construction Act
of 1970, 219
Developmental Disabilities
Assistance and Bill of
Rights Act of 1975, 219–20
Amendments of 2000, 220
Devolution, 48, 83, 85, 254, 264
Disability and work, 204–11
eliminating work
disincentives, supporting
work, 205–6
keeping more cash benefits
and health benefits, 206
Plan to Achieve Self-Support
(PASS), 207–8
Ticket to Work, 209–11
vocational rehabilitation
and employment
services, 204–5
Disability Determination
Services (DDS), 198
Disability insurance (DI),
155
Disability policy, 192–225. *See
also* Civil rights for individuals with disabilities;
Supplemental Security
Income (SSI)
for children, 219–22
civil rights for individuals
with disabilities, 211
fair definition of disabled,
193
future, 222–23
public assistance for the
deserving poor and,
193–95
Veterans Administration
and, 203–4
Dissimilarity index, 463
Domestic violence. *See also*
Intimate partner violence.
Domestic violence courts
in New York, 436–37
Drug abuse prevention
programs, 62–63
Drug Abuse Resistance
Education (D.A.R.E.)
program, 62–63
Drug control, 44

by selected characteristics, 115–18 2008, 116f
Self-Sufficiency Standard and, 113
as structure, 126–27
thresholds, 109, 110, 110t
U.S. government's definition of, 109–10
problems with, 110–12
welfare as cause of, 140–41
women and, 115, 116f, 416
Poverty gap, 110
Preferred provider organization (PPO), 291
Prefunded retirement system, 173–74
Pregnancy Discrimination Act of 1978, 424
Pre-K Now, 337
Pretest-posttest design, 60, 61f
Preventive Health and Health Services (PHHS) Block Grant, 290
Primary care case management (PCCM), 290
Privatization
of child support enforcement, 243–44
of government services, 86
of prisons, 402
of Social Security, 173
Program process or implementation, assessment of, 49, 50
Program theory, assessment of, 49
Progressive price indexing, 172
Project MATCH, 48, 50
Promoting Safe and Stable Families (PSSF), 373, 374
Proposition, 36, 402
Proxy groups, 19, 20
Prussian educational system, 325
Public assistance, 4. *See also* Publicly supported housing, Temporary Assistance for Needy Families (TANF), Supplemental Nutrition Assistance Program (SNAP), Supplemental Security Income (SSI)

adult categorical public assistance programs, 194
for the deserving poor, 193–94
government intervention, 194–95
reducing, ideas for, 141–43
vs. social insurance, 154
Public hearings, 56–57
Publicly supported housing, 132–35, 139
Public mental health system, 399–401
Public opinion, 23–24
Public policy
changing (Eight Ps), 19–20
implementing, 25
legitimizing, 24
private pensions and, 175–76
Public policy theorists, 23
Public Works and Economic Development Act of 1965, 76, 345

Q

Quasiexperimental designs, 60

R

Race norming, 468
Racial and ethnic targeting, 477–80
hate crimes, 480
racial profiling, 477–78
War on terror, 479–80
Racial equality, 456–57
affirmative action, 466–70
Civil Rights Acts, 457–58
housing and racial discrimination, 462–66
Native Americans, 474–76
school desegregation, 458–62
voting rights, 470–74
Racketeer Influenced, Corrupt Organization (RICO) Act of 1970, 429
Rational activity, policy evaluation as, 48–50, 49, 52
Rationalism in policymaking, 4–5
limits of, 5–6

Really Simple Syndication (RSS) feeds, 23
Reapportionment, 472–73
Redistricting, 472–73
Redlining, 463–65
Reductionistic experiments, 59
Reefer Madness (film), 23
Rehabilitation Act of 1973, 215, 216, 217
Rehabilitation Services Administration (RSA), 204
Representative payee, 199
Republican Contract with America, 1984, 15
Research designs, formal, 57–62
classic experimental design, 58, 58f
logic model of teen parent program, 59f
pretest-posttest design, 60, 61f
quasiexperimental design, 60
theoretical evaluation, 59–60
time series design, 60–62, 61f
Research Triangle Institute, 63
Residual programs, 4
Respecting Accuracy in Domestic Abuse Reporting (RADAR), 438
Retiring, amount of Social Security needed for, 164–65
Robert Wood Johnson Foundation, 63

S

Safe and Timely Interstate Placement of Foster Children Act of 2006, 376
Sales tax, 27
Sanctuary cities, 483
Scholastic Aptitude Test (SAT), 337
School desegregation, 458–62
busing and mandatory desegregation, 459
educational quality, 461–62
future desegregation policy, 462
resegregation, 461